**GLENCOE
LATIN 1**

LATIN
FOR AMERICANS

B.L. ULLMAN

CHARLES HENDERSON, JR.

McGraw Hill **Glencoe**

New York, New York   Columbus, Ohio   Chicago, Illinois   Peoria, Illinois   Woodland Hills, California

About the Authors

B. L. Ullman (Ph.D., University of Chicago) enjoyed a distinguished career of teaching and scholarship at the Universities of Pittsburgh, Iowa, Chicago, and North Carolina. An internationally recognized authority on all aspects of the Roman world, ancient, medieval, and Renaissance, he was also a pioneer in modern methods of teaching Latin.

Charles Henderson, Jr. (Ph.D., University of North Carolina) collaborated with Professor Ullman on several revisions of this book. He has taught at New York University, the University of North Carolina, and Smith College, where he served as Chairman of the Classics Department and Assistant to the President.

Acknowledgments

The authors would like to thank the following individuals for their assistance in this revision of **Latin for Americans.**

Contributing Writers

David Driscoll (Ph.D., University of North Carolina) is Head of Latin and Classical Studies at The Masters School in Dobbs Ferry, NY. He has taught Latin and Greek at Gustavus Adolphus College, the University of Mississippi, and at schools in the Boston area.

Frances Knapp Clawson (A.B., Smith College; M.S., Nazareth College) has taught Latin in the Pittsford, NY, schools and lectured at Xiamen University, China.

Reviewer

Sue Wood, Indianapolis, Indiana

Front cover:

The Coliseum, everlasting symbol of the grandeur that was Rome.
Photo by A. & L. Sinibaldi/Getty Images

The McGraw·Hill Companies

Send all inquiries to:
Glencoe/McGraw-Hill
8787 Orion Place
Columbus, OH 43240

ISBN-13: 978-0-07-874251-4
ISBN-10: 0-07-874251-X

Printed in the United States of America.

4 5 6 7 8 9   027/055   12 11 10 09

CONTENTS

THE ROMAN WORLD: ROMAN ITALY

Larry Lee/Westlight

UNIT II

ROMAN INFLUENCE

Wayne Rowe

National Trust/Art Resource, NY

ROMANS AT HOME AND ABROAD

ROMAN SOCIETY

Carmen Redondo/CORBIS

The Metropolitan Museum of Art, Gift of Henry Walters, 1925. (25.41)

UNIT V

ROMAN POETS, GODS, AND HEROIC JOURNEYS

MISSION TO A NEW WORLD: AENEAS AND ROME

Scala/Art Resource, NY

Lawrence Migdale/Photo Researchers

UNIT VII

SCHOOLS, SITES, AND SIGHTS IN THE ROMAN EMPIRE

UNIT VIII

ADVENTURES ABROAD AND LIFE AT HOME

Department of Antiquities, Ashmolean Museum, Oxford

The Metropolitan Museum of Art, Fletcher Fund, 1930. (30.11.9). Copyright © 1982 By the Metropolitan Museum of Art.

THE ADVENTURES OF ULYSSES, ROMULUS, REMUS, AND PYRRHUS

MYTHS, LEGENDS, AND HISTORY OF EARLY GREECE AND ROME

Ronald Sheridan/Ancient Art & Architecture Collection

Scala/Art Resource, NY

ROMAN GODS AND ROMAN HEROES

CLASSICAL MYTHS AND PORTRAITS OF ROMAN HEROES

Dagli Orti/The Art Archive

UNIT XIII

ROMAN LEGENDS: PORTRAITS OF PERSEVERANCE, PATRIOTISM, AND COURAGE

OUR ROMAN HERITAGE

The Romans used great arches as monuments to celebrate military victories or famous heroes. All over
the world, other people have built triumphal arches
in imitation of this Roman custom.

Arches are also gateways, and the Latin language is the arch through which countless generations of Western people have been able to enter
their past and discover the ideas and traditions that
have shaped their lives. All over the world, for centuries, people have
studied Latin because of their curiosity about the ancient world. Now you,
too, stand before the arch. Step right ahead! Just through that arch is the
rich inheritance the Romans have left to all of us.

The first thing you will notice as you begin the study of Latin is the
close resemblance between many Latin and English words, since the
English language owes a great debt of vocabulary to Latin. However,
the Roman heritage is not just one of vocabulary; equally important are
the ways in which the ancient Romans have influenced our forms of government, our social institutions, and our habits of thinking and have
inspired statesmen, writers, artists, architects, engineers, and almost all
educated people.

Your own greatest reward beyond the arch will be the broadened vision
you will find in yourself. Some things in the ancient world will be strikingly
familiar to you; others, totally new; some things will seem primitive; others,
remarkably modern. How did an ancient Roman live? What was life like in
his or her family? What were their ideas about government and religion?
How could they believe in both freedom and slavery? What were the moral
qualities and the skills that made the Romans, once simple farmers, the
masters of the world? To all these questions you will discover the answers,
and the comparisons between the Roman experience and yours will help
to broaden your view of the world. As so many others before you have
learned, you will see that "to learn another language is to gain another soul."

Why study Latin and Rome rather than a modern language and a modern
city? No other language and no other city have had so much influence—and
for so long a time—upon our own culture. More than twenty-seven hundred
years ago Rome was an insignificant settlement on the Tiber River in a central district of Italy called Latium[1]. From small beginnings, the military,

---

[1]Pronounce as *Lay´shum.*

The Arch of Titus was begun by the emperor Vespasian to honor his son Titus' victory over Jerusalem in A.D. 70. It was completed in A.D. 81. It is located on the Sacred Way in Rome and is one of the best examples of a distinctively Roman style of architecture, the triumphal arch.

The Emperor Justinian (sixth century) was responsible for establishing the Justinian Code, a collection of Roman laws, edicts, and decisions of the previous one thousand years. It is still the basic law of many nations. In this mosaic, we see the Emperor Justinian with his court.

political, and cultural power of Rome spread, first throughout Latium, then through Italy and over the Mediterranean. By the second century after the birth of Christ, the Romans dominated almost the entire civilized world; Rome itself was at the same time **urbs et orbis**—*city and world*.

The Romans' language, Latin (which gets its name from Latium), came to be used everywhere, largely displacing the languages of the conquered peoples. Only Greek, a language much older than Latin, successfully resisted the invasion, mainly because it was the vehicle of great literature and culture that the Romans admired and imitated. Just as we today study Latin, so did the Romans then study Greek, and for similar reasons.

From the map on pages 54–55, you can see the stages of growth of the Roman Empire, and you can also see why the languages of Spain, Portugal, France, Italy, and Romania are called Romance languages: they are the living descendants of the Latin spoken by the Romans who conquered and colonized these lands. Although English is basically a Germanic language, Latin has influenced it so much through the centuries that it would be almost fair to call it a Romance language also. More than sixty percent of our English vocabulary has been derived or taken intact from Latin!

Thus the Latin language and the ideas it conveys have actually survived the Roman Empire itself. As the centuries passed and as the empire was gradually transformed into the beginnings of modern Europe, Latin continued to be the international language of all educated men and women, living a sort of parallel existence with the different national languages that were growing up from and alongside it. When the Middle Ages ended, interest in the classical Latin of Cicero, Caesar, and Vergil increased with the discovery of more works of the ancient authors in the monasteries and libraries of Europe. This rebirth of interest in the ancient world was one of the major causes for the Renaissance, the period that marks the transition to the modern world. From their deeper knowledge of the past, the people of the Renaissance found a new confidence in themselves and new horizons to explore. Since the colonization of the New World was the work of Europeans who were the heirs of the Roman tradition, Latin was transplanted to the Western Hemisphere. Even today, the people of Mexico, Central America, and South America are called Latins, and the region they live in is called Latin America.

Our own country was settled under the same influences. The men who led the Revolutionary War and drafted the Constitution cherished the classical ideals of liberty and the dignity of the individual. The two names by which we refer to our country, America and the United States, are both derived from Latin. Our nation's motto, **E pluribus unum,** is Latin. In one sense, there could have been no Declaration of Independence without Latin; its first sentence would have looked like this: "We hold these truths to be self-____, that all men are ____ ____, that they are ____ by their ____ with ____ ____ rights; that among these are life, ____, and the ____ of happiness." The Romans not only gave us the omitted words but the ideas themselves, which they in turn had borrowed from the Greeks. There is hardly a page in this book that does not show you a specific example of the way in which classical literature, mythology, art, history, or social custom is still part of our lives in the twenty-first century.

To be sure, Latin itself is seldom written or spoken today outside of ecclesiastical circles. However, its immense influence upon English and other languages makes its study a very practical one. Most of the difficult words in English come from Latin (or Greek)—in a short time you will see how even an elementary knowledge of Latin makes it easy to figure out the meaning and spelling of such words as *impecunious, equanimity, collaborate, obdurate,* and many others. Latin abbreviations, words, mottos, and phrases that are common in English will no longer be a mystery. Latin will help build the technical vocabulary you will need if you are to become a doctor, lawyer, teacher, or scientist. Translating Latin will give polish

Roman influence was far flung. The well-preserved Roman amphitheater at El Jem, Tunisia, is still standing today. Equipment, wild animals, and gladiators were kept in the vast area under the amphitheater floor until they were needed for the show.

and precision to your English style and will help avoid the narrow prejudice that our way of saying something is always the easiest or best.

Nevertheless, the best reason for passing through the arch is that you will enter a new and different world that will tell you much about your own. It will also help educate you, for understanding what you owe to the past is a major part of being educated. As the famous Roman orator Cicero said, "Not to know what happened before you were born is to be forever a child."

Questions

1. How many events of Roman history can you list?
2. Which famous Romans can you name?
3. What Roman gods and goddesses can you recall?
4. What do you know about the city of Rome as it is today?
5. Make a list of the Latin words, phrases, legal terms, scientific terms, mottos, proverbs, and abbreviations you already know.

ALPHABET

Without writing, the continuity of civilization would be impossible. People can pass on hard-won experience and ideas by word of mouth, but only to a few individuals, in a limited area, and only for a brief time. What is only heard can be easily misunderstood. Whatever is written down, however, can be read by people far and wide, preserved for long periods of time, and changed if it is proven wrong by later experience. Since writing gives permanence and wide distribution to knowledge and ideas, it is a more effective way to move people's minds than such violent means as war, slavery, and torture. This is what we mean when we say that the "pen is mightier than the sword."

There are many forms of writing, some better than others. The earliest, used long ago by prehistoric humans, was *pictographic,* meaning that it told stories by using pictures. The ancient Egyptians and Chinese, and even modern Native Americans, have used pictographic writing. Although the pictures are often quite beautiful, they are difficult to draw, leave a lot out of the story and, as they become more numerous and complicated, are too much for any one person to remember. *Ideographic* writing is similar to pictographic: the pictures have gradually been standardized into simpler characters that convey an idea. They, too, are often difficult for the untrained reader to understand; for example, a foreign

Scala/Art Resource, NY

A wax-covered tablet, called an *abecedarium.* **The alphabet was scratched on the wooden rim as a model to imitate. The letters run from right to left as in the earlier Semitic alphabets.**

visitor driving along a highway might think that the signpost **+** stood for a gravestone instead of a crossroad (and in his case indeed it might!). In *logographic* writing the characters are associated with the sounds of the words of which they were originally pictures: if a wavy line represents the

sea and the figure of a small boy represents a *son,* then

becomes *season*. When, in this way, a limited number of characters become firmly fixed as the standard signs for the sounds of the syllables of a language, *syllabic* writing is the result. Many ancient people used syllabic writing, often together with the other types; this is the form the Japanese use today.

The simplest and clearest system of writing is the *alphabetic,* which developed from the syllabic system and in which there is a single character for almost every vowel or consonant sound. This system helps people hear more easily the sounds they see and thus simplifies learning to read and write. Furthermore, in the alphabetic system the sounds of one language can be represented almost exactly in the writing of another language, and this makes learning the new language that much simpler. Not even the alphabetic system is perfect; in English we still have difficulty learning to spell because custom often requires us to use a different set of characters for the same sound: compare *debt* and *let,* or *there* and *their.*

Nevertheless, the Roman alphabet that we use and share with so many other countries is the best yet invented and is one of the Romans' greatest contributions to our culture. Its history is an excellent example of the way in which valuable inventions are passed from one civilization to another. Sometime before 1500 B.C., the Semites, a people of western Asia, developed a syllabic script from Egyptian pictographic characters and gave these characters names from their own language. The first letter was *aleph* (*ox,* because the character looked like the head of an ox, although upsidedown); the second was *beth (house),* and so forth. The Phoenicians, a seafaring Semitic people related to the Jews and Arabs, passed this set of characters to the Greeks, who adapted it to their own language and made the signs for the vowels *(a, e, i, o, u)* separate and distinct (the Semitic alphabet had not done this). *Aleph* became *alpha,* and *beth* became *beta,* and thus the alphabet was born, because *alpha* and *beta* no longer had anything to do with *ox* and *house* but were simply signs for the sounds *a* and *b*. From the Greeks the alphabet was passed to the Etruscans, northern neighbors of the Romans in Italy. When the Romans in turn borrowed it from the Etruscans, they made some changes in the values and forms of the letters, and passed it on to the modern world, where it is used almost universally today. Both of the Americas, all of Australia, and all of Europe

The Bettmann Archive

IMP · CAES · DIVI
M · ANTONINI · PII · GERMANICI
SARMATICI · FILIVS · DIVI
COMMODI · FRATER ·
DIVI · ANTONINI · PII · NEPOS · DIVI · HADRIANI
PRONEPOS · DIVI · TRAIANI · PARTHICI
ABNEPOS · DIVI · NERVAE · ADNEPOS ·
L · SEPTIMIVS · SEVERVS
PIVS · PERTINAX · AVG ·
ARABICVS · ADIABENICVS · P · MAX ·
TR · POT · IIII · IMP · VIII · CoS · II · P · P
COLVMNAM · VII · TEMPESTATE ·
CONFRACTAM · RESTITVIT ·

This inscription is a decree issued by the emperor Septimius Severus, who was emperor from A.D. 193 to 211. He expanded the empire in a war against the Parthians but died in an attempt to take Scotland. Do you recognize any words?

(except Bulgaria, Serbia, and Russia, which use a modified Greek alphabet, and Greece itself) write in Latin letters. In 1928 Turkey, as one symbol of its emergence into the modern world, abandoned the Arabic alphabet (a descendant of the ancient Semitic one) in favor of the simpler Latin alphabet. Even in places where it has not already displaced the system of native characters—Israel and the Middle East, Africa, Japan, China, and the rest of Asia—"our" Roman alphabet is widely understood and used as a secondary writing system. As the modern world becomes more of a global community and as the knowledge of English and other western languages (especially French and Spanish) increases, so does the use of the ancient Roman system become more prevalent. Here is that splendid tool the Romans have bequeathed to us:

Roman   A B C D E F G H I   K L M N O P Q R S T   V   X Y Z
English A B C D E F G H I J K L M N O P Q R S T U V W X Y Z

You can see that the alphabet has changed little since Roman days. The Romans used *i* for both *i* and *j*. Four centuries ago it became the custom in English to use a long form of *i* for *j*, and thus our *j* was formed. Similarly, the Romans used only one character for *u* and *v*, but we have introduced the useful distinction between them, even in Latin, and in this book *u* is printed for the vowel, *v* for the consonant. The original identity of the two is shown by another modern letter, *w*, which is a double *u* in name and a double *v* in form. (The letters *j* and *w* are not found in Latin words in this textbook.)

The Romans made no distinction between capitals and small letters. Our small letters gradually developed out of capitals in late antiquity.

A Roman school

PRONUNCIATION

The pronunciation of Latin has naturally changed in the course of centuries. During the Middle Ages it varied from country to country in accordance with the rules for pronouncing the everyday languages of those countries, and this practice has continued in some places even to the present time. A century ago scholars discovered in various ways how Latin was pronounced in the days of Caesar and Cicero. This "new" ancient pronunciation first came into general use in the United States. It is now fairly general everywhere except in Italy and Vatican City. According to the ancient pronunciation, Cicero pronounced his name **Ki´kero,** and so you are taught in this book—but once it was pronounced **Si´sero** in England and the United States, **See´sero** in France, **Tsi´tsero** in Germany and Austria, **Chee´chero** in Italy, **Thi´thero** in Spain. But we know that **Kikero** is most nearly correct because, for example, Greek writers spell his name **ΚΙΚΕΡΩΝ (Kikerōn),** and the **k** sound in Greek cannot be confused with the **s** sound, for which there is an entirely different letter. Caesar pronounced his own name **Kysar.** We used to pronounce it in Latin as in English *(Seezer),* and each of the other languages had its own way of saying the word.

Ronald Sheridan/Ancient Art & Architecture Collection

Messages were scratched into wax that covered wooden writing tablets. Often, two tablets were placed with their right sides together, tied, and sealed with sealing wax to preserve the integrity of the message.

The system of pronunciation that you are taught in this textbook is thus ancient, "modern," and standard. Pronouncing Latin is not difficult: the rules are few and simple, and unlike English, each consonant (except **b**) has only one sound, and each vowel at most only two sounds. The best way to get started is by imitating your teacher carefully and by listening to the audio CDs which accompany this book. Pay particular attention to the length (quantity) and sound (quality) of the vowels and to the position of the stress (´). You will find that Latin is a sonorous and almost musical language.

Pronunciation Exercises

1. Each of the first five columns drills a different vowel, either long or short; the sixth column is devoted to the different diphthongs. Pronounce:

ā	ē	quī	nōn	iūs	aes
Mārs	mē	hīc	prō	cūr	quae
pār	pēs	vīs	mōns	lūx	Aet´nae
ab	ex	in	nox	nunc	aut
iam	sed	quid	post	cum	cau´sa
dat	per	fit	mors	dux	clau´sae
nār´rat	cer´tē	di´gitī	cō´gor	iūs´tus	poe´nae
ma´lā	lē´ge	mī´litis	ro´gō	cur´rū	moe´nia

2. Read the verse. Can you tell from the rhythm and arrangement of words what it is?

Mi´cā, mi´cā, par´va stēl´la!
Mī´ror quae´nam sīs, tam bel´la,
Splen´dēns ē´minus in il´lō,
Al´ba ve´lut gem´ma, cae´lō.

3. This is a translation by George D. Kellogg of the first two stanzas of *America.*

Tē ca´nō, Pa´tria,	**Tē ca´nō, Pa´tria,**
Can´dida, lī´bera	**Sem´per et ā´tria**
Tē re´feret	**Inge´nuum;**
Por´tus et ex´ulum	**Lau´dō viren´tia**
Et tu´mulus se´num;	**Cul´mina, flū´mina;**
Lī´bera mon´tium	**Sen´tiō gau´dia**
Vōx re´sonet.	**Caeli´colum.**

4. Here is part of a translation of Lincoln's Gettysburg Address made by Monsignor Edwin Ryan for the Vatican Library:

Octōgin´tā et sep´tem ab´hinc iam an´nōs rem pū´blicam no´vam, lībertā´te incep´tam at´que homi´nibus nātū´rā pa´ribus dēdicā´tam, maiō´rēs hīs in regiō´nibus ēdidē´runt.... Sēn´sū ta´men altiō´re hanc ter´ram dēdicā´re, cōnsecrā´re, sānctificā´re, nō´bīs nōn com´petit... Quō fī´et ut cī´vitās haec De´ō adiuvan´te lībertā´tī renāscē´tur; et di´ciō in po´pulō fundā´ta, ā po´pulō ges´ta, ad po´pulī salū´tem dīrēc´ta, nēquā´quam dē mun´dō tābēs´cēns interī´bit.

5. These are ancient Latin quotations, some of which you may have seen:

• **Vē´nī, vī´dī, vī´cī.** *I came, I saw, I conquered.* (Caesar's famous dispatch to the senate after a victory)

• **In hōc sig´nō vin´cēs.** *In this sign* (the cross) *you will conquer.* (motto of Constantine, the first Christian emperor)

• **Pos´sunt qui´a pos´se viden´tur.** *They can because they think they can.* (Vergil)

• **Aman´tium ī´rae amō´ris integrā´tiō est.** *The quarrels of lovers are the renewal of love.* (Terence; quoted by Winston Churchill in a message to Franklin D. Roosevelt)

6. The two verses that follow were used by Roman children in some of their games:

• **Ha´beat sca´biem quis´quis ad mē vē´nerit novis´simus.** *May he have the itch who comes to me last.*

• **Rēx e´rit quī rēc´tē fa´ciet; quī nōn fa´ciet nōn e´rit.** *He will be king who does right; he who does not will not be king.*

7. Here is the most famous sentence of President John F. Kennedy's Inaugural Address, translated into Latin:

Ī´taque concī´vēs me´ī Americā´nī, nē rogē´tis quid pa´tria ves´tra prō vō´bis fa´cere pos´sit, im´mo quid vōs prō pa´triā fa´cere possī´tis, id rogā´te.

UNIT
I

THE ROMAN WORLD: ROMAN ITALY

Unit Objectives

- To read and understand simple Latin sentences, dialogues, and narratives
- To understand and apply the concepts of declension, case, number, gender; noun–adjective agreement; subject–verb agreement; conjugation of verbs, present tense; person and number of verbs; principal parts of verbs; the present stem and present infinitive of verbs; the nominative, genitive, and accusative cases
- To learn about the geography of the Roman world

This view looking across the Roman Forum from the Capitoline Hill sweeps over three thousand years of history. In the foreground, the ancient columns of the Temple of Castor and Pollux *(right)* and the round Temple of Vesta *(left)*. In the middle ground, the Church of Santa Maria Nova (tenth century A.D.); and the Temple of Venus and Rome (second century A.D.). In the background, the vast mass of the Coliseum (first century A.D.) and, if you look closely, an object clearly from the twentieth century. Even in ruins, the Forum remains to all the world an inspiration as one of the wellsprings of civilization.

Stephen Studd/©Tony Stone Images

13

LESSON I

RŌMA ET ITALIA

LESSON OBJECTIVES
- To learn the uses of the nominative case and the endings of first declension nouns
- To understand Latin word order

Rōma est in Italiā. Italia est in Europā. Britannia est in Eurōpā. Britannia est īnsula. Italia nōn est īnsula. Italia paene[1] est īnsula. Italia paenīnsula est. Sicilia et Sardinia sunt īnsulae. Īnsulae in aquā sunt. Austrālia īnsula est, sed Āsia nōn est īnsula.

[1] *almost*

Sunt viae et silvae in paenīnsulā Italiā. Viae et silvae et paenīnsulae in 5 Eurōpā sunt. Italia et Graecia et Hispānia paenīnsulae sunt. Rōma nōn in Graeciā sed in Italiā est. Est Graecia in Eurōpā?

Est aqua in Antarcticā, sed nōn sunt silvae in Antarcticā. Silvae in Africā sunt. Est America īnsula?

Questions

1. Can you use other islands, countries, states, and cities whose names end in -*a*, such as Bermuda, India, Virginia, Philadelphia, to make up additional Latin sentences?
2. What do we call an "almost-island" in English?
3. Which words in the reading seem totally unrelated to English?

VOCABULARY

Nota·Bene

In the vocabularies, the words in brackets are not needed now, but soon will be, so it may be simpler and easier for you to learn the whole vocabulary entry now.

The words in parentheses are English derivatives of Latin words. An English derivative is any word descended from an original Latin word.

Nouns
a´qua, [a´quae f.] *water* (aqueduct, aqueous)
īn´sula, [īn´sulae f.] *island* (insulate, isolate)
sil´va, [sil´vae f.] *forest, woods* (Pennsylvania, sylvan)
vi´a, [vi´ae f.] *road, way, street* (viaduct, deviate)

Verbs
est *is, there is, he/she/it is*
sunt *are, there are, they are*

Adverb
nōn *not* (nonentity, nonsense)

Conjunctions
et *and* (et cetera)
sed *but*

In the vocabulary list, the nominative singular and genitive singular forms of each noun, and its gender, are provided.

Reading and Understanding Latin

Following are hints to help you understand the meaning of a Latin sentence.

1. Read aloud through the entire sentence, word for word, in Latin. Pronounce the parts of each word (syllables) distinctly and accurately, remembering that there are no silent letters in Latin. Reading aloud is better, since you are less likely to skip over words or their important endings.

2. Work on your pronunciation, since changes in Latin word spelling often result in changes of meaning: **lĭ´ber** *(book)*, **lī´ber** *(free)*; **dū´cēs** *(you will lead)*, **dŭ´cēs** *(leaders)*; **mă´la** *(bad)*, **mā´la** *(apples)*. Be especially attentive to the endings, since these regularly change the meaning.

3. Try to grasp the meaning of each Latin word in the order in which it appears in a sentence. Do not jump around. Your goal is to understand Latin as the Romans did. Direct comprehension of a sentence, rather than writing (translating) into English, should always be your ultimate goal.

4. If you cannot understand the meaning of a word, try to connect its spelling with an English word you do know. **A´qua** is related to *aquatic* which means *having to do with water*. By using the derivative *aquatic*, you may be able to see that the meaning of **a´qua** is *water*. Look up the meaning of a Latin word in the vocabulary list only as a last resort.

5. Be attentive not only to the root meaning of every word in a Latin sentence but also to its form (spelling) and position: **īnsula** = *island,* but **īnsulae** = *islands*. As you will learn, the meaning of a Latin word depends greatly on its exact spelling. A change in the form of a word (its inflection) almost always results in a change in meaning. In Latin, word position is more important for emphasis than for meaning.

6. Learn as many meanings as possible for each vocabulary word, starting with the most basic: **via** = *road*, also *way* and *street*. If none of the meanings you have learned makes sense, try a synonym. However, do not change the part of speech.

7. Supply the article *a, an,* or *the* with the nouns that need one.

GRAMMAR

Nouns

In English and in Latin, *nouns* name persons, places, things, qualities, or actions. In addition to their meanings, nouns in Latin display the following features: *case, number, gender,* and *declension.*

Case Latin nouns, by changing their endings, show various *cases,* which tell you how the word is to be understood in its sentence. You will learn about each case as you continue your Latin studies.

Number *Number* simply means whether the noun is singular or plural. A noun is *singular* in *number* when it names one person, place, or thing.

Larry Lee/Westlight

In the Forum of Julius Caesar, a short distance from the Roman Forum, are the three surviving columns of the Temple of Venus Genetrix, the goddess of love whom Caesar claimed as the founder of the Julian clan. In the background are the arched remains of numerous shops, and behind them the Capitoline Hill.

It is *plural* when it names more than one. The ending of the noun shows whether it is singular or plural.

īnsula	*island*	**īnsulae**	*islands*
vīta	*life*	**vītae**	*lives*

Gender *Gender* refers to whether the noun is *masculine, feminine,* or *neuter* in Latin. In English, you are used to calling female people and animals "she," and male people and animals "he." You normally refer to everything else using the neuter word "it." In Latin, every noun has a gender that must be learned.

Declensions Nouns are divided into groups called *declensions.* There are five declensions in Latin. The nouns grouped together within a single declension share the same general pattern of case endings. Nouns in the first declension all end in **-a** in the nominative singular. Most first declension nouns are feminine.

To decline a noun, add the case endings to the word's stem (base). To find the stem, drop the **-ae** from the genitive singular form. First declension nouns are declined like the model **silva** (*forest*).

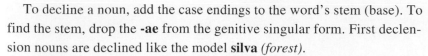

FIRST DECLENSION NOUNS		
CASE	SINGULAR	PLURAL
Nominative	**sil´va** (*forest*)	**sil´vae** (*forests*)
Genitive	**sil´vae**	**silvā´rum**
Dative	**sil´vae**	**sil´vīs**
Accusative	**sil´vam**	**sil´vās**
Ablative	**sil´vā**	**sil´vīs**

Sentences: Subject and Predicate

The word "sentence" comes from the Latin word **sententia,** which means *thought*. In both Latin and English, sentences are words grouped together to express thoughts. Every sentence has two parts: the *subject,* about which something is said, and the *predicate,* which says something about the subject and includes the verb and everything that goes with it to complete the statement.

Italy (subject) *is a peninsula* (predicate).   **Italia paenīnsula est.**
The girls (subject) *carry water* (predicate).   **Puellae aquam portant.**

In Latin, the subject of a sentence is always in the nominative case. After a linking verb (*is, are, seem,* etc.), a noun or adjective used in the predicate is also in the nominative case. This is called the *predicate nominative.* A linking verb is really nothing more than an equals sign (=). The use of the nominative case makes the identity between the subject and predicate clear.

A   =   B   A   =   B
Britannia est īnsula.   *Britain is an island.*

isolation = insulation

Did You Know?

The Romans often gave names to their racing horses. Sometimes a horse was named after a legendary figure like **Ajax** or **Daedalus.** Sometimes the name described its appearance or character like **Maculōsus** *(Spotty),* **Candidus** *(Snowy),* or **Hilarus** *(Good-tempered).* Often it represented the hopes of the owner like **Advolāns** *(Flier),* **Callidromus** *(Gorgeous Runner),* or **Sagitta** *(Arrow).*

WORD STUDY

Loan Words Many Latin words have become part of the English language. Many times the spelling of these words does not change, but meaning does. For example, the Latin first declension noun **larva**, which means *ghost,* is used in English to name the just-hatched egg of many insects because, in a pale and formless way, the larva "masks" the form of the future insect. The larva grows into a **pūpa** (the Latin word for *doll),* which looks like a small version of the adult form. The plural of each of these words in English is the same as in Latin: *larvae, pupae.* However, the **-ae** ending is pronounced like *e* in *me,* not like the *y* in *my.*

Other words of this sort are *alumna, antenna, penna, minutiae* (singular is rare). But others have adopted the English plural in *-s: area, arena, camera, formula, scintilla.* In an English dictionary, look up the present and the former meanings of each of these italicized loan words.

Nota•Bene

In Latin, word order is more flexible than in English. For example, the predicate nominative can be put anywhere in the sentence in Latin, while in English it comes after the verb.

Britannia īnsula est.
Britain is an island.

Britannia est īnsula.
Britain is an island.

LESSON OBJECTIVES

- To learn the nominative and accusative endings of first declension adjectives
- To learn the main use of the accusative case
- To understand the forms and uses of Roman numerals

[1] *of Sicily*
[2] *dolls*

SICILIA

Sicilia est magna īnsula in Eurōpā. Magna est fāma Siciliae[1], sed fortūna Siciliae nōn bona est. In Siciliā vīta est dūra. Terra et aqua sunt bonae, sed familiae sunt magnae. Magnae silvae in Siciliā nōn sunt. Viae parvae et nōn bonae sunt. Vīta est dūra in Siciliā, et fortūna nōn bona est.

5   In Siciliā sunt parvae et magnae puellae. Parvae puellae pūpās[2] amant. Magnae puellae aquam portant. Familiae puellās bonās amant. Familiae Siciliam et fāmam Siciliae amant, sed fortūnam dūram nōn amant.

Questions

1. With what continent is Sicily associated?
2. Why is life hard in Sicily?
3. What is wrong with Sicilian roads?
4. Who carries water?
5. How do Sicilians feel about their daughters?
6. How do Sicilians feel about their country?

Sicily, earlier colonized by the Greeks who subdued the native tribes in the eighth century B.C., later fell under Carthaginian influence and then became an important stepping-stone for the Romans as they extended their domain. These remains of the Greek Temple of the Dioscuri (Castor and Pollux) stand, along with five others, in the Valley of the Temples in Agrigento. Sicily was the first Roman province (235 B.C.) and a critical source of food for Rome.

Australian Picture Library/Westlight

VOCABULARY

Nouns

fā´ma, [fā´mae f.] *report, fame*   (defamation, famous)
fami´lia, [fami´liae f.] *family*   (familial, familiar)
fortū´na, [fortū´nae f.] *fortune, luck*   (fortunate, misfortune)
puel´la, [puel´lae f.] *girl*
ter´ra, [ter´rae f.] *earth, land*   (terrain, territory)
vī´ta, [vī´tae f.] *life*   (vital, vitamin)

Adjectives

[bo´nus], bo´na, [bo´num] *good*   (bonbon, bonus)
[dū´rus], dū´ra, [dū´rum] *hard*   (durable, duress)
[mag´nus], mag´na, [mag´num] *great,*   (magnify, magnitude)
  large, big
[par´vus], par´va, [par´vum] *small, little*   (parvovirus)

Verbs

a´mant *they love, like*   (amateur, amatory)
por´tant *they carry*   (portable, porter)

Nota·Bene

In the vocabulary list, each adjective is presented with three forms: the masculine, feminine, and neuter nominative singular forms, respectively.

bonus (masculine)
bona (feminine)
bonum (neuter)

GRAMMAR

Adjectives

An *adjective* is a word used to describe a noun or tell about its character: *good people*, *long road*. Any adjective that describes a noun is said to *modify* that noun. Pick out the adjectives in the second paragraph of the reading on Sicily.

In English, the spelling of an adjective almost never changes to show the number or case (function) of the noun it describes. For example, we say *good dogs*, not *goods dogs*. In Latin, an adjective changes its ending to agree with the gender, number, and case of the noun it modifies. The adjective most often follows the noun.

Silva est bona.   *The forest is good.*
                             (nominative singular)

Silvae sunt bonae.   *The forests are good.*
                                (nominative plural)

Puellae amant silvam bonam.   *The girls like the good forest.* (accusative singular)

Nota·Bene

Adjective comes from Latin **ad + iaciō**, meaning *add to*.

An adjective may be used directly with a noun, as in the third example on page 21, or it can form part of the statement made about a subject, as in the first two examples. When it is used as part of a statement about the subject, it is called a *predicate adjective*. Predicate adjectives appear after a linking verb in English, separated from the noun they describe. In Latin, the position of the predicate adjective can vary.

- Matching the case, number, and gender of an adjective with the noun it describes is called adjective–noun agreement.

- Since an adjective in Latin must agree with the noun it modifies in gender, number, and case, its position is less restricted than in English.

Magna familia bona est.   *A large family is good.*
Viae sunt longae et dūrae.   *The roads are long and hard.*

When translating a sentence from Latin to English, be sure to place the adjectives before the nouns they modify, unless the adjective is part of the predicate. In that case, put it after the linking verb.

Viae bonae sunt longae.   *The good roads are long.*
Magna est familia.   *The family is large.*

It is important to analyze a Latin sentence first to decide how you will reorder the sentence into English. Determine which adjectives are predicate adjectives and which are not. Be careful not to match an adjective with a noun with which it does not belong.

Puellae bonam vītam amant.   NOT   *The good girls love life.*
   BUT   *The girls love the good life.*

Accusative Case: Direct Object

The *accusative* case is used to indicate the *direct object* of the verb. A direct object is the word or words directly acted upon by the verb. The direct object answers the question *what* or *whom*. For example, in the sentence, *My best friend likes vegetables*, *vegetables* answers the question *Likes what?* In other words, the word *vegetables* is the direct object (target of the action) of the verb; *my best friend* is the doer or subject of the action. The direct object in English is usually placed after the verb; the subject is usually placed before it. Note the direct objects below.

The girl loves the family.
The family loves the girl.

Note how a change in the position of words in an English sentence greatly affects its meaning. In Latin, the subject and direct object are not shown by word position but by case ending.

Puella amat familiam. /   *The girl loves the family.*
   Familiam amat puella.
Familia amat puellam. /   *The family loves the girl.*
   Puellam amat familia.

A Roman mother and child.

Did You Know?

The Roman **familia** does not correspond exactly to our concept of family. It consisted of all individuals under the authority of the **paterfamiliās** *(male head of the household):* his wife, unmarried daughters, sons, clients, and slaves.

Only a change in spelling from **familiam** (accusative case) to **familia** (nominative case) makes the family love the girl. The sentences show that you must always rely on your knowledge of case endings, not word position, to make sense of a Latin sentence.

The accusative endings of first declension nouns are **-am** in the singular and **-ās** in the plural.

Familia īnsulam amat.	*The family loves the island.*
Familia īnsulās amat.	*The family loves the islands.*

Word Order in Latin and English: A Summary

- One major difference between English and Latin is the concept of word order. In English, the word order shows the connection between words in a sentence. In Latin, that connection is shown by using endings. **Anna dūcit Clāram** or **Clāram dūcit Anna** both mean *Anna leads Clara.* In English, however, a change in word order from *Anna leads Clara* to *Clara leads Anna* results in a completely different meaning.

- Adjectives in English almost always precede the noun they modify; only rarely do we use such expressions as *lady fair, Captain Courageous, Prince Charming.* In Latin, the adjective generally follows its noun. Adjectives indicating quantity and size usually precede the noun. **Magnam fāmam amat.** *She* (or *He*) *likes great fame.*

Sometimes in English the spelling of a word changes (is inflected) to reflect a change in how it functions in relation to the verb.

He watched me. (not I)
I watched him. (not he)
It is his.

📖 *Exercises*

A. Translate the following sentences. Pay careful attention to case and number.
1. Via est bona.
2. Silva parva est.
3. Īnsula magna est.
4. Familiae sunt magnae.
5. Fāmam et vītam amant.
6. Familiae īnsulam amant.
7. Puellae Siciliam amant.
8. Parvae puellae sunt bonae.
9. Puellae aquam bonam portant.
10. Crēta et Sicilia sunt magnae īnsulae.

B. Complete each sentence with the correct case endings.
1. Vi__ sunt bon__.
2. Vīt__ est dūr__.
3. Puell__ est parv__.
4. Puell__ sunt parv__.
5. Terr__ nōn bon__ est.
6. Puellae aqu__ portant.
7. Via et silva sunt magn__.
8. Familiae vīt__ bon__ amant.
9. Familiae fortūn__ bon__ amant.
10. Puell__ terr__ dūr__ nōn amant.

C. Give the Latin for the italicized words. Be sure to use the correct endings. Then translate the sentences into English.
1. Puellae *(the land)* amant.
2. Familiae *(water)* portant.
3. Puellae *(the good roads)* amant.
4. *(Large)* familiae *(small lands)* nōn amant.

Roman Numerals in English   Roman numerals are used often in English. Dates on inscriptions, on the title screens of movies, and (in lowercase) on the first few pages of many textbooks are just a few places Roman numerals are found. There are seven symbols used to indicate numbers.

I = 1	L = 50	D = 500
V = 5	C = 100	M = 1000
X = 10		

The other numbers are formed by combining these seven numerals. To add, place one or more numerals of equal or lesser value after a numeral.

III = 3	VII = 7	CCLVI = 256

To subtract, place a smaller numeral before a larger one.

IV = 4	IX = 9	XCV = 95

A smaller numeral placed between two larger numerals subtracts from the numeral that follows it.

LXXIX = 79	CCCXLV = 345	MMIX = 2009

Try writing your birth date as well as these numbers, using Roman numerals: 53, 178, 29, 543, 2010

Ball III, Strike II

ANNA ET RĀNA

LESSON OBJECTIVES

- To learn personal endings of verbs and their functions
- To learn the forms and meanings of present infinitives and the present stem of verbs
- To learn the formation and English meanings of the first conjugation, present tense
- To understand the formation of English derivatives from Latin words

Agricolae in[1] Sardiniā labōrant. Fēminae[2] etiam[3] labōrant. Sardinia magna īnsula est et terra ibi[4] dūra est. Agricolae terram exarant et irrigant[5]. Parvae puellae agricolās spectant et temptant[6] adiuvāre[7]. Puella nōmine[8] Anna magnam urnam[9] portat.

5 **Fēmina nōmine Claudia:** Salvē,[10] Anna. Quid[11] portās?
Anna: Salvē, Claudia. Urnam portō.
Fēmina nōmine Sophia: Salvēte,[10] Anna et Claudia! Quid[11] in urnā est, Anna?
Anna: Aquam in urnā portō.
10 **Agricola nōmine Sylvester:** Mactē![12] Aquam bonam amāmus. In terrā dūrā labōrāmus.
(Agricolae et fēminae aquam bonam spectant. Exclāmant.[13])
Agricola nōmine Labōriō: Quid in aquā est, puella?
Anna: Parva rāna[14] in aquā est.
15 **Claudia:** Rānās amās, Anna?
Anna: Sīc! Rānās amō. In silvā multa aqua est. In aquā multae rānae sunt. Rānās amātis?
Sophia: Minimē!
(Rāna subsultat[15] et Sophia exclāmat. Sylvester rīsitat[16].)
20 **Labōriō:** Rānās in aquā amāmus, Anna, sed nōn in urnā.
(Anna etiam rīsitat.)
Claudia: Valē,[17] Anna.
Anna: Valēte,[17] Claudia et Sophia.
(Urnam novam parat.)
25 **Claudia:** Valē, Sophia!

[1] *on*
[2] *women; wives*
[3] *also*
[4] *there*
[5] *plow and irrigate*
[6] *try*
[7] *to help*
[8] *by the name of, named*
[9] *water jar*
[10] *hello*
[11] *what*
[12] *Well done!*
[13] *They shout!*
[14] *frog*
[15] *jumps up*
[16] *laughs*
[17] *good-bye*

Questions

1. Where are the farmers working?
2. What do the women do? The small girls?
3. Why is work difficult for farm families?
4. What is Anna carrying?
5. What is wrong with the water in Anna's jar?
6. How many farmers are there in the dialogue?
7. What are their names?
8. How many women are there in the dialogue?
9. What are their names?
10. Who likes frogs? Who does not?
11. What does the name **Labōriō** suggest?

Quid puella spectat? What is this beautiful young woman gazing at so wistfully? A fresco like this is created by quickly blending colored pigments into the plaster while it is still fresh and wet. This one, once on a wall in Herculaneum, has been removed by an equally delicate process to be kept safe from damaging sunlight in a Naples museum.

VOCABULARY

Noun

agri´cola, agri´colae m. *farmer* (agriculture, agribusiness)

Adjectives

[lon´gus], lon´ga, [lon´gum] *long* (elongate, longitude)
[mul´tus], mul´ta, [mul´tum] *much* (multitude, multiply)
[no´vus], no´va, [no´vum] *new, strange* (novel, novelty)

Verbs

a´mō, amā´re, [amā´vī, amā´tus] *love, like* (amateur, amatory)
labō´rō, labōrā´re, [labōrā´vī, labōrā´tus] *work* (labor, laborious)
pa´rō, parā´re, [parā´vī, parā´tus] *get, get ready, prepare* (preparation)
por´tō, portā´re, [portā´vī, portā´tus] *carry* (import, portable)
spec´tō, spectā´re, [spectā´vī, spectā´tus] *look (at), watch* (inspect, spectacle)

Adverbs

mi´nimē *no, not at all*
sīc *yes, thus, so*

In the vocabulary list, each verb is listed with four forms. These represent the four principal parts of the verb. The first form is the first person singular present tense and the second form is the present infinitive. You will not use the bracketed third and fourth principal parts for a while, but their regularity of form makes them easy to learn now.

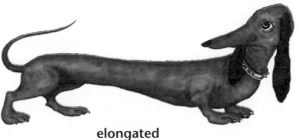

elongated

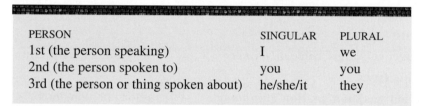

GRAMMAR

Verbs

Verbs tell what a subject is or does. The verb expresses either the whole predicate or part of it.

Puella parva est.	*The girl is small.* (part)
Puellae labōrant.	*The girls work.* (whole)

Verbs also indicate the time or *tense* of an action, that is, whether the action is in the past, present, or future. In English, the verb usually, but not always, changes to show the tense. In Latin, verbs always change to show tense.

videō *I see*	**vīdī** *I saw*
audiō *I hear*	**audīvī** *I heard*
pōnō *I put*	**posuī** *I put*

Verbs have three *persons* in both the singular and the plural. English indicates the persons by the use of personal pronouns.

PERSON	SINGULAR	PLURAL
1st (the person speaking)	I	we
2nd (the person spoken to)	you	you
3rd (the person or thing spoken about)	he/she/it	they

However, in Latin personal pronouns are usually omitted. Personal endings show the person and number of the subject. In a sense, they are the equivalent of personal pronouns. The most common personal endings are:

	SINGULAR		PLURAL
I	**-ō** (or **-m**)	we	**-mus**
you	**-s**	you	**-tis**
he/she/it	**-t**	they	**-nt**

These endings must become as familiar to you as the personal pronouns in English. Memorize them in the order shown above.

Present Infinitive

In English, the infinitive is the verb form that is introduced by *to*: *to go*, *to be*, *to prepare*. It does not show person or number. In Latin, there is no separate word corresponding to the English word *to*. The present infinitive of all regular Latin verbs ends in **-re**.

parāre *to get*	**ponere** *to put*
vidēre *to see*	**audīre** *to hear*

The word *tense* comes from the Latin **tempus** meaning *time*.

Present Stem

The present stem of a verb is used as the building block to form three tenses, including the present. To form the stem, you drop the infinitive ending -**re**.

parā~~re~~	parā-	pone~~re~~	pone-
vidē~~re~~	vidē-	audī~~re~~	audī-

Present Tense: First Conjugation

Latin verbs are divided, according to the present stem, into four classes called *conjugations*. Verbs with a present stem ending in **-ā** belong to the first conjugation. A first conjugation verb is *conjugated* in the present tense by adding the personal endings to the present stem.

Sometimes verbs change in English to show differences of person, for example, *he is* (not *he are*); *she writes* (not *she write*).

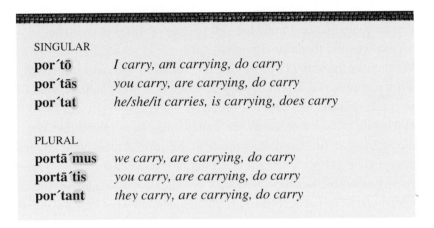

SINGULAR

por´tō	*I carry, am carrying, do carry*
por´tās	*you carry, are carrying, do carry*
por´tat	*he/she/it carries, is carrying, does carry*

PLURAL

portā´mus	*we carry, are carrying, do carry*
portā´tis	*you carry, are carrying, do carry*
por´tant	*they carry, are carrying, do carry*

Note that all vowels are shortened before final -**t, -nt,** or -**m.** In the first person singular, the stem vowel -**ā** disappears entirely before the personal ending -**ō,** and the ending -**m** is not used in this instance.

Observe the three ways to translate the Latin present tense: *I carry* (common present), *I am carrying* (progressive present), and *I do carry* (emphatic present). Unlike English, Latin does not use "do" and "am" as auxiliary (helping) verbs. For example, in English one says, *Do you carry? Are you carrying?* In Latin, one simply says, **Portās?** Latin does not have progressive and emphatic verb forms corresponding to English. Do not say **Est portat** for *He is carrying.* **Portat** is enough.

Remember that when a noun (in the nominative case) is used as the subject, the personal pronoun should not be expressed: **Puella portat.** *The girl carries*, not *The girl she carries.*

The change in a verb's personal ending to show the person and number of its subject is called subject–verb agreement: **Puella labōrat** *(The girl is working),* but **Puellae labōrant** *(The girls are working).* It is important that verbs always agree in person and number with their subject, both in English and in Latin.

Two singular subjects connected by **et** *(and)* require a plural verb, just as in English when *and* joins two singular subjects: **Puella et agricola aquam portant** *(The girl and the farmer carry [not carries] water).*

C. M. Dixon

Public water systems that supplied this fountain in Pompeii were common alternatives to private wells. Members of the familia were often sent here to fetch water for use at home. Aqueducts brought the water down by gravity from mountain springs far away, and an underground piping system distributed it throughout the city.

Translating Latin

To translate a language means to communicate the meaning and expression of one language in the words of another. A good translation should accurately reflect not only the meaning of the original writer's words but something of his or her manner of speaking as well. Translating effectively is in great part a skill that can be learned. Following are some procedures to follow to translate Latin into English successfully.

1. Begin by reading the Latin sentence aloud, trying to get some idea of its meaning from the words you know. If necessary, read the sentence again to get a clearer idea of its parts and how they may relate to each other. Go slowly, taking each word in the order you find it, until you reach the end of the sentence. Do you see any words that might be nominatives (and that have nouns and adjectives in agreement with them)? Are they singular or plural? Do you see any words that could be accusatives and therefore direct objects?

2. What about the verb? Even though it is regularly the most important word in a sentence, it will usually be at the end, and you must wait for it. Is the verb singular or plural; first, second, or third person? Does it agree with the word or words you believe may be nominatives? Would the accusatives fit in as direct objects of the verb? At this point you will have a good grasp of the basic meaning of the sentence.

3. Even in a simple sentence there may be other words or phrases for which you have not accounted. If you understand what they mean, you can fit them in, even if they appear to be out of the order you would expect in English.

4. Now when the whole sense of the sentence in all its parts becomes clear to you, write or speak all of it in good English, using good English word order.

Well-to-do Romans often decorated the rooms of their houses with fresco wall paintings. Wallpaper was unknown. This scene from the Palatine house of the Empress Livia (the wife of Augustus) creates the effect of an indoor garden.

David J. Driscoll

5. This process requires that you know not just the Latin vocabulary but also the forms the words may take. Your recognition of these forms must, and eventually will, become automatic. Then your translations, which will be slow at first, will eventually become nearly as fast as writing or speaking English.

EXAMPLE:	**In Siciliā, īnsulā magnā in Eurōpā, terram bonam agricolae amant.**
THINK:	The sentence has something to do with Sicily, an island, Europe, farmers, and love.
THINK:	**In Siciliā**—Easy! Just like English! The long **ā** means it cannot be nominative, nor can **īnsulā magnā in Eurōpā**, for the same reason.
THINK:	**terram bonam**—*earth* is accusative singular feminine, probably the direct object, and *good,* also accusative singular feminine, very likely goes with it.
THINK:	**agricolae**—*farmers* could be nominative plural and the subject of the sentence
THINK:	**amant**—*love,* third person plural, fits with **agricolae** as its subject
AND THINK AGAIN:	*In Sicily, island large in Europe, earth good farmers love* or *In Sicily, a large island in Europe, the farmers love good earth.*
THINK:	The sentence makes sense. I've got it!

Now finally say aloud, and with a certain freedom if you wish:

In Sicily, a large island in Europe, the farmers like good soil.

In English, direct objects almost always follow the action verb. In Latin, direct objects usually precede the verb, so you should change the order in converting to English.

The Art Archive/Museo Civico Trieste/Dagli Orti

A modern artist's recreation of a Roman wedding, corresponding in only a few details to what we know of the actual event. Here the bride, in a white tunic and orange veil (for which brides today substitute an orange-blossom bouquet) appears to be making a sacrifice before a cult statue at an altar in a temple (perhaps of Juno, the patron goddess of marriage). Behind the bridal pair, a man plays a lyre. A formal Roman wedding was as elaborate as one today, but the wedding vow was beautifully simple. The bride merely said **Ubi tū Gāius, ego Gāia,** *Wherever you are John Doe, I am Mary Doe,* and that was it.

Did You Know?

The early Romans had three forms of marriage. The first, **coemptiō,** was a symbolic bride-purchase during which the bridegroom paid a penny to the father or guardian in exchange for his bride. The second form, **ūsus,** involved a couple's living together for at least one year. The third form, **confarreatiō,** was the most elaborate wedding ceremony (even including a sort of wedding cake).

🁢 *Exercises*

A. Read the words aloud; then translate them.
1. Amō; parās; spectat
2. Spectās; parō; labōrat
3. Portāmus; amātis; parant
4. Portant; amāmus; parātis
5. Labōrāmus; parat; est; sunt

B. Read the sentences aloud; then translate them. Pay attention to the endings.
1. Puella terram spectat.
2. Multam aquam portant.
3. Puella bona viam dūram spectat.
4. Puellae et agricolae aquam parant.
5. Agricola et puella silvam spectant.

C. Give the Latin for the italicized words. Be sure to use the correct endings.
1. Puella *(is working)*.
2. Agricolae *(carry)* aquam.
3. Multās īnsulās *(I am looking at)*.
4. *(You* [sing.] *like)* parvam puellam.
5. Terram bonam *(we like)*.
6. Parat *(to carry)* aquam.
7. *(Are they watching)* agricolam?
8. *(We do love)* puellās; bonae *(they are)*.

D. Complete each sentence with the correct endings.
1. Vīt__ dūr__ est.
2. Vi__ nov__ sunt bon__.
3. Puellae silv__ amant.
4. Agricol__ aquam bonam spectant.
5. Long__ īnsul__ agricolae amant.

WORD STUDY

Derivatives An *amiable* person is "lovable." What is a *portable* computer? A *respectable* job? Why do we use *insulation*? What does a *porter* do? An *elaborate* carving is one that required a lot of *work*. An *amateur* pursues his interest for the *love* of it. What is *durum* wheat? What sort of person is *introspective*? What is meant by *amity* among nations?

As we have already seen, many scientific terms in English are borrowed directly from the Latin first declension as loan words. Here are a few more: *amoeba, amoebae* (or *amoebas*); *nebula, nebulae* (or *nebulas*); *nova, novae* (or *novas*); *scapula, scapulae* (or *scapulas*); *vertebra, vertebrae* (or *vertebras*). Look up the meanings of these words if they are unfamiliar.

LESSON IV

VIAE

LESSON OBJECTIVES
- To learn the case endings of second declension masculine nouns ending in **-us**
- To distinguish masculine and feminine genders and to learn to form second declension adjectives
- To understand the Latin origins of English derivatives

Multae viae in Italiā erant et sunt. Multae viae Rōmānae erant bonae. Via Appia in Italiā erat et est. Ōlim[1] Via Appia erat via Rōmāna. Nōn nova est sed fāma eius[2] est magna, quod longa et bona via est. Multae viae Americānae ōlim erant malae, sed nunc bonae sunt. In Italiā et in Americā bonās viās laudāmus. Viās malās nōn amāmus. Viās dūrās amātis?

Multī carrī et equī erant in viīs[3] Rōmānīs. Agricolae in Viā Appiā erant. Servī magnī et parvī in viīs erant. Ubi nunc equī sunt? Ubi carrī sunt? Nunc servī nōn sunt.

Agricola carrum bonum parat. Agricola carrum laudat, quod novus et magnus est. Puellae carrōs nōn amant, quod dūrī sunt. Puellae equōs amant, quod bonī sunt. Agricola equōs amat, quod in terrā labōrant. Servum malum nōn laudat, quod nōn labōrat.

5 [1] *once*
[2] *its*
[3] *on the roads*

Questions

1. Where is the Appian Way?
2. Why is the Appian Way famous?
3. How are roads in the United States similar to Roman roads?
4. Who were some of the people who used the Appian Way?
5. What people or animals are no longer found on the Appian Way?
6. Why don't the girls like traveling by wagon?
7. What do both the girls and the farmer like?
8. Do they like them for the same reasons? Explain.
9. Why doesn't the farmer like the slave?

The **Via Appia** first connected Rome and Capua, and it later extended as far as Brundisium. See the map on page 14.

A mail coach was one means of delivering messages and parcels throughout Rome and the empire. An earlier system in which both private citizens and public officials used hired messengers called **tabellārī** was replaced by a public service under Augustus. Relays of messengers changing horses and carriages at way stations could average about fifty miles a day, and more if the need were urgent. What discovery and inventions have made this ancient version of the Pony Express obsolete?

Erich Lessing/Art Resource, NY

VOCABULARY

Nouns

car´rus, [car´rī] m. *cart, wagon*   (car, carriage)
e´quus, [e´quī] m. *horse*   (equestrian, equine)
ser´vus, [ser´vī] m. *slave*   (servile, servitude)

Adjective

ma´lus, ma´la, [ma´lum] *bad*   (malice, malign)

Verbs

e´rat *was, there was, he/she/it was*
e´rant *were, there were, they were*
lau´dō, laudā´re, [laudā´vī, laudā´tus] *praise*   (laudatory)

Adverbs

nunc *now*
u´bi *where*   (ubiquitous)

Conjunction

quod *because*

The Romans built a highly efficient road system throughout the empire. This one, still in use in Vetulonia, Italy, shows how well the top layer of stones fitted together. The various layers of sand, stone, and pebbles provided a stable foundation.

SEF/Art Resource, NY

GRAMMAR

Second Declension Nouns

Nouns that belong to the second declension have an **-ī** ending in the genitive case; the nominative singular ending varies. Nouns and adjectives of this declension whose nominative ends in **-us,** like **servus**, are declined as follows.

	SECOND DECLENSION NOUNS	
CASE	SINGULAR	PLURAL
Nominative	ser´vus *(slave)*	ser´vī *(slaves)*
Genitive	ser´vī	servō´rum
Dative	ser´vō	ser´vīs
Accusative	ser´vum	ser´vōs
Ablative	ser´vō	ser´vīs

Gender

In English, and sometimes in Latin, *gender* is a distinction in the form of words corresponding to a distinction of sex (natural gender). It is shown by change of word (*father*, **pater**; *mother*, **māter**), by change of endings (*master*, **dominus**; *mistress*, **domina**), or by use of a prefix *(he-goat, she-goat)*. *Father*, *master*, *he-goat* are masculine words; *mother*, *mistress*, *she-goat* are feminine words.

In English, nouns that are the names of sexless things are neuter. However, many nouns that would be considered neuter in English are masculine or feminine in Latin: **via** (f.), *way*; **carrus** (m.), *cart*. In these cases, the gender is usually indicated not by the meaning of the word but by its ending or declension (grammatical gender).

Nouns of the first declension ending in **-a** are feminine (except a few that name males); those of the second declension ending in **-us** are regularly masculine. Other nouns in the second declension ending in **-um** are regularly neuter. For nouns of other declensions, the gender assigned to a noun does not obey any rule and must be memorized: **virtus** (f.) *courage;* **finis** (m.) *end*.

Adjectives have forms to match the gender of the nouns they modify: **parva puella, parvus equus, servī bonī.** They agree in this way with their nouns in number, case, and gender. In many instances, *but not always,* the endings of the adjectives will match the spelling of the nouns they modify, as the preceding examples illustrate.

WORD STUDY

Loan Words Most know that a *bonus* is something *good*. *Genius (inborn talent)* and *bonus* are just two of many loan words the Latin second declension has given to English in their original forms. Here are others: *alumnus, alumni; bacillus, bacilli; circus, circuses; focus, focuses* (or *foci*); *stimulus, stimuli* (or *stimuluses*).

Look up the meanings and the plurals of *campus, fungus, gladiolus, humus, locus, quietus.*

Names of some American cities and towns with Latin names that show the influence of Rome on the building of this country are Alma, Americus, Augusta, Aurora, Cincinnati, Columbia, Columbus, Concordia, Emporia, Pomona, Urbana, and Utica. Perhaps your hometown has a classical name.

Oral Practice

1. Give the nominative plural of **īnsula, equus, fortūna, carrus** together with the adjective *good* in Latin.
2. Give the accusative plural of **aqua, servus, fāma, carrus, via** together with the adjective *bad* in Latin.
3. Give the Latin for *you* (sing.) *get, they are carrying, we do praise, she is working.*

Did You Know?

Slaves in Roman times were sometimes slave owners themselves. A cashier named Musicus Scurranus, who was employed in one of the provincial treasuries of Emperor Tiberius, was very wealthy and had at least sixteen household slaves of his own. These slaves evidently admired Scurranus, because they dedicated a funeral monument in his honor.

Exercises

A. Translate the following sentences.

1. Viae sunt malae.
2. Servus erat parvus.
3. Servus nōn est malus.
4. Equī magnī sunt et bonī.
5. Carrī magnī sunt sed equī sunt parvī.
6. Servī aquam laudant.
7. Servus malus in terrā labōrat.
8. Agricola magnōs carrōs spectat.
9. Ubi servī multōs carrōs parant?
10. Puella et agricola longam vītam laudant.

B. Give the Latin for the italicized words.

1. *(Wagons)* nunc nōn sunt.
2. Nunc fortūna *(bad)* est.
3. *(The farmer)* equōs bonōs parat.
4. Agricolae *(the good slaves)* laudant.
5. Ubi est *(the large island)?*
6. Amāmus *(the girl)* quod bona est.
7. Aquam *(the large slaves)* portant.
8. *(Large wagons)* spectātis.

C. Complete each sentence with the correct endings.

1. Bon__ est equus.
2. Carrī long__ sunt.
3. Serv__ aqu__ portant.
4. Ubi sunt vi__ long__?
5. Puella est parv__ et bon__.
6. Puellae īnsulam ama__.
7. Serv__ agricola specta__.
8. Servus equum mal__ nōn ama__.
9. In īnsulā terr__ dūr__ erat.
10. Bon__ serv__ et puellam bon__ laudās.

GLIMPSES OF ROMAN LIFE

ROMAN ROADS AND TRAVEL

ROMAN BUILDING SKILLS

Perhaps nothing demonstrates the industry, thoroughness, and engineering skill of the Romans better than the system of roads with which they linked their empire. Built like walls as much as three feet deep into the ground and running in straight lines across all but the most difficult terrain, many of these roads are still in use today. They are more than monuments to Roman building skills; they are testimony to the practical vision of a people who quickly saw that their military conquests would be made permanent and that commerce and colonization would flourish only with an extensive and efficient means of communication. The Roman army, under the supervision of engineers, built much of the nearly fifty thousand miles of hard-surface highways—enough to circle the globe twice—radiating out from Rome through Italy and beyond. For a faster means of travel, the world had to wait until the eighteenth century when the invention of the steam engine made railroads and steamships possible.

The construction of our railroads is a better parallel to the Romans' efforts than our present system of superhighways, for westward expansion was supported initially by the railway system. Even now, well over two thousand years after the Romans built many of their roads, America's system of interstate highways is still being completed.

Remains of the **milliārium aureum**, the Golden Milestone. The Emperor Augustus erected the column in the Forum to signify the beginning of all the roads of the Empire. Milestones giving the distance from this reference point were placed along the roads themselves.

APPIAN WAY

The queen of Roman highways (**rēgīna viārum,** as the Roman poet Statius said) was the Appian Way, built in 312 B.C., just after the Romans had subdued Latium. Like most Roman roads, it took its name from its builder, the statesman Appius Claudius. The **Via Appia** stretched about 130 miles from Rome to Capua, the most important city in southern Italy, and brought all Campania close to the capital. Later it was extended more than two hundred miles across Italy to Brundisium, the important seaport and gateway to Greece and the Orient. The first part of its course, just outside the boundaries of ancient Rome, was lined by family tombs. Much of the **Via Appia** is still in use today.

It is not difficult to imagine the bustle and confusion of these great arteries of commerce, crowded with travelers and vehicles. People traveled by foot, on horses and mules, or in carriages. Along the roads were milestones to indicate distances from the **milliārium aureum,** the golden milestone erected by Augustus in Rome. Footpaths often were constructed along the roadside. There were benches and fountains where the weary might refresh themselves and watering troughs for the animals. Still, travel was slow and difficult (the word *travel* basically means *torture;* compare the related word *travail).* Fifty to sixty miles a day was a fast rate for people in a great hurry. Half that speed was average.

Hotel accommodations were often poor. Those who could afford it avoided the cramped, dirty, and uncomfortable inns (where horses were sheltered under the same roof) and stayed overnight instead at country villas belonging to themselves or to their friends. A wealthy Roman might have half a dozen or more villas scattered throughout Italy, and he was always prepared to extend hospitality to friends.

TRAVEL BY WATER

Travel by water was avoided if possible, but there were fortunes to be made in overseas trade. Merchants swallowed their fears of the unpredictable sea and weather and took their cargoes to sea in small vessels propelled by sails and oars. Sailing was often dangerous, and ships without compasses for guidance skirted the coast as much as possible. Sailors almost never put to sea during the winter months.

All these roads, by land or sea, led back to Rome. Along them came not just people and goods but ideas: Greek art and literature, Eastern religions, and Christianity, which was to have a major effect on European history during and after the last years of the Roman Empire.

QUESTIONS

1. Why were the Romans great road builders?
2. What effect has rapid transportation had on the development of the United States, Canada, and Europe?
3. For many centuries, people could travel no faster than the horses they rode. What discoveries have enabled us to move faster?

Larry Mulvehill/Photo Researchers

The Roman system of roads and road building, still a wonder in the modern world, was originally designed to move troops rapidly to the various frontiers. Commerce and Roman culture inevitably followed. This section of the Appian Way, still in use south of Rome in Vetulonia, Italy, shows how carefully the basalt paving stones were fitted over a solid foundation of sand, pebbles, and large rocks.

VOCABULARY

Nouns

Pronounce the following nouns aloud, and provide the genitive, gender, and meaning of each.

agricola	fāma	puella	via
aqua	familia	servus	vīta
carrus	fortūna	silva	
equus	īnsula	terra	

Adjectives

Pronounce the following adjectives. Then provide the feminine nominative form and meaning of each.

bonus	longus	malus	novus
dūrus	magnus	multus	parvus

Verbs

Pronounce the following verbs, and provide their meanings and first two principal parts (for **erat**, **erant**, **est**, and **sunt**, just provide the meanings).

erat, erant	amō	laudō	portō
est, sunt	labōrō	parō	spectō

Adverbs

Pronounce the following adverbs, and provide the meaning of each.

minimē	nunc	ubi
nōn	sīc	

Conjunctions

Pronounce the following conjunctions, and provide the meaning of each.

et	quod	sed

GRAMMAR SUMMARY

Nouns

In Latin, nouns:
- regularly show case and number by their endings: **fēmina** *(woman)* (nom. sing.), **fēminae** *(women)* (nom. pl.), **fēminam** (acc. sing.), **fēminās** (acc. pl.);
- can be placed before or after the verb without changing the meaning of the sentence: **Equus agricolam spectat** or **Agricolam spectat equus.** *The horse watches the farmer;*
- can have feminine or masculine gender for things: **īnsula** (f.), **carrus** (m.).

In English, nouns:
- regularly show number but not case, by endings: *woman, women; puppy, puppies* (number); *he, him; she, her* (case);
- regularly must appear before a verb to indicate the subject and after the verb to indicate the object or target of an action;
- show only natural gender: masculine for male persons or animals, feminine for female persons or animals, neuter for things: *it is large* (referring to an island), but *he is big* (referring to a man).

Adjectives

In Latin, adjectives:
- change in form to agree in number, gender, and case with the noun they modify: **fāma bona, multī equī, parvam silvam;**
- generally follow the noun (except when showing quantity or size, or positioned in the predicate): **Terrae novae sunt dūrae.**

In English, adjectives:
- generally do not change form to agree with the noun they modify: *large forest, large forests;*
- usually precede the noun: *good reputation, many horses, small forest.*

Verbs

In Latin:

- verb endings show person and number: **amō** (first person singular); **amant** (third person singular); an exception is the infinitive (**amāre** *to love*), which does not show person or number;
- subject pronouns are usually omitted: **amō** *I love;* **amant** *they love;*
- verbs agree with their subject in person and number: **Agricola et servus labōrant.**

In English:

- some verb endings show person and number: *carries* (third person singular); *carry* (all other persons and numbers);
- subject pronouns are regularly used: *he carries, we carry;*
- verbs agree with their subjects in person and number: *The farmer and the slave are working.*

ENDINGS AND STEMS

1. What are the singular and plural endings of the nominative case in the first declension? In the second declension?
2. What are the singular and plural endings of the accusative case in the first declension? In the second declension?
3. How do you find the present stem of a Latin verb? With what letter does the stem of a first conjugation verb end? What are the six personal endings?

UNIT PRACTICE

A. In each sentence, identify the subject, the verb, and the object or predicate nominative. Then translate each sentence.
   1. Equus est parvus.
   2. Longam viam nunc parātis.
   3. Carrī parvī equōs nōn portant.
   4. Agricola fortūnam bonam laudat.
   5. Servus et puella multam aquam portant.
   6. Anna puellās spectat.
   7. In Siciliā viae sunt parvae.
   8. Virginia et Anna equōs amant.
   9. Silvae magnae et longae erant.
   10. In silvā aquam bonam parātis?

B. Give the Latin for the italicized words.
   1. Anna loves *horses*.
   2. It is *a long road*.
   3. My slaves are *small*.
   4. Anna is *a good girl*.
   5. I look at the *large wagons*.
   6. These horses are *small*.
   7. He looks at *a small island*.
   8. We get *good water*.

C. Identify the case and number of the following: **fortūna, īnsulam, equī, servōs, via.** Give the correct form of **magnus** with each of the preceding words.

WORD STUDY

1. What is a loan word?
2. What is a derivative?
3. Judging from the meaning of their Latin roots, determine the meaning of the following italicized words: a *laudable* success, *a subservient* manner, to live in *amity*, a *multitude* of errors, *aquatic* sports.

UNIT I ASSESSMENT · LESSONS I–IV

VOCABULARY

Circle the word that best completes each sentence.

1. _____ in aquā sunt.
   a. Viae
   b. Silvae
   c. Īnsulae
   d. Rōma

2. _____ aquam portant.
   a. Puellae
   b. Terrae
   c. Fortūnae
   d. Fāmae

3. Familia longam _____ nōn amat.
   a. silvā
   b. viam
   c. vītam
   d. fāma

4. Agricola equum _____ laudat.
   a. bonum
   b. longum
   c. dūram
   d. malum

5. Carrus multōs servōs _____.
   a. spectant
   b. portat
   c. amant
   d. parat

GRAMMAR

Complete each sentence with the correct case endings.

6. Puell___ est parv___.
7. Familiae fortūn___ bon___ amant.
8. Agricol___ terram bonam spectant.
9. Carrī long___ sunt.
10. In īnsulā terr___ dūr___ erat.

TRANSLATION

Translate the following sentences.

11. Britannia est īnsula.
12. Magna est familia.
13. Agricola et puella silvam spectant.
14. Ubi sunt magnī equī?
15. Servus malus in terrā nunc labōrat.

INVESTIGATION

Find the answers to these questions from any lesson in Unit I.

16. Arrange these Roman numerals in ascending order: M I X V D L C.
17. MDCCLXXVI dates the year _____.
18. XXXVIII et XLIV sunt _____.
19. Write these years in Roman numerals:
    1812   1964   2010.
20. Subtract 3,384 from 5,387. Write the answer in Roman numerals.

CULTURE

Vērum aut Falsum? Indicate whether each statement is true or false.

21. The Romans built enough miles of roads to circle the globe three times.
22. Roman roads were constructed much like walls.
23. The Appian Way was named for its destination.
24. There is no evidence of the Appian Way today.
25. Romans preferred travel by land to travel by sea.

A young Roman girl gets ready to spin. In the early days, mothers taught their daughters such skills as cooking and spinning. Later, wealthy women handed over the care of their children to nurses and slaves.

FROM LATIN TO ENGLISH

Apply your knowledge of Latin roots to determine the best meaning of the italicized words.

26. It was clear to the audience that his speech was a *laudable* success.
    a. interesting
    b. praiseworthy
    c. stimulating
    d. timely
27. The politician regarded the *conservation* of energy as a topic of great importance.
    a. destruction
    b. misuse
    c. wise use
    d. location
28. The kingdoms on opposite sides of the river lived for many years in *amity*.
    a. fear
    b. dread
    c. happiness
    d. friendly terms
29. After reading the paper, the professor could not believe the *multitude* of errors.
    a. large number
    b. small number
    c. severity
    d. stupidity
30. Although she had played tennis for many years, her passion was *aquatic* sports.
    a. team
    b. winter
    c. contact
    d. water

ROMAN INFLUENCE

Unit Objectives

- To learn the primary uses of the genitive, dative, and ablative cases
- To learn the future active and present imperative of the first conjugation
- To learn about the expansion of Roman influence

The Temple of Hadrian at Ephesus, on the southwest coast of Turkey, is a good example of the way Roman influence spread. Founded by Greek colonists around 1000 B.C. on a major trade route and near an important religious center, Ephesus was a prize for which many nations fought until the King of Pergamum left it to Rome in his will in 133 B.C. The Temple of Artemis here was one of the Seven Wonders of the World, and it was here that St. Paul caused a riot among the populace by preaching against idolatry. The Temple of Hadrian (second century B.C.) gave the people a place to worship the spirit of the emperor. Ephesus, rich in ruins, temples, libraries, gymnasia, theaters, mosques, churches, and history, remains one of the most important tourist sites in modern Turkey.

Robert Frerck/© Tony Stone Images

RŌMA

¹ *at first*
² *Romans*
³ *on account of its seven hills*
⁴ *city*
⁵ *square*
⁶ *afterwards*
⁷ *once*
⁸ *not now; no longer*
⁹ *ancient*
¹⁰ *even, also*

Rōma prīmō¹ parva erat et Rōmānī² nōn multī erant. Propter Septimontium,³ urbs⁴ nōn plāna erat, sed fōrma Rōmae quadrāta⁵ erat. Posteā⁶ magna et clāra urbs erat; rēgīna terrārum erat. Fortūna Rōmae et Rōmānōrum bona erat.

5   Viae Rōmānae multae et longae erant. Rēgīna viārum erat Via Appia. Ōlim⁷ magnus numerus carrōrum et equōrum in viīs Rōmae erat; nunc in viīs Italiae nōn multī carrī et equī sunt. Ōlim multī servī erant in viīs Rōmānīs, sed nōn iam⁸ servī in Rōmā sunt.

Quod aqua bona erat magna cūra Rōmānōrum, erant multī et longī
10 aquaeductūs in Latiō antīquō⁹. Etiam¹⁰ nunc cōpia aquae clārae est cūra multōrum Italōrum et multōrum Americānōrum.

Fāma Rōmae magna est. Fāma Americae etiam magna est. Americānī viās bonās et architectūram Rōmānōrum amant.

Multī Americānī Rōmam laudant; ruīnās antīquās Rōmae spectant et
15 laudant. Fōrmam Rōmae antīquae et novae spectant. Pictūrās ruīnārum Rōmānārum amātis?

A model of ancient Rome as it appeared in A.D. 300. This view across the Tiber River shows warehouses along its banks and the Circus Maximus (the long oval in the center). To the left above it are the Palatine Hill and the Coliseum. In the far upper left, only partially visible, is the Roman Forum. This model is in the Museum of Roman Civilization in Rome.

Scala/Art Resource, NY

Questions

1. What was Rome's original size and shape?
2. Did good luck have anything to do with its growth?
3. The Romans built many long aqueducts. Why?
4. What concern do Italians and Americans today all have in common?
5. What attraction does Rome have now for sightseers?
6. Just as the **Via Appia** was called *queen of the roads,* Rome was called queen of what?
7. Answer the final question in the passage in Latin.

VOCABULARY

Nouns

ci´bus, ci´bī m. *food*
cō´pia, cō´piae f. *supply, abundance*　　(copious, cornucopia)
cū´ra, cū´rae f. *worry, care, concern*　　(curator, curious)
fōr´ma, fōr´mae f. *shape*　　(formal, reformatory)
nu´merus, nu´merī m. *number*　　(enumerate, numerical)
rēgī´na, rēgī´nae f. *queen*　　(regina, *a loan word*)

Adjectives

clā´rus, clā´ra, [clā´rum] *clear, famous*　　(clarinet, Clara)
plā´nus, plā´na, [plā´num] *level, flat*　　(aquaplane, plain)

Remember that the vocabulary entry gives a lot of information for each noun: the nominative singular, the genitive singular, the gender, and the meaning. These four things and your knowledge of the standard endings of the declension to which a noun belongs give you control over that noun and knowledge of its meaning.

GRAMMAR

The Genitive Case

In English, the objective case following the preposition *of* shows various relationships between nouns, including the idea of possession or ownership. (There is also a possessive case in English indicated by the addition of *-'s,* or *-s',* or sometimes by the apostrophe alone, to the word indicating the owner.)

In Latin, these various relations between nouns are expressed by endings in the genitive case. No separate word meaning *of* or punctuation mark like the apostrophe is needed.

Possession in English

the father of the boy	=	the boy's father
the wagons of the slave	=	the slave's wagons
the father of the boys	=	the boys' father
the wagons of the slaves	=	the slaves' wagons

Possession in Latin (Genitive of Possession)

Latin expresses the relationship of possessor and possessed (two nouns) by attaching the genitive case ending to the word indicating the possessor. The endings of the genitive case for nouns and adjectives of the first and second declensions are:

	SINGULAR	PLURAL
FIRST DECLENSION	**-ae**	**-ārum**
	viae *road's;*	**viārum** *roads';*
	of (the) road	*of (the) roads*
SECOND DECLENSION	**-ī**	**-ōrum**
	servī *slave's;*	**servōrum** *slaves';*
	of (the) slave	*of (the) slaves*

equus agricolae   *the horse of the farmer, the farmer's horse*

fāma multōrum Italōrum   *the fame of many Italians, many Italians' fame*

The genitive case word (possessor) in Latin usually follows the word it possesses. Notice also that any adjectives that describe or limit the genitive case word will agree with it in case, number, and gender.

Dave Bartruff/CORBIS

Not all genitives are genitives of possession. There are a number of other uses of the genitive which you will eventually learn, but they all can almost always be translated with *of*. The genitive's basic function is to limit or define the other noun, almost like an adjective. *The farmer's wagon* limits all the wagons in the world to that one wagon the farmer owns; *a coat of wool (= a wool coat),* distinguishes it from all coats made of other materials.

Oral Practice

Give the Latin nominative, genitive, and accusative case forms, both singular and plural, of *water, supply, wagon, land, number.* Translate the genitives.

Did You Know?

The early Romans ate more vegetables and fish than meat and often ate their food cold. There was originally little difference between the meals of the wealthy and the poor. However, these frugal eating habits contrasted sharply with those of wealthy Romans of later times, who relished such delicacies as sow's udder in tuna sauce, raw sea urchins, peacock, flamingos, and jellyfish.

Roman cultural influence extended throughout Europe far beyond Italy, even to England (Britannia), which was under Roman control for nearly five centuries. These well-preserved Roman baths at Bath reflect the typical Roman concern for water, both as a commodity and as a convenience.

Translation hint: In English, when the subject follows the verb, the sentence (unless it is a question) begins with *there*. In Latin, no such word is used.

Sunt multae viae.
There are many roads.

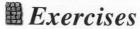

Exercises

A. Translate the following sentences. Pay careful attention to the endings.

1. Equōs amāmus.
2. Est cōpia aquae bonae.
3. Fōrma terrae in Siciliā plāna nōn est.
4. Cūrae puellārum nōn parvae sunt.
5. Numerus servōrum in īnsulā erat magnus.
6. Silvās clārās īnsulae magnae spectātis.

B. Give the Latin for the italicized words.

1. Cōpiam *(of good water)* portāmus.
2. Terram novam *(we are looking at).*
3. *(There is not)* rēgīna Americae.
4. Parvus est numerus *(of girls).*
5. Cibus *(of the slaves)* parvus erat.

C. Translate the following sentences.

1. Where is the slaves' water? The slaves' water is in the cart.
2. Where are the carts of the farmers? The carts of the farmers are on the land.
3. Where are the horses of the girls? The horses of the girls are in the forest.
4. Where are the lands of the queen? The lands of the queen are in Britain.
5. Where is the frog of the slave? The frog of the slave is in the water.

WORD STUDY

Borrowed Phrases Many Latin phrases and abbreviations are used regularly in English.

i.e. (id est)	*that is*
e.g. (exempli gratia)	*for example*
etc. (et cetera)	*and the rest, and so forth*
cf. (confer)	*compare*
magna cum laude	*with great praise, honor*
in loco parentis	*in place of a parent*
carpe diem	*seize the day,* i.e. *enjoy the moment*
Magna Carta	the *Great Paper,* the document signed in 1215 that is one of the cornerstones of English civil liberties

A detail of the Magna Carta, the charter of English political and civil liberties, written in 1215. Can you find a word you already know? (Try line 6.)

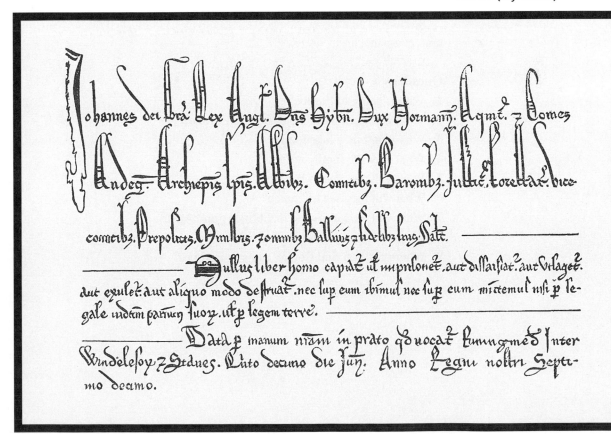

LESSON OBJECTIVE
- To learn the future tense of first conjugation verbs

EURŌPA

Ad Eurōpam crās nāvigābō; tōta[1] familia nāvigābit. Nautae nāvem[2] novam parābunt. Magnam pecūniam ad Eurōpam portābimus. Cibum nōn parābimus, quod in nāvī[3] magna cōpia cibī bonī est.

Magnās undās crās spectābimus; sed aquam plānam, nōn magnās undās,
5 amāmus. Ad īnsulam clāram Britanniam nāvigābimus. In Britanniā familia domum[4] rēgīnae spectābit. Ruīnās Rōmānās in Britanniā spectābō. Tum tōta familia ad Galliam nāvigābit. In Galliā rēgīna nōn est, sed familia multās pictūrās spectābit. Ruīnās Rōmānās in Galliā spectābō.

Tum ad Germāniam et ad Austriam ībimus[5]. Familia pictūrās et statuās in
10 Germāniā et in Austriā spectābit, sed ego[6] ruīnās Rōmānās spectābō. Tum ad Italiam ībimus. In Italiā tōta familia ruīnās Rōmānās spectābit.

Rēgīnās et pictūrās et statuās et terrās novās spectābō, sed ruīnās Rōmānās amō et amābō.

1 *entire, whole*
2 *ship* (acc. sing.)
3 *ship* (abl. sing.)
4 *home*
5 *we shall go*
6 *I* (for emphasis and contrast)

Questions
1. Who is going to Europe?
2. What is the family going to take to Europe?
3. Why won't they take food?
4. What does the family not like?
5. What will they see in Britain?
6. What will they see in France?
7. What will the family see in Germany and Austria?
8. What does the narrator prefer to see?
9. Where can you find Roman ruins in Europe?

Wayne Rowe

Rome's empire outside Italy was divided into provinces (see map, pages 54–55). All of Gaul (ancient France and part of northern Italy) was finally made a Roman province by Julius Caesar in the first century B.C. This Roman amphitheater in Nîmes, France, is sometimes used for bullfights, not unlike the shows held there in ancient times.

▦ VOCABULARY

Nouns

nau´ta, nau´tae m. *sailor*   (astronaut, nautical)
pecū´nia, pecū´niae f. *money*   (impecunious, pecuniary)
un´da, un´dae f. *wave*   (surround, undulate)

Verb

nā´vigō, nāvigā´re, [nāvigā´vī,   (navigation, navy)
nāvigā´tus] *sail*

Adverbs

crās *tomorrow*   (procrastinate)
tum *then, next*

Preposition

ad followed by noun in accusative   (adapt, adduce)
case, *to, toward* (with verbs of
motion); *near* (with verbs of rest)

50°

20°   10°   0°   10°

MARE
GERMANICUM

HIBERNIA   Eboracum

BRITANNIA
Londinium

MARE SUEVICUM

GERMANIA

Saxones
Albis   Vistula

Belgae   GERMANIA
Rhenus
Sequana   Remi
Lutetia   Matrona
RAETIA   NORICUM   PANNONIA
Liger   GALLIA
Celtae   Genava   ALPES
Lugdunum   Helvetii
Mediolanum   ILLYRICUM
40°   AQUITANIA   Rhodanus   Padus
Garunna   Narbo   Genua   Rubico
Numantia   Hiberus   PYRENAEI   Massilia   ITALIA
HISPANIA   Tarraco   CORSICA   Roma
LUSITANIA   Saguntum   Ostia   Cannae
Tagus   Corduba   Neapolis   Dyrrachium
Anas   Nova Carthago   BALEARES   Pompeii   Tarentum
Gades   SARDINIA

MARE

OCEANUS ATLANTICUS

MAURETANIA
ATLAS
NUMIDIA   Utica   SICILIA   Aetna
Zama   Carthago   Syracusae
AFRICA   MELITA
Thapsus
30°   MEDIT

Leptis Magna

<table>
<tr><td>〜〜〜〜</td><td>Roman Walls</td></tr>
<tr><td>▓▓▓</td><td>Roman Territory 264 B.C. Before Punic Wars</td></tr>
<tr><td>⧸⧸⧸</td><td>Added Territory 238-201 B.C. After First and Second Punic Wars</td></tr>
<tr><td>▒▒▒</td><td>Added Territory 133 B.C.</td></tr>
<tr><td>░░░</td><td>Added Territory 44 B.C. Death of Caesar</td></tr>
<tr><td>□□□</td><td>Added Territory 14 A.D. Death of Augustus</td></tr>
<tr><td>▓▓▓</td><td>Added Territory Second Century A.D.</td></tr>
</table>

0°   10°   20°

IMPERIUM ROMANUM

SARMATIA

SCYTHIA

Tanais

DACIA

Danuvius

MOESIA

THRACIA

MACEDONIA
Phillipi
Pydna
Thessalonica
EPIRUS
Pharsalus
Actium
Corinthus
GRAECIA
Sparta
CRETA

Byzantium   *Bosporus*

Troia

ASIA

LYDIA

PAMPHYLIA

LYCIA

RHODUS

Mare

Aegaeum

ERRANEUM

Cyrene

Alexandria

AEGYPTUS

Nilus

BITHYNIA

GALATIA

CILICIA

CYPRUS

Tyrus

PONTUS EUXINUS

CAUCASUS

MARE CASPIUM

PONTUS

ARMENIA

CAPPADOCIA

Antiochia

PHOENICIA

SYRIA
Palmyra
Damascus

PALAESTINA

Hierosolyma

ARABIA

MESOPOTAMIA

Euphrates

ASSYRIA

PARTHIA

Tigris

Babylon

Scale of Miles

0   100   200   300   400   500

GRAMMAR

The Future Tense

The future tense refers to something that will or is going to happen at a future time. In Latin, the future of the first conjugation is formed by adding the tense sign **-bi-** (which corresponds to *shall* and *will* in English) to the present stem and then attaching the present tense endings. The future tense sign **-bi-** drops the **-i-** before **-ō** in the first person singular and changes to **-bu-** in the third person plural.

SINGULAR		PLURAL	
portā´bō	*I shall carry*	**portā´bimus**	*we shall carry*
portā´bis	*you will carry*	**portā´bitis**	*you will carry*
portā´bit	*he/she/it will carry*	**portā´bunt**	*they will carry*

Aquam bonam parābō. *I shall get good water.*
Agricolae terram spectābunt. *The farmers will look at the land.*

Oral Practice

1. Conjugate **labōrō** and **nāvigō** in the future tense and translate.
2. Translate **labōrātis, portābit, nāvigāmus, parant, spectābitis.**

🔲 *Exercises*

A. Translate the following sentences.
   1. Ad silvam cibum crās portābunt.
   2. Nunc carrum rēgīnae spectāmus.
   3. Ad terram novam nāvigābimus.
   4. Magnae undae ad īnsulam sunt.
   5. Ubi magnam cōpiam cibī parābis?
   6. Nautae ad īnsulam plānam nāvigābunt.
   7. Anna ad familiam cōpiam aquae portābit.
   8. Ubi undae erant, fōrma terrae plāna est.
   9. Ad īnsulam nāvigābis.

B. Give the Latin for the italicized words.

    1. Ad terrās novās *(we shall sail).*

    2. Multōs carrōs *(he will prepare).*

    3. Undās magnās *(they will look at).*

    4. Ad familiam nautae crās pecūniam *(I shall carry).*

    5. Numerus undārum magnus *(was).*

C. Complete each sentence with the correct endings.

    1. Est cōpia cib__ bon__ *(of good food).*

    2. Ubi sunt silv__ insul__ *(the forests of the island)?*

    3. Cōpiam pecūni__ *(of money)* parā__ *(we shall get).*

    4. Familia naut__ *(sailor's)* ad īnsul__ *(island)* nāvigā__ *(will sail).*

    5. Agricolae terr__ plān__ *(the flat land)* amā__ *(will like).*

Did You Know?

Rome's equivalent to Wall Street was the **Via Sacra.** The banking houses there provided money-changing and money-lending services; handled deposits and checking accounts; sold bills of exchange on distant banks; negotiated loans; made sales, purchases, and investments for their clients; and collected debts. The banks also provided music and wine to customers while doing business!

Photodisc

Obverse: The Father of His Country **(Pater Patriae)** on a U.S. coin, in a typically classical pose. *Reverse:* How many words on this coin are neither Latin nor derived from Latin? What do the arrows in the eagle's claws symbolize? The olive branches?

WORD STUDY

Derivatives The vocabulary words in this lesson provide the root of several words in English. Find the Latin root in each of the following words, and look up the actual definitions. Then use them in English sentences.

impecunious	abundant	navigable
inundate	nautilus	redundant

impecunious

COLUMBUS

LESSON
OBJECTIVE
• To learn the use of the
dative case

Columbus ad Hispāniam nāvigat. Isabellae, rēgīnae Hispāniae, nūntiat: "Terra nōn plāna est; id[1] probābō et terrās novās mōnstrābō. Ad Indiam nāvigābō; viam novam mōnstrābō." Sed Isabella pecūniam nōn dōnat. Tum amīcus Columbī litterās ad Isabellam portat, et Isabella Columbō pecūniam mandat. Columbus grātus amīcō fortūnam bonam nūntiat.

Annō Dominī[2] MCCCCXCII Columbus nāvigat, sed via longa est et cūrae multae sunt. Vīta nautārum dūra est. Magnus numerus nautārum malōrum Columbum accūsat[3]: "Īnsānus est! Ubinam gentium sumus?[4] Terra plāna est. Indiam numquam[5] spectābimus."

Columbus nautīs malīs nūntiat: "Ad terrās novās nāvigābimus. Vōbīs[6] praedam magnam dōnābō."

Sed subitō[7] nauta terram grātam Columbō mōnstrat. Columbus cūram nāvis[8] nautīs mandat et terram novam spectat. Īnsula parva est, sed grāta nautīs, quod terra firma est. Tum Columbus litterās ad Isabellam portat et Isabellae praedam dōnat. Nautīs praedam dōnat?

[1] *it*

[2] *in the year of our Lord.* What abbreviation is used in English?

[3] *criticize*

[4] *Where in the world are we* (literally, *where of nations*)?

[5] *never*

[6] *to you*

[7] *suddenly*

[8] *of the ship*

Columbus probably used this kind of map, based on a fifteenth-century Latin edition of the geography of the ancient Greek Ptolemy. Note the prominence of India, which Columbus thought he had reached; hence he called the American natives Indians.

Questions

1. What did Columbus wish to prove?
2. Where did Columbus intend to sail?
3. What caused the queen to grant Columbus' request?
4. When did Columbus' ships sail?
5. Why did his sailors criticize him?
6. What did Columbus promise the sailors?
7. According to the passage, what did he discover?
8. To whom did he give the loot?
9. Find in an encyclopedia where Columbus got the idea that the earth was round.

Did You Know?

Roman children played with dolls made of rags, clay, or wax, often with jointed arms and legs. Roman children also enjoyed hitching tame mice or rats to tiny carts, building model houses, riding on hobbyhorses, spinning tops, playing hide-and-seek and blindman's bluff, and rolling hoops with a stick. These hoops even had bits of metal attached to warn people to get out of the way.

When a new word in the vocabulary is related to a word previously studied, the latter is given in brackets instead of an English derivative.

VOCABULARY

Nouns

amī´cus, amī´cī m. *friend*   **[amō]**

lit´tera, lit´terae f. *letter (of the alphabet);*   (literal, literary)
    pl. *a letter (epistle); letters (if modified by*
    an adjective such as **multae**)

prae´da, prae´dae f. *loot, booty*   (predator, prey)

Adjective

grā´tus, grā´ta, [grā´tum] *pleasing, grateful*   (grateful, gratitude)

Except for *letter*, all the English derivatives of **littera** have one *t*, based on an older spelling **lītera**.

Verbs

dō′nō, dōnā′re, [dōnā′vī, dōnā′tus] *give,* (donate, pardon)
  present to (as a gift)

man′dō, mandā′re, [mandā′vī, mandā′tus] (mandate, mandatory)
  entrust, give to (to keep safe)

mōn′strō, mōnstrā′re, [mōnstrā′vī, (demonstrate)
  mōnstrā′tus] *point out, show to*

nūn′tiō, nūntiā′re, [nūntiā′vī, nūntiā′tus] (pronunciation,
  announce, report to renunciation)

pro′bō, probā′re, [probā′vī, probā′tus] (probation, probe)
  test, prove, approve

GRAMMAR

The Dative Case: Indirect Object

As you learned in Lesson II, the *direct object* takes the force of the verb directly: *He tells a story.* The direct object answers the question *Tells what?* In English, the "target" of the action is normally indicated by its placement after the verb.

With some verbs (*give, show, tell,* etc.), the action of the verb may be transferred not only to a direct object but also to an *indirect object.* In such instances, the indirect object is the person(s) to or for whom an action is

Archivo Iconografico, SA/CORBIS

In this relief from Praeneste near Rome, now in the Vatican Museum, you can see a warship with its company of marines ready for battle. Some stand behind a raised bulwark designed to protect them and the rowers. The structure in the bow is a turret from which stones could be hurled. The sail has been lowered and the mast rests against the curved bowsprit. In the actual fighting, the most effective weapon was the ram, seen beneath the bow, but using it to sink an enemy ship took skillful maneuvering, at which the Romans were not very practiced. More often the tactic was to come alongside and board the enemy for hand-to-hand combat. The crocodile is probably a figurehead; perhaps it represents some connection of the ship with Egypt.

done. For example, *He tells the girl a story.* The position of the word *girl* in the sentence shows that the action (telling) is done to or for the girl: *He tells the girl a story = He tells a story to (for) the girl.*

In Latin, the indirect object of a sentence is marked by the dative case ending. These endings for the first and second declension are:

	SINGULAR	PLURAL
FIRST DECLENSION	-ae	-īs
	puel´lae	puel´līs
SECOND DECLENSION	-ō	-īs
	ser´vō	ser´vīs

In the reading selection, notice that the direct objects (**pecūniam, litterās**) are in the accusative case, while the indirect objects are in the dative case (**nautae, nautīs**). Also note that in the first declension, the dative case ending (**-ae**) is identical in spelling to the genitive singular and nominative plural (**pecūniae**). Therefore, great care must be exercised in writing and understanding sentences with words ending in **-ae.** Here are some tips:

- The genitive case word in **-ae** usually comes after another noun.
- The dative case word in **-ae,** like the indirect object in English, usually precedes the direct object noun(s) in a sentence.
- Any plural nominative case word must be matched by a verb with a plural ending. The subject (the nominative case word) normally stands first or near the beginning in a sentence.

Sentences containing nouns in different cases require patient and careful analysis to find out the correct relationship between them. Withhold your judgment until you decide which of the various possibilities makes the best sense in the context in which you find it.

When translating English *to* into Latin, if *to* really means *toward* (after a verb indicating motion), do not use the dative. Instead, translate using **ad** plus a word in the accusative.

Columbus isn't sailing to Britain. **Columbus ad Britanniam (not Britanniae) nōn nāvigat.**

He went to the city
as fast as he could.
(accusative with ad*)*

He told his story to the
officer and showed him his
driver's license. *(datives of
indirect object)*

UBI IGNIS EST?

Oral Practice

1. Put the following phrases in the dative: *to the horses, for the family, to the sailors, for the friends.*
2. Tell the case you would use if you were translating the italicized words into Latin.
   a. Give *me* the horses.
   b. I showed *Anna* the book.
   c. I told my *friend* the whole story.
   d. We carried our bags to the *station.*
   e. He presented his library to the *president.*
   f. He told *me* how to go to the *wharf.*
   g. They moved to *California.*
   h. Promise *me* the *truth.*
   i. Show *him* to *me.*
   j. Forgive *us* our *debts.*

Nota•Bene

Remember that after verbs of motion like *come* and *go,* the word *to* is expressed in Latin by the preposition **ad** followed by the accusative.

📖 *Exercises*

A. Translate the following sentences. Pay careful attention to the endings.
1. Familiae pecūniam dōnābit.
2. Puellae litterās mandāmus.
3. Servō praedam nōn mōnstrābimus.
4. Amīcīs bonīs litterās mandābis.
5. Anna Clarae magnam pecūniam dōnābit.
6. Carrī ad longam silvam aquam clāram portant.
7. Rēgīna puellae magnam pecūniam mandat.
8. Annae viās silvae mōnstrābō.

B. Give the Latin for the italicized words. Then translate the sentences into English.
1. *(To many lands)* nāvigābimus.
2. *(To the sailor)* litterās mandābō.
3. *(To the sailors)* viam mōnstrant.
4. *(To Anna)* fortūnam bonam nūntiābit.
5. *(Many families)* pecūniam dōnat.

C. Give the Latin for the italicized words.
1. *(To the slave)* litterās mandābō.
2. *(To the girls)* pecūniam dōnābimus.
3. Nautae *(to the islands)* nāvigābunt.
4. *(To Clara)* cibum *(she gives)*.
5. *(To Anna)* litterās *(she will carry)*.

WORD STUDY

Derivatives Try to see the relation between the meaning of the English derivative and the Latin word from which it comes. Then use the derivative in a sentence.

- A *literary* person is a person of letters; a *literal* translation is one that is almost letter for letter.

- A *mandate* is something entrusted to a person or a group.

- A *novelty* is something new.

- A person who is on *probation* is being tested.

In the same way, explain a *familiar* friend, an *undulating* river, an *amicable* attitude, an interested *spectator*.

LESSON VIII

GALLIA

LESSON OBJECTIVE
- To learn the ablative of means or instrument

Consisting of three tiers of arcades, the Pont du Gard near Nîmes, France, is a fine example of a Roman aqueduct. It was built in 19 B.C. over a deep gorge to carry water to the city from a freshwater source about 15 miles away.

Rōmānī Galliam occupant et magnam praedam parant. Gallī silvīs fortūnās et familiās mandant. Rōmānī Gallīs[1] magnās poenās parant. Poenae dūrae sunt. Tum memoria iniūriārum prōvinciam Galliam ad pugnam incitat. Gallī Rōmānīs nūntiant:

"Terram nostram[2] pugnīs occupātis. Praedam magnam ad Italiam multīs 5 carrīs portātis. Poenae nostrae[2] dūrae sunt. Sed crās pugnābimus et victōriīs nostrīs[2] vītās et pecūniam nostram servābimus. Iniūriīs et poenīs nōs[3] ad pugnam incitātis. Pugnāre parāmus. Familiīs nostrīs victōriās grātās nūntiābimus, sed victōriās grātās Rōmae nōn nūntiābitis."

Gallī diū et fortiter[4] pugnant, sed multae et clārae sunt victōriae 10 Rōmānōrum. Pugnīs Gallī vītās et terram nōn servant.

Ubi est prōvincia Gallia? Gallōs accūsātis quod pugnāvērunt[5]? Animum[6] Gallōrum nōn laudātis? Memoriae pugnās Gallōrum mandābitis?

[1] for the Gauls, i.e., the people of Gaul (Gallia, modern France, Belgium, and northern Italy)
[2] our
[3] us (acc.)
[4] long and bravely
[5] they fought
[6] spirit

Questions

1. What do the Gauls do with their families and fortunes?
2. What do the Romans do to Gaul?
3. What incites the Gauls to fight?
4. According to the Gauls, who will announce pleasing victories? Will they be pleasing to Rome?
5. Whose victories were famous?
6. By what means do the Gauls intend to save their lives and property? Did they succeed?
7. Answer the questions of the last paragraph in Latin.

Did You Know?

Before the conquest of Gaul by Julius Caesar, its regions were named after the appearance of their inhabitants. The region north of Rome but south of the Alps was called **Gallia Togāta** because the men there were Roman citizens and wore togas. The region northwest of the Alps was called **Gallia Bracāta** because the men there wore long pants (cf. English *breeches*). The northernmost area, near present-day Belgium, was named **Gallia Comāta** because of the long hair of the people who lived there.

▦ VOCABULARY

Nouns

iniū´ria, iniū´riae f. *injustice, wrong, injury*	(injurious, injury)
memo´ria, memo´riae f. *memory*	(memorable, memorial)
poe´na, poe´nae f. *punishment, penalty*	(penal, penalize)
prōvin´cia, prōvin´ciae f. *province*	(provincial)
pug´na, pug´nae f. *fight, battle*	(pugnacious, repugnant)
victō´ria, victō´riae f. *victory*	(victorious)

Verbs

in´citō, incitā´re, [incitā´vī, incitā´tus]   (incitement)
   excite, stir up, incite

oc´cupō, occupā´re, [occupā´vī, occupā´tus] (occupant, occupation)
   seize (hold of)

pug´nō, pugnā´re, [pugnā´vī, pugnā´tus]   (impugn, pugnacity)
   fight

ser´vō, servā´re, [servā´vī, servā´tus]   (conservation,
   save, guard   preservation)

▦ GRAMMAR

Ablative Case: Ablative of Means

A word or words in Latin having an ablative case ending can be used to express a number of different relationships to the verb in a sentence. In English, these relationships are summed up in the prepositions *with*, *by*, *in*, *on*, or *from*. Like the genitive and dative cases, the ablative case alone often expresses the relations *with*, *by*, *in*, or *from,* in Latin, no separate word is required. The ablative case endings for the first and second declensions are as follows.

	SINGULAR	PLURAL
FIRST DECLENSION	-ā	-īs
	vi´ā	vi´īs
SECOND DECLENSION	-ō	-īs
	ser´vō	ser´vīs

Compare the following.

Genitive	**Fōrmam terrae amō.**	*I like the shape of the land.*
Dative	**Amīcīs cōpiam cibī donās.**	*You are giving a supply of food to friends.*
Ablative	**Victōriīs nostrīs vītās et pecūniam servābimus.**	*We shall save lives and money by means of (with, through) our victories.*

The English word *preposition* comes from the Latin **praepōnō,** *place in front.*

Therefore, when you see a word or words in the ablative case in Latin, you should use an English preposition like *with*, *by (means of)*, *from*, *in*, *on*, or *through*. Together, these words make up what is called a prepositional phrase in English; the words that follow *with* or *by* are called *objects of the preposition (with the money, by means of letters).*

In Latin, when the ablative word expresses the instrument or means by which a person does something, it is called an *ablative of means.* The position of the ablative case word in a Latin sentence is flexible, like English prepositional phrases. Changing position often results only in a change in emphasis. Compare the following examples:

For the Gauls living north of Italy, the fertility of Italian land was irresistible and the cause of many attempts at invasion. In 387 B.C. they succeeded in besieging, capturing, and burning most of Rome, holding the Romans hostage for an outrageous ransom. Even after the Romans had weighed out the amount of gold agreed upon, the Gallic leader Brennus demanded more, tipping the scales and crying **Vae victīs!** *(Woe to the conquered!),* a saying the Romans never forgot. In this painting by Mariano Rossi (1730–1807), the Roman general Camillus, summoned from exile to the rescue, is breaking the terms of the treaty and driving the Gauls down from the Capitol.

Dagli Orti/Galleria Borghese, Rome/The Art Archive

FOR EMPHASIS	**Pugnīs Rōmānī Galliam occupant.**
	By fights (i.e., *making war) the Romans seize Gaul.*
NORMAL	**Rōmānī Galliam pugnīs occupant.**
	The Romans seize Gaul by fights.

Note that the ablative and dative have some identical endings (**-ō** in the second declension singular, **-īs** in the first and second declensions plural). To avoid confusion, consider that:

- if the verb means *give, allow, show, entrust,* etc., it will most likely have an indirect object in the dative;
- the dative is used for people (less often, for animals or things), the ablative of means for things;
- the dative will often come before an accusative direct object, as in English.

Oral Practice

Translate the phrases in italics into Latin: he was pushed (*by waves*), we carried the load (*with wagons*).

📖 *Exercises*

A. Translate the following sentences.
  1. Pugnīs īnsulam occupātis.
  2. Cibō multās familiās servābitis.
  3. Victōriīs vītam et prōvinciam servant.
  4. Memoriā iniūriae nautās incitās.
  5. Aquā vītam equōrum servābimus.
  6. Puella memoriae litterās mandābit.
  7. Litterīs rēgīnae magnam victōriam nūntiābit.

B. Give the Latin for the italicized words. Then translate the sentences.
  1. *(With money)* nautās incitāmus.
  2. *(To friends)* victōriam nūntiābō.
  3. *(With care)* vītam amīcī servābō.
  4. *(With many wagons)* praedam portābitis.
  5. Memoria iniūriārum et poenārum nautās *(incites)*.

C. Complete each sentence with the correct endings.
  1. Pecūni__ *(with money)* nautās incitā__ *(I shall excite).*
  2. Poenam serv__ *(of the slaves)* nōn probāmus.
  3. Mult__ aqu__ *(with much water)* silvam serva__ *(they save).*
  4. Victōri__ *(by victory)* prōvinciam servā__ *(they will save).*
  5. Amīc__ *(to friends)* pecūniam dōnā __ *(I shall give).*

WORD STUDY

- From what Latin words are *curator, reservoir, incite, conservation, injury, vitality, vitamin,* and *commemoration* derived?

- Use the following words in a good English sentence that shows you know the Latin root of each: *penal, pugnacious, occupy, impugn.*

- Study the following Latin phrases that are used in English.

persona non grata	*an unacceptable, unwelcome person*
ad nauseam	*to [the point of] seasickness* or *disgust*
Nova Scotia	*New Scotland, a province in Canada*
aqua et ignis	*water and fire,* i.e., *the necessities of life*

LESSON
OBJECTIVES
• To review the first and
  second declensions
• To learn the singular
  and plural forms of the
  present imperative

CORNĒLIA ET NAUTA

Māter[1]:	Fīliae, fīliae meae, paene quīnta hōra est. Portāte aquam ad casam[2] et cibum bonum parāte. Anna, ubi est soror[3] tua Cornēlia?
Anna:	Aquam portābō, māter. Cornēlia in arēnā[4] est. Nautam in undīs spectat.
5 **Māter:**	Mala puella est. Anna, nūntiā Cornēliae cūram meam.
	(*Nunc quīnta hōra est.*)
Anna:	Māter! Pater![5] Spectāte, Cornēlia in aquā est! Sed ubi est nauta? Nunc sub[6] aquā est, sed eum[7] Cornēlia servābit!
Pater:	Ubi sunt, Anna? Mōnstrā eōs[8].
10	(*Anna nautam et Cornēliam mōnstrat.*)
Anna:	Nunc, pater! Servā eōs!
Nauta:	Servā mē! Undae magnae sunt!
Māter:	Pater tuus ad nautam et sorōrem[3] tuam natat[9]. Eōs fūne[10] servābit.
Anna:	Spectāte! Nauta et Cornēlia fūnem[11] prēnsant[12]. Nunc ad arēnam
15	natābunt[13]. (*Nunc sexta[14] hōra est.*)
Māter:	Mala puella es[15], Cornēlia. Cūra mea magna erat. Nunc portā aquam ad casam. Anna soror tua labōrat.
Nauta:	Semper familiam et fīliam tuam laudābō; grātus sum[16], amīcī.
Cornēlia:	Dūra es[15], māter. Nōn aquam sed nautam amō; est bonus et grātus.
20 **Māter:**	Nōn dūra sum, sed grāta. Nunc familiae meae magnam cōpiam cibī parābimus. Gaudeāmus![17]

[1] mother
[2] house
[3] sister
[4] sand, seashore
[5] father
[6] under
[7] him
[8] them
[9] is swimming
[10] with a rope (abl.)
[11] rope (acc.)
[12] are grabbing
[13] will swim
[14] sixth
[15] you are
[16] I am
[17] Let's be happy!

A scene from the **Āra Pācis Augustae** (*Augustan Altar of Peace*) in Rome. In the center sits **Terra Māter** (*Mother Earth* or perhaps **Italia**), with children, livestock, and crops to symbolize the fertility of Italy. On each side is a nymph, probably *(left)* a goddess of the winds and *(right)* one of the seas, so that the whole panel represents Roman peace over sky, earth, and sea. The altar is a supreme example of Roman sculpture.

Franz-Marc Frei/CORBIS

Questions

1. How are Cornelia and Anna related?
2. What does Anna's mother tell her and Cornelia to do?
3. Where does Anna say Cornelia is?
4. Where is Cornelia when Anna goes to look for her?
5. Why is the sailor yelling?
6. By what means was the sailor saved?
7. What will the sailor always do and why?
8. What does Cornelia's mother say she and the others will do?
9. How long did the whole incident last?

VOCABULARY

Nouns

fī´lia, fī´liae f. *daughter*   (affiliate, filial)

hō´ra, hō´rae f. *hour*   (horologium, hour)

Adjectives

me´us, me´a, [me´um] *my, mine*

quīn´tus, quīn´ta, [quīn´tum] *fifth*   (quintet, quintuplet)

tu´us, tu´a, [tu´um] *your, yours* (referring to one person)

Adverbs

pae´ne *almost*   (peninsula)

sem´per *always*

GRAMMAR

Summary of First and Second Declensions

	FIRST DECLENSION		SECOND DECLENSION		USE
	SING.	PL.	SING.	PL.	
NOM.	**-a**	**-ae**	**-us**	**-ī**	subject; pred. nom
GEN.	**-ae**	**-ārum**	**-ī**	**-ōrum**	possessive, etc.
DAT.	**-ae**	**-īs**	**-ō**	**-īs**	indirect object
ACC.	**-am**	**-ās**	**-um**	**-ōs**	direct object
ABL.	**-ā**	**-īs**	**-ō**	**-īs**	means, etc.

FIRST DECLENSION

	SINGULAR	PLURAL
NOM.	**via nova**	**viae novae**
	new road	*new roads*
GEN.	**viae novae**	**viārum novārum**
	of the new road	*of the new roads*
DAT.	**viae novae**	**viīs novīs**
	(to/for) the new road	*(to/for) the new roads*
ACC.	**viam novam**	**viās novās**
	new road (D.O.)	*new roads (D.O.)*
ABL.	**viā novā**	**viīs novīs**
	by/with the new road	*by/with the new roads*

SECOND DECLENSION

	SINGULAR	PLURAL
NOM.	**equus meus**	**equī meī**
GEN.	**equī meī**	**equōrum meōrum**
DAT.	**equō meō**	**equīs meīs**
ACC.	**equum meum**	**equōs meōs**
ABL.	**equō meō**	**equīs meīs**

NOUN–ADJECTIVE AGREEMENT

	SINGULAR	PLURAL
NOM.	**nauta bonus**	**nautae bonī**
GEN.	**nautae bonī**	**nautārum bonōrum**
DAT.	**nautae bonō**	**nautīs bonīs**
ACC.	**nautam bonum**	**nautās bonōs**
ABL.	**nautā bonō**	**nautīs bonīs**

Find all the endings that are the same in the first and second declensions.

Because of the frequency of **-a** in its endings, the first declension is also called the **-a** *declension*. Similarly, the second declension is the **-o** *declension* (in the nominative and accusative singular the **-o** changed to **-u**).

In a Latin sentence, how do you know which case is indicated? You must decide which of the various possibilities makes the best sense in each sentence. The secret of rapid reading is to know the endings so well that the recognition of case endings becomes almost automatic. Note: In the first declension, short **-a** (nominative singular) and long **-ā** (ablative singular) are not the same ending.

Agreement of Adjectives and Nouns

Notice in the final section of the preceding chart that **nauta,** because it is a masculine noun, requires its modifiers to be masculine also. Clearly, the agreement of nouns and adjectives is not based upon the use of identical endings. Agreement of adjectives and nouns is based upon case, number, and gender. When a noun belongs to the first declension and is masculine (e.g. **agricola, nauta**), adjectives that describe it will have masculine (second declension) endings. The declension of **nauta bonus** is a good example of the principle that an adjective agrees with the noun it modifies in gender, number, and case, but not necessarily in its ending.

Oral Practice

Decline in all cases, singular and plural, the following: **amīcus meus, numerus magnus, victōria parva, nauta malus.**

Present Imperative

The verbs you have studied so far have been either in the *infinitive* form or in the *indicative* mood. The indicative mood is used to make statements or ask questions. You have studied both the present indicative and the future indicative.

Commands are expressed in both Latin and English by the *imperative* mood. In Latin, the present imperative singular is the same as the present stem of the verb: **portā,** *carry.* The plural is formed with the ending **-te: portāte,** *carry.* An imperative usually stands at or near the beginning of the sentence. Do not confuse the present imperative singular ending **-ā** (e.g., **pugnā:** *fight)* with the ablative singular ending **-ā** (**pugnā:** *with a fight).* The imperative is used only with verbs; the ablative ending is used only with nouns and adjectives.

Oral Practice

1. Form the singular imperatives of *love, praise, report, prepare.*
2. Form the plural imperatives of *give, sail, save, entrust, point out.*

Did You Know?

Rome's equivalent to Broadway in New York City was the **Via Lāta.** Traffic on this busy thoroughfare caused so much congestion that heavy vehicles were ordered to move only during the night. On the other hand, some busy streets in Rome were so narrow that residents had to knock on the inside of their doors before leaving, so as not to collide with passersby.

▦ *Exercises*

A. Translate the following sentences.

   1. Mōnstrāte amīcīs viam.

   2. Nunc quīnta hōra est; nāvigābimus.

   3. Amā fīliam tuam et fīlia tua tē *(you)* amābit.

   4. Servā pecūniam tuam et pecūnia tua tē *(you)* servābit.

   5. Nautae vītam servōrum laudant et servī vītam nautārum laudant.

B. Give the imperative form of the words in italics. Decide whether the singular or plural or both forms of the imperative are appropriate. Then translate the sentence.

   1. *(Show)* puellīs litterās meās.

   2. *(Stir up)* servum et pugnābit.

   3. Puellae, *(look at)* magnōs equōs.

   4. *(Entrust)* fāmam tuam fortūnae.

   5. Nunc, nautae, ad prōvinciam *(sail)*.

   6. *(Praise)*, amīcī, fīliās bonās.

   7. *(Watch)* agricolās bonōs, fīliae meae.

   8. *(Give)* pecūniam tuam amīcīs.

   9. *(Seize)* prōvinciam.

  10. *(Save)* vītam puellae cibō.

C. Work with a partner. Write a two-line dialogue according to the model. The first person gives a command (use the imperative) to the second person, who responds that it will be done. Remember to add a preposition, if necessary, to make sense.

   women / praise / farmers

   —Fēminae, laudāte agricolās!

   —Fēminae agricolās laudābunt.

   1. farmers / save / girls

   2. slaves / get ready / wagons

   3. daughter / prepare / food

   4. sailors / sail / island

D. Work with a group. In Latin, command one person to carry food or water to another person. Then command more than one person (plural imperative) to do the same. Take turns giving and following commands.

WORD STUDY

Latin Words in the Romance Languages Like English, the Romance languages, which are derived from Latin, have also borrowed many words with little or no change. Compare the following list.

FRENCH	SPANISH	PORTUGUESE	ITALIAN
aimer	amar	amar	amare
ami	amigo	amigo	amico
bon	bueno	bom	buono
char	carro	carro	carro
famille	familia	familia	famiglia
forme	forma	forma	forma
heure	hora	hora	ora
lettre	letra	letra	lettera
province	provincia	provincia	provincia
terre	tierra	terra	terra

Judging from the Latin, what does each of these French, Spanish, Portuguese, and Italian words mean? Make a parallel column of English words.

BONUM   bon   bueno   bom   buono

"Good," isn't it?

GLIMPSES OF ROMAN LIFE

THE ETERNAL CITY

Although modern archaeology shows that the site of Rome was inhabited many centuries earlier, the Romans put the founding of their city in 753 B.C. The first settlement was on the Palatine Hill, named after Palēs, the goddess of shepherds, who was worshipped by the first settlers. As the city grew from a group of small village governments, it spread to the nearby hills and along the valleys between the banks of the Tiber River. In time, it came to be known as the "City of the Seven Hills." These hills are neither high nor extensive; the Palatine is only 142 feet above the level of the Tiber River—about the height of a modern ten-story building.

Below the Palatine Hill was the valley that came to be known as the **Forum Rōmānum.** At first a marshy district, it became the marketplace of Rome, then the chief shopping and business district, and finally the civic center. The Forum eventually evolved into a rectangular paved space surrounded by temples, law courts, a senate house, and other public buildings. At one end was a speakers' platform called the *rostra* because it was ornamented with the beaks of ships (**rōstrum** = *beak*) captured in a war fought in the fourth century B.C.[1] Modern excavations are still uncovering many of the ancient levels of the Forum.

The Palatine, because of its nearness to the Forum, became the residential district for the wealthy and the site of a number of temples. The first emperors had their homes there. Eventually, the whole imperial administration came to be centered on this hill during Augustus' rule, and the emperor's buildings covered it completely. Thus, the hill that had been named for the lowly goddess of shepherds (**Palēs**) who lived in huts came to be the site of *palatial* buildings.

Another hill near the Forum, the Capitoline, got its name from the famous temple of Jupiter known as the Capitolium. It was so named because it was the *head* (**caput**) or main temple of that god. From this, the Capitol in Washington, D.C., or any other state capitol building, gets its name. Also on the Capitoline was the temple of Juno Moneta. Why the goddess Juno was called Moneta is not certain. In connection with this temple, a mint for coining money was later established, and thus from the word **monēta** we derive our words *money* and *mint.* The other hills were the Aventine, Caelian, Esquiline (which was originally a paupers' graveyard and later a park), Quirinal, and Viminal. In the valley between the Palatine and the Aventine lay the Circus Maximus, a racecourse for chariots.

To the northwest of the Forum in a bend of the Tiber River stretched the Campus Martius, which enclosed a park and drill ground. It also was covered with temples, theaters, public baths, and other buildings. In the Middle Ages, this was the most densely populated district in Rome, as can

Vanni/Art Resource, NY

The Roman Forum, where business was transacted, laws were made, and a strong civilization took hold. The remains of the temple of Vesta are in the center; the three columns of the Temple of Castor and Pollux are on the right with the Arch of Titus just behind them, and the remains of the Coliseum are in the background.

[1] The fourth century B.C. (before Christ) covers 400–301 B.C.; the first century is 100–1 B.C. Then comes the first century A.D. (**Annō Domini**), A.D. 1–100, etc.

be seen from its many narrow, twisting streets. Of the many temples, baths, and shops constructed here, only the Pantheon is visible today, along with fragments of other Roman buildings.

The streets of Rome were narrow and crooked, and there existed over two hundred of them. In the early days they were unpaved, but during the last part of the first century B.C., there was a program to beautify the city.

The early people of Rome got their water from wells, springs, and the Tiber River, which winds its way along one side of the city in the shape of the letter "s." In about 313 B.C., Appius Claudius (the man also responsible for the **Via Appia**) built the first aqueduct, which brought pure water from springs about seven miles east of the city. Later, other aqueducts were built, some having their sources nearly forty miles away. Rome had fourteen aqueducts at its peak, and several of them are still in use today. There were many street fountains, and eventually running water was piped into the public baths and many of the private houses of the wealthy.

For better administration, the Emperor Augustus divided the city into fourteen regions, or wards. One feature of this arrangement was the reorganization and extension of the police and fire department (**vigilēs,** *watchmen*), the latter force numbering about seven thousand. Earlier fire protection had been so poor that private fire companies were organized, but these companies were criticized for buying burning houses at bargain prices before they extinguished the fires.

In early days the Servian Wall was built around the city for protection; parts of this wall may still be seen in the busy modern city. Rome soon outgrew this wall, and in the third century A.D., Emperor Aurelian constructed a new wall, which had fifteen gates and still stands today.

At its height, ancient Rome had a population of more than one million people. The modern city has recovered from its severe decline in the Middle Ages, growing rapidly with a population of about three million, and is once again the largest city in Italy.

Rome has been an important city for a longer time than any other city in the western world. It was first a kingdom, then a republic, and later the capital of the great Roman Empire. It continued its importance as the seat of the Catholic Church, and in recent generations, it has become the capital of one of the leading nations of modern Europe. The name given to it during ancient times—"Eternal City" (**urbs aeterna**)—has been justified.

QUESTIONS

1. What is a civic center? Describe a modern one that you have visited, and compare and contrast it with that of ancient Rome.
2. Compare the development of Rome and that of Washington, D.C. or some other large city.
3. What factors cause a community to grow until it reaches the status of a city? A megalopolis?

VOCABULARY

Practice saying the following vocabulary words aloud with a partner. In addition to the meaning, for the nouns, give the genitive and gender; for the adjectives, give the three nominative forms; for the verbs, give the four principal parts; and for the prepositions, give the case they take.

Nouns

amīcus	fōrma	nauta	prōvincia
cibus	hōra	numerus	pugna
cōpia	iniūria	pecūnia	rēgīna
cūra	littera	poena	unda
fīlia	memoria	praeda	victōria

Adjectives

clārus	meus	quīntus
grātus	plānus	tuus

Verbs

dōnō	mōnstrō	occupō	servō
incitō	nāvigō	probō	
mandō	nūntiō	pugnō	

Adverbs

crās	paene	semper	tum

Preposition

ad (acc.)

GRAMMAR SUMMARY

Case Uses

	LATIN	ENGLISH
Subject	Nominative	Nominative
Possession, etc.	Genitive	Possessive
Indirect Object	Dative	Objective with *to*
Direct Object	Accusative	Objective
Various Uses	Ablative with or without preposition	Objective with various prepositions

The Genitive Case The genitive case is used to make one noun modify another. An important use is to show possession.

iniūriam puerī   *the injury of the boy (the boy's injury)*

memoria agricolārum *the memory of the farmers (the farmers' memory)*

The genitive is also used after the preposition *of* to show the whole from which a part is drawn.

cōpia aquae   *a supply of water*

The Dative Case The dative case is used to indicate the indirect object of the verb. The indirect object is most commonly used after such verbs as *give, show, tell,* and *entrust.* In English, we often use the prepositions *to* or *for* to show this relationship. The preposition can be dropped in English with a change in word order, but the dative case is always used in Latin.

Pecūniam puellae dōnābō.	*I shall give money to the girl.*
	I shall give the girl money.

Ablative of Means The ablative is used to express the means or instrument by which something is done. In English, we almost always use the preposition *by* or *with* to express this, but in Latin, no preposition is used.

Litterīs victōriam nūntiant.	*They report the victory by (means of) a letter.*
Nautās praedā incitābit.	*He will stir up the sailors with booty.*

Verbs

The Future Tense The future tense is formed in Latin by adding the tense sign **-bi-** to the stem. The **-i-** is dropped before the **-ō** in the first person singular and becomes **-u-** in the third person plural.

Undās spectābimus.	*We shall look at the waves.*
Nautās puellīs mōnstrābō.	*I shall point out the sailors to the girls.*
Equōs laudābunt.	*They will praise the horses.*

The Present Imperative The present imperative is used to give commands. The singular is the present stem of the verb. The plural is formed by adding **-te** to the singular.

Occupā prōvinciam!	*Seize the province!*
Occupāte Rōmam!	*Seize Rome!*

UNIT PRACTICE

A. Decline **vīta mea, nauta malus** in the singular and plural.

B. State the case required and then give the following in Latin.
1. *level land* (direct object)
2. *your daughter* (possessive)
3. *little girl* (indirect object)
4. *my wagons* (means)
5. *large horses* (direct object)

C. This is a rapid-fire drill to be answered as quickly as possible.
1. Translate **occupābō, mōnstrās, dōnā, amīcōrum, pecūniā, laudābunt, servāre, nāvigātis, incitant.**
2. Translate *of the victory, with money, we report, he will entrust, you will be showing, they give, he fights.*
3. Give the cases of nouns and adjectives and tenses of verbs: **iniūriīs, numerō, undās, pugnābunt, grātam, spectātis, bonō, tua, mandās.**

WORD STUDY

Give the nominative, genitive, gender, and meaning of the Latin noun suggested by each of the following derivatives: *copious, curator, informal, injure, literature, memorable, pecuniary, penalize, predatory, undulating, pugnacity, vitamin.*

VOCABULARY

Circle the word that best completes each sentence.

1. _____ mea nautam in viā spectābit.
   a. Poena
   b. Cūra
   c. Fīlia
   d. Hōra

2. Rēgīna litterās _____ mandat.
   a. cōpiae
   b. pecūniae
   c. servō
   d. equō

3. Victōriam Rōmānam familiae meae crās _____.
   a. incitābō
   b. servābō
   c. pugnābō
   d. nūntiābō

4. In īnsulā puellae aquam _____ semper portant.
   a. carrō
   b. formā
   c. undā
   d. prōvinciā

5. _____ praedam amīcō nunc!
   a. Nāvigāte
   b. Amā
   c. Pugnāte
   d. Dōnā

GRAMMAR

Complete each sentence with the correct case endings.

6. Cōpia cib___ bon___ erat magn___.
7. Nauta ad Americam crās nāvigā___.
8. Mōnstrā serv___ vestr___ fōrmās litterārum novārum.
9. Multās prōvinciās pugn___ occupābunt.
10. Memoriam pugnae magn___ cūr___ servābimus.

TRANSLATION

Translate the following sentences.

11. Rēgīna clāra poenam malam probat.
12. Fōrma silvae minimē plāna erat.
13. Iniūriae nautārum Rōmānōrum parvae sunt.
14. Tum litterīs fortūnam bonam servōrum in prōvinciā tuā nūntiābis.
15. Incitā, agricola, equōs meōs ad aquam.

INVESTIGATION

Find the answers to these questions from any lesson in Unit II.

16. Which of the following is not a Romance language?
    a. French
    b. Spanish
    c. German
    d. Portuguese
    e. Italian

17. The name of the river on which Rome was built is _____.

18. True or false? From the earliest days, the Romans were big meat eaters.

19. Tell the English meaning of these three common Latin abbreviations.

i.e.

e.g.

etc.

20. The Latin name for what is now France was _____.

CULTURE

Vērum aut Falsum? Indicate whether each statement is true or false.

21. The traditional founding date of Rome was 753 B.C.

22. The Circus Maximus, Rome's famous racecourse, was on top of the Palatine Hill.

23. The Capitolium was the Latin name for the speakers' platform.

24. The Campus Martius was an area used for military drill.

25. Twenty-five aqueducts brought water to the city of Rome in ancient times.

FROM LATIN TO ENGLISH

Apply your knowledge of Latin roots to determine the best meaning of the italicized words.

26. The student realized he needed to improve his *pecuniary* habits.
  a. study
  b. social
  c. exercise
  d. financial

27. There was a *copious* amount of water in the irrigation ditch.
  a. unusual
  b. small
  c. plentiful
  d. typical

28. The myth told the story of a *predatory* creature.
  a. huge
  b. plundering
  c. ancient
  d. foreign

29. The town was *inundated* that month.
  a. flooded
  b. deserted
  c. settled
  d. burned

30. The professor became the *curator* of a famous museum.
  a. founder
  b. treasurer
  c. supporter
  d. caretaker

ROMANS AT HOME AND ABROAD

Unit Objectives

- To learn the present and future active tenses and present imperatives of the second conjugation

- To learn the present tense of the linking verb **sum**

- To learn the perfect active tense of the first and second conjugations

- To learn second declension nouns and adjectives ending in **-r,** neuter nouns and adjectives ending in **-um**; the use of the vocative case, ablative of place from which construction, and the accusative of place to which construction

- To learn about daily life and class society in ancient Rome

Street musicians in actors' masks play their instruments: double flute, finger cymbals, and tambourine. The smaller person at the left may be playing a stringed instrument. Notice how tiles of a darker color have been used to create shadows. This mosaic from the Villa of Cicero in Pompeii is now in the National Museum in Naples.

Araldo de Luca/CORBIS

LESSON OBJECTIVES
- To learn the present and future tenses of the second conjugation
- To learn the Latin origins of English derivatives

LINGUA LATĪNA

Lingua Rōmānōrum Latīna erat. Lingua patriae nostrae[1] nōn Latīna est, sed Anglica[2]. Linguā Latīnā scientiam[3] linguae nostrae augēmus. Lingua Latīna prīmō[4] nōbīs[5] nova erat, sed nunc nōn terret. Disciplīna nōs[6] nōn terret, quod magistrum[7] bonum habēmus. Linguam Latīnam semper in memoriā habēbimus.

In Britanniā, in Italiā, in Galliā, in Americīs, in multīs terrīs et prōvinciīs multī magistrī linguam Latīnam nunc docent et semper docēbunt. In patriā nostrā lingua Latīna fāmam magnam habet. Magistrī magnum numerum discipulōrum[8] docent. Disciplīna semper scientiam nostram augēbit. Magistrī nōs probābunt, sī[9] cūram habēbimus. Patria nōs probābit et laudābit, sī scientiam et fāmam bonam parābimus.

[1] our
[2] English
[3] knowledge
[4] at first
[5] to us (dat.)
[6] us (acc.)
[7] teacher (If the teacher is a woman, read **magistram bonam** instead.)
[8] pupils (The form **discipulārum** may also be needed if the class is all or mostly girls.)
[9] if

Part of a handsome inscription of A.D. 17, in the market of Lepcis Magna, Libya, on an arch dedicated by the governor, Gaius Vibius Marsus, to the Roman empress as Augusta Health-Giver. **AVGVSTA [SALVTARIS] [C. VI] BIVS MARSVS P[RO CONSVL (governor)...] AFRICAE DEDICAVIT.**

Roger Wood/CORBIS

Questions

1. By what means (how) can we increase our knowledge of English?
2. How did Latin appear to us at first?
3. Where is Latin taught?
4. Do many students study Latin?
5. Do you agree that the study of Latin helps your knowledge of English and the Romance languages? Count the number of different Latin words in this passage from which an English word is derived.
6. When will our teachers approve of us?
7. When will our country praise our accomplishments?

▦ VOCABULARY

Nouns

disciplī´na, -ae f. *training, instruction*   (discipline)
lin´gua, -ae f. *tongue, language*   (bilingual, linguistic)
pa´tria, -ae f. *fatherland, country*   (expatriate, patriotic)

Verbs

au´geō, augē´re, [au´xī, auc´tus] *increase*   (auction, augment)
do´ceō, docē´re, [do´cuī, doc´tus] *teach*   (document, indoctrinate)
ha´beō, habē´re, [ha´buī, ha´bitus]   (habit, inhabitant)
   have, hold
ter´reō, terrē´re, [ter´ruī, ter´ritus]   (terrific, terrify)
   scare, frighten

▦ GRAMMAR

The Second Conjugation: Present and Future Tenses; Present Imperative

The verbs you studied in previous lessons all contain the stem vowel **-ā-** and belong to the first conjugation. Verbs that have the stem vowel **-ē-** in the present and future tenses belong to the second conjugation. The only difference from the present and future tenses of the first conjugation is in the stem vowel (ē or ĕ for ā or ă). Note that in the present tense of the second conjugation the stem vowel is shortened in three places and is kept in the first person singular (**doceō**).

Anna puerōs terret.	*Anna frightens the boys.*
Disciplīnam nautārum augēbis.	*You will increase the training of the sailors.*

Now that you are more familiar with nouns, the second entry will be the genitive ending only, not the full form, whenever possible. To get the stem of a noun, simply drop the genitive ending.

Note that the last two principal parts of second conjugation verbs are not quite so regular as those of the first conjugation.

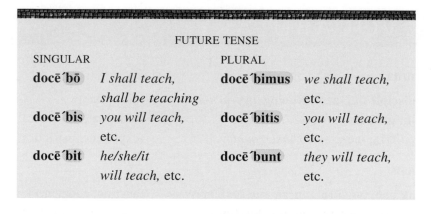

PRESENT TENSE

SINGULAR		PLURAL	
do´ceō	*I teach, am teaching, do teach*	docē´mus	*we teach, are teaching, do teach*
do´cēs	*you teach,* etc.	docē´tis	*you teach,* etc.
do´cet	*he/she/it teaches,* etc.	do´cent	*they teach,* etc.

FUTURE TENSE

SINGULAR		PLURAL	
docē´bō	*I shall teach, shall be teaching*	docē´bimus	*we shall teach,* etc.
docē´bis	*you will teach,* etc.	docē´bitis	*you will teach,* etc.
docē´bit	*he/she/it will teach,* etc.	docē´bunt	*they will teach,* etc.

IMPERATIVE

do´cē!	*teach!*	docē´te!	*teach!*

The present imperative of second conjugation verbs is formed according to the same rules as the first conjugation. **Augē fortūnam tuae familiae!** *Increase your family's fortune!*

Oral Practice

1. Conjugate **habeō** *(have, hold)* in the present tense and **augeō** *(increase)* in the future tense and then translate.
2. Give the singular imperative of *have, increase, teach;* give the plural imperative of *hold, scare.*
3. Translate: *they will have, he increases, we show, he will teach, you* (pl.) *scare, fight!* (sing.), *fight!* (pl.).

Did You Know?

Besides the **lūdī** or **scholae** where basic instruction was given to both male and female Roman students, there were special schools for music, cooking, and barbering. However, no provision was made for formal training in certain subjects like law, administration, diplomacy, and military tactics. For practical on-the-job training, a young man would apprentice himself to an older man distinguished in one of these areas.

Ronald Sheridan/Ancient Art & Architecture Collection

Magister discipulum tardum terret. While one boy begins to read from his roll, the teacher rebukes a latecomer *(far right).* From a relief now in Trier, Germany.

📖 *Exercises*

A. Translate the following sentences. Pay particular attention to the endings.
1. Docē linguās, Anna.
2. Multās linguās nōn docēbō.
3. Magnae undae servōs terrēbunt.
4. Magnae undae cūrās nautārum augent.
5. Victōria numerum servōrum nōn semper augēbit.
6. Pecūniam servāre est semper fortūnam augēre.
7. Prōvinciīs victōriam magnam patriae nūntiābimus.
8. Amīcus meus magnam pecūniam et parvam disciplīnam habet.

B. Identify the person, number, and tense required. Then give the Latin for the italicized words.
1. Fīlia linguās *(will teach).*
2. Nautae Annam *(are scaring).*
3. *(Love)* linguam patriae tuae.
4. Cibum multum nōn *(we do have).*
5. *(Increase)* fortūnam tuam disciplīnā.
6. Memoriam Rōmae linguā Latīnā *(we shall preserve).*
7. Patriam *(to seize)* et familiam meam *(to scare)* parābunt.

C. Say what the following people are doing today (**hodiē**); then say that they will do it again tomorrow (**crās**); finally, say what they do or will do always (**semper**). Follow the model.

> **fīlia / amāre / familia**
> **Hodiē fīlia familiam amat.**
> **Crās fīlia familiam amābit.**
> **Semper fīlia familiam amat (amābit).**

1. nauta / nāvigāre
2. agricola / augēre / fortūna
3. magister / docēre / discipulī
4. dominī / spectāre / equī
5. servī / portāre / cibus
6. rēgīna / habēre / magna pecūnia

WORD STUDY

Derivatives

- From what Latin words are *accurate, doctrine, document* derived? When is the word *doctor* used to mean *one who teaches?* What is a *linguist?* What does the word *discipline* usually mean? What was its original meaning?

- Which one of these words does not belong with the others? Why?

  terrible   subterranean   deter   terrified

- A number of Latin verb forms are preserved as loan words. First conjugation: **vetō, habitat, ignorāmus, mandāmus.** Second conjugation: **tenet.** Look these words up in a dictionary to see if their English meanings are the same as they used to be in Latin.

- The Latin ablative of the first declension is preserved in English in the word *via:* "I am going to Toronto *via* (by way of) New York." The ablative plural is found in *gratis,* a shortened form of **grātiīs:** "He is doing this *gratis*" (for thanks, for nothing).

The U.S. Capitol reflects the classical influence of Rome on those who, in the eighteenth century, imagined a Roman temple, with its high podium and massive dome, as the central symbol of American government. Although it has taken almost two hundred years to complete the design, the Capitol remains true to its original conception and has become the model for most state capitols and many other public buildings.

LESSON XI

CAESAR IN BRITANNIĀ

LESSON OBJECTIVES
- To learn prepositions of place
- To learn how to analyze sentences

Magna īnsula Britannia in amīcitiā Galliae manet. Caesar in Galliā pugnat et amīcitiam Britanniae et Galliae videt. Ibi māteriam et cibum parat et ad Britanniam nāvigat. In Britanniā amīcōs Gallōrum pugnīs terret, sed in Britanniā nōn manet.

Īnsulam videt, nōn occupat, sed glōriam suam[1] auget. Semper prō[2] patriā et 5 prō glōriā suā[1] labōrat. Caesar grātiam et amīcitiam Rōmānōrum meret[3] quod magnae sunt victōriae. Multīs litterīs Rōmae victōriās nūntiat. In Rōmā magnam pecūniam amīcīs dōnat. Magna est grātia patriae quod Caesar patriam auget. Multam praedam carrīs et equīs ad patriam portat. Nunc Caesar glōriam magnam habet et semper habēbit. 10

[1] *his own*
[2] *for, on behalf of*
[3] *earns*

Photo Bulloz/Louvre, Paris

A portrait bust, now in the Louvre, of C. Julius Caesar, the man whose name is always associated with Roman authority, wearing the laurel wreath of a conquering general. The period from 133 to 31 B.C. was one of great civil turmoil, during which one strong man after another sought power by either attacking or defending the conservative policies of the Senate. Caesar, although he was an aristocrat, adopted measures favored by the common people. His campaigns in Gaul (and briefly Britain) were not only for territorial conquest and propaganda purposes, but also to acquire the resources and followers necessary for his political ambitions. He succeeded in making himself the sole master of Rome in 46 B.C. but was assassinated in 44 B.C.

Questions

1. What relationship do Great Britain and Gaul have before Caesar's arrival?
2. In which country does Caesar fight first?
3. What does Caesar do in Gaul?
4. What does Caesar do to Britain?
5. Whose friendship and gratitude does Caesar earn?
6. By what means does Caesar announce his victories?
7. Why do Caesar's victories win his country's gratitude?
8. How are the war spoils transported back to Rome?

VOCABULARY

Nouns

amīci´tia, -ae f. *friendship*	**[amō]**
glō´ria, -ae f. *glory*	(glorify, glorious)
grā´tia, -ae f. *gratitude, influence*	**[grātus]**
māte´ria, -ae f. *matter, timber*	(material, materialism)

Verbs

ma´neō, manē´re, [mān´sī, mānsū´rus[4]] *remain*	(manor, mansion)
vi´deō, vidē´re, [vī´dī, vī´sus] *see*	(provide, visual)

Preposition

in with abl. *in, on*

Adverb

i´bi *there*

GRAMMAR

Prepositions of Place: *In*

In the preceding lessons, the various uses of the prepositions *with, of, to, for, by* with nouns have been expressed in Latin by case endings without prepositions. But some English expressions require the use of prepositions in Latin.

In with the ablative (ablative of place where – *in, on*)

in silvā	*in a forest*
in viīs	*on the streets*

---

[4] This form in **-ūrus** instead of **-us** will be explained at a later time.

Hadrian's Wall, an ancient fortified wall, crosses northern England at its narrowest point. After the Romans abandoned their attempt to conquer Scotland, the wall became the permanent northern boundary of the Roman empire as a barrier against the Scottish barbarians. Begun in A.D. 121, it stretched 73.5 miles. The wall varied from 6.5 to 11.5 feet thick and was 23 feet tall in places. It was protected on both sides by a ditch. Large portions of the wall are still standing.

National Trust/Art Resource, NY

Sentence Analysis

Before writing the Latin translation of an English sentence, you may find it helpful to write the case and number required for each noun and the person, number, and tense for each verb in the Latin sentence. Study the following.

NOM. SING.	3RD SING., PRES.	ACC. SING.	DAT. SING.
The man	gives	a book	to the boy.

GEN. SING.	NOM. SING.	3RD SING., FUT.	ACC. SING.	ABL. SING.
My friend's	son	will save	his life	by flight.

Oral Practice

1. Decline **amīcus tuus, vīta longa,** and **agricola clārus.**
2. Give in Latin: *good friendship* in the accusative singular and plural; *good food* in the genitive singular and plural; *a small number* in the ablative singular and plural; *a famous language* in the dative singular and plural.
3. Analyze the following English sentence by labeling each noun's case and number: *On many islands the sailors carry the queen's timber.*
4. Analyze the following Latin sentence: **In Gallōrum terrā multōs equōs spectō.**

Did You Know?

Each year it took fourteen million bushels of wheat, representing the produce of millions of acres of wheat fields, to feed the people of Rome in Augustus' time. Most of this grain was imported specifically for the city of Rome. One third of it came from Egypt; most of the rest came from Sicily and North Africa and was unloaded at Ostia, the coastal city that served as the seaport for Rome.

▦ Exercises

A. Analyze the nouns and verbs and translate.
1. Laudāte amīcitiam.
2. Magna est grātia puellārum.
3. In silvīs māteriam vidēbis.
4. Nautae in terrā nōn manēbunt.
5. In viīs multōs servōs nōn videō.
6. Multās hōrās nōn habētis. Labōrāte!
7. Disciplīnā glōriam patriae augēbimus.
8. In patriā magnam pecūniam nunc habēmus.

B. Give the Latin for the italicized words. Then translate the sentences.
1. *(On the streets)* carrōs vidēmus.
2. Multa māteria *(in the forest)* est.
3. Equī *(on the island)* nōn manēbunt.
4. *(In the provinces)* multōs servōs vidēbimus.
5. *(In my country)* magnum numerum amīcōrum habeō.

C. Translate into Latin.
1. Remain and see my friends.
2. They will remain on the islands.
3. I shall see your daughter on the street.
4. By friendship you will increase your influence.
5. Through (by) injustice they will seize the land of the provinces.

WORD STUDY

Latin Forms of English Names

• Many English names of boys and girls are taken from Latin words, such as Alma, *kindly;* Clara, *clear, bright;* Leo, *lion;* Stella, *star;* Sylvester, *belonging to the woods.* Some have been changed slightly: Mabel, from **amābilis**, *lovable;* Belle, from **bella,** *beautiful;* Florence, from **flōrentia,** *flourishing;* Grace, from **grātia,** *grace;* Margaret, from **margarīta,** *pearl;* Rose, from **rosa,** *rose.*

• Commonly used by the Romans were the names August, Augustus, *venerable;* Rufus, *red-haired;* Victor, *conqueror;* Vincent (**vincēns**), *conquering.*

• Other Roman names still used in English include: Emil and Emily (**Aemilius, Aemilia**), Cecilia (**Caecilia**); Claudia; Cornelius, Cornelia; Horace (**Horātius**); Julius, Julia; Lavinia; Mark and Marcia (**Mārcus**); Paul and Paula (**Paulus**).

• How many older brothers and sisters do you think a boy named Quintus has?

• Do any members of your class have Latin names not included here?

LESSON OBJECTIVES

- To learn the perfect tense of the first and second conjugations
- To learn the English derivatives from some Latin roots

PUERĪ RŌMĀNĪ

Lūcius, puer[1] Rōmānus, in Viā Altā amīcum Mārcum videt.

Lūcius: Ubi est socius tuus Quīntus?

Mārcus: Ad īnsulam nāvigāvit.

Lūcius: Cūr[2] ad īnsulam nāvigāvit?

5 **Mārcus:** Īnsulam amat. Ibi in aquā diū[3] manet; in silvā altā ambulat[4]. In īnsulā multōs amīcōs habet.

Lūcius: Cūr nōn cum[5] sociō tuō ad īnsulam nāvigāvistī? Cūr hīc[6] mānsistī?

Mārcus: In casā labōrāre dēbeō[7] quod servōs līberāvimus.

10 **Lūcius:** Magnum numerum servōrum habēmus et semper habuimus. In casā, in viā, in silvā labōrant. Māteriam portant. Agricolae sunt. Servī grātiam nostram meruērunt, sed eōs[8] tenēbimus.

Mārcus: Quod servī nostrī agricolae bonī erant et semper labōrāvērunt, eōs nōn tenuimus sed līberāvimus. Nunc amīcī et sociī sunt et 15 amīcitiam eōrum[9] semper memoriā tenēbō.

[1] boy
[2] why
[3] a long time
[4] walks
[5] with
[6] here
[7] I have to (ought)
[8] them
[9] their

Roman slaves, like these who are threshing or sifting grain, worked for their Roman masters and lived with them as part of the **familia**. Slaves did not only do manual labor, but some also taught the master's children or served as a personal secretary to their master. Some were allowed to conduct their own businesses and eventually bought their freedom.

Ronald Sheridan/Ancient Art & Architecture Collection

Questions

1. Where does Lucius see Marcus?
2. Where did Marcus' friend go?
3. What is Quintus doing on the island?
4. Why didn't Marcus go to the island?
5. Why must he work?
6. What sorts of work do Lucius' slaves do?
7. Why did Marcus' family free his slaves?
8. What relationship do the slaves have to Marcus' family now that they are free?

VOCABULARY

Nouns

ca´sa, -ae f. *house*
so´cius, so´cī m. *ally, comrade*   (associate, social)

Adjective

al´tus, al´ta, [al´tum] *high, tall, deep*   (altimeter, altitude)

Verbs

lī´berō, līberā´re, līberā´vī, [līberā´tus] *free* (liberal, liberator)
me´reō, merē´re, me´ruī, [me´ritus]   (merit, meritorious)
   deserve, earn
te´neō, tenē´re, te´nuī, [ten´tus] *hold, keep* (retain, retentive)

GRAMMAR

The Perfect Tense

In English, the past tense refers to an action that is completed: *He went yesterday.* The present perfect refers to an action that is completed, but from the point of view of the present: *He has just gone.* One does not say *He has gone yesterday.*

In Latin, the perfect tense is used like both the past and the present perfect of English, though it more often corresponds to the past.

Grātiam meruimus.	*We deserved (have deserved) gratitude.*
Magister puellās docuit.	*The teacher taught (has taught) the girls.*
Viam spectāvimus.	*We looked (have looked) at the road.*

Second declension nouns (not adjectives) that end in **-ius** usually shorten the **-iī** of the genitive singular to **-ī. So´ciī** becomes **so´cī** and the accent is not changed. The stem is **soci-** and the nominative plural always ends in **-iī**.

Remember that each verb has four principal parts. The third principal part, which shows you the perfect stem, is introduced in this lesson.

This wall painting (first century B.C.) appears to be Nausicaa, princess on the island of Phaeacia, with her laundry on her head, welcoming a bedraggled Ulysses, who was shipwrecked there while returning from Troy. (See Lesson XLV.) This picture does not quite match all the details of the story as told by Homer.

Perfect Tense and Perfect Stem

Verbs of the first conjugation studied so far form the perfect stem by adding **-v-** to the present stem: **līberā-, līberāv-.** To find the perfect stem of verbs of the second conjugation, drop the **-ī** of the perfect first person singular, which is the third principal part of the verb (as listed in your lesson vocabulary list), **doceō, docēre, docuī, doctus: docu-.** Add the perfect tense endings to the perfect stem to form the perfect tense. Learn the following forms.

ENDINGS	FIRST CONJUGATION	SECOND CONJUGATION
-ī	**portā´vī** *I carried, have carried, did carry*	**do´cuī** *I taught, have taught, did teach*
-istī	**portāvis´tī** *you carried*, etc.	**docuis´tī** *you taught*, etc.
-it	**portā´vit** *he/she/it carried*, etc.	**do´cuit** *he/she/it taught*, etc.
-imus	**portā´vimus** *we carried*, etc.	**docu´imus** *we taught*, etc.
-istis	**portāvis´tis** *you carried*, etc.	**docuis´tis** *you taught*, etc.
-ērunt	**portāvē´runt** *they carried*, etc.	**docuē´runt** *they taught*, etc.

The perfect tense endings are not used in any other tense.

Oral Practice

1. Conjugate the following in the perfect tense: **labōrō (labōrāv-), teneō (tenu-), mereō (meru-), maneō (māns-), mōnstrō (mōnstrāv-), augeō (aux-), habeō (habu-), videō (vīd-).**
2. Translate: *he has praised, we entrusted, they scared, we did teach, I saw.*

📖 Exercises

A. Translate the following sentences.

1. Servō litterās mandāvī.
2. Multōs sociōs habuistis.
3. Agricola in terrā labōrābit.
4. Undae altae puellās terruērunt.
5. Cōpiam aquae clārae parāvistī.
6. Multōs servōs in casā vīdimus.
7. Agricolae, grātiam patriae meruistis.
8. Amīcus meus in prōvinciā nōn mānsit.

B. Translate the following sentences into Latin.

1. The slave held the horses.
2. We saw a large number of horses.
3. The farmers have got the food ready.
4. The girls will carry the food to my house.
5. My comrade has deserved your friendship.

Gianni Dagli Orti/Museo Palazzo dei Conservatori Rome/The Art Archive

Magister discipulōs docet. In this relief the master, seated and holding a roll, reads to four bearded disciples. The beards, dress, and crude portrayal of hair all suggest a late date, probably the fourth century A.D.

Did You Know?

The Romans saw their Greek subjects as rebellious and untrustworthy, yet they were keenly aware that the Greeks were their cultural superiors. This love-hate relationship was central to Roman social life and history. The Greeks provided a great deal of the art, architecture, medicine, and teaching to the Roman world, and Greek culture was fashionable among the educated Romans.

WORD STUDY

Derivatives

• Using their meanings as a guide, tell which of the following words come from **servāre** and which from **servus:** *serf, conserve, serve, servant, reserve.*

• What does the derivation tell us about the meaning of *social, social service, social security, socialism?* What is an *equestrian?* A *copious* amount? A *nautical* mile?

• The Latin perfect tense of the first conjugation is preserved in English *affidavit.*

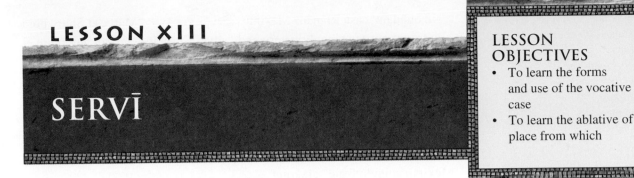

LESSON XIII

SERVĪ

LESSON OBJECTIVES
- To learn the forms and use of the vocative case
- To learn the ablative of place from which

Servī Rōmānī erant captīvī. Rōmānī multīs pugnīs singulas terrās occupāvērunt, et magnus erat numerus captīvōrum. Captīvōs ē Graeciā, ē Galliā, ex Asiā, ex Āfricā in Italiam mōvērunt. In familiā Rōmānā erant multī servī, bonī et malī.

Servī aquam in[1] casās portāvērunt; medicī[2] et agricolae erant; dē vītā, dē gloriā, dē amīcitiā docuērunt. Multī Graecī clārī erant servī et amīcī Rōmānōrum. Litterae[3] Rōmānōrum memoriam servōrum servāvērunt. Poena servī malī magna erat. Servōs bonōs multī Rōmānī līberāvērunt.

[1] *into*
[2] *doctors*
[3] *literature*

This costly and elaborate tombstone of Q. Fabius Diogenes and Fabia Primigenia, who shared forty-seven years together, was set up by their freedmen, freedwomen, and slaves (familia). Obviously, these freedmen and slaves thought highly of their former master and mistress.

In quādam[4] casā Rōmānā Maximus servōs vocāvit: "Mārce et Stātī[5], hōra
10 quīnta est; portāte singulī māteriam dē silvā; Cornēlī, vocā socium tuum et
movēte carrum ā viā et equōs ab aquā. Tum parāte cēnam; amīcōs meōs in
Altā Viā vīdī et ad cēnam vocāvī."

Servī māteriam portāvērunt, carrum et equōs mōvērunt. Tum cibum
parāvērunt et ad mēnsam[6] portāvērunt. Post[7] cēnam amīcī mānsērunt, et
15 Maximus amīcīs pictūrās mōnstrāvit. Interim[8] servī in culīnā[9] labōrāvērunt.
Tum amīcī Maximī servōs laudāvērunt et eīs[10] pecūniam dōnāvērunt.
Maximō singulī "valē" dīxērunt[11].

Questions

1. How and from what places did the Romans get their slaves?
2. Name four things that slaves did.
3. What did they teach?
4. How do we know about the lives of slaves?
5. What reward was given to slaves for good service?
6. What were the names of Maximus' slaves?
7. What tasks did he assign them?
8. What did Maximus show his friends after dinner?
9. What did the slaves do in the meantime?
10. What reward did they get? From whom?

VOCABULARY

Nouns

captī´vus, -ī m. *prisoner* (captivate, captivity)
cē´na, -ae f. *dinner*

Adjective

sin´gulī, sin´gulae, [sin´gula] *one at a time,* (single, singular)
one by one (always plural)

Verbs

mo´veō, movē´re, mō´vī, [mō´tus] *move* (movement, motive)
vo´cō, vocā´re, vocā´vī, [vocā´tus] *call* (evocative, vocal)

Prepositions

ā, ab with abl., *away from, from* (abduct, abjure)
dē with abl., *down from, from, about,* (destroy, derive)
concerning
ē, ex with abl., *out from, from, out of* (exit, export)

▣ GRAMMAR

The Vocative Case

In Latin, the vocative case is used to address people directly or to get a person's attention. It has the same form as the nominative in all declensions, except that the vocative singular of **-us** nouns and adjectives of the second declension ends in **-e**; in **-ius** nouns (but not adjectives) **-ie** becomes **-ī**.

Līberā captīvōs, amīce Mārce.	*Free the captives, friend Marcus.*
Spectāte undās, fīliī meī et fīliae meae.	*Look at the waves, my sons and my daughters.*

Upon their return from market, the slaves took food purchases to the kitchen for preparation or storage. Fruits and fish were an important part of the Romans' diet. This boy named Junius appears in a mosaic from Pompeii.

Unless used for special emphasis, the vocative does not stand first in a sentence. It is regularly separated from the rest of the sentence by commas, as in the preceding sentences.

Oral Practice

1. Give the vocative forms of the following: **Lūcius, agricolae, Cornēlia, Quīntus, Tullius, Anna, varius** (adj.).
2. Translate the following into Latin using the vocative case: *Slave! Maximus! Clara! Romulus and Remus! Publius!*

Ablative Expressing Place From Which

The ablative of place from which uses one of three prepositions, together with the ablative, to express the concept *from*.

ā, ab	*away from (the outside)*
dē	*down from, from*
ē, ex	*out from (the inside), out of*

Although all three prepositions mean *from*, **ab** means *away from the outside*, **ex** means *out from the inside*, and **dē** means *from*, when it is not important to distinguish *where from*. Sometimes **dē** means *down from*, sometimes it means *about*.

Cicerō dē amīcitiā scrīpsit.	*Cicero wrote about (concerning) friendship.*

ā viā   dē silvā   ex aquā

The shorter forms **ā** and **ē** are used only before words beginning with a consonant (except **h**); **ab** and **ex** are used before words beginning with vowels and sometimes before consonants.

Ā viā ambulant.	*They are walking away from the road.*
Equī dē Galliā ambulāvērunt.	*The horses walked (down) from Gaul.*
Ē silvā ambulāvit.	*He walked out of (from) the forest.*

Oral Practice

Give the Latin for the following phrases: *out of the water, away from the house, from Italy, down from the horse, from the islands, about glory.*

🏛 *Exercises*

A. Translate the following sentences.
1. Vocā, Mārce, servōs ē casā.
2. Sociī equōs ē Viā Quīntā movēbunt.
3. In fortūnā malā amīcōs bonōs habuimus.
4. Movē, Cornēlī, carrōs singulōs dē silvā altā.
5. Portāte, captīvī, māteriam dē silvīs ad aquam.
6. Servī malī multam praedam ab īnsulīs portāvērunt.

B. Translate the following sentences into Latin.
1. We have called the girls to dinner.
2. My daughter had a large number of friends.
3. Brutus, move the prisoners one at a time from the island.
4. One at a time they sailed from the island to the new land.

C. Tell the following people to move something from somewhere. Follow the model.

>**Anna / rāna / aqua**
>**Movē, Anna, rānam ex aquā.**

1. Mārcus / carrus / via
2. Clāra / Mārcus / Gallia
3. Servī / familia / casa
4. Quīntus / captīvī / undae
5. Fīlius bonus / māteria / silvae

Did You Know?

Roman medicine was largely imported from Greece, taught and practiced by Greek physicians. It included many of the features we have adapted into modern medicine: careful observation of the patient, diagnosis and prognosis, and clinical treatment. Cures through diet, the use of herbal drugs, and surgery were important features. Surgical procedures were quite sophisticated for those times, but other areas of ancient medicine we would put in the realm of magic and superstition, and there was little of what we would call research and experimentation.

WORD STUDY

Word Formation Many Latin words are formed by joining prefixes (**prae** *in front;* **fīxus** *attached*) to root words. These same prefixes, most of which are prepositions, are those chiefly used in English. With these prefixes we are continually forming new words.

- Examples of the prefixes **ab-, dē-** and **ex-** are:
  ab- (abs-, ā-): *a-vocation, ab-undance, abs-tain*
  dē-: *de-fame, de-form, de-ter, de-viate, de-portation*
  ex- (ē-, ef-): *ex-alt, ex-patriation, ex-pect* (from **spectō**),
      e-voke, ex-president.

- Define the words above according to prefix and root. For root words, see previous lesson vocabularies.

- Look up the difference between *vocation* and *avocation*.

- Other examples of English words having the prefix **ex-** are:
  ex-cuse, e-dict, ex-empt, ef-fect, ef-fervescent, e-gress, ex-tend.
  Look up their meanings in a dictionary.

LESSON XIV

ARISTOTELĒS ET ALEXANDER

[1] Aristotle (nom.)
[2] king of Macedonia
[3] Aristotle (acc.)
[4] Aristotle (dat.)
[5] Homer
[6] I am
[7] of Achilles (gen.) hero of Homer's Iliad
[8] anger
[9] reverence, respect
[10] we owe
[11] he will be

Aristotelēs[1] magister bonus multōrum virōrum erat. Philosophiam et scientiam nātūrālem docuit. Quod Aristotelēs erat clārus et magister bonus, Philippus, rēx Macedoniae,[2] Aristotelem[3] probāvit.

Philippus fīlium habuit, Alexandrum, puerum bonum et amīcum.
5 Philippus clārō magistrō Aristotelī[4] puerum Alexandrum mandāvit:

"Docē fīlium meum, philosophe."

Aristotelēs semper amīcus Alexandrō erat, et Alexandrum nōn terruit. Aristotelēs Alexandrum dē philosophiā et dē Homērō[5], poētā clārō, docuit. Alexander Homērum amāvit et laudāvit, sed philosophia erat disciplīna dūra
10 et longa.

In agrō Alexander equum novum habuit. Alexander agrum et equum spectāvit, et Aristotelī[4] nūntiāvit:

"Vidē, magister, agrum grātum. Casam tuam nōn amō. Docē mē in agrō. Puer sum[6], nōn vir. Puer līber sum, fīlius Philippī, nōn captīvus tuus. In agrō
15 Homērum et glōriam virī magnī Achillis[7] memoriae mandābō."

Aristotelēs in agrō Alexandrum docēre parat. Sed ubi est puer Alexander? Alexander ad silvam equum incitat. Līber est!

Magna erat īra[8] Philippī, sed in philosophō amīcō nōn erat īra. Philippō Aristotelēs nūntiat:
20 "Puer nōn malus est. Puerī nostrī sacrī sunt; puellae nostrae sacrae sunt. Puerīs nostrīs reverentiam[9] magnam dēbēmus[10]. Alexander bonus est et magnus erit[11]."

Et erat Alexander magnus. Multās terrās occupāvit. Semper fāmam Achillis[7] memoriā tenuit.

Questions

1. What did Aristotle teach?
2. Why did Philip put Aristotle in charge of teaching his son?
3. What was Philip's son's name and what kind of boy was he?
4. What did Aristotle teach him about?
5. What subject(s) did the boy prefer?
6. What did Alexander watch while studying?

7. What reasons did he give for wanting to study outside?
8. Where did Alexander go?
9. What was his father's reaction?
10. How did Aristotle try to persuade Philip not to punish his son?
11. What promise did Alexander make to Aristotle? Did Alexander keep it?

VOCABULARY

Nouns

a´ger, a´grī m. *field*	[agricola]
fī´lius, fī´lī m. *son*	[fīlia]
magis´ter, magis´trī m. *teacher*	(Mr., master)
pu´er, pu´erī m. *boy*	(puerile)
vir, vi´rī m. *man, hero*	(virile, triumvirate)

Adjectives

amī´cus, amī´ca, [amī´cum] *friendly*	[amō]
lī´ber, lī´bera, [lī´berum] *free*	[līberō]
nos´ter, nos´tra, [nos´trum] *our*	(nostrum)
sa´cer, sa´cra, [sa´crum] *sacred*	(consecrate, sacrifice)

GRAMMAR

The Second Declension: Nouns and Adjectives in *-r*

Nouns and adjectives of the second declension whose stem ends in **-r** omit the ending **-us** in the nominative singular. Therefore, such words end in **-er** or **-r** in the nominative. The genitive singular of nouns and the feminine nominative singular of adjectives both show whether **-e-** is retained before **-r-** in the other case forms.

Alexander the Great (356–323 B.C.) was the son of Philip II of Macedon. Even as a young boy, Alexander was a skilled horseman, a talented musician, and an avid reader. He was taught by the Greek philosopher Aristotle until called to duty at his father's side at age sixteen. When his father was murdered, Alexander became king. One of his most famous victories was the Battle of Issus in Asia Minor (333 B.C.), in which King Darius of Persia was put to flight. Later, Alexander succeeded in conquering Egypt and Persia.

Erich Lessing/Art Resource, NY

STEM	AGR-	NOSTR-		
	SINGULAR		PLURAL	
Nominative	**a´ger**	**nos´ter**	**a´grī**	**nos´trī**
Genitive	**a´grī**	**nos´trī**	**agrō´rum**	**nostrō´rum**
Dative	**a´grō**	**nos´trō**	**a´grīs**	**nos´trīs**
Accusative	**a´grum**	**nos´trum**	**a´grōs**	**nos´trōs**
Ablative	**a´grō**	**nos´trō**	**a´grīs**	**nos´trīs**
Vocative	**a´ger**	**nos´ter**	**a´grī**	**nos´trī**

STEM	VIR-	LĪBER-		
	SINGULAR		PLURAL	
Nominative	vir	lī'ber	vi'rī	lī'berī
Genitive	vi'rī	lī'berī	virō'rum	liberō'rum
Dative	vi'rō	lī'berō	vi'rīs	lī'berīs
Accusative	vi'rum	lī'berum	vi'rōs	lī'berōs
Ablative	vi'rō	lī'berō	vi'rīs	lī'berīs
Vocative	vir	lī'ber	vi'rī	lī'berī

Several Latin nouns and adjectives of the **-er** type are used in English: *arbiter, cancer, minister, vesper, integer, miser, neuter, sinister.*

In memorizing vocabularies, always note carefully the nominative, the genitive, and the gender of every noun.

- Nouns and adjectives like **puer** and **līber** have the **-e-** throughout; those like **ager** and **noster** have it only in the nominative singular, while **vir** has no **-e-** at all. Most **-er** words are like **ager;** no others are like **vir.**
- The English derivative will usually show whether **-e-** is retained or not; for example, *pu-e-rile, lib-e-ral, mis-e-rable;* but *agriculture, sacred, magistrate.*
- Adjectives agree with their nouns in gender, number, and case but not always in ending: **puer bonus, nauta līber.**

Oral Practice

1. Decline **magister novus, fīlius sacer.**
2. Tell the form or forms of **equīs, agrum, virō, nostrī, līberōs, sacrā, plānōrum, singulī, casārum.**

Did You Know?

Giving a slave his freedom could mean that he could become a Roman citizen. In other words, he was entitled to inherit part or all his former master's estate, and his sons were even eligible for the senate, knighthood, or high rank in the army. The manumission of slaves made upward social mobility possible within the rigid Roman hierarchical society.

🏛 *Exercises*

A. Translate the following sentences.

1. Incitā, Mārce, equum amīcum ex agrīs.
2. Magister noster linguam clāram docet.
3. Memoria clārōrum virōrum nostrōrum sacra est.
4. Magister tuus puerō malō pecūniam nōn dōnāvit.
5. In Americā magnōs agrōs et virōs līberōs vidēbitis.
6. Virī nostrī agrōs sociōrum amīcōrum nōn occupāvērunt.

B. Translate the following sentences into Latin.

1. Give Anna the boy's money.
2. Our country is free and sacred.
3. A friend of my son teaches boys.
4. I saw many horses in the fields of our friends.
5. The men moved the timber out of the forest with horses.
6. He is our little boy.

C. Answer each question using the word in parentheses. Make all necessary changes. Follow the model.

Mārcus fīlius tuus est? (sīc)

Sīc, Mārcus meus fīlius est.

1. Ubi undae sunt? (aqua)
2. Casa in aquā est? (ager)
3. Equum meum vīdistī? (silva)
4. Sunt virī līberī? (captīvī)
5. Est casa tua in terrā plānā? (alta)

WORD STUDY

Assimilation Some prefixes change their final consonants to make them like the initial consonants of the words to which they are attached. This is called assimilation (**ad** *to;* **similis** *like*).

The prefix **ad-** is generally assimilated. Identify the roots and define the following words—all of them formed from Latin words in the earlier vocabularies: *ac-curate, af-filiate, al-literation, an-nounce, ap-paratus, a-spect, as-sociate, ad-vocate.*

Additional examples are: *ab-breviate, af-fect, ag-gressive, ac-quire, ar-rogant, at-tend,* and the word *as-similation* itself.

LESSON OBJECTIVES
- To learn the present tense of **sum**
- To learn the accusative of place to which

COLŌNĪ RŌMĀNĪ

¹ *city*

² *grain*

³ *you*

Puella Rōmāna sum. Fīlia sum agricolae. Colōnī sumus et in prōvinciā Galliā habitāmus. Ex Italiā in prōvinciam migrāvimus. In prōvinciā sunt agrī novī et magnī. Agrī nostrī sunt bonī, sed casa nostra parva est. In agrīs multās hōrās labōrāmus. Līberī sumus, sed labōrāmus; multōs servōs nōn
5 tenēmus. Pecūniam nōn habēmus. Vīta agricolārum dūra est, sed agricolae et colōnī magnum animum habent.

Multī agricolae ad urbem¹ Rōmam migrāvērunt, sed familia mea ad urbem nōn migrābit. Rōmam vīdī, sed ibi nōn mānsī. Agricolae in urbem equīs et carrīs māteriam et frūmentum² portant, sed ibi nōn manent. Multī virī in viīs
10 Rōmae sunt: agricolae, colōnī, nautae, magistrī, captīvī, servī.

Estis colōnī, puerī et puellae? Ubi habitātis? Ad urbem migrāvistis? Vīta dūra in agrīs vōs³ terruit? Animōs agricolārum nōn habētis.

Questions
1. Who is the narrator of the story?
2. From where did she move?
3. Why do the settlers move to the province?
4. Describe the life of colonists based on the first paragraph.
5. Has the narrator been to Rome?
6. What types of people can you find in Rome?
7. What do the farmers go to Rome for?
8. In Latin, answer the questions found at the end of the story.

Gianni Dagli Orti/Museo Concordiese Portogruaro/The Art Archive

A bronze statuette (first century A.D.) of a farmer sowing grain. Although the life of farm families was often hard, Roman writers and politicians were fond of praising its virtues.

VOCABULARY

Nouns

    a´nimus, -ī m. *mind, courage, spirit*   (unanimous)

    colō´nus, -ī m. *settler, colonist*   (colonize)

Verbs

    ha´bitō, habitā´re, habitā´vī,   (habitation)
        [habitā´tus] *live, dwell*

    mi´grō, migrā´re, migrā´vī,   (migration)
        [migrātū´rus] *depart, migrate*

    sum, es´se, fu´ī, [futū´rus] *be*   (essence, future)

Preposition

    in with acc., *into, onto, to, against;*
        with abl., *in, on*

GRAMMAR

Present of *sum*

    The verb *to be* is irregularly formed in English and Latin as well as in other languages; thus, it does not belong to one of the "regular" conjugations. The present indicative of **sum** is conjugated as follows.

sum	*I am*	**su´mus**	*we are*
es	*you are*	**es´tis**	*you are*
est	*he/she/it is*	**sunt**	*they are*

Note that it is the stem, not the personal endings, that are irregular.

Sum is a linking verb and cannot have a direct object. It links adjectives or nouns in the predicate with the subject of the sentence. If an English (progressive) verb form showing *-ing* (e.g., *I am working*) is called for, do not use a form of **sum.** Remember that **labōrō** by itself can mean *I work, I do work,* and *I am working.*

Oral Practice

Give the Latin for the italicized words. Tell which are predicate nominatives and which are direct objects.

1. They are *sailors*.
2. We are *settlers*.
3. They are moving the *prisoners*.
4. He is a *slave*.
5. I like *my friend*.
6. You are *boys*.

Accusative of Place To Which: *Ad, In + Accusative*

All prepositions in Latin are followed by either the accusative or ablative case. When used with verbs of motion, **ad** means *to, toward* and **in** means *into, onto,* and they are followed by the accusative case. Note the difference in meaning as captured in the following sentences.

Carrōs ad aquam movent.	*They move the carts to the water.*
Carrōs in aquam movent.	*They move the carts into the water.*

However, when the preposition **in** is followed by the ablative case, it means *in* or *on.* Note the difference in meaning as captured in the illustrations below.

The preposition **ad** without a verb of motion can mean *near* or *at.*

Ad aquam sedet.	*She is sitting near (at) the water.*

In a way, **ad** is the opposite of **ab,** and **in** is the opposite of **ex.**

ad aquam

in aquam

in aquā

🏛 *Exercises*

A. Translate the following sentences into English.

1. Animus virōrum est magnus.
2. Servī estis et in agrīs labōrātis.
3. Colōnī ex Eurōpā migrāvērunt.
4. Ad līberam Americam nāvigāvērunt.
5. Multī līberī virī in īnsulā magnā habitant.
6. Sociī nostrī in īnsulam captīvōs mōvērunt.
7. Carrīs dē silvīs ad aquam māteriam portābitis.

B. Translate the following sentences into Latin.

1. Give the loot to the settlers.
2. Are you the sons of settlers?
3. The teacher's horse is in our field.
4. The prisoners will carry the timber into the fields.
5. The settlers will depart from the island and live in the province.

WORD STUDY

Derivatives and Assimilation The preposition **in,** used as a prefix, is common in English derivatives. Define the following, formed from words found in recent vocabularies: *in-gratiate, in-habitant, in-spect, in-undate, in-voke, in-form.*

The prefix **in-** is often assimilated (see Word Study, page 107). Define the following words: *im-migrant, im-port.* Other examples of assimilation are *il-lusion, ir-rigate.* Words that have come into English through French often have **en-** or **em-** for **in-** or **im-:** *enchant, inquire,* or *enquire.* Our word *envy* comes from Latin **in-vidia** (from **in-videō,** *look into* or *against, look askance at*).

What is meant by the *colonial* period of a nation's history? What is a *magnanimous* person? What is the difference between *immigration* and *emigration?*

TRŌIA

¹ *the Trojans*
² *near Troy*
³ *who*
⁴ *Asia* (modern Turkey)
⁵ *tenth*
⁶ Ulys'sēs
⁷ *to them*
⁸ *climbed*
⁹ *wrote*
¹⁰ *Minerva, a goddess who favored the Greeks*
¹¹ *deserted*
¹² *town*
¹³ *at night*
¹⁴ *returned*
¹⁵ *one of the Greeks*

Graecī et Trōiānī[1] ad Trōiam[2] pugnāvērunt. Trōiānī barbarī erant, quī[3] in Asiā[4] habitāvērunt. Trōiānī et Graecī annōs IX pugnāvērunt. Decimō[5] annō Ulixēs[6], clārus Graecus, cōnsilium novum in animō habuit. Graecōs singulōs signō vocāvit et eīs[7] cōnsilium mandāvit: "Multam māteriam ex silvā ad
5 castra portāte. Ex māteriā equum altum parāte. Barbarīs praemium novum dōnābimus."

Graecī equum parāvērunt et in equum virī singulī ascendērunt[8]. In equō scrīpsērunt[9]: "Graecī Minervae[10] praemium dōnant." Tum ad Trōiānōs equum mōvērunt. Ad īnsulam parvam nāvigāvērunt et frūmentum
10 parāvērunt. Barbarī equum et castra dēserta[11] Graecōrum vīdērunt. Equum vocāvērunt signum sacrum et in oppidum[12] mōvērunt. Nocte[13] Graecī ab īnsulā revertērunt[14] et ūnus ex Graecīs[15] signō ex equō virōs ēvocāvit. In oppidum sociōs vocāvērunt. Graecī Trōiam occupāvērunt. Fortūna Trōiānōrum mala erat.

The legend of the Trojan Horse
and the capture of Troy have
inspired artists and storytellers
from Homer (ca. 750 B.C.) down
to the present day. In this 1994
painting by Tomas Galamoros,
the fall of Troy is told as much by
color symbolism as by narrative
detail. The gold, silver, and
elaborate design suggest the
wealth of Troy; the red and
black, the fire and ashes of its
destruction. In the center, most
of the Trojans gladly welcome
the horse, ignoring the ghoulish
figure in the lower right who
urges them not to trust the
Greeks, even when they bear
gifts.

Questions

1. Where did the Greeks fight and with whom?
2. Name the modern country where the Trojans once lived.
3. How long did the Greeks fight?
4. Who masterminded the plot to take Troy?
5. What plan did he formulate?
6. What did the Greeks put inside the horse?
7. What did they write on the outside and why?
8. Where did the Greeks go after that?
9. What did the Trojans do with the horse? Why?
10. When did the Greeks return to Troy and what did they do then?
11. From what material did the Greeks build the horse?
12. Can you give an example of a modern "Trojan Horse" trick?

VOCABULARY

Nouns

an´nus, -ī m. *year*	(annual, biennial)
bar´barus, -ī m. *foreigner, barbarian*	
cas´tra, -ō´rum n. (pl. in form; sing. in meaning), *camp*	(Lancaster)
cōnsi´lium, cōnsi´lī n. *plan, advice*	(counsel)
frūmen´tum, -ī n. *grain*	(fruit)
prae´mium, prae´mī n. *reward*	(premium)
sig´num, -ī n. *sign, standard, signal*	(sign, significant)

Adjective

bar´barus, -a, -um *foreign*	(barbaric)

Verb

ē´vocō, ēvocā´re, ēvocā´vī, [ēvocā´tus] *call out, summon*	[vocō]

Nota•Bene

Latin adjectives such as **barbarus** can regularly be used as nouns. You have already seen **amīcus** used as a noun to mean (a male) *friend* and **amīcus, -a, -um** to mean *friendly*. **Amīca,** the feminine form of the adjective, is used as a noun to mean *girlfriend*.

GRAMMAR

Neuters of the Second Declension

The second declension contains, in addition to masculine nouns ending in **-us (-ius)**, **-er**, and **-r**, neuter nouns ending in **-um (-ium).** The difference between the neuter and the masculine nouns of the second declension is that the neuter noun in the nominative and accusative plural ends in short **-a** rather than in **-ī** and **-ōs.**

Nota•Bene

Nouns (not adjectives) that end in **-ium** usually shorten **-iī** to **-ī** in the genitive singular: **cōnsi´liī** becomes **cōnsi´lī,** but the accent is not changed.

The column of Trajan (A.D. 113) in Rome records the military campaigns of the emperor in Dacia (modern Romania) in A.D. 100–102 and 105–106 and provides a unique illustration of the organization and activities of the Roman army. The marble column, standing in the Forum of Trajan, rises to exactly 100 Roman feet and can be ascended by an internal spiral staircase. On their death, Trajan and his wife Plotina were buried beneath the column in a golden casket.

Scala/Art Resource

Neuter nouns and adjectives are presented in this lesson. Remember that neuter nouns are listed with an *n.* and the neuter adjective form is listed third.

Adjectives also have neuter forms. Thus, the full nominative form of an adjective like **barbarus** is **barbarus** (masculine), **barbara** (feminine), **barbarum** (neuter) and is listed in your lesson vocabulary as **barbarus, -a, -um.** From now on, adjectives will appear in the vocabularies in this abbreviated form.

NEUTER: SECOND DECLENSION				
STEM	**SIGN-**	**PARV-**		
	SINGULAR		PLURAL	
Nominative	sig´num	par´vum	sig´na	par´va
Genitive	sig´nī	par´vī	sig´nōrum	parvō´rum
Dative	sig´nō	par´vō	sig´nīs	par´vīs
Accusative	sig´num	par´vum	sig´na	par´va
Ablative	sig´nō	par´vō	sig´nīs	par´vīs

All neuters have the same ending in the accusative as they have in the nominative.

Oral Practice

1. Decline **frūmentum bonum** and **praemium grātum.**
2. Give in Latin: *a new standard* in the accusative singular and plural; *a famous reward* in the ablative singular and plural; *a great plan* in the genitive singular and plural; *a small camp* in the dative plural.

▣ *Exercises*

A. Translate the following sentences into English.
1. Amīcus meus multa praemia merēbit.
2. Nūntiā, Fabī, signō victōriam amīcīs tuīs.
3. Litterīs ad castra virōs barbarōs ēvocāvit.
4. Cōnsiliō bonō vītam amīcī nostrī servābimus.
5. Castra sociōrum nostrōrum in magnā īnsulā sunt.
6. Agricolae ex agrīs in castra frūmentum portāvērunt.
7. Captīvī singulī virīs nostrīs cōnsilium nūntiāvērunt.

B. Translate the following sentences into Latin.
1. We shall give our friends great rewards.
2. The colonists will sail from Europe to America.
3. The new year will increase the supply of grain.
4. The settlers then moved the grain with horse and wagon.
5. The strange shape of the horse did not scare the prisoners.

WORD STUDY

- The following are Latin words of the **-um** and **-ium** type preserved in their original form in English.

SINGULAR	PLURAL	SINGULAR	PLURAL
addendum	addenda	delirium	deliria (or -ums)
	agenda	dictum	dicta (or -ums)
bacterium	bacteria	maximum	maxima (or -ums)
candelabrum	candelabra	memorandum	memoranda (or -ums)
curriculum	curricula	minimum	minima (or -ums)
datum	data	stratum	strata (or -ums)

There is a common tendency among people unfamiliar with Latin to turn neuter plurals into singulars. You, knowing the correct forms from your Latin, should remember to say *these data, those agenda, many strata,* etc.

- What is a *signatory* to a treaty? How did **barbarus,** meaning *foreigner,* come to mean *barbarian?*

- More than twenty-five states have towns named *Troy;* South Dakota has both a *Troy* and a *Trojan*. There is a town called *Roma* in Texas and ten towns named *Rome* in other states. *Gallia* is in Ohio.

SLAVERY

In the earliest days the Romans had few slaves, but as prosperity and colonization spread the Romans increasingly depended on them. Slaves did much of the work on the farms and in the trades and in the growing number of businesses. Slaves worked as unskilled laborers, mechanics, artisans, carpenters, bricklayers, seamen, and assistants to merchants and to shopkeepers. Most slaves were prisoners of war who were won in battles with foreign nations. Some of those who came from less developed countries may actually have profited from their exposure to Roman culture. Many from Greece and the Near East, however, were more knowledgeable than their masters because of their backgrounds and early education. They became the teachers, doctors, musicians, actors, and bookkeepers in Roman society. Although the educated and skilled slaves were given much personal freedom, they were still the master's property and could be bought and sold at will. A highly educated slave might cost as much as one hundred twenty thousand dollars at today's prices, a trained farm worker slightly more than ten thousand dollars, a common laborer, still less. Desired attributes of a slave included physical strength, beauty, education, and special skills.

Wealthy Romans kept large numbers of slaves, many of whom had specialized tasks in the household (**familia urbāna**). One slave might be in charge of polishing the silver; another, of writing letters; and another, of announcing the guests or the hour of the day. Great landholders sometimes had hundreds of slaves on their estates where they tended the herds and did the work of growing grapes, olives, or wheat.

A Greek red-figured vase shows two women, matron and maid, as they begin the work of weaving with the spinning of thread. The spindle, loaded with wool, can be seen above and between them.

Gift of Dr. Lloyd E. Hawes, Courtesy, Museum of Fine Arts, Boston

SLAVES AND THEIR MASTERS

The lot of the slave was not always as hard as we might imagine. Businesslike Romans realized that a slave was valuable property, although he was often mistreated by a cruel master or by a foreman who might himself be a slave. Disobedient slaves were punished in various ways. The master had the legal right to kill a slave, but naturally he was rarely inclined to do so, because he would be destroying his own property. Flogging with a whip was a common punishment for minor offenses. Another more feared punishment was to send a city slave to the farm or to the mines where the work was harder. Runaway slaves were branded on the forehead with the letter F, for **fugitīvus,** when they were caught. Sometimes a former runaway slave wore a metal collar around the neck on which was inscribed the name of his owner. Between 73 and 71 B.C., a slave named Spartacus led a mass revolt that seriously disturbed the peace of southern Italy until it was ruthlessly suppressed.

On the other hand, some slaves and their masters became close friends. A fine example of the close relationship between master and slave is that of Cicero and his secretary Tiro, a brilliant man who invented a system of shorthand. Many of Cicero's letters show the great affection and esteem he had for Tiro.

Most slaves were given allowances, and the thrifty slave could hope to save enough over the course of several years to buy his own freedom. Masters often granted freedom or released their slaves out of gratitude for services rendered, many from a genuine feeling that slavery was evil. Others freed their slaves in their wills and left them sums of money so that they might begin new lives.

A few of these freedmen became rich and influential. From the time of the Emperor Augustus in the first century A.D. until the rule of Hadrian, some freedmen took over highly important secretaryships in the imperial administration. Narcissus, the freedman secretary of the Emperor Claudius, made a tremendous fortune. He was even sent to hasten the Roman invasion of Britain in A.D. 48.

QUESTIONS

1. What differences are there between Roman slavery and the slavery that existed in the Americas?
2. Does slavery still exist today? Where?

North Wind Picture Archives

Educated slaves were often an important part of their Roman master's entourage. In this illustration a slave is bringing a document to his master.

UNIT III REVIEW

LESSONS X–XVI

VOCABULARY

Nouns

ager	castra	glōria	puer
amīcitia	cēna	grātia	signum
animus	colōnus*	lingua	socius*
annus	cōnsilium	magister*	vir
barbarus*	disciplīna	māteria	
captīvus*	fīlius*	patria	
casa	frūmentum	praemium	

Adjectives

altus	barbarus	noster	singulī
amīcus	līber	sacer	

Verbs

augeō	habitō	migrō	terreō
doceō	līberō	moveō	videō
ēvocō	maneō	sum	vocō
habeō	mereō	teneō	

Adverb

ibi

Prepositions

ā, ab	ē, ex
dē	in

*Like **fīlius,** *son,* and **fīlia,** *daughter,* these masculine nouns can be changed into feminines of the first declension when they are applied to females: **captīva, -ae; colōna, -ae; magistra, -ae; socia, -ae,** etc.

GRAMMAR SUMMARY

Nouns
The Genitive Always Shows the Declension

	FIRST DECLENSION	SECOND DECLENSION	
Nominative	**-a**	**-us**	
		-er	masculine
		-r	
		-um	neuter
Genitive	**-ae**	**-ī**	

Second Declension Neuter Neuter nouns of the second declension end in **-um** in the nominative and accusative singular. Otherwise they share the same second declension endings as the masculine nouns, except that the nominative and accusative plural end in **-a.**

> **Nautae multa praemia dōnāvit.**
> *He gave the sailor many rewards.*

The Ablative of Place From Which The ablative is used with certain prepositions (**ab, ex, dē**) to express movement from a place. **Ab** is shortened to **ā** and **ex** to **ē** before a consonant.

> **Equum ā viā movet.**
> *She moves the horse away from the road.*

The Accusative of Place To Which The accusative is used after certain prepositions (**in** *into*, **ad** *toward*) to indicate the endpoint or target of a verb of motion. That endpoint of motion can be a person but is usually a place.

> **Colōnae migrāvērunt in Italiam.**
> *The colonists migrated into Italy.*

> **Ad magistrum litterās portāvī.**
> *I carried the letter to the teacher.*

The Vocative Case The vocative case is used to address people directly. It has the same endings as the nominative except for second declension masculine nouns ending in **-us** and **-ius.** In these nouns, the **-us** changes to **-e** and the **-ius** changes to **-ī.** The vocative is regularly separated from the rest of the sentences by commas and rarely appears first.

> **Nāvigā ad īnsulam, Mārce.**
> *Sail to the island, Marcus.*

> **Servā pecūniam tuam, fīlī.**
> *Save your money, son.*

Agreement of Adjectives and Nouns An adjective in Latin must agree with its noun in gender, number, and case. Therefore, in order to modify nouns of different genders, every adjective studied so far has a threefold declension; for example: **magnus, magna, magnum.** (For full declension, see the Grammar Appendix.)

Caution: Since **nauta** and **agricola** are masculine—although they belong to the first declension—to agree with them, an adjective must have the second declension forms, such as **nauta bonus, nautae bonī.**

Adjectives Ending in **-er**

Adjectives of the first and second declensions ending in **-er** have the same case endings as nouns of the first and second declensions (except in the nominative and vocative singular). It is important to learn all three nominative forms in order to know whether the vowel **e** is lost or retained in the stem: **sacer, sacra, sacrum,** but **līber, lībera, līberum.** A knowledge of English derivatives (*sacred, liberty*) and their spellings is helpful here.

> **Fīlia nostra in casā est.**
> *Our daughter is in the house.*

> **Nautae sunt līberī.**
> *The sailors are free.*

Verbs

Present and Future Tenses, Second Conjugation Verbs that belong to the second conjugation have an **-e** in their present stem. The first principal part always ends in **-eō** and the infinitive always ends in **-ēre.**

> **Magister scientiam docet.**
> *The teacher teaches science.*

> **In casā manēbimus.**
> *We shall remain in the house.*

UNIT III REVIEW

LESSONS X–XVI

The Perfect Tense The perfect tense is formed by adding the perfect endings (**-ī, -istī, -it, -imus, -istis, -ērunt**) to the perfect stem. To find the perfect stem, drop the **-ī** from the third principal part. To translate it, use the past tense of the verb or the helping verbs *has, have,* or *did.* Do not use *do* or *does,* which are used for the present.

The Verb *To Be* The principal parts of the verb *to be* are **sum, esse, fuī, futūrus.** It is irregular in the present tense (**sum, es, est, sumus, estis, sunt**). It is also a linking verb, which means it never takes a direct object. Remember that nouns or adjectives that are part of the predicate of a linking verb are put in the nominative.

> ### Medicus vir bonus est.
> *The doctor is a good man.*

Sentence Analysis

It is a good idea to identify mentally the attributes of each word or phrase before translating. This means that for nouns and adjectives, the gender, number, and case are important; for verbs, the person, number, and tense are important. With practice, the process will become automatic.

UNIT PRACTICE

Oral Practice

1. Decline **socius noster, agricola novus, signum nostrum.**
2. Conjugate in full and translate: **migrō** in the present, **maneō** in the perfect, **doceō** in the future.
3. What forms are **tenent, sociī, tenuistis, fīliī, docēbitis, linguīs, fīlī, habēbis, habitāre, amīce?**
4. Translate into Latin: *he increases, they have, we have lived, he taught, I shall remain, they are calling, you* (sing.) *deserve, we work, you* (pl.) *will see, call out* (sing.).

Exercises

A. Choose the right words in parentheses to complete the sentences. Identify the construction and translate each sentence.
   1. Agrī sunt (magnī, magnōs).
   2. Agricola (agrōs, agrī) habet.
   3. Agricolae (in agrōs, in agrīs) labōrant.
   4. In īnsulā (multī colōnī, multōs colōnōs) vidēbō.
   5. In patriā nostrā (multās, multōs) agricolās habēmus.

B. Complete the sentences with the correct endings. Then translate the sentences.
   1. Agricola est bon__.
   2. Portā aquam, serv__.
   3. Colōnī multōs servōs habu__.
   4. Amīcī meī sunt mult__ et bon__.

WORD STUDY

1. Give prefix and Latin root word from which the following words are derived and define: *defame, approve, advocate, invocation, immigrant, emigrant, avocation, vocation, deter.*

2. Choose the word in parentheses that most nearly gives the meaning of the italicized word. Tell why you selected it.

   a. *amicable* relations (friendly, social, free, hostile)

   b. a *puerile* act (poor, childish, manly, effeminate)

   c. a *docile* creature (wild, giant, stubborn, easily taught)

   d. an animal's *habitat* (habit, appearance, living place, color)

   e. a *migratory* bird (singing, wandering, tame, nocturnal)

VOCABULARY

Circle the word that best completes each sentence.

1. Glōriam patriae nostrae _____ augēbimus.
   a. cēnīs
   b. agrō
   c. annīs
   d. disciplīnā

2. Magister multōs puerōs ē viīs _____.
   a. terruit
   b. habitāvit
   c. mānsit
   d. ēvocāvit

3. Memoria parvae puellae in _____ meō manet.
   a. animō
   b. signō
   c. annō
   d. praemiō

4. Singulī _____ ad terram barbaram migrābunt.
   a. captīvus
   b. puellae
   c. agricolae
   d. fīliōs

5. Colōnī līberī in Americā _____. Ibi manēbimus.
   a. sum
   b. sumus
   c. es
   d. estis

GRAMMAR

Complete each sentence with the correct endings.

6. Movē, Luc___, māteri___ ē silv___ ad cas___.
7. Crās colōnī magnōs agr___ in patri___ barbar___ vidē___.
8. Docē___, vir___, servōs nostr___ dē lingu___ nostr___.
9. Castra sociōrum tu___ viās plān___ hab___.
10. Cōpiam frument___ in prōvinci___ me___ augēbō.

TRANSLATION

Translate the following sentences.

11. Lingua barbara nautārum multōs colōnōs nōn terruit.
12. Puerī praemium tuum in casā meā vidēbunt.
13. Mōnstrā, Mārce, cōnsilium tuō amīcō bonō in castrīs.
14. In Viā Sacrā multī carrī rēgīnam et captīvōs ē pugnā magnā portāvērunt.
15. Familia nostra amicītiam servōrum nostrōrum cūrā et grātiā semper augēbit et servābit.

INVESTIGATION

Find the answers to these questions from any lesson in Unit III.

16. What is the meaning of the English word *ignoramus,* and what Latin verb form is it?
17. Julius Caesar and other famous Romans who celebrated a triumph sometimes are shown wearing a wreath made from what plant?

18. The name of the Emperor who built a great defensive wall in Britain was   .
19. True or false? Most of the grain consumed by the ancient Romans was imported from Gaul.
20. The Trojan Horse was said to be a gift for the goddess _____.
    a. Venus
    b. Minerva
    c. Vesta

CULTURE

Vērum aut Falsum? Indicate whether each statement is true or false.

21. A Roman master had the legal right to kill his slave if he chose to do so.
22. Some Roman slaves were able to save money to buy their freedom.
23. The term **familia urbana** referred to a landholder's team of slaves on his agricultural estate.
24. Most Roman slaves were prisoners of war.
25. Roman slaves often were better educated than their masters.

FROM LATIN TO ENGLISH

Apply your knowledge of Latin roots to determine the best meaning of the italicized words.

26. Roman culture put great emphasis on *filial* obedience.
    a. of officials
    b. of children
    c. of visitors
    d. of citizens
27. At the party he acted in a *puerile* way.
    a. cheerful
    b. strange
    c. quiet
    d. childish
28. She wanted to *augment* her income from that job.
    a. save
    b. record
    c. increase
    d. spend
29. They did not approve of his *counsel*.
    a. assembly
    b. reason
    c. request
    d. advice
30. We all thought the man *merited* the trophy.
    a. stole
    b. deserved
    c. disliked
    d. desired

ROMAN SOCIETY

Unit Objectives

- To learn the future and perfect tenses of the verb **sum**
- To learn the uses of the infinitive (as subject and as object)
- To learn the present and perfect active tenses and present imperatives of the third and fourth conjugations
- To learn how questions are asked in Latin
- To learn about apposition
- To learn to develop "word sense" and the ability to translate and comprehend Latin sentences
- To learn more about Roman history, daily life, and some famous Romans

The House of Neptune and Amphitrite (Neptune's sea goddess wife) in Herculaneum gets its name from the figures framed by a giant seashell on the right wall. The room served as a summer dining room, or **triclinium**. The water motif is continued by seashells embedded in the walls, by a fountain and shallow pool in the center, and, at the rear, by a **nymphaeum**, an artificial grotto for water-nymphs, framed by elaborate vines and hunting scenes. Diners reclined on pillows around the three sides of the **triclinium** and were served from a table placed at its end.

LESSON
OBJECTIVES
- To learn the future and perfect of **sum**
- To learn uses of the infinitive

LESSON XVII

RŌMULUS ET NUMA ET TULLUS

[1] *the first king*

[2] *refuge, sanctuary*

[3] *said*

[4] *second*

[5] *the goddess Egeria*

[6] *the gods*

[7] *if*

[8] *third*

[9] *reverence*

[10] *sacrifices*

[11] *stirred up*

[12] *with a lightning bolt*

Prīmus rēx[1] Rōmae Rōmulus fuit. Armīs et cōnsiliīs bonīs glōriam Rōmae auxit. Virī Rōmulum amāvērunt quod multīs familiīs asȳlum[2] dōnāvit et ad victōriam sociōs incitāvit. "Rōma magna erit," inquit[3] Rōmulus. "Clārī eritis."

Secundus[4] rēx Rōmae fuit Numa Pompilius. Numa bellum nōn amāvit.

5 Deam Ēgeriam[5] amāvit. Ēgeria Numam dē cūrīs sacrīs docuit. Tum rēx Rōmānōs docēre mātūrāvit. "Deī[6] amīcī Rōmae erunt," inquit[3] Numa, "sī[7] bonī et grātī erimus. Multam grātiam deīs habēre dēbēmus."

Tertius[8] rēx Rōmae fuit Tullus Hostīlius. Tullus inquit[3], "Bonus vir et rēx erō." Sed reverentiam[9] parvam habuit et concordiam nōn amāvit. Sacra[10] nōn

10 tenuit et multa bella mōvit[11]. Sed Iuppiter vītam Tullī nōn probāvit et Tullum fulmine[12] exstinguit.

A marble relief of Romulus and Remus. According to legend, these twins were the offspring of the god Mars and a Vestal Virgin, Rhea Silvia. Ordered to be exposed and left to die by her wicked uncle, they were nursed by a she-wolf until they were found and reared by a shepherd. Later, as they quarreled over who should name and rule the new city, Remus was killed; in 753 B.C. Romulus became the first of Rome's seven kings.

Questions

1. Why was Romulus a popular king?
2. How did he increase the glory of Rome?
3. How did Numa learn so much about the gods?
4. What was his lesson for the Roman people?
5. What did Tullus neglect and what was the result?

VOCABULARY

Nouns

ar´ma, -ō´rum n. pl. *arms, weapons*   (arms, army)

auxi´lium, auxi´lī n. *aid, help*   (auxiliary)

bel´lum, -ī n. *war*   (bellicose, belligerent)

concor´dia, -ae f. *harmony*   (concord)

nūn´tius, nūn´tī m. *messenger*   **[nūntiō]**

Verbs

dē´beō, dēbē´re, dē´buī, [dē´bitus]   (debtor, indebtedness)
ought, owe

mātū´rō, mātūrā´re, mātūrā´vī,   (mature, maturity)
[mātūrātū´rus] *hasten*

GRAMMAR

The Future and Perfect of the Verb *to be:* sum

The future tense of **sum**, like the present tense, is slightly irregular though the personal endings remain regular.

e´rō *I shall be*   **e´rimus** *we shall be*

e´ris *you will be*   **e´ritis** *you will be*

e´rit *he/she/it will be*   **e´runt** *they will be*

The perfect tense of **sum** is conjugated like all regular verbs, although it is based on a different stem (**fu-**).

fu´ī *I have been, was*   **fu´imus** *we have been, were*

fuis´tī *you have been, were*   **fuis´tis** *you have been, were*

fu´it *he/she/it has been, was*   **fuē´runt** *they have been, were*

Oral Practice

1. Translate into English: **es, erit, fuērunt, sunt, erimus, fuistī.**
2. Translate into Latin: *we have been, you* (pl.) *are, I am, she has been, you* (sing.) *will be, they will be.*

Infinitive Used as Subject

The infinitive form of a verb can be used as a noun and can function as the subject of a verb.

Errāre est hūmānum.	*To err is human.*
Amīcōs habēre est grātum.	*To have friends is pleasing.*

Though the infinitive is used as a noun, it is not declined and does not show case and number. Its gender is neuter. Therefore the predicate adjective must also be neuter, as **hūmānum** and **grātum** are in the preceding examples.

The infinitive may be used as a predicate nominative.

Vidēre est crēdere.   *To see is to believe.*

Infinitive Used as Object

The infinitive form of a verb may also be used as a direct object, like other nouns.

Servōs līberāre parat.   *He prepares to free the slaves.*

Being a verbal noun, the infinitive may also have an object; note **servōs** and **amīcōs** in the examples above.

Oral Practice

Translate the italicized phrases and state whether you are using the infinitive as a subject, predicate nominative, or direct object: I deserve *to remain; To love* is great; He prepared *to praise;* It is pleasing *to announce* good things.

🔲 Exercises

A. Translate the following sentences.
1. Puellae et puerī cēnam bonam parāre dēbent.
2. Multōs equōs in agrīs vidēre grātum fuit.
3. Pecūniam habēre est semper multās cūrās habēre.
4. Rēgīnae praemium nostrum mōnstrāre mātūrāmus.
5. Bonum erit concordiam et auxilium in bellō habēre.
6. Nūntiī praemiīs animōs nautārum incitāre parābunt.
7. Signa et arma ad terram novam portāre mātūrāvimus.

B. Give the Latin for the italicized words.
1. Es *(my friend).*
2. Erit *(a farmer).*
3. Erat *(a sailor).*
4. Fuimus *(comrades).*
5. Erunt *(our friends).*

C. Translate the following sentences into Latin.
1. It is bad to owe money.
2. Farmers, hasten to increase the supply of grain.
3. We ought to report the plan of war to the men.
4. It was pleasing to see the courage and harmony of the messengers.
5. The messenger will hasten to report the victory to the settlers.

J. A. Cash/Photri

The story of the founding of Rome by Romulus was spread throughout the Roman empire. This reproduction of the famous Etruscan statue of the she-wolf is in Spain. Romulus was the first of the seven kings of Rome.

Did You Know?

In 509 B.C., after 244 years of monarchy, the Romans expelled the last of their seven kings. He was Tarquin the Proud, really an Etruscan from north of Rome, urged on to tyranny by his ambitious and ruthless wife. Long after his expulsion, even the very mention of the word **rēx** raised fear in the minds of the citizens of republican Rome.

WORD STUDY

Borrowings

- What is meant by large *armaments?* When is a person called *bellicose?* What is an *auxiliary* engine on a yacht? What is a *debenture?* a *debit?* a *premature* judgment?
- The following English phrases are borrowed from Latin.

multum in parvo	*much in little*
de novo	*anew*, literally, *from a new (start)*
in memoriam	*to the memory (of), in memory of*

SPARTACUS

Spartacus fuit clārus servus, captīvus Rōmānōrum. Sociōs ēvocāvit et ad bellum incitāvit: "Ō sociī, Rōmānī nōn sunt aequī. Puer fuī in oppidō meō, et vīta grāta semper erat. Magna erat concordia in patriā nostrā. Populus aequus erat. Silvās magnās et agrōs lātōs amāvī. Dominum nōn habuī; līber
5 ibi fuī. Vērum amīcum habuī, puerum bonum et grātum. Sed Rōmānī patriam meam occupāvērunt; mē et amīcum meum ex patriā portāvērunt.

Nunc post[1] multōs annōs vir sum, et in arēnā pūblicā pugnō. Hodiē[2] in hōc[3] oppidō virum quem[4] nōn cognōvī[5] occīdī[6]—et erat amīcus meus!

Estisne virī? Populum Rōmānum et dominōs malōs nōn amātis. Iniūriās
10 nōn merēmus. Causa nostra est aequa. Nōnne nunc hōra est? Ad arma! Pugnāte! Animum vestrum mōnstrāte! Vocāte sociōs vestrōs ad auxilium! Servōs līberābimus, līberī erimus, ad patriam nostram sacram migrāre mātūrābimus et ibi in agrīs nostrīs labōrābimus et in concordiā habitābimus."

[1] after
[2] today
[3] this
[4] whom
[5] I did not recognize
[6] I killed

This amphitheater near Capua in southern Italy, now in ruins but once rivaling the Roman Coliseum in size, testifies to the popularity of gladiatorial games even after the revolt of Spartacus and his followers in 73 B.C. Gladiatorial combat was originally a solemn Etruscan ceremony intended to honor a great warrior with sacrifices to his memory. Under the Romans it became a spectacle of lavish and ingenious acts of cruelty, until it was finally outlawed in the fourth century A.D.

Mimmo Jodice/CORBIS

Questions

1. Who was Spartacus?
2. Why did he object to the Romans and what they did?
3. What was Spartacus' life as a boy like? Give details.
4. What was the incident that made Spartacus hate gladiatorial combat?
5. To what people did Spartacus deliver his speech?
6. What did he want his listeners to do?
7. What was the aim (objective) of the speech?

VOCABULARY

Nouns

cau´sa, -ae f. *cause, reason, case* (because, causal)
do´minus, -ī m. *master* (dominion, dominate)
op´pidum, -ī n. *town*
po´pulus, -ī m. *people* (populace, popular)

Adjectives

ae´quus, -a, -um *even, just, calm* (equality, equate)
lā´tus, -a, -um *wide* (latitude)
pū´blicus, -a, -um *public* (publish)
vē´rus, -a, -um *true, real, not false* (verify, verity)
ves´ter, ves´tra, ves´trum *your*
   (referring to two or more persons)

Pronouns

quis *who?*
quid *what?* (quid pro quo)

Adverb

u´bi *where? when?*

Enclitic Syllable

-ne (introduces questions)

GRAMMAR

Asking Questions

In Latin, as in English, there are two main types of questions: the first type asks for information; the second expects only a *yes* or *no* answer. To ask for information in Latin, use an interrogative word—either a pronoun (**quis**, *who?* **quid**, *what?*) or an adverb (**ubi**, *where?*).

Ubi est Italia? *Where is Italy?*
Quis in viā ambulat? *Who is walking in the street?*
Quid spectās? *What are you watching?*

Nota•**B**ene

Think of the syllable **-ne** as a kind of question mark. Remember: it is not translated into English and it is never used alone.

Since the syllable **-ne** becomes part of the word, the word accent may shift: **īnsulam´ne.** If a word like **Corsica** ends in a short vowel and if the syllable before it is also short (see Grammar Appendix), begin the sentence with some other word and attach the **-ne** to it.

---

[7] *Empire*

[8] This whole sentence can be translated very simply: *Yes.*

[9] eyes

[10] *I.*

If the answer can be either *yes* or *no,* add the syllable **-ne** to the end of the first word in the sentence. If you expect the answer to be *yes,* begin the sentence with **nōnne (nōn + ne).**

Mārcusne Clāram amat?	*Does Marcus love Clara?*
Nōnne Mārcus Clāram amat?	*Marcus loves Clara, doesn't he?*

Conversation: A Geography Lesson

M = **Magistra** (or **Magister**) *teacher*
D = **Discipulae** (or **Discipulī**) *pupils*

M:	Spectāte, discipulae (discipulī).
D:	Spectāmus, magistra (magister).
M:	Ubi est Italia?
D:	In Eurōpā Italia est.
M:	Estne Italia lāta?
D:	Italia longa sed nōn lāta est.
M:	Īnsulamne vidētis?
D:	Corsicam vidēmus.
M:	Estne Corsica magna īnsula?
D:	Parva, nōn magna, īnsula est Corsica.
M:	Quid in Siciliā vidētis?
D:	Aetnam vidēmus.
M:	Magnam īnsulam mōnstrō; Britannia est. Colōnī ex Britanniā ad Americam et ad Austrāliam migrāvērunt.
M:	Fuitne Gallia prōvincia?
D:	Gallia fuit prōvincia imperī[7] Rōmānī.
M:	Nōnne magna fuit glōria Galliae?
D:	Magna fuit glōria Galliae.[8]
M:	Quis oculōs[9] bonōs habet?
Maria:	Ego.[10]
M:	Mōnstrā discipulīs Rōmam.
Maria:	Rōma in Italiā est.

Oral Practice

Ask the following questions in Latin: *Is the field wide? Where is your town? He prepared the dinner, didn't he? What are they carrying?*

 *Exercises*

A. Answer the following questions in Latin.

    1. Estne Eurōpa in Italiā?   **4.** Estne Italia prōvincia?

    2. Estne Italia īnsula?   **5.** Nōnne erat causa vēra?

    3. Ubi est Rōma?

Did You Know?

 The "newspaper" of the ancient Romans was written on a series of tall boards attached to pillars in the Forum. The **Acta Diurna** (*Daily Happenings*) posted the latest news from war fronts, the provinces, different sections of Rome, senate proceedings and government regulations, and news of personal interest. There were also "For sale" and "For rent" sections of the "newspaper."

WORD STUDY

Vocabulary

- What is *popular* government? Use *depopulate* in a sentence. What is meant by the sentence: "I listened to his attacks with *equanimity*"? Give three more derivatives of **aequus**.
- Give three derivatives each from **nūntiō, portō, spectō,** and **vocō** by attaching one of the prefixes **ad-, dē-, ex-,** or **in-**.

The Supreme Court building in Washington, D.C., modeled after a classical temple, houses one of the three cornerstones of popular government in the United States. Notice the high podium, the Corinthian columns, and the elaborate sculpture in the pediment (the triangular area at the top).

Mel Curtis/PhotoDisc

LESSON OBJECTIVES

- To learn the third conjugation: present, present imperative, and perfect tenses
- To learn about apposition

PATRŌNUS ET CLIENTĒS[1]

This artist's rendition of an ancient Roman house is based on existing archaeological remains in Pompeii. The view looks through the **ātrium** to the interior. Note the **impluvium**, a central pool, often located under an opening left in the roof to catch rainwater. At the upper right, drapes may conceal second-floor rooms. The lower sections of some columns are painted red (to hide fingerprints!).

North Wind Picture Archives

[1] *a patron and his clients*
[2] *central hall*
[3] *soon will be present*
[4] *meanwhile*
[5] *his office*
[6] *leisure*
[7] *for other*
[8] *him*
[9] *never*
[10] *often*
[11] *therefore*
[12] *his*
[13] *so many*

In ātriō[2] multī clientēs exspectant. Patrōnus, vir clārus, mox aderit[3]. Interim[4] clientēs dē officiīs agunt. Patrōnum laudant quod amīcus et generōsus est.

Cliēns prīmus: "Salvē, amīce! Vīdistīne patrōnum nostrum?"

5 Cliēns secundus: "Minimē. Multa officia habet et in tablīnō[5] labōrat."

Cliēns prīmus: "Parvum ōtium[6] habet quod prō aliīs[7] vītam agit. Cūrae aliōrum virōrum semper eum[8] movent."

Cliēns secundus: "Ab officiīs novīs et dūrīs numquam[9] cēdit. Nōnne saepe[10] auxilium ad familiās nostrās mīsit?"

10 Cliēns prīmus: "Sīc. Ergō[11] dēbēmus eum laudāre et grātiā nostrā fāmam eius[12] augēre. Ssst! Patrōnus accēdit!"

Nunc patrōnus in atriō est. Patrōnō grātum est vidēre tot[13] virōs—amīcōs, fīliōs, clientēs, servōs. Familiam salūtat, et familia eum salūtāre matūrat.

Magnus servus sportulās[14] in atrium portat et in sportulās pecūniam et cibum pōnit. Sportulae praemia sunt. Quod clientēs fīdī[15] fuērunt et erunt, patrōnus[15] sportulās ad familiās clientium[16] mittit. Tum patrōnus ad Forum excēdit.

Aliquandō[17] clientēs patrōnum spectant dum[18] causās in Forō agit. Aliquandō patrōnus clientēs dēfendit. Aliquandō clientēs ad cēnam vocat. Clientēs nōn servī sunt, sed patrōnus paene dominus est. "Manus manum lavat."[19]   20

14 *little baskets*
15 *loyal*
16 *of the clients*
17 *sometimes*
18 *while*
19 *"One hand washes the other."*

Questions

1. Where is the patron at the start of the story?
2. In what part of the house are the two clients waiting for him?
3. Why is the patron always so busy?
4. What are the clients discussing while they are waiting?
5. What do the clients take home from the visit to their patron?
6. In what other ways did Roman patrons provide for their clients?
7. What do clients provide in return for the support given them by patrons?

VOCABULARY

Noun

offi´cium, offi´cī n. *duty*   (official, officiate)

Verbs

a´gō, a´gere, ē´gī, [āc´tus] *do, drive,*   (action, active)
discuss, live, spend (time)

cē´dō, cē´dere, ces´sī, [cessū´rus] *move*   (cede)
(away from), retreat, yield, give way

accē´dō, accē´dere, acces´sī,
[accessū´rus] *approach*

excē´dō, excē´dere, exces´sī,
[excessū´rus] *depart*

dēfen´dō, dēfen´dere, dēfen´dī,   (defensive, indefensible)
[dēfēn´sus] *defend*

exspec´tō, exspectā´re, exspectā´vī,   [spectō]
[exspectā´tus] *look out for, await*

mit´tō, mit´tere, mī´sī, [mis´sus] *let go, send*   (missile, transmit)

pō´nō, pō´nere, po´suī, [po´situs] *put, place*   (postpone, position)

Carefully inspect the verbs in the vocabulary to the left to see how often verbs of the third conjugation, unlike most verbs of the first and second conjugations, change their stem in the third and fourth principal parts, e.g. **agō → ēgī, āctus; pōnō → posuī, positus,** etc. Pronouncing them aloud as you memorize them is a great help.

The elegant interiors of upper-class Roman houses continue to influence the taste of wealthy builders and landowners in Europe and America. The use of frescoed wall paintings, statuary, fluted columns, painted and paneled ceilings, colored tiles, and marble floor mosaics mark this classical style, which had its origins in second-century B.C. Greece. Note that the artist has included the customary watchdog, fierce but chained.

Gianni Dagli Orti/Musée des Arts Decoratifs Paris/The Art Archive

GRAMMAR

The Third Conjugation

Verbs of the third conjugation have the stem vowel **-ĕ-** (short e). Note the difference of stem vowels in the verb conjugations.

CONJUGATION		PRESENT STEM
FIRST	long **-a** verbs	**portā-** (from infinitive **portāre**)
SECOND	long **-ē** verbs	**docē-** (from infinitive **docēre**)
THIRD	short **-e** verbs	**pōnĕ-** (from infinitive **pōnere**)

To get the present stem, drop the **-re** of the infinitive.
The short vowel **-ĕ-** of the third conjugation changes to **-ĭ-**, except in:
    the first person singular, where it disappears before **-ō**;
    the third person plural, where it becomes **-u-**; and
    the second person singular of the imperative, where it remains **-ĕ-**.

Study the following forms.

PRESENT TENSE

pō´nō *I put, do put, am putting,* etc.
pō´nis
pō´nit

pō´nimus *we put, do put, are putting,* etc.
pō´nitis
pō´nunt

PRESENT IMPERATIVE

pō´ne *put!*   **pō´nite** *put!*

The *endings* of the perfect tense are the same in all conjugations. (See page 96.) However, the perfect *stem* of third conjugation verbs, like that of the second conjugation, is often quite different from the present stem.

PERFECT TENSE

po´suī *I placed, have placed, did place,* etc.
posuis´tī
po´suit

posu´imus *we placed, have placed, did place,* etc.
posuis´tis
posuē´runt

Oral Practice

1. Conjugate **agō** and **dēfendō** in the present and perfect tenses.
2. Form the present imperative, singular and plural, of **cēdō, mittō, agō.**
3. Give the Latin for *he departs, he moves, he hastens, we are defending, you* (pl.) *approach.*

Apposition

Dominum meum, Lūcium Cornēlium, exspectō.
 I am waiting for my master, Lucius Cornelius.
Nautīs, amīcīs nostrīs, pecūniam dōnāvimus.
 We gave money to the sailors, our friends.

You will note in the first example on page 137 that **Lūcium Cornēlium** identifies the object **dominum,** stands in direct relation to it, and is in the accusative like **dominum. Amīcīs nostrīs** in the second example identifies **nautīs,** the indirect object, and is in the dative, as is **nautīs.** This construction is called *apposition.* A noun in apposition to (**ad + pōnō,** *place next to*) another noun (or pronoun) is in the same case as that other noun (or pronoun) and is frequently set off from the rest of the sentence by commas.

Oral Practice

Translate the words in italics into Latin: I saw John, *my friend.* Have you heard the story of Spartacus, *the slave?* We lived in England, *a large island.* I told it to Mr. Jones, *my teacher.*

 # *Exercises*

A. Translate the following sentences.
1. Litterāsne ad amīcōs vērōs mīsistī?
2. Semper, puerī, agite vītam bonam.
3. Equōsne tuōs, Cornēlī, in aquam agis?
4. Ubi praedam pōnitis? In viā praedam pōnimus.
5. In Americā, patriā nostrā, semper habitābimus.
6. Ad īnsulam cessimus et castra dēfendere parāvimus.

B. Translate the following sentences into Latin.
1. Is he not living a long life?
2. Send aid to our allies, the Roman people.
3. It is the duty of the prisoner to work in the fields.
4. Ought we not (Shouldn't we) increase the number of settlers in the province?
5. The slave, a prisoner of the Romans, is preparing to put the grain into the wagon.

Did You Know?

Many of our common and useful pieces of furniture were unknown to the Romans. No mirrors hung on their walls; there were no chests of drawers or desks; there were no glass door cabinets to show objects of value and beauty. Even the houses of the wealthy were simply furnished with essential items such as chairs, tables, couches, chests, wooden cabinets with doors, olive oil lamps, and an occasional brazier for heating rooms. The walls, however, were covered with colorful paintings.

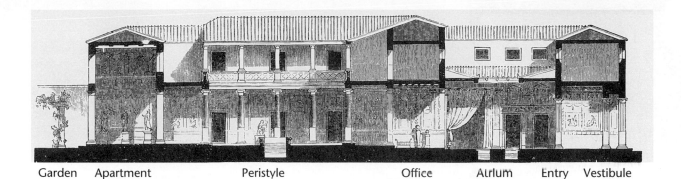

Garden　　Apartment　　　　　　　Peristyle　　　　　　　Office　　Atrium　　Entry　Vestibule

C. Can you describe your own house as if you were living in Roman times? You may find the following nouns and prepositions helpful. Draw a floor plan of your house and label the rooms in Latin.

āla *side room*

ātrium *central hall*

cubiculum *bedroom*

culīna *kitchen*

vestibulum *entranceway*

hortus *garden*

impluvium *pool*

peristȳlium *courtyard (porch)*

tablīnum *den, study*

trīclīnium *dining room*

latrīna *bathroom, toilet*

cella *storeroom, attic*

apud mē *at my house*

ante (+ acc.) *in front of, before*

post (+ acc.) *behind, after*

super (+ acc.) *above*

sub (+ abl.) *below*

prope (+ acc.) *near*

In this section of a Roman house, you can visualize the rectangular shape as you enter from the street at the right into the vestibule. Rooms on each side of the vestibule served as shops. Guests were received in the atrium and the master of the house often had his office in the **tablīnum.** Often an **impluvium** would be found in the center of the atrium.

WORD STUDY

Latin Roots We have seen that many English nouns and adjectives have preserved their original Latin forms. A great many more nouns or verbs have preserved the base of the Latin word. Others again consist of the Latin stem plus silent *-e.* The following are examples. Stem: *defend, form, laud, public, sign;* stem plus *-e: cause, cede, fortune, fame, cure.*

The same rules are illustrated in the following words in which changes in the base have taken place. Stem: *letter* (**littera**), *number* (**numerus**), *car* (**carrus**), *clear* (**clārus**); stem plus *-e:* evoke (**ēvocō**), *single* (**singulī**).

Give ten other examples from nouns, adjectives, and verbs already studied.

RŌMĀNĪ

LESSON OBJECTIVES
- To learn the present tense, present imperative, and perfect tense of the third conjugation **-iō** and fourth conjugation verbs
- To learn certain idiomatic expressions and develop word sense in Latin

¹ *once*
² *to the gods*
³ *other*
⁴ *justly*
⁵ *for many years* (acc. of duration of time)

Quondam¹ Rōma, oppidum Italiae, parva erat. Rōmānī, populus firmus, oppidum mūnīvērunt quod arma capere et patriam dēfendere parāvērunt. Victōriīs magnīs patriam servāvērunt et auxērunt. Ex multīs terrīs praedam ēgērunt. Deīs² grātiās ēgērunt et templa magna et alta fēcērunt. Magna
5 praemia Rōmānī meruērunt et accēpērunt, quod officium fēcērunt. Magnum numerum colōnōrum in aliās³ terrās mīsērunt. Multās terrās barbarās cēpērunt, prōvinciās fēcērunt, et aequē⁴ rēxērunt. Barbarī linguam Latīnam accēpērunt. Rōmānī frūmentum ex aliīs³ terrīs in Italiam portāvērunt. Ad Britanniam, Hispāniam, Āfricam, Graeciam, Āsiam nāvigāvērunt et oppida
10 mūnīvērunt. Rōma multōs annōs⁵ multōs populōs rēxit.

Nunc Rōma magna et pulchra est. Multī ad Italiam veniunt et viās antīquās et templa pulchra inveniunt. Mātūrābisne in Italiam venīre et ruīnās Rōmānās invenīre?

The ruins of this theater in Djemila, Algeria, show the extent of Roman culture throughout the Mediterranean world. Many ancient theaters were situated in such a way that they stood in front of some strikingly dramatic natural background, like mountains or the sea.

The beautiful circular Temple of Vesta in the Forum, partially restored, once housed the sacred flame that symbolized the eternal life of the city. The fire was kept alive by six priestesses (the Vestals) but was extinguished and relit on March 1 to mark each new year. The round form of the Temple recalls the earliest Roman dwellings on the Palatine Hill, seen to the right.

Questions

1. By what means did the Romans increase their power?
2. Whom did they thank for their success and how?
3. Why were the Romans rewarded?
4. Whom did they send to other countries?
5. What did they obtain from other lands?
6. What did foreigners receive from them in return?
7. In what manner did they rule?
8. What do visitors find in Italy today?

Did You Know?

One of the oldest and most famous priestly colleges of Rome was located in the temple dedicated to Vesta, the goddess of the hearth. The worship of this goddess was directed by six women called **Vestālēs** *(Vestals),* who tended the sacred fire on the altar and took part in Roman festivals. Each Vestal spent ten years learning her duties, ten years performing them, and then ten years training younger women.

VOCABULARY

Noun

tem´plum, -ī n. *temple*   (contemplate, temple)

Adjective

pul´cher, -chra, -chrum *beautiful*   (pulchritude)

Verbs

ca´piō, ca´pere, cē´pī, [cap´tus] *take, seize*   (recipient, captive)
   acci´piō, acci´pere, accē´pī, [accep´tus]
     receive
fa´ciō, fa´cere, fē´cī, [fac´tus] *do, make*   (efficient, manufacture)
mū´niō, mūnī´re, mūnī´vī, [mūnī´tus] *fortify* (ammunition)
re´gō, re´gere, rē´xī, [rēc´tus] *rule, guide*   (regent, rectitude)
ve´niō, venī´re, vē´nī, [ventū´rus] *come*   (convene, adventure)
   inve´niō, invenī´re, invē´nī, [inven´tus]
     find, come upon

GRAMMAR

Third (-iō) and Fourth Conjugation Verbs

In a few important verbs of the third conjugation, a short **-ĭ-** is inserted before the stem vowel in the first person singular and in the third person plural of the present tense. They are often called "**-iō** verbs" of the third conjugation and are conjugated like **capiō,** *take*.

But most verbs ending in **-iō** belong to the fourth conjugation and have as a stem vowel long **-ī-.** They retain this long **-ī-** throughout their conjugation except where long vowels are regularly shortened (see page 29). Fourth conjugation verbs are conjugated like **mūniō,** *fortify*.

THIRD CONJUGATION		FOURTH CONJUGATION	
ca´piō *(I take, etc.)*	**ca´pimus**	**mū´niō** *(I fortify, etc.)*	**mūnī´mus**
ca´pis	**ca´pitis**	**mū´nīs**	**mūnī´tis**
ca´pit	**ca´piunt**	**mū´nit**	**mū´niunt**

The imperative shows similar differences: **cape, capite** (but the imperative singular of **faciō** is **fac**); **mūnī, mūnīte.**

The perfect tense is conjugated regularly: **cēpī, munīvī,** etc. (See the Grammar Appendix.)

Oral Practice

1. Conjugate and give all possible meanings in the present tense: **accipiō, capiō, veniō.**
2. Give the present imperatives of: **mūniō, accipiō, regō.**
3. Conjugate and give all possible meanings in the perfect tense: **inveniō, incipiō, faciō.**

Christie's/SuperStock

A portrait of Julius Caesar (100–44 B.C.) as imagined by Peter Paul Rubens (1577–1640). Rubens has followed the tradition that Caesar's vanity made him constantly wear his victory crown to conceal his thinning hair.

Hints for Developing "Word Sense"

Few words in any language, except prepositions, etc., have exactly the same meaning at all times. While words usually have one general meaning, they may have several shades of meaning, which depend entirely upon their context. Therefore, in translating a Latin word it is necessary to get its exact meaning (as opposed to its general or "vocabulary" meaning) from the context or setting it has in a sentence. Let's look at one verb, **agō,** to see how its meaning can vary.

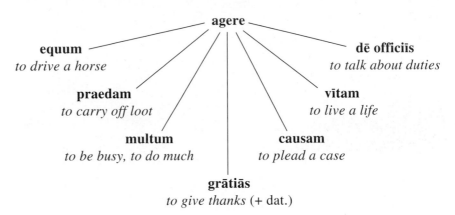

agere

equum — *to drive a horse*

praedam — *to carry off loot*

multum — *to be busy, to do much*

grātiās — *to give thanks* (+ dat.)

causam — *to plead a case*

vītam — *to live a life*

dē officiīs — *to talk about duties*

The preceding are only a few of the meanings of **agō.** When translating, do not blindly follow the meanings given to words in the vocabulary; figure out one best suited to the context. In this way you will develop good judgment and "word sense."

 *Exercises*

A. Translate the following sentences.
1. Castra mūniunt et virōs ēvocant.
2. Ubi estis, puerī et puellae? Venīmus, magister.
3. Nōnne aequum est semper amīcōs dēfendere?
4. In agrīs frūmentum, magnum auxilium, invenīmus.
5. Virī singulī praemia accipiunt quod officium fēcērunt.
6. Mārcus multum agit. In agrōs equōs agit, in bellō praedam agit, in Forō causās agit, amīcō prō *(in exchange for)* cēnā grātiās agit, cum *(with)* amīcīs dē officiīs agit. Vītam bonam agit.

B. Translate the following sentences into Latin.

1. We are fortifying the camp.
2. It is pleasing to find money.
3. We did not find our friend Marcus.
4. Marcus is not receiving a reward because he did not come.
5. A beautiful queen rules the people.

WORD STUDY

Latin and English Word Formation: Vowel Changes When a Latin word is compounded with a prefix, short **-ă-** or short **-ĕ-** in the root is usually "weakened" to short **-ĭ-** before a single consonant except **-r-.** The English derivatives show the same change. Long **-ā-** and long **-ē-** are not affected. Study these examples.

From **agō,** Latin **ex-igō, ab-igō,**   English *exigency*
    red-igō, etc.

From **habeō,** Latin **pro-hibeō,**   English *prohibit, exhibit*
    ex-hibeō, etc.

From **teneō,** Latin **con-tineō,**   English *continent, retinue*
    re-tineō, etc.

(But **veniō** and its compounds do not follow this rule; English *convene.*)

Illustrate the rule further by compounding **capiō** and **faciō** with **ad-, dē-, ex-,** and **in-,** giving English derivatives where possible.

Mārcus, amīcus meus, fīlius est vīcīnī[1] nostrī. Nōn in oppidō sed in agrīs habitāmus. Causam amīcitiae nostrae nārrābō.

Mārcus praemium accēpit: equum et carrum. Carrus parvus erat et pretium carrī nōn magnum erat. Prīmō[2] equus carrum dūcere nōn voluit[3]. Sed Mārcus
5 equum docuit et disciplīnā multum effēcit. Nunc Mārcus equum dūcit et equus carrum dūcit.

Quōdam diē[4] Mārcus ad casam nostram vēnit et mē[5] ēvocāvit: "Ad terminum agrōrum māteriam carrō portābō. Auxilium tuum rogō[6]. Venī."

Māteriam in carrō posuimus. Prīmō in viā plānā, tum ad locum altum,
10 terminum agrōrum, Mārcus equum agere mātūrāvit. Ibi vir malus dē locō nōn cessit et equum terruit et ego[7] ex carrō paene cecidī[8]. Sed aequus erat animus Mārcī, quī[9] equum tenuit et mē[5] servāvit. Ad terminum vītae meae nōn vēnī. Nōnne Mārcō, vērō amīcō, grātus esse dēbeō et praemium dōnāre? Perīculum[10] semper amīcōs firmōs efficit.

1 *neighbor*
2 *at first*
3 *did not want*
4 *one day*
5 accusative of **ego**
6 I ask
7 I
8 *fell*
9 *who*
10 *danger*

What do you imagine these three women are talking about? From a wall painting in Herculaneum.

Gianni Dagli Orti/Archaeological Museum Naples/The Art Archive

Questions

1. What relation does Marcus have to the narrator?
2. Why did the wagon cost little?
3. What did Marcus teach and how did he accomplish that?
4. What is he asking of his friend?
5. What did the two of them put in the wagon and where did they go?
6. Why was the narrator grateful to Marcus?

VOCABULARY

Nouns

lo´cus, -ī m. *place;* pl., **lo´ca** n.[11]   (local)

pre´tium, pre´tī n. *price*   (precious, appreciate)

ter´minus, -ī m. *end, boundary*   (term, terminal)

[11] Note that **locus** changes gender and declensional endings in the plural.

[12] The imperative sing. is **dūc.**

Verbs

dū´cō, dū´cere,[12] dū´xī, [duc´tus] *lead, draw*   (reduce)

effi´ciō, effi´cere, effē´cī, [effec´tus]   **[faciō]**
   bring about, produce, effect

nār´rō, nārrā´re, nārrā´vī, [nārrā´tus]
   tell, relate   (narrate)

GRAMMAR

Word Order

We have seen that the words in a Latin sentence show their connection with one another by means of endings, regardless of position (unlike English). Therefore, they may be shifted rather freely without obscuring the relationship. Even so, the "regular" order is as follows.

SUBJECT	PREDICATE
noun / adj. (gen., appositive)	abl. / indir. obj. / dir. obj. / adv. / verb

Remember:

• Adjectives usually follow their nouns, but adjectives indicating quantity and size usually precede: **virī bonī; multī virī.**

• Possessive adjectives (**meus, tuus,** etc.) follow their nouns, unless used for emphasis.

• A genitive often follows its noun.

• An indirect object often stands before a direct object.

• A word used to ask a question usually stands first, as in English. **Nōnne,** for example, is put first in the sentence.

• The verb generally stands last. However, forms of the linking verb are often placed in the middle of a sentence, as in English.

But this normal order is far less strict in Latin than the normal order in English. Shifting the word order in Latin serves to bring out varying shades of emphasis. This is done also in English, though to a lesser degree, largely in imitation of the Latin. Emphasis is gained in Latin particularly by:

- Putting the emphatic words first in the sentence: **Magna erat glōria Romae!,** also common in English: *Great was the glory of Rome!*
- Separating the emphatic word from the word to which it belongs: **Magnās puer amīcō grātiās ēgit,** *The boy thanked his friend very much.*

Oral Practice

1. Decline **pretium vestrum** and **locus pulcher.**
2. Conjugate **dūcō** and **efficiō** in present tense, with meanings.

Exercises

A. Translate the following sentences.
1. Magnum fuit pretium victōriae.
2. Invēnī in viā pecūniam, sed nōn cēpī.
3. Ubi est terminus agrōrum Mārcī, amīcī nostrī?
4. Virōs ad arma vocā, Lūcī, et mūnī loca pūblica.
5. Ad locum pulchrum vēnērunt et magnam silvam vīdērunt.
6. Multōs habēre dēbēmus equōs, sed magnum est pretium.

B. Translate the following sentences into Latin.
1. Great is the fame of your (pl.) teacher.
2. Have you seen many beautiful places?
3. Are you coming to our friend's dinner?
4. They are hastening to send the horses to the boundary of our territory (lands).
5. The price of instruction is small, but the rewards are great.

WORD STUDY

Explain by derivation: *admit, equity, demote, location, efficiency, terminate, invention.*

The following English phrases are borrowed from Latin.

ex animo   *from the heart (sincerely)*
Experientia docet.   *Experience teaches.*
ad infinitum   *to infinity,* i.e., *without limit*

Many state mottoes are also English phrases borrowed from Latin.

Ad astra per aspera   *To the stars through difficulties*
                           (used by Kansas as its state motto)

SIGNS OF THE TIMES

Perhaps nothing gives us quite so intimate a glimpse of a civilization as signs and posters on walls, in windows, and on posts. We are fortunate in being able to catch such a glimpse of the everyday life of ancient cities through the signs found at Pompeii and Herculaneum, two cities near Naples that were buried by a shower of volcanic ash and mud from Mt. Vesuvius in A.D. 79. For more than two hundred years, excavation has been going on in the ruins, and hundreds of notices painted or scratched on walls have been uncovered. Among them are the scribblings of small children who practiced writing the alphabet. In the women's waiting room of the Forum Baths in Herculaneum, the Latin alphabet through the letter *q* is written on the wall. Sometimes the writer started a fable, as "Once upon a time, a mouse . . ." Sometimes lines were quoted from Vergil and other poets. In a shop in Herculaneum, a quotation from Diogenes, a Greek philosopher, is neatly written in Greek. A kind of "pig Latin" is represented by **anumurb** for **urbānum,** like "eesay" for "see."

In Pompeii, there are messages to sweethearts; in one, greetings are sent to a girl whom the lover calls his "little fish." Another girl is called the "queen of Pompeii," evidently meaning *the beauty queen*. To another, who is unnamed, there is merely the message **Venus es.** Several run like this: **Helena amātur ā Rūfō,** *Helen is loved by Rufus*. But another tells about a girl who cannot stand a certain boy. In the House of Telephus in Herculaneum, someone has penned "Portumnus loves Amphianda, Januarius loves Veneria, We pray, Venus, that you should hold us in mind—this only we ask you."

The wall of this popular Pompeian fast-food establishment is covered with election posters. You may be able to make out the name of the candidate LVCRETIUM in the left center. In the lower left corner a notice harder to read: Asellina, the owner of the shop, asks the passerby to vote for Ceius Secundus. Sign painters were paid to whitewash the walls and create new slogans.

Ronald Sheridan/Ancient Art & Architecture Collection

Erich Lessing/Art Resource, NY

A busy market in Ostia. The customer at the far left has just bought a dressed fowl, and the owner offers him another from the rack while his wife hands the customer's son (or slave?) a loaf of bread (or is it an apple?) from her baskets. There may be small birds in the cage to her left. Geese (?) poke their heads through their cage beneath the counter, and two monkeys, probably used to attract customers, sit on the rabbit cage.

Some of the messages are not very complimentary: *thief* occurs several times. One reads **Stronnius nīl scit,** *Stronnius knows nothing.* In another, one person says hello to another and adds **Quid agit tibi dexter ocellus?** *How is your right eye?*—apparently having some fun about a black eye. The owners of houses in Pompeii tried to keep away idlers with such signs as **Ōtiōsīs locus hic nōn est. Discēde, morātor,** *This is no place for idlers. Go away, loafer.*

Sometimes there are New Year's greetings or holiday greetings (**Iō Sāturnālia**). In some cases a record is kept of special events, such as a birthday or the arrival of the emperor. One writer indicates that he has a cold. One says that he (or she) baked bread on April 19; another, that he put up olives on October 16; still another tells of setting a hen on April 30. One wall lists daily expenditures for cheese, bread, oil, and wine. A laundry list mentions a tunic and a cloak on April 20, underwear on May 7, and two tunics on May 8. No wonder that some unknown writer scribbled: "Wall, I wonder that you have not collapsed from having to bear the tiresome stuff of so many writers."

When we come to formal notices, we find that election posters play a prominent part. Advertising in Pompeii was less restrained than in Herculaneum, and both politicians and shopkeepers went in for the "hard sell." These ask support for this man or that because he is deserving or respectable or honest or because he delivers good bread, etc. The supporters include teamsters, tailors, barbers, dyers, and many other groups. One inscription advocates giving away the money in the public treasury!

Another group of notices advertises the shows of gladiators, similar to our prizefights. Besides mentioning the number of matches, they often name other attractions for the fans, such as awnings for sun protection, sprinklers for dust control, animal fights, and athletic contests.

Hotels and shops are advertised frequently. One hotel in Pompeii offers a dining room with three couches and all conveniences (**commoda**). An apartment house (**īnsula**) advertises shops on the ground floor from July 1. The advertisement suggests "see agent of the owner" for the luxurious (**equestria,** suitable for an upperclass tourist) upstairs apartments. A wine shop in Herculaneum advertised its different wines with a picture of the god Bacchus and the expression, "Come to the sign of the bowls [of wine]!"

Signs in Pompeii and Herculaneum offer rewards for return of lost or stolen articles. On one Pompeian sign, a man says that he found a horse on November 25 and asks the owner to claim it on a farm near the bridge.

QUESTIONS

1. Why are billboards an effective means of advertising?

2. Why did both the ancient Romans and colonial Americans use symbols to advertise to the common people?

3. What is the difference between advertising and graffiti?

Inscribed milestones, stationed at every Roman mile (4,862 feet), often gave the distance covered and the distance to go between two towns, the name of the emperor who subsidized the road, and the workers (usually legionary soldiers) who built it. Thousands have been found along roads all over the Roman Empire. This one still stands in Capernaum, by the Sea of Galilee in Israel. Imagine the thoughts of the weary trader or soldier who passed it as he began his long trek back to Italy.

Richard T. Nowitz/CORBIS

LESSONS XVII–XXI

VOCABULARY

Nouns

arma	dominus	populus
auxilium	locus	pretium
bellum	nūntius	templum
causa	officium	terminus
concordia	oppidum	

Adjectives

aequus	pūblicus	vērus
lātus	pulcher	vester

Verbs

accēdō	dūcō	mittō
accipiō	efficiō	mūniō
agō	excēdo	nārrō
capiō	exspectō	pōnō
cēdō	faciō	regō
dēbeō	inveniō	veniō
dēfendō	mātūrō	

Pronouns

quis	quid

Adverb

ubi

Enclitic Syllable

-ne

GRAMMAR SUMMARY

Future and Perfect of Sum

Sum is irregular in the present and future but regular in the perfect. The present stem is **es-** or **s-**, the future **er-**, the perfect stem **fu-**. All tenses of **sum** regularly use the predicate nominative construction.

Dominī erunt bonī.
The masters will be good.
Nūntiī fuērunt in casā nostrā.
There have been (were) messengers in our house.

Uses of the Infinitive

The infinitive can be used as the subject of a sentence or as a direct object. It is a verbal noun, always neuter and singular.

Laudāre magistrōs est bonum.
To praise teachers is good.
Litterās scrībere dēbeō.
I ought to write a letter.

The Third Conjugation/Third Conjugation -iō

The third conjugation is idéntified by an infinitive ending in **-ere.** It must be distinguished from the second conjugation, which has infinitives in **-ēre.** The stem vowel is a short **-ĕ,** seen only in the present infinitive and the singular imperative, because it is elsewhere absorbed, weakened, or modified by the personal endings. Third conjugation verbs whose first principal part ends in **-iō** retain the short **-ĭ** in the first person singular, the third person plural, and the plural imperative (**accipiō, accipiunt, accipite**). Both types of third conjugation verbs form the perfect tense regularly by adding perfect personal endings to the third principal part minus its final **-i.**

Caesar virōs in Galliam dūcit.
Caesar is leading the men into Gaul.
Loca pulchra capiunt.
They take beautiful places.
Accēdite ad oppidum, puerī!
Approach the town, boys!
Multa praemia accipimus.
We are receiving many rewards.

The Fourth Conjugation

The fourth conjugation verbs all have long **ī** as part of the present stem, but it is shortened to **-ĭ** before the personal endings **-ō**, final **-t,** and **-unt.** The perfect is formed regularly.

Ad templum venīmus.
We are coming to the temple.
Pretium invēnistī.
You found the prize.
Viās in Galliā mūnīte.
Build (fortify) roads in Gaul!

Conjugations

The four conjugations are distinguished by the stem vowel, easily found by detaching the **-re** ending of the infinitive. They may be called the **ā, ē, ě,** and **ī** conjugations.

First conjugation	port **Ā** re
Second conjugation	doc **Ē** re
Third conjugation	pōn **Ě** re
Third conjugation (**-iō** verbs)	cap **Ě** re
Fourth conjugation	mūn **Ī** re

Apposition

A noun put in apposition to another merely adds new information about it. In Latin, the case of the two nouns so identified will normally be the same.

Vērum amīcum, Mārcum, habuī.
I had a true friend, Marcus.
Rōma, oppidum Italiae, erat pulchra.
Rome, a town of Italy, was beautiful.

Asking Questions

To ask for information, begin your sentence with an interrogative adverb or pronoun. To ask a *yes/no* question, add **-ne** to the end of the first word. If you expect the answer to be *yes,* begin with **nōnne.**

Quis dūcit?
Who is leading?
Agisne officium pūblicum tuum?
Are you doing your public duty?
Nōnne dominus vester est aequus?
Your master is fair, isn't he?
OR *Isn't your master fair?*

WORD STUDY

1. Give the prefix and Latin root word from which the following are derived: **excipiō, adigō, ērigō, afficiō;** allocation, depopulate, exigency, efficient, accessory.
2. Make Latin words out of **ad-** and **capiō, in-** and **pōnō, ad-** and **teneō, dē-** and **mereō.**
3. The bold word in each of the following lines is a Latin word. Pick the one correct derivative from the English words in each line below it.
    pōnō
    pone   pony   exponent   put
    mittimus
    mitten   meet   send   remit
    populus
    poplar   population   pope   pop
    capit
    cap   cape   decapitate   recipient
    aequum
    equestrian   equine   equity   equip

LESSONS XVII–XXI

UNIT PRACTICE

Noun and Adjective Drill

A. Decline **multum auxilium, populus clārus, concordia vēra.**

B. Provide the Latin singular and plural of the following in the cases indicated.
1. (nom.) my public duty
2. (dat.) a good boundary
3. (abl.) our friend
4. (gen.) your true reason
5. (acc.) a beautiful and wide place
6. (nom.) a just man

Verb Drill

A. Decide which form of **sum** translates the italicized words.

1. *they were*	fuimus	sunt	erant	sumus
2. *you will be*	erō	eris	estis	fuistis
3. *you are*	eris	fuistī	fuistis	es
4. *he was*	erant	erat	erit	fuērunt
5. *we are*	sunt	sumus	estis	erimus
6. *they will be*	erunt	erant	erit	sunt
7. *we were*	erant	erimus	sumus	fuimus
8. *they've been*	sunt	erunt	erant	fuērunt

B. Give the third plural of the following verbs in the present, future, and perfect.
1. sum
2. exspectō
3. dēbeō
4. mātūrō
5. ēvocō

C. Translate the verb forms. Then provide the person, number, and tense.
1. regunt
2. pōnit
3. erunt
4. mātūrātis
5. mīsit
6. fuit
7. fēcistī
8. es
9. exspectābimus
10. eris
11. dūxērunt
12. invenīmus
13. veniunt
14. accēdit
15. laudābunt
16. invēnimus

D. Translate into Latin.
1. he will be
2. I fortified
3. they approached
4. you (sing.) yield
5. we are
6. they do
7. they received
8. you (pl.) came
9. we shall be
10. they will hasten
11. they will be
12. he leads
13. we are defending
14. he departed
15. he takes

E. Reread the *Glimpses of Roman Life*. Then work with a partner or in a small group and create similar slogans, sayings, and graffiti in Latin that would be appropriate now. Use your imagination!

VOCABULARY

Circle the word that best completes each sentence.

1. _____ novum viās lātās et aquam bonam habet.
   a. Officium
   b. Praemium
   c. Pretium
   d. Oppidum

2. Ibi populus concordiam et amīcitiam in terrā pulchrā _____.
   a. mātūrāvit
   b. mīsit
   c. invēnit
   d. vēnit

3. Dominus servōs ad templum _____ nunc dēbet.
   a. dūcere
   b. mānēre
   c. excēdere
   d. venīre

4. Agricolae ā fortūnā dūrā vītae nōn _____.
   a. ēgērunt
   b. cessērunt
   c. exspectāvērunt
   d. posuērunt

5. Virī clārī templum in īnsulā parvā _____ dēfendere mātūrābunt.
   a. locīs
   b. causīs
   c. frūmentīs
   d. armīs

GRAMMAR

Complete each sentence with the correct endings.

6. Mātūrāte, Anna et Mārce, litterās dē bell___ magnō ad familiās vestr___ mitt___.

7. Nūnti___ ad termin___ viae longae vēnērunt, et ibi templ___ pulchra invēnērunt.

8. Domin___ meus pretium aequ___ accip___.

9. Agi___, puerī, vītam vestr___ in loc___ grātō.

10. Offici___ servōrum puellās et puer___ in casā dēfend___ est.

TRANSLATION

Translate the following sentences.

11. Barbarī loca alta et pūblica pugnā cēpērunt.

12. Nōnne vīta bona concordiam et amīcitiam in patriā nostrā efficit?

13. Socius meus erit amīcus vērus in bellō.

14. Rōmānī prōvinciās multās in Eurōpā rēxērunt. Nunc terrae līberae sunt.

15. Lūcius, fīlius meus, carrum novum et dūrum ē māteriā silvae altae facit.

INVESTIGATION

Find the answers to these questions from any lesson in Unit IV.

16. Identify the following parts of a Roman house:
    ātrium   culīna   impluvium   trīclīnium

17. True or false? The rules for word order in a Latin sentence are less strict than the rules in English.

18. According to legend, the parents of Romulus and Remus were Rhea Silvia and _____.

19. True or false? During its years of monarchy, Rome was ruled by ten kings.

20. The priestesses who tended Rome's sacred hearth were dedicated to which goddess?
  a. Juno
  b. Vesta
  c. Minerva
  d. Venus

CULTURE

Vērum aut Falsum? Indicate whether each statement is true or false.

21. **Iō Saturnalia** is the way to say *Happy Birthday* in Latin.

22. Both Pompeii and Herculaneum were buried in an eruption of Mt. Vesuvius.

23. From the graffiti on the walls in Pompeii it is clear that only the very wealthy were concerned with politics.

24. A great eruption of Mt. Etna took place in the year A.D. 79.

25. The signs on the walls of Pompeii reveal that its citizens had great interest in athletics.

FROM LATIN TO ENGLISH

Apply your knowledge of Latin roots to determine the best meaning of the italicized words.

26. The team immediately sensed the *bellicose* mood of the opponents.
  a. serious
  b. quarrelsome
  c. friendly
  d. nervous

27. Some say Cleopatra was famous for her *pulchritude.*
  a. wealth
  b. power
  c. cunning
  d. beauty

28. The principal questioned the *veracity* of the students' remarks.
  a. timing
  b. purpose
  c. truth
  d. source

29. Her goal was to have an *auxiliary* role in the project.
  a. leading
  b. helping
  c. teaching
  d. temporary

30. The committee is going to *accede* to that demand.
  a. return
  b. move on
  c. say no
  d. yield

ROMAN POETS, GODS, AND HEROIC JOURNEYS

Unit Objectives

- To learn the future active tense of the third and fourth conjugations
- To learn how to form adverbs from first and second declension adjectives
- To learn about the ablatives of accompaniment and agent
- To learn the imperfect active tense of all conjugations
- To learn the passive voice of the present, imperfect, and future tenses of all conjugations
- To learn about transitive and intransitive verbs
- To learn some Roman myths and legends about the founding of Rome
- To learn about Roman dress

The poet Vergil (70–19 B.C.) is known as one of the world's greatest writers. His masterpiece was the *Aeneid,* an epic poem that tells of the wanderings of the Trojan Aeneas and his attempts to find a new home after the capture of Troy by the Greeks in the twelfth century B.C. It also describes Aeneas' arrival in Italy where his descendants were said to have founded Rome. In this painting by Jules Guérin (1866–1946), we see Aeneas and Queen Dido in the palace at Carthage.

Scala/Art Resource, NY

159

LESSON OBJECTIVES
- To learn more Roman mythology
- To learn the future tense of third conjugation verbs

CERĒS ET PRŌSERPINA[1]

Both this woodcut of Pluto kidnapping Proserpina as well as the smaller one on page 162 were illustrations from editions of Ovid. This one was printed in 1501.

[1] *Proserpina*

[2] *once*

[3] *other*

[4] *flowers*

[5] *picked*

[6] *those below,* i.e., the ghosts of the dead in Hades

[7] *her*

[8] *at night*

Cerēs, dea frūmentī, et fīlia Prōserpina in Siciliā habitāvērunt. Quondam[2] Prōserpina et aliae[3] puellae in agrīs erant. Locum commodum invēnērunt et flōrēs[4] variōs lēgērunt[5]. Ōtium grātum erat; magnum erat studium puellārum.

Plūtō, deus īnferōrum[6], Prōserpinam vīdit et amāvit. Equōs incitāvit et ad
5 locum ubi puellae erant accessit. Puellae fūgērunt. Prōserpina fugere mātūrāvit, sed Plūtō valuit et eam[7] cēpit, in carrō posuit, ad īnferōs dūxit.

Cerēs nocte[8] ex agrīs vēnit. Fīliam exspectāvit, sed Prōserpina nōn vēnit. Magna erat cūra deae. Ad multa loca, ad terminōs terrae Cerēs accessit. Ōtium nōn invēnit.

10 Quod Cerēs Prōserpinam nōn invēnit, in agrīs nōn labōrāvit. Flōrēs[4] nōn erant, frūmentum in agrīs nōn erat. Populus vītam dūram ēgit et deam accūsāvit quod pretium cibī magnum erat. Multī agricolae dīxērunt:

"Quid agēmus? In agrīs labōrāmus sed frūmentum nōn habēmus. Nōn valēmus. Deī nōn aequī sunt; officium nōn faciunt."

Iuppiter, quī deōs et virōs regit, iniūriās populī vīdit et deae agrōrum nūntiāvit:

"Prōserpina valet sed Plūtō eam habet. Mercurium nūntium ad īnferōs mittam. Mercurius fīliam tuam ad tē[9] dūcet. Sed nōn semper in terrā Prōserpina manēbit. Ita commodum erit: partem[10] annī in terrā, partem sub terrā aget."

Ita Iuppiter concordiam effēcit. Cerēs fīliam accēpit. Prōserpina partem annī in terrā, partem sub terrā ēgit. Cum[11] lībera in terrā est, multōs flōrēs et magnam cōpiam frūmentī vidēmus, quod Cerēs grāta in agrīs est et magnum est studium deae. Sed cum[11] Prōserpina ad īnferōs excēdit, Cerēs trīstis[12] est, et flōrēs variī nōn sunt.

15

20

25

⁹ *you*
¹⁰ *part* (acc. sing.)
¹¹ *whenever*
¹² *sad*

Questions

1. What was Proserpina doing when Pluto came?
2. How did Pluto take her away?
3. Where did Ceres go looking for Proserpina?
4. What happened in the fields while Ceres mourned for her daughter?
5. What did the farmers say?
6. How did Ceres learn where her daughter was?
7. What was Mercury's role in solving the issue?
8. What solution did Jupiter devise to resolve the conflict?
9. How does the earth reflect Ceres' joy and grief?

VOCABULARY

Nouns

de´a, -ae f. *goddess*
de´us, -ī m. *god* (deity, deism)
ō´tium, ō´tī n. *leisure, peace* (otiose)
stu´dium, stu´dī n. *eagerness, interest;* (studio, studious)
   pl. *studies*

Adjectives

com´modus, -a, -um *suitable, convenient* (accommodate, commodious)

va´rius, -a, -um *changing, various* (variable, variety)

Verbs

[13] The present imperative sing. is **dic**.

dī´cō, dī´cere, dī´xī, [dic´tus][13] *say, tell* (dictionary, dictum)

fu´giō, fug´ere, fū´gī, [fugitū´rus] (fugitive, refugee)
run away, flee

va´leō, valē´re, va´luī, [valitū´rus] *be strong,* (valiant, valid)
be well

Adverb

i´ta *so*

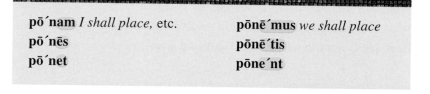

GRAMMAR

Third Conjugation: Future Tense

You know that the future sign of verbs of the first and second conjugations is **-bi-** (pages 56, 86). The future sign of verbs of the third and fourth conjugations, however, is long **-ē-**. The **-ō** verbs of the third conjugation substitute this long **-ē-** for the stem vowel, **-ĕ-**, except in the first person singular which uses **-a-**, and in the third person singular and plural, short **-ĕ.**

Except in the first person singular, the present of **doceō** will look just like the future of **pōnō.** Therefore, it is critical to know to which conjugation a verb belongs by memorizing its principal parts.

pō´nam *I shall place,* etc.	**pōnē´mus** *we shall place*
pō´nēs	**pōnē´tis**
pō´net	**pōne´nt**

Be careful to distinguish the future tense of the third conjugation from the present tense of the second conjugation. They look much alike.

This version of the abduction of Proserpina from her mother and her companions, a woodcut from a 1539 edition of Ovid, portrays Pluto and his horse in dark tones, presumably because he was the god of the dark kingdom of the underworld.

Oral Practice

1. Conjugate **dūcō** and **regō** in the future.
2. Conjugate **mittō** in the present, **cēdō** in the future, and **dēfendō** in the perfect.
3. Identify precisely the form of **fūgit, valēbis, efficit, dūcēmus, docēmus, accipitis, mūniunt, migrāvit, agent.**

▦ Exercises

A. Translate the following sentences.
1. Cēdētisne puerīs malīs?
2. Valēsne, fīlia mea? Valeō.
3. Captīvī ab oppidō in silvās lātās fugiunt.
4. Litterās ad Mārcum, amīcum meum, mittam.
5. Puerī bonī ex studiīs magnam fāmam accipiunt.
6. Virī ex oppidō nōn excēdent sed puellās dēfendent.
7. Multās hōrās in ōtiō nōn agēmus sed semper labōrābimus.

B. Translate the following sentences into Latin.
1. They fortify the camp.
2. They will rule the province.
3. Did you approve the shape of the wagon?
4. It is not convenient to send a letter.
5. We shall remain in the town and send a messenger.

Ceres, the goddess of grain and the harvest, is often shown with food items, as she is here, carrying a fruit basket and accompanied by a wild boar. The Romans identified her with the Greek goddess Demeter.

Erich Lessing/Art Resource, NY

WORD STUDY

- What are *commodities* and why are they so called? Why does a good student "pursue" his or her *studies?* Can you explain the word *cereal?* Give three more derivatives of **varius.**

- Here are some Latin phrases in English.

auxilio ab alto	*by aid from (on) high*
victoria, non praeda	*victory, not loot*
ex officio	*out of (as a result of) one's duty or office;* for example, a president of an organization may be a member of a committee *ex officio* simply from holding the office of president.

- Here is another state motto.

    Montani semper liberi. *Mountaineers (are) always free.* (motto of the state of West Virginia)

Did You Know?

The Romans often celebrated holidays, as many as 132 days each year during the rule of Augustus. Popular forms of holiday entertainment were games, the circus, or the theater. The great public games (**lūdī**) were free entertainment originally provided by the state to honor a god or goddess. They consisted of **lūdī scaenicī** (dramas and comedies at theaters), **mūnera gladiātōria** (staged combat between gladiators), and **lūdī circēnsēs** (chariot races and other exhibitions in the circus).

LŪCIUS ET MĀRCUS

LESSON OBJECTIVES
- To learn how to form adverbs from first and second declension adjectives
- To learn about the ablative of accompaniment

Rōmānī cum Germānīs, populō firmō et dūrō, bella perpetua gessērunt. Ōtium semper bellō cēdit, et nunc quoque[1] bella perpetua gerimus. Variae sunt bellōrum causae.

Quondam[2] Rōmānī et Aquītānī, sociī Rōmānōrum, cum Germānīs pugnābant[3]. Germānī pugnam nōn aequē incipiunt, et Rōmānī cum sociīs lātē 5 fugiunt. Lūcius, clārus Aquītānus, ex equō virōs Rōmānōs et Aquītānōs in Germānōs incitāvit. Servus Lūciō clārē nūntiāvit: "Germānī frātrem[4] tuum Mārcum capiunt!" Lūcius frātrem amāvit. Perīculum Mārcī Lūcium magnā cūrā affēcit. Lūcius equum incitāvit, armīs Germānōs terruit, frātrem servāvit. Quod equus nōn valuit, Lūcius frātrem sōlum[5] in equō posuit et ad 10 castra Aquītānōrum et Rōmānōrum equum incitāvit. Tum sōlus Germānōs exspectāvit. Multī Germānī accessērunt. Lūcius firmus cēdere incipit, auxilium exspectat—sed auxilium nōn venit—ē vītā excēdit. Mārcus vīdit et equum in Germānōs incitāvit et vītam āmīsit[6].

Varia et dūra est fortūna bellī et variē hominēs[7] afficit, sed glōriam semper 15 laudāmus.

1 *too*
2 *once*
3 *were fighting*
4 *brother*
5 *alone*
6 *lost*
7 *people*

Erich Lessing/Art Resource

A bareheaded and long-haired barbarian defends his homestead against a well-groomed and well-armored Roman soldier (notice his engraved metal helmet and cheek protector and the cuirass with its overlapping plate). The European tribes north of Italy often built conical thatched huts on piles in swamps as a defense against human and animal enemies. From a relief in the Louvre, in Paris.

Questions

1. Who was fighting with the German people?
2. Which side won the first battle and why?
3. What was Lucius' role before Marcus was captured?
4. Who was Marcus?
5. How did the danger affect Lucius?
6. What did he use to scare the Germans?
7. Why didn't Lucius ride back with Marcus?
8. Describe Lucius' next encounter with the Germans.
9. What happened to Marcus after this?

▧ VOCABULARY

Adjectives

fir´mus, -a, -um *strong, firm*   (firmness, affirm)

perpe´tuus, -a, -um *constant*   (perpetual)

Verbs

affi´ciō, affi´cere, affē´cī, [affec´tus]   **[faciō]**
  affect, afflict with

ge´rō, ge´rere, ges´sī, [ges´tus] *carry on, wage* (belligerent)

inci´piō, inci´pere, incē´pī, [incep´tus]   **[capiō]**
  take on, begin

Preposition

cum (+ abl.) *with*   (company, convert)

▧ GRAMMAR

Formation of Adverbs

In English, adverbs are usually formed from adjectives by adding the suffix *-ly: clear; clearly.*

In Latin, adverbs are formed from first and second declension adjectives by adding **-ē** to the base.

ADJECTIVE		ADVERB	
clārus	*clear*	**clārē**	*clearly*
līber	*free*	**līberē**	*freely*
pulcher	*beautiful*	**pulchrē**	*beautifully*

Oral Practice

1. Form adverbs from **pūblicus, grātus, commodus, aequus** and translate.
2. Give the Latin for *harshly, truly, firmly, deeply.*

Ablative of Accompaniment

As you already know, the means *by* or *with which* something is done is expressed by the ablative without a preposition (page 67): *They fought with arms,* **Armīs pugnāvērunt.** However, when *with* means *together with* or *along with,* the preposition **cum** is used with the ablative. This expresses *accompaniment:* **Cum servīs pugnat,** *He is fighting with the slaves.* Do not use **cum** (*with*) unless the *with* signifies accompaniment or association. If the *with* really means *by means of,* do not use **cum.** In the following English sentences, decide when **cum** should be used and when it should be omitted.

1. Come *with me.*
2. Walk *with us,* Jane.
3. John writes *with ink.*
4. Anna is *with the teacher.*
5. George fights *with snowballs.*
6. Play *with these toys,* Grace.

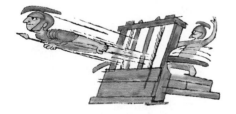

Virō pugnat.

(The man is used as a weapon.)

Cum virō pugnat.

■ *Exercises*

A. Translate the following sentences.

1. Nautae, pūblicē līberāte captīvōs.
2. Nautae terram firmam clārē vidēre incipiunt.
3. Cum populō barbarō bellum perpetuum gerēmus.
4. Armīs templa dēfendent et cum sociīs pugnābunt.
5. Magister dūrus poenā puerōs malōs aequē afficit.
6. In amīcitiā firmā et perpetuā cum sociīs nostrīs manēbimus.
7. Servus cum magnā cōpiā pecūniae fūgit; nōn ōtium sed cūrās invēnit.

B. Translate the following sentences.

1. We shall send the slave with food.
2. They will defend the island with arms.
3. It is not just to carry on war with friends.
4. By your (pl.) constant help I am beginning to be strong.
5. The settlers are beginning to flee with (their) families.

WORD STUDY

Latin and English Word Formation The preposition **cum** is often used as a prefix in Latin and English but always in the assimilated forms **com-, con-, col-, cor-, co-.** In compounds it usually means *together* rather than *with.*

Define the following words, all formed from verbs that you have studied: *convoke, collaborate, commotion, convene.* What is a political *convention?*

Give five other English words formed by attaching this prefix to Latin verbs, nouns, or adjectives already studied.

PLĀGŌSUS ORBILIUS

LESSON OBJECTIVES
- To learn about a famous Roman schoolmaster
- To learn the meaning and use of the adjectival suffix **-ōsus**
- To learn the future tense of third conjugation **-iō** and fourth conjugation verbs

Multa[1] dē Rōmānīs clārīs ā magistrō tuō audiēs et ex librīs trahēs. Venīte, puerī et puellae! Nunc audiētis fābulam novam dē magistrō Orbiliō et dē discipulō eius[2] Quīntō.

Orbilius grammaticus[3] dūrus erat; saepe[4] discipulōs tardōs poenā afficiēbat. Quīntus saepe tardus erat, quod in viīs Rōmānīs pater eius multa[1] 5 dē vītā mōnstrābat.

In scholā[5] Orbilius discipulīs nūntiāvit: "Librī vestrī multa adiectīva[6] continent, quae litterīs -ōsus fīniuntur[7]. Litterae -ōsus sunt signum plēnitūdinis[8]. Spectāte; mōnstrāre incipiam:

"Verbum—verb-ōsus. Liber multa verba continet. Liber est plēnus 10 verbōrum. Liber verbōsus est. Spectāte.

[1] *many things*
[2] *his*
[3] *schoolteacher*
[4] *often*
[5] *school*
[6] *adjectives*
[7] *which end with the letters -ōsus*
[8] *of fullness*

Museo Provinciale Campano, Capua

A teacher poses with his pupils, perhaps members of a chorus. Their stiff attitude looks like a lot of modern class pictures!

"Glōria—glōri-ōsus. Patria glōriam magnam accipiet. Patria plēna glōriae erit. Patria glōriōsa erit. Spectāte.

"Iniūria—iniūri-ōsus. Bellum plēnum iniūriārum est. Bellum iniūriōsum est.

"Sed ubi est Quīntus Horātius? Tardusne est? Nōnne est semper tardus? Studiōsus nōn est—ōtiōsus est. Poenā Quīntum afficiam—multās plāgās[9] dōnābō."

Et poenā nōn grātā Quīntum miserum[10] affēcit. Sed nunc Orbilius famōsus est. Cur? Quod discipulus tardus Quīntus erat Quīntus Horātius Flaccus, clārus poēta Rōmānus. Posteā[11] Horātius poēta magistrum Orbilium "plāgōsum Orbilium" in librō appellāvit[12] quod Orbilius plēnus plāgārum fuerat[13]. Quod Horātius verbum novum "plāgōsum" invēnit, multī discipulī plāgōsum Orbilium memoriā tenuērunt et semper tenēbunt.

[9] whacks (with a stick or whip)
[10] poor
[11] afterwards
[12] named
[13] had been

Questions

1. Who was Orbilius and what was he like?
2. Who was Quintus and what did he do to deserve punishment?
3. What was Quintus' full name and later occupation?
4. Why was he late so often?
5. What is the teacher's lesson to the class and how does he teach it?
6. How did Orbilius become famous?
7. What does **plāgōsus** mean and whom does it describe?
8. Who invented the word **plāgōsus**?
9. What English derivatives can you form by adding **-ōsus** to **victōria, cōpia, cūra?**

▦VOCABULARY

Nouns

lí´ber, lí´brī m. *book*	(library, libel)
ver´bum, -ī n. *word*	(verbal, verbose)

Adjectives

plē´nus, -a, -um *full*	(plenty, plenary)
tar´dus, -a, -um *late, slow*	(retardant, tardy)

Verbs

au´diō, audī´re, audī´vī, [audī´tus] *hear*	(audience, auditorium)
conti´neō, continē´re, conti´nuī, [conten´tus] *hold (together), contain*	**[teneō]**
tra´hō, tra´here, trā´xī, [trāc´tus] *draw, drag*	(attraction, tractor)

GRAMMAR

The Future of Third (-iō) and Fourth Conjugation Verbs

Verbs of the fourth conjugation form the future by adding **-ē-** (**-a-** in the first person singular) and the personal endings directly to the present stem. Long **-ī-** of the stem is shortened, however, since it precedes another vowel. The future of verbs of the third conjugation ending in **-iō** is the same as that of the fourth conjugation verbs.

THIRD CONJUGATION (–iō)		FOURTH CONJUGATION	
ca´piam	capiē´mus	mū´niam	mūniē´mus
I shall take, etc.		*I shall fortify*, etc.	
ca´piēs	capiē´tis	mū´niēs	mūniē´tis
ca´piet	ca´pient	mū´niet	mū´nient

Oral Practice

1. Give the future tense of **incipiō** and **audiō.**
2. Give the Latin for *they will affect, we shall hear, you* (pl.) *will receive, they will draw, it will contain.*
3. Translate and tell the form of **inveniētis, audīs, faciam, vidēbunt, parāvistī.**

Exercises

A. Translate the following sentences.
1. Equī carrōs agricolārum tardē trāxērunt.
2. Carrī magnam cōpiam frūmentī continent.
3. Equōs in locō lātō et commodō continēbimus.
4. Magister puerōs tardōs poenā pūblicē afficiet.
5. Nautae nostrī ex aquā virōs trahent et servābunt.
6. Colōnī ex agrīs frūmentum portābunt et magnam pecūniam accipient.

B. Translate the following sentences into Latin.
1. Will you come to my house?
2. We shall save the people with food.
3. Anna, a friendly girl, will receive a book.
4. The late girls will not hear the words of the famous man.
5. The boys will not receive a reward because they are late.

Discipulus ad scholam accēdit.
A young Roman schoolboy, ready to listen to his teacher, carries his tablet and stylus to school. The Greeks were the first to encourage universal literacy, and, by the first century A.D., it had reached remarkable levels in the Roman cities of Italy, as the graffiti at Pompeii testify.

Did You Know?

The Romans adopted Greek ideas of education beyond the elementary level. Schools were established soon after the Punic Wars. The curriculum was based on study of the Greek poets. The main subject was **ars grammatica** (skill in writing), which included both Latin and Greek grammar, literature, and some literary criticism. Students were also taught geography, mythology, antiquities, history, and ethics by the **grammaticus** (grammar teacher).

WORD STUDY

Prefixes Most prefixes are also used as prepositions, but a few are not. **Re-** is found only as a prefix in both Latin and English; it means *back* or *again*. It sometimes has the form **red-,** especially before vowels. Examples: **retineō,** *hold back;* **reficiō,** *make again;* **redigō,** *drive back;* **recipiō,** *take back.*

- In English, *re-* is freely used with many verbs: *remake, revisit, rehash, refill.*

- Give seven examples of the prefix *re-* in English words derived from Latin. What are the meanings of *revoke, refugee, refectory?*

AENĒĀS

LESSON OBJECTIVES
- To learn about the Trojan War
- To understand the relationship between the Romans and their household gods
- To learn about idioms

[The Trojan War was fought more than three thousand years ago at Troy, in Asia Minor, near the Dardanelles in what is now Turkey. The story of the war is told by the Greek poet Homer in the *Iliad*. Vergil, the Roman poet, tells part of the story in his *Aeneid* and goes on to tell of the Trojan Aeneas, said to be the son of the goddess Venus. After the fall of Troy Aeneas eventually reached Italy and, according to the story, he and his companions were the ancestors of the Romans.]

Trōiānī cum Graecīs multōs annōs bellum gessērunt. Graecī Trōiam occupāvērunt. Aenēās Trōiānus arma cēpit et cum multīs virīs oppidum dēfendere mātūrāvit. Sed Venus dea, māter Aenēae[1], eum[2] in mediō oppidō invēnit et verba fēcit:

"Audī sententiam meam. Tenē memoriā familiam tuam. Convocā familiam 5 et amīcōs firmōs et fuge. Novam patriam veniēs. Cēde fortūnae. Deī Trōiānōs poenā dūrā afficient."

Aenēās cōnsilium nōn grātē audīvit, sed officium fēcit. Virōs redūxit et amīcōs convocāvit. Amīcī convēnērunt et excēdere parāvērunt. Tum Aenēās ex oppidō patrem[3] portāvit et fīlium parvum dūxit. Cum multīs servīs et 10 sociīs fūgit. Singulī in locum commodum convēnērunt et ibi castra posuērunt. Māteriam ex silvā portāvērunt et nāvēs[4] parāvērunt. Tum nāvēs in aquam trāxērunt et undīs mandāvērunt et migrāvērunt. Ad multās īnsulās et terrās novās vēnērunt sed patriam novam nōn invēnērunt. Vītam dūram ēgērunt. Īra Iūnōnis[5], rēgīnae deōrum, hoc[6] effēcit. 15

In īnsulā Crētā castra posuērunt. Tum in mediō somnō[7] Aenēās Penātēs[8] vīdit et sententiam audīvit:

"Crēta patria vestra nōn erit. Excēdite, Trōiānī. Locus est quem[9] Graecī Hesperiam, aliī[10] Italiam vocant. Ibi terminum cūrārum perpetuārum inveniētis. Ibi in ōtiō et concordiā habitābitis et magnum oppidum pōnētis et 20 mūniētis."

Ita Trōiānī cōnsilium novum cēpērunt. Castra mōvērunt et ad Italiam nāvigāvērunt.

[1] *of Aeneas (gen. sing.)*
[2] *him*
[3] *father (acc. sing.)*
[4] *ships (acc. pl.)*
[5] *the anger of Juno*
[6] *this (acc. sing.)*
[7] *sleep*
[8] *household gods (acc. pl.)*
[9] *which (acc.)*
[10] *others*

A mosaic from Tunisia shows the poet Vergil holding a roll on which is written one of the opening lines of the *Aeneid:* "**Mūsa mihi causās memorā...**" On either side are two of the nine Muses, the goddesses associated with the arts. Clio, the Muse of History, holds a scroll, while Melpomene, the Muse of Tragedy, displays a tragic mask.

The Bettmann Archive

Questions

1. What was Aeneas' reaction once the Greeks had seized hold of Troy?
2. Venus gives Aeneas five specific instructions and makes two predictions. What are they?
3. What is Aeneas' first reaction to this advice about his future?
4. What preparations did Aeneas make before leaving Troy?
5. What caused the Trojans to wander over the seas so long and with such hardship?
6. From whom did Aeneas next receive advice?
7. What final destination did Aeneas and the Trojans have?
8. What were the Trojans to obtain or find in their new homeland?

VOCABULARY

Noun

senten´tia, -ae f. *feeling, opinion, motto*   (sentence)

Adjective

me´dius, -a, -um *middle, middle of*   (mediator)

Verbs

conve´niō, convenī´re, convē´nī,   [veniō]
   [**conventū´rus**] *come together*
con´vocō, convocā´re, convocā´vī,   [vocō]
   [**convocā´tus**] *call together*
redū´cō, redū´cere, redū´xī, [**reduc´tus**]   [dūcō]
   lead back

GRAMMAR

Idioms

Every language has expressions whose full meanings are lost when they are translated word for word into another language. The French for *How are you?* (**Comment allez-vous?**) literally means *How do you go?* which doesn't sound right to us. Such expressions are called *idioms.* Every language has hundreds of them. The following are some of the common ones in Latin.

grātiās agō *thank,* with dat. (literally, *act gratitude*)

grātiam habeō *feel grateful,* with dat. (lit., *have gratitude*)

vītam agō *live a life* (lit., *act life*)

bellum gerō *wage* or *carry on war*

castra pōnō *pitch camp* (lit., *place camp*)

viam mūniō *build a road* (lit., *fortify a road;* roads were built like walls)

verba faciō *speak, make a speech* (lit., *make words*)

memoriā teneō *remember* (lit., *hold in memory*)

cōnsilium capiō *adopt a plan* (lit., *take a plan*)

Oral Practice

Give the Latin for the following: *we are waging war, you* (sing.) *will remember, they built the roads, they spoke, I will adopt your plan, live your life in leisure, she will thank the gods, you* (pl.) *are grateful to the goddess.*

Sicily was the first land outside of Italy to become Roman territory (241 B.C.). Centuries earlier, the Trojan hero Aeneas is said to have landed his ships near Drepana and established funeral games in honor of his dead father, Anchises. See pages 204–205 for an elaborate painting depicting these events.

A Roman house had a special area set aside in which to place its household gods, the **Larēs**. Off the courtyard of this large home, the figures are displayed in a recess in a wall behind the altar. Aeneas fled with his household gods, the **Larēs** and **Penātēs**, from Troy to Italy.

Werner Forman/Art Resource, NY

Exercises

A. Translate the following sentences.
1. Puerōsne ex mediā silvā in oppidum redūcam?
2. Virī ex multīs terrīs convenient et verba facient.
3. Rōmānī multās (et) longās viās in Italiā mūnīvērunt.
4. Puerōs singulōs convocābimus et sententiās audiēmus.
5. Pōnite castra, puerī, in agrīs, et ibi agite līberam vītam.
6. Magistrō nostrō grātiam habēmus et līberē grātiās agēmus.

B. Translate the following sentences into Latin.
1. The boys will find water and pitch camp.
2. We ought to feel grateful to your friends.
3. The girls feel grateful and will thank the teacher.
4. We shall remember the teacher's words about duties.
5. You will not lead your comrades back to your fatherland.

C. Work with a partner to translate the following story and to learn more about the **Larēs** (m., nom. and acc. pl.) and **Penātēs** (m., nom. and acc. pl.) of the Romans.

Aeneas heard the Penates in (his) sleep. They said, "Depart from Crete." So he heard them (**eōs**) and he did his duty. The Lares and Penates were not big gods, but small. A Roman family had two (**duōs**)

Lares and two Penates. The Lares and Penates protected (**dēfendō**) the family. The family worshipped (**coluit**) the Lares and Penates because the gods protected the family's food and fortune. The family gave food to the gods. If (**sī**) a family departed from the house to a new house, it took the Lares and Penates with it (**sēcum**).

Did You Know?

Did your partner do a good job? Say **Euge!** *Well done! Bravo!* Did you win the game? Say **Evax!** *Hurrah!* Did you lose? Say **Hēu** or **Ehēu!** *Alas!* Do you want someone's attention? Say **Ecce**, or **En**, or **Em!** *Look!* Or are you calling for silence? Say **Au** or **Pāx** *(Peace)* or **St!** *Shh!* Surprised? Say **Ō**, or **Ōh**, or **Proh!** Amazed? Say **Vah!** *Wow!* Afraid? Let your teeth chatter a bit: **Attatae!** Scornful? Say **Hui!** *Phooey!* or **Apage!** *Get out of here!* Interjections, words of exclamation or high emotion, are remarkably similar from language to language. Many of those common among the Romans were borrowed from the Greeks.

WORD STUDY

Prefixes and Roots Often a careful *inspection* of a familiar English word will reveal an *unexpected aspect* of meaning. A "sentence" in grammar is a single complete *opinion* or expression. A judicial "sentence" is a judge's *opinion*. A "convention" *comes together* in an "auditorium" to *hear* the speaker. A "mediator" settles disputes by taking a *middle* position. A spiritualistic "medium" is supposed to take a *middle* position between the unseen spirit and the "audience" who *hears*. A "studious" person is one who is *eager* to learn. An "alarm" is a call *to arms* (**ad arma**). To "repatriate" a person is to bring him or her *back to the fatherland*.

• What is *verbosity?* A *convocation?* An *audition?*

• In the United States there are towns named Aeneas, Virgil, Juno, Venus, and Crete. Many firms dealing with women's clothes, cosmetics, etc., are called *Venus*. Why is this a popular name?

Mediator and belligerents

LESSON OBJECTIVES

- To learn about the early life and work of Vergil
- To learn hints for understanding Latin
- To learn how to form and translate the imperfect tense

POĒTA CLĀRUS

Quondam puer parvus Pūblius prope¹ Mantuam, oppidum Italiae, habitābat. Fīlius erat agricolae. In agrīs Pūblius nōn labōrābat quod numquam valuit, sed agrōs, silvās, frūmentum, et equōs amābat. In lūdō² multōs librōs legēbat, multās fābulās dē glōriā patriae et dē locīs clārīs
5 Italiae audiēbat, verba sententiāsque magistrī memoriā tenēbat.

Reliquī puerī in patriā mānsērunt, sed Pūblius, nunc vir, in urbe³ Rōmā studia coluit⁴. In Forō Rōmānō verba numquam fēcit quod timidus erat et populus eum⁵ terrēbat. Bella armaque semper fugiēbat, concordiam ōtiumque amābat. Agrōs et casam familiae āmīsit⁶, sed auxiliō amīcōrum recēpit.
10 Magnam grātiam amīcīs semper habēbat. Amīcōs nōn multōs sed firmōs habēbat. Tum carmina⁷ varia dē agrīs agricolīsque scrībere incēpit. Tardē scrībēbat multumque labōrābat, sed nōn multa carmina effēcit. Posteā⁸ magnum carmen⁹ dē bellō Trōiānōrum et dē glōriā Rōmae scrīpsit.

¹ near
² school
³ city
⁴ cultivated, carried on
⁵ him
⁶ lost
⁷ songs, poems (acc. pl.)
⁸ afterwards
⁹ song, poem (acc. sing.)

Dagli Orti/Museo della Civilta Romana, Rome/The Art Archive

Publius Vergilius Maro, or simply Vergil (70–19 B.C.), was one of Rome's greatest poets. He created the *Eclogues,* ten poems in the forms of pastoral poetry dealing with the social, political, and literary questions of his day. Next came his *Georgics,* four poems devoted to different aspects of farming, and finally his masterpiece, the *Aeneid,* in twelve books, left slightly unfinished at his death. The simple prose selections in this textbook will tell you at least the plot of this great Roman epic.

Audīvistisne dē Pūbliō, puerī puellaeque? Erat Pūblius Vergilius Marō[10], [10] *nominative singular*
clārus poēta Rōmānus, quī reliquōs poētās Rōmānōs superāvit[11]. 15 [11] *was superior to*
Lēgistis legētisque fābulam pulchram Vergilī dē Aenēā.

Questions

1. What things did Vergil like as a boy?
2. Why didn't he work with his father in the fields?
3. What sort of stories did Vergil hear as a boy?
4. Why didn't Vergil plead cases in the Roman Forum?
5. Would he have made a good soldier? Explain.
6. What were the subjects or themes of his first poems?
7. What was his **magnum opus** (*great work*) about?
8. Did he write much?
9. What was Vergil's full name and from what town did he come?

VOCABULARY

Noun

poē´ta, -ae m. *poet*   (poetry)

Adjective

re´liquus, -a, -um   (relic)
   remaining, rest (of)

Verbs

le´gō, le´gere, lē´gī, [lēc´tus]   (legible)
   gather, choose, read
scrī´bō, scrī´bere, scrīp´sī, [scrīp´tus]   (scribe)
   write

Adverb

num´quam *never*

Enclitic Conjunction

-que *and* (translated before the word to which it is joined)

GRAMMAR

Hints for Understanding Latin

First read the sentence aloud. As your eyes move across the page, following the order of words, separate them into groups according to their sense and grammatical relation. Since this grammatical relation is shown primarily by word endings—not by word order, as in English—watch the endings carefully. Each word group, or phrase, should be read and understood as a unit. When you come to the end of the sentence, translate in the English word order.

Here are the first four sentences of **Poēta Clārus** separated into groups of words according to their grammatical relation. Each division represents the words your eye should take in at each stop.

Quondam ‖ puer parvus Pūblius ‖ prope Mantuam, ‖ oppidum Italiae, ‖ habitābat. ‖ Fīlius erat agricolae. ‖ In agrīs ‖ Pūblius ‖ nōn labōrābat ‖ quod numquam valuit, ‖ sed agrōs, silvās, frūmentum, et equōs ‖ amābat. ‖ In lūdō ‖ multōs librōs ‖ legēbat, ‖ multās fābulās ‖ dē glōriā patriae ‖ et dē locīs clārīs Italiae ‖ audiēbat, ‖ verba sententiāsque magistrī ‖ memoriā tenēbat.

The Imperfect Tense

The Latin imperfect tense is called *imperfect* because it often represents incomplete, repetitive, or habitual actions in the past. It is formed by adding the tense sign **-bā-** to the present stem and then attaching the personal endings, which you already know. It is translated into English by *was, were, used to, kept, would,* or sometimes even *tried to.*

Observe that the personal ending for the first person singular is **-m,** not **-ō** as in the present tense. For the short vowels see page 29.

SINGULAR		PLURAL	
portā´bam	*I was carrying*	**portābā´mus**	*we were carrying*
portā´bās	*you were carrying*	**portābā´tis**	*you were carrying*
portā´bat	*he/she/it was carrying*	**portā´bant**	*they were carrying*

Similarly, **docēbam, pōnēbam, mūniēbam, capiēbam.** (For full conjugations, see the Grammar Appendix.)

The imperfect of **sum** is given below. You are already familiar with the third person singular and plural.

e´ram *I was, used to be*	**erā´mus** *we were, used to be*
e´rās *you were, used to be*	**erā´tis** *you were, used to be*
e´rat *he/she/it was, used to be*	**e´rant** *they were, used to be*

Uses of the Perfect and Imperfect Tenses: How They Differ

The imperfect tense always refers to action or being as *repeated, customary,* or *continuous,* like the English progressive past, and must be carefully distinguished from the perfect. In the following sentences the first group would be in the perfect in Latin, the second in the imperfect.

PERFECT	IMPERFECT
I saw John yesterday.	*I saw John frequently.*
I went to camp last year.	*I used to go to camp every year.*
Did you ever play football?	*Did you play football long?*
The alarm clock rang and I got up.	*The alarm clock kept on ringing, but I stayed in bed.*

Latin has two past tenses: perfect and imperfect; English has six ways of translating them: past, present perfect, emphatic past, progressive past, customary past, repeated past. Notice the difference in the following.

Vēnī, *I came* (past), or *I have come* (present perfect), or *I did come* (emphatic past).

The translation will depend on the context, but the first is much more common.

Veniēbam, *I was coming* (progressive past), or *I used to come* (customary past), or *I kept on coming* (repeated past).

Sometimes, however, the imperfect is best translated by the simple past; this is especially true of the imperfect of **sum.**

In Latin, the perfect is used much more often than the imperfect. In translating the English past into Latin, use the perfect unless there is a clear reason for using the imperfect.

Did You Know?

Libraries were another Roman borrowing from the Greeks, whose rulers assembled massive collections of papyrus or parchment rolls in great cities like Alexandria in Egypt (ca. 200,000 volumes) or Pergamum in Asia. There were no public libraries in Rome until the end of the first century B.C., but some wealthy collectors had extensive collections, either bought from Rome's many booksellers or looted from conquered lands. Books as we know them, in **cōdex** form, came to replace rolls (**volūmina**) in the third and fourth centuries A.D.

▦ *Exercises*

A. Translate the following sentences.
1. Multōsne librōs lēgistis?
2. Puellae puerīque litterās scrībēbant.
3. In casam veniēbam; ibi amīcum meum vīdī.
4. Mārcus amīcum vocābat sed amīcus nōn vēnit.
5. Multōs equōs in viīs vidēbāmus, sed nunc ubi sunt equī?
6. Multī virī in agrīs habitābant sed nunc ad oppida migrāvērunt

B. Translate the following sentences into Latin.
1. Have you never received letters?
2. We were leading the horses to water.
3. We kept waiting but they did not come.
4. Marcus, did you read about the causes of the war?
5. Marcus came to dinner but the rest of the boys did not come.

C. Work with a partner to ask questions and answer them, following the cues. Refer to page 139 if you need help with the vocabulary.
1. What were you doing in your house?
   (I was reading a book.)
2. What were you doing in the fields?
   (I was working with the farmers.)
3. What were Clara and your friend doing in the den?
   (They were writing a letter.)
4. What were the servants doing in the kitchen?
   (They were preparing dinner.)
5. What were you doing in the entrance hall?
   (I was waiting for my friend.)

WORD STUDY

- How did the *Mediterranean* Sea get its name? The English word *deficit* preserves the third person singular present of Latin **dēficiō.** What is the literal (Latin) meaning of *deficit?*

deficit

- Here are some Latin phrases in English.

magnum bonum	*a great good*
via media	*a middle way* or *course*
amicus curiae	*a friend of the court*
consilio et armis	*by counsel and by arms*

AD ITALIAM

LESSON OBJECTIVES
- To learn about Aeneas' trip toward Italy
- To learn the passive voice and the passive forms of the present, imperfect, and future tenses

In magnīs undīs nāvēs[1] Trōiānōrum volvuntur[2]. Sed Trōiānī ex mediīs undīs servantur et ad Actium[3] properant; ibi inveniunt Helenum Trōiānum, quī[4] terram regēbat. Helenus Trōiānōs convocat et verba pauca facit:

"Longa est via ad Italiam, ad quam[5] accēdere parātis. Accēdite ad Siciliam et nāvigāte ab Siciliā ad Italiam fīnitimam. Dūrum est semper nāvigāre, sed 5 Fāta viam invenient."

Sententia Helenī grātē accipitur, et Aenēās Helenō grātiās agit. Castra moventur nāvēsque undīs committuntur. "Italiam, Italiam videō!" clāmat nauta et terram mōnstrat. In terrā equī clārē videntur. "Signum proeliī sunt equī," dīcit Anchīsēs[6]; "equīs bellum geritur. Proelium committere nōn 10 dēbēmus." Nōn ibi manent sed ad Siciliam fīnitimam properant. Aetna eōs[7] terret et ā Siciliā fugiunt.

Tum Iūnō, rēgīna deōrum, quae[8] Trōiānōs nōn amābat, ad Aeolum, quī ventōs regit et continet, venit dīcitque:

"Sī ventī dūrī in nāvēs[9] Trōiānōrum mittentur, magnam grātiam habēbō et 15 magna praemia tibi[10] dōnābō."

Aeolus ventōs in nāvēs mittere mātūrat. Altīs undīs Trōiānī terrentur. Arma virīque in undīs sunt. Tum Neptūnus, deus undārum, ventōs audit et ad locum venit ubi nāvēs sunt. Īra Neptūnī magna est; ventī lātē fugiunt. Paucī Trōiānī āmittuntur[11]; reliquī ad terram fīnitimam veniunt et servantur. Sed in 20 quā[12] terrā sunt? Nōn sciunt[13], sed castra pōnere nōn dubitāvērunt[14].

[1] *ships (nom. pl.)*
[2] *are tossed*
[3] *Actium (Ak´shium)*
[4] *who*
[5] *which*
[6] *father of Aeneas; pronounced Ankī´sēs*
[7] *them*
[8] *who*
[9] *ships (acc. pl.)*
[10] *to you*
[11] *are lost*
[12] *what*
[13] *know*
[14] *did not hesitate*

Questions
1. Where do the Trojans land first and whom do they meet?
2. Where does their host tell them to go before going to Italy?
3. What will help the Trojans get there?
4. Is Helenus' advice accepted?
5. Who spots Italy first and what does he see there?
6. How does Anchises interpret what is seen?
7. Do the Trojans stop in Italy?
8. What scares them about Sicily?

Vanni/Art Resource, NY

Īra Neptūnī magna est.
Neptune, god of the sea, angry because the storm stirred up by Juno and Aeolus has disturbed his kingdom, drives the raging winds away from the Trojans' ships, calms the sea, and leaves Aeneas headed in the opposite direction from Italy.

9. Who is Juno and what is the trouble she causes?
10. Are any Trojans lost at sea?
11. At the end of this passage, where are the Trojans?

▣ VOCABULARY

Nouns

fīni´timus, -ī m. *neighbor*
proe´lium, proe´lī n. *battle*
ven´tus, -ī m. *wind*   (vent, ventilate)

Adjectives

fīni´timus, -a, -um *neighboring*
pau´cī, -ae, -a *few* (pl. only)   (paucity)

Verbs

commit´tō, commit´tere, commī´sī, [commis´sus]   [mittō]
   join together, commit, entrust
  proe´lium commit´tō *begin battle*
pro´perō, properā´re, properā´vī,
  [properātū´rus] *hasten, hurry*

▉ GRAMMAR

Voice: Active and Passive

When the verb shows that the subject acts (is doing something), it is in the *active voice*.

Vir dūcet. *The man will lead.*

When the verb shows that the subject is acted upon, it is in the *passive voice*.

Vir dūcētur. *The man will be led.*

Observe that voice is shown in Latin by endings. The linking verb **sum** has no voice, for it merely indicates existence or a state of being.

Progressive and Passive Verb Forms in English

Distinguish in English between active progressive forms and passive verb phrases, both of which use some form of the verb *to be*.

Active (progressive): *He is seeing* **(videt).** *They were calling* **(vocābant).**

Passive: *He is (being) seen* **(vidētur).** *They were being called* **(vocābantur).**

In Latin it is not difficult to distinguish active and passive.

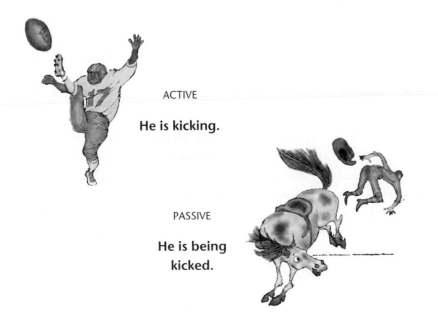

ACTIVE

He is kicking.

PASSIVE

He is being kicked.

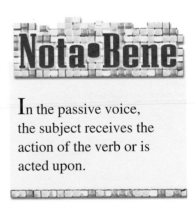

Nota•Bene

In the passive voice, the subject receives the action of the verb or is acted upon.

The word *being* is often important in the English translation of the imperfect passive, since it underscores the incomplete nature of that tense.

Oral Practice

Tell which of these verbs are passive: *he called, we were cold, he was laughing, they were found, you are being taught, he is fighting, they will be scolded, he will praise, you will be invited, it was being written, we were reading, she was sent, they were free, they were freed.*

Passive Voice of the Four Conjugations

In all conjugations, form the passive voice by adding the passive personal endings to the appropriate stem.

ENDINGS		FIRST CONJUGATION PRESENT PASSIVE	
-r	**-mur**	**por´tor** *I am (being) carried*	**portā´mur** *we are (being) carried*
-ris	**-minī**	**portā´ris** *you are (being) carried*	**portā´minī** *you are (being) carried*
-tur	**-ntur**	**portā´tur** *he/she/it is (being) carried*	**portan´tur** *they are (being) carried*

THIRD CONJUGATION PRESENT PASSIVE	
pō´nor *I am (being) put*	**pō´nimur** *we are (being) put*
pō´neris *you are (being) put*	**pōni´minī** *you are (being) put*
pō´nitur *he/she/it is (being) put*	**pōnun´tur** *they are (being) put*

Similarly, **doceor, capior, mūnior** (see the Grammar Appendix).

FIRST CONJUGATION IMPERFECT PASSIVE	
portā´bar *I was (being) carried, was carried, used to be carried*	**portābā´mur** *we were (being) carried, etc.*
portābā´ris *you were (being) carried, etc.*	**portābā´minī** *you were (being) carried, etc.*
portābā´tur *he/she/it was (being) carried, etc.*	**portāban´tur** *they were (being) carried, etc.*

THIRD CONJUGATION IMPERFECT PASSIVE

pōnē´bar *I was (being) put, was put, used to be put*

pōnēbā´mur *we were (being) put, etc.*

pōnēbā´ris *you were (being) put, etc.*

pōnēbā´minī *you were (being) put, etc.*

pōnēbā´tur *he/she/it was (being) put, etc.*

pōnēban´tur *they were (being) put, etc.*

Similarly, **docēbar, mūniēbar, capiēbar** (see the Grammar Appendix).

FIRST CONJUGATION FUTURE PASSIVE

portā´bor *I shall be carried*

portā´bimur *we shall be carried*

portā´beris *you will be carried*

portābi´minī *you will be carried*

portā´bitur *he/she/it will be carried*

portābun´tur *they will be carried*

THIRD CONJUGATION FUTURE PASSIVE

pō´nar *I shall be put*

pōnē´mur *we will be put*

pōnē´ris *you will be put*

pōnē´minī *you will be put*

pōnē´tur *he/she/it will be put*

pōnen´tur *they will be put*

Similarly, **docēbor, mūniar, capiar** (see the Grammar Appendix).

Observe that **-r** occurs in five of the six passive endings.

In forms ending in **-ō** in the active (as **portō** and **portābō**), the passive ending **-r** is added to, not substituted for, the active ending. The **-ō-** becomes short (see page 29).

Oral Practice

1. Conjugate **accipiō** in the present passive, **dēfendō** in the imperfect passive, and **inveniō** in the future passive.

2. Translate into Latin: *we shall be called, he is being taught, it is not approved, they were being sent, it will be received, he will be heard, you (sing.) are moved, they are ruled, you (pl.) will be seen, we are awaited.*

Nota•Bene

Notice the slight but important difference: **dūceris** (short **-e-**), 2nd pers. sing. pres. passive, *you are led,* and **dūcēris** (long **-ē-**), 2nd pers. sing. fut. passive, *you will be led.*

📖 *Exercises*

A. Translate the following sentences.
1. Amā fīnitimum tuum.
2. Litterae in ōtiō scrībentur.
3. Reliquī nautae ad prōvinciam mittentur.
4. Rōmānī proelium cum barbarīs nunc committunt.
5. Paucī virī in fīnitimīs agrīs oppidīsque vidēbantur.
6. Multa praemia reliquīs puerīs puellīsque dōnābuntur.
7. Captīvī ad oppidum redūcentur et proelium committētur.

B. Translate the following sentences into Latin.
1. Few books were being read in camp.
2. They will find food in the house.
3. Food will be found in the kitchen (**culīna**) of the house.
4. The rest of the men will be sent to the island.
5. Are the rest of the boys working in the fields?

WORD STUDY

- **Roots** We have seen how Latin and English words are formed from others. It is important to recognize the roots that words have in common. Note the relationship and review the meanings of the following words that have occurred in previous vocabularies.

  amīcus and **amīcitia, nāvigō** and **nauta, nūntiō** and **nūntius, capiō** and **captīvus** (a *captive* is *one who is taken*), **pugna** and **pugnō, puer** and **puella, habeō** and **habitō** (*to inhabit* a place is *to keep on having it*)

  Try to associate new Latin words with those you have already studied, as well as with English derivatives that you find.

- Towns named Neptune are in New Jersey and Tennessee; Neptune Beach is in Florida. The four cities in the United States which have more firms named Neptune listed in their telephone directories than other cities are New York, Boston, Seattle, and Los Angeles. Why do you think this name is popular in these cities?

AENĒĀS IN ĀFRICĀ

LESSON OBJECTIVES

- To learn more about the travels of Aeneas
- To learn the difference between transitive and intransitive verbs
- To learn the ablative of agent construction

Aenēās sociōs convocāvit et verba fēcit:

"In terrā novā sumus. Sed deī praesidium nostrum sunt. Deīs vītam committite. Neque terra neque aqua nōs[1] terret. Inveniēmus viam aut faciēmus. Italia nostra erit. Ibi et terminus malōrum nostrōrum et ōtium perpetuum ā Trōiānīs invenientur. Ibi patria erit et nova Trōia. Ē patriā novā numquam excēdēmus."

Tum Aenēās cum ūnō sociō ē castrīs excessit. Loca explōrāre mātūrāvit. Venus māter eum[2] vīdit et appellāvit. Nōmen[3] oppidī, quod[4] appellātur Carthāgō et in Āfricā est, et nōmen rēgīnae, quae[5] est Dīdō, Aenēae[6] Venus nūntiat. Via Aenēae ā deā mōnstrātur; Aenēās prōcessit et magnum oppidum 10

[1] *us*
[2] *him*
[3] *name* (acc.)
[4] *which*
[5] *who*
[6] *dative*

5

The Metropolitan Museum of Art, Gift of Henry Walters, 1925. (25.41)

In Carthage, Dido, sympathetic to the Trojans' woes, welcomed them and had a great banquet prepared. Afterwards, Aeneas, at Dido's insistence, reluctantly told of the havoc of the fall of Troy and his pain at having to flee in obedience to the will of the gods. Can you identify some of the events connected with the Trojan War as shown in this sixteenth-century enamel?

vīdit. In mediō oppidō templum erat. Ad templum rēgīna Dīdō cum paucīs sociīs vēnit. Ibi erant reliquī Trōiānī quōs[7] undae ab Aeneā[8] sēparāverant[9].

Dīdō mala Trōiānōrum audit et dīcit:

"Auxiliō meō aut in Italiam aut in Siciliam commodē veniētis, amīcī. Sed
15 sī grātum est in nostrā patriā manēre, oppidum nostrum est vestrum et praesidium habēbitis."

Tum magna cēna et cibī ēgregiī[10] ā rēgīnā parantur. Aenēās nūntium ad fīlium, quī Iūlus[11] appellātur, mittit; nūntius dīcit:

"Properā ad oppidum, Iūle. Pater tē[12] exspectat."

20 Sed in locō Iūlī Venus deum Amōrem[13] mittit. Sed et Aenēās et reliquī Trōiānī deum crēdunt esse Iūlum[14]. Tum Amor rēgīnam afficit, et Dīdō Aenēam amāre incipit.

Questions

1. What does Aeneas tell his comrades about the gods?
2. How does he express his determination to get to Italy?
3. What will be found in Italy and why does he speak of a **nova Trōia** (line 5)?
4. Why did Aeneas leave the camp?
5. Who saw him leave and met him?
6. What information did he receive from her?
7. Who was at the temple when Aeneas and his comrade got there?
8. What choices did Dido offer Aeneas after hearing his troubles? Were they helpful?
9. To whom does Aeneas send a message, and what was it?
10. What is the paradoxical (unexpected) result?

▥ VOCABULARY

Noun

praesi´dium, praesi´dī n. *guard, protection*

Verb

appel´lō, appellā´re, appellā´vī, [appellā´tus] (appellate)
  call, name

Conjunctions

aut *or*
aut... aut *either . . . or*
et... et *both . . . and*
ne´que (or **nec**) *and not, nor*
ne´que... ne´que *neither . . . nor*

⊞ GRAMMAR

Transitive and Intransitive Verbs

When the action of a verb is carried over to a direct object, i.e., when the action affects a person or a thing or produces a result, then that verb is *transitive*, literally, "going across" (**trāns**) to an object.

Puerum amat.	*She loves the boy.* (transitive)
Viam mūnīvērunt.	*They built a road.* (transitive)

An *intransitive* verb is one that does not have a direct object.

Mārcus excēdit.	*Marcus departs.* (intransitive)
In aquā Claudia mānsit.	*Claudia stayed in the water.* (intransitive)

In English and normally in Latin, transitive verbs are the only verbs used in the passive voice.

Some Latin verbs that are intransitive can be used either transitively or intransitively in English.

Anna labōrat.	*Anna is working.* (intransitive)
(not in Latin)	*He works the brakes.* (transitive)
In casam currit.	*He runs into the house.* (intransitive)
(not in Latin)	*She runs the sideshow.* (transitive)

Ablative of Agent

Let us see what happens when the two sentences containing transitive verbs are turned around and the verb becomes passive.

Anna aquam portat.	*Anna is carrying the water.*
Aqua ab Annā portātur.	*The water is carried by Anna.*
Virōs videō.	*I see the men.*
Virī ā mē videntur.	*The men are seen by me.*

Observe that in both English and Latin: (a) the direct object of the active verb becomes the subject of the passive verb; (b) the subject of the active verb becomes the object of a preposition (**ā, ab,** *by*), indicating the *agent;* (c) the verb ending changes from active to passive and may change person (the second example) to agree with the new subject. However, its tense remains the same.

Distinguish carefully between the ablative of agent and the ablative of means, both of which are often translated with *by.* Remember that *"means"* refers to a *thing,* while *"agent"* refers to a *person.* Besides, the ablative of *means* is never used *with* a preposition, but the ablative of *agent*

Nota Bene

In English and Latin, if the verb has a direct object, it is *transitive* in that sentence. If it does not, it is *intransitive.* A verb that can be used in the passive can also be called transitive. Experience and common sense will tell you the intransitive Latin verbs that cannot be used in the passive.

The banquet in Carthage was followed by a hunt. Young Iulus *(upper right),* eager for big game, charges ahead. Dido is in the center, while Aeneas *(lower left)* points to the stag in the clearing.

is never used *without* the preposition **ā (ab).** This preposition means *by* only when used before nouns referring to persons and with passive verbs.

Puella poenā terrētur.   *The girl is scared by punishment.*
                              (means)

Puella ā puerīs terrētur.   *The girl is scared by the boys.*
                              (agent)

Oral Practice

A. Tell whether the words in italics require the ablative of means or the ablative of agent construction.

1. I was hit *by a stone.*
2. He was liked *by everybody.*
3. The game will be won *by our team.*
4. This book was bought *by me with my own money.*
5. John will be sent for *by messenger,* Mary *by letter.*
6. The note had been written *by hand* and not *with a word processor.*

B. Change the following from active to passive, or from passive to active. Then translate each sentence.

1. Vir librum videt.
2. Puerī verba tua exspectābant.
3. Oppida ā populō reguntur.
4. Reliqua pecūnia ab amīcō meō accipiētur.
5. Multī sociī ad medium oppidum ā nūntiō convocābantur.

Agreement

In both English and Latin, when two subjects are connected by *or* (**aut**), *either . . . or* (**aut... aut**), *neither . . . nor* (**neque... neque**), the verb agrees with the nearer subject: *Neither the boys nor the girl is in the forest.*
Neque puerī neque puella in silvā est.

▦ *Exercises*

A. Translate the following sentences.

1. Aut puerī aut virī equōs ad agrōs redūcent.
2. Neque servus neque equus in viīs vidēbitur.
3. Equus puerum trahit; puer ab equō trahitur.
4. Mārcus amīcus vērus ā multīs virīs appellābātur.
5. Neque praemia neque auxilium ā sociīs nostrīs mittitur.
6. Multa praemia ā reliquīs puerīs puellīsque grātē accipientur.
7. Magister puerōs puellāsque docēbat; puerī puellaeque ā magistrō docēbantur.

B. Translate the following sentences into Latin.

1. The letter was (being) written by my friend.
2. Friendly words were (being) spoken by the foreign queen.
3. The grain will be dragged by wagon to the town.
4. The men see few houses; few houses are seen by the men.
5. Neither water nor grain is carried by the rest of the settlers.

Did You Know?

The Roman **mātrōna** (*matron*) enjoyed high respect and influence in the ancient world. Upon marriage, a Roman woman acquired a social position never attained by the women of ancient Greece. A Roman matron was not kept at home in special quarters as were Greek women. She directed the management of the household to include the early education of her children, supervised the tasks of the household slaves, and even on occasion exercised political influence.

WORD STUDY

- What is meant by taking an *appeal* to a higher court? Why is such a court called an *appellate court?* What is meant by an *appellation? Carthage* is a town name in eleven states; *Cartago* is in California.

- Study the following English phrases borrowed from Latin.

  terra firma *solid earth* (as opposed to water and air)

  In Deo speramus. *In God we trust.* (motto of Brown University)

  Pauci quos aequus amat Iuppiter. *(Only) the few whom fair-minded Jupiter loves (succeed).*

- Explain **Elizabeth regina,** abbreviated **ER** on British coins.

Terra nōn firma

DRESS AND APPEARANCE

Probably the most obvious difference between ancient and modern clothing was that civilized men did not wear long pants or trousers. These garments were worn only by barbarians. After the barbarians invaded the Roman Empire, their dress became the fashion for all of Europe. The same is true of the mustache (without beard). No early Roman citizen ever wore one, and it was just as much the mark of the barbarian as long pants were. Most Roman men were smooth shaven until the second century A.D., when beards and hair worn across the forehead came into fashion.

Over a sort of pair of trunks, Roman men wore a long shirt called a **tunica,** made of white wool, as an outer garment. Senators and knights had crimson stripes down the front and back, the senators' stripes being broader than those of the knights. A belt was worn around this, and the upper part was bloused out over the belt. When a Roman was engaged in some active occupation, he pulled his tunic up to his knees. In the house, the tunic was usually sufficient clothing.

Over the tunic the Roman citizen might wear a **toga.** This garment was the official dress of Roman citizens, the symbol of their civic life, and only citizens were allowed to wear it. It was also made of white wool and was quite bulky. The toga worn by boys and government officials had a crimson border. When boys grew up, they changed to the plain white toga.

Important citizens always wore this garment when appearing in public, but the ordinary Roman wore it much less frequently. The poorer classes and slaves wore only a tunic. For parties and special occasions, brightly colored togas were often worn, but clothing styles changed very slowly.

The toga was really a sort of blanket that was thrown over the left shoulder, pulled across the back and under the right arm, and again thrown over the left shoulder. Even though the unwrapped length of a toga was 10 to 15 feet, it was not fastened in any way, and it must have been quite a trick to learn to wear it properly!

Roman women also wore woolen tunics. Over the **tunica,** married women wore a **stola,** a long dress with a protecting band sewn around the bottom. A **stola** for parties often had embroidery around the hem. For street wear, a shawl often reaching down to the ankles, called a **palla,** was added.

Erich Lessing/Art Resource, NY

The fact that the ancient Roman matron in the modern-looking wicker chair has three hairdressers testifies to her wealth and position. The mirror shown was probably of highly polished bronze. The girl in the middle holds a jar of unguents. This relief is now in Trier, Germany.

Wool was thus the chief material for clothing; next came linen, made from the flax plant. Silk was rare and expensive and ranked with gold in value; cotton, which was imported from the East, was almost unknown.

In the house men and women wore slippers or sandals without heels; outdoors they wore shoes. The shoes of officials were red. No stockings were worn, although in cold weather old and sickly people sometimes wound cloth around their legs.

Hats were rarely worn except on journeys. Such hats as there were had broad brims and were flat. Women often wore ribbons and elaborate pins in their hair. Styles in hairdressing changed constantly as they do in modern times, but women did not cut their hair short as they sometimes do now.

For jewelry, both men and women of the richer classes wore rings, usually made of gold. Women also occasionally wore a decorative pin, or **fibula,** to fasten tunics or shawls. They were often decorated with semiprecious stones and cameos. Women also wore necklaces, chains, bracelets, and earrings.

Cosmetics and perfumes also played an important role in the lives of the wealthy Romans. For example, the women of the Roman upper class often blackened their eyelids, eyelashes, and eyebrows with charcoal. The herb henna was used to dye the nails and, often, the palms and soles of the feet. White lead or chalk whitened the face, while rouge was applied to the cheeks and lips. Balsam perfume and rosewater were popular with both men and women.

QUESTIONS

1. What was the distinctive garment of Roman men? Of women?

2. When did the Roman men begin to grow mustaches and wear long pants?

North Wind Picture Archives

A most important moment in a Roman boy's life was the time, at about age seventeen, when, at the Capitoline temple, he exchanged the **toga praetexta** with its crimson border for the all-white **toga virīlis** (the toga of manhood) and became a full Roman citizen. Later, when as a grown man he became a candidate for public office, he would whiten his toga with chalk (the **toga candida**) to make himself stand out in the crowd as he campaigned.

GLIMPSES OF ROMAN LIFE

PUT YOURSELF IN A ROMAN'S SHOES

Work in a small group. In Latin, describe the clothing, jewelry, and hairstyle you are wearing.[1] Use **gerō** and **habeō** for *wear*. Your teacher will help with strange forms.

Articles of Clothing
cap – **pīleus, -ī** m., **petasus, -ī** m. (brimmed), **mitra, -ae** f. (women's)
clothes – **vestis, -is** f., **vestimentum, -ī** n.
coat (cloak) – **lacerna, -ae** f., **tunica, -ae** f., **paenula, -ae** f. (with hood)
dress – **stola, -ae** f.
pants – **brācae, -ārum** f., **brācae praecīsae** (shorts)
sandal – **solea, -ae** f.
scarf – **mitella, -ae** f.
shirt – **tunica, -ae** f., **camisia, -ae** f.
shoe – **calceus, -ī** m.
skirt – **limbus, -ī** m.
stockings – **tibiālia, -ium** n.
style – **habitus, -ūs** m.
sweater – **thōrācium, -ī** n.
undershirt (T-shirt) – **subūcula, -ae** f.

Clothing Materials
(Use the adjective or say **factus, -a, -um ex** + noun in the abl.)
cotton – **xylinus, -a, -um**
leather – **corium, -ī** n., **scoricus, -a, -um**
linen – **linum, -ī** n., **linteus, -a, -um**
silken – **sēricus, -a, -um** (really "Chinese")
wool – **lāna, -ae** f., **lāneus, -a, -um**

Colors
black – **āter, -ra, -rum**
blue – **caeruleus, -a, -um**
bright – **lūcidus, -a, -um**
brown (or dark) – **fuscus, -a, -um**
faded – **dēcolōrātus, -a, -um**
gray – **glaucus, -a, -um**
green – **viridis, -e**
pink – **puniceus, -a, -um**
plaid – **colōribus quadrātīs variegātus, -a, -um**
purple – **purpureus, -a, -um**
red – **ruber, -ra, -rum**
yellow – **flāvus, -a, -um** (golden)
tan, khaki – **lūteolus, -a, -um**
white – **albus, -a, -um**

Jewelry
bracelet – **armilla, -ae** f.
earrings – **inaurēs, -ium** f.
eyeglasses – **perspicillia, -ōrum** n.
necklace – **torquēs, -is** m., **monīle -is** n.
pin, brooch – **fībula, -ae** f.
ring – **ānulus, -ī** m.
watch – **hōrologium, -ī** n.

Hairstyles
braided – **nexus, -a, -um**
combed – **comptus, -a, -um**
crewcut – **capillī dēsectī** m.
curled – **cincinnātus, -a, -um**
curly (natural) – **crispus, -a, -um**
hair – **capillī, -ōrum** m., **comae, -ārum** (usu. women's)
long – **prōmissus, -a, -um**
long flowing – **caesariātus, -a, -um**
shaved – **dērāsus, -a, -um**
short – **brevis, -ĕ**
straight – **rēctus, -a, -um**
uncombed – **horridus, -a, -um**

[1]Do not worry if many of these items do not fit or exactly match (their modern equivalents). The Romans will never know, and you need not memorize this vocabulary.

VOCABULARY

Nouns

dea	ōtium	sententia
deus	poēta	studium
fīnitimus	praesidium	ventus
liber	proelium	verbum

Adjectives

commodus	medius	plēnus	varius
fīnitimus	paucī	reliquus	
firmus	perpetuus	tardus	

Verbs

afficiō	conveniō	incipiō	trahō
appellō	convocō	legō	valeō
audiō	dīcō	properō	
committō	fugiō	redūcō	
contineō	gerō	scrībō	

Adverbs

ita	numquam

Preposition

cum

Conjunctions

aut	neque (or nec)
aut... aut	neque... neque
et... et	-que

Idioms

grātiās agere	viam mūnīre
grātiam habēre	verba facere
vītam agere	memoriā tenēre
bellum gerere	cōnsilium capere
castra pōnere	

GRAMMAR SUMMARY

Formation of Adverbs

Adverbs in Latin can easily be formed by taking the base of a first or second declension adjective and adding an **-ē** to it.

Poēta verba dīxit clārē. *The poet said the words clearly.*

Convocābuntur tardē. *They will be called together slowly.*

Future of Third Conjugation Verbs

Present stem + tense sign **ē/e** + personal endings (**-am** in first person singular)

Reliquōs poētās redūcam. *I shall lead back the rest of the poets.*

Perpetuē Italiam regēs. *You will rule Italy constantly.*

Future of Third (-iō) and Fourth Conjugation Verbs

Formed identically: Present stem (with **i**) + tense sign **ē/e** + personal endings (**-am** in first personal singular)

Pauca verba commoda audiet. *He will hear few suitable words.*

Aut bellum gerere incipiētis aut fugiētis. *Either you will begin to wage war or (you will) run away.*

The Imperfect Tense

Present stem + **bā/a** or **ēbā/a** + personal endings
(**-m** in first person singular)

Deōs deāsque appellābāmus.	*We kept calling the gods and goddesses.*
Librōs scribēbās.	*You used to write books.*

Past Tenses

In Latin	In English
1. Perfect (**Vēnī.**)	1. **a.** Past *(I came.)*
	b. Present perfect *(I have come.)*
	c. Emphatic past *(I did come.)*
2. Imperfect (**Veniēbam.**)	2. **a.** Progressive past *(I was coming.)*
	b. Customary past *(I used to come, would come.)*
	c. Repeated past *(I kept on coming.)*

The Passive Voice

The passive voice is used to show that the subject of the sentence is receiving the action of the verb rather than doing it. The present, imperfect, and future passive tenses are formed like the active voice, but a different set of personal endings is used.

In proelium vocātur.	*He is called into battle.*
Ā magistrō continēbantur.	*They were being kept (held) together by the teacher.*
Sententiīs firmīs tuīs nōn afficiar.	*I will not be affected by your strong feelings.*

Transitive and Intransitive Verbs

Transitive verbs are those that have a direct object. Intransitive verbs are those that do not. Many intransitive verbs are followed by a prepositional phrase. Generally, only transitive verbs are used in the passive voice.

Verba fēcit.	*She made a speech.* (transitive)
Ad Italiam Trōiānī properant.	*The Trojans are hurrying to Italy.* (intransitive)

Ablative of Agent

The doer of an action in a sentence with a passive verb is expressed by using the preposition **ā/ab** + the ablative case. This construction is called the ablative of (personal) agent.

Proelium numquam ā fīnitimīs populīs committitur.
Battle is never begun by the neighboring peoples.

Litterae ā multīs neque scrībentur neque legentur.
Letters will neither be written nor read by many.

If the means of the action is a thing, **ā/ab** is not used and the ablative is an ablative of means.

Firmīs armīs dēfendētur.
He will be protected by stout armor.

Ablative Uses

LATIN		ENGLISH
No prep.	MEANS	Prep. *with* or *by*
cum	ACCOMPANIMENT	Prep. *with*
ā/ab	AGENT	Prep. *by*

UNIT PRACTICE

Sentence Drill

A. Give the Latin for the italicized words.
1. *(We are called)* amīcī bonī.
2. Multī virī in proeliō *(will be called)*.
3. Patria *(will be saved)* quod valet.
4. Verba magistrī in scholā *(are being heard)*.
5. Puer ex aquā *(will be dragged)*.
6. Multa bella in Galliā *(were being carried on)*.

B. Translate the following sentences into Latin.
1. Few find leisure; leisure is found by few.
2. The men will receive aid; aid will be received by the men.
3. The boy scares the horses; the horses are scared by the boy.
4. Many will never read my words; my words will never be read by many.
5. The teacher will praise the girls; the girls will be praised by the teacher.

WORD STUDY

Derivatives

1. Define according to derivation: *relic, digest, Mr., doctor, libel, audiovisual, mediation*. Look these words up in the dictionary if necessary.

2. Give the prefix and Latin root word from which each of the following is derived: **redigō, concipiō, attrahō, committō;** *respect, component, incorrigible, exhibit.*

VOCABULARY

Circle the word that best completes each sentence.

1. Poēta sententiās multās in casā vestrā crās

   _____.

   a. audīvit

   b. legēbat

   c. dīcet

   d. scrīpsit

2. Rōmānī virōs ē castrīs in _____ cum armīs convōcāvērunt.

   a. praemium

   b. ōtium

   c. pretium

   d. proelium

3. Quis _____ deōrum audīre properat?

   a. ōtia

   b. verba

   c. ventōs

   d. praedās

4. _____, servī, carrōs ē viā lātā et in loca commoda.

   a. Trahite

   b. Valēte

   c. Venīte

   d. Afficite

5. Nautae ad terrās fīnitimās ventīs accēdere

   _____.

   a. incipiēbant

   b. appellābant

   c. continēbant

   d. augēbant

GRAMMAR

Complete each sentence with the correct endings.

6. Populī in prōvinciā bellum longum gerēba___; nunc oppidum firm___ mūnī___ dēbe___.

7. Cōpia cib___ bonī ā serv___ meīs parā___.

8. Fāmam amīcōrum pauc___ memori___ perpetu___ grātē tenēbimus.

9. Agricola cum soci___ multīs equ___ parvōs ē medi___ oppidō in agr___ crās redūc___.

10. Puellae reliquae litterās long___ familiīs dē ōti___ in īnsul___ pulchrā tard___ scrībēba___.

TRANSLATION

Translate the following sentences.

11. Liber pulcher verbōrum sacrōrum ā fīliā fīliōque captīvī in castrīs barbarīs servābātur.

12. Quis auxilium et praesidium populīs mittet, vir aut rēgīna?

13. "Vītae nostrae undīs deīsque committuntur," nautae publicē dīxērunt.

14. Multī Rōmānī fugiēbant; neque signīs variīs neque ā nūntiīs convocābantur.

15. Poēta novus scrīpsit: "Numquam verbum dūrum in librō meō continēbitur."

INVESTIGATION

Find the answers to these questions from any lesson in Unit V.

16. Match the Roman poet with his work.

Vergil   Horace   Ovid

  a. *Odes* and *Satires*

  b. *Metamorphoses*

  c. *Aeneid*

17. The Romans explained the change of seasons by the mythological story of _____ and _____.

18. Who were the **Larēs** and **Penātēs?**

19. True or false? **Lūdī scaenicī** were gladiatorial games in the arena.

20. Identify the following names from the *Aeneid.*

Aeneas   Anchises

Dido   Iulus

CULTURE

Vērum aut Falsum? Indicate whether each statement is true or false.

21. A toga with a crimson border was worn only by elected officials.

22. From statues we learn that most Roman men regularly wore beards and moustaches.

23. The basic item of Roman clothing for men and women of all classes was the tunic.

24. A **fībula** was a long shawl worn by Roman women.

25. The natural fibers wool and linen were most often used for Roman clothing.

FROM LATIN TO ENGLISH

Apply your knowledge of Latin roots to determine the best meaning of the italicized words.

26. We were amazed that the manuscripts were so *legible.*

  a. ancient

  b. valuable

  c. colorful

  d. readable

27. The committee was unable to predict the *paucity* of supplies.

  a. shortage

  b. cost

  c. destruction

  d. surplus

28. The senator was famous for his *verbose* speeches.

  a. powerful

  b. brief

  c. wordy

  d. critical

29. After the destruction of the village he became a *fugitive.*

  a. one ruling

  b. one fighting

  c. one helping

  d. one fleeing

30. The disease was in its *incipient* stage.

  a. contagious

  b. beginning

  c. final

  d. most serious

Gianni Dagli Orti/Biblioteca Estense Modena/The Art Archive

MISSION TO A NEW WORLD: AENEAS AND ROME

Unit Objectives

- To learn how adjectives may be used as nouns
- To learn the past perfect and future perfect active tenses
- To learn the perfect, past perfect, and future perfect passive tenses
- To learn personal pronouns and review possessive adjectives
- To learn about the perfect passive participle
- To learn about the present passive infinitive
- To read more stories from the *Aeneid*
- To learn about the Roman house and its furnishings

A scene by an unknown artist showing many of the events in Book V of the *Aeneid*. Aeneas has left Carthage and stops in Sicily to preside over funeral games for his father, Anchises, who had died there. The artist has followed Vergil's narrative in great detail. Have your teacher tell you the story and see how many of the events you can identify.

AENĒĀS ET DĪDŌ

¹ *sister* (acc.)
² *to him* (dat.)
³ *this*
⁴ *ships* (acc. pl.)
⁵ *why*
⁶ *commands (me)*
⁷ *killed herself*

Dīdō ad Annam sorōrem[1] properāvit: "Anna soror," dīxit, "animus meus miser perīculīs terrētur; Aenēam amō. Quid agam?"

Anna respondit: "Aenēās est bonus et amīcus vir. Prō Trōiā pugnāvit sed patriam āmīsit; nunc prō nostrā patriā multōs annōs pugnābit. Fīnitimī nōn
5 sunt amīcī. Terminī nostrī ab Aenēā proeliīs dēfendentur."

Aenēās in Āfricā cum rēgīnā pulchrā mānsit. Dīdō Trōiānum per medium oppidum dūxit et eī[2] oppidum mōnstrāvit.

Tum Iuppiter Mercurium nūntium ad Aenēam mīsit. "Annum in hōc[3] locō ēgistī," Mercurius dīxit. "Verba deī memoriā nōn tenēs; properā in
10 Italiam cum sociīs tuīs, ubi fīlius tuus reget. Ibi ōtium habēbis."

Aenēās sociōs convocāvit. Sociī frūmentum in nāvēs[4] portāvērunt. Dīdō Aenēam appellāvit:

"Cūr[5] fugis? Dūrus es; iniūriam facis. Magnum est perīculum nostrum. Ā populīs fīnitimīs agrī nostrī occupābuntur, oppidum āmittētur. Praesidium
15 nostrum esse dēbēs. In concordiā perpetuā habitābimus."

Aenēās respondit: "Deum Mercurium vīdī. Officium meum est ad Italiam nāvigāre. Dūrum est, sed deus imperat[6]."

Aenēās tardē excessit et ad nāvēs vēnit. Sociī convēnērunt et nāvēs in aquam trāxērunt. Tum nāvēs undīs ventīsque commīsērunt. Dīdō misera
20 nāvēs vīdit et sē interfēcit[7].

Trōiānī ad Italiam migrāvērunt et patriam novam invēnērunt. Dīdō vītam āmīsit; Aenēās patriam invēnit. Ita in librīs poētārum scrībitur.

Questions

1. Why was Dido troubled?
2. Why did Anna and Dido both think that Aeneas should stay?
3. What does Mercury tell Aeneas to do?
4. What arguments did Dido use to try to persuade Aeneas to stay in Carthage?
5. What did Dido do after Aeneas left?
6. Where did Aeneas go?
7. How long did Aeneas stay with Dido?

VOCABULARY

Noun

perī´culum, -ī n. *danger*   (perilous)

Adjective

mi´ser, mi´sera, mi´serum *unhappy, poor*   (miserable)

Verb

āmit´tō, āmit´tere, āmī´sī, [āmis´sus] *let go, lose*

Preposition

prō (with abl.) *in front of, before, for*   (provide, pronoun)

GRAMMAR

Words Used as Nouns

A pronoun is a word used instead of a noun *(pro-noun)*. For example, *he* or *she* can take the place of the name of a person. *It* or *that* takes the place of the name of a thing.

We have seen that the infinitive form of the verb may be used as a noun, as subject or object. (See page 128.)

An adjective also may be used as a noun. In Latin, the masculine and feminine adjectives refer to persons, the neuter to things. The usage, although common in English, is limited to adjectives of certain meanings. For example:

Bonī laudantur.	*The good (good men) are praised.*
Multum facit.	*He does much.*

But Latin can use almost any adjective as a noun.

Nostrī veniunt.	*Our (men) are coming.*
Multa facit.	*He does many (things).*
Fīnitimī nōn sunt amīcī.	*The neighboring (men, peoples) are not friendly (men, peoples).*
	The neighbors are not friends.

The god Mercury, often shown with a winged hat and sandals, was not only the messenger of the gods, but also the god associated with merchants, commerce, science, astronomy, thieves, travelers, and cleverness.

The Arch of Diocletian at now-deserted Sbeitla in northern Africa. After the destruction of Carthage in 146 B.C., Africa became a Roman province. Roman colonists later built a new Carthage, which became a flourishing provincial capital and educational center. Sbeitla, about 30 miles away, was in a fertile area important for the production of grain and olive oil.

Conversation

(See the map of the Roman world on pages 54–55.)

M = Magister aut Magistra   **D** = Discipulī et Discipulae

M: Spectāte, puerī et puellae.

D: Spectāmus, magister.

M: Ubi oppida vidētis?

D: In Eurōpā multa oppida spectāmus.

M: In mediā terrā aquam vidētis? Illam[8] aquam "Mediterrāneum Mare[9]" appellāmus. Ibi est Lūsitānia—vidētisne?

D: Vidēmus.

M: Ubi est Hibernia?

D: Hibernia est īnsula in Ōceanō Atlanticō.

M: Ubi pugnābat Caesar?

D: Caesar in Galliā pugnābat.

M: Ubi Dīdō habitābat? Respondēte, puellae puerīque.

D: _____

M: Ad quās *(which)* terrās Aenēās nāvigat?

D: _____

M: Multī virī multōrum populōrum in Eurōpā habitant. Ubi habitant Italī? Graecī? Helvetiī? Belgae?

D: _____

[8] *that*
[9] *sea*

Questions

Answer in Latin.

1. Ubi habitāmus?
2. Ubi agricolae multum frūmentum parant?
3. Ubi loca nōn plāna vidētis?
4. Ubi est Londīnium? Rōma? Lutetia? Corduba? Hierosolyma?

 *Exercises*

A. Translate the following sentences.
   1. Magna in proeliō fēcit.
   2. Nōnne bonum facere dēbēmus?
   3. Puer miser in viā librum āmīsit.
   4. Vīta ā multīs in bellō āmittētur.
   5. Nostrī prō patriā et familiīs pugnābant.
   6. Multōs annōs in perīculō ēgimus; nunc ōtium habēmus.

B. Translate the following sentences.
   1. Were the girls being scared by the horses?
   2. The people will be called together by the queen.
   3. I have entrusted the care of the money to the teacher.
   4. The boys saw the danger clearly and fled to the woods.
   5. By harsh discipline the master ruled the unhappy slaves.

Did You Know?

Books were published in ancient Rome by copying each one individually onto rolls of papyrus. If the author was wealthy, his manuscript was distributed for reproduction among his copyists and proofreaders. Commercial publishing was essentially similar except that more copyists were employed. After copies went on the market, they could be reproduced by anyone.

WORD STUDY

- As a prefix, **prō-** has its prepositional meanings, with the additional one of *forward*. Define the following derivatives of words that you have already studied: *provoke, prospect, produce, proceed, promote.*

- Tell which of the following are derived from **liber**, **librī**, and which from **līber**, **-a**, **-um**: *liberty, librarian, liberal, liberate.*

- Study the following English phrases borrowed from Latin.

pro patria	*for (one's) country*
pro forma	*(only) for (the sake of) form*
pro bono publico	*for the public good*

AENĒĀS AD ĪNFERŌS[1]

LESSON OBJECTIVES
- To learn about Aeneas in Hades
- To learn how to form and translate the past perfect and future perfect active tenses

Aenēās fīlius Anchīsae[2] fuit, quī in Siciliā ē vītā excesserat. Tum Anchīsēs in somnō ad fīlium vēnerat et fīlium vocāverat: "Venī, fīlī, ad īnferōs, ubi sum. Sibylla[3] viam nōvit et tē[4] dūcet."

Ita Aenēās in Italiam prōcessit, ubi Sibylla habitābat. Cōnsilium Sibyllae erat: "Sī in silvā rāmum aureum[5] inveniēs, ad īnferōs tē prōdūcam et sine 5 perīculō redūcam; sed sine rāmō numquam tē prōdūcam." Ita Aenēās in silvam properāvit. Auxiliō Veneris[6] rāmum invēnit et cum Sibyllā ad īnferōs dēscendit. Ibi multa nova vīdit et nōvit.

Tum ad magnam silvam vēnērunt. Ibi erat Dīdō. Aenēās rēgīnam vīdit et vocāvit: "Nūntiusne vērum nūntiāvit? Vītamne āmīsistī? Causane fuī? 10 Invītus[7] ē patriā tuā excessī, sed ita deus imperāvit[8]." Sed rēgīna, nunc inimīca, verbīs lacrimīsque[9] Aenēae nōn movētur. Neque Aenēam spectāvit neque respondit, sed in silvam fūgit.

Aenēās tardē ē silvā excessit et locum vīdit ubi malī poenā afficiēbantur. Tum Aenēās Sibyllaque in Ēlysium[10] prōcessērunt. Ibi animae[11] bonōrum in 15 concordiā vītam agēbant. Iniūriae et pugnae aberant. Ibi Anchīsēs erat.

[1] the Lower World (See footnote 6, p. 160)
[2] Anchises (Ankī´ses, gen.)
[3] the Sibyl (a prophetess)
[4] you (acc.)
[5] golden branch
[6] genitive of Venus
[7] unwilling(ly)
[8] has commanded
[9] tears
[10] Elў´sium, Greek and Roman heaven
[11] souls

Scala/Art Resource, NY

Ever obedient to the will of Fate, Aeneas reluctantly abandons Troy to fulfill his destiny as the founder of Rome. On his shoulder, he carries his father Anchises, who grasps a lion skin, and at his side is Ascanius (Iulus). Also with him are his household gods, brought along to serve as a vital link between the past and the future. Following is Creusa, his Trojan wife, who represents the past he must leave behind.

[12] *grateful(ly)*
[13] *will overcome*

Grātus[12] fīlium accēpit et nūntiāvit: "Clārōs Rōmānōs quī posteā in terrā erunt et glōriam populī tuī mōnstrābō. Rōmānī malōs superābunt[13] et populōs aequē regent." Aenēās ab Anchīse nōn retinētur et ā Sibyllā in terram redūcitur. Tum loca commoda in Italiā occupāre mātūrāvit. .

Questions

1. Where did Aeneas' father die?
2. What did Aeneas' father ask him to do?
3. Whom did Aeneas need to lead him into the Lower World?
4. What did Aeneas need to find in order to go into the Lower World and come back safely?
5. What questions did Aeneas ask of Dido?
6. What reason did he give for leaving her country?
7. How did Dido react and where did she go?
8. Where did Aeneas go after leaving Dido?
9. Whom did he see next and what was he shown?

▦ VOCABULARY

Adjective

inimī´cus, -a, -um *unfriendly, hostile;*   **[amīcus]**
    as noun, *personal enemy*

Verbs

ab´sum, abes´se, ā´fuī, [āfutū´rus]   **[sum]**
    be away, be absent
nōs´cō, nōs´cere, nō´vī, [nō´tus]
    learn; in perfect tense, *have learned, know*
prōcē´dō, prōcē´dere, prōces´sī,   **[cēdō]**
    [processū´rus] *go forward, advance*
prōdū´cō, prōdū´cere, prōdū´xī,   **[dūcō]**
    [prōduc´tus] *lead out*
reti´neō, retinē´re, reti´nuī, [reten´tus]   **[teneō]**
    hold back, keep

Adverb

iam *already, now*

Preposition

si´ne (with abl.) *without*   (sinecure)

GRAMMAR

The Past Perfect and Future Perfect Active

The *past perfect tense* (sometimes called the *pluperfect*) refers to an action that was completed before a certain time in the past: *He had gone* (before something else happened).

In Latin, the past perfect is formed by adding the tense sign **-erā-** (or **-erǎ-**) to the perfect stem, together with the personal endings of the present (but **-m,** not **-ō,** in the first person). The tense signs and personal endings together are the same as the various forms of the imperfect tense of **sum: portāv-eram, docu-eram, fu-eram,** etc. (For full conjugation see the Grammar Appendix.)

Iam excesserat.	*He had already left.*
Puellam laudāveram.	*I had praised the girl.*

The *future perfect tense* refers to an action completed before a certain time in the future: *He will have gone* (before something else will happen). In Latin, it is formed by adding the tense sign **-eri-** (first person **-erō**) to the perfect stem, together with the personal endings of the present: **portāv-erō, docu-erō, fu-erō,** etc. (For full conjugation see the Grammar Appendix.)

Verba fēcerit (fut. perf.) **antequam castra movēbimus** (fut.).	*He will have finished (his) speech before we (will) move the camp.*
Multum nōveris.	*You will know (have learned) a lot.*

The past perfect and the future perfect are used much less frequently than the perfect.

The Sibyls were prophetesses whose pronouncements were supposed to be inspired by Apollo. This painting, called *Augustus and the Sibyl,* was done by Antoine Caron in the sixteenth century and now hangs in the Louvre in Paris. Augustus is pictured kneeling before the Sibyl, who points to a vision of the future in the sky.

Oral Practice

1. Conjugate in the perfect: **videō**, **legō**, **efficiō**; in the past perfect: **moveō**, **incipiō**; in the imperfect: **retineō**, **prōcēdō**; in the future perfect: **laudō**, **faciō**.
2. Give the tense of **āfuimus**, **prōdūxerat**, **retinuistī**, **nōvērunt**, **prōcesserimus**, **āmīserātis**, **docēbās**.

Did You Know?

Roman schools of rhetoric were similar to our colleges and universities. The students were young men, usually wealthy, who studied Greek and Latin prose authors, philosophy, and the practice of composition. These studies began with the simple form of narratives and continued with public speaking. Often students would role-play a famous Roman who had to make an important decision and then would discuss his possible courses of action.

Exercises

A. Translate the following sentences.
1. Parvī puerī linguam retinēre dēbent.
2. Multī puerī aberant. Nōnne valēbant?
3. Carrī ex silvā vēnerant et ad oppidum tardē prōcēdēbant.
4. Fīliī et fīliae agricolārum multa dē agrīs et equīs nōvērunt.
5. Magister puerōs retinuit, quod fōrmās verbōrum nōn nōverant.
6. Paucī labōrābant sed reliquī puerī in castrīs semper manēbant.
7. Fīlius magistrī multa dē librīs nōvit, sed fīlium agricolae agrī docent.

B. Translate the following sentences.
1. We know much about many lands and peoples.
2. The poor woman will not have had much leisure.
3. Marius had fought in Gaul for (his) native land.
4. We are the daughters of free (men) and love our native land.
5. The slave deserved a large reward, because he had saved the life of our son.

C. One Sibyl was a prophetess who resided in a cave in Cumae near Naples in Italy. People went to visit her for her predictions and to ask for her advice. Sometimes they wrote down their request and had a messenger deliver it to her because she often frightened people while prophesying in a trance. Work with a small group and write a short note in Latin to the girl playing the Sibyl. Your note might be about Aeneas and the founding of Rome or a more present-day concern. The Sibyl's Latin responses are best if they are possible but ambiguous.

WORD STUDY

Prefixes

- We have seen that the preposition **in** is used as a prefix. There is another prefix **in-**, used chiefly with adjectives and nouns, which has an entirely different meaning and must be carefully distinguished from the former. It is a *negative* prefix, as in *injustice*. It is assimilated like the other prefix **in-**, as in *il-legal, im-moral, ir-regular*. Identify the Latin roots and define the following derivatives of words that you have already studied: *immemorial, immaterial, inglorious, ingratitude, illiberal, illiteracy, infirm.*

- Tell which of the two prefixes (preposition or negative) is used in each of the following words: *inhabit, invalid, invoke, induce, invariable, inequality, inundate, immovable, impecunious.*

- The prefix **dis-** in English and Latin means *apart*, but sometimes it is purely negative like **in-**. It is either assimilated or left unchanged, as follows: *dis-inter, dis-locate, dis-arm, dif-fuse, di-vert, di-stant, dis-similar*. Define the first three of these words, derived from words in previous lesson vocabularies.

AENĒĀS IN ITALIĀ

[1] *king*

[2] *afterwards*

[3] *also*

[4] *outside*

[5] *Arcadians* (acc.)

[6] *who*

[7] *why*

[8] *please*

[9] *story*

[10] *with us.* For the joining of **cum** to the abl. of personal pronouns, see footnote 18, p. 219.

Ōlim in Latiō erat oppidum appellātum Pallanteum. Rēx[1] oppidī, Ēvander, cum multīs colōnīs ab Arcadiā in Graeciā mīgrāverat. In Italiā oppidum mūnīverant in locō ubi posteā[2] Rōmulus Rōmam mūnīvit. Cum fīnitimīs populīs Latīnīs Ēvander Graecīque bellum semper gerēbant.

5   Aenēās et colōnī Trōiānī etiam[3] in Italiā habitābant et etiam cum Latīnīs pugnābant. Quod sociōs cupiēbant, Aenēās et paucī virī ad Pallanteum accessērunt. Extrā[4] oppidum virī Trōiānī fīlium Ēvandrī et paucōs Arcadēs[5] invēnērunt. Dīxērunt.

Pallas: Pallas sum, fīlius Ēvandrī. Ego et amīcī meī vōs salūtāmus. Quī[6] 10 estis? Cūr[7] tū et virī tuī ad Pallanteum vēnistis?

Aenēās: Appellor Aenēās. Ego et virī meī ad Italiam vēnimus quod Fāta nōs dūxērunt. Nunc auxilium vestrum cupimus. Accipite nōs, quaesō,[8] et historiam[9] nostram audīte.

Pallas: Vōs nōn dīmittam. Multa dē vōbīs audīvī. Ad oppidum nōbīscum[10] 15 prōcēdite.

(Rēx Ēvander grātē Aenēam accipit.)

Rēx Ēvander grātē Aenēam accēpit. At Pallanteum, the town on the site of what was to become Rome, King Evander *(center)* receives Aeneas *(right)* who is escorted by Evander's son Pallas. The artist, Pietro da Cortona, has kept the tradition that the Arcadians, exiles from Greece, lived in rustic and peaceful harmony.

Araldo de Luca/CORBIS

Ēvander: Ubi puer eram in Arcadiā, Aenēas, pater tuus ad patriam meam vēnit. Is mihi multa grāta dōnāvit. Virum grātē memoriā teneō. Tū etiam vidēris[11] vir bonus et pius[12]. Tē probō et tibi auxilium dōnābō.

    Aenēās: Grātiās tibi agō, Ēvander. Firmī sociī erimus.   20

    Ēvander: Quod ego nōn iam[13] iuvenis[14] sum, vōbīscum pūgnāre dubitō. Tibi, Aenēae, fīlium meum mandābō. Is integer est et prō mē pugnābit. Pallas, mī[15] fīlī, tē cum Trōiānīs nunc dīmittam. Prōdūce tēcum[10] multōs virōs.

    Pallas: Valē, pater! Nōs fortiter[16] bellum gerēmus   25
Et fortiter pugnāvit Pallas. Sed miser Ēvander numquam fīlium vīvum iterum[17] vīdit.

[11] *seem to be·*
[12] *loyal*
[13] *not now, no longer*
[14] *young*
[15] The vocative of **meus** is irregular.
[16] *bravely*
[17] *alive again*

Questions

1. Where did the king of the town Pallanteum come from originally?
2. What is particularly interesting about the site of Pallanteum?
3. What common enemy did the Trojans and the Arcadians have?
4. Who is Pallas?
5. What did Aeneas ask Pallas for?
6. Where did the two talk?
7. Why did Evander decide to give Aeneas help?
8. Did Pallas keep his promise to Evander?
9. Why didn't Evander himself lead his men into battle alongside Aeneas?

VOCABULARY

Pronouns

  eʹgo, meʹī *I, of me*   (egoist, egocentric)
  nōs, nosʹtrum *we, of us*
  tū, tuʹī *you, of you* (sing.)
  vōs, vesʹtrum *you, of you* (pl.)
  is *he, it* m.; **eʹa** *she, it* f.; **id** *it* n.

Adjective

  inʹteger -gra, -grum   (integral, integrity)
    fresh, whole, untouched

Nota·Bene

The word *it* is used to translate **is** and **ea** when the noun referred to is masculine or feminine in Latin and the noun is a thing: **Carrum vīdī, et is magnus erat**. *I saw the wagon, and it was large.*

I...I...I....
..now let's talk about
me for awhile..

egoist

Verbs

cu´piō, cu´pere, cupī´vī, [cupī´tus]   (cupidity, Cupid)
  desire, wish, want
dīmit´tō, dīmit´tere, dīmī´sī, [dīmis´sus]   [mittō]
  let go, send away
du´bitō, dubitā´re, dubitā´vī, [dubitā´tus]   (indubitable)
  hesitate, doubt

Adverbs

ō´lim *formerly, once (upon a time)*
u´bi *when, where*   (ubiquitous)

█ GRAMMAR

Personal Pronouns

In English, nominative forms of personal pronouns are used to show the person and subject of the verb: **I** am, **you** are. In Latin, as we have seen (p. 28), personal endings are used instead. When, however, emphasis or sharp contrast in subjects is desired, Latin uses the personal pronouns **ego** *(I)* and **tū** *(you)*. **Is, ea,** and **id** serve as the personal pronouns of the third person *(he, she,* and *it)*. The full declension of **is, ea,** and **id** will be given later. For now, memorize the declensions of **ego** and **tū.**

PERSONAL PRONOUNS

	SINGULAR	PLURAL
Nom.	**e´go** *I*	**nōs** *we*
Gen.	**me´ī** *of me*	**nōs´trum** *of us*
Dat.	**mi´hi** *to (for) me*	**nō´bīs** *to (for) us*
Acc.	**mē** *me*	**nōs** *us*
Abl.	**mē**[18] *with (from, etc.) me*	**nō´bīs**[18] *with (from, etc.) us*

	SINGULAR	PLURAL
Nom.	**tū** *you*	**vōs** *you*
Gen.	**tu´ī** *of you*	**ves´trum** *of you*
Dat.	**ti´bi** *to (for) you*	**vō´bīs** *to (for) you*
Acc.	**tē** *you*	**vōs** *you*
Abl.	**tē**[18] *with (from, etc.) you*	**vō´bīs**[18] *with (from, etc.) you*

Possessive Adjectives

The *possessive adjectives* **meus** *(my, my own, mine),* **noster** *(our, our own, ours),* **tuus** *(your, your own, yours),* and **vester** *(your, your own, yours)* are derived from the bases of their corresponding personal pronouns: **ego (me-), nōs (nostr-), tū (tu-),** and **vōs (vestr-).**

The possessive adjective follows its noun except when emphatic.

Cautions: To show *possession,* use the possessive adjectives **meus, tuus, noster,** and **vester,** not the possessive pronouns. Say **amīcus meus,** not **amīcus meī.**

If, however, the *of*-idea is *partitive* (see Genitive of the Whole, Grammar Appendix), use the genitive of the pronoun. **Pars meī** (pronoun) means *part of me,* while **pars mea** (adjective) means *my part.*

Remember that an adjective agrees with the noun it modifies in gender, number, and case. A man referring to his daughter would say **Est fīlia mea;** a woman referring to her husband would say **Est vir meus.** In other words, the ending of the possessive adjective depends upon what is possessed, not upon the possessor.

Oral Practice

1. Decline **equus vester** and **familia mea.**

2. Give the Latin for the italicized words.

    a. *I* shall give *you* a present.

    b. *I* criticize *you; you* criticize *me.*

    c. *She* showed *us* beautiful flowers.

    d. *She* is *my* friend; *he, my* enemy.

    e. I shall show *you* (sing.) the house.

f. We'll love *you* (pl.) if you'll love *us*.

g. He came *to us* and showed *us* many pictures.

h. Come *with us* and we shall go *with you* (pl.).

i. *He* was mentioned *by me*, but *she* told *me* nothing.

j. *Your* daughter was seen *by us with you* (sing.) on the street.

🎞 *Exercises*

A. Translate the following sentences.

1. Multa ā tē, amīce, accēpī.
2. Liber tuus ā mē nōn retinēbitur.
3. Cupītisne vidēre nōs, amīcōs vestrōs?
4. Ego sum amīcus tuus; is est inimīcus.
5. Ego sum miser sine tē; tū misera es quod tēcum nōn maneō.
6. Fīlius meus in perīculum mēcum properāre numquam dubitāverat.

B. Translate the following sentences into Latin.

1. We are foreigners; you are Romans.
2. My words are not (being) heard by you.
3. I want to present the reward to you (sing.).
4. They had not hesitated to free the unfriendly prisoners.
5. Come (pl.) with us; we are your friends, not your enemies.

Did You Know?

The Roman army had several ways of capturing a gated, fortified city. Their first task was to fill up the ditches around the city walls with small tree branches mixed with soil and thrown into the ditches. Then the Roman soldiers would make their own trenches, roads, and tunnels to undermine the walls. Lastly, they would unleash heavy missiles against the walls and towers of the beseiged city with the **catapulta** and **ballista**.

Bettmann/CORBIS

WORD STUDY

Suffixes

• We have seen that prefixes are so called because they are attached to the beginnings of words. *Suffixes* (**sub**, *under, after;* **fixus**, *attached*) are attached to the ends of words. Like Latin prefixes, Latin suffixes play a very important part in the formation of English words.

• The Latin suffix **-ia** usually has the form *-y* in English. Give the English forms of the following words found in the preceding vocabularies: **memoria, glōria, familia, iniūria, victōria, cōpia** (with change of meaning in English).

• What are the Latin words from which are derived *elegy, history, industry, infamy, Italy, luxury, misery, perfidy, philosophy, Troy?*

• Some **-ia** nouns drop the **-ia** entirely in English: *concord, vigil, matter* (from **māteria**).

A city under siege, illustrating the various types of weaponry known to Romans of Caesar's time. *From left to right:* the **turris ambulātōria** (movable tower) used to overcome the advantage in height the city walls provided; the **testūdō arietāria** (a battering ram concealed under a shed like the shell of a tortoise) used to dislodge masonry; the **testūdō** (a cover of interlocking shields) and **scālae** (ladders); the **onager** ("donkey," so nicknamed from its "kick") and the **ballista**, machines for throwing heavy and light missiles, stones, or spears.

LESSON OBJECTIVES

- To read the story of a famous Roman general
- To learn the use of the present infinitive as direct object

Q.¹ FABIUS MAXIMUS

¹ Q. = Quīntus

² ablative: *in __.*

³ *was able*

⁴ ablative

⁵ *Livius,* the Roman general responsible for defending the city

⁶ *this* (abl.)

⁷ *citadel* (acc.)

⁸ *effort*

⁹ *it*

Bellō² Pūnicō secundō Hannibal virōs cum Rōmānīs pugnāre iubēbat sed Q. Fabius Maximus semper discēdēbat neque in ūnō locō manēbat. Sine victōriīs Hannibal Italiam in prōvinciam redigere nōn poterat³.

Maximus perpetuō labōre⁴ etiam Tarentum, oppidum Italiae, recēpit. 5 Līvius⁵ in hōc⁶ oppidō fuerat sed oppidum āmīserat et ad arcem⁷ virōs remōverat. Maximus ad portās oppidī virōs prōcēdere iussit et oppidum recēpit; tum is etiam ad arcem prōcessit. Ibi Līvius, superbus quod arcem retinuerat, Fabiō dīxit: "Meā operā⁸ Tarentum recēpistī." Fabius respondit: "Vērum est, Līvī: ego recēpī oppidum quod tū id⁹ āmīsistī."

10 Statuās deōrum ex oppidō Tarentō Maximus nōn remōvit sed, quod deī inimīcī Tarentīnīs erant, Tarentīnōs in oppidō statuās retinēre iussit.

Questions

1. How did Maximus weaken Hannibal?
2. How did Maximus recover Tarentum?
3. How did Livius help in recovering Tarentum?
4. What did Maximus say to Livius' claim?
5. Why didn't Maximus remove the statues of the gods from the town?

Elephants, both African and Indian, were the "tanks" of ancient warfare. At first they terrified the Romans in the early encounters with Pyrrhus before the First Punic War (third century B.C.). This sixteenth-century painting by Jacopo Ripanda shows Hannibal routing a troop of Roman cavalry during the Second Punic War (218–201 B.C.). Later, even the Romans used elephants, but only rarely.

Gianni Dagli Orti/CORBIS

VOCABULARY

Noun

por´ta, -ae f. *gate*   (portal)

Verbs

discē´dō, discē´dere, disces´sī, [discessū´rus] [cēdō]
   go away, depart

iu´beō, iubē´re, ius´sī, [ius´sus] *order*

reci´piō, reci´pere, recē´pī, [recep´tus]   **[capiō]**
   take back, recover

red´igō, redi´gere, redē´gī, [redāc´tus]   **[agō]**
   drive back, reduce; **in prōvinciam**
   redigere *to reduce to the status of a*
   province

remo´veō, removē´re, remō´vī, [remō´tus]   **[moveō]**
   remove, move back

Adverb

e´tiam *also, even*

GRAMMAR

Object Infinitive with Accusative Subject

Virōs discēdere iussī.	*I ordered the men to go away.*
Mē labōrāre nōn cupīvistī.	*You did not want me to work.*
Vōs amāre concordiam docuērunt.	*They taught you to love harmony.*

Hannibal on horseback reviews his army as it moves through an Alpine pass. Leading this large force of men, horses, and elephants all the way from Spain across the Alps and down into the boot of Italy remains one of the greatest feats in military history.

Observe that with such English verbs as *order, teach* (also *wish, forbid,* etc.), the infinitive object is often used with a noun or pronoun in the objective case, which may be regarded as its subject. In Latin, too, certain verbs of similar meaning have an *object* infinitive with its *subject* in the accusative case. In the first sentence above, the phrase **virōs discēdere** is the object of **iussī,** while the word **virōs** is the subject of **discēdere.** In the second sentence, the phrase **mē labōrāre** is the object of **cupīvistī,** with **mē** as the subject of **labōrāre.** As the third sentence shows, the infinitive may have its own subject and direct object, each in the accusative case. In such instances, the infinitive's subject usually stands first.

▦ *Exercises*

A. Translate the following sentences.
1. Māteria ā servīs removēbitur.
2. Librī nōs etiam inimīcōs amāre docent.
3. Librīne bonī, puerī, ab amīcīs vestrīs leguntur?
4. Fīliās nostrās bonōs librōs semper retinēre docēmus.
5. Magister nōs amīcōs nostrōs dīmittere et ā viā discēdere iussit.
6. Nōnne bonum est inimīcōs in amīcitiam et concordiam redigere?

B. Translate the following sentences.
1. It was good to see our friends.
2. They had hesitated to remove the grain without wagons.
3. The sons of farmers are beginning to go away from the farms (use **ager**).
4. Lucius, order the boy to lead out fresh horses to the gates of the town.

WORD STUDY

- The Latin suffix **-ia** usually has the form -*y* in English, as we have seen (page 221). When it is preceded by **-t-**, the combination **-tia** generally has the form -*ce* in English.

- Give the English forms of the following words found in the preceding vocabularies: **grātia, sententia.**

- What must be the Latin words from which are derived *science, diligence, prudence, absence?*

- The *tarantula* (a spider) and the *tarantella* (a dance) both got their names from *Tarentum*. Look them up in the dictionary.

- *Fabius* is the name of towns in three states. Missouri, New York, Ohio, and Wisconsin have towns named *Hannibal*. Pennsylvania has a *Tarentum*.

AENĒĀS ET TURNUS

LESSON OBJECTIVES
- To read how the Fates bring about the end of Aeneas' struggles
- To learn about the perfect passive participle and how to form the perfect passive tenses

Trōia ā Graecīs capta erat et Aenēās cum paucīs Trōiānīs ad Italiam vēnerat et per terrās barbarōrum virōs prōdūxerat. Sed Iūnō inimīca mānsit et contrā Aenēam miserum multōs populōs barbarōs Italiae incitāvit. Lāvīnia, fīlia rēgis Latīnī[1], ā Turnō amābātur sed Aenēae[2] in mātrimōnium dōnāta est. Turnus bellum gerere nōn dubitāvit. Ab Aenēā bellum nōn grātē susceptum est; ad terminum vītae sub armīs esse nōn cupīvit. 5

Sed causa Trōiānōrum ā Fātīs suscepta erat. Aenēās etiam ā Graecīs quī in Italiā habitābant beneficium et auxilium accēpit, quod Turnō inimīcī erant. Per multōs diēs bellum gestum est et multa ēgregia exempla virtūtis[3] in proeliīs clārīs prōposita sunt. 10

Tandem Turnus sōlus Aenēam sōlum ad pugnam ēvocāvit, quod reliquīs exemplum prōpōnere cupīvit. In locō commodō sub portīs oppidī pugnāvērunt. Nōn longa fuit pugna, quod Venus, māter Aenēae, fīliō arma ēgregia dōnāverat quae[4] deus Vulcānus fēcerat. Fāta iusserant auxilium ad Turnum nōn mittī[5]; itaque Iūnō, socia Turnī, aberat. Vīta Turnī fūgit et 15 Aenēās ad terminum perīculōrum vēnit et ōtium invēnit.

[1] *King Latinus* (gen.)
[2] *dative*
[3] *of courage* (gen.)
[4] *which*
[5] *to be sent*

David J. Driscoll

A painted frieze found in 1875 on the outskirts of Rome shows an episode of the Aeneas legend outside of Vergil's *Aeneid*. Here a winged Victory crowns Aeneas during the final fatal struggle between Trojans and Rutulians near the river Numicus. According to the poet Ovid, it was at this moment that Aeneas was transformed into a god to be worshipped by succeeding generations of Romans.

Questions

1. What goddess was still hostile to the Trojans?
2. Who was Lavinia?
3. Why was Turnus' love for her a problem for Aeneas?
4. Why wasn't Aeneas glad to engage in a fight with Turnus?
5. Who gave Aeneas help?
6. When did Turnus call Aeneas out to fight one-on-one?
7. Where did they fight?
8. Was the fight fair? Why or why not?

VOCABULARY

Nouns

benefí´cium, benefí´cī n. *kindness, benefit*　　**[faciō]**
exem´plum, exem´plī n. *example*　　(exemplify, sample)

Adjective

ēgre´gius, -a, -um *distinguished, excellent*　　(egregious)

Verbs

prō´pōnō, prōpō´nere, prōpo´suī, prōpo´situs [pōnō]
　　put forward, offer
susci´piō, susci´pere, suscē´pī, suscep´tus　　**[capiō]**
　　undertake, take up, start

Prepositions

per with acc. *through*　　(perforate, permit, percolate)

sub *under, close up to;* with acc. after verbs of motion, with abl. after verbs of rest　　(suspicion)

GRAMMAR

Perfect Participle

A *participle* is that form of a verb which is used as an adjective. The past *participle* in English usually ends in *-ed: carried*. With other verbs, it is "irregular": *shown, eaten, seen, heard*. The *perfect passive participle* in Latin regularly ends in **-tus** (**portātus**, *having been carried, carried*) or **-sus** (**missus**, *sent*) and is declined like the adjective **magnus, -a, -um**. It agrees, like an ordinary adjective, with a noun or pronoun in gender, number, and case: **litterae receptae**, *the recovered letter*. The perfect participle represents an act as having taken place before the time indicated by the main verb and from now on will be given in the vocabularies without brackets.

Perfect Passive Tense

In English, the perfect passive tense is formed by using the past tense of *to be (was, were, has been* or *have been)* as an auxiliary (helping) verb with the past participle: *he was carried, he has been carried.*

In Latin, the perfect passive tense is formed by using the present tense of **sum** (i.e., **sum,** etc.) as an auxiliary with the perfect participle: **portātus est,** *he has been carried.* The participle really modifies the subject and therefore agrees with it in gender, number, and case.

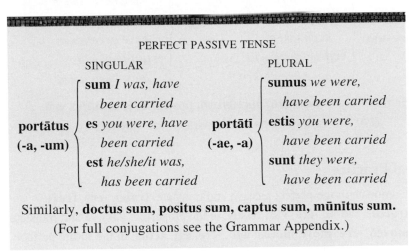

PERFECT PASSIVE TENSE

	SINGULAR		PLURAL
portātus (-a, -um)	**sum** *I was, have been carried*	**portātī** (-ae, -a)	**sumus** *we were, have been carried*
	es *you were, have been carried*		**estis** *you were, have been carried*
	est *he/she/it was, has been carried*		**sunt** *they were, have been carried*

Similarly, **doctus sum, positus sum, captus sum, mūnītus sum.**

(For full conjugations see the Grammar Appendix.)

Past Perfect Passive and Future Perfect Passive

In English, the past perfect (pluperfect) passive is formed by using the past perfect tense of *to be* (i.e., *had been*) as an auxiliary with the past participle: *he had been carried.*

In Latin, the past perfect passive is formed by using the imperfect tense of **sum** (i.e., **eram,** etc.) as an auxiliary with the perfect participle: **portātus erat,** *he had been carried.*

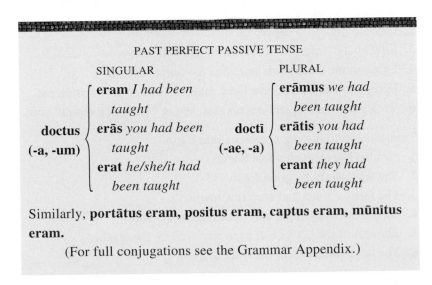

PAST PERFECT PASSIVE TENSE

	SINGULAR		PLURAL
doctus (-a, -um)	**eram** *I had been taught*	**doctī** (-ae, -a)	**erāmus** *we had been taught*
	erās *you had been taught*		**erātis** *you had been taught*
	erat *he/she/it had been taught*		**erant** *they had been taught*

Similarly, **portātus eram, positus eram, captus eram, mūnītus eram.**

(For full conjugations see the Grammar Appendix.)

The future perfect passive is formed by using the future tense of **sum** (i.e., **erō,** etc.) as the auxiliary with the perfect passive participle: **portātus erit,** *he will have been carried.*

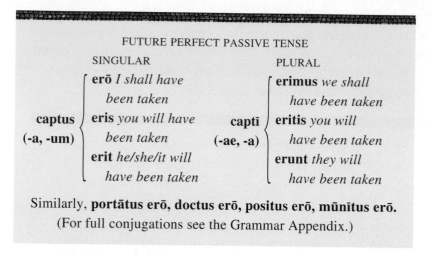

FUTURE PERFECT PASSIVE TENSE

	SINGULAR		PLURAL
captus **(-a, -um)**	**erō** *I shall have been taken*	**captī** **(-ae, -a)**	**erimus** *we shall have been taken*
	eris *you will have been taken*		**eritis** *you will have been taken*
	erit *he/she/it will have been taken*		**erunt** *they will have been taken*

Similarly, **portātus erō, doctus erō, positus erō, mūnītus erō.**
(For full conjugations see the Grammar Appendix.)

Oral Practice

1. Conjugate in the perfect passive and translate: **trahō, -ere, trāxī, trāctus; videō, -ēre, vīdī, vīsus;** in the pluperfect passive and translate: **moveō, -ēre, mōvī, mōtus; agō, -ere, ēgī, āctus;** in the future perfect passive and translate: **prōpōnō, prōpōnere, prōposuī, prōpositus; laudō, laudāre, laudāvī, laudātus.**

2. Translate: *they have been seen, I had been dragged, you* (sing.) *have been moved, having been driven, they will have been ordered.*

📖 *Exercises*

A. Translate the following sentences into English.
1. Arma carrīs ad castra portāta erant.
2. Causam populī suscipere est officium bonōrum.
3. Equī ab agricolā per silvam ad aquam āctī sunt.
4. Ēgregiumne exemplum amīcitiae memoriā tenētis?
5. Ēgregium exemplum beneficī ā magistrō vestrō prōpositum est.
6. Vir ā puerō sub aquam trāctus erat, sed et vir et puer servātī[6] sunt.

B. Translate the following sentences into Latin.
1. He also knew much about horses.
2. She was taught by good teachers.
3. The farmer's son had seen few towns.
4. An excellent example was presented to my son.
5. The rest of the books had been removed by the teacher.
6. The boys were absent but were praised.

[6] Note that the participle is plural because it refers to both **vir** and **puer.**

C. According to Roman mythology, the Fates, or **Parcae**, were three women who decided everyone's destiny. They were present at the birth of every child and decided how long each person would live. Each of the Fates had a specific job. Clotho spun the thread of life; Lachesis decided the length of each thread; Atropos cut the thread when it was long enough. Create a dialogue that the **Parcae** might have had as they decided the fate of some real or imaginary individual. The following vocabulary may be useful.

filum, -ī n. *thread*
longitūdō, longitūdinis f. *length*
secō, secāre, secuī, sectus *cut*
neō, nēre, nēvī, nētus *spin*
constituō, constituere, constituī, constitūtus *decide*

WORD STUDY

Prefixes

- The preposition **sub**, used as a prefix in Latin and English, means *under, up from under*: **sus-tineō** hold *up*; **suc-cēdō**, *come up*. It is regularly assimilated before certain consonants: *suc-ceed, sus-ceptible, suf-fer, sug-gest, sus-pend, sup-port, sur-rogate, sus-tenance*, but *sub-mit, sub-trahend*. We use it freely in English to form new words: *sub-lease, sub-let, sub-orbital*. Look up these words in a dictionary.

- **Per** usually remains unchanged when used as a prefix.

- Explain by derivation the meaning of *permanent, permit, sustain, suspect*. What is meant by being *susceptible* to colds?

A medieval artist's portrayal of Vergil in the process of composing his *Georgics*. The mood of peace and tranquility, remote from the civil wars and bloodshed which had occupied the Romans in most of the first century B.C., is one Vergil himself would have appreciated. His family farm in northern Italy had been confiscated and distributed to veterans; Italian agriculture was in ruins. It was only Augustus who finally restored peace (and Vergil's land) who could give hope.

Dagli Orti/Bibliotheque Municipale Dijon/The Art Archive

NIOBĒ[1]

Niobē, rēgīna superba, in Graeciā habitābat. Avus[2] erat Iuppiter, quī deōs virōsque rēxit, et hoc[3] superbiam rēgīnae auxit. Niobē erat superba etiam quod septem fīliōs et septem fīliās habuit.

Apollō deus erat fīlius deae Lātōnae, et Diāna erat fīlia. Aliōs[4] līberōs Lātōna nōn habuit.

Sacra[5] Lātōnae ā populō suscipiēbantur. Superba Niobē adfuit et rogāvit:

"Cūr[6] mātrī[7] duōrum līberōrum sacra suscipitis? Hoc[8] nōn permittam. Etiam Niobē dea est; XIV, nōn II, līberōs habeō. Lātōna glōriam nōn meret—Niobē esse prīma dēbet. Vōbīs līberīsque vestrīs exemplum ēgregium prōpōnō. Sī[9] sententia mea ā vōbīs nōn probāta erit, poenā[10] afficiēmini."

[1] Nǐ´obē
[2] grandfather
[3] this (nom.)
[4] other
[5] sacred rites
[6] why
[7] for the mother
[8] this (acc.)
[9] if

The god Apollo, twin brother of Diana, was born on the island of Delos. His particular areas of influence were prophecy, archery, medicine, courage, and wisdom. He presided over the shrine of the Delphic Oracle in Delphi, Greece.

Scala/Art Resource, NY

Superba verba rēgīnae ā Lātōnā audīta sunt. Novum cōnsilium cēpit: fīlium vocāvit et officium eī[10] permīsit:

"Tē iubeō septem fīliōs Niobae interficere."

15   Prīmus fīlius adfuit et interfectus est, tum reliquī. Niobē septem fīliōs nunc per linguam superbam āmīserat, tamen remānsit superba quod fīliae remānsērunt. Itaque Lātōna iussit etiam fīliās septem ēdūcī et ā Diānā interficī. Singulae fīliae ē vītā discessērunt, et Niobē misera in saxum[11] dūrum mūtāta[12] est. Poenā magnā affecta erat. Niobae exemplum memoriā tenēre dēbēmus.

[10] *to him* (dat.)
[11] *rock*
[12] *changed*

Questions

1. Where did Niobe live and to whom was she related?
2. Give three reasons for Niobe's pride.
3. Who was Latona and who were her children?
4. What threat did Niobe make?
5. Who killed Niobe's sons? Who killed her daughters?
6. What happened to Niobe?
7. What is the moral of the story?

▦ VOCABULARY

Nouns

lī´berī, -ō´rum m. *children*   [līber]
super´bia, -ae f. *pride, arrogance*

Adjectives

prī´mus, -a, -um *first*   (primary, primitive)
super´bus, -a, -um *proud, arrogant*   (superb)

Verbs

ad´sum, ades´se, ad´fuī, adfutū´rus[13]   [sum]
     be near, be present
ēdū´cō, ēdū´cere, ēdū´xī, ēduc´tus *lead out*   [dūcō]
interfi´ciō, interfi´cere, interfē´cī,   [faciō]
     interfec´tus *kill*
permit´tō, permit´tere, permī´sī,   [mittō]
     permis´sus *let go through, allow,*
     entrust (with dat.)
rema´neō, remanē´re, remān´sī,   [maneō]
     remānsū´rus[13] *stay behind, remain*

Adverb

ta´men *nevertheless*

[13] A few verbs lack the perfect passive participle; most intransitive verbs have a future active participle in **-ūrus,** which, from Lesson XI on, has been substituted as the fourth principal part.

GRAMMAR

How to Study a Latin Paragraph

Do not turn at once to the dictionary at the end of the book for a word you do not know. Try to read an entire paragraph before you look up a word. There are three good ways to find the meaning of a word without looking it up:

1. English derivatives. Nearly every Latin word has at least one English derivative.
2. Related Latin words. If you know the meaning of **re-** and **dūcō**, you know the meaning of **redūcō.**
3. Sensible guessing from the context.

Do not become a slave to the dictionary at the end of the book.

Developing "Word Sense"

Do not become a slave to a single meaning for a word. Choose English equivalents that sound natural. Give a different translation for **incitat** in each of the following sentences.

1. Agricola equōs incitat.
2. Caesar animōs sociōrum incitat.
3. Dominus servum tardum incitat.
4. Concordia ōtium incitat.
5. Magister bonus discipulōs ad studia incitat.
6. Memoria poētam incitat.

Oral Practice

1. Conjugate in the perfect passive and translate: **āmitto, -ere, āmīsī, āmissus; retineō, -ēre, retinuī, retentus; redigō, -ere, redēgī, redāctus; cupiō, -ere, cupīvī, cupītus**; in the past perfect passive: **iubeō, -ēre, iussī, iussus; nōscō, -ere, nōvī, nōtus**; in the future perfect passive: **interficiō, -erē, -fēcī, -fectus.**
2. Translate: **ēductī sumus, susceptum erat, permissum erit, trāctī estis, mōtus es, āctī erant, vīsae estis, iussae sunt, portātus erō, prōpositum est.**

Present Passive Infinitive

In English, the present passive infinitive is formed by using the auxiliary *to be* with the perfect passive participle: *to be seen, to be heard.*

In Latin, in the first, second, and fourth conjugations, the present passive infinitive is formed by changing the final **-e** of the present active infinitive to long **-ī.**

ACTIVE	PASSIVE
portāre *to carry*	**portārī** *to be carried*
docēre *to teach*	**docērī** *to be taught*
mūnīre *to fortify*	**mūnīrī** *to be fortified*

In the third conjugation, final **-ĕre** is changed to long **-ī.**

ACTIVE	PASSIVE
pōnere *to place*	**pōnī** *to be placed*
capere *to take*	**capī** *to be taken*

Diana was the goddess of the woods and the hunt as well as the protector of women. She is often represented as young, lean, and athletic and is accompanied by a deer. She was the twin sister of Apollo.

The present passive infinitive, like the active infinitive, may be used either as a subject or direct object.

Publicē laudārī est grātum.	*To be praised publicly is pleasing.*
Nōn cupiō līberōs vidērī.	*I do not want the children to be seen.*

▦ *Exercises*

A. Translate the following sentences.
1. Nōnne dūrum est sub aquā remanēre?
2. Equī ex oppidō per agrōs lātōs ēductī erunt.
3. Pecūnia merērī et servārī ā puerīs puellīsque dēbet.
4. Puerī adfuērunt prīmī, quod puellae tardae fuērunt.
5. Tibi vītam līberōrum meōrum permittere nōn dubitāvī.
6. Verbīs bonōrum virōrum semper incitārī et regī dēbēmus.

B. Translate the following sentences.
1. We have ordered the boys to be dismissed.
2. The boys are absent, but the girls are present.
3. The men had been ordered to seize the fortified town.
4. The children ought to be called together by the teacher.

Did You Know?

Sandals were customarily worn only inside the house by the Romans. If a Roman rode to dinner in a litter, he wore sandals; if he walked, he wore shoes while his sandals were carried by a personal slave. Sandals were not worn during meals and were taken by slaves when the guest arrived. Thus, the phrase **soleās poscere** *(to ask for one's sandals)* came to mean "to prepare to leave."

WORD STUDY

- What is a *primary* school? A political *primary*?

The word *education* is often wrongly said to be derived from **ēdūcere**. As you can see, the derivative of **ēdūcere** would be *eduction*. *Education* comes from a related word, **ēducāre**, *to bring up*. According to derivation, if you are well educated, you are well brought up.

- Study the following English phrases borrowed from Latin.

Deo Gratias	*thanks to God*
per annum	*by (through) the year*
sub rosa	*under the rose (in concealment)*
Dei gratia	*by the grace of God* (seen on Canadian coins)

- Here is another state motto.

Sic semper tyrannis	*Thus* (i.e., *death*) *always to tyrants* (motto of the state of Virginia)

THE HOUSE AND ITS FURNITURE

ROMAN ARCHITECTURE

The Pompeian town house was different from ours, more like the kind one finds in southern Europe and Latin America today. It was usually built of concrete covered with stucco. For privacy and security, and because glass was expensive, there were few windows on the street. The typical house consisted of two parts, front and rear. The front contained a large room, called the atrium (**ātrium**, the "black room," from the smoke of the hearth). It was surrounded by small bedrooms. The atrium had an opening in the roof for light and air. The roof sloped down to the opening. Below the opening there was a basin into which the rain fell. This cistern (**impluvium**) furnished the soft water for washing, necessary in a country where most of the water is hard. At the corners of the basin there were often columns extending to the roof.

Since the house was built directly on the street, it had no front yard. The heavy front door opened into a hall leading into the atrium. On one side of the hall there might be a small shop, usually rented out by people who did not live in the house. On the other side there was the room of the doorkeeper (**iānitor**). Very often there was a place for a watchdog. Sometimes a fierce dog was painted on the wall or depicted in a mosaic on the floor of the hall.

The impressive interior of the "House of the Silver Anniversary" is framed by four fluted Corinthian columns. They surround the **impluvium**, which had its ornamental value as well as the practical purpose of catching rainwater for washing.

Alinari/Art Resource, NY

Smithsonian Institution

These earthenware jugs, excavated from Troy and now located in the Smithsonian Museum in Washington, D.C., belong to a common type of pottery widely dispersed in Turkey and Greece and dating from the third millennium B.C. They probably belonged to people who lived on the site of Troy perhaps a thousand years before Aeneas and his companions left its smoking ruins to follow a new destiny.

Opposite the entrance was the study or office (**tablīnum**) of the master of the house, placed so that he could keep an eye on what was going on. Here he kept his safe. Often there were also upstairs rooms.

The rear of the house surrounded a garden. Because of the columns which ran all the way around the garden this part was called the peristyle (**peristȳlium,** "columns around"); today we might call it a colonnade. It was often very pretty. Charming fountains and statuary were usually to be seen in the garden. Kitchen, bathroom, and dining rooms were in this part of the house. There were often two dining rooms, one on the shady side for summer, the other on the sunny side for winter use.

ACCESSORIES

The walls were covered with elaborate paintings. Rugs and draperies were in common use. The floors were usually made of tile or flagstone, as in Italy today, instead of wood. Chairs were few, and many of them were without backs. On the other hand, there were many couches, used like easy chairs, not only for reading and resting but also at the dinner table. There were many kinds of tables and stands, often beautifully made. Many small lamps of bronze or clay were placed everywhere, some on stands, some on large elaborate candelabra. These burned olive oil. Glass chimneys were unknown. Candles were also used. The light was so poor that people went to bed early and got up early. Portable charcoal heaters were common. In northern Italy central heating was sometimes used.

Kitchen utensils and dishes were made of bronze, silver, or earthenware. Those made of earthenware were chiefly red in color and were decorated with engraved lines.

GLIMPSES OF ROMAN LIFE

HOUSES VERSUS APARTMENTS

The size of the population and the scarcity and cost of land within Rome's city limits prevented all but the wealthy from living in houses such as these from Pompeii. Instead, the Romans expanded vertically and lived in apartment houses, called **īnsulae** because they were "islands" surrounded by narrow streets. Often they were five or six stories high, and in design remarkably like apartment houses today. In fact, in exterior decoration and the imaginative use of varied building materials (concrete, brick, stone, stucco, and wood) they were probably more interesting. But in safety and convenience they left a good deal to be desired; many were flimsily built by speculators during the period of Rome's greatest growth (100 B.C. to A.D. 100) and stood in constant danger of fire or collapse. Unlike the Pompeian house, the apartment dwelling did not have rooms designed for specific functions; they were just spaces for the tenant to use as he chose. The filth, smoke, and noise must often have been nearly intolerable.

Many of the rich and socially prominent, and those who wanted to be, lived in individual houses or luxurious ground floor apartments on or near the Palatine Hill, an area that was eventually taken over by the imperial family. The wealthy also had country houses (**villae**) in other parts of Italy, which they used to escape the heat and bustle of the city, or as places to stop overnight when traveling.

QUESTIONS

1. In what ways did Roman houses differ from ours?
2. How did the poor lighting facilities affect the daily living of the people?
3. How does climate affect the types of houses?

VOCABULARY

Nouns

beneficium	perīculum
exemplum	porta
līberī	superbia

Pronouns

ego	is, ea, id	vōs
nōs	tū	

Adjectives

ēgregius	integer	prīmus
inimīcus	miser	superbus

Verbs

absum	dubitō	prōcēdō	removeō
adsum	ēdūcō	prōdūcō	retineō
āmittō	interficiō	prōpōnō	suscipiō
cupiō	iubeō	recipiō	
dīmittō	nōscō	redigō	
discēdō	permittō	remaneō	

Adverbs

etiam	iam	ōlim	tamen	ubi

Prepositions

per (+ acc.)	sine (+ abl.)
prō (+ abl.)	sub (+ acc. or abl.)

GRAMMAR SUMMARY

Words Used as Nouns (Substantives)

1. Pronouns
   Ego (in place of a person's name), **tū**, etc.
2. Infinitives
   As subject: *Cēdere* **nōn est grātum**. *To yield is not pleasant.*
   As object: **Viam novam** *mūnīre* **dēbēmus**. *We ought to build a new road.*
3. Adjectives
   Miser (nom. sing. masc.) **terrētur**. *The unhappy (man) is scared.*
   Aequae (nom. pl. fem.) **praemia merent**. *The just (women) deserve rewards.*
   Multum (acc. sing. neut.) **facimus**. *We do much.*
   Multa (acc. pl. neut.) **facimus**. *We do many (things).*

Principal Parts

Verbs generally form the perfect passive participle by adding **-tus** or **-sus** to the stem. Review the following first conjugation verbs, whose principal parts are regular.

amō, appellō, convocō, dōnō, dubitō, ēvocō, exspectō, habitō, incitō, labōrō, līberō, mandō, mōnstrō, nāvigō, nūntiō, oppugnō, parō, portō, probō, pugnō, servō, spectō, vocō

Past Perfect and Future Perfect Tenses

The past perfect (pluperfect) and future perfect active tenses are formed by adding a tense sign to the perfect stem. The tense sign of the past perfect (pluperfect) is **-era-**; the tense sign of the future

LESSONS XXIX–XXXIV

perfect is **-eri-**, except in the first person. The regular personal endings are then added (**-eram** for the first person pluperfect, **-erō** for the first person future perfect).

Discēdere dubitāverant.	*They had hesitated to depart.*
Mē salūtāveris.	*You will have greeted me.*

Personal Pronouns

The personal pronouns **ego, nōs, tū,** and **vōs** are used just as they are in English, except that it is not necessary to use them as the subject unless it is for emphasis or clarity.

Tē dīmīsī.	*I sent you (and not your sister) away.*
Ea nōbīscum discessit.	*She left with us.*

Possessive Adjectives

The possessive adjectives **meus, noster, tuus,** and **vester** are derived from the personal pronouns. Like all adjectives, they must agree with the noun they modify in gender, number, and case. The number and gender have no necessary relation to the number and gender of the possessor.

Puellae fuerant amīcae meae.	*The girls had been my friends. (my might refer to a single man or woman)*
Equōs tuōs in agrīs videō.	*I see your horses in the fields. (the possessor referred to by your is singular and may be either male or female)*

Infinitives as Objects

Certain verbs, including *teach, order, wish, forbid,* and *force* are often followed by an object infinitive. The subject of such an infinitive must be in the accusative case.

Inimīcōs accēdere iubet.	*He orders the enemies to approach.*
Nōs nārrāre fābulās docuit.	*She taught us to tell stories.*

The Perfect Passive Tenses

The perfect passive tenses are all formed by using the fourth principal part (the perfect passive participle) and a form of **sum** as a helping verb. Because the participle modifies the subject, it must agree with it in gender, number, and case.

Susceptum est prō nōbīs.	*It was undertaken for us.*
Retenta erat.	*She had been held back.*
Ēductī erimus ē perīculō.	*We shall have been led out of danger.*

Present Passive Infinitive

The present passive infinitive is formed by changing the final **-e** on the present infinitive to **-ī**, except for all third conjugation verbs, where the **-ere** changes to **-ī**.

Laudārī ā tē amant.	*They love to be praised by you.*
Capī nōn cupīvērunt.	*They did not want to be taken.*

UNIT PRACTICE

A. Give the Latin for *I, me, we, us, with me, with us, you* (as sing. subject and object), *you* (as pl. subject and object), *of you* (sing. and pl.), *with you* (sing. and pl.).

B. Give in Latin the singular and plural of *great danger* and *my son* used as subject, used as direct object, and used as indirect object.

C. Give the present passive infinitive of **appellō, āmittō, removeō,** and **audiō.** Translate into Latin: *to undertake, to be undertaken; to order, to be ordered; to lead out, to be led out.*

D. Give in six tenses, translating each tense form: the active first singular of **iubeō,** and the passive third plural of **permittō.**

E. Translate **fuerant, fuistī, iusserāmus, discessit, remōvī, retinuistis, cupīvimus, ēdūxit, prōpositum est, remōtī sunt, dubitāverō.** Provide in Latin: *he had been, she has been seen, it has been presented, he has remained, undertaken, it will be entrusted, they have been, we had been sent away.*

WORD STUDY

1. Find and use in sentences as many English derivatives as possible from **servō, moveō, dūcō, capiō.** For example: from **servō** is derived *conservation,* which could be used as follows: *The conservation of our soil and of our forests is a necessity.*

2. Identify Latin words from which each of the following is derived: *primitive, permission, beneficiary, exemplary, proposition, librarian, inimical, integration, commiserate, retention, reproduce.*

VOCABULARY

Circle the word that best completes each sentence.

1. Cupiēbāmus nōn _____ ē casā, quod perīculum in viā novā magnum erat.
   a. dēfendī
   b. dubitārī
   c. dīmittī
   d. incipī

2. Captīvus superbus sub portā oppidī ā rēgīnā _____.
   a. trācta erat
   b. ēvocātī erant
   c. prōductum erat
   d. retentus erat

3. Iubēbisne nōs officia dūra sine auxiliō _____?
   a. interficere
   b. suscipere
   c. abesse
   d. adesse

4. Nūntius amīcus līberōs parvōs _____ loca nōta ad magistrum dūxit.
   a. per
   b. prō
   c. dē
   d. ā

5. Ōlim Mārcus vītam fīlī prīmī meī servāvit; _____ amīcus vērus est.
   a. ego
   b. tū
   c. is
   d. ea

GRAMMAR

Complete each sentence with the correct endings.

6. Aud___ verb___ pulchra poēt___ ēgregiōrum semper grāt___ est.

7. Vent___ perpetuus paucōs naut___ Trōiānōs ad īnsūlam miseram redēg___, tamen multī in mediīs undīs āmiss___ ___.

8. Ego crās ab___ (be absent), quod familia me___ ē prōvinciā prōcēd___, sed Lūcius migr___ numquam cupiet.

9. Benefici___ disciplīn___ bonae etiam ā mult___ amīc___ me___ recept___ erunt.

10. Venus dīxit: "Nōsc___, fīlī, verb___ cōnsiliaque deōrum. Reman___ in Trōiā nōn est officium tu___."

TRANSLATION

Translate the following sentences.

11. Tū ē locīs variīs clārīsque litterās multās mihi scrīpseris, et semper grātē sententiās tuās legam.

12. Multa exempla superbiae inimīcīs nostrīs ā vōbīs in pugnā longā prō oppidō mōnstrāta sunt.

13. Agricolae singulī cum amīcīs in agrum lātum convenīre incēperant, et nōbīscum dīcēbant.

14. Dōnā mihi librum bonum dē linguā barbarā; nunc verba nova legam et memoriā semper tenēbō.

15. Servus meus librum parvum fīliae meae in aquā invēnerat, et is praemium pecūniae ā nōbīs recēpit.

UNIT VI ASSESSMENT

INVESTIGATION

Find the answers to these questions from any lesson in Unit VI.

16. Who were the Sibyls, and what did one of them do to help Aeneas?

17. True or false? The Carthaginian general Hannibal was able to capture Rome and make Italy a province of his country.

18. Latin nouns ending in **-ia** often become English nouns ending in _____, while those ending in **-tia** often end in the letters _____ in English. Give two examples of each.

19. A wealthy college-age student in ancient Rome would need to be able to read and understand what two languages?

20. Which Roman deities were twins, and in what aspects of life was each one powerful?

CULTURE

Vērum aut Falsum? Indicate whether each statement is true or false.

21. Romans often had a garden with fine statues in front of their homes.

22. Fire and collapse were both serious problems in ancient Roman apartment buildings.

23. The **impluvium,** a basin for collecting rainwater, usually was found in the kitchen.

24. Among Rome's seven hills, the Palatine was the favorite for homes of the wealthy.

25. Ancient Romans heated their rooms with charcoal fires.

FROM LATIN TO ENGLISH

Apply your knowledge of Latin roots to determine the best meaning of the italicized words.

26. Telling bad jokes as he introduced the speaker was an *egregious* mistake.
  a. common
  b. minor
  c. outstandingly bad
  d. deliberate

27. The emigrants had embarked on a *perilous* journey.
  a. unknown
  b. long
  c. joyous
  d. dangerous

28. The official's *cupidity* surprised the citizens.
  a. statement
  b. greed
  c. generosity
  d. attitude

29. Our team *indubitably* will win the championship game.
  a. certainly
  b. hopefully
  c. possibly
  d. never

30. Throughout her career the senator displayed great *integrity*.
  a. authority
  b. wisdom
  c. determination
  d. incorruptibility

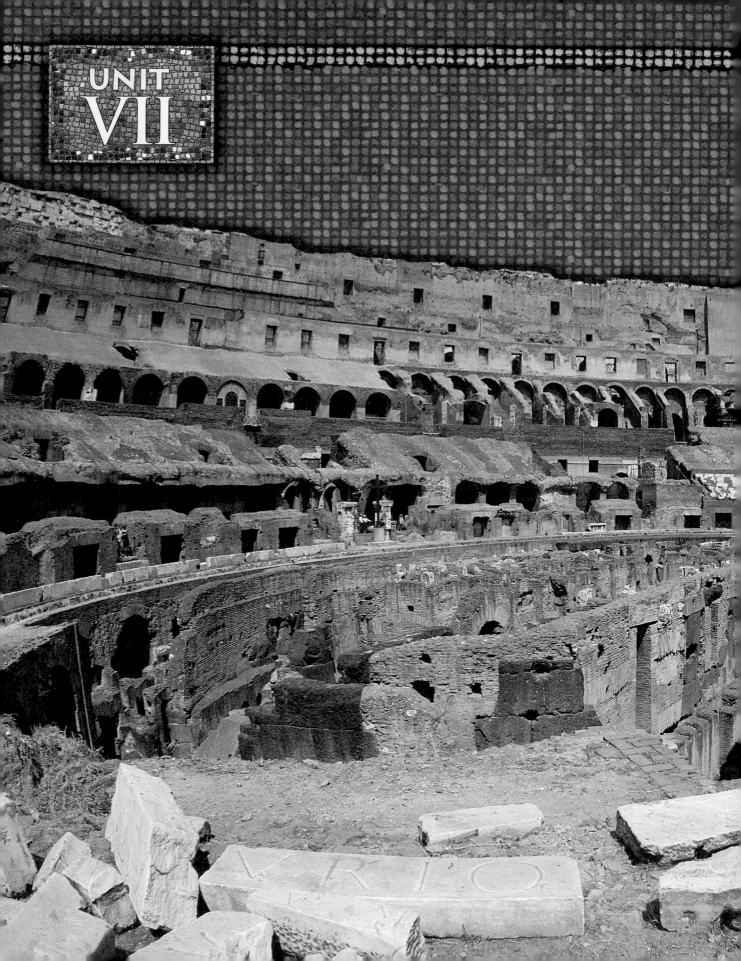

SCHOOLS, SITES, AND SIGHTS IN THE ROMAN EMPIRE

Unit Objectives

- To master the principal parts of verbs of the four conjugations and of **sum**

- To learn the forms and uses of relative and interrogative pronouns and interrogative adjectives

- To learn about Roman schools, temples, and daily life

- To learn the ablative of manner

The Roman Coliseum, built between A.D. 72 and 80, is constructed of limestone blocks called travertine. It was built for large-scale gladiatorial combats, fights with wild animals, and naval battles, for which it could be flooded. The seating capacity was fifty thousand. The seats were divided into three tiers: the lowest tier was for the senators, Vestals, and ambassadors; the second tier for the wealthy citizens; and the upper tier for the general public.

Here you can see the subterranean passages that were used for keeping wild animals and through which scenery and props were brought into the arena for the spectacles. Over the centuries, nearly two-thirds of the Coliseum was removed for use in the construction of various other Roman buildings.

S. Vidler/SuperStock

245

LŪDĪ RŌMĀNĪ ET NOSTRĪ

LESSON OBJECTIVE

• To review and master the concept of principal parts, the present, perfect, and participial stems and their uses

A boy with his box of writing instruments stands before his teacher. Roman children were taught by a **magister**, who was often a slave captured from one of the provinces. Young children learned reading, writing, and simple arithmetic. Older children, taught by a **grammaticus**, studied Greek, history, and literature among other subjects.

C. M. Dixon/Photo Resources

[1] *likeness* (nom. fem.)

[2] *no* (Girls were usually taught at home.)

[3] *on foot*

[4] *all* (nom.)

Inter lūdōs Rōmānōs et nostrōs similitūdō[1] nōn magna est. In lūdīs Rōmānīs inter puerōs erant nūllae[2] puellae, in nostrīs sunt multae; puerī Rōmānī ad lūdum ā servīs ductī sunt; nōs pedibus[3] aut in carrīs venīmus; magistrī Rōmānī servī erant, nostrī līberī sunt; lingua lūdōrum Rōmānōrum
5 erat Latīna, lingua lūdōrum nostrōrum est Anglica. Lūdī Rōmānī nōn erant pūblicī. Ob dīligentiam et studium puerīs Rōmānīs praemia pulchra data sunt; nunc puerī puellaeque ob dīligentiam "A" merent. Malī discipulī Rōmānī poenā affectī sunt, sed malī discipulī poenā semper afficiuntur. Ob variās causās vīta discipulōrum nostrōrum grāta est, sed etiam puerī Rōmānī
10 lūdum librōsque amāvērunt. Magna pecūnia lūdīs nostrīs datur et beneficia disciplīnae pūblicae omnēs[4] puerī puellaeque accipiunt. Nōnne est officium pūblicum pecūniam dare et lūdīs auxilium submittere? Rōmānī lūdīs auxilium nōn submīsērunt, neque beneficia disciplīnae pūblicae puerī Rōmānī accēpērunt. Lūdus Rōmānōrum prīmus "lūdus litterārum" appellātus
15 est quod ibi magistrī litterās docēbant. Etiam nostrī lūdī sunt lūdī litterārum.

Questions

1. How do our schools differ from Roman schools?
2. How did the boys get to school?
3. What was the **lūdus litterārum** and why was it so named?
4. What is the biggest difference between the Roman and our systems of education?

■ VOCABULARY

Nouns

dīligen′tia, -ae f. *diligence*   (diligent)
lū′dus, -ī m. *game, play, show, school*   (ludicrous)

Verbs

dō,[5] da′re, de′dī, da′tus *give*   (dative, data)
submit′tō, -mit′tere, -mī′sī, -mis′sus   **[mittō]**
     let down, furnish

[5] **Dō** is irregular: it has perfect **dedī**, and short **ă** in all forms except the present tense, second person singular (**dās**), the imperative singular (**dā**), and the present participle (**dāns**) (to be studied later).

Prepositions

in′ter with acc. *between, among*
ob with acc. *(facing toward), on account of, for, because of*

Conversation: School

Magister/-tra:	Discipulōs discipulāsque appellābō. Anna.
Anna:	Adsum.
Magister:	Marīa.
Marīa:	Adsum.
Magister:	Mārcus.
Discipulī:	Abest.
Magister:	Ubi est Mārcus? Ubi est ___?
Discipulī:	Ad lūdum vēnit/nōn vēnit. Adest/Abest.
Magister:	Grātane erat vīta puerōrum Rōmānōrum?
Discipulī:	Nōn grāta erat vīta puerōrum Rōmānōrum, quod puerī Rōmānī ante lūcem *(daylight)* in lūdum dūcēbantur.
Magister:	Ubi puerī Rōmānī labōrābant?
Discipulī:	In lūdō puerī Rōmānī labōrābant.
Magister:	Multīne puerī in lūdō fuērunt?
Discipulī:	Paucī puerī in lūdō fuērunt.

Questions

Answer in Latin.

1. Ubi nunc estis?
2. Pecūniamne tuam āmīsistī? Pēnsum *(homework)* tuum?
3. Estne grātum in lūdō esse?
4. Tardusne/Tardane in lūdum vēnistī?
5. Semperne tardus/tarda in lūdum veniēs?
6. Ubi librum tuum Latīnum āmīsistī?

GRAMMAR

Verbs: Principal Parts

The principal parts of the model verbs of the four conjugations and of **sum** are as follows.

CONJUGATION	PRESENT INDICATIVE	PRESENT INFINITIVE	PERFECT INDICATIVE	PERFECT PARTICIPLE
First	**portō**	**portāre**	**portāvī**	**portātus**
Second	**doceō**	**docēre**	**docuī**	**doctus**
Third	**pōnō**	**pōnere**	**posuī**	**positus**
	capiō	**capere**	**cēpī**	**captus**
Fourth	**mūniō**	**mūnīre**	**mūnīvī**	**mūnītus**
Irregular verb	**sum**	**esse**	**fuī**	**futūrus**

Tense Stems

The forms of every Latin verb are built upon three stems. These are formed from the principal parts.

- PRESENT STEM: drop **-re** from the present infinitive active: **portā-**
- PERFECT STEM: drop **-ī** from the perfect indicative active: **portāv-**
- PARTICIPIAL STEM: drop **-us** from the perfect participle: **portāt-**

What tenses are formed (a) upon the present stem, (b) upon the perfect stem, (c) with the perfect participle?

Exercises

A. Translate the following sentences into English.
1. Puerōs poenā nōn afficī iussimus.
2. Ob amīcitiam auxilium submīsimus.
3. Castra in locō plānō inter oppidum et silvam erant.
4. Ob multās causās concordia inter līberōs esse dēbet.
5. Officium pūblicum est puerīs puellīsque disciplīnam dare.

B. Translate the following sentences into Latin.
1. The fields had been seized by the slaves.
2. He has been aroused by the messenger's harsh words.
3. We have furnished help to the scared provinces.
4. On account of the danger we did not desire to sail to Europe.

WORD STUDY

Prefixes As a prefix in Latin and English, **inter-** has its usual meanings. It is rarely assimilated. It is used rather freely in English to form new words: *inter-class, inter-state, inter-scholastic*, etc.

As a prefix, **ob-** has the meaning *toward* or *against*. It is regularly assimilated before certain consonants: *oc-cur, of-ficial, o-mission, op-ponent; but ob-tain, ob-serve, ob-durate, ob-vious.*

Explain by derivation the meanings of *intercede, opponent, intervene, obvious.* What are *data?*

opponents

LESSON
OBJECTIVES
• To learn more about
  Roman mythology
• To learn the forms
  and uses of relative
  pronouns

LESSON XXXVI

TEMPLA DEŌRUM

¹ *at first*
² *worshipped*
³ *afterwards*
⁴ *these* (nom.)
⁵ *people*
⁶ *daily news, newspapers*

Silvae erant prīma templa deōrum. Prīmō¹ virī in agrīs habitābant et Nātūram colēbant². Posteā³ virī quī in oppidīs habitābant templa pulchra in altīs locīs ad glōriam deōrum pōnēbant. Templa saepe in locīs altīs posita sunt. Cūr? Quod haec⁴ loca caelō fīnitima erant, in quō deī habitābant.

5 "Nātūra est pulchra," hominēs⁵ dīxērunt. "Etiam loca sacra ad quae convenīmus et in quibus beneficia deōrum petimus pulchra esse dēbent. Deī nōbīs fortūnam bonam dedērunt. Deīs grātiam habēmus ob frūmentum quō vītam sustinēmus et ob auxilium perpetuum quod nōbīs submīsērunt."

Itaque Graecī et Rōmānī ob beneficia deōrum magna et pulchra templa
10 faciēbant quae deīs erant grāta. Statua aut deī aut deae semper in templō pōnēbātur.

In Graeciā et in Italiā ruīnae templōrum multōrum et pulchrōrum videntur. Templum clārum Athēnae, appellātum Parthenōn, ob fōrmam pulchram semper laudātum est. Nōnne fuērunt multa templa Rōmāna inter pictūrās
15 quās vīdistī? Cūr pictūrās templōrum et Graecōrum et Rōmānōrum, quae in multīs librīs inveniuntur, nōn spectātis? Etiam in actīs diurnīs⁶ pictūrās templōrum antīquōrum inveniētis.

Pulchrum templum Bacchī.
A Roman temple dedicated to Bacchus still stands at Baalbek in Lebanon. Baalbek *(City of the Sun God,* Heliopolis to the Greeks and Romans) was a rich and important trading center for spices and luxury items on the route from the eastern Mediterranean to India.

Explorer/Photo Researchers

In templīs virī auxilium deōrum petēbant. Virī malī quōrum vīta[7] in perīculō erat saepe[8] ad templa fugiēbant, quod neque ex templīs removēbantur neque ibi poenam sustinēbant.

[7] We use the plural in English.
[8] *often*

20

Questions

1. What were the first temples?
2. After men moved into towns, where were the first temples located? Why?
3. Why did ancient peoples show gratitude to the gods?
4. What did ancient builders regularly put inside their temples?
5. What and where is the Parthenon, and why has it been praised?
6. In addition to being places of worship, what other uses did temples have?

VOCABULARY

Noun

nātū´ra, -ae f. *nature*　　　　　　　　　(natural, naturalize)

Pronoun

quī, quae, quod *who, which, that*　　　　(quorum)

Verbs

pe´tō, pe´tere, petī´vī, petī´tus *seek, ask*　(compete, petition)

susti´neō, sustinē´re, -ti´nuī, -ten´tus　　[teneō]
　　hold up, maintain, endure

Adverb

cūr interrogative *why?*

GRAMMAR

Relative Pronouns

The English pronouns *who, which, what,* and *that* are called *relative* pronouns because they relate or refer to some preceding word, called the *antecedent: The boy who lives next door collects stamps.* The word *boy* is the antecedent of the relative pronoun *who.*

In Latin there is only one relative pronoun. It is declined as follows and, with its English meanings, must be thoroughly learned.

	SINGULAR			PLURAL		
	M.	F.	N.	M.	F.	N.
Nom.	quī	quae	quod	quī	quae	quae
Gen.	cu´ius	cu´ius	cu´ius	quō´rum	quā´rum	quō´rum
Dat.	cui	cui	cui	qui´bus	qui´bus	qui´bus
Acc.	quem	quam	quod	quōs	quās	quae
Abl.[9]	quō	quā	quō	qui´bus	qui´bus	qui´bus

[9] In combination with **cum**:
quōcum, quācum, quibuscum.

ENGLISH MEANINGS IN SINGULAR AND PLURAL

	M., F.	N.
Nominative	*who, which, that*	*which, that, what*
Genitive	*whose, of whom, of which*	*whose, of which,*
Dative	*to (for) whom, which*	*to (for) which*
Accusative	*whom, which, that*	*which, that, what*
Ablative	*by, with etc., whom, which*	*by, with etc., which*

Temples dedicated to the cult of the emperor were common throughout the Empire as an effective form of imperial propaganda. The ruins of Hadrian's temple at Ephesus, Turkey, show several of the architectural features that Hadrian, an architect at heart as well as emperor, used in his designs: curved walls, colonnades, and vaults.

E. Streichan/SuperStock

Study the forms and note which ones are alike. The accusative singular, masculine and feminine, ends in **-m,** as in the English *whom.* The nominative singular feminine is like the nominative plural feminine and neuter.

Relative Pronouns in English

That as a relative pronoun can be used to refer to both persons and things, but *who* always refers to persons; *which* always refers to things. In other words, *which* is the neuter of *who. Which* and *that* do not change form to indicate case, while *who* does.

Nominative *who*   Possessive *whose*   Objective (Accusative) *whom*

Relative Pronouns in Latin

When a sentence contains two or more subjects and predicates, the separate parts are called *clauses.* A *relative clause* is introduced by a relative pronoun. In the following sentences, the antecedent and relative are highlighted. Give the number and gender of each.

Vīdī **rēgīnam quae** Britanniam regit.	I saw the queen who rules Great Britain.
Puer cuius librum habeō est amīcus noster.	The boy whose book I have is our friend.
Virum cui librum dedī vīdistī.	You saw the man to whom I gave the book.
Oppidum quod vīdit erat parvum.	The town that he saw was small.
Lūdī ex quibus vēnimus erant magnī.	The schools from which we came were large.
Inīmīcī erant **virī quibuscum** pugnābātis.	Enemies were the men with whom you used to battle.

Now compare the case of the relative pronoun and its antecedent in these same sentences. You will see that the relative pronoun agrees with its antecedent in gender and number, *but its case depends upon its use in its own clause.*

Finally, check each one of the sentences once more. What function does the relative clause serve? What does it do for its antecedent? To what part of speech would you compare the relative clause?

Oral Practice

Identify the antecedent and the gender, number, and case of the italicized relative pronoun. Then give the Latin for the italicized words.

1. The boy *whom* I visited was my cousin.
2. I saw the horses *that* were on the road.
3. I know the town *in which* the president was born.
4. Have you seen the girl *to whom* I gave the books?
5. The man *by whom* we were robbed has been arrested.
6. The land *from which* our parents came was beautiful.
7. Have you seen the islands *to which* we sailed two years ago?
8. All the men *to whom* we spoke were pleased by your action.
9. All the girls (*whom*)[10] I have invited have accepted, but one girl *whose* mother is sick may not be able to come.
10. That is not *what* I mean.

Understanding Relative Clauses

As you come across a relative pronoun in reading a Latin sentence, you must be alert to its *antecedent,* the word which (usually immediately) precedes it. What follows the relative pronoun is a clause that can be understood as a unit and further describes or defines the antecedent. **Vīdī rēgīnam** [antecedent] **quae** [relative pronoun] **Britanniam regit,** *I saw the queen who rules Great Britain.* The relative clause **quae Britanniam regit,** like a giant adjective, modifies **rēgīnam** and tells what the queen does. The relative clause, with its own verb, is subordinate to the main verb **vīdī.** Here is the same sentence, meaning exactly the same thing, in a more normal Latin order: **Rēgīnam quae Britanniam regit vīdī.**

> Think: **rēgīnam** acc. sing. fem., must be an object;
> **quae** relative pronoun, could be nom. sing. fem. and refer to **rēgīnam** *the queen*
> **quae Britanniam regit** relative clause, probably *who rules Great Britain*
> **vīdī** *I saw.* Yes, I've got it!
> Say: *I saw the queen who rules Great Britain.*

Resist the temptation to jump around. Expect the relative pronoun to agree with its antecedent in gender and number, but not necessarily in case, which it takes from its use in its own clause. Expect the relative clause (from **clausus,** *closed*) to close with a verb. Bracket the whole relative clause in your mind until you understand the whole sentence. Stick with the words in the order in which they come, paying careful attention to their endings. Finally, put all the elements of the sentence together in the natural English order.

Relative clauses are one means Latin and English have of creating *complex* sentences, sentences that have a *main* or *independent* clause that

[10] The relative pronoun may be omitted in English but is never omitted in Latin: *The man (whom) I saw,* **Vir quem vidī.**

can make sense by itself and other *subordinate* or *dependent* clauses that cannot stand alone. The preceding example of the British queen is a complex sentence. Let's try a more complicated example.

Deīs grātiam habēmus ob frūmentum quō vītam sustinēmus et ob auxilium perpetuum quod nōbīs submīsērunt.

Think: **Deīs grātiam habēmus** *To the gods we have gratitude*
   ob frūmentum prep. with an acc. object, *on account of the grain*
   quō vītam sustinēmus relative pronoun, abl. sing. neut., probably abl. of means referring back to **frūmentum**, *grain by which;* **vītam sustinēmus** *we sustain life*
   et *and*
   ob auxilium perpetuum a second parallel prepositional phrase, *on account of the perpetual aid*
   quod nōbīs submīsērunt Is **quod** *because* or the relative pronoun? Most probably the relative, since it has a possible noun antecedent (**auxilium**) modified by the following **perpetuum** and since **ob** has already indicated *because;* **nōbīs submīsērunt** probably a dat. pl. indirect object plus the 3rd pers. pl. perfect of **submittō.** Oops! The person and the tense have changed, *which to us they have sent down.*

Say: *We feel gratitude to the gods on account of the grain with which we sustain our lives and because of the constant help which they have furnished us.*

Note how the finished English translation means almost exactly what the Latin says and yet is smoother and freer than a perfectly literal translation. *Sustain* does precisely catch the Latin idea of "holding up life," but *our lives* (pl.) is the natural way we say it in English. Finally, if you think of the gods as living on high, *sent down* for **submīsērunt** would be fine, but *submitted* would not. That is why translation is both a difficult and creative art.

Did You Know?

Because of their location on high promontories along the Mediterranean coastline, some ancient temples were important aids to navigation, especially if the fires on their altars were kept burning continuously and thus made them "lighthouses" by night. Sailors who had made a safe passage or survived shipwreck could then give their thanks (and offerings) to the god or goddess presiding over the temple.

▓ *Exercises*

A. Translate the following sentences into English.
1. Via quā vēnimus pulchra erat.
2. Librōs quī dē fāmā et fortūnā agunt puerī amant.
3. Vir cui pecūniam permīsī amīcus meus vērus erat.
4. Cūr pecūniam puerō vīsō ā tē in Viā Quīntā nōn dedistī?
5. Cūr nōn fortūnam quam nātūra vōbīs dedit sustinētis?

B. Translate the following sentences into Latin.
1. I saw the boy whose book I had lost.
2. The friendly girl whom I saw in the woods is approaching.
3. You endured constant dangers on account of your enemies.
4. I departed from the province on account of the unhappy life that I led there.

C. Working with a partner or in a small group, identify in Latin what you know about the functions and spheres of influence of various gods and goddesses: Jupiter, Juno, Neptune, Pluto, Minerva, Venus, Ceres, Apollo, Diana, Mercury, Vesta, Lares, and Penates.

WORD STUDY

Prefixes Most of the Latin prepositions that are used as prefixes in Latin and English may have intensive force, especially **con-, ex-, ob-, per-.** They are best translated either by an English intensive, such as *up* or *out*, or by an adverb, such as *completely, thoroughly, deeply.* Thus **commoveō** means *to move greatly;* **permagnus,** *very great;* **obtineō,** *to hold on to;* **concitō,** *to rouse up;* **excipiō,** *to catch, receive;* **cōnservō,** *to save up, preserve;* **complicō,** *to fold up.*

Explain *component, confirmation, evident, elaborate.* What is meant by *conservation* of natural resources? What is a political *conservative?* What is a *contract?*

LESSON XXXVII

COLOSSĒUM

LESSON OBJECTIVES

- To learn about Roman games
- To learn the ablative of manner
- To review the principal parts of the second conjugation

The Flavian amphitheater at Rome, one of the largest in the Roman Empire. This closeup of the Coliseum shows the three orders of Greek columns: Doric on the ground level, Ionic on the second level, and Corinthian on the third. The fourth level had Corinthian pilasters (rectangular columns attached to a wall) that were used to anchor a large canvas cloth that shielded spectators from the sun.

Lawrence Migdale/Photo Researchers

Lūdōs et pompās[1] populus Rōmānus magnō studiō spectābat. In Italiā, in Āfricā, in Galliā cōnservantur theātra[2] et amphitheātra[2] Rōmānōrum, in quibus lūdī etiam nunc habentur. Nātūra virōrum varia est sed paucī lūdōs nōn amant.

Captīvī et servī malī quōs dominī in amphitheātrum mīserant in mediā 5 arēnā pugnāre cōgēbantur. Populus Rōmānus studium lūdōrum numquam intermīsit. Multī captīvī magnō cum animō pugnābant et lībertātem[2] obtinēbant. Multī virī malī etiam prō vītā pugnābant et poenam in arēnā sustinēbant.

Quondam duo gladiātōrēs[2] in arēnā Rōmānā pugnābant. Tum inter 10 gladiātōrēs vēnit sine armīs vir bonus aequusque, quī petīvit: "Cūr pugnātis? Proelium intermittite, nam amīcī estis. Malum exemplum prōpōnitis." Sed gladiātōrēs verbīs nōn permōtī sunt et virum bonum interfēcērunt. Servī virum ex arēnā trahere incipiēbant. Tum populus īrā permōtus est, quod vir erat Tēlemachus, quī amīcus miserīs semper fuerat et fāmam magnam obtinuerat. 15 Numquam posteā gladiātōrēs in Colossēō pugnāvērunt, et Colossēum cum cūrā cōnservātum est. Hodiē[3] ruīna magna pulchraque manet.

Scrīptum est:

"Quamdiū stat Colisaeus,[4] stat et[5] Rōma. Quandō[6] cadet[7] Colisaeus, cadet et Rōma. Quandō cadet Rōma, cadet et mundus[8]." 20

[1] games and parades
[2] Use English derivative.
[3] today
[4] as long as the Colossēum stands
[5] also
[6] when
[7] will fall
[8] world

Questions

1. How are some ancient theaters used today?
2. What two classes of people fought in the amphitheaters?
3. Who interrupted a fight between two combatants?
4. What was the effect of his condemnation of blood sport?
5. What was the effect on the spectators?
6. According to the passage, was the Coliseum well preserved afterwards?
7. According to the last sentence, how long will the world last?

VOCABULARY

Verbs

cōnser´vō, cōnservā´re, cōnservā´vī, cōnservā´tus *save, preserve*	[servō]
intermit´tō, intermit´tere, intermī´sī, intermis´sus *stop, interrupt, let go*	[mittō]
obtin´eō, obtinē´re, obti´nuī, obten´tus *hold, obtain*	[teneō]
permo´veō, permovē´re, permō´vī, permō´tus *move (deeply), upset*	[moveō]

GRAMMAR

Second Conjugation: Principal Parts

These are verbs already studied, given here with their principal parts for review.

Three orders of classical architecture illustrated here, Doric *(top)*, Corinthian *(center)*, and Ionic *(bottom)*, are notably different in the capitals of their columns. The Doric is the simplest, the Corinthian the most ornate. The Ionic capital is distinguished by its rolled shape.

PRESENT INDICATIVE	PRESENT INFINITIVE	PERFECT INDICATIVE	PERFECT PARTICIPLE
habeō	habēre	habuī	habitus
teneō	tenēre	tenuī	tentus
contineō	continēre	continuī	contentus
sustineō	sustinēre	sustinuī	sustentus
augeō	augēre	auxī	auctus
iubeō	iubēre	iussī	iussus
maneō	manēre	mānsī	mānsūrus
moveō	movēre	mōvī	mōtus
videō	vidēre	vīdī	vīsus

No general rule can be given for forming the perfect and participial stems of verbs of the second conjugation. There are three general types, as can be seen above. **Habeō** represents the most common type. Like it are **dēbeō, doceō, mereō, terreō, valeō** (participle, **valitūrus**). **Retineō** and **obtineō** are like **contineō; removeō,** like **moveō.**

Oral Practice

Give the first singular of **augeō** and the third plural of **videō** in all tenses of the active voice.

Ablative of Manner

In English, the *manner* of an action is expressed by an adverb or by a phrase (a group of words) answering the question *how? in what manner?* When a phrase is used, a preposition, such as *with,* introduces it. In Latin, manner is similarly expressed.

Cum studiō labōrat.	*He labors with eagerness (eagerly).*
(Cum) magnō studiō labōrat.	*He labors with great eagerness (very eagerly).*

The Roman theater at Jerash (ancient Gerasa), Jordan. The semicircular area is called the orchestra (originally, "dancing ground"). The actors performed on the raised rectangular platform or stage. In the near background is the ancient forum, enclosed by columns, and in the distance, the modern city.

Hubertus Kanus/Photo Researchers

Nota•Bene

When the adjective and **cum** are used with the noun, the order is often *adjective*–**cum**–*noun,* as in **magnā cum laude.**

Note that when an adjective is used, **cum** may be omitted. Be careful to distinguish this latest use of *with* from the ablatives of accompaniment (page 167) and means (page 67) studied earlier. The ablative of manner always refers to a behavior, not to a person or thing. Distinguish the three different uses of *with* in the following sentences.

With the greatest pleasure I shall go with him.
With this equipment we can work with greater success.
With my car I can cover the distance with you with ease.

Exercises

A. Translate the following sentences into English.
1. Magnā cum cūrā silvās nostrās cōnservābimus.
2. Cibō et pecūniā colōnōs miserōs līberē sustinuimus.
3. Multī puerī ob bellum studia intermīsērunt.
4. Puer quī prīmum locum obtinuit magnā cum cūrā studiōque labōrāverat.
5. Amīcus noster nōn permōtus est, sed animō firmō ad casam nostram prōcēdere mātūrāvit.

B. Translate the following sentences into Latin.
1. He has been deeply moved by my words.
2. The teacher carefully taught the boys to save money.
3. Why did you give a reward to the boy who was absent?
4. The teacher very carefully removed the girls' and boys' books.

C. Another English spelling of *Coliseum* is *Colosseum.* There are several well-known modern coliseums. How many can you name?

Did You Know?

The Romans' passion for gladiatorial games was so strong that Augustus had to pass laws that limited them. He announced that gladiators could not fight without permission of the Senate; that gladiatorial contests were to be limited to two annually; and not more than sixty pairs could be in combat at one time. During his reign, however, he gave eight **mūnera** (*offerings to the people, i.e., games*) in which no less than ten thousand men fought.

WORD STUDY

Derivatives Many ordinary English words have very interesting stories locked up within them. The key to these stories is Latin.

The *efficient* person is the one who accomplishes (**efficiō**) something—remember this when you hear people talk about *efficiency*. A *traction* company is engaged in drawing or hauling vehicles. What is a *tractor?* What sort of person is a *tractable* person? Politicians should remember that a public *office* is a duty. An *office* is also a place where one does his duty or daily work.

Find the stories in *petition, competition, promotion, demotion, condone, conservative.*

competition

LESSON OBJECTIVES
- To read the story of Dentatus
- To learn the forms and functions of the interrogative pronoun **quis, quid** and the interrogative adjective **quī, quae, quod**

VĒRUS RŌMĀNUS

Audīvistīne dē Dentātō? "Quis fuit et quid fēcit?" rogās. Quod Dentātum nōn nōvistī aut memoriā nōn tenēs, tē monēbō.

Dentātus fuit Rōmānus clārus quī patriam dēfendit et variīs modīs inimīca oppida castraque cēpit. Modus eius[1] vītae et ab amīcīs et ab inimīcīs
5 probābātur ac laudābātur, nam Rōmānus bonus erat. Cum[2] officia pūblica intermittēbat, agricola erat atque in agrīs labōrābat.

Samnītēs[3], quōs Dentātus cēdere coēgerat, magnam pecūniam ad virum clārum mīsērunt et nūntiāvērunt: "Pecūnia quam coēgimus est tua. Auxilium tuum atque amīcitiam petimus." Tum Dentātus permōtus eōs[4] monuit: "Quod
10 aurum[5] mihi datis? Cōnservāte aurum vestrum. Nam vērus Rōmānus pecūniam obtinēre nōn cupit sed eōs[6] quī aurum habent superāre[7]."

[1] his
[2] whenever
[3] the Sam´nites
[4] them
[5] gold
[6] those
[7] conquer

Questions
1. Why was Dentatus famous?
2. What did Dentatus do when he was not in public service?
3. What did the Samnites send to Dentatus? Why?
4. How did Dentatus respond?
5. What is the point of Dentatus' answer to the Samnites?

VOCABULARY

Noun

mo´dus, -ī m. *manner, way*　　　(mood, mode)

Pronoun

quis, quid *who? what?*

Adjective

quī, quae, quod *which? what?*

Gianni Dagli Orti/Archaeological Museum, Naples/The Art Archive

The Samnites, a people who lived in central Italy, were known for their bravery and fierce love of freedom. They fought against Rome from 343 B.C. until finally defeated in 290 B.C., in the consulship of Dentatus. The armor tells us that these men are Samnites; they are from a tomb painting of the third century B.C.

Verbs

cō´gō, cō´gere, coē´gī, coāc´tus   [agō]
   drive together, collect, compel
mo´neō, monē´re, mo´nuī,   (monitor)
   mo´nitus *remind, warn*

Conjunctions

at´que (ac) *and, and even*
nam *for* (in the sense of "because," introducing a new verb)

GRAMMAR

Interrogatives

Interrogative pronouns and adjectives are used to ask questions.

Pronoun In English, the interrogative pronoun *who* refers only to persons, *what* refers only to things. In Latin, the interrogative pronoun corresponding to *who?* and *what?* is **quis?** or **quid?,** declined as follows.

	SINGULAR		PLURAL		
	M., F.	N.	M.	F.	N.
Nominative	**quis** *who?*	**quid** *what?*	**quī**	**quae**	**quae**
Genitive	**cuius** *whose?*	**cuius** *of what?*	**quōrum**	**quārum**	**quōrum**
Dative	**cui** *to whom?*	**cui** *to what?*	**quibus**	**quibus**	**quibus**
Accusative	**quem** *whom?*	**quid** *what?*	**quōs**	**quās**	**quae**
Ablative[8]	**quō** *by whom?*	**quō** *by what?*	**quibus**	**quibus**	**quibus**

The plural is declined like the singular.

Lapsūs Linguae *(Slips of the Tongue).* Have you ever said, *Who did you see?* Why is *who* incorrect? Give the correct form and translate the sentence into Latin.

Adjective In English, the interrogative pronoun *who* is not used as an adjective; we cannot say, *who man?* But *what* may be used as an adjective, referring to either persons or things: *What man? What thing?* In Latin, the interrogative adjective is **quī, quae, quod,** declined like the relative pronoun (see page 252). Compare the interrogative **quis** with the relative **quī** and note the differences in the singular. The interrogative adjective is used to ask the question *what x?* or *which x?* where x is any person or thing. The interrogative pronoun stands alone and simply asks *who?* or *what?* Study the following examples.

Interrogative Pronoun
Quae monitae erant?   *Who* (fem. pl.) *had been warned?*
Interrogative Adjective
Quī librī āmissī sunt?   *What books were lost?*

Oral Practice

1. Decline *what comrade? What price?*

2. Determine whether to use the interrogative adjective or the interrogative pronoun for each word in italics. Then translate the words into Latin.
  a. *What* girls came?
  b. *What* did he say?
  c. *Whose* book is that?
  d. To *whom* shall I go?
  e. *Who* were those men?
  f. *What* boys do you mean?
  g. To *whom* shall I give this?
  h. *What* towns were destroyed?
  i. By *whom* (sing.) was he seen?

[8] In combination with **cum: quōcum, quibuscum.**

Exercises

A. Translate the following sentences into English.

1. Quis mē petit?
2. Quō modō sociī praedam coēgērunt?
3. Quī puer verbīs bonī virī nōn permōtus est?
4. Cui puerō, cui puellae, Nātūra nōn vītam grātam dedit?
5. Ā quō vōs puerī magnā cūrā dē perīculīs monitī erātis?
6. Quid amīcī tuī fēcērunt atque quod praemium accipient?
7. Quod cōnsilium, puellae, ā magistrō vestrō vōbīs datum est?

B. Translate the following sentences into Latin.

1. Whom did you seek?
2. To whom shall we give the books?
3. By what street did you girls come?
4. In what manner did you obtain the money?
5. In what place is he preparing to make a speech?

WORD STUDY

- What is a *cogent* reason for doing something? What is an *intermission* in a play? Explain the meaning of *modal, model, admonition.*

- Study the following English phrases that are borrowed from Latin.

inter nos	*between us*
in absentia	*in absence*
Pax vobiscum!	*Peace (be) with you!*
in perpetuum	*(into perpetuity) forever*
sine qua non	*a necessity* (literally, *without which not*)
Cui bono?	*For whose benefit (is it)? What good is it?* (literally, *To whom [is it] for a good?*)
Ilium fuit.	*Ilium has been (no longer exists).* (said of Troy [Ilium] after its destruction; now applied to anything that is past and gone)

LESSON OBJECTIVES

- To learn about battlefield life with Julius Caesar
- To review the principal parts of third conjugation verbs

PŪBLIUS PŪBLIAE SAL.[1]

[A letter that a young Roman with Caesar's forces in Gaul in 55 B.C. might have sent to his sister in Rome.]

[1] For **salūtem dīcit:** *Publius says "greetings" to Publia,* the usual form of beginning a letter.

[2] *that's good (it is well)*

[3] *ask*

[4] *soon*

[5] *them*

[6] *his*

[7] *perhaps*

[8] *our friend*

[9] *farewell*

Sī valēs, bene est[2]; ego valeō. Magnō studiō litterās tuās lēgī quae cum cūrā scrīptae et plicātae erant.

Dē Galliā rogās[3] ac dē nōbīs cognōscere cupis. Vīta nostra nōn dūra est et integrī sumus. Magnus numerus captīvōrum in castrīs iam coāctus est.
5 Caesar multās pugnās iam pugnāvit et multa oppida mūnīta cēpit, quae praesidiīs tenet. In paucīs oppidīs, numerō, nōn animō superāmur. Victōria nostra erit. Mox[4] Caesar erit dominus Galliae; Gallia in prōvinciam redigētur et viae novae mūnientur. Sed dominus aequus erit. Tum virōs nostrōs trāns Rhēnum flūmen ēdūcet et Germānōs terrēbit. Iam eōs[5] monuit. Modum quō
10 bellum gerit probō. Sententia eius[6] est: "Veniō, videō, vincō." Magnus et ēgregius vir est. Fortasse[7] trāns aquam in Britanniam prōcēdēmus, quae est magna īnsula dē quā nōn ante lēgī aut cognōvī.

Quid Quīntus noster[8] agit? Quae nova officia suscēpit? Cūr nōn ante scrīpsit? Litterās tuās cum studiō exspectābō. Valē.[9]

Questions

1. Did Publius have an easy time in Gaul?
2. By what means is Caesar holding towns in Gaul?
3. What progress is Caesar making in his conquest of Gaul?
4. Does Publius approve of Caesar's method of conducting war?
5. What is Caesar's motto?
6. Has Publius seen Germany yet? Has he seen Britain?
7. What does the writer of the letter know about Britain?

VOCABULARY

Verbs

cognōs´cō, cognōs´cere, cognō´vī,　　　　　[noscō]
　cog´nitus *learn,* perf. *have
　learned, know*
pli´cō, plicā´re, plicā´vī, plicā´tus *fold*　　(application, pleat)

Adverb

an´te *before*　　　　　　　　　　　　　(antebellum)

Prepositions

an´te (+ acc.) *before*　　　　　　　　　(antediluvian,
　(of time or place)　　　　　　　　　　　　antecedent)
trāns (+ acc.) *across*　　　　　　　　　(transparent, transmit)

GRAMMAR

Third Conjugation: Principal Parts

Review the principal parts of the following verbs of the third conjugation already studied. No rule can be given for the formation of the third and fourth parts, but in the most common type the perfect ends in **-sī** or **-xī**. The perfect participle normally ends in **-tus** or **-sus**.

Scala/Art Resource, NY

A Roman general *(top center),* with arm outstretched, leads a cavalry charge against the barbarians. Sculpted with great skill and extraordinary detail, the panel gives an excellent example of the confusion and savagery of battle. At the top right, above all the weapons, horsemen, and fallen enemy, stands the bugler **(cornicen)**, blowing his circular trumpet **(cornū)**, which has lost a section to later damage.

PRESENT INDICATIVE	PRESENT INFINITIVE	PERFECT INDICATIVE	PERFECT PARTICIPLE
1. cēdō	cēdere	cessī	cessūrus
dīcō	dīcere	dīxī	dictus
(Similarly accēdō, discēdō, excēdō, prōcēdō)			
dūcō	dūcere	dūxī	ductus
(Similarly ēdūcō, prōdūcō, redūcō)			
gerō	gerere	gessī	gestus
mittō	mittere	mīsī	missus
(Similarly āmittō, committō, dīmittō, intermittō, permittō, submittō)			
regō	regere	rēxī	rēctus
scrībō	scrībere	scrīpsī	scrīptus
trahō	trahere	trāxī	trāctus
agō	agere	ēgī	āctus
cōgō	cōgere	coēgī	coāctus
redigō	redigere	redēgī	redāctus
legō	legere	lēgī	lēctus
nōscō	nōscere	nōvī	nōtus
(Similarly cognōscō)			
petō	petere	petīvī	petītus
pōnō	pōnere	posuī	positus
(Similarly prōpōnō)			
2. capiō	capere	cēpī	captus
accipiō	accipere	accēpī	acceptus
incipiō	incipere	incēpī	inceptus
suscipiō	suscipere	suscēpī	susceptus
cupiō	cupere	cupīvī	cupītus
faciō	facere	fēcī	factus
afficiō	afficere	affēcī	affectus
efficiō	efficere	effēcī	effectus
fugiō	fugere	fūgī	fugitūrus

The meditative and intense expression of the young girl holding wax tablets and a stylus shows the artist's interest in the psychology of his subject. Sometimes called **Sappho** after the Greek poet of that name, the painting from Pompeii dates from the first century A.D.

Erich Lessing/Art Resource, NY

The change or lengthening of the vowel in the perfect and participial stems may be compared with the change of vowel in English: *sing, sang, sung; swim, swam, swum.*

Oral Practice

Give the third singular of **committō** and the first plural of **accipiō** in all tenses of the passive voice.

Did You Know?

Although there was no official postal service, slaves called **tabellāriī** (*couriers*) were employed by the wealthy or important Romans to deliver letters. These slaves could cover twenty-six miles by foot or forty to fifty miles in carts daily. Letters could be sent to Athens from Rome in twenty-one days and to Britain from Rome in thirty-three days. In colonial America in the winter, it took one month for mail to travel from the northeastern to the southern states!

📖 *Exercises*

A. Translate the following sentences.

1. Quid iam cognōvistis?
2. Bella trāns ōceanum cum victōriā gessimus.
3. Litterae ā tē scrīptae cum cūrā plicātae erant.
4. Captīvī, quī ante portam positī erant, līberātī sunt.
5. Litterās quās scrīpsī plicābō et ad familiam meam mittam.
6. Quī librī ā magistrā nōn ante coactī erant?
7. Linguam Latīnam cum studiō legere incipimus; nova verba iam cognōvimus.

B. Translate the following sentences into Latin.

1. The new words ought always to be learned.
2. Is it Marcus who wrote the letter that you are reading?
3. The poor prisoners had been dragged across the fields.
4. I do not know the small boy who lives across the street.

WORD STUDY

- **Prefixes** **Ante-** has its regular meaning and form when used as a prefix. **Trāns-** (or **trā-**, as in **trā-dūcō**) means *through* or *across*.

- **Importance of the Verb** The most important part of speech in Latin for English derivation is the verb. The most important part of the verb is the *perfect participle*. This form is also the most important for Latin word formation. Therefore, you must carefully learn the principal parts of every verb.

By associating a Latin word with its English derivative, you can make the English help your Latin, and vice versa. You can often tell the conjugation or the perfect participle of a Latin verb with the help of an English derivative. The English word *mandate* shows that **mandō** has **mandātus** as its perfect participle and is therefore of the first conjugation. Similarly *migrate, donation,* and *spectator* follow this pattern. The word *vision* helps one remember that the perfect participle of **videō** is **vīsus.** Similarly *motion* from **mōtus,** *missive* from **missus,** *active* from **āctus.**

Give the derivatives from **lēctus, nōtus, ductus.** Explain *election, deposit, complication, domineer.*

In compounds short **-a-** becomes short **-e-** before two consonants: **captus, acceptus.** Give two examples each from compounds of **capiō** and **faciō.**

EDUCATION

Even before they went to school, some Roman children learned the alphabet by playing with letters cut out of ivory—just as children today do with their blocks. They started school at about the same age as children in the United States. However, the schools were quite different. They were small private schools, usually run by Greek slaves for small fees and attended by children of the middle and professional classes and government officials. (The children of the very rich were taught at home by educated slaves.) Schoolwork began early in the morning. The children were taken to and from school by slaves called **paedagōgī,** a Greek word which means *those who lead children.* They did no teaching but merely kept the children in order. However, some pedagogues of Greek heritage were able to tutor their charges in Greek.

In the elementary (**elementa,** *letters of the alphabet*) school, called the **lūdus litterārum,** reading, writing, and arithmetic formed the basis of the curriculum, which, like the teaching, was fairly unimaginative. For reading, the Romans had to depend at first on the Twelve Tables of the law, which were the first set of laws that the Romans put in writing. In the third century B.C., a schoolteacher by the name of Livius Andronicus translated the *Odyssey* from Greek for the use of his pupils. Later, other works of Greek and Roman literature were used. Children learned to read by loudly pronouncing the words and sentences after their teacher. Unlike English, Latin is written phonetically, so spelling did not need to be taught as a subject.

The students wrote on wax tablets that consisted of wooden boards covered with a thin layer of wax. They wrote by scratching the wax with a pointed stylus made of metal, wood, or bone. The other end was flat for erasing or, rather, smoothing over the wax.

Roman students also learned to write with a reed pen and ink on papyrus, a kind of paper made of thin strips of reed that grew in Egypt. Most books were made by hand out of rolls of this material. Papyrus was expensive, and schoolchildren used only the backs of old books and loose sheets for their scratch paper. For tablets, parchment came to be used instead of wax-covered wood. Eventually, a number of these were put together to form a book of the kind familiar to us, and the papyrus roll went out of style.

Ronald Sheridan/Ancient Art and Architecture Collection

A Roman inkwell, pen, and stand. The pen, or **stylus,** could also be used to write in wax on wooden tablets.

Arithmetic was complicated by the fact that the Romans did not have the Arabic system of numerals, with its zero, that we use. Multiplication and division were virtually impossible because the system of Roman numerals does not have "place value," as our system does. The Romans had two aids in their arithmetic: an elaborate system of finger counting and the **abacus,** or *counting board.*

More advanced education prepared boys for the one respected profession in ancient Rome, that of law and public life. Hence the secondary school, called the **schola grammaticī** *(school of the grammarian),* specialized in language, composition, rhetoric, and public speaking. But the course was also a broadly cultural one and included both Greek and Latin literature, especially the epics of Homer. Most educated Romans also learned to speak and write Greek fluently.

Physical fitness was also important, especially as preparation for the army. When academic lessons were over, boys took part in such sports as running, wrestling, and fencing.

The college course in the **schola rhētoricī** *(school of the rhetorician)* was still more technical in preparation for a career in which public speaking, whether in a law court or a legislative body, played a very important role. For graduate work, wealthy students could go to such university centers as Athens or Rhodes and listen to lectures by famous philosophers and professors of rhetoric.

Although the aim of the schools beyond the elementary level was the relatively narrow one of preparing male citizens for public service, the practical Romans felt that a liberal training in literature and philosophy was the best educational system.

QUESTIONS

1. What educational advantages do you have that a Roman boy or girl did not have?
2. Compare books and writing materials then and now.
3. What sort of education should our lawyers and government officials have?

Scala/Art Resource, NY

Oratory was one of the important subjects of every well-educated young Roman. Young men from affluent families even went to Greece to study under the masters there.

VOCABULARY

Nouns

dīligentia lūdus modus nātūra

Pronouns

quī, quae, quod (relative)
quis? quid? (interrogative)

Adjective

quī? quae? quod? (interrogative)

Verbs

cognōscō intermittō petō
cōgō moneō plicō
cōnservō obtineō submittō
dō permoveō sustineō

Adverbs

ante cūr

Prepositions

ante (+ acc.) ob (+ acc.)
inter (+ acc.) trāns (+ acc.)

Conjunctions

atque, ac nam

GRAMMAR SUMMARY

Verbs: Principal Parts

Remember that the four principal parts are the present indicative, present infinitive, perfect indicative, and the perfect participle. Concentrate on learning these forms when you learn a new verb.

Relative Pronoun

The relative pronoun **quī, quae, quod** agrees with its antecedent in gender and number, but takes its case from its use in its own clause.

Interrogative Pronoun

The interrogative pronoun **quis, quid** is used to ask about the identity of the person(s) or thing(s) related to an action.

Cui litterās mandāvistī?	*To whom did you entrust the letter?*
Quid facis?	*What are you doing?*

Interrogative Adjective

The interrogative adjective **quī, quae, quod** is declined like the relative pronoun but is used to ask a question about the kind of person(s) or thing(s) under discussion. It agrees with the noun it modifies in gender, number, and case. Translations include *which?* or *what?,* but not *who* or *that.*

Quae puella tēcum vēnit?	*Which girl came with you?*

Ablative of Manner

The manner in which an action is performed is expressed by the ablative with **cum. Cum** may be omitted if an adjective is used.

Magnā (cum) diligentiā pugnāvērunt.	*They fought with great diligence (very diligently).*
Cum studiō litterās lēgēbam.	*I was reading the letter with eagerness (eagerly).*

UNIT PRACTICE

A. Give the four principal parts of the following verbs: **committō, cedo, dūcō, agō, efficiō.**

B. Give the principal parts of the following verbs in Latin: *defend, flee, have, be, see, remain, increase, learn.*

C. Give in all tenses the second singular active of **moveō;** the third singular passive of **agō;** the third plural passive of **accipiō.**

D. Decline **quae nātūra, quod signum, quī dominus.**

E. Supply the words in italics and translate the questions.
1. *(Whom)* petis?
2. *(What)* librōs lēgistī?
3. *(Who)* litterās scrīpsit?
4. *(To whom)* librum dabō?
5. *(By whom)* litterae scrīptae sunt?

F. Review pages 67, 167, 259 and then decide whether the "with" phrase in each of the following sentences expresses means, manner, or accompaniment.
1. Say it *with flowers.*
2. My uncle farms *with a mule.*
3. I spent the evening *with friends.*
4. The soloist sang *with deep feeling.*
5. We shall talk over matters *with him.*
6. All supported the cause *with enthusiasm and money.*

WORD STUDY

1. Write sentences using as many English derivatives as you can find from the Latin **vocō, videō, mittō,** and **faciō.** (Remember the importance of the perfect participle.)
2. In the groups below, choose the one English word that is derived from each Latin word. You may need to check in an English dictionary.

dō	dough	dote	do
	dot	dative	
moneō	month	remain	admonition
	moan	remind	
cōgō	cog	incognito	cognate
	cogency	concoct	
petō	pet	compete	petal
	petite	impede	
legō	leg	log	collect
	lag	lick	

VOCABULARY

Circle the word that best completes each sentence.

1. Multī virī proelium inter puerōs reliquōs
   _____ incipiēbant.
   a. dare   c. monēre
   b. intermittere   d. plicāre

2. Lingua nova ā Rōmānīs paucīs in terrā barbarā
   _____ erat.
   a. sustentus   c. submissus
   b. territa   d. obtenta

3. Migrābatne ad Americam _____ modum
   novum vītae aut magnam fortūnam?
   a. prō   c. dē
   b. sine   d. ob

4. Captīvī dīxērunt: "_____ auxilium nōbīs et tum
   oppidum tuum semper dēfendēmus."
   a. submitte   c. plicā
   b. monē   d. intermitte

5. Ante lūdum longās litterās fīliae meae _____
   dēbeō.
   a. monēre   c. permovēre
   b. plicāre   d. prōcēdere

GRAMMAR

Complete each sentence with the correct endings.

6. Fām___ agricolae dē qu___ librum recēpistī
   magn___ cum studi___ semper laudābitis.

7. Aenēās cum pauc___ soci___ patri___ nov___
   in qu___ sine iniūri___ perpetu___ vītam
   agēbat invēnerat.

8. Spectāte, līber___, rēgīn___ pulchram qu___
   populōs variōs regit, sed tamen superb___
   nōn est.

9. Qu___ mod___ vīt___ puerōrum in īnsulā sine
   aqu___ aut cib___ sustent___ erat?

10. Nautae magna praemi___ qu___ recēperant ad
    port___ templī posu___ atque grāti___
    Neptūnō ēgērunt.

TRANSLATION

Translate the following sentences.

11. Cui librum novum et parvum magnā cum
    dīligentiā scrīptum dabō?

12. In fīnitimā prōvinciā poenā dūrā miserōrum et
    nātūrā locī permotae sunt.

13. Dominus servōs quī equum pulchrum virī
    superbī cēperant monuit.

14. Petēbātisne cēnam bonam et hōram ōtī quod
    dominus vester ē casā aberat?

15. Cūr magnō studiō līberī trāns agrum lātum
    properāvērunt et ad templum deī convēnērunt?

INVESTIGATION

Find the answers to these questions from any lesson
in Unit VII.

16. The seating capacity of the Roman Coliseum is
    said to have been _____.
    a. 25,000   c. 100,000
    b. 50,000   d. 150,000

17. True or false? The most important part of a
    Latin verb for furnishing us with English
    derivatives is the perfect participle.

18. In an ancient theater, what was the original meaning of the word *orchestra?*

19. Match the description of the capitals' columns to the name of the order.

Doric	**a.** recognized by the scrolled curlicue decoration
Ionic	**b.** the plainest, with smooth surfaces
Corinthian	**c.** very elaborate, with carved leaves

20. What is the Latin name for slaves who were hired to deliver letters?

CULTURE

Vērum aut Falsum? Indicate whether each statement is true or false.

21. A **stylus** was a wax tablet used for practicing letters in a Roman school.

22. Two famous centers of higher education in the Roman world were the city of Athens and the isle of Rhodes.

23. It is easier to do multiplication and division problems with Roman numerals than with Arabic numerals.

24. Roman children generally began their schooling at about the age of ten.

25. A **lūdus litterārum** was equivalent to a high school in which language, composition, and public speaking were taught.

FROM LATIN TO ENGLISH

Apply your knowledge of Latin roots to determine the best meaning of the italicized words.

26. The bruise was found in the *anterior* part of the organ.
   a. upper
   b. lower
   c. front
   d. back

27. Her father's recommendation was a *cogent* reason for selecting that book.
   a. unusual
   b. compelling
   c. minor
   d. ridiculous

28. Why was the chieftain so *obdurate* in his treatment of the captives?
   a. hard-hearted
   b. kind
   c. hasty
   d. secretive

29. The students had no *cognizance* of the committee's decision.
   a. fear
   b. report
   c. dislike
   d. knowledge

30. It was difficult to ignore her best friend's *admonition.*
   a. problem
   b. warning
   c. success
   d. kindness

UNIT
VIII

ADVENTURES ABROAD AND LIFE AT HOME

Unit Objectives

- To learn the forms of third declension masculine and feminine nouns
- To review principal parts of fourth conjugation verbs
- To learn the forms of **possum**
- To learn the use of participles as clauses
- To learn the ablative absolute construction
- To read about the adventures of Ulysses
- To learn about Roman amusements

Homer's *Odyssey* was popular among the Romans, either in the original Greek or translated into Latin as a school reader. This epic poem tells the story of Ulysses, king of Ithaca, and his many adventures as he attempts to return to his homeland after the Trojan War. In this painting by Stradano, we see Ulysses descending into the Lower World where he will learn news of his wife, Penelope, and his homeland from his deceased mother. You may recall a similar episode from Vergil's epic, the *Aeneid*, in which Aeneas goes to the Lower World. Vergil echoed many other episodes from Homer's *Odyssey*.

LESSON
OBJECTIVES
• To learn about the
  adventures of Ulysses
• To learn the forms of
  the third declension
  masculine and femi-
  nine nouns

ULIXĒS

(Ulysses [or Odysseus] was a Greek who fought in the Trojan War. His many wanderings before he returned home to Ithaca, an island west of Greece, are described by the Greek poet Homer in the *Odyssey*.)

Ulixēs, dux Graecus quī in bellō Trōiānō pugnāverat, post pācem ad Ithacam, in quā īnsulā habitāverat, properāvit. Sed multa mala miser sustinuit nec salūtem invēnit. Cūrīs dūrīs pressus, decem annōs in multīs terrīs ēgit.

Ulysses and his companions escape the blinded Cyclops Polyphemus. The sixteenth-century artist P. Tibaldi has differed from Homer's account of the episode in one important detail. Read this lesson carefully and discover what that detail is. (Hint: It is not just the panpipe on the bench beside the giant; Polyphemus was a shepherd and naturally played tunes to his flocks.)

Scala/Art Resource, NY

Post pācem ā Trōiā cum multīs mīlitibus Ulixēs migrāverat. Ad terram
Lōtophagōrum[1] accessit. Paucī mīlitēs Graecī lōtum ēdērunt[2] et amāvērunt; 5
nec ducem nec sociōs memoriā tenuērunt. Ulixēs mīlitēs ad nāvēs[3] redūxit,
quās undīs commīsit.

Tum ad Siciliam ventīs āctus est. In Siciliā habitāvērunt Cyclōpēs[4], gigantēs
altī et dūrī quī singulōs oculōs[5] habuērunt. Lēgēs neque deōrum neque hominum
timuērunt. Ulixēs cum paucīs mīlitibus in hōc[6] locō frūmentum petīvit. Magnam 10
spēluncam[7] invēnērunt, quae magnam cōpiam frūmentī continuit. Tum vēnit
Cyclōps appellātus Polyphēmus. Ovēs[8] in spēluncam ēgit. Polyphēmus Graecōs
vīdit et clāmāvit: "Ā quō locō venītis? Quī hominēs estis? Quid petitis?" Ulixēs
respondit: "Nōs Graecī sumus. Ego Nēmō[9] appellor. Auxilium tuum petimus."

Polyphēmus duōs hominēs cēpit et ēdit[10]; tum somnum cēpit[11]. Reliquī 15
Graecī sude[12] oculum Polyphēmī pressērunt, quī clāmāvit et sociōs ēvocāvit.
"Quid est?" rogant. "Quis tē vulnerāvit?" Polyphēmus respondit, "Nēmō[9] mē
vulnerāvit." Itaque reliquī Cyclōpēs discessērunt. Polyphēmus Graecōs
petīvit sed nōn invēnit quod sub ovibus[8] ligātī[13] ē spēluncā excesserant.
Līberātī ad nāvēs properāvērunt atque ibi salūtem invēnērunt. 20

[1] Lotus-eaters
[2] ate the lotus
[3] ships (fem. pl.)
[4] Cȳclōpēs, round-eyed ones (nom. pl.)
[5] one eye apiece
[6] this
[7] cave
[8] sheep
[9] No-man, no-body
[10] ate
[11] fell asleep
[12] with a stake
[13] tied (perf. passive part.)

Questions

1. How long did it take Ulysses to reach home?
2. What happened to people who ate the lotus?
3. Who was Polyphemus?
4. Where did he live?
5. What did he do to two of the Greeks?
6. What did the Greeks do to him?
7. How did the Greeks escape from the cave?
8. Why didn't the other Cyclopes help Polyphemus?
9. Why did Ulysses and his men go in the cave in the first place?

▦ VOCABULARY

Nouns

dux, du´cis m. *leader, general*	[dūcō]
ho´mō, ho´minis m. *man, person, human being*	(homicide, hominid)
lēx, lē´gis f. *law*	(legal, legislature)
mī´les, mī´litis m. *soldier*	(militant, military)
pāx, pā´cis f. *peace*	(pacifist, pacify)
sa´lūs, salū´tis f. *health, safety*	(salubrious, salutary)

Ulixēs sub ove ligātus ex spēluncā excessit. From a Greek vase dating from 475 B.C. This type of vase painting is called red-figured because the subjects were left in the natural red color of the clay, and a black background was painted in around them.

Anonymous Gift in memory of L.D. Caskey, Courtesy, Museum of Fine Arts, Boston

Verbs

clā´mō, clāmā´re, clāmā´vī, clāmā´tus *shout, cry out*	(claim, clamor)
pre´mō, pre´mere, pres´sī, pres´sus *press, press hard*	(impression, pressure)
vul´nerō, vulnerā´re, vulnerā´vī, vulnerā´tus *wound*	(invulnerable, vulnerable)

▦ GRAMMAR

The Third Declension: Masculine and Feminine Nouns

In nouns of the third declension, the genitive singular ends in **-is.** As with other nouns, you must find the base by dropping the genitive singular ending.[14]

All three genders occur in nouns of the third declension; no general rule for gender can be given. Therefore, the gender, as well as the nominative and genitive singular, must be learned from the vocabulary. Masculine and feminine nouns are declined with the same set of case endings.

---

[14]The ending of the nominative singular varies but often is a vowel + **s**, e.g., **miles**; a stem ending in **c** or **g** combines with **s** to make **x**, e.g., **duc + s = dux.**

	ENDINGS		EXAMPLES			
			mīles *soldier*		**lēx** *law*	
	SINGULAR	PLURAL	SINGULAR	PLURAL	SINGULAR	PLURAL
Nominative	—	-ēs	mīles	mīlitēs	lēx	lēgēs
Genitive	-is	-um	mīlitis	mīlitum	lēgis	lēgum
Dative	-ī	-ibus	mīlitī	mīlitibus	lēgī	lēgibus
Accusative	-em	-ēs	mīlitem	mīlitēs	lēgem	lēgēs
Ablative	-e	-ibus	mīlite	mīlitibus	lēge	lēgibus

The dative and ablative plural are alike, as is true in all declensions. The nominative and accusative plural are also alike in the third declension. The vocative, singular and plural, is like the nominative.

S. Vidler/SuperStock

Every year thousands of visitors climb up into this large wooden replica of the Trojan Horse at Truva, Turkey, to pretend that they are the Greeks who once hid inside, to look over the ruins of ancient Troy nearby (not shown) and, of course, to have their pictures taken.

No End to Endings?

With the addition of the third declension to your repertoire, the multiplicity of word endings may now seem bewildering. Eventually distinguishing among them should and will become automatic, but for now it may help to make for yourself a table of all their various possibilities of meaning. For example, how many things (not counting verb endings) can a form ending in **-īs** be? Answer: ablative or dative plural in the first and second declensions, but not the **-is** genitive singular in the third declension, because its **-i** has no long mark (called a *macron*).

Do the same thing for nouns or adjectives ending in **-a, -ā, -am, -ās, -e, -ē, -em, -es, -ēs, -ibus, -ī, -is, -ō, -um.**

Paying careful attention to the long marks (macrons) will help, but the real solution is to be thoroughly familiar with the vocabulary and the declensional endings and finally to interpret the word's function and meaning in its context.

Did You Know?

Almost everything about Homer, whom we suppose to be the author of both the *Iliad* and the *Odyssey,* is a mystery. Where was he born? Seven Greek cities claimed to be his birthplace. When did he live? Perhaps in the eighth century B.C. Was he really blind? Quite possibly. Did he compose both poems? Most probably. Did he dictate them orally or write them down? Perhaps he did both. It has even been suggested that Homer was a woman. The answers to these elements of what is known as "the Homeric Question" have been debated for centuries.

Oral Practice

1. Decline **homō magnus, pāx aequa.**
2. Give the case and number of **salūtem, ducum, lūdīs, mīlitibus, lēgī, modum, ducem, mīlite.**

▦ *Exercises*

A. Translate the following sentences into English.
1. Sine pāce vīta dūra est.
2. Dux mīlitēs ad pugnam dūxit.
3. Valet populus ubi lēgēs valent.
4. Salūtem patriae in armīs mīlitum nostrōrum pōnimus.
5. Sine bellō pācem et ōtium et salūtem obtinēre cupimus.
6. Magna est glōria mīlitum quī bellō pressī nōn cessērunt.

B. Translate the following sentences into Latin.

  1. The prepared soldiers began battle.

  2. "Safety first!" is a good motto on the roads.

  3. The general ordered the soldiers to be called together.

  4. Many books sent by boys and girls were received by the soldiers.

C. Both Aeneas and Ulysses encountered good and bad experiences during the Trojan War and afterwards. Pretend you were a soldier (either Greek or Trojan) and write a journal entry in Latin (similar to the following fictitious entry) about your experiences during this period of history.

We fought for ten years. Our leaders were great men; they were strong and they prepared many soldiers to withstand many injuries. The Trojans/Greeks pressed hard, but we took many victories. I will always remember my friends. After many battles and many wounds, there was peace. Then we sailed from Troy. We saw many foreign people and they aroused our spirits and memories of our fatherland. To find my house soon will be pleasing.

WORD STUDY

- Explain *illegal, impressive, depression, ducal, militant.* To *salute* a person is to wish him or her *health,* as we say *good morning.* To *pay* a person is to *pacify* him or her. What is a *pacifist?*

- Four states have towns named *Ithaca.* Can you name these states? Four states have towns named *Ulysses.* Can you name these states?

- Study the following English phrases borrowed from Latin.

lex scripta	*the written law*
pax in bello	*peace in (the midst of) war*
novus homo	*a new man (in politics);* hence, *an upstart*
Dux femina facti.	*A woman (was) leader in (of) the deed.*

LESSON OBJECTIVES
- To review the principal parts of fourth conjugation verbs
- To learn numerals

LESSON XLI

COLŌNĪ

[1] *afterwards*

Dē colōnīs quī ē Britanniā ad Americam vēnērunt multa fortasse nōvistī. Patriam relīquērunt et terram novam petīvērunt. Multī antecessērunt; reliquī posteā[1] ad terram petītam trānsportātī sunt. In locīs altīs stetērunt et terram novam grātē spectāvērunt. Etiam puerī puellaeque Rōmānae dē colōnīs
5 cognōvērunt.

In the foreground is the excavation of a 32-room Roman villa, complete with a full Roman bath, at Chedworth, England. It was occupied ca. A.D. 180–350, and its walls, now exposed, have been roofed over to protect them from the damage caused by sun, wind, and rain.

Mīlitēs ā Rōmānīs in Britanniam trānsportātī sunt et bella ibi gessērunt. Vālla² fēcērunt atque viās mūnīvērunt. Tum colōnōs trādūxērunt et colōnīs agrōs captōs et oppida occupāta dedērunt. Per colōnōs in Britanniam trāductōs lingua Latīna et lēgēs Rōmānae Britanniae datae sunt. Semper mīlitēs antecēdunt, tum colōnī veniunt et in pāce salūteque vīvunt.   10

² *walls*

Rōmānī oppida in Britanniā mūnīvērunt—Londīnium, Eborācum, Lindum; nunc appellantur London, York, Lincoln. Multae ruīnae Rōmānae etiam nunc in Britanniā stant. Quis nōn cupit ad Britanniam nāvigāre et ibi ruīnās relīctās vidēre?

Questions

1. Thc writer of this passage assumes the reader may already know many things about what topic?
2. What did the settlers do when they arrived?
3. Roman colonization in Great Britain was preceded by what actions and events?
4. What long-term effects did Roman colonization have on Britain?
5. What would be the Latin name for New York?
6. Compare the Roman colonization of Britain with the British, French, and Spanish colonization of the Americas.

▓ VOCABULARY

Verbs

antecē´dō, antecē´dere, anteces´sī, antecessū´rus *go before, go earlier*	[cēdō]
relin´quō, relin´quere, relī´quī, relīc´tus *leave (behind), abandon*	(relinquish, derelict)
stō, stā´re, ste´tī,³ stātū´rus *stand*	(station)
trādū´cō, trādū´cere, trādū´xī, trāduc´tus *lead across*	[dūcō]
trānspor´tō, trānsportā´re, trānsportā´vī, trānsportā´tus *transport, carry across*	[portō]
vī´vō, vī´vere, vī´xī, vīc´tus *live*	(vivacious, victuals)

Adverb

fortas´se *perhaps*	[fortūna]

³ The perfect stem of **stō**, like that of **dō**, (**ded-**), is "irregular" if compared to that of the ordinary verbs of the first conjugation.

GRAMMAR

Fourth Conjugation: Principal Parts

Review the principal parts of the following verbs, which were presented in earlier lessons.

audiō	audīre	audīvī	audītus
veniō	venīre	vēnī	ventūrus
conveniō	convenīre	convēnī	conventūrus
inveniō	invenīre	invēnī	inventus

Numerals

Ūnus puer et ūnus puer sunt **duo** puerī; duo ducēs et ūnus dux sunt **trēs** ducēs; duo equī et duo equī sunt **quattuor** equī; trēs carrī et duo carrī sunt **quīnque** carrī; quattuor oppida et duo oppida sunt **sex** oppida; sex mīlitēs et ūnus mīles sunt **septem** mīlitēs; quīnque nautae et trēs nautae sunt **octō** nautae; septem hominēs et duo hominēs sunt **novem** hominēs; sex puellae et quattuor puellae sunt **decem** puellae.

Summary: **ūnus, duo, trēs, quattuor, quīnque, sex, septem, octō, novem, decem.**

Trick Question

⁴ *how many*

Quīnque mīlitēs et trēs rēgīnae sunt octō hominēs. Quot⁴ virī sunt trēs dominī et quattuor dominae?

Exercises

A. Translate the following sentences into English.
1. Ubi pecūnia quam āmīserās inventa est?
2. Ob quās causās hominēs agrōs relīquērunt?
3. Servī trāns agrōs equōs territōs trādūxērunt.
4. Multī mīlitēs in Āsiam iam trānsportātī sunt.
5. Nūntium mīsimus ad Marium, quī sine multīs mīlitibus antecesserat.
6. Cum cūrā carrum age; tua fortasse erit vīta quam cōnservābis.

B. Translate the following sentences into Latin.
1. We ought to work with eagerness.
2. How did you hear about your (sing.) friend's health?
3. Marius ordered our soldiers to be led across.
4. Why do you stand in the middle (of the) street?

Did You Know?

Roman soldiers were required to make a regular or fortified camp every night while on the march. This was done to avoid the ever-present possibility of a surprise attack by the enemy. The disciplined Roman army rarely engaged in battle until they were fully entrenched. Such practices made the Roman legion an extremely capable fighting force in the ancient world.

WORD STUDY

Derivatives Latin words have been adopted into English continuously from the beginning of our language to the present moment. Julius Caesar twice invaded Britain, and a century later the Romans conquered the island. For the next four hundred years the Romans ruled Britain, and the language, at least in the towns, came to be Latin. When the Angles and Saxons invaded Britain in the fifth century and gave their name *(Angle-land, Eng-land)* and language to the island, they adopted a number of Latin words. Even before that they had come into contact with the Romans in northern Germany and borrowed some Latin words. So you might say that Latin affected English even before English existed as a separate language. Among such early borrowings probably are *wine* from **vīnum,** *cheese* from **cāseus,** and *pound* from **pondus.**

As the Romans in Britain found it necessary to build many military camps that developed into towns, the word **castra** can be found in a number of town names, many of which have been used elsewhere also. So *Chester* (PA), *Ro-chester* (NY, MN, Australia), *Man-chester* (NH, IA, NC), *Wor-cester* (South Africa, MA, pronounced *Wooster* and so spelled in Ohio), *Lan-caster* (PA). What other names with these endings can you give?

We have seen a similar evolution in North America where frontier forts, erected originally as defenses against the American Indians, became trading posts, out of which have grown such cities as Fort Dodge (IA), Fort Scott (KS), Fort Worth (TX), and Fort Frances (Canada).

PLĪNIUS ET PUER

Plīnius,[1] cuius facta bona vōbīs fortasse nōn ante nōta fuērunt, multās litterās scrīpsit quās etiam nunc legere possumus. Audīte factum pulchrum Plīnī. Quondam[2] ad oppidum parvum in quō nātus[3] erat vēnit. Ibi inter multōs hominēs stābat et dē salūte familiārum rogābat. Tum amīcum nōtum cum
5 fīliō cernit. Plīnius puerum rogāvit: "Discipulusne es?" Puer respondit: "Discipulus Mediōlānī[4] sum." Plīnius, commōtus quod puer patriam relīquerat, rogāvit: "Cūr nōn hīc[5]? Cūr patriam relīquistī?" Puer respondit: "Nōn possum hīc manēre, nam magistrōs nōn habēmus." Tum Plīnius verba fēcit: "Verbīs puerī commōtus sum. Certē lūdum hīc habēre potestis atque
10 dēbētis. Cognōscite cōnsilium meum. Ego nōn līberōs habeō sed tertiam partem pecūniae quam dabitis parātus sum dare. Vōsne parātī estis reliquam partem dare, sī[6] ego tertiam partem dabō?"

[1] *Pliny*

[2] *once*

[3] *born* (The town is Como in North Italy.)

[4] *at Milan* (25 miles south of Como)

[5] *here*

[6] *if*

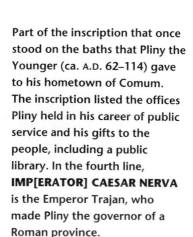

Part of the inscription that once stood on the baths that Pliny the Younger (ca. A.D. 62–114) gave to his hometown of Comum. The inscription listed the offices Pliny held in his career of public service and his gifts to the people, including a public library. In the fourth line, **IMP[ERATOR] CAESAR NERVA** is the Emperor Trajan, who made Pliny the governor of a Roman province.

Questions

1. The purpose of this story is to illustrate what character trait of Pliny?
2. Where does the dialogue take place?
3. Why did Pliny object to the boy's choice of place to pursue his studies?
4. What was the boy's reply to the objection?
5. What was Pliny's reaction to this?
6. What was Pliny's offer to the town's people?

VOCABULARY

Noun

fac´tum, fac´tī n. *deed*	[faciō]

Adjectives

cer´tus, cer´ta, cer´tum *fixed, sure*	[cernō]
nō´tus, nō´ta, nō´tum *known, familiar*	[nōscō]
parā´tus, parā´ta, parā´tum *prepared, ready*	[parō]
ter´tius, ter´tia, ter´tium *third*	(tertiary)

Verbs

cer´nō, cer´nere, crē´vī, crē´tus *(separate), discern, see*	(discretion)
commo´veō, commovē´re, commō´vī, commō´tus *disturb, alarm*	[moveō]
pos´sum, pos´se, po´tuī, — *can, be able* (with infinitive)	[sum]
ro´gō, rogā´re, rogā´vī, rogā´tus *ask*	(interrogate)

GRAMMAR

Participles Used as Adjectives and Nouns

Perfect participles of many verbs came to be used as simple adjectives just as in English: **parātus,** "prepared," *ready;* **nōtus,** "known," *familiar.* A participle, like any adjective, may also be used as a noun: **factum** (n.), "a thing (having been) done," *a deed;* **nōtūs** (m.), "a man (having been) known," *an acquaintance.*

This is called the substantive use of an adjective. A *substantive* is a noun or any word that functions as a noun.

Conjugation of *Possum*

Possum is a compound of **sum** and is therefore irregular. It has no passive voice. Review the conjugation of **sum. Possum = pot(e) + sum. Pot-** becomes **pos-** before all forms of **sum** which begin with **s-.**

PRESENT

pos´sum	*I can, am able*	**pos´sumus**	*we can, are able*
po´tes	*you can, are able*	**potes´tis**	*you can, are able*
po´test	*he/she/it can, is able*	**pos´sunt**	*they can, are able*

IMPERFECT

po´teram	*I could, was able*	**poterā´mus**	*we could, were able*
po´terās	*you could, were able*	**poterā´tis**	*you could, were able*
po´terat	*he/she/it could, was able*	**po´terant**	*they could, were able*

FUTURE

po´terō	*I shall be able*	**pote´rimus**	*we shall be able*
po´teris	*you will be able*	**pote´ritis**	*you will be able*
po´terit	*he/she/it will be able*	**po´terunt**	*they will be able*

Potuī (perf.), **potueram** (plup.), and **potuerō** (fut. perf.) are conjugated like other regular verbs.

Complementary Infinitive

Possum is regularly used with an infinitive that completes its meaning: **Paucōs hominēs in īnsulā cernere poteram.** *I was able to (could) discern few people on the island.* **Certē bellum ac perīculum nōn possunt sustinērī.** *Surely war and danger cannot be endured.* Infinitives that complete the meaning of another verb are often called *complementary.*

Oral Practice

1. Give the form and the meaning of **potuerās, poterātis, potuērunt, possunt, poterit, posse.**
2. Translate *you could* (sing.), *they had been able, we shall be able, he can, they could.*

◼ *Exercises*

A. Translate the following sentences into English.

1. Amīcus certus in malā fortūnā cernitur.
2. "Facta, nōn verba" sententia nostra esse dēbet.
3. Linguam Latīnam et legere et scrībere possum.
4. Perīcula vītae bonum hominem commovēre nōn poterunt.
5. Facta clārārum semper nōta erunt et laudābuntur.
6. Ante bellum patria nostra nōn parāta erat, nam paucōs mīlitēs habēbāmus.

B. Translate the following sentences into Latin.

1. Few (people) can neither read nor write.
2. My motto is: "Always ready." Is it yours (sing.)? I ask you.
3. They had not been able to come on account of the bad streets.
4. We came across the level fields, because the road was not familiar.

WORD STUDY

- Explain *commotion, certificate, notorious, tertiary.*

- Study the following English words and phrases borrowed from Latin.

datum (pl. **data**)	*a given point or fact*
erratum (pl. **errata**)	*error*
terra incognita	*an unknown land*
Te Deum.	*Thee, God (we praise);* the name of a hymn
Et tu, Brute.	*You too, Brutus.* (said by Caesar on receiving the deathblow from his friend Brutus)
de facto	*from* or *according to fact, actual;* as a **de facto** government, one which is actually in operation, even if not recognized as legal

- Translate **ante bellum.**

LESSON OBJECTIVES

- To read a letter from Rome to a soldier in Caesar's army
- To learn about participles used as clauses

PŪBLIA PŪBLIŌ SAL.

[An answer to the letter in Lesson XXXIX]

Adducta litterīs ā tē, Pūblī, in Galliā scrīptīs, respondēbō, nam multa rogāvistī. Multa nova sunt. Quid putās[1]? Quīntus noster fīliam tertiam Rūfī in mātrimōnium dūxit! Ego hoc[2] nōn prōvīdī; Quīntus mē nōn cōnsuluit. Tūne hoc prōvīdistī? Tenēsne memoriā puellam, parvam ac timidam? Nōn
5 iam timida est; nunc pulchra est, ā multīs amāta.

De Caesaris ducis ēgregiīs victōriīs scrīpsistī. Magnō cum studiō litterās tuās lēgī, nam ultima Gallia semper fuit terra nova et nōn mihi nōta. Dē Galliā paucī nūntiī vēnērunt, quī fugam Gallōrum nūntiāvērunt. Caesar victōriīs suīs[3] glōriam et fāmam mīlitum Rōmānōrum auxit et pācem effēcit.
10 Caesarī grātiam habēmus quod prō salūte nostrā pugnāvit. Gallōs in fugam datōs nōn iam timēbimus. Alpēs, quae inter nōs et Gallōs stant, nunc Rōmam ā perīculō dēfendunt, nam Gallī timidī trāns Alpēs mīlitēs nōn trānsportābunt. Gallīs mīlitēs trāductōs redūcere dūrum erit.

Sī Caesar mē cōnsulit, librum "Dē Bellō Gallicō" scrībere dēbet. Sī liber
15 ab eō[4] scrībētur, ā multīs hominibus legētur; etiam post spatium multōrum annōrum, cum cūrā et dīligentiā legētur.

Litterae tuae nōn longae erant. Cūr longās litterās nōn scrībis? Multa nova in terrīs ultimīs vīdistī atque vidēbis. Valē.

Footnotes:
[1] *think*
[2] *this*
[3] *his*
[4] *him*

Questions

1. What reasons does Publia give for replying to Publius' letter?
2. What girl does Quintus marry and what was she like?
3. What has Caesar accomplished in Gaul?
4. What does Publia think Caesar should do now and why?
5. What geographical barrier serves to protect Rome from her northern neighbors?
6. What complaint does Publia have about Publius' letters?

An illustration from a fifteenth-century French manuscript shows Julius Caesar's expeditionary force landing on the coast of Britain. The soldiers carry ladders with which to scale the high cliffs of white chalk visible in the background. Caesar's two invasions in Britain, in 55 and 54 B.C., did not result in permanent occupation but did reduce the threat to Rome from the Gauls, who had close alliances with the Britons.

▦ VOCABULARY

Nouns

fu´ga, -ae f. *flight*   [fugiō]
  in fu´gam dō, *put to flight,*
    cause to run away, make run
spa´tium, spa´tī n. *space, time*   (spacious, spatial)

Adjectives

ti´midus, -a, -um *shy*   (intimidate)
ul´timus, -a, -um *farthest, last*   (ultimate, ultimatum)

Verbs

addū´cō, addū´cere, addū´xī,   [dūcō]
  adduc´tus *lead to, influence*
cōn´sulō, cōnsu´lere, cōnsu´luī,   (consultant,
  cōnsul´tus *consult*   consultation)
prōvi´deō, prōvidē´re, prōvī´dī,
  prōvī´sus *foresee, see ahead*   [videō]

Adverb

nōn iam *no longer*

GRAMMAR

Participles Used as Clauses

The participle, although not used much in English, is very common in Latin. Often it is best translated by a subordinate clause, introduced in English by *who* or *which, when* or *after, since* or *because, although* or *if.* The sense of the Latin sentence as a whole must be considered in choosing which conjunction *(when, since, after,* etc.) or pronoun *(who* or *which)* to introduce before the participle. Think of the participle's literal meaning before trying to expand it into a clause. The translations in the following sentences show various ways a Latin participle can be translated.

Relative	**Pecūniam amissam invēnit.**	*He found the money which had been lost.* (literally, *the lost money*)
Temporal (time)	**Convocātī puerī verba magistrī audient.**	*After they have been called together,* the boys *will hear the words of the teacher.* (literally, *having been called together*)
	Librum lēctum tibi dabō.	*Once it has been read, I shall give the book to you.* (literally, *the book read*)
Causal	**Territī nōn processērunt.**	*Because they were scared, they did not advance.* (literally, *having been scared*)
Adversative	**Territī nōn fūgērunt.**	*Although they were scared, they did not flee.* (literally, *having been scared*)

Observe that the perfect participle denotes time before that of the main verb. Like an adjective, it agrees with a noun or pronoun (sometimes not expressed) in gender, number, and case.

Oral Practice

Give the Latin for the italicized words.

1. Nūntiōs *(who had been sent away)* petīvistī.
2. Liber bonus *(if read)* semper amīcus vērus erit.
3. Numerus librōrum *(which I had consulted)* magnus fuit.
4. Multōs librōs lēgī *(because I had been influenced)* ā magistrīs meīs.
5. Nōnne magnum est pretium ultimae casae *(which was shown to me by you)?*

▦ *Exercises*

A. Translate the following sentences into English.

1. Perīculum prōvīsum nōs nōn terruit.
2. Rōmānī multa oppida occupāta relīquērunt.
3. Monitī vōs dē perīculō cōnsulere nōn poterāmus.
4. Pecūnia, ā mē in viā āmissa, ab amīcō meō inventa est.
5. Malus puer, ab amīcīs monitus, verbīs addūcī nōn potest.

B. Translate the following sentences into Latin.

1. I have read the letter written by my son.
2. I saw the girl who had been scared by you. (Express in two ways.)
3. The boys read the book because they had been influenced by the teacher's words. (Express in two ways.)

Did You Know?

Out of eighty high-quality wines known to the Romans, two-thirds of them were produced in Italy. The best grapes were grown south of Rome in Latium, Campania, and on the rich volcanic slopes of Mt. Vesuvius. Much agricultural knowledge was devoted to winemaking and viticulture, and by the first century A.D. Italian wines had become famous as far away as India.

WORD STUDY

Roots In Lesson XLI we saw that a number of Latin words came into English as a result of the Roman occupation of Britain. Other examples are *wall* (from **vāllum**), together with place names like *Walton* (Walltown); *port* (from **portus,** *harbor*) together with place names like *Portsmouth; street* (from **strāta**); *Lincoln* (from **colōnia,** *colony);* cf. *Cologne,* the name of a German city that was an ancient Roman colony.

A century and a half after the Angles and Saxons settled in England, Pope Gregory sent missionaries to convert the island to Christianity. Since the missionaries spoke Latin, they introduced a number of new Latin words into English, especially words dealing with the Church, as *temple* (**templum**), *disciple* (**discipulus**), *bishop* (**episcopus**).

Explain *cologne, Stratford, antecedent, relic, providence.*

Ultima Thule was a phrase the Romans used for the "Farthest North." This explains why a major United States base on Greenland was named Thule. Columbus was inspired by a prophecy of the Roman poet Seneca that *new worlds* (**novōs orbēs**) would be discovered and Thule would no longer be **Ultima Thule.**

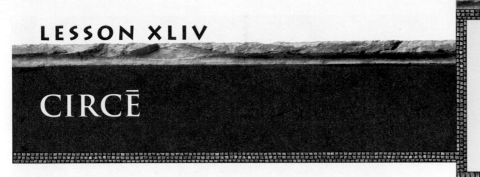

CIRCĒ

[After Ulysses left the land of the Lotus-eaters and the Cyclopes, he encountered the sorceress Circe *(Sir´se)*.]

Siciliā relīctā, Ulixēs ad rēgnum Aeolī, rēgis ventōrum, nāvigāvit, quī Ulixī ventōs malōs in saccō ligātōs dedit et dīxit: "Malīs ventīs ligātīs, nōn iam impediēris et in patriā tuā salūtem inveniēs."

Itaque multōs diēs[1] Graecī sine impedīmentō et sine cūrā nāvigāvērunt. Ūnō ventō amīcō āctī sunt, reliquīs ligātīs. Iam Ithacam clārē cernunt. Sed 5 nautae dē saccō cūrā affectī sunt quod dē ventīs quī in saccō erant nihil[2] audīverant. "Praemia et pecūnia in saccō sunt," nauta dīxit. "Rēx Ulixēs nautīs quī mala sustinuērunt pecūniam dare dēbet." Itaque, saccō apertō[3], ventī expedītī Graecōs ad rēgnum Aeolī redēgērunt. Sed nōn iam Aeolus auxilium dat. Ūnam nāvem[4] Graecī nunc habent, reliquīs āmissīs. 10

Nunc, impedīmentīs relīctīs, ad īnsulam veniunt quam Circē pulchra regēbat. Vīgintī[5] hominēs, ab Ulixe ad rēgīnam missī, pācem praesidiumque lēgum petīvērunt. Ab Eurylochō[6] duce per silvam pedibus ductī sunt ad rēgīnam, quae eōs[7] in animālia[8] vertit. Eurylochus sōlus[9] in animal nōn versus ad nāvem fūgit et Ulixī omnia[10] dē sociīs impedītīs nūntiāvit. Ulixēs 15 commōtus cum reliquīs auxilium sociīs pressīs dare mātūrāvit. In viā Mercurium deum vīsum cōnsuluit. Mercurius eum[11] monuit et herbam eī[12] dedit. "Hāc[13] herbā," inquit,[14] "vītam tuam servāre et mīlitēs tuōs expedīre poteris." Ulixēs rēgīnam iussit sociōs in hominēs vertere. Circē, Ulixis verbīs et factīs territa, animālia in hominēs vertit. Rēgīna, quae nōn iam 20 inimīca fuit, magnam cēnam ac cibum bonum parāvit; ita concordiam amīcitiamque redūxit. Sociīs expedītīs, annum ibi Ulixēs mānsit et vītam grātam ēgit. Tum, ā sociīs adductus, discessit.

[1] *days*
[2] *nothing*
[3] participle of **aperiō**, *open*
[4] *ship*
[5] *twenty*
[6] *Eurylochus (Ūrĭl´okus)*
[7] *them*
[8] acc. pl. n.
[9] *alone*
[10] *everything*
[11] *him*
[12] *to him*
[13] *with this*
[14] *he said*

Circe turns some of Ulysses' men into pigs.

The Bettmann Archive

Questions

1. What did Aeolus give Ulysses and why was it useful?
2. Why was Ulysses prevented from reaching Ithaca? What or who was responsible?
3. How many ships survived the storm?
4. How many people were sent to Circe and what was their mission?
5. What happened to them?
6. What was Eurylochus' role in the story?
7. How did Ulysses avoid being turned into an animal?
8. Who instructed Ulysses about how to deal with Circe?
9. What was Circe's response to Ulysses' request?
10. How long did Ulysses spend with Circe?

VOCABULARY

Nouns

impedīmen´tum, -ī n. *hindrance;*   [pēs]
   pl. *baggage*

pēs, pe´dis m. *foot*   (pedal, pedestrian)

rēg´num, -ī n. *kingdom, realm*   (interregnum)

rēx, rē´gis m. *king*   (regal, royal)

Verbs

expe´diō, expedī´re, expedī´vī,   [pēs]
   expedī´tus *set free*

impe´diō, impedī´re, impedī´vī,   [pēs]
   impedī´tus *hinder, obstruct*

li´gō, ligā´re, ligā´vī, ligā´tus *bind, tie*   (ligament, ligature)

ver´tō, ver´tere, ver´tī, ver´sus *turn*   (vertigo, versus)

GRAMMAR

Ablative Absolute

In English, we sometimes say, "This being the case, there is nothing I can do." Since such phrases as "This being the case" are used loosely and have little direct connection with either the subject or the predicate of the sentence, they are said to be in the *nominative absolute* (from Latin **absolūtus,** *untied, set free*), i.e., they are *free* in a grammatical sense from the rest of the sentence. The nominative absolute, in other words, outlines the circumstances or background against which the main action of the sentence takes place, like an adverbial clause.

In Latin, this construction is very common, with this difference: the ablative is used instead of the nominative. This loose use of the participial phrase in which its noun is not the same as the subject, object, or other word dependent upon the main verb, is therefore known as the *ablative absolute.* The perfect participle is most frequently used in this construction. Occasionally a noun, adjective, or present participle is used (examples follow).

Consider the participle's literal meaning before attempting to expand it into a clause beginning with *when, once, since, after, because, if, although* (see page 294) or an active participle.

1. **Officiō factō** (lit., *the duty having been done*), **dominus discessit.**   *After he did his duty, the master departed.*

2. **Puer, litterīs nōn missīs** (lit., *the letter not having been sent*), **pecūniam nōn accēpit.**   *Because he did not send the letter, the boy did not receive the money.*

3. **Dux, signō datō** (lit., *the signal having been given*), **prōcessit.**   *Having given the signal, the general advanced.*

4. **Oppidīs nostrīs captīs** (lit., *our towns captured*), **bellum gerēmus.**   *If our towns are captured, we shall wage war.*

In the first three sentences above, a natural English translation is achieved by converting from the Latin perfect passive participle to the English perfect active participle (which Latin does not have).

The sorceress Circe tries to drug the weary Ulysses, who looks fairly disoriented already. To the right is Circe's loom, showing the shuttle and the vertical strands of the weave, weighted down with loom weights. A cartoon on a vase of the fourth century B.C.

Department of Antiquities, Ashmolean Museum, Oxford

When forms other than the perfect passive participle are used in the ablative absolute, the conversion to English is even simpler. Often you must supply a form of the verb *to be*. Understand the literal translation before attempting to expand the participial phrase into a clause.

Numā rēge, pācem habuimus.	*(When) Numa (was) king*, we had peace. (noun + noun)
Populō līberō, vīta grāta erit.	*(If) the people (are) free*, life will be pleasant. (noun + adjective)

How the Ablative Absolute Construction Differs From Other Uses of the Perfect Participle

When the participle can agree with (modify) a noun or pronoun in the main sentence, it does so, and the ablative absolute is not used. Compare the following sentences.

Servus monitus territus est.	*The slave, having been warned, was terrified.*
Dominus servum monitum terruit.	*The master terrified the slave he had warned* (lit., *the having-been-warned slave*).

But with the ablative absolute:

Servō monitō et territō, dominus familiam dīmīsit.	*Having warned and terrified the slave* (lit., *the slave having been warned and terrified*), *the master dismissed the household.*

It is always better to begin by considering the literal meaning of the words in their context. Often by inserting the words *being* or *having been,* you can determine the general meaning of the sentence. The next step, if necessary, is to turn the idea into the English clause that makes the best sense.

Oral Practice

Identify which of the following are ablative absolutes and which are not. Then translate the words in italics.

1. This boy, *sent* to visit his aunt, lost his way.
2. After the boy *had been freed,* everyone was happy.
3. *After* the money *was given,* the boy was returned to his parents.
4. The boys *having been compelled* to stop fighting, the principal went back to her office.
5. *Having read* the books, we returned them to the library.
6. *After putting* the prisoner in jail, the policewoman went home.

▦ *Exercises*

A. Translate the following sentences. Distinguish the ablative absolute from other uses of the participle.

1. Librō āmissō, puella legere nōn potuit.
2. Dux servōrum, signō datō, equōs ēdūcī iussit.
3. Expedītī ē perīculō, deīs grātiās agere dēbēmus.
4. Rōmānī, castrīs positīs, Gallōs ad fugam vertērunt.
5. Captīvī miserī, trāctī ad pedēs rēgis, pācem timidē petēbant.
6. Impedīmentīs in oppidō relīctīs, mīlitēs salūtem petīvērunt.
7. Librīs lēctīs, discipulī magistrum aequō animō exspectāvērunt.
8. Hominēs, praedā armīsque impedītī, properāre nōn poterant.

B. Translate the following sentences into Latin. Which of the four does not require the ablative absolute?

1. Having written good letters, the boys will receive rewards.
2. Hindered on account of bad roads, we did not wish to come on foot.
3. Since the advice of the teacher has been heard, we shall read the book.
4. After sending a messenger to the gate, the king shouted: "My kingdom for (**prō** + abl.) a horse!"

Did You Know?

The Romans enjoyed many of the herbs and spices that we enjoy today. Poppy seeds were eaten with honey for dessert or sprinkled over a mushroom-shaped bread before baking. Indian pepper and cinnamon were also important to the Roman haute cuisine. A dish from an existing Roman cookbook lists these herbs for a roast meat sauce: pepper, lovage, parsley, celery seed, dill, asafoetida root, hazelwort, turmeric, caraway, cumin, and ginger.

WORD STUDY

Derivatives Latin words should not always be studied individually but can often be grouped together by *families,* so to speak. This is much easier, much more useful, and much more interesting. For example, there is the word **pēs,** the father of its family. **Pēs** has many derivatives in both English and Latin. **Im-pediō** means *to entangle the feet.* An *impediment* is a *tangle,* something in the way. Transportation is still a big problem with an army; it is no wonder that the Romans, without railroads, aircraft, or trucks, called the baggage train of the army **impedīmenta. Ex-pediō** means *to free the foot from a tangle;* therefore in English an *expedient* is a means of solving a difficulty. To *expedite* matters is to hurry them along by removing obstacles.

You have already become acquainted with several other "families" of words. Other words which should be studied in groups are **rēgīna, regō, rēgnum,** and **rēx; dō** and **dōnō; dūcō** and **dux; ager** and **agricola; cōnsulō** and **cōnsilium.** Show how the members of these families are related.

What is the meaning of *ligature, ligament, obligation, pedestrian?* Why was *Aeolus* chosen as the name of a company dealing in ventilators? What do you really mean when you say "I am much *obliged*"?

AMUSEMENTS AND SPORTS

Roman children enjoyed playing games just as children do today. Babies had their rattles; girls had their dolls; and boys played various kinds of marble games with nuts. The phrase **rēlinquere nucēs** (*to give up nuts*) meant to grow up, but adult men, even the Emperor Augustus, sometimes played such games. Vacation was the time for marble games. The poet Martial says: "Sadly the boy leaves his marbles and is called back to school by the teacher—the Saturnalia (December) vacation is all over."

Other amusements for children included spinning tops, walking on stilts, flying kites, rolling hoops, and playing with toy wagons and toy soldiers. Among Roman children's games were also blindman's buff, hide and seek, leapfrog, and jacks. Ball games, some like today's tennis and handball, were favorites, especially for men who played them at the large public baths.

For indoor amusement the Romans had a board game which was something like chess and checkers, and another like the many games we have in which the throwing of dice controls the number of moves made on a board. A game called knucklebones, **tālī,** was played with knucklebones and dice-like pieces, **tesserae,** that had numbers on each side.

Roman boys and men had their sports: swimming, fishing, hunting, as well as athletic contests—running, jumping, throwing the discus and javelin, boxing, wrestling, and fencing. Most of these activities were useful training for a soldier.

Araldo de Luca/CORBIS

A toy horse and rider, designed to be pulled by a string. It hardly differs from a modern version, except in longevity.

The chief amusements for the Roman people as a whole were the circus, the gladiatorial shows, and the theater. The oldest and most popular was the circus with its races. Although the races were the main event, gradually various side shows and acrobatic exhibitions were added to entertain between races. The modern circus is a revival of the ancient circus, but the chariot races no longer have the same prominence. Even the circus parade that precedes the performance today is borrowed from the Romans, who called it a **pompa.**

The circus games were held at public expense on holidays. They took place in the valley between the Palatine and Aventine hills. Originally the people sat on the hillsides; later, magnificent stands seating as many as two hundred thousand people were built. Other circuses were built in Rome and elsewhere, but the original Circus Maximus remained the chief one.

The games created as much interest as our professional baseball, football, tennis, and hockey. There were various racing companies, distinguished by their colors, like those in modern schools and colleges and professional teams. Successful drivers were slaves or freedmen who became popular heroes and often won their freedom and became rich. Their records and those of the horses were carefully kept. One man, Pompeius Muscosus, is said to have won 3559 races. This attention is much like that we give to the number of home runs made by famous major league baseball players today.

The theater was another important place for outdoor amusement. Adaptions of Greek custom, Roman theaters were semicircular. The actors usually wore masks that indicated what part each actor was playing. As in Shakespeare's time, women's parts were played by men. Comedies, tragedies, farces, and pantomimes were given. The most famous Roman writers of comedies were Plautus and Terence, whose plays are not only still being performed but also have been turned into Broadway hits—*The Boys from Syracuse* and *A Funny Thing Happened on the Way to the Forum*.

The Roman amphitheater in France, at Arles, where the magistrates held athletic contests and games in its arena estimated to have held about twenty thousand people. It is still in use. Arles was one of the most important cities of Roman Gaul.

GLIMPSES OF ROMAN LIFE

AMUSEMENTS AND SPORTS (CONTINUED)

The gladiatorial contests were rather late importations from Etruria, the region to the north of Rome. At first, they consisted of sword fights at funerals between two men who were often slaves. Later on they became very popular, and fights between men and animals (like Spanish bull-fights) were added, as well as fights between animals. Sometimes very elaborate shows were staged in open-air amphitheaters. The most famous amphitheater was the Coliseum at Rome that had room for fifty thousand spectators. It was not built until A.D. 80 and was large enough and durable enough to eliminate the need for another amphitheater in the city.

QUESTIONS

1. What modern sports compare with the circus games of the Romans in popular appeal?
2. In what ways did the Roman theater differ from ours?
3. What were the good and bad features of the gladiatorial contests?

This stone relief shows Roman children playing a game. One game they liked to play was similar to bowling, but they rolled a walnut at walnut "castles" built up on the ground.

Erich Lessing/Art Resource, NY

VOCABULARY

Nouns

dux	lēx	rēx
factum	mīles	salūs
fuga	pāx	spatium
homō	pēs	
impedīmentum	rēgnum	

Adjectives

certus	parātus	timidus
nōtus	tertius	ultimus

Verbs

addūcō	cōnsulō	premō	trādūcō
antecēdō	expediō	prōvideō	trānsportō
cernō	impediō	relinquō	vertō
clāmō	ligō	rogō	vīvō
commoveō	possum	stō	vulnerō

Adverbs

fortasse	nōn iam

GRAMMAR SUMMARY

Third Declension: Masculine and Feminine Nouns

Third declension nouns that are masculine or feminine in gender are declined with the following case endings:

(sing.) —, **-is, -ī, -em, -e**; (pl.) **-ēs, -um, -ibus, -ēs, -ibus**. These endings are added to the base of the word, obtained by taking the case ending **-is** off the genitive singular. The nominative (often ending in **-s** or **-x**) must be learned separately, as must the gender of third declension words.

Salūtem mīlitum nostrōrum auxit.	*He increased the safety of our soldiers.*
Salūs rēgis timidī erat certa.	*The safety of the timid king was assured.*
Tertius homō ducem meum antecessit.	*A third man went before my leader.*

The Conjugation of Possum

The verb **possum**, a compound of **sum**, is somewhat irregular in the present, where its stem (**pot-**) changes to **pos-** before a following **s**: **possum, possumus, possunt**. The imperfect and future use the **pot-** stem plus forms of **sum**. The perfect tenses are regular.

Ad casam tuam venīre nōn possum.	*I am not able to (cannot) come to your house.*
Rēx multa perīcula prōvidēre poterat.	*The king was able to (could) see many dangers ahead.*

Participles Used as Clauses

The perfect passive participle is often used to replace a whole clause in Latin. The English equivalent uses a clause beginning with *when, after, because, since, if, although*—whatever conjunction makes the best sense. The participle agrees with the noun that it is describing in gender, number, and case.

| **Ventīs territī, nautae relinquī cupīvērunt.** | *(Since they were) terrified by the winds, the sailors wanted to be left behind.* |
| **Pūblius rogāvit dē captīvīs expedītīs.** | *Publius asked about the captives (who had been) freed.* |

Ablative Absolute

The ablative absolute construction most often consists of two words: a noun and a noun, a noun and an adjective, or a noun and a participle (usually a perfect passive participle). These two words are in the ablative case, set off from the rest of the sentence by commas, and only loosely connected to it grammatically.

| **Portā clausā, hostēs fugere nōn potuērunt.** | *After the gate was closed, the enemies were unable to flee.* |
| **Nāvibus āmissīs, Ulixēs miser erat.** | *Since the ships had been lost (The ships having been lost), Ulysses was unhappy.* |

Absolute Construction

IN LATIN	IN ENGLISH
1. Ablative	1. Nominative
2. Perfect passive participle usually	2. Present or past active or passive participle
3. Construction very common	3. Construction much less common

UNIT PRACTICE

A. Give the Latin for the italicized words.
1. Perīcula *(if foreseen)* mē nōn terrent.
2. Librum *(after I had read it)* amīcō dōnāvī.
3. Puerī *(although they were called)* nōn vēnērunt.
4. Puellae *(because they had been scared)* fūgērunt.
5. Auxilium *(which had been furnished)* ā sociīs nostrīs patriam cōnservāvit.

B. Translate the ablative absolute in each of the following sentences into natural English.
1. **Litterīs scrīptīs,** I took a walk.
2. **Rēgnō āmissō,** he was still king.
3. **Auxiliō missō,** they can still win.
4. **Agrīs occupātīs,** the people were starving.

C. Do the following.
1. Decline **rēx magnus, lēx bona, spatium lātum.**
2. What is the case of **ducum, hominī, mīlitibus, disciplīnae, pācem?**
3. Give in all tenses the third plural of **possum,** translating each tense form.
4. Give the principal parts of **commoveō, dō, expediō, submittō, absum, prōpōnō, premō.**

Numerals Review

1. The teacher assigns a number—**Ūnus, Duo, Trēs,** etc., to each of ten students. The following questions and others like them should be answered by the student whose number furnishes the correct answer.

> **MAGISTER:** Quot *(how many?)* sunt trēs et quattuor?
> **DISCIPULUS "SEPTEM":** Trēs et quattuor sunt septem.
> **M.:** Quot sunt quattuor et quīnque?
> **D. "NOVEM":** Quattuor et quīnque sunt novem.
> (A competitive game can be made by having two sets of ten or less and scoring one for the side whose representative answers first.)

2. Give the Latin word for the missing numeral represented by the question mark.
   a. III + V = ?
   b. XII ÷ III = ?
   c. IV + ? = X
   d. II × V = ?
   e. X − ? = VIII
   f. VI − I = ?

WORD STUDY

1. Make a sketch map of England (not including Scotland) and indicate on it all the names you can of towns derived from Latin **castra.** Then see how many of these town names are found in the United States.

2. The first word in each of the following groups is a Latin word. From among the last five words pick the one which is an English derivative of the first word.

stāre	status	stair	stare
	star	staff	
hominī	homely	home	hominy
	homicide	hum	
mīles	mile	militant	mill
	millinery	million	
premō	supreme	premises	premonition
	express	prime	
clāmō	clam	clamp	clammy
	inclement	exclaim	
pāx	pace	packs	Pacific
	impact	pass	

UNIT VIII ASSESSMENT

LESSONS XL–XLIV

VOCABULARY

Circle the word that best completes each sentence.

1. Dux in viā _____ et mīlitēs spectāre poterat.
   a. ligāre
   b. premere
   c. relinquere
   d. stāre

2. Homō in parvō oppidō _____ erat, quod prō populō multa bona fēcerat.
   a. certus
   b. nōtus
   c. tertius
   d. ultimus

3. _____ vulnerātīs, servī portam mūnīre et locum dēfendere mātūrābant.
   a. Rēgis
   b. Rēgīnā
   c. Dominō
   d. Mīlitibus

4. Quid studium līberōrum _____?
   a. clāmābit
   b. cōnsulet
   c. impediet
   d. cernet

5. Populus _____ magnā cum dīligentiā cūrāque cōnservāre dēbet.
   a. fugam
   b. lēgēs
   c. pāce
   d. salūs

GRAMMAR

Complete each sentence with the correct endings.

6. Adductī fām___ locī, pauc___ nautae ad ultim___ īnsul___ antecesserant, et ibi in animō reman___ habuērunt.

7. Verb___ poetae audītīs, quae puellae lingu___ pulchrā nōn commōt___ ____?

8. Post spati___ quattuor ann___ dux octō mīlit___ in castr___ relīquit et reliquōs ē prōvinci___ trādūxit.

9. Certē, mea fīli___, perīcul___ prōvidēs et crās cum amīc___ tuīs salūt___ pet___.

10. Qu___ cūrae nunc vōs prem___? Poteritisne ad oppid___ ven___ et hōram pāc___ nōbīscum inven___?

TRANSLATION

Translate the following sentences.

11. Cōnsiliīs parātīs, per terram barbaram impedīmenta trānsportāre nōn dubitāmus.

12. "Vulnerāvistīne pedem tuum in proeliō aut fugā?" mīles timidum amīcum rogābat.

13. Fortasse puellam quae in tertiā casā habitat dē officiīs novīs cōnsulam.

14. Expedīta ex officiīs, tibi longās litterās scrībere poterō; tē dē rēgnō et factīs rēgis docēbō.

15. Verbīs deae commōtī erant et nōn iam in īnsulā manēre sed ad patriam novam migrāre cupīvērunt.

INVESTIGATION

Find the answers to these questions from any lesson in Unit VIII.

16. A long narrative poem, such as the *Aeneid* or *Odyssey,* that tells the tale of a hero struggling against odds is called an _____ poem.

17. City names such as Rochester, Lancaster, Worcester, and Chester are based on the Latin word _____ meaning _____ because the Romans established these places throughout England.

18. Briefly identify these characters from the *Odyssey.*
   a. Polyphemus
   b. Aeolus
   c. Circe

19. True or false? The ancient Romans enjoyed adding spices and herbs to their food.

20. Who were Plautus and Terence?

CULTURE

Vērum aut Falsum? Indicate whether each statement is true or false.

21. Gladiatorial contests began as a part of funeral ceremonies.

22. Among the spectator entertainments of gladiatorial games, chariot races, and theater, chariot racing was most popular.

23. Many personal Roman sports were introduced because they helped train men in military skills.

24. Most parts in the Roman theater were played by women.

25. **Tālī** was a Roman marble game.

FROM LATIN TO ENGLISH

Apply your knowledge of Latin roots to determine the best meaning of the italicized words.

26. Her committee tried to *expedite* the process.
   a. hinder
   b. begin
   c. accelerate
   d. understand

27. We will *relinquish* our claim to that land.
   a. insist upon
   b. give up
   c. bargain for
   d. reestablish

28. After the accident he experienced several periods of *vertigo.*
   a. dizziness
   b. depression
   c. fear
   d. soreness

29. Cornelia wished to *discern* the importance of the letter.
   a. disregard
   b. argue about
   c. explain
   d. see clearly

30. Does the new exercise have any *salutary* effect?
   a. healthful
   b. long-lasting
   c. harmful
   d. controversial

THE ADVENTURES OF ULYSSES, ROMULUS, REMUS, AND PYRRHUS

Unit Objectives

- To learn the forms of third declension neuter nouns
- To learn the third declension **i**-stem nouns of all genders
- To learn the forms of third declension adjectives
- To learn how the context of a Latin word can change its basic meaning
- To learn about the ablative of respect
- To learn more about Greek and Roman legends and history
- To learn about Roman food and meals

Ulysses at the court of King Alcinous in Phaeacia. At the left, King Alcinous commands the blind minstrel Demodocus to stop recounting the woes of the Greeks at Troy, since Ulysses *(center)* cannot control his grief. The rest of the court is amazed to see so brave a hero weep.

Gianni Dagli Orti/Palazzo Reale Milan/The Art Archive

SĪRĒNĒS ET PHAEĀCIA

LESSON OBJECTIVES
- To learn more about the travels of Ulysses
- To learn the forms of third declension neuter nouns

Annō in īnsulā quam Circē rēxit āctō, Ulixēs ad Sīrēnēs[1] vēnit. Sīrēnēs corpora avium[2] et capita puellārum habuērunt. Carmina pulchra canēbant[3], quibus nautae mōtī nāvēs ad saxa[4] vertēbant. Hōc[5] modō vītam āmittēbant.

Sed Ulixēs dē Sīrēnibus ā Circē[6] monitus erat. Perīculō prōvīsō, aurēs[7]
5 sociōrum cērā[8] clausit sed nōn suās[9]. Iussit manūs[10] pedēsque suōs[9] ad nāvem ligārī. Hōc modō carmina Sīrēnum clārē audīvit neque vītam āmīsit.

Posteā sociī Ulixis interfectī sunt, et Ulixēs sōlus ad īnsulam parvam āctus est in quā habitābat rēgīna pulchra cui[11] nōmen erat Calypsō. Rēgīna Ulixem nōn dīmīsit. Itaque Ulixēs ibi octō annōs—longum temporis
10 spatium—remānsit. Sed tum Iuppiter rēgīnam iussit Ulixī nāvem parāre. Hōc factō, Ulixēs expedītus rēgīnam relīquit.

Sed nāvis undīs frācta est ad īnsulam cui[11] nōmen erat Phaeācia[12]. Vulneribus impedītus, homō miser vix[13] corpus in silvam fīnitimam ad flūmen trahere potuit, ubi somnum[14] cēpit.

15 Interim Nausicaa[15], fīlia rēgis Phaeāciae, cum aliīs[16] puellīs carrō ad flūmen prōcēdēbat, quod in flūmine vestēs lavāre[17] cupīvit; nam tempus mātrimōnī Nausicaae aderat. Ubi vestēs in flūmine lāvērunt, labōre intermissō, Nausicaa pilam[18] ad reliquās puellās in ōrdine iaciēbat. Sed puella quaedam[19] in flūmen pilam iēcit. Clāmōribus puellārum ab Ulixe
20 audītīs, Ulixēs nōn dubitāvit sed pilam ex aquā servāvit. Puellae timidae fugere incipiunt quod is ob mala atque vulnera quae sustinuerat nōn iam pulcher erat. Sed Nausicaa nōn territa ante Ulixem stetit et eī[20] grātiās ēgit. Vestibus plicātīs, ad oppidum in ōrdine prōcessērunt. Ulixēs ab rēge Alcinoō[21] acceptus est, cui factīs clārīs nōtus fuit. Paucōs diēs Ulixēs in
25 Phaeāciā mānsit. Tum Alcinous Ulixem ad patriam Ithacam mīsit. Itaque post vīgintī annōs Ulixēs sōlus sine sociīs ad patriam vēnit.

Ulixe in Ithacā vīsō, Neptūnus nāvem in quā Ulixēs trānsportātus erat ante portum Phaeāciae in saxum[22] vertit. Portus īnsulae hōc[5] impedīmentō clausus est neque posteā Alcinous et hominēs īnsulae nāvigāre potuērunt.

1 the Sī´rens
2 of birds
3 would sing
4 rocks (acc. pl. neut.)
5 this (abl.)
6 ablative
7 ears (fem.)
8 wax
9 his (own)
10 hands
11 whose (lit., to whom, to which)
12 Fēā´shia
13 barely
14 sleep
15 Nausic´ää
16 other
17 wash clothes
18 ball
19 one girl
20 to him
21 Alcinous (Alsin´ous) (abl.)
22 a rock

Questions

1. What did the Sirens look like?
2. What special power did their songs have?
3. By whom had Ulysses been warned?
4. How did Ulysses manage to hear the Sirens without danger?
5. Whose island was Ulysses driven to next?
6. How long did he remain there?
7. Who ordered the queen to get a ship ready for Ulysses?
8. What happened to the ship and where?
9. Who found Ulysses and in what condition was he?
10. What was the special occasion for which the king's daughter was washing clothes?
11. What were the girls doing when they encountered the man?
12. Why did Nausicaa thank Ulysses?
13. How long did Ulysses remain with King Alcinous?
14. For how many years had Ulysses been away from Ithaca?
15. What happened to the Phaeacian ship in which Ulysses sailed? What happened to the Phaeacians' port?

Ulysses, tied to his mast by his men, listens to the Siren's song. (You can see, to the right, the flute played by one Siren.) To the left, another Siren, her body covered with feathers, holds up a tempting delicacy, a lobster. Around the ship swim fish and dolphins. Part of a mosaic from Cherchel, Tunisia.

Ronald Sheridan/Ancient Art & Architecture Collection

Puellae timidae fugere incipiunt. The helmeted goddess Minerva watches Ulysses come out of the water. Nausicaa looks ready to run.

VOCABULARY

Nouns

ca´put, ca´pitis n. *head*   (capital, chief)

car´men, car´minis n. *song*

clā´mor, clāmō´ris m. *noise, shouting*   **[clāmō]**

cor´pus, cor´poris n. *body*   (corporation, corpse)

flū´men, flū´minis n. *river*   (fluid, flume)

nō´men, nō´minis n. *name*   (nominate, nominative)

ōr´dō, ōr´dinis m. *order, rank, row*   (inordinate, ordinary)

tem´pus, tem´poris n. *time*   (temporal, temporary)

vul´nus, vul´neris n. *wound*   (vulnerable)

Verbs

clau´dō, clau´dere, clau´sī, clau´sus *close*   (clause, include)

ia´ciō, ia´cere, iē´cī, iac´tus *throw, hurl*   (project, subject)

GRAMMAR

Third Declension: Neuter Nouns

	ENDINGS		EXAMPLE	
	SINGULAR	PLURAL	SINGULAR	PLURAL
Nominative	—	-a	corpus	corpora
Genitive	-is	-um	corporis	corporum
Dative	-ī	-ibus	corporī	corporibus
Accusative	—	-a	corpus	corpora
Ablative	e	-ibus	corpore	corporibus

In the third declension, as in the second, the nominative and accusative singular forms of neuter nouns are alike. The nominative and accusative plural both end in **-a.** These two rules hold true for all neuter nouns, regardless of their declension. The vocative, singular and plural, is like the nominative.

Oral Practice

1. Decline **nōmen clarum.**
2. Tell the form(s) of **flūminum, capita, tempus, lēgēs, vulnerī, nōmine, carminis.**

Did You Know?

The Romans had several kinds of bread but did not eat bread with butter. Some of these breads were suet bread, honey and oil bread, cheese bread, large, grainy Cilician loaves, wafer bread, a soft and salty raised bread called Cappadocian, pancakes, rolls baked on a spit, and square loaves flavored with oil, aniseed, and cheese. Roman bakers even made cookies for dogs!

▦ *Exercises*

A. Translate the following sentences into English.
  1. Quae nōmina flūminum Galliae cognōvistis?
  2. Corpore hominis inventō, mīles ducem vocāvit.
  3. Ob tempus annī frūmentum trānsportāre nōn poterāmus.
  4. Litterae variae quās scrīpsistī mittī crās poterunt.
  5. Rēx, victōriā barbarōrum territus, mīlitēs trāns flūmen trādūxit.

B. Translate the following sentences into Latin.
  1. The river that you see is wide.
  2. Horses have large bodies but small heads.
  3. There were many wounds on the farmer's body.
  4. Since the river is closed, grain can no longer be transported.

WORD STUDY

- Many English words preserve the original Latin forms of the third declension.

SINGULAR	PLURAL
amanuensis	*amanuenses*
apex	*apexes* or *apices*
appendix	*appendixes* or *appendices*
genus	*genera*
index	*indexes* or *indices*
insigne (rare)	*insignia*
stamen	*stamens* or *stamina* (with difference in meaning)
vertex	*vertexes* or *vertices*
	viscera (singular rare)

Nouns with their plurals in **-s** are *consul, ratio,* and many nouns in **-or**: *doctor, actor, factor, labor, victor,* etc.

- Explain *contemporary, invulnerable, decapitate, capitalism, capital punishment.* What is a *corporation?* What is meant by *incorporated*? State two ways in which *siren* is used today.

- There is a town named *Calypso* in North Carolina.

PĒNELOPĒ

LESSON OBJECTIVES
- To read about Ulysses' return to Ithaca and Penelope
- To learn the forms of third declension **i**-stem nouns

Ulixēs, nāvī et sociīs āmissīs, corpore vulneribus cōnfectō, in patriam pervēnerat. Ad fīnem itineris sed nōn labōrum perpetuōrum vēnerat. Et cīvēs et hostēs crēdidērunt[1] Ulixem nōn iam vīvum esse.

Prīmus quī Ulixem vīdit sed nōn cognōvit erat pāstor cuius nōmen erat Eumaeus. Ab Eumaeō Ulixēs nōn pauca dē uxōre[2] Pēnelopē et fīliō 5 Tēlemachō audīvit. Tēlemachus ab īnsulā tum aberat quod Pēnelopē eum[3] trāns mare ad ultima rēgna cīvitātēsque[4] Gracciae mīserat, in quibus locīs itinera faciebat et Ulixem petēbat. Per multōs annōs nūllam fāmam dē Ulixe Pēnelopē accēperat. Interim[5] multī ducēs rēgēsque, cupiditāte[6] rēgnī Ulixis adductī, dē montibus Ithacae et ē īnsulīs fīnitimīs convēnerant et rēgīnam in 10 mātrimōnium petēbant. Cīvēs hōs[7] hostēs ē fīnibus Ithacae sine auxiliō ad montēs redigere nōn poterant. Itaque Pēnelopē, capite submissō, dīxit:

"Ubi vestem quam faciō cōnfēcerō, nōn iam dubitābō in mātrimōnium darī."

Itaque exspectāvērunt. Sed cōnsilium Pēnelopae fuit tempus trahere. 15 Itaque nocte retexēbat[8] vestem quam multā dīligentiā texuerat. Post trēs

[1] *believed*
[2] *wife*
[3] *him*
[4] *states, city-states*
[5] *meanwhile*
[6] *by desire (for)*
[7] *these*
[8] *unwove*

National Gallery, London/SuperStock

Post trēs annōs hominēs cōnsilium Penelopae cognōvērunt, et Pēnelopē vestem cōnficere coācta est. A steadfast Penelope works at her loom while several suitors, dressed as Renaissance dandies, express their impatience and dissatisfaction at her progress. Above her head is Ulysses' deadly bow, and outside the window is the ship that has brought him back to Ithaca.

annōs hominēs cōnsilium Pēnelopae cognōvērunt, et Pēnelopē vestem cōnficere coācta est.

Hōc[9] tempore Ulixēs nāvī ad īnsulam Ithacam trānsportātus est. Eōdem[10]
20 tempore Tēlemachus, ā Minervā monitus, in patriam properāvit. Ibi ad mare ab Ulixe vīsus atque cognitus est. Ulixēs Tēlemachum ad oppidum antecēdere iussit. Ab Ulixe monitus, Tēlemachus neque mātrī neque aliīs[11] dē patre nūntiāvit.

[9] at this
[10] at the same
[11] to others, i.e., anyone else

Questions

1. How many allies did Ulysses have when he reached Ithaca?
2. What was the prevailing belief about Ulysses at the time of his arrival?
3. Who was the first to meet him?
4. For what purpose had Telemachus been sent away from Ithaca?
5. What motive did kings and leaders on the island have for seeking the hand of Penelope in marriage?
6. What did local citizens attempt to do about the aggressive steps taken by these suitors?
7. What promise did Penelope make to hold them off and how long did that work?
8. What caused Telemachus to return?
9. Whom did Telemachus meet upon his return?
10. What instructions did Ulysses give his son?

▦ VOCABULARY

Nouns

***cī´vis,**[12] **cī´vis, cī´vium** m. or f. *citizen*	(civic, civil)
***fī´nis, fī´nis, fī´nium** m. *end;* pl. *borders, territory*	(final, finite)
***hos´tis, hos´tis, hos´tium** m. *enemy, national enemy* (usually pl.), differing from **inimīcus,** *personal enemy*	(hostile, hostility)
i´ter, iti´neris n. *journey, route, march*	(itinerant, itinerary)
***ma´re, ma´ris, ma´rium** n. *sea*	(marine, submarine)
***mōns, mon´tis, mon´tium** m. *mountain*	(mount)
***nā´vis,**[13] **nā´vis, nā´vium** f. *ship*	(naval, navy)
pās´tor, pāstō´ris m. *herdsman, shepherd*	(pastor, pastorale)
***ves´tis, ves´tis, ves´tium** f. *garment, clothes*	(vest)

[12] Nouns marked with an asterisk (*) are **i**-stem nouns. The genitive plural of such nouns is always provided.
[13] The ablative singular of **nāvis** and a few other masculine and feminine **i**-stem nouns end in **-i**, not **-e.** An alternate form of the accusative plural, **-is** instead of **-ēs,** is occasionally found.

Verb

cōnfi´ciō, cōnfi´cere, cōnfē´cī, cōnfec´tus *complete, exhaust, do thoroughly*	[faciō]

▦ GRAMMAR

Third Declension: i–Stem Nouns

A group of third declension nouns called **i**-stems have **-ium** instead of **-um** in the genitive plural and may show other differences from the regular third declension which you will see below. The major classes of **i**-stem nouns are:

1. Masculine and feminine nouns with a nominative ending in **-is** and **-ēs** and having the same number of syllables in the genitive as in the nominative: **cīvis, cīvis** (gen. sing.), **cīvium** (gen. pl.); some, like **nāvis,** have an **-ī** instead of an **-ě** in the ablative singular, and some will occasionally show **-īs** for **-ēs** in the accusative plural.

2. Masculine and feminine nouns with only one syllable in the nominative and a base which ends in two consonants: **mōns, montis** (gen. sing.), **montium** (gen. pl.).

3. Neuter nouns whose nominatives end in **-al, -ar,** or **-ě** regularly have **-ī** in the ablative singular, **-ia** in the nominative and accusative plural, and **-ium** in the genitive plural. See the declension of **mare** below.

	MASCULINE OR FEMININE		NEUTER	
	SINGULAR	PLURAL	SINGULAR	PLURAL
Nominative	cī´vis	cī´vēs	ma´re	ma´ria
Genitive	cī´vis	cī´vium	ma´ris	ma´rium
Dative	cī´vī	cī´vibus	ma´rī	ma´ribus
Accusative	cī´vem	cī´vēs	ma´re	ma´ria
Ablative	cī´ve	cī´vibus	ma´rī	ma´ribus

Oral Practice

1. Decline **nāvis pulchra**.
2. Give the singular and plural in Latin in the case indicated: *high mountain* (gen.), *level sea* (acc.), *small mountain* (dat.), *neighboring enemy* (abl.), *our end* (nom.).

▦ *Exercises*

A. Translate the following sentences into English.
 1. Ad fīnem itineris longī vēnērunt.
 2. Montēs altōs et flūmina alta in Eurōpā vīdī.
 3. Cīvēs bonī officia pūblica suscipere nōn dubitant.
 4. Parvā nāvī colōnī trāns mare lātum ad prōvinciam migrāvērunt.
 5. Ob numerum hostium quī in montibus erant, cīvēs in castrīs remānsērunt.

B. Translate the following sentences into Latin.
  1. By whom was a ship seen on a mountain?
  2. We have made a long journey but can now see the end.
  3. A large number of citizens was called together by the leader.
  4. If the sea is closed, the enemy's ships will not be able to transport soldiers. [Hint: Use ablative absolute.]

WORD STUDY

- Many Latin **i**-stem nouns ending in **-is** are preserved in their original form in English. The original plural in **-es** is pronounced like *ease: axis, axes; basis, bases.*
  Distinguish *axēs* from *axĕs* (plural of *ax*), *basēs* from *basĕs* (plural of *base*).

- Study the following English phrases borrowed from Latin.

Tempus fugit.	*Time flies.*
per capita	*by heads or individuals*
me iudice	*in my judgment* (lit., *I being judge*)
Fata viam invenient.	*The Fates will find a way.*
pro tem (pro tempore)	*for the time (being), temporarily*
de jure	*according to right*, as a **de jure** government; cf. **de facto** (p. 291)

Tempus fugit.

Did You Know?

Some of our marriage customs originated in Roman times. The Roman bridegroom carried his bride over their threshold in order to avoid the bad omen of having her slip on the doorsill. The groom also gave his bride an iron ring for the third finger of her left hand. It was believed that a vein to the heart was located here and by encircling the finger with iron, the heart was made "captive" and the marriage binding.

LESSON XLVII

FĪNIS LABŌRUM

LESSON OBJECTIVES
- To read the final chapter of Ulysses' story
- To learn the forms of third declension adjectives

Ulixēs, rēx fortis Ithacae, ad portās oppidī quod rēxerat stābat, ā multīs cīvibus vīsus, sed nōn cognitus, quod vestēs sordidās¹ gerēbat. In oppidum itinere facilī prōcessit. Multōs servōs vīdit ā quibus nōn cognitus est. Canis² tamen Ulixis dominum cognōvit et gaudiō³ affectus ē vītā excessit. Ubi Ulixēs ad rēgīnam adductus est, omnēs procī⁴ eum⁵ hostem appellāvērunt et 5 eum discēdere iussērunt. Sed tamen Pēnelopē, quae eum nōn cognōverat, vestibus sordidīs permōta eum manēre iussit et eī⁶ cibum dedit.

Pēnelopē vestem cōnfēcerat et nunc tempus aderat quō⁷ iūs erat marītum dēligere⁸. Magnum arcum⁹ ante procōs⁴ pōnī iussit quem Ulixēs clārus ante vīgintī annōs tetenderat. Tum nūntiāvit: 10

"Homō quī arcum Ulixis fortis tendere poterit marītus meus erit; marītus novus pār Ulixī esse dēbet. Ita iūs est."

Itaque singulī in ōrdine arcum cēpērunt sed tendere nōn potuērunt quod Ulixī parēs nōn fuērunt. Tum Ulixēs arcum petīvit. Omnēs rīsērunt¹⁰, sed Pēnelopē arcum Ulixī darī iussit, nam iūs erat. Id¹¹ quod reliquī nōn facere 15

¹ dirty
² dog
³ joy
⁴ suitors
⁵ him
⁶ to him
⁷ at which
⁸ to choose a husband
⁹ bow
¹⁰ laughed
¹¹ that

Canis dominum cognōvit. A dog joyfully greets his careworn master. Did the sculptor of this relief have in mind the famous scene from the *Odyssey,* when Odysseus' favorite hound died upon recognizing his long-absent master? From a second-century A.D. sarcophagus now in a Naples museum.

poterant—arcum tendere—Ulixī facile erat. Tum in procōs arcum tetendit, quōs in fugam dedit. Tēlemachus et Eumaeus auxilium dedērunt. Ulixēs omnēs portās oppidī claudī iusserat, ob quam causam procī ex oppidō ad montēs fugere nōn potuērunt. Salūte petītā, nōn inventā, omnēs interfectī
20 sunt. Hōc[12] modō rēgnum et uxōrem Ulixēs recēpit et in lībertāte pāceque vītam ēgit. Nōn iam nāvibus itinera trāns maria faciēbat.

Questions

1. Why was Ulysses not recognized when he returned?
2. Who managed to recognize Ulysses first?
3. Why did Ulysses choose not to reveal his identity immediately?
4. How was the man wearing dirty clothes treated by Penelope?
5. What contest did Penelope propose to determine who would be fit to marry her? What would it prove?
6. How well did the suitors meet the challenge?
7. Why did everyone laugh when Ulysses asked for the bow?
8. Why was their laughter out of place?
9. How did Eumaeus and Telemachus help Ulysses? What was the result?
10. How did Ulysses' dog die?

▦ VOCABULARY

Nouns

iūs, iū´ris n. *right*	(jury, justice)
līber´tās,[13] **lībertā´tis** f. *freedom, liberty*	**[līber]**
u´xor, uxōr´is f. *wife*	(uxorious)

Adjectives

ce´ler, ce´leris, ce´lere *swift, quick*	(accelerate)
fa´cilis, fa´cile *easy, doable*	**[faciō]**
for´tis, for´te *strong, brave*	(fort, fortitude)
om´nis, om´ne *all, every*	(omnipotent, omniscient)
pār, pa´ris (gen.) *equal; equal to* (+ dat.)	(parity, peer)

Verb

ten´dō, ten´dere, teten´dī, ten´tus *stretch*	(intent, tendon)

[13] All nouns ending in -**tās** (nom. sing.) are feminine.

The Metropolitan Museum of Art, Fletcher Fund, 1930. (30.11.9). Copyright © 1982 By the Metropolitan Museum of Art.

Ulysses, in the guise of a beggar, offers consolation to Penelope as she despairs of ever seeing her husband again. Behind Penelope is Ulysses' son Telemachus; seated is the swineherd Eumaeus. A relief in the Metropolitan Museum of Art, New York.

GRAMMAR

Third Declension Adjectives

The adjectives studied so far, such as **magnus, -a, -um** and **sacer, -cra, -crum,** have been declined like nouns of the first and second declensions. Many adjectives, however, belong to the third declension. With the exception of one important class, which will be presented in a later lesson, almost all adjectives of the third declension are **i**-stems. They are divided into classes according to the number of forms that are used in the nominative singular to show gender.

1. Two endings[14]—masculine and feminine in **-is**, neuter in **-e: fortis, forte.**
2. One ending—one form for all genders: **pār.**

Adjectives of the third declension have **-ī** in the ablative singular, **-ium** in the genitive plural, identical neuter nominative and accusative singular, and **-ia** in the neuter nominative and accusative plural. [See Lesson XLVI.] Note particularly that the ablative singular, unlike that of most **i**-stem nouns, ends in **-ī,** not in **-e.**

---

[14] A few adjectives in -er have three endings in the nominative singular, one for each gender: **celer** (m.), **celeris** (f.), **celere** (n.). These are called adjectives of three endings. With the exception of the nominative singular form, the declension of the masculine forms is exactly the same as the feminine forms. See the Grammar Appendix for a full declension.

Two-ending adjectives are declined like **fortis, forte** *(strong)*.

	SINGULAR		PLURAL	
	M. + F.	N.	M. + F.	N.
Nominative	fortis	forte	fortēs	fortia
Genitive	fortis	fortis	fortium	fortium
Dative	fortī	fortī	fortibus	fortibus
Accusative	fortem	forte	fortēs[15]	fortia
Ablative	fortī	fortī	fortibus	fortibus

One-ending adjectives are declined like **pār, paris** *(equal)*.

	SINGULAR		PLURAL	
	M. + F.	N.	M. + F.	N.
Nominative	pār	pār	parēs	paria
Genitive	paris	paris	parium	parium
Dative	parī	parī	paribus	paribus
Accusative	parem	pār	parēs[15]	paria
Ablative	parī	parī	paribus	paribus

Did You Know?

Although the Romans built a variety of ships, they were not very capable sailors. Most Roman ships used oars as well as sails because they could only run before a favorable wind. For reasons of economy, **nāvēs onerāriae** *(merchant ships)* relied on sails. **Nāvēs longae** *(warships)* used sails in transit, but as soon as a sea battle started, the masts were lowered and the sails stored. Victory often depended on skillful maneuvering and ramming, not on firepower.

Oral Practice

1. Decline **lībertās pār, iter facile.**
2. Give in Latin: *swift boys* (acc.), *brave citizen* (abl.), *all towns* (gen.), *equal right* (acc.), *few enemies* (dat.).

[15] As with **i**-stem nouns, occasionally -**is** is the case ending used instead of -**ēs**. Do not confuse this with the genitive singular of the third declension (-**is**) or dative and ablative plural of the second declension (-**is**).

📖 *Exercises*

A. Translate the following sentences into English.
1. Quid est pretium lībertātis?
2. Servus factīs fortibus lībertātem obtinuit.
3. Omnia maria nāvibus hostium clausa erant.
4. In patriā nostrā omnēs cīvēs sunt līberī et parēs.
5. Nōvistīne, amīce bone, hominem quem in nāvī vīdimus?
6. Itinere facilī inventō, dux omnēs mīlitēs dē montibus dūcere mātūrāvit.

B. Translate the following sentences into Latin.
1. All free men love peace.
2. Nature has given us many beautiful things.
3. We ought not to undertake a long journey now.
4. It will not be easy to defend the freedom of our country on the sea.

C. After ten long years of war and ten more years of travel, Aeneas founded Lavinium, and Ulysses arrived home in Ithaca. Work with a partner or a small group and write a brief paragraph in English explaining which one of the heroes, in your opinion, had the more difficult time. Do not forget that both suffered mental as well as physical hardships. Both endured, for better or for worse, the interference of one or more gods, and both were responsible for the people traveling with them.

WORD STUDY

Derivatives A number of English nouns and adjectives preserve the nominative singular, and a few the nominative plural, of Latin adjectives of the third declension: *par, pauper, simplex, duplex,* etc.; *September,* etc. Neuter forms occur in *simile, facsimile, regalia* (singular rare), *forte* (singular only). The dative plural is seen in *omnibus* (a vehicle *for all);* in the common shortened form *bus,* only the ending is left.

LESSON OBJECTIVES

- To learn the story of Romulus and Remus
- To learn how the context of a Latin word can change its meaning

RŌMULUS ET REMUS

Silvius Proca, rēx fortis Albānōrum[1], Numitōrem et Amūlium fīliōs habuit. Numitōrī rēgnum relīquit. Sed Amūlius, Numitōre ē cīvitāte pulsō, rēxit. Rhēa Silvia, fīlia Numitōris, geminōs[2] Rōmulum et Remum habuit. Pater geminōrum deus Mārs erat; itaque Mārs auctor populī Rōmānī
5 appellābātur. Amūlius puerōs in Tiberī flūmine pōnī iussit. Sed aqua geminōs in siccō[3] relīquit. Lupa[4] accessit et puerōs aluit[5]. Posteā Faustulus, pāstor rēgis, puerōs invēnit. Post multōs annōs Rōmulō et Remō dīxit: "Numitor est avus[6] vester." Verbīs pāstōris adductī, geminī Amūlium

[1] the Albans, a people of Latium
[2] twins
[3] on dry ground
[4] wolf
[5] fed
[6] grandfather

In this primitive mosaic, now in the Leeds Museum in England, the she-wolf feeds Romulus and Remus, the twins she has rescued from the flooded Tiber. Above her is pictured the site of the legend, the **Ficus Rūminālis,** or the sacred fig tree of Rome. Yet there are questions: Why is she baring her teeth? Is she standing or lying down? Why does she look so much like a horse? Had the artist never seen a wolf?

Leeds Museums and Art Galleries (City Museum)/The Bridgeman Art Library

interfēcērunt. Numitōrī, quem Amūlius ē cīvitāte pepulerat, rēgnum
mandāvērunt.   10

Posteā oppidum mūnīvērunt in locō in quō inventī erant, quod dē nōmine
Rōmulī Rōmam appellāvērunt.

Rōmulus Remusque parēs erant, sed tamen Remō cēdere Rōmulō nōn
facile erat. Remō interfectō, Rōmulus sōlus Rōmānōs rēxit et omnibus iūra
dedit.   15

Questions

1. How were Numitor and Amulius related?
2. What happened to Numitor?
3. Numitor's daughter gave birth to twins with divine ancestry. How could
   they claim divinity?
4. What action did Amulius take in response to this birth?
5. How were the twins saved?
6. Who persuaded Romulus and Remus to kill Amulius?
7. Whom did they establish as rightful ruler of the Albans?
8. What did the twins do next?
9. What does the conclusion of the story suggest about the original character
   of the Roman people?

▦ VOCABULARY

Nouns

auc´tor, auctō´ris m. *maker, author*	[augeō]
cī´vitās, cīvitā´tis f. *citizenship, state*	[cīvis]
pa´ter, pa´tris m. *father*	(paternal)

Verb

pel´lō, pel´lere, pe´pulī, pul´sus	(impel, repulsive)
beat, drive, defeat	

Adverb

post´eā *afterwards*

Preposition

post with acc. *behind (of place); after (of time)*

Developing "Word Sense"

By now it should be clear that a Latin word may have many shades of meaning which are suggested by the context. In translating, therefore, do not adhere strictly to the "vocabulary" meaning of the word, but use the one required by the context—the particular passage in which the word occurs. Note the varying translation of **magnus** when used with the following nouns.

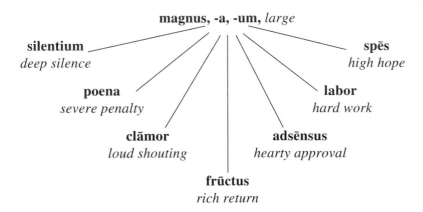

magnus, -a, -um, *large*

silentium
deep silence

spēs
high hope

poena
severe penalty

labor
hard work

clāmor
loud shouting

adsēnsus
hearty approval

frūctus
rich return

Oral Practice

1. Combine **magnus** with each of the following nouns already studied and translate freely: **perīculum, studium, pecūnia, pretium.**
2. How does **altus** differ when applied to rivers and mountains?
3. Translate **puella pulchra** and **homō pulcher.**

Exercises

A. Translate the following sentences into English.
1. Ego aut viam inveniam aut faciam.
2. Dēbēmusne, pāce factā, numerum nāvium augēre?
3. Flūmina omnia Italiae ex montibus ad mare tendunt.
4. Auctōrēs librōrum nōn semper magnam pecūniam merent.
5. Poteruntne hostēs, montibus occupātīs, posteā iter facere?
6. Post multōs annōs Rōmānī iūra cīvitātis omnibus dedērunt.
7. Post oppidum erat mōns altus, in quō fortēs mīlitēs hostium pulsī erant.

B. Translate the following sentences into Latin.
1. Is it not pleasing to all men to see friends?
2. The road stretches through the mountains.
3. Equal rights of citizenship were given to many Gauls.
4. My father made many journeys across high mountains and deep seas.
5. After a long journey my friend is approaching (**ad**) the end of life.

WORD STUDY

- The suffix **-tās** is usually found in nouns formed from adjectives. Its English form is -*ty*, which is to be distinguished from -*y*.

  What must be the Latin words from which are derived *commodity, integrity, liberty, publicity, timidity, variety?* Note that the letter preceding the ending is usually -*i*-.

- Study the following English phrases borrowed from Latin.

  ad fin. (ad finem)   *near the end (of the page)*

  ex libris   *from the library (of)*

  P.S. (post scriptum) *written after (at the end of a letter)*

What is the sense behind the motto of the University of Texas, **Disciplina praesidium civitatis**? The inscription **In libris libertas** on the Los Angeles Public Library?

CĪNEĀS ET PYRRHUS

[1] *Epī´rus,* a region in northwest Greece

[2] *Cineas (Sin´eas)*

[3] *lieutenant*

[4] = **cum multā libertāte**; the **cum** in the ablative of manner often stands between the adjective and the noun (p. 260).

[5] **quid... animō** *what do you intend?*

[6] *said*

Pyrrhus erat rēx Ēpīrī[1]. Cīneās[2], quī erat lēgātus[3] in Pyrrhī castrīs et reliquōs lēgātōs auctōritāte et virtūte superābat, cōnsiliīs Pyrrhī nōn probātīs, multā cum lībertāte[4] rēgem monēbat. Quondam Pyrrhus Cīneae familiārī dīxit: "In Italiam prōcēdere et cīvitātem Rōmānam cum celeritāte superāre
5 parō."

Cīneās, "Superātīs Rōmānīs," rogāvit, "quid est tibi in animō[5] facere, rēx fortis?"

"Italiae fīnitima est īnsula Sicilia," inquit[6] rēx, "quam facile erit armīs occupāre."

10 Tum Cīneās, "Occupātā Siciliā," rogāvit, "quid posteā faciēs?"

Pyrrhus tum respondit: "Posteā trāns mare in Āfricam mīlitēs meōs celerēs trānsportābō et hostēs, quī celeritāte et virtūte mīlitibus meīs nōn parēs sunt, pellam."

Cavalry attack an elephant whose face and trunk are protected by special armor and even a spear for offensive action.

North Wind Picture Archives

Cīneās, "Pulsīs hostibus," rogat, "quid tum faciēs?" "Post haec[7] bella,
Cīneā[8]," inquit Pyrrhus, "pāce cōnfirmātā, vītam in ōtiō agam."   15

    Celer Cīneās respondit: "Familiāris meus es. Cūr nōn etiam nunc pācem   [7] *these*
cōnfirmāre potes atque mēcum in ōtiō vītam agere? Quid tē impedit?"   [8] *vocative*

Questions

1. What were Pyrrhus' plans? List them in order.
2. What did Cineas want Pyrrhus to do?
3. How was Cineas used to talking with the king?
4. In what respects did Pyrrhus think his soldiers were superior to the
   Africans?
5. In what respect was Cineas superior to Pyrrhus' other lieutenants?
6. What is the duty of a close friend?

VOCABULARY

Nouns

auctō´ritās, auctōritā´tis f.   [**auctor**]
  authority, influence
cele´ritās, celeritā´tis f. *swiftness, speed*   [**celer**]
vir´tūs, virtū´tis f. *manliness, courage*   [**vir**]

Adjective

familiā´ris, -e *of the family, friendly;*   [**familia**]
  as noun, *(close) friend*

Verbs

cōnfir´mō, -ā´re, -ā´vī, -ā´tus   [**firmus**]
  make firm, encourage, establish
respon´deō, -ē´re, respon´dī, respōn´sus   (response)
  answer, reply
su´perō, -ā´re, -ā´vī, -ā´tus *overcome,*   (insuperable)
  excel, surpass

GRAMMAR

Ablative of Respect

Notice the use of the ablative in the following sentences.

Equī et hominēs nōn sunt parēs celeritāte.	*Horses and men are not equal in swiftness.*
Puer erat vir factīs.	*The boy was a man in deeds.*
Numerō, nōn animō, superāmur.	*We are surpassed in number, not in courage.*

Observe the following points.

- The ablative specifies the *respect* in which the meaning of an adjective, a noun, or a verb is true.
- No preposition is used in Latin, but in English we use a preposition, chiefly *in*.
- The ablative of respect construction answers the questions *in what respect? in what specific way? how?*

Exercises

A. Translate the following sentences into English.

1. Omnēs hostēs ē fīnibus nostrīs certē pellēmus.
2. Servī magnā cum celeritāte ad flūmen fūgērunt.
3. Nōn omnēs puellae dīligentiā et celeritāte parēs sunt.
4. Puer erat celer pede sed studiīs ab omnibus superābātur.
5. Sex familiāribus vīsīs, ad oppidum fīnitimum iter fēcimus.
6. Colōnī ex patriā migrant et in variīs terrīs cīvitātem petunt.
7. Pāx et amīcitia cum cīvitātibus fīnitimīs ā Rōmānīs cōnfirmātae sunt.

B. Translate the following sentences into Latin.

1. We cannot all be swift footed (swift in respect to foot).
2. Does a horse excel a boy in swiftness?
3. He was king in name; nevertheless he did not have a kingdom.
4. (Now that) peace has been established, free citizens will maintain the state.

WORD STUDY

- Study the following English phrases borrowed from Latin.

in omnia paratus	*prepared for all things*
Dominus providebit.	*The Lord will provide.*
Fortes Fortuna adiuvat.	*Fortune aids the brave.*
extempore	*without preparation* (lit., *from the moment*)
Vanitas vanitatum et omnia vanitas	*Vanity of vanities, and all (is) vanity* (from the Vulgate, or Latin translation of the Bible, *Ecclesiastes, I,2*)
Arma non servant modum.	*Armies do not show (preserve) restraint,* i.e., *War observes no limit.*

- Here are more state mottoes.

Virtute et armis	*By courage and by arms* (Mississippi)
Ense petit placidam sub libertate quietem.	*With the sword she seeks quiet peace under liberty.* (Massachusetts)
Audemus iura nostra defendere.	*We dare to defend our rights.* (Alabama)
Ditat Deus.	*God enriches us.* (Arizona)
Regnat populus.	*The people rule.* (Arkansas)

FOOD AND MEALS

The Romans ate a variety of foods, although some foodstuffs that we take for granted such as corn, potatoes, tropical fruits, and tomatoes were unknown to them. Butter was rarely used, except externally as a sort of salve or cold cream, but other dairy products like cheese were common foods. Instead of sugar, which was also unknown, honey served as a sweetener, and the extensive use of honey made beekeeping a very important occupation. Fine wheat bread baked in flat, round loaves was the "staff of life." Breads of coarse wheat flour, of flour and bran, or bran alone were also popular. Cabbage, onions, beans, carrots, and peas were among the chief vegetables. Apples, pears, grapes, raisins, figs, plums, and olives were among the chief fruits. The **mālum Persicum** (from which our word *peach* is derived) was, as its name shows, originally brought from Persia.

Canning and freezing were unknown, but salted fish in a fermented fish sauce was put up in earthenware jars; one of the best brews, commercially produced, came from Pompeii. This practice led to a wider consumption of fish. The lack of refrigeration restricted the importation and preservation of many foods except those, such as grapes and figs, that could be preserved by drying. Ice, in the form of snow, was a great luxury available to only a few.

Archivo Incongrafico, SA/CORBIS

Hardly appetizing after two thousand years, these Roman eggs make a better still life than a breakfast.

Scala/Art Resource, NY

A bakery in Pompeii. A huge freestanding oven can be seen at the left, while a row of grain mills to keep the baker well supplied with raw ingredients runs across the center.

A marble-covered counter or bar, in an inn at ancient Pompeii, near Naples. Here travelers could buy warmed-up wine, bread, and cheese.

Salads of cress and lettuce were as common then as they are today. This was one reason for the importance of olive oil, which was used also in cooking instead of butter and was the fuel for lamps. It was also used to rub the body after bathing, especially by athletes, and it was even a base for perfume.

The favorite meat was pork; beef was less important than mutton. At least six kinds of sausage with pork as a base were popular, and one can read in Roman cookbooks of at least fifty different ways to cook pork. Various kinds of fowl and birds like chickens, ducks, geese, and pigeons were eaten; the wealthy classes even ate peacocks. Oysters and exotic fish became extremely popular.

Besides milk and water the chief drink of the Romans was wine. There were many grades of native and imported wines. They were usually mixed with water when served at meals. **Mērum**, or unmixed wine, was important to the soldiers because it was concentrated and less cumbersome to pack. The Romans also made and enjoyed apple cider as well as mulberry and date wines. Coffee and tea were unknown.

The working class primarily ate a porridge of boiled wheat. Meat, fish, and vegetables were often expensive extras.

Breakfast (**ientāculum**), for even the wealthier Romans, was a simple meal, consisting chiefly of bread, although raisins, olives, and cheese were sometimes added. In the country, dinner (**cēna**) was at noon, but in the city this was postponed until early evening. Instead there was a luncheon

GLIMPSES OF ROMAN LIFE

FOOD AND MEALS
(CONTINUED)

(**prandium**) at midday or somewhat earlier. This consisted of bread, salad, olives, cheese, fruit, nuts, and cold meat from the previous dinner. Dinner began with a course of appetizers like lettuce, onions, eggs, oysters, asparagus, etc., called the **gustus** *(taste),* followed by the chief course of meat, fish, or fowl and vegetables, then the dessert, called the **secunda mēnsa** *(second table),* of fruit, nuts, pastry, and sweets. The Latin expression **ab ōvō usque ad māla,** *from eggs to apples* (cf. English *from soup to nuts*), meaning *from beginning to end,* shows what the usual relishes and desserts were.

The guests at banquets reclined on couches instead of sitting in chairs. Slaves removed the guests' sandals and bathed their feet, which were often sore and dusty from their journey. The couches, each with room for three people, were placed along the three sides of the rectangular table. As the guests reclined on their left elbows, only their right hands were free. Forks were rarely used; food was eaten with fingers or with spoons. Meat was cut up before being served. Although much use was made of the fingers, we may well imagine that people of culture ate just as neatly as those of us who use forks today. They also had finger bowls and napkins, as well as slaves, to wipe their hands.

QUESTIONS

1. Where did we originally get some of the important foods that the Romans knew nothing about?
2. Name the order of meals and describe a Roman dinner.
3. Compare the usual diet of the ancient Romans with our own.
4. How would you arrange a Roman banquet in your Latin club or school?

UNIT IX REVIEW

VOCABULARY

Nouns

auctor	clamor	lībertās	pater
auctōritās	corpus	mare	tempus
caput	fīnis	mōns	uxor
carmen	flūmen	nāvis	vestis
celeritās	hostis	nōmen	virtūs
cīvis	iter	ōrdō	vulnus
cīvitās	iūs	pastor	

Adjectives

celer	familiāris	omnis
facilis	fortis	par

Verbs

claudō	cōnfirmō	pellō	superō
cōnficiō	iaciō	respondeō	tendō

Adverb

posteā

Preposition

post (+ acc.)

GRAMMAR SUMMARY

Third Declension Neuter Nouns

Ordinary third declension neuter nouns have the same endings as other third declension nouns except for the accusative singular, which always has the same form as the nominative, and the nominative and accusative plurals, which always end in **-a.**

In flūmine quīnque corpora erant.	*In the river there were five bodies.*
Nōmen meum Anna rogāvit.	*Anna asked my name.*

Third Declension I-Stem Nouns

A group of third declension nouns, called **i-stems,** have **-ium** in the genitive plural instead of **-um.** Many third declension nouns can be identified as **i-**stems if: 1) they are masculine or feminine singular in **-is** or **-ēs** and have the same number of syllables in the genitive singular; or 2) they are masculine or feminine monosyllables with a base ending in two consonants; or 3) they are neuter with a nominative ending in **-al, -ar,** or **-e.**

Dux multārum nāvium pulsus est.	*The admiral (the leader) of many ships was beaten.*
Fīnēs cīvitātis ā marī ad montēs tetendērunt.	*The boundaries of the state stretched from the sea to the mountains.*

Third Declension Adjectives

Ordinary third declension adjectives are declined like third declension **i**-stem nouns except that they have **-ī**, not **-ĕ**, in all three genders of the ablative singular. The stem is obtained by dropping the **-is** of the genitive singular.

Ā fortī mīlite servātae sumus.	*We (women) were rescued by a brave soldier.*
Omnia iūra cīvium cōnfirmāta erant.	*All the rights of citizens had been strengthened.*

Ablative of Respect

To show in what respect an adjective, noun, or verb is true, use the ablative without a preposition.

Virtūte Tēlemachus patrī pār erat, nōn tamen auctōritāte.	*Telemachus was equal to his father in courage, not, however, in authority.*
Certus sententiīs tuīs es.	*You are fixed in your opinions.*

Ablative Uses

The ablative case really is a combination of three cases and that is why it has so many different uses.

When an ablative is used with a preposition we generally do not need a special name for it. One exception is the ablative of agent, because the preposition **ab** with this ablative cannot be translated in its usual sense of *from*. We also use a name ("accompaniment") for the ablative with **cum**. This is to distinguish it from the ablative of means, since both are expressed by *with* in English.

Pay particular attention to the ablatives used without a preposition because their translation depends on a correct analysis of the type of ablative used. Which are the three ablatives of this type that you have studied? Which ablative have you studied with which a preposition is sometimes used, sometimes not? Which of the prepositions studied so far are used with the ablative?

UNIT PRACTICE

A. 1. Decline **dux fortis, lībertās nostra, omnis mīles, rēx magnus.**

2. Give the following in Latin: *a small ship*, in the nom., sing. and pl.; *an easy journey*, in the gen., sing. and pl.; *a good citizen*, in the dat., sing. and pl., *a brave enemy*, in the acc., sing. and pl.; *the deep sea*, in the abl., sing. and pl.

3. Give the genitive and accusative, singular and plural, of **tempus, casa, mōns, corpus, fīnis, celeritās, mare, ōrdō, flūmen.**

4. Give in all tenses the third plural active of **impediō;** the first plural passive of **claudō;** the third singular active of **līberō;** the second plural passive of **teneō;** the second singular active of **cōnficiō.**

WORD STUDY

- Give the Latin noun suggested by each of the following: *civil, finish, submarine, navigate, corpulent, legislate, nominal, decapitate.*

corpulent

- Give the Latin verb suggested by each of the following: *expedite, press, verse, attention, repellent.*

- Give the Latin adjective suggested by each of the following: *omnipresent, celerity, facilitate, disparity, fortitude.*

- Find and use in sentences as many English derivatives as possible from **parō, teneō, agō,** and **scrībō.**

- The first word, printed in boldface type, in each of the following lines is a Latin word. From among the last five words in each group pick the one which is an English derivative of the first word.

dō	dough	dote	do	dot	dative
moneō	month	remain	admonition	moan	remind
cōgō	cog	incognito	cognate	cogency	concoct
petō	pet	compete	petal	petite	impede
legō	leg	log	collect	lag	lick

VOCABULARY

Circle the word that best completes each sentence.

1. Ulixēs virōs _____ portam iussit.
   a. claudere
   b. iacere
   c. respondēre
   d. superāre

2. In proeliō equī nostrī _____ esse dēbent.
   a. celerēs
   b. facilēs
   c. fortem
   d. parēs

3. Pater multa _____ in corpore fīlī nōn invēnit.
   a. carmina
   b. iūra
   c. verba
   d. vulnera

4. Gallī trāns _____ iter facere et in Italiam venīre nōn cupīvērunt
   a. agrīs
   b. flūminis
   c. maribus
   d. montēs

5. Puella _____ pulchrās quās cōnfēcerat rēgīnae dedit.
   a. auctōritās
   b. cīvitās
   c. vestēs
   d. virtūs

GRAMMAR

Complete each sentence with the correct endings.

6. Auctor qu___ ē Britanniā vēnerat omn___ fāmā superāvit, et post cēn___ carmin___ lēgit.

7. Bellō cōnfect___, dux mīlitēs ē prōvinciā host___ trāns flūmin___ et mar___ ad fīn___ familiār___ redūxit.

8. Magnus equ___ ā cīv___ Trōiae per port___ puls___ ___, et posteā mīlit___ host___ bellum gerere incēpērunt.

9. Lībertāt___ cōnfirmāt___, serv___ līberātī dominum nōn iam timēbant, et magn___ cum grāti___ excēdēbant.

10. Quī homin___ Ulixem virtūt___ superāba___ aut par___ virō fact___ erant?

TRANSLATION

Translate the following sentences.

11. Terra patris meī ē montibus altīs ad flūmen pulchrum tendit; tamen superbus nōn est sed fortūnam bonam semper laudat.

12. Clāmōrēs puerōrum puellārumque ā magistrīs quae līberīs auxilium dedērunt clārē audītī erant.

13. Post longum tempus in agrīs pastor vestem in capite posuit et tardē discessit ad parvam casam quam amāvit.

14. Magister rogāvit, "Potestisne nōmina officiaque omnia deārum deōrumque Rōmānōrum mihi nārrāre?"

15. Cīvitās sociōrum nostrōrum habet multās nāvēs longās et nautās quī magnīs undīs in marī numquam terrentur.

INVESTIGATION

Find the answers to these questions from any lesson in Unit IX.

16. Name at least three ways in which the Romans used olive oil.

17. Briefly identify the following characters from the *Odyssey*.
    a. Sirens
    b. Telemachus
    c. Penelope

18. Translate the Latin phrase **ab ōvō usque ad māla** and explain its meaning.

19. Where can the motto **In Librīs Libertās** be found, and what does it mean?

20. What was the difference between **nāvēs ōnerāriae** and **nāvēs longae**?

CULTURE

Vērum aut Falsum? Indicate whether each statement is true or false.

21. Ancient Romans could not enjoy a pizza like ours because they did not have cheese.

22. More pork than beef was eaten by the ancient Romans.

23. A wealthy Roman might eat three meals a day: **ientāculum** *(breakfast)*, **prandium** *(lunch)*, and **cēna** *(dinner)*.

24. **Secunda mēnsa** *(second table)* was the name given to the main course at a Roman dinner.

25. Sugar was unknown, but honey was used regularly to sweeten food.

FROM LATIN TO ENGLISH

Apply your knowledge of Latin roots to determine the best meaning of the italicized words.

26. He thought they had spent an *inordinate* amount of time on that topic.
    a. insufficient
    b. reasonable
    c. excessive
    d. typical

27. People came to the town hall to see works by the *itinerant* artist.
    a. famous
    b. well-trained
    c. traveling
    d. unknown

28. The decision created greater *parity* between the schools.
    a. cooperation
    b. equality
    c. communication
    d. distance

29. In that time of crisis my friend showed great *fortitude*.
    a. fear
    b. selfishness
    c. indecision
    d. bravery

30. The change of terrain made the king's troops feel *vulnerable*.
    a. well protected
    b. powerful
    c. discouraged
    d. open to attack

MYTHS, LEGENDS, AND HISTORY OF EARLY GREECE AND ROME

Unit Objectives
- To learn the forms and use of the demonstratives **hic, ille, is, īdem,** and the intensive **ipse**
- To learn the ablative of time when
- To learn more about Greek and Roman religion, legends, and history

A dramatic event from early Greek mythology. Zeus, astride his eagle and with fiery thunderbolts in hand, banishes the Giants to Tartarus, while his fellow Olympians watch the victory. The Romans, giving Latin names to the Greek deities, adapted this story to their own mythology. Notice the circle of the zodiac encircling Zeus. At the left, notice Juno's peacock, Venus' son Cupid, and Mars. At the right are the Muses and other Olympians. At the bottom, the artist Pierino del Vaga (sixteenth century), in his vision of Hell, has included not just humans but also a view of Rome and even his own self-portrait *(bottom right)*.

Scala/Art Resource, NY

345

OBJECTIVE

• To survey the main deities in Roman religion

DEĪ DEAEQUE RŌMĀNŌRUM

Rōmānī multōs deōs quōrum officia erant varia habuērunt. Deōs in omnibus locīs vīdērunt—in terrā, in agrīs, in frūmentō, in montibus, in silvīs, in undīs maris, in aquā flūminum, in omnī nātūrā. Nōn omnēs parēs auctōritāte erant, nam magnī deī erant et parvī deī, deī deaeque. Inter magnōs
5 deōs prīmus auctōritāte erat Iuppiter, rēx atque pater deōrum hominumque, quī in caelō habitābat et fulmine[1] malōs terrēbat. Iūnō erat uxor Iovis[2] et rēgīna deōrum. Venus erat pulchra dea amōris. Mārs, deus bellī, arma et pugnās et exercitūs[3] amābat. Auctor populī Rōmānī vocābātur, et fortasse ob hanc[4] causam Rōmānī semper bella gerēbant. Mercurius, celer nūntius
10 deōrum, omnēs celeritāte superābat. Neptūnus erat deus maris, quī equōs in undīs regēbat. Reliquī magnī deī erant Cerēs, dea frūmentī, Minerva, dea sapientiae[5], Diāna, dea silvārum, Vulcānus, deus ignis, Apollō, quī omnia prōvidēbat et quem hominēs cōnsulēbant, Bacchus, deus vīnī. Rōmānī nōmina omnium magnōrum deōrum et multōrum parvōrum cognōverant—
15 quod nōn facile erat, nam magnus erat numerus deōrum deārumque. Etiam "terminus[6] agrōrum" deus erat.

[1] lightning bolt
[2] genitive singular of **Iuppiter**
[3] armies
[4] this
[5] wisdom
[6] Terminus, the minor god who, represented by a boundary stone, protected property limits

Giraudon/Art Resource, NY

This frieze in Rome shows a ritual sacrifice, called a **lustrum**, which was performed after the **cēnsus** was taken (every five years). The **lustrum** was intended to purify the citizens of their sins, ward off evil, and protect the good. To the left the **cēnsor** enrolls a line of citizens; in the center stands the **pontifex** at the altar, and to the right the sacrificial animals, a bull, a sheep, and a pig. The censor's main function was to count the people and divide them into classes, but the fact that he could deny citizenship or even expel a senator from the Senate for immoral conduct is an indication of just how closely tied together were religion and politics in ancient Rome.

Bill Roberts/PhotoEdit

A **larārium**, or private chapel for the **Lārēs**, in the House of the Vettii in Pompeii. Between the **Lārēs** is the **Genius**, or guardian spirit of the family (the **gēns**), with his head covered in prayer. This **genius** resides in the **paterfamiliās**, the head of the family, during his lifetime. The snake, a symbol of renewal and longevity, represents the guardian spirit as well.

Questions

1. In what places did the Romans observe divine powers?
2. Describe the Roman goddesses and their powers.
3. Describe the Roman gods and their powers.
4. Why was Mercury the messenger of the gods?
5. Which god, in your view, would be most important for the Romans and why?
6. Which god was called the founder of the Roman people and how did this affect them?

LESSON OBJECTIVES
- To learn more about the twelve Olympian gods and goddesses
- To learn the demonstratives **hic** and **ille**

Auctor et prīmus rēx deōrum Ūranus erat. Hunc fīlius Sāturnus ex rēgnō expulit. Ūranus hīs verbīs Sāturnum monuit: "Tempus auctōritātis tuae nōn longum erit; nam tū ā fīliō tuō expellēris." Hīs verbīs territus Sāturnus omnēs fīliōs in ōrdine dēvorābat. Sed māter illum quem ante[1] reliquōs amābat
5 servāvit. Hic fuit Iuppiter, ad īnsulam Crētam ā mātre missus. Post paucōs annōs hic patrem expulit et rēgnum illīus occupāvit. Sāturnus reliquōs fīliōs reddere coāctus est. Rēgiam[2] in monte Olympō Iuppiter posuit, ex quō in omnēs partēs spectāre poterat. Frātrēs convocāvit. Neptūnō maris rēgnum, Plūtōnī rēgnum īnferōrum[3] permīsit.

10 Sed posteā Gigantēs[4], fīliī Terrae, cum deīs bellum gessērunt. Illī ad Olympum praecipitēs cucurrērunt sed, ā deīs proeliō superātī, poenīs dūrīs affectī sunt. Posteā multa templa in terrā deīs ab hominibus posita sunt.

[1] *more than* (lit. *before*)
[2] *palace*
[3] *of those below,* i.e., the dead
[4] *the Giants*

Iuppiter pater deōrum hominumque. Under Jupiter, the Olympian sky-gods, after fierce battles, defeated the monstrous earthborn Giants and introduced greater order into a violent universe. All the names of this supreme sky-god, Zeus, Iuppiter (Diespiter the Day Father in archaic Latin), and Jupiter in English, have the word "day" hidden in their base.

Araldo de Luca/CORBIS

Questions

1. Who was the first king of the gods?
2. How was Saturn related to him?
3. What was the warning Uranus gave?
4. What did Saturn then do?
5. How was Jupiter saved?
6. What did Jupiter do to establish his rule?
7. Who were Jupiter's brothers and what area did each control?
8. Who were the Giants and what became of them?

▦ VOCABULARY

Noun

mā´ter, mā´tris f. *mother*   (matron, maternal)

Demonstratives

hic, haec, hoc *this;* (pl.) *these*
   (as pronoun: *he, she, it, they, this man,* etc.)
il´le, il´la, il´lud *that;* (pl.) *those*
   (as pronoun: *he, she, it, they, that man,* etc.)

Adjective

prae´ceps, (gen.) **praeci´pitis**   (precipice, precipitate)
   headfirst, steep, straight (down)

Verbs

cur´rō, cur´rere, cucur´rī, cursū´rus *run*   (cursive, precursor)
expel´lō, expel´lere, ex´pulī,   [pellō]
   expul´sus *drive out*

▦ GRAMMAR

The Demonstratives *Hic* and *Ille*

In English, *this* (plural, *these*) and *that* (plural, *those*) are called *demonstratives* because they "point out" persons or objects. They may be used as either adjectives or pronouns. *This* (adjective) *man certainly did not write that* (pronoun). *That* (pronoun) *could not have been done by these* (adjective) *boys.*

Hic vir illud nōn scrīpsit.	*This man did not write that.*
Illud ab hīs puerīs nōn	*That was not done by these boys.*
factum est.	

Pluto, god of the
underworld, rests
on the river Styx.
Under his left arm
is Cerberus, the
watchdog of Hell.

Ronald Sheridan/Ancient Art & Architecture Collection

In Latin, **hic** means *this* (near the speaker in place or thought), while **ille** means *that* (more distant from the speaker).

	THIS SINGULAR			*THESE* PLURAL		
	M.	F.	N.	M.	F.	N.
Nominative	hic	haec	hoc	hī	hae	haec
Genitive	hu´ius	hu´ius	hu´ius	hō´rum	hā´rum	hō´rum
Dative	huic	huic	huic	hīs	hīs	hīs
Accusative	hunc	hanc	hoc	hōs	hās	haec
Ablative	hōc	hāc	hōc	hīs	hīs	hīs

	THAT SINGULAR			*THOSE* PLURAL		
	M.	F.	N.	M.	F.	N.
Nominative	il´le	il´la	il´lud	il´lī	il´lae	il´la
Genitive	illī´us	illī´us	illī´us	illō´rum	illā´rum	illō´rum
Dative	il´lī	il´lī	il´lī	il´līs	il´līs	il´līs
Accusative	il´lum	il´lam	il´lud	il´lōs	il´lās	il´la
Ablative	il´lō	il´lā	il´lō	il´līs	il´līs	il´līs

Ille is declined regularly, like **bonus,** in the plural (**illī, illae, illa**); likewise **hic** (**hī, hae, haec**) except for its nominative and accusative plural neuter. The **-c** which appears in many forms of **hic** in the singular is the remnant of an intensive suffix **-ce** which makes *this* emphatic: *this one here!* The form **illud** of the nominative and accusative neuter of **ille** is also irregular.

From such expressions as *this man, that woman,* the demonstrative adjectives **hic** and **ille** came to be used as a third person pronoun *he, she, it.* These personal pronouns, however, are usually not required in Latin, except for emphasis or contrast.

Position of Demonstratives

Demonstrative adjectives regularly precede their nouns in English and Latin: *these boys,* **hī puerī;** *that girl,* **illa puella.** In English, when *that* precedes its noun, it is the demonstrative adjective **(ille);** when it follows, it is the relative pronoun **(quī),** equivalent to *who* or *which. The man that I saw was famous.* **Vir quem** (not **illum**) **vīdī clārus erat.**

Oral Practice

Supply the correct forms of **hic** and **ille.**
1. *(This)* flūmen altum est, *(that)* nōn altum est.
2. *(These)* hominēs laudō, *(those)* numquam probābō.
3. *(This)* puerī patrem et *(that)* puellae mātrem vīdī.
4. Studia ab *(this)* puerō intermissa sunt, nōn ab *(that).*

🔲 *Exercises*

A. Translate the following sentences into English.
1. Ille erat dux ducum.
2. Hunc cognōvī sed illum ante hoc tempus nōn vīdī.
3. Hī hominēs sunt patris meī amīcī; illī sunt inimīcī.
4. Haec est mea patria; nam ego cīvis in hōc locō sum.
5. Praeceps in illud flūmen cucurrī quod illōs nōn vīdī.
6. Māter mea huic hominī grātiam habet, quod hic patrem meum servāvit.

B. Translate the following sentences into Latin.
1. This is my money; that is yours.
2. This girl excels that (one) in discipline.
3. What names did the mother give to the children?
4. When this prisoner has been bound[5], I shall bind that (one).
5. The enemy of this man is strong; the enemy of that one (is) equal in speed.

---

[5] Use the ablative absolute.

Did You Know?

There was a building in ancient Rome called the **Rēgia** *(palace)* near the **Ātrium Vestae** *(precinct of Vesta)*. It was located on the **Via Sacra** near the Temple of Vesta. A sacred grove separated the **Rēgia** from the building which housed the Vestals. The **Rēgia** was the office of the **Pontifex Maximus** *(chief priest)* and also the assembly area where the **pontificēs** *(priests)* gathered.

WORD STUDY

Derivatives More English words are derived from nouns and adjectives of the third declension than from any other. The English word is usually derived from the stem, not from the nominative. It is therefore doubly important to memorize the genitive, from which the stem is obtained. It would be difficult to see that *itinerary* is derived from **iter** if you did not know that the genitive is **itineris.** See how many of the third declension words you have studied have derivatives from the base. Note the help given for English spelling: *temporal, corporal, military, nominal,* etc.

On the other hand, the English derivative will help you remember the genitive. In the following list of words, a derivative is placed after each. Give the genitive: **religiō** *(religion),* **sermō** *(sermon),* **latus** *(lateral),* **rādīx** *(radical),* **orīgō** *(original),* **ēruptiō** *(eruption),* **custōs** *(custody),* **dēns** *(dental),* **mōs** *(moral).*

Many towns are named after the Roman gods: *Jupiter, Juno, Mars, Mercury, Minerva, Bacchus, Ceres.* Many firms or their products are also named after them.

The major planets too are named after Roman gods: *Mercury, Venus, Mars, Jupiter, Saturn, Neptune, Pluto. Uranus* is from the Greek.

Here are two more state mottoes.

Nil sine numine *Nothing without the divine will* (Colorado)

Qui transtulit sustinet. *He who transplanted (still) sustains.* (Connecticut)

CAEDICIUS FORTIS

LESSON OBJECTIVES
- To learn the story of Caedicius
- To learn how Latin expresses time when

Prīmō bellō Pūnicō hostēs locum nātūrā mūnītum occupāverant, et perīculum mīlitum Rōmānōrum magnum erat. Aestās erat, nam Rōmānī semper aestāte, nōn hieme, bella gerēbant. Dux nihil facere poterat. Rogāvit: "Quod cōnsilium capere dēbeō?" Tribūnus[1] mīlitum Rōmānus cui[2] nōmen Caedicius[3] erat, ad ducem hōc tempore vēnit et sententiam prōposuit, locō 5 quōdam[4] mōnstrātō:

"Virōs tuōs servāre poteris sī ad illum locum CCCC mīlitēs currere iubēbis. Hostēs, ubi hōs mīlitēs vīderint, proelium committent et hōs omnēs interficient. Dum[5] haec faciunt, facile erit reliquōs mīlitēs ex hōc locō ēdūcere. Haec est sōla via salūtis." 10

"Bonum tuum cōnsilium probō," inquit dux, "sed tamen quis illōs praecipitēs in mortem certam dūcet?"

"Cūr mē nōn mittis? Mors mē nōn terret," respondit tribūnus. Itaque dux tribūnō magnās grātiās ēgit et hunc cum CCCC mīlitibus contrā hostēs mīsit. Fortēs illī Rōmānī nihil timuērunt. Neque cessērunt neque fūgērunt sed 15 magnō numerō hostium superātī sunt. Omnēs aut vītam āmīsērunt aut vulnera accēpērunt. Interim reliquī mīlitēs Rōmānī integrī salūtem petīvērunt.

Deī praemium tribūnō Caediciō ob ēgregium exemplum dōnāvērunt; nam vītam nōn āmīsit. Vulnera multa accēpit sed neque in capite neque in corde. 20 Illā aestāte hostēs expulsī sunt, et hieme Rōmānī hostēs nōn iam timuērunt.

[1] *tribune,* a junior officer
[2] *whose* (lit., *to whom*)
[3] *Caedicius (Sēdish´us)*
[4] *a certain* (abl.)
[5] *while*

Questions

1. In what war did the battle take place?
2. What danger did the Romans face?
3. At what time of year did the battle take place and why?
4. What was Caedicius' suggestion?
5. How many Roman soldiers were wounded or died in the battle?
6. What happened to Caedicius?
7. What reward did he receive and from whom?
8. Which part of this story is hardest to believe and why?

A highly imaginative seventeenth-century rendition of Scipio Africanus' triumph at the end of the First Punic War (241 B.C.). In the background, the mountainous seaport town on a river is meant to be Rome.

Gianni Dagli Orti/CORBIS

VOCABULARY

Nouns

aes´tās, aestā´tis f. *summer*	(estivate)
cor, cor´dis n. *heart*	(cordial, record)
hi´ems, hi´emis f. *winter*	(hibernate)
***mors, mor´tis, mor´tium** f. *death*	(mortal)
ni´hil, *nothing* (indeclinable)	(annihilate, nil)

Verb

ti´meō, -ē´re, ti´muī, —, *fear, be afraid (of)*	(timid)

GRAMMAR

Ablative of Time When

In English, time is expressed with or without the prepositions *in, on,* etc.; for example, *last summer, in winter, on Friday, at one o'clock.* In Latin, the *time when* something happens is regularly expressed by the ablative but without a preposition.

Illō annō in oppidō mānsimus.	*(In) that year we remained in town.*
Aestāte agrī sunt pulchrī.	*In summer the fields are beautiful.*
Illō tempōre nihil timuimus.	*At that time we feared nothing.*

Compare with the ablative of *place where*: when *at, in,* or *on* denotes time instead of place, no preposition is used.

■ *Exercises*

A. Translate the following sentences into English.

1. Hic puer et aestāte et hieme in agrīs labōrat.
2. Mīlitēs nostrī, paucī numerō sed corde fortēs, prōvinciam illō tempore occupāvērunt.
3. Illā hieme decem librōs lēgī sed hāc aestāte nihil fēcī.
4. Quīntā hōrā omnēs servī cum magnā celeritāte fūgērunt.
5. Hōc annō nihil timēmus, quod cōpiam frūmentī habēmus.
6. Prō Deō et patriā! Haec clāra verba corda hominum semper incitāvērunt.

B. Translate the following sentences into Latin.

1. In summer the rivers are not deep.
2. In that year we had many ships on every sea.
3. Good citizens love their country and do not fear an enemy.
4. Our country contains brave sons and beautiful daughters.
5. If[6] Marcus is our leader, nothing will scare us this winter.

WORD STUDY

- An *excursion* is a little *run out of* town. What is a *current* of water? *Cursive* writing? A *recurrent* illness? *Concurrent* powers of the federal government and the states? *Discord* is *hearts apart; concord, hearts together.* What is a *cordial* welcome? An apple *core?*

- Study the following English phrases borrowed from Latin.

primus inter pares	*first among (his) equals*
A.D. (anno Domini)	*in the year of the Lord*
aut Caesar aut nihil	*either Caesar or nothing*
Alma Mater	*nurturing mother* (applied to a school or college)

- Here are more state mottoes.

Dirigo.	*I direct.* (Maine)
Iustitia omnibus	*Justice for all* (District of Columbia)

---

[6] Use ablative absolute, omitting *is.*

CĪVITĀS RŌMĀNA

Duae partēs cīvitātis Rōmānae, Trōiānī et Latīnī, contrā perīcula commūnia pugnāvērunt. Ubi cīvitās nova concordiā aucta est, rēgēs populīque fīnitimī, cupiditāte praedae adductī, partem agrōrum Rōmānōrum occupābant. Paucī ex sociīs auxilium Rōmānīs submittēbant quod perīculīs
5 territī sunt. Sed Rōmānī properābant, parābant, cum hostibus proelia committēbant, lībertātem patriamque commūnem armīs dēfendēbant, mortem nōn timēbant. Dum pāx incerta est[1], dum eī nē spīrāre quidem[2] sine perīculō possunt[1], cūram perpetuam nōn remittēbant.

Dum haec geruntur[1], eī Rōmānī quōrum corpora ob annōs nōn iam firma
10 erant sed quī bonō cōnsiliō valēbant dē rē pūblicā[3] cōnsulēbantur; ob aetātem[4] patrēs aut senātōrēs appellābantur. In senātū convēnērunt.

Prīmō rēgēs erant, quī lībertātem cōnservābant et rem pūblicam[3] augēbant, sed posteā, quod eōrum rēgum duo ex Etrūriā superbī fuērunt, Rōmānī rēgēs pepulērunt et fēcērunt duōs cōnsulēs[5]. Eī cōnsulēs appellābantur quod
15 senātōrēs dē rē pūblicā[3] cōnsulēbant.

[1] use the past tense
[2] **nē... quidem** not even
[3] *republic*
[4] *age*
[5] *consuls,* the two officials jointly holding the supreme power in Rome

Once little more than marshy pastureland for shepherds, the Roman Forum slowly evolved into the chief civic and religious center of the city. It reached its greatest glory in the first and second centuries A.D., but, with Rome's gradual decline, it suffered so from fire, invasion, pilfering, and neglect that by the seventeenth century it was once again a Campo Vaccino, a *cow pasture.* Archaeological investigation and reconstruction under the supervision of experts from many nations began in the eighteenth century and continues to this day.

Stephen Studd/Getty Images

Eō tempore corda omnium Rōmānōrum glōriam spērāvērunt. Virī fortēs bella amābant, in castrīs aestāte atque hieme labōrābant, nihil timēbant: virtūs vēra eōrum omnia superāverat. Itaque populus Rōmānus magnum numerum hostium paucīs mīlitibus in fugam dabat, oppida nātūrā mūnīta pugnīs capiēbat. Hostibus superātīs et perīculō remōtō, Rōmānī aequē 20 regēbant. Iūra bellī pācisque cōnservābant; hōc modō auctōritās eōrum cōnfirmāta est. In ultimās partēs mīlitēs colōnīque eōrum missī sunt. Lingua Latīna in omnibus terrīs docēbātur. Post tertium Pūnicum bellum Rōmānī fuērunt dominī omnium terrārum mariumque. Nunc sine cūrā spīrāre et animōs remittere potuērunt. 25

Sed tum fortūna, semper incerta, eōs superāvit. Rōmānī pecūniam imperiumque[6], nōn iam glōriam, spērāvērunt. Superbī, nōn iam aequī fuērunt; iūra lēgēsque nōn iam cōnservāvērunt. Sēnsim[7] virtūtem auctōritātem fīnēs prōvinciās āmīsērunt et post longum tempus ā barbarīs superātī sunt. 30

[6] *empire, power*
[7] *gradually*

Questions

1. What caused the Roman state to grow?
2. What two peoples originally were parts of the Roman state?
3. Were their neighbors friendly?
4. What motivated neighboring kings to occupy Roman territory?
5. What character traits enabled the early Romans to survive?
6. How did the old men serve the state?
7. Why did the Romans expel their kings for good?
8. After the expulsion of the kings, how was the power shared?
9. What developments occurred as Roman dominion was extended?
10. When did they begin to relax and not feel anxiety?

VOCABULARY

Noun

*pars, par´tis, par´tium f. *part,*
  direction, side
  (partition, party)

Demonstrative

is, e´a, id, (adj.) *this, that;* (pron.) *he, she, it;*
  (pl.) *they*

Adjectives

commū´nis, -e *common* (commune, communism)
incer´tus, -a, -um *uncertain* [certus]

When the verb in a **dum** clause *(while)* is in the present tense and the main verb is in a past tense, translate the verb in the **dum** clause as if it were past.

Dum haec geruntur, Caesar discessit. *While these things were going on, Caesar left.*

Verbs

remit´tō, remit´tere, remī´sī, remis´sus　　　　**[mittō]**
　　relax, send back, (lit., *let back*)

spē´rō, spērā´re, spērā´vī, spērā´tus　　　　(despair)
　　hope (for), hope (that)

spī´rō, spīrā´re, spīrā´vī, spīrā´tus *breathe*　　(inspiration, spirit)

Conjunction

dum *while*

GRAMMAR

The Demonstrative *Is*

		SINGULAR	
	M.	F.	N.
Nominative	**is** *he, it*	**e´a** *she, it*	**id** *it*
Genitive	**e´ius** *his, its; of him*	**e´ius** *her, its; of her*	**e´ius** *its; of it*
Dative	**e´ī** *(to/for) him*	**e´ī** *(to/for) her*	**e´ī** *(to/for) it*
Accusative	**e´um** *him, it*	**e´am** *her, it*	**id** *it*
Ablative	**e´ō** *(by/with) him, it*	**e´ā** *(by/with) her, it*	**e´ō** *(by/with) it*

		PLURAL	
	M.	F.	N.
Nominative	**e´ī (i´ī)** *they*	**e´ae** *they*	**e´a** *they*
Genitive	**eō´rum** *their, of them*	**eā´rum** *their, of them*	**eō´rum** *their, of them*
Dative	**e´īs (i´īs)** *(to/for) them*	**e´īs (i´īs)** *(to/for) them*	**e´īs (i´īs)** *(to/for) them*
Accusative	**e´ōs** *them*	**e´ās** *them*	**e´a** *them*
Ablative	**e´īs (i´īs)** *(by/with) them*	**e´īs (i´īs)** *(by/with) them*	**e´īs (i´īs)** *(by/with) them*

Oral Practice

Decline **ea pars; id iter; is vir.**

Is as a Demonstrative Pronoun

Instead of pointing out a particular person or thing near or far away from the speaker, as **hic** and **ille** do, the demonstrative pronoun **is** usually refers less emphatically to someone or something just mentioned. The thing or person just referred to by the pronoun **is** is called its antecedent. When the antecedent of a form of **is** is a thing, that form is translated as *it* or (genitive) as *its*. On the other hand, when the form of **is** refers to a person, it is translated as *he, she* (nominative), *his, her* (genitive), or *him* or *her* (dative, accusative, ablative) depending on the case and gender (masculine or feminine) of the pronoun.

Mātremne tuam vidēre cupīvistī?	*Did you wish to see your mother?*
Sīc, eam vidēre cupīvī.	*Yes, I wished to see her.*

(Antecedent of **eam** is a person.)

And:

Lūdumne Mārciae vidēre cupīvistī?	*Did you wish to see Marcia's school?*
Sīc, lūdum eius vidēre cupīvī.	*Yes, I wished to see her school (the school of her).*

But:

Casamne vidēre cupīvistī?	*Did you wish to see the house?*
Sīc, eam vidēre cupīvī.	*Yes, I wished to see it.*

(Antecedent is a thing; **eam** is therefore translated as *it*.)

Is as a Demonstrative Adjective

Like **hic** and **ille, is,** although less emphatic, can also be used to modify nouns, agreeing with the noun it modifies in case, number, and gender and regularly standing before it.

Eam nāvem vīdī.	*I saw this* (or *that*) *ship*
Eārum partium nōmina cognōvī.	*I learned the names of those* (or *these*) *parts.*

Forms of **is** often serve as antecedents of the relative pronoun **quī, quae, quod** (pages 251 ff.).

Is quī videt probat.	*He who sees approves.*
Id quod dīcit probō.	*I approve that which she says. (I approve what she says.)*

 *Exercises*

A. Translate the following sentences into English.
1. Dum spīrō spērō. (the state motto of South Carolina)
2. Is cui librōs dedī eōs nōn remīsit.
3. Certa āmittimus dum incerta petimus.
4. Puellās et mātrem eārum in lūdō vīdī.
5. Commūne perīculum concordiam facit.
6. Eī puerī quōs aestāte vīdimus erant eius fīliī.
7. Hostibus pulsīs, tamen disciplīnam nostram nōn remittēmus.

B. Translate the following sentences into Latin.
1. Her father and mine are away.
2. Give him a part of the money.
3. We shall see him and his mother this summer.
4. This man is my teacher; that man is her father.

The Roman ruins at Dougga, Tunisia, are among the best-preserved in all Roman Africa. The Temple of Jupiter shown here dates from the second century A.D. The high platform is characteristic of Roman temples.

Did You Know?

In order to finance wars in an emergency, Rome often needed to borrow money from both landowners and wealthy businessmen. Sometimes, when the lenders' patriotism wore thin and they demanded repayment, the government, i.e, the Senate, was obliged to mortgage public lands to them.

WORD STUDY

- **The Names of the Months** In early Roman times the year began on March 1, and February was the last month. We still use the ancient Roman names of the months. *March* was named after Mars. *April* was the *opening* month (**aperiō**), when the earth seems to open up with new growth. *May* is the month when things become *bigger* (**maior**), *June* is Juno's month, *July* was originally called **Quīnctīlis**, the *fifth* month, but was renamed in honor of Julius Caesar after he had the calendar changed to our present system. Similarly, *August* was originally **Sextīlis**, the *sixth* month, but was renamed after the Emperor Augustus. *September* was originally the *seventh* month and kept its name even after it later became the ninth; similarly, *October, November, December. January* was named after Janus, the god of beginnings. *February* was the month of purification (**fēbrua**), a religious period vaguely similar to Christian Lent, Muslim Ramadan, and Jewish Yom Kippur.

- Here are more state mottoes.

  Joannes est nomen eius.   *John is his name.* (honoring St. John the Baptist, patron saint of Puerto Rico)

  Esto perpetua.   *May she live forever.* (Idaho)

LESSON OBJECTIVES
- To learn the story of King Midas
- To learn the demonstrative **īdem**

MIDĀS

Midās, nōbilis genere, rēx Phrygiae[1], multīs oppidīs expugnātīs, magnam auctōritātem habuit. Quondam Sīlēnus, magister deī Bacchī, in agrīs Phrygiae interceptus, ad eum rēgem ductus est. Quod Sīlēnus ab eōdem rēge multa beneficia accēpit, Bacchus parātus fuit rēgī dare id quod spērāvit.
5 Midās dīxit: "Sī omnia quae parte corporis meī tetigerō in aurum[2] vertentur, mihi grātum erit."

Hōc praemiō datō, omnia commūnia quae rēx tangēbat in aurum vertēbantur. Terram tangit: nōn iam terra est sed aurum. Aquam tangit: eōdem modō in aurum vertitur. Tum grātiās Bacchō prō magnō praemiō ēgit.

10 Tum rēx magnam cēnam parārī iussit et omnia genera cibōrum in mēnsā pōnī. Haec mēnsa ab eōdem tācta in aurum versa est. Dum magnā celeritāte servī cēnam parant, Midās familiārēs nōbilēs convocāvit. Grātō animō cēnam bonam quae parāta erat spectāvit. Dum cibum capit, cibus in aurum versus est. Vīnum in mēnsā pōnī iubet. Hoc tangit et nōn iam idem est sed in aurum
15 vertitur. Omnibus amīcīs ēgregia cēna grāta fuit sed nōn rēgī. Inter multōs cibōs Midās tamen nihil edere[3] potuit.

Tandem[4] ad Bacchum, auctōrem malōrum, rēx miser prōcēdere mātūrāvit et fīnem supplicī petīvit—nam supplicium et impedīmentum, nōn iam praemium, erat id quod ā deō accēperat. Bacchus iussit eum in mediō
20 flūmine Pactōlō[5] sē[6] lavāre. Praeceps rēx ad flūmen cucurrit, ubi sē lāvit, sē remīsit, sine cūrā spīrāvit, nam aurum remōtum erat. Arēna[7] flūminis in aurum versa est, et etiam nunc in hōc eōdem flūmine aurum est.

Questions
1. Who was Midas and why did he have great authority?
2. Who was caught and brought to the king?
3. Who was ready to give Midas exactly what he wished for and why?
4. What gift did Midas request?
5. Describe the "golden" feast and what happened.
6. What is meant by the expression "the Midas touch"?
7. Why was the gift given to Midas eventually a punishment?
8. What did Midas beg Bacchus for? What were the god's instructions to him?
9. According to the story, why is there gold in the river Pactolus today?

VOCABULARY

Nouns

ge´nus, ge´neris n. *birth, kind*   (generation, genus)

suppli´cium, suppli´cī n. *punishment*   (supplication)

Demonstrative

ī´dem, e´ădem, ĭ´dem (adj.) *the same;*   (identify, identity)
(pron.) *the same man, woman, thing*

Adjective

nō´bilis, -e *noble*   (nobility, noblewoman)

Verbs

expug´nō, expugnā´re, expugnā´vī,   [pugnō]
    expugnā´tus *capture by assault*

interci´piō, interci´pere, intercē´pī,   [capiō]
    intercep´tus *intercept, cut off, catch*

tan´gō, tan´gere, te´tigī, tāc´tus *touch*   (tactile, tangent)

Adverb

quon´dam *once (upon a time)*

Did You Know?

The Romans valued gold so highly that they banned the burial of any gold with the corpse, except for gold cavity fillings. Cavities were also filled with silver by barbers who often practiced as dentists. Gold wire was used to attach wooden false teeth to the jaws of wealthy Romans. Some well-to-do Romans even had a decayed tooth replaced by a healthy tooth from a slave's mouth, which was then hammered into the jaw and kept in place by a gold wire.

An illustration by Walter Crane testifies to the vitality of ancient legend. King Midas had no daughter in the original version of the story, so in 1852 Nathaniel Hawthorne, the famous American novelist, invented one for him, named her Marygold, and turned her to gold at her father's affectionate kiss. (But, of course, Hawthorne also brought her back to life.) Now Marygold too has become part of the legend.

Bettmann/CORBIS

GRAMMAR

The Demonstrative *Īdem*

The demonstrative **īdem,** meaning *(the) same,* is a compound of **is** and
-dem, with slight changes in spelling for ease of pronunciation.

	SINGULAR		
	M	F	N
Nominative	ī´dem	e´ădem	ĭ´dem
Genitive	eius´dem	eius´dem	eius´dem
Dative	eī´dem	eī´dem	eī´dem
Accusative	eun´dem	ean´dem	ĭ´dem
Ablative	eō´dem	eā´dem	eō´dem

	PLURAL		
	M	F	N
Nominative	eī´dem	eae´dem	e´ădem
Genitive	eōrun´dem	eārun´dem	eōrun´dem
Dative	eīs´dem	eīs´dem	eīs´dem
Accusative	eōs´dem	eās´dem	e´ădem
Ablative	eīs´dem	eīs´dem	eīs´dem

Oral Practice

Give the Latin in the singular and plural for *the same body* in the
accusative, *the same summer* in the ablative, *the same year* in the genitive,
the same punishment in the nominative, *the same part* in the dative.

▦ *Exercises*

A. Translate the following sentences.

1. Eōdem annō lībertās captīvīs data est.
2. Dux eum ad idem supplicium trahī iussit.
3. Dum omnia timēmus, glōriam spērāre nōn possumus.
4. Oppidō expugnātō, Caesar impedīmenta hostium intercēpit.
5. Hic homō nōbilī genere sed nōn magnīs factīs illum superat.
6. Hominēs līberī parēsque esse dēbent, quod eadem iūra habent.

B. Translate the following sentences into Latin.

1. His punishment scared the rest.
2. He will not send back the same book.
3. When I saw the same boy[8], I was no longer afraid.
4. Their towns were captured one at a time the same year.

C. Imagine the conversation the god Bacchus may have had with King Midas. Work with a partner to create a scene wherein Bacchus offers Midas the golden touch because he had done many kind things for people. King Midas then goes about touching and naming objects and rendering them useless even if they are gold.

This armband and ring from Pompeii are fine examples of Roman workmanship in gold.

[8] Change to passive in English; then use ablative absolute.

WORD STUDY

- Explain the meaning and etymology of the word *community*. **Supplicium** literally means *folding* (or *bending*) *down for punishment* (**sub + plicō**). Explain *supplication*.

- Study the following English phrases borrowed from Latin.

ibid. (ibidem)	*in the same place*
id. (idem)	*the same* (i.e., as mentioned above)
quid pro quo	*something for something*
Homo proponit, sed Deus disponit.	*Man proposes, but God disposes.*
Genus homo, semper idem.	*The human race, always the same.*

- Here are more state mottoes.

Scuto bonae voluntatis tuae coronasti nos.	*You have encircled us with the shield of your goodwill.* (seal of Maryland)
Si quaeris peninsulam amoenam, circumspice.	*If you seek a lovely peninsula, look about you.* (Michigan)

North Wind Picture Archives

Ubi sumus?

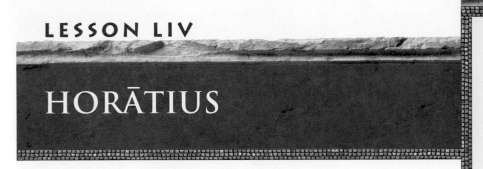

LESSON LIV

HORĀTIUS

LESSON OBJECTIVES
- To learn about Roman commitment to the community
- To learn the intensive pronoun/adjective **ipse**
- To learn about words often confused

Nunc in locīs commodīs sedēbimus et legēmus dē Horātiō[1], virō fortī nōbilīque genere. Sī haec fābula, nōn tibi nōta, tē dēlectābit[2], tū ipse lege eandem sorōribus frātribusque tuīs parvīs (sī frātrēs sorōrēsque habēs), quī circum tē sedēbunt et magnō cum studiō audient.

Tarquiniī[3], ā Rōmānīs pulsī, auxilium petīvērunt ā Porsenā[4], rēge 5 Etrūscōrum. Itaque Porsena ipse cum multīs mīlitibus Rōmam[5] vēnit. Rōmānī, dē salūte commūnī incertī, territī sunt, quod magna erat potestās Etrūscōrum magnumque Porsenae nōmen. Rōmānī quī agrōs colēbant in oppidum migrāvērunt; portās clausērunt et oppidum ipsum praesidiīs dēfendērunt. Pars urbis Tiberī[6] flūmine mūnīta est. Pōns sublicius[7] iter 10 hostibus dabat, sed ēgregius vir prohibuit, Horātius Coclēs[8], illō cognōmine appellātus quod in proeliō oculum āmīserat. Is, extrēmā pontis parte occupātā, sōlus sine auxiliō mīlitēs hostium intercēpit et sustinuit et Rōmānōs quī fugiēbant pontem frangere iussit. Ipsa audācia[9] hostēs terruit. Ponte frāctō, Horātius nōn dubitāvit sed armīs impedītus praeceps in Tiberim 15 dēsiluit[10] et per multa tēla[11] integer ad Rōmānōs trānāvit[12]. Eius virtūte oppidum nōn expugnātum est et potestās Porsenae frācta est. Grāta ob factum clārum eius cīvitās fuit. Multī agrī eī pūblicē datī sunt, quōs ad terminum vītae coluit. Exemplum virtūtis ab eō prōpositum Rōmānī semper memoriā retinuērunt. 20

[1] *Horatius (Horā´shus)*
[2] translate by the present: *pleases*
[3] *the Tar´quins,* Etruscan rulers of Rome in the sixth century B.C.
[4] *Por´sena*
[5] *to Rome*
[6] *Tiber River* (**Tiberis, -is** m. is a "pure" **i**-stem; its acc. sing. ends in **-im** [see line 15].)
[7] *bridge made of wooden pilings*
[8] *Cō´clēs ("One-Eye")*. Many Romans acquired a nickname (**cognōmen**) from some exploit or physical characteristic (see page 467).
[9] *boldness*
[10] *jumped down*
[11] *spears*
[12] *swam across*

Questions
1. What does the narrator of this passage want his audience to do?
2. If the reader enjoys the story, what is he or she asked to do then?
3. Why did Porsena go to Rome?
4. Why were the Romans frightened?
5. How was Porsena prevented from entering the city?
6. What natural barrier prevented the Etruscans from attacking Rome?
7. Who saved Rome? How?
8. How did the hero escape?
9. What was his reward?
10. How did Cocles get his name?

The single arch *(left center)* is all that remains of the **Pōns Aemilius** (second century B.C.), the first stone bridge built within the city of Rome. Many think that the wooden **Pōns Sublicius** (Horatius' Bridge) stood nearby. This ancient bridge stood almost intact until the sixteenth century, when floods destroyed most of it.

Did You Know?

The Latin word **pontificēs** *(priests)* comes from the two Latin words **pōns** *(bridge)* and **faciō** *(make)*. As *bridgemakers,* priests had the magical powers needed to cross the boundary a river formed. The first wooden bridge across the Tiber River dated from the seventh century B.C. This and other early bridges served as models for the later stone structures. Julius Caesar had two bridges erected across the Rhine, and the Emperor Trajan built a five-thousand-foot-long bridge across the Danube.

VOCABULARY

Nouns

frā´ter, frā´tris m. *brother*   (fraternal, fraternity)

*pōns, pon´tis, pon´tium m. *bridge*   (pontoon, pontificate)

potes´tās, potestā´tis f. *power*   **[possum]**

so´ror, sorō´ris f. *sister*   (sorority)

Intensive Pronoun

ip´se, ip´sa, ip´sum (pron. and adj.)
   -self, the very

Verbs

co´lō, co´lere, co´luī, cul´tus   (cult, cultivate)
   till, cultivate, worship, inhabit

fran´gō, fran´gere, frē´gī, frāc´tus *break*   (fracture, fraction)

se´deō, sedē´re, sē´dī, sessū´rus *sit*   (preside, session)

GRAMMAR

The Intensive in English and the Latin *Ipse*

In English, compound pronouns are formed by joining *-self* to *my, your, him, her, it* and the plural *-selves* to *our, your, them.* These compounds may be used in an intensive or emphatic sense, such as, *I saw the man myself.*

In Latin, the pronoun **ipse** is a compound of **is** and the intensive ending **-pse** and therefore has purely intensive force; its meaning depends on the person, number, and gender of the word modified.

Ipse hominem vīdī.	*I saw the man myself.*
Hominem ipsum vīdī.	*I saw the man himself.*
Puellae ipsae ad oppidum cucurrērunt.	*The girls themselves ran to the town.*

Note that **ipse** may also be used alone in the nominative to emphasize an omitted subject. It is declined like **ille,** except in the neuter nominative and accusative singular, where it has the regular **-um** ending. The plural is regular: **ipsī, -ae, -a.** Plural meanings: *ourselves, yourselves, themselves.*

Oral Practice

Translate **frātris ipsīus, suppliciō ipsō, partēs ipsae, hic cīvis ipse, illārum nāvium ipsārum, meae sorōrī ipsī, eiusdem generis, eōrundem auctōrum.**

The English words *himself, herself, themselves,* etc., are used in a variety of ways. To test whether these would be translated as a form of Latin **ipse,** ask yourself: Can the word *-self* be omitted from the sentence and still make sense? Does *-self* mean *on (his, her, its, their) own?* If the answer to either of these two questions is *yes,* the form *-self* is probably intensive, requiring a form of **ipse.**

	SINGULAR		
	M.	F.	N.
Nominative	**ip´se** *myself, yourself, himself, itself*	**ip´sa** *myself, yourself, herself, itself*	**ip´sum** *itself*
Genitive	**ipsī´us** *of myself, yourself, himself, itself,* etc.	**ipsī´us** *of myself, yourself, herself, itself,* etc.	**ipsī´us** *of itself*
Dative	**ip´sī**	**ip´sī**	**ip´sī**
Accusative	**ip´sum**	**ip´sam**	**ip´sum**
Ablative	**ip´sō**	**ip´sā**	**ip´sō**
	PLURAL		
	ip´sī	**ip´sae**	**ip´sa,** etc.

🔲 *Exercises*

A. Translate the following sentences into English.
1. Nōnne idem ipsī cernitis, puerī?
2. Quae officia soror vestra ipsa suscipiet?
3. Deī quōs Rōmānī colēbant multī erant.
4. Quis est ille puer quī cum sorōre meā sedet?
5. Ille homō agricola appellātur quod agrōs colit.
6. Frātrēs et sorōrēs eiusdem familiae iūra paria habēre dēbent.

B. Translate the following sentences into Latin.
1. These (men) are standing; those are sitting.
2. These letters were written by the king himself.
3. We ourselves shall get much money in a few years.
4. The same winter they saw and heard him themselves.

WORD STUDY

The Norman–French Influence in English In previous lessons, we saw how Latin words were introduced into the English language at its very beginning. A very important later period of influence followed the Norman invasion of England (1066). The language of the Norman conquerors was an old form of French, and thus itself descended from Latin. In a few centuries, it had introduced many new words that often show great variation from the original Latin spellings. Especially common is the change from one vowel to two. Look up the Latin originals of *captain, courage, duke, homage, peer, prey, reign, treason, villain, visor.*

The opening pages of Sir Walter Scott's *Ivanhoe* reveal in language the changed cultural situation that followed the Norman conquest. The animals that the defeated and oppressed Saxons must tend are referred to by the Anglo-Saxon names *swine* and *kine.* But when these animals are served on the tables of the Norman masters, they are referred to by their Latin-derived names, *pork* and *beef.*

GLIMPSES OF ROMAN LIFE

RELIGION

Cerēs, dea frūmentī.

The earliest Romans believed that for almost every object and activity—the sky, the flow of rivers, the ripening of crops, even the hinges of a door—there was a mysterious and protective spirit or power **(anima).** This is the *animism* common in primitive agricultural societies, filled with what we would call superstitions, magic, and taboos. Gradually these spirits began to take on clearer forms and personalities as Roman gods and goddesses. Worship was centered in the family around various household gods: the **Lār Familiāris** (plural, **Larēs Familiārēs**), originally a field spirit who had been domesticated to protect the entire homestead; **Vesta,** goddess of the hearth; the **Penātēs,** gods of the food supply; and the **Genius,** the guardian spirit of the head of the household. The family's simple offerings and prayers to these deities long remained the most vital part of Roman religion. Offerings were most often made to the household deities at dinner, although devout Romans prayed every morning.

As Rome grew as a political community, public religious activity became an integral part of state affairs and rapidly assimilated other gods, goddesses, and forms of worship from people throughout the Empire. From the Etruscans the Romans learned a style of building temples and foretelling the future. The first temple in Rome was built by the Etruscans and was dedicated to Jupiter, Juno, and Minerva. When Greek influence on Rome increased, the Romans identified their native gods with the chief Greek deities: the sky god Jupiter with Zeus, the war god Mars with Ares, the love goddess Venus with Aphrodite, the grain goddess Ceres with Demeter, and so on. Still later, as much of the world flocked to Rome, new religions were introduced from Egypt, Asia Minor, and Persia, while the official state cult turned more toward emperor worship. Mystery religions, such as the worship of the Egyptian goddess Isis and the Babylonian cult of Zoroaster, became popular among the common people. Worship of Mithras, an Eastern god representing the beneficent power of light over darkness, gained great influence in the Roman army. Judaism had been known to the Romans since their conquest of Palestine in the first century B.C.

The generally tolerant and *polytheistic* (believing in many gods) Romans found *monotheism* (belief in a single god) strange. For nearly three centuries they persecuted the Christians because they scorned the pagan gods of the state and would not admit the divinity of the emperor. Christianity itself was officially recognized by Emperor Constantine in A.D. 313. As Christianity grew in strength, the great pagan gods and goddesses faded from the ceremonies of the state, and the simple family rituals retreated to the peasant folk from whom they had originally sprung.

Just as remarkable as the variety and ability of the Roman religion to borrow other forms of worship was the closeness of its tie with politics. Originally the chief priest **(pontifex maximus)** had been the king himself; later the chief priest was elected, and he and all other priests or **pontificēs** were government officials. The duties of the **pontifex maximus** included inaugurating the **pontificēs,** caring for public records, and overseeing the sacred rites of Vesta. The state had charge of the building and restoration of temples, which, in addition to being centers of worship, were public treasuries, record offices, museums, and meeting places.

Another political feature of the ancient religion was the attempt to determine the will of the gods in various ways. The duty of priests who were called **augurēs** *(augurs)* was to determine whether a certain important act (such as a military expedition) would be successful. They did this by observing the behavior and flight of birds. Certain movements were supposed to indicate success; others, failure. Another practice, borrowed from the Etruscans, was to determine the will of the gods by inspecting the entrails of sacrificial animals. These methods were considered official and were used before important public matters were undertaken. Such acts of interpretation were called the "taking of the auspices." Eventually, many educated Romans lost faith in these types of practices, but they continued them in order to influence the more ignorant classes. Private persons also resorted to numerous unofficial fortune-tellers, such as astrologers, as some people do today.

With so many gods to worship, the Romans naturally had many holidays. Some of these were celebrated with amusements as well as with religious observances, as is true of our holidays today. For example, the festival called Consualia was celebrated on August 18 and was given in honor of Consus who presided over the storage of the harvest. In the Saturnalian revels of late December, masters and slaves exchanged roles. The Palilia festival in honor of Pales, the goddess of flocks, occurred on April 21. This was also the official day honoring the founding of Rome.

QUESTIONS

1. What part did family worship play in Roman life?
2. In what countries today is religion directly connected with the state?

VOCABULARY

Nouns

aestās	hiems	pars	supplicium
cor	māter	pōns	
frāter	mors	potestās	
genus	nihil	soror	

Demonstrative Pronouns/Adjectives

hic	ille	is
īdem	ipse	

Adjectives

commūnis	nōbilis
incertus	praeceps

Verbs

colō	frangō	spērō
currō	intercipiō	spīrō
expellō	remittō	tangō
expugnō	sedeō	timeō

Conjunction

dum

Adverb

quondam

GRAMMAR SUMMARY

The Demonstratives Hic, Ille, Is, Īdem

Demonstratives are used to point out things. As adjectives they are translated by *this* or *that* in the singular, *these* or *those* in the plural. As pronouns, they are translated by *he, she, it, his, her, its, him,* *her, it, they, their,* or *them,* according to case, number, and gender. **Īdem** means *the same.* When used as adjectives, demonstratives agree with the noun they modify—even if it is not expressed—in gender, number, and case. As pronouns, forms of **is, ea, id** agree in gender and number, but not necessarily in case, with their antecedent, just as relative pronouns do.

Haec fēmina in agrō labōrat.	*This woman is working in the field.* (adjective)
Illa aquam portat.	*That (woman) is carrying water.* (pronoun)
Eum et eam in Forō vīdimus.	*We saw him and her in the Forum.* (pronoun)
Eundem equum vīdī.	*I saw the same horse.* (adjective)

The Intensive Ipse

The intensive is used to emphasize any noun or pronoun in the sentence. It is translated as *-self* or *-selves* added to *my, your, him, her, it, our, your,* or *them.*

Ipsī eōs vīdimus.	*We saw them ourselves.*
Rōmānī rēgem ipsum ex oppidō expellere cupīvērunt.	*The Romans desired to drive the king himself out of the town.*

Ablative of Time When

The time when an action takes place is expressed by the ablative without a preposition. In English, the preposition *in* or *on* is often used.

Cēnam decimā horā ēdimus.	*We ate dinner at the tenth hour.*
Aestāte natāre amō.	*In the summer I like to swim.*

SUMMARY OF CASE USES

	THE ABLATIVE WITH LATIN	THE OBJECTIVE WITH ENGLISH
Place	1. Preposition **in**	1. Preposition *in*
Means	2. No preposition	2. Preposition *with* or *by*
Accompaniment	3. Preposition **cum**	3. Preposition *with*
Agent	4. Prep. **a/ab**	4. Preposition *by*
Manner	5. No preposition or preposition **cum**	5. Preposition *with*
Respect	6. No preposition	6. Preposition *in*
Time	7. No preposition	7. No preposition or preposition *at, in,* or *on*

UNIT PRACTICE

A. Make **hic, ille,** and **īdem** agree as demonstrative adjectives with the following nouns in the case required.

Example:

māteriae (genitive): **huius, illīus, eiusdem māteriae**

aestāte	**partī**
capita (nominative)	**patris**
cor (accusative)	**pretium** (accusative)
frātrēs (nominative)	**sorōrem**
mortium	

B. Give the correct form of **is.** Then translate the sentences.

1. *(Him, her, it)* vīdī.
2. *(By him, by her)* ēvocātus sum.
3. Fīlium *(his, her)* docēbō.
4. Nōvistīne *(their)* patrem?
5. Hunc librum *(to him, to her, to them)* mandābō.

WORD STUDY

1. Give the Latin words suggested by the derivatives: *cordial, partial, sedentary, fraternity, inspiration, cult, generation, sorority, cursive, remiss, maternal, intercept, infinite, sediment.*

Intercept

2. Write sentences using as many English derivatives as you can find from the Latin **trahō, audiō,** and **premō.**

VOCABULARY

Choose the word that best completes each sentence.

1. Illō annō frāter meus agrōs patris nostrī sub monte _____.
   a. remittēbat
   b. sedēbat
   c. intercipiēbat
   d. colēbat
2. "Viā numquam mōnstrātā, dē itinere _____ sum," nūntius dīxit.
   a. commūnis
   b. incertus
   c. nōbilis
   d. praeceps
3. Magnae undae nāvēs Ulixis _____, et nautae miserī vītam āmīsērunt.
   a. spērāverant
   b. spīrāverant
   c. frēgerant
   d. timuerant
4. Fortēs puellae praecipitēs in perīculum mātūrāvērunt; nihil _____.
   a. timuērunt
   b. spīrāvērunt
   c. sēdērunt
   d. cucurrērunt
5. Puellae quae in eādem familiā sunt _____ semper appellantur.
   a. frātrēs
   b. mātrēs
   c. patrēs
   d. sorōrēs

GRAMMAR

Complete each sentence with the correct endings.

6. Illā aestāt___ mīlitēs ad flūmen alt___ labōrāba___, nam inter oppid___ pōns mūniēbā___.
7. In cord___ rēx nātūr___ vēram captīv___ illīus crēv___, itaque illum līberāv___.
8. Ill___ quī in ultimam part___ prōvinci___ ab h___ duce nunc trānsportantur cūrās remitt___ hiem___ dūrā nōn poterunt.
9. "Mort___ ips___ nōn timeō," nōbilis nūntiāba___. "Etiam supplici___ huius gener___ sustinēbō."
10. Host___ expulsīs, omnēs magnā cum celeritāt___ ad templ___ cīvitāt___ currēba___ et nōmin___ deōrum ipsōrum laudābant.

TRANSLATION

Translate the following sentences.

11. Caesare duce, Rōmānī Gallōs expugnāvērunt, et illīs barbarīs populīs lēgēs linguamque dedērunt.
12. "Quondam potestātem glōriamque spērāvimus; hōc tempore, pāce cōnfirmātā, omnia quae cupīveramus obtinuimus," Rōmānus dīxit.
13. Hic, adductus exemplō ēgregiō magistrī clārī, omnia verba pulchra carminum illōrum cognōvit et ea nōbīs docet.
14. Dum ipsae ad mare sedent et magnō studiō librōs legunt, ille ā frātre eārum ad portam interceptus est.
15. Eādem hōrā cīvēs ad medium oppidum properāvērunt et patrēs dē salūte commūnī cōnsuluērunt.

INVESTIGATION

Track down the answers to these questions from any lesson in Unit X.

16. Explain the difference between monotheism and polytheism.

17. Tell the main area of influence for the following Roman deities.

Venus	Ceres
Mars	Minerva
Mercury	Diana
Neptune	Vulcan

18. True or false? According to the original Roman calendar, the first month of the year was February.

19. In ancient Rome, what was the **Rēgia,** and where was it located?

20. In the government of the Roman republic, who were the **cōnsulēs?**

CULTURE

Vērum aut Falsum? Indicate whether each statement is true or false.

21. From the Greeks the Romans learned to inspect animal entrails to determine the will of the gods.

22. The word **anima** refers to the protecting spirit of an object or activity.

23. One of the important household deities was Vesta, goddess of the hearth.

24. The Romans believed in the complete separation of religion and government.

25. Religions from Persia, Asia Minor, and Egypt were all practiced in Rome.

FROM LATIN TO ENGLISH

Apply your knowledge of Latin roots to determine the best meaning of the italicized words.

26. The tribe had *annihilated* that species of bird on the island.
  a. protected
  b. destroyed
  c. worshipped
  d. introduced

27. That general was the *precursor* of several fine governors in our province.
  a. descendant
  b. teacher
  c. forerunner
  d. enemy

28. Some animals have a highly developed *tactile* sense.
  a. of sight
  b. of hearing
  c. of taste
  d. of touch

29. Writing the letter was an act of *supplication.*
  a. begging
  b. forgiving
  c. refusing
  d. explaining

30. A *mortiferous* chemical had been spilled into the river.
  a. harmless
  b. deadly
  c. discarded
  d. liquid

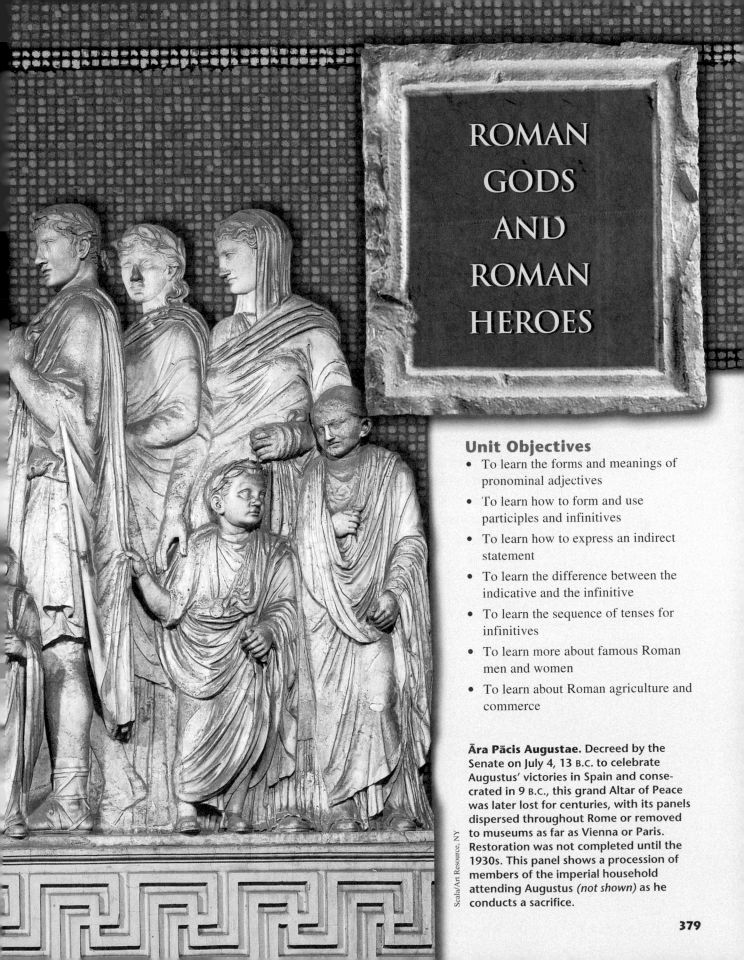

ROMAN GODS AND ROMAN HEROES

Unit Objectives

- To learn the forms and meanings of pronominal adjectives
- To learn how to form and use participles and infinitives
- To learn how to express an indirect statement
- To learn the difference between the indicative and the infinitive
- To learn the sequence of tenses for infinitives
- To learn more about famous Roman men and women
- To learn about Roman agriculture and commerce

Āra Pācis Augustae. Decreed by the Senate on July 4, 13 B.C. to celebrate Augustus' victories in Spain and consecrated in 9 B.C., this grand Altar of Peace was later lost for centuries, with its panels dispersed throughout Rome or removed to museums as far as Vienna or Paris. Restoration was not completed until the 1930s. This panel shows a procession of members of the imperial household attending Augustus *(not shown)* as he conducts a sacrifice.

Scala/Art Resource, NY

LESSON OBJECTIVE

- To learn more about Roman gods and goddesses, particularly those worshipped by the family

ALIĪ DEĪ DEAEQUE

Dē magnīs deīs, quōs Rōmānī ā Graecīs accēperant, iam lēgimus. Nunc dē multīs parvīs deīs, vērē Rōmānīs, legēmus. Concordiam, Victōriam, Salūtem, Pācem, Fortūnam, Virtūtem Rōmānī deās vocāvērunt, quod sacrae erant et ā Rōmānīs amābantur. Etiam Pecūnia ā Rōmānīs amābātur et dea
5 erat, sed tamen (ita scrībit auctor Rōmānus Iuvenālis[1]) nōn in templō habitāvit.

Aliī deī erant deī familiārēs, quōs prīmōs puerī puellaeque cognōverant. Lār familiāris erat is deus quī familiam cōnservābat. Penātēs erant eī deī quī cibum servābant. Vesta erat dea focī[2] in quō cibus parābātur. Ad focum
10 erant parvae fōrmae deōrum. Ibi, omnibus līberīs et familiāribus convocātīs, paterfamiliās[3] ipse deīs grātiās agēbat et cibum dōnābat. Quondam nōn multus cibus erat, sed tamen pater deīs partem cibī dōnābat. Līberī patrem rogāvērunt: "Cūr ille cibus deīs hōc tempore ā tē datur? Nōn multum habēmus." Pater respondit: "Cibō hōc datō, deī hominibus magna beneficia
15 et longam vītam dabunt."

[1] *Jū´venal,* a poet of the second century A.D.
[2] *of the hearth*
[3] *father of the household* (**familiās** is an old form of the genitive)

Questions

1. What surprising fact about Roman worship did you learn in the first paragraph?
2. What is meant by the term **deī familiārēs**?
3. What role and function did the **Lār familiāris** have?
4. What role and function did the **Penātēs** have?
5. What was the central location for religious ceremony and sacrifice in the household?
6. What reasons did the father have for sacrificing and giving food to the gods?

▦ *Exercises*

A. Translate the following sentences into English.

   1. Hoc genus potestātis ipsum frangī nōn potest.
   2. Cor eius sententiīs nōbilibus tāctum est dum deōs deāsque colit[4].   [4] Translate as if imperfect tense.
   3. Frātrēs rēgis ipsīus hāc hieme ē cīvitāte expellentur.
   4. Pars eōrum supplicium mortis timēbat, pars tempus virtūtis et fīnem omnium malōrum exspectābat.
   5. Posteā omnia iūra magnā cum celeritāte cōnfirmābuntur.

B. Translate the following sentences into Latin.

   1. The gods of the family will overcome a common enemy.
   2. The land of our fathers and mothers stretched from the mountains to the sea.
   3. The founder of the Roman people was a god of war who was strong both in name and in influence.
   4. It is not easy for them to find courage when the citizens themselves sit and do nothing.
   5. The same people who hope for freedom are the very ones who are afraid when peace has been established.

CICERŌ ET TĪRŌ

LESSON OBJECTIVES

- To learn about the special friendship between Cicero and Tiro
- To learn the declension and use of numeral and pronominal adjectives

Cicerō et Tīrō fuērunt Rōmānī clārī, alter maximus[1] ōrātor tōtīus Ītaliae, alter servus fīdus[2]. Quod Tīrō dīligentiā sapientiāque[3] Cicerōnī magnum auxilium dabat, Cicerō eum tōtō corde amābat et posteā līberāvit. Neutrī grātum erat sine alterō ūllum iter facere.

5 Cicerō cum Tīrōne in Graeciā fuerat. Ubi ille in Ītaliam revertit, Tīrō sōlus in Graeciā relīctus est quod aeger[4] fuit. Cicerō ad eum trēs litterās in itinere ūnō diē[5] scrīpsit. Inter alia haec ipsa scrīpsit:

"Variē litterīs tuīs affectus sum, prīmā parte territus, alterā cōnfirmātus. Hōc tempore tē[6] neque marī neque itinerī committere dēbēs. Medicus tuus 10 bonus est, ut[7] scrībis et ego audiō; sed eum nōn probō; nam iūs[8] nōn dēbet stomachō aegrō darī. Sed tamen et ad illum et ad Lysōnem[9] scrīpsī. Lysōnis nostrī neglegentiam nōn probō, quī, litterīs ā mē acceptīs, ipse nūllās remīsit; respondēre dēbet. Sed Lysō Graecus est et omnium Graecōrum magna est neglegentia. In nūllā rē[10] properāre dēbēs.

15 "Curium[11] iussī omnem pecūniam tibi dare quam cupis. Sī medicō pecūniam dabis, dīligentia eius augēbitur. Magna sunt tua in mē officia[12]; omnia superāveris, sī, ut spērō, salūtem tuam cōnfirmātam vīderō. Ante, dum magnā dīligentiā mihi auxilium dās[13], nōn salūtem tuam cōnfirmāre potuistī; nunc tē nihil impedit. Omnia dēpōne; salūs sōla in animō tuō esse dēbet."

20 Nōnne Cicerō dominus aequus amīcusque erat? Aliī dominī erant bonī, aliī malī. Omnī aetāte[14] et in omnibus terrīs bonī et malī hominēs fuērunt et sunt et fortasse semper erunt.

[1] greatest
[2] loyal
[3] wisdom
[4] ill
[5] ablative
[6] yourself
[7] as
[8] soup
[9] Tiro was staying at Lyso's house.
[10] thing, circumstance
[11] Cu´rius, a banker
[12] services
[13] Translate as imperfect.
[14] age

Questions

1. What was Tiro's relationship to Cicero?
2. Why was Cicero so fond of Tiro?
3. To whom did Cicero write about Tiro?
4. Why was Tiro left behind in Greece?
5. What things did Cicero recommend for Tiro's recovery?
6. What prejudices does the writer show toward Greeks?
7. What does the letter say about the cost of medical care?

The Acropolis in Athens sits atop the highest point in the city (acropolis means *high city* in Greek) at 500 feet above sea level. The Doric style Parthenon, dedicated to Athena, patron deity of the city and goddess of wisdom, is the largest of the group of temples located there. It is made entirely of white marble.

Scala/Art Resource, NY

VOCABULARY

Adjectives

a´lius, a´lia, a´liud[15] *other, another*   (alias)
   a´lius... a´lius *one . . . another*
   a´liī... a´liī, *some . . . others*
al´ter, al´tera, al´terum[16] *the other* (of two)   (alternate)
   al´ter... al´ter *the one . . . the other*
neu´ter, neu´tra, neu´trum *neither* (of two)[17]   (neutral)
nūl´lus, nūl´la, nūl´lum *no, none*   (nullify)
sō´lus, sō´la, sō´lum *alone*   (sole, solitary)
tō´tus, tō´ta, tō´tum *whole, entire*   (total)
ūl´lus, ūl´la, ūl´lum *any*
ū´nus, ū´na, ū´num *one*   (unify)

[15] The neuter nominative and accusative singular end in **-d**, not **-m** (cf. **ille**).

[16] The genitive singular of **alter** ends in **-ĭus** (short -ĭ).

[17] **Uter,** *which (of two),* and **uterque,** *each (of two),* *both,* are likewise irregular and belong to this group but are comparatively rare.

All the adjectives above, except **alter**, have **-īus** in the genitive and **-ī** in the dative singular of all genders.

Did You Know?

Doctors, doctors' assistants, and nurses in Rome were often Greek slaves or freedmen. Such medical personnel had been imported from Greece since the second century B.C. Although Greek physicians were not generally well regarded by the Romans because they were foreigners and/or slaves, Julius Caesar made citizens of Greek physicians who practiced in Rome, and Augustus later granted them additional privileges.

Declension of *Ūnus* and Pronominal Adjectives

The numeral **ūnus** and the other adjectives in the vocabulary of this lesson are "irregular" in the genitive singular (**-īus,** but **alter** has **-ĭus**) and dative singular (**-ī**), like **ipse. Alius,** like **ille,** has the neuter nominative and accusative singular ending in **-ud** and uses **alterĭus** as its genitive singular. Elsewhere in the singular and everywhere in the plural, these adjectives are regularly declined like **magnus.** Like **hic** and **ille,** they are emphatic and usually precede their nouns.

Oral Practice

1. Decline in the singular **alius frāter tuus.**
2. Give the Latin for the following in the genitive and dative singular: *neither sister, the whole town, the other leader, no winter, safety alone, one citizen.*

Words Often Confused

alius = *another*, one of a group of *three or more*
alter = *(the) one* or *the other*, i.e., *of two* and no more

tōtus = *whole*, i.e., no part missing, not capable of being divided
omnis (sing.) = *every*
omnēs (pl.) = *all*, i.e., a complete collection of units or parts

nūllus = *not any, no*—an adjective
nihil = *not a thing, nothing*—always a noun
nēmō = *no man, no one*—always a noun
nōn = *not*—an adverb

Marcus Tullius Cicero was Rome's most outstanding orator. Born in 106 B.C. in the nearby town of Arpinum, he held all the positions in the **cursus honōrum** (the successive offices in the political career), including the consulship. He suppressed an internal conspiracy and was an honest provincial governor. No other Roman was so devoted to Greek culture, and his writings were very important in transmitting Greek thought to later Europe. His letters, some eight hundred of which exist, give us a full picture of Roman daily life in the first century B.C. His later career brought many disappointments: political eclipse, even exile, domestic troubles, the death of his beloved daughter Tullia; and his speeches against the opponents of republican principles eventually cost him his life.

▦ *Exercises*

A. Translate the following sentences into English.

1. Rēx neutrī fīliō potestātem committet.
2. Cōnsilia alterius ducis alterī nōn erant grāta.
3. Sorōrēs meae agrōs montēsque tōtīus īnsulae vīdērunt.
4. Is homō ipse ab aliīs dēfēnsus est sed nūllō modō ab aliīs.
5. Quīnque amīcī eius iam discessērunt et is sōlus nunc manet.
6. Accēpistīne ipse ūlla praemia prō meritīs tuīs? Nūlla accēpī neque ūlla exspectō.

B. Translate the following sentences into Latin.

1. Every man in our whole country ought to work.
2. To one sister I shall give money, to the other this book.
3. Did you (sing.) see my mother and sister? I saw neither.
4. My brother spent part of that same summer alone in the woods.

WORD STUDY

- Latin phrases in English:

  inter alia　*among other things*
  alter ego　*the other I,* i.e., *an intimate friend*
  in toto　*entirely, altogether*
  una voce　*with one voice,* i.e., *unanimously*

- When is a nation *neutral?* A gearshift in *neutral?*

- Assimilation: Many prefixes bring about the doubling of consonants by assimilation. The most important are **ad-, con-, in-, ob-, ex-,** and **sub-.** If you will analyze the English word, you can often tell whether the consonant is to be doubled: **con-** and **modus** form **commodus**; add the prefix **ad-** and you get the English derivative *ac-com-modate* with two *c*'s and two *m*'s. Similarly, *commend* has two *m*'s; *re-com-mend* has two *m*'s but only one *c* because **re-** cannot be assimilated. Other examples of doubling through assimilation are *im-material, ac-celerate, suf-ficient, ef-ficient* (but *de-ficient,* for **dē-** is not assimilated).

QUĪNTUS CICERŌ ET POMPŌNIA

Pompōnius Atticus erat firmus amīcus M. Cicerōnis. Pompōnia, soror Atticī, erat uxor Quīntī, frātris M. Cicerōnis. Sed inter Pompōniam Quīntumque nōn semper concordia erat. Ūna gravis causa inter aliās erat haec, quod apud[1] Quīntum auctōritās Stātī[2] valēbat; quem Pompōnia domō[3]
5 expellere nūllō modō potuit; aliēnae auctōritātī cēdere nōn cupīvit. Neuter alterī cēdere potuit; neuter alterum movēre potuit. Cicerō Pompōniam accūsāvit; Atticus, Quīntum. Cicerō ad Atticum hōc modō scrīpsit:

"Frātrem meum vīdī. Tōtus sermō[4] inter nōs dē tē et sorōre tuā fuit. Verba Quīntī nōn inimīca fuērunt. Tum ad Pompōniam contendimus. Quīntus eī

[1] *with*
[2] *Statius (Stā´shus), a freedman of Quintus*
[3] *from the house*
[4] *conversation*

In this frontispiece of an eighteenth-century edition of the complete works (**Opera Omnia**) of Cicero we see what claims to be a portrait of the author at work in his study. Behind him there appears to be a bust of Homer. The publishers also offer the complete notes (**cum integrīs nōtīs**) of Petrus Victorius, a prominent sixteenth-century scholar, and of others, as an incentive to buyers. The Venetian blinds on each side of the bookcase prove that they are not a modern invention. What is wrong about the books themselves? (See page 182.)

amīcā vōce dīxit: 'Pompōnia, tū rogā mulierēs⁵ ad cēnam, ego puerōs 10 ⁵ *women*
rogātūrus sum.' (Hī puerī erant fīliī Cicerōnis et frātris eius.) Sed illa, ⁶ *hostess* (but see Exercise C, p. 392)
audientibus nōbīs, 'Ego ipsa sum,' respondit, 'in hōc locō hospita⁶.' Hoc ⁷ *he said*
dīxit quod īdem Stātius cēnam parārī iusserat. Tum Quīntus, 'Audīsne?' ⁸ *It is a serious matter.*
inquit⁷ mihi, 'haec semper sustinēre cōgor.' Dīcēs: 'Haec vōx nihil est.' Sed
magnum est;⁸ vōce dūrā atque animō aliēnō eius oppressus et commōtus 15
sum. Ad cēnam illa nōn adfuit; Quīntus tamen ad eam sedentem sōlam
cibum mīsit; illa remīsit. Grave vulnus Quīntus accēpit neque ipse ūllam
iniūriam fēcit. Cupiēns eam plācāre nōn potuit. Gravibus cūrīs opprimor
Quid factūrī sumus? Contendere dēbēmus inter sorōrem tuam et frātrem
meum pācem efficere." 20

Questions

1. Who was Atticus' brother-in-law?
2. Of whom was Pomponia jealous? Why?
3. What action did she try to take against him?
4. Who blamed whom?
5. Whose boys was Quintus going to call to dinner?
6. What did Pomponia say to protest?
7. What further offense, according to Cicero, did Pomponia show toward her husband?
8. What solution does Marcus Cicero propose to Pomponius Atticus?
9. What relationship do Pomponius Atticus and Pomponia have to one another?

▦VOCABULARY

Noun

vōx, vō´cis f. *voice, remark*　　　　　[**vocō**]

Adjectives

aliē´nus, -a, -um *another's, unfavorable*　　[**alius**]
gra´vis, -e *heavy, severe*　　　　　　(gravitation, gravity)

Verbs

conten´dō, conten´dere, conten´dī,　　[**tendō**]
　contentū´rus *struggle, hasten*
op´primō, oppri´mere, oppres´sī,　　[**premō**]
　oppres´sus *overcome, surprise*

GRAMMAR

The Present Active Participle

Formation

In English, the present active participle is a verbal adjective ending in *-ing: I saw your brother reading a book* (*reading* describes what the brother is doing).

In Latin, the present active participle is formed by adding **-ns** (nominative singular) or **-ntis** (genitive singular) to the present stem of any verb (see pages 29, 248): **por´tāns, portan´tis,** *carrying;* **mo´vēns, moven´tis,** *moving;* **du´cēns, ducen´tis,** *leading,* etc. It is declined like an adjective of the third declension (cf. **pār,** page 326), except in the ablative singular, which regularly ends in **-e.**

1. The ablative singular ending is regularly **-e,** but **-ī** is used whenever the participle is used simply as an adjective.
2. In verbs of the fourth conjugation, and **-iō** verbs of the third, **-ie-** appears throughout, forming the base **-ient-,** as **audiēns, audientis; capiēns, capientis.**
3. **Sum** has no present participle in common use; that of **possum** is **potēns.**

PRESENT ACTIVE PARTICIPLE OF CAPIŌ

SINGULAR		PLURAL	
M., F.	N.	M., F.	N.
cap´iēns	cap´iēns	capien´tēs	capien´tia
capien´tis		capien´tium	
capien´tī		capien´tibus	
capien´tem	cap´iēns	capien´tēs (īs)	capien´tia
capien´te (ī)		capien´tibus	

Oral Practice

Form and translate the present active participles of **vocō, moneō, dīcō, faciō, mūniō.**

A Roman matron sits comfortably reading a book (or is it her shopping list?) while the butcher expertly carves ribs. Note what else he has for sale and the scales behind his back. It is easy to see that butchers' blocks have not changed in two thousand years.

Usage

In English, the participle is used as a verbal adjective, as in *the conquering hero,* and also to form the *progressive* forms of verbs: *he is watching me, he had been watching me.*

In Latin, the present active participle is used as a verbal adjective, agreeing in gender, number, and case with the noun it modifies, like any other adjective. It is not used to form progressive forms of verbs. Remember that the single form **audit** can be translated *he listens, he does listen* (emphatic), or *he is listening* (progressive). (See page 29.) Do not say, **Est audiēns!** Latin has no present passive participle, so if you wish to say *he is being heard,* you need merely say **audītur.**

Participles, like other adjectives, may be used as substantives: **ab audiente**, *by (the one) listening,* is virtually equivalent to *by the listener.*

Important: Although it is called the *present* participle, it always indicates an action going on at the same time as that of the main verb, no matter what the tense of the main verb is. It may help to imagine the word *while* as accompanying the participle. Note this carefully in the example that follows.

Mīlitēs in viā currentēs videt.   *He sees soldiers running in the street.*

Currentēs (acc. pl. masc.) must modify **mīlitēs** (acc. pl. masc.) and not go with **videt,** which is singular. So the subject sees the soldiers while (at the moment that) they are running in the street.

Because the participle has verbal properties, it can take direct or indirect objects or it can be modified by adverbs or by prepositional phrases acting as adverbs. For example, **in viā** above tells where the running is occurring. Latin often puts these objects or modifiers between the word and the participle that modifies it.

Agricola equum trāns pontem agēns hominem in viā currentem impedīvit.	*A farmer driving a horse across a bridge got in the way of a man running in the road.*

When did this happen? In the past. Who was doing what? **Agēns** (nom. sing. masc.) must go with **agricola** (nom. sing. masc.); so it was the farmer driving his horse (**equum,** acc. sing. masc, the direct object of **agēns**) across the bridge (**trāns pontem,** a prepositional phrase modifying **agēns**) who blocked the jogger's way. **Currentem** (acc. sing. masc.) agrees with **hominem** (acc. sing. masc.—the object of **impedīvit**) and **in viā** is a prepositional phrase telling you where he was running. The whole phrase **hominem in viā currentem** acts as a giant direct object to **impedīvit,** and all the action occurred concurrently.

The Future Active Participle

Unlike English, Latin has a future active participle which we have already seen in the vocabularies as the fourth principal part of some intransitive verbs like **currō, cēdō,** etc. It is formed by dropping the **-us** of the perfect participle and adding **-ūrus: portāt-ūrus,** *going to (about to) carry,* **fact-ūrus,** *going to (about to) make.* A single English word will not translate it, so we must use a phrase. It is declined like **magnus, -a, -um** and is often combined with forms of **sum** to make an alternate type of future tense: **dictūrus est,** *he is about to speak.* It expresses an action that will take place in the future, i.e., later than the time of the main verb.

Oral Practice

Form and translate the future active participles of **nāvigō, obtineō, prōdūcō, accipiō, veniō.**

Variety in Translating Participles

Latin participles allow great flexibility in translation into English. Here are some examples of correct translations available to you for individual cases.

Puellam trāns viam currentem vocō.

I call to the girl running across the road.

I call to the girl as she runs across the road.

I call to the girl who is running across the road.

I call to the girl while she runs across the road.

Perīculum prōvidēns, puellam trāns pontem ambulantem vocābam.

Foreseeing the danger, I kept calling to the girl walking across the bridge.

Because I foresaw danger, I kept calling to the girl as she was walking across the bridge.

Nōs moritūrī tē salūtāmus!

We who are about to die salute you!

We, men about to die, salute you!

We salute you as we are (soon) about to die!

Illum ipsum librum lectūrī estis.

You are going to read that very book (someday).

You will read that very book.

Exercises

A. Translate the following sentences into English.

1. Duo puerī pugnantēs ā magistrō captī sunt.
2. Rōmānīs tardē prōcēdentibus, barbarī fūgērunt.
3. Hieme nūllōs agricolās in agrīs labōrantēs vidēbimus.
4. Cūr in hōc locō sine frātribus tuīs remānsūrus es?
5. Hī nūntiī, suppliciō gravī affectī, ā rēge malō dīmissī sunt.
6. Vōcēs amīcōrum auxilium rogantium ā nōbīs numquam audītae sunt.
7. Oppressī in aliēnō locō, hostēs cum impedīmentīs ad montēs contentūrī erant.

B. Translate the following sentences into Latin using participles wherever possible.

1. The arms given to the other soldiers are heavy.
2. The number of (those) approaching was not large.
3. He is going to fold the letter (which he has) written.
4. He was dragged to death by you (while he was) defending the public cause.

C. In this lesson's reading you have learned about the strained relationships between Quintus Cicero, his trusted freedman Statius, and his wife Pomponia. Now read the *Did You Know?* below. Which do you believe Pomponia meant when she called herself **hospita:** *hostess, guest,* or *stranger?* Was she simply complaining or really and justifiably angry? Carefully analyze the context and the behavior of the three individuals and defend your answer.

Did You Know?

Hospes (m.) or **hospita** (f.) can mean both *host(ess)* and *guest* (or even *stranger*). Each individual was bound to provide food and shelter, legal protection, medical assistance, and personal contacts when visiting the other. The **hospitēs** exchanged tokens, which were passed on to descendants, as a means of identification. It was considered an honor to continue the **hospitium** tradition in a Roman family.

WORD STUDY

- What is an *alien?* What is meant by the statement in the Declaration of Independence "that all men . . . are endowed by their Creator with certain *unalienable* rights [usually misquoted *inalienable*]; . . . life, liberty, and the pursuit of happiness"?

- Latin present participles give us proper names like **Vincent,** *conquering;* **Clement,** *showing mercy;* **Dante,** *giving,* etc.

- **Timeo Danaos et dona ferentes** (Vergil) *I fear the Greeks even bearing gifts* (what the priest said when he saw the Trojan Horse left at Troy by the Greeks) i.e., *I am suspicious.*

- Study the following English phrases borrowed from Latin.

ipso facto	*by the fact itself, thereby*
in loco parentis	*in place of a parent*
obiter dictum	*(something) said by the way* (**ob iter**), *incidentally*
vox humana	*the voice of humanity*
vox populi	*the voice of the people*

LESSON LVIII

CINCINNĀTUS

LESSON OBJECTIVES
- To learn the story of Cincinnatus
- To learn how to form and use the perfect active infinitive

Hostēs Minucium[1], ducem Rōmānum, et mīlitēs eius in locō aliēnō magnā vī premēbant. Ubi id nūntiātum est, omnēs Rōmānī timentēs vim hostium cupīvērunt Cincinnātum[2] dictātōrem facere, quod is sōlus Rōmam ā perīculō nōn levī prohibēre et cīvitātem servāre poterat. Ille trāns Tiberim eō tempore agrum parvum colēbat. Nūntiī ā senātū missī eum in agrō labōrantem 5 invēnērunt et cōnstitērunt. Salūte[3] datā acceptāque, Cincinnātus uxōrem parāre togam iussisse dīcitur; nam nōn oportēbat[4] sine togā nūntiōs audīre.

Hī nūntiī eum dictātōrem appellant et dīcunt: "Mīlitēs nostrī ab hostibus premuntur et cīvēs terrentur. Perīculum nostrum nōn leve est. Hostēs nōn cōnsistent sed mox[5] ad portās nostrās ipsās venient. Auxilium tuum rogāmus." 10 Itaque Cincinnātus, vōcibus eōrum adductus, contrā hostēs contendit. Rōmānī, tēlīs[6] iactīs, hostēs opprimunt et castra expugnant. Minuciō servātō, Cincinnātus dīcitur hostēs sub iugum[7] mīsisse. Tum, nūllīs hostibus prohibentibus, mīlitēs ad urbem redūxit et triumphāvit. Vīs hostium frācta erat. Ductī sunt in pompā[8] ante eum ducēs hostium, capta arma ostenta sunt; 15 post eum mīlitēs vēnērunt praedam gravem ostendentēs. Et haec omnia Cincinnātus magnā celeritāte gessit: potestāte dictātōris in[9] sex mēnsēs acceptā, sextō decimō diē[10] ad agrōs discessit, nōn iam dictātor sed triumphāns agricola. Eōdem mēnse agricola et dictātor et iterum[11] agricola fuit.

[1] *Minucius (Minū´shus)*
[2] *Cincinnatus (Sinsinā´tus)*
[3] *greeting*
[4] *it was not proper*
[5] *soon*
[6] *weapons, spears*
[7] *under the yoke*, i.e., an arch of spears. This act signified surrender.
[8] *procession, parade*
[9] *for*
[10] *on the sixteenth day*
[11] *again* (adv.)

Kaveler/Art Resource, NY

Cincinnatus, a Roman patriot and ex-consul in the fifth century B.C., was chosen to help defend Rome against the Aequi, a nearby Latin tribe. Given the supreme command as dictātor, he left his farm, drove off the enemy, celebrated a triumph, laid down his power and returned to his plow, all in only sixteen days, unwilling to hold his absolute power any longer than was necessary. His example served as a model for early U.S. presidents, who voluntarily limited themselves to two terms in office.

Questions

1. Why did the Romans elect Cincinnatus as dictator?
2. Where was Cincinnatus' farm?
3. What did he tell his wife to do as the messengers arrived? Why?
4. How long did he stay away from his farm?
5. What did Cincinnatus accomplish?
6. What did the military parade (triumph) look like?
7. What was Cincinnatus doing when the messengers found him? What did he end up doing at the end of the story?
8. What lesson should the story teach about holding the extraordinary, all-powerful position of dictator?

VOCABULARY

Nouns

* **mēn´sis, mēn´sis, mēn´sium** m. *month*   (semester)
* **vīs, vīs, vīrium**[12] f. *force, violence;*   (vim)
   pl. *strength*

Adjective

le´vis, -e *light* (in weight)   (levitate, levity)

Verbs

[12] This is an irregular noun. It is declined (sing.) **vis, vis, vi, vim, vi;** (pl.) **virēs, virium, viribus, virēs, viribus.**

cōnsis´tō, cōnsis´tere, cōn´stitī, cōnstitū´rus *stand still, stop*	[stō]
osten´dō, osten´dere, osten´dī, osten´tus *show, stretch out before, present*	[tendō]
prohi´beō, prohibē´re, prohi´buī, prohi´bitus *prevent, keep from*	[habeō]

GRAMMAR

The Perfect Active Infinitive

The perfect active infinitive is formed by adding **-isse** to the perfect stem.

portāvisse	*to have carried*	**cēpisse**	*to have taken*
docuisse	*to have taught*	**audīvisse**	*to have heard*
posuisse	*to have put*	**fuisse** (from **sum**)	*to have been*

Society of the Cincinnati, insignia. *(Left)* As a third senator runs up, two others present a sword to Cincinnatus at his plow. *(Right)* Cincinnatus returns to his plowing, while over his head winged Fame **(Fāma)** trumpets his victory. Note, in the background, ships and cities, signs of commerce and peace.

The perfect active infinitive is used to indicate an action completed before the time of the main verb.

> **Rēgīna terram occupāvisse**   *The queen is said* (NOW) *to have*
>   **dīcitur.**   *seized the land* (EARLIER).
> **Dux hostēs superāvisse**   *The general is said* (NOW) *to have*
>   **dīcitur.**   *conquered the enemy* (AT A
>   PREVIOUS TIME).

In these examples, note that the subjects of the perfect infinitives are the same as those of the main verbs, which are in the passive voice. In cases like these, no accusative subject for the infinitives is needed (compare page 223).

Oral Practice

Form the perfect active infinitive of **dīmittō, intercipiō, videō, expediō, laudō, cernō.**

▓ *Exercises*

A. Translate the following sentences into English.
1. Ostendite omnibus exemplum bonum.
2. Vim prohibēre et pācem cōnservāre est nōbile.
3. Rēgis fīlia librum scrīpsisse sine auxiliō dīcitur.
4. Quis dīxit, "Dā mihi lībertātem aut dā mihi mortem"?
5. Rōmānī paucās nāvēs ad Britanniam mīsisse dīcuntur.
6. Mīlitēs cōnsistentēs arma levia magnā cum vī iēcisse dīcuntur.
7. Homō malus mē cōnsistere iussit et omnem meam pecūniam dare.

B. Translate the following sentences into Latin.
1. We cannot breathe under water.
2. I saw your mother folding a letter.
3. That king is said to have tilled the fields himself.
4. Those men are said to have come together in a strange land.

C. The leading citizens of Rome sought out Cincinnatus at his farm because they had such respect for him and his ability to be a leader. He had once been a consul, holding the highest position in the Roman state. In times of extraordinary danger, however, the Romans appointed a dictator who had supreme power, even over the consuls. Work with a partner to create the dialogue that you imagine took place that day in which the citizens persuaded Cincinnatus to lead the troops against the enemy and save Minucius, despite the fact that the former consul was now a simple farmer. Then create a monologue, imagining what Cincinnatus said to the citizens as he was laying down his dictatorial powers after only sixteen days.

Did You Know?

Julius Caesar gave us almost exactly the version of the calendar that we use today. As Pontifex Maximus, he corrected the Roman calendar, then almost 3 months out of phase with the solar year, by taking the 360-day Egyptian solar calendar, and adding 5 days to it, so that the year 45 B.C. would have 365 days, and the months would come out as we know them, including the extra day in February in leap years. The Julian reform worked so well that only a very minor adjustment by Pope Gregory XIII was needed in 1582.

WORD STUDY

- The suffix **-or** is added to the stem of the past participle and, therefore, is preceded by **-t** or **-s**. It indicates the doer of an action: **monitor** *(one who warns)*, **scrīptor** *(one who writes)*, **inventor** *(one who finds)*. It is used in English in the same way.

- A different suffix **-or** is added to the present base of a verb (minus the stem vowel); it usually indicates a state of being or condition: **timor, amor, terror.**

- Find five English words which are formed by adding one of these **-or** suffixes to the stems of verbs that you have studied.

- Explain the meanings and etymologies of *consistent, dictionary, ostentation, prohibition.*

- The city of *Cincinnati,* Ohio, was named from the Society of the Cincinnati, formed by the regular officers of the Continental Army at the end of the Revolutionary War. Why do you suppose the society took that name? What does its motto **Omnia reliquit servare rem publicam** mean? There is also a town named *Cincinnatus* in New York.

eject

BELLA

Quae sunt causae bellī? Variī auctōrēs ostendērunt multās esse causās. Multa bella aut ob iniūriās aut prō lībertāte gesta esse vidēmus. In aliīs bellīs lībertās sociōrum dēfēnsa est. Haec bella iūsta fuērunt. Multī populī pugnāvērunt quod putāvērunt potestātem imperiumque vī bellōque augērī
5 posse. Hī cupīvērunt patriam esse nūllī secundam. Sī superātī sunt, omnia saepe āmīsērunt; sī superāvērunt, aliēnās terrās occupāvērunt, quās in fōrmam prōvinciārum redēgērunt. Putāsne bella huius generis iūsta esse? Multī dīcunt omnia bella iūsta esse, aliī putant nūlla esse iūsta. Quid dē hōc putās? Nōvimus aliōs prō lībertāte, aliōs prō glōriā bella gessisse. Quae
10 fuērunt causae bellōrum nostrōrum? Audīvistīne dē bellō frīgidō? Etiam nunc nova bella et novōs hostēs timēmus.

Horātius,[1] poēta Rōmānus, scrībit dulce esse prō patriā vītam āmittere. Sī patria in perīculō est, nōnne putās mūnus nostrum esse eam dēfendere?

[1] *Horace.* The exact words of his famous phrase are: **Dulce et decōrum est prō patriā morī,** *Sweet and fitting it is to die for one's country.* The Latin words appear on the gates leading into Arlington National Cemetery near Washington, D.C.

Roman soldiers used different instruments of war, depending on the situation. Here, a battering ram (arēs) is used to weaken or break into the walls of the fortification.

Mary Evans/Photo Researchers

Scīmus nōn levēs esse labōrēs mīlitum, gravia eōs accipere vulnera, multōs ad mortem mittī; etiam scīmus eōs tamen nōn dubitāre omnēs labōrēs prō 15 patriā grātō animō suscipere et sustinēre. Prō hīs mūneribus praemia aequa eīs solvere nōn possumus. Sed nec praemia nec beneficia exspectant; spērant cīvēs facta sua memoriā tentūrōs esse et aliōs semper parātōs futūrōs esse patriam dēfendere. Hōc modō praemia solvere possumus.

Bellane ūllō tempore cōnstitūra sunt? Possuntne bella prohibērī? Quis 20 scit? Sed spērāmus parvō spatiō temporis nōn iam bella futūra esse; spērāmus omnēs hominēs aliōrum iūra cōnservātūrōs esse.

Questions

1. What are three reasons for war that many people consider just?
2. Why else, according to the passage, did many peoples wage war?
3. What have been the risks and potential benefits of these wars?
4. What did the poet Horace have to say about dying in battle?
5. If your country is in danger, according to this passage, what should you do?
6. The passage reminds us of certain facts about soldiers in war. Name three.
7. What do brave soldiers undertake on behalf of their country?
8. What do these soldiers expect in return for their service?
9. What does the writer express about his hopes for the future?
10. What are your answers to the questions asked in the Latin reading?

VOCABULARY

Nouns

la´bor, labō´ris m. *work, hardship*   (laboratory, laborious)
mū´nus, mū´neris n. *duty, service, gift*   (munificent)

Adjectives

iūs´tus, -a, -um *just*   (justice, justify)
secun´dus, -a, -um *second*   (secondary)

Verbs

pu´tō, -ā´re, -ā´vī, -ā´tus *think, suppose*   (reputation)
sci´ō, scī´re, scī´vī, scī´tus *know*   (science)
sol´vō, sol´vere, sol´vī, solū´tus *loosen, pay*   (solution, resolve)

Conjunction

sī *if*

Defeat in war usually meant enslavement. This relief shows chained captives carried along in Trajan's triumph of A.D. 107.

Remember that the present passive infinitive of third conjugation verbs ends in a single **-ī,** *not* in **-erī.**

GRAMMAR

The Perfect Passive and Future Active Infinitives

The *perfect passive infinitive* is formed by using the perfect passive participle and **esse,** the present infinitive of **sum.**

> **portātus, -a, -um esse,** *to have been carried;* **doctus, -a, -um esse,** *to have been taught;* **ductus, -a, -um esse,** *to have been led;* **captus, -a, -um esse,** *to have been taken;* **audītus, -a, -um esse,** *to have been heard*

The *future active infinitive* is formed by using the future active participle and **esse,** the present infinitive of **sum.**

> **portātūrus, -a, -um esse,** *to be about to (going to) carry;* **doctūrus, -a, -um esse,** *to be about to teach;* **ductūrus, -a, -um esse,** *to be about to lead;* **captūrus, -a, -um esse,** *to be about to take;* **audītūrus, -a, -um esse,** *to be about to hear*

The future active infinitive of **sum** is **futūrus, -a, -um esse.**

Transitive verbs can have a future passive infinitive, but it is formed differently, is quite rare, and can be omitted here.

Oral Practice

1. Form and translate the perfect passive and future active infinitives of **putō, prohibeō, solvō, faciō, impediō.**
2. Give the five infinitives you have learned so far for: **probō, terreō, mittō, cupiō, inveniō.**

Infinitive with Verbs of *Saying, Knowing,* Etc.

In English, after verbs of *saying, knowing, thinking, believing,* and many others describing some mental action, if the words are not quoted directly, we regularly use a clause introduced by *that: He says (that) the boys are fighting.* But often we use the infinitive: *he knows it to be true; I believed her to be a good person; the boys are said to be fighting.*

In Latin, the infinitive is *always* used after such words. **Dīcit puerōs pugnāre. Puerōs** is accusative because it is the subject of the infinitive **pugnāre** (page 223). No introductory word like *that* is used.

Direct and Indirect Statement

1. **Dīcit, "Puerī pugnant."** Direct statement: *He says, "The boys are fighting."*
2. **Dīcit puerōs pugnāre.** Indirect statement: *He says (that) the boys are fighting.*

In the first sentence the exact words of the speaker are given, as indicated by the quotation marks. It is a *direct statement.* In the second sentence, the exact words are not quoted, but merely reported. This is called *indirect statement* (or *indirect discourse*). After verbs of *saying, knowing,* etc., Latin converts the form of the direct statement's verb into an infinitive and its subject from the nominative into the accusative. The indirect statement (the infinitive and its accusative subject) is considered the object of the introductory main verb.

Who or *Whom?* You can see how a knowledge of indirect statement in Latin will help you to use *who* and *whom* in English.

1. Dr. Truman is a man, *who,* I believe, *is* honest.
2. Dr. Truman is a man *whom* I believe *to be* honest.

Oral Practice

Give the Latin for the italicized words.
1. I know *him to be* wise.
2. I know the *signal was given.*
3. They say the *wagon was drawn* by mules.
4. I hear that your *sister will live* in town.
5. I believe the *men have been led across* the river.

When compound forms like perfect passive or future active infinitives, i.e., one composed of a participle + **esse,** are used in indirect statement, the participle must agree with the subject in gender, number, and case (which will be accusative).

🁢 *Exercises*

A. Translate the following sentences into English.
1. Dīcunt, "Cīvis iūstus lībertātem amat."
2. Cīvis iūstus lībertātem amāre dīcitur.
3. Dīcunt cīvem iūstum lībertātem amāre.
4. Putāmus mūnera nostra futūra esse levia.
5. Nōs omnēs scīmus in spatiō vītae esse cūrās et labōrēs.
6. Putāsne hunc pecūniam dēbitam solvisse aut solūtūrum esse?
7. Sciō et dīcō pecūniam ab illō homine dēbitam nōn solūtam esse.
8. Putō, Mārce, illam numquam futūram esse prīmam aut secundam ōrdine.

B. Translate the following sentences into Latin.
1. Galba said, "My father is a soldier."
2. We all know that his father is a soldier.
3. I think that Galba himself will be a soldier.
4. I hear that Galba's brother was a sailor and was not scared by the sea.
5. He himself said, "I am going to be a soldier, for my father is a soldier."

C. Iūdicium Paridis (The Judgment of Paris or The Cause of the Trojan War)
1. Dīcō "Iūdicium Paridis causa bellī Trōiānī erat."
2. Tū dīcis causam bellī Trōiānī nōn inventam esse.
3. Sed multī auctōrēs scrībunt iūdicium Paridis causam bellī Trōiānī fuisse.
4. Auctōrēs veterēs *(ancient)* scrīpsērunt iūdicium Paridis causam bellī esse.
5. Paris, fīlius rēgis Priamī, pulcherrimus *(very handsome)* fuisse dīcitur.
6. Venus, dea amōris, putābat sē *(she herself)* omnium deārum pulcherrimam *(most beautiful)* esse.
7. Sed et Minerva, dea sapientiae *(of wisdom),* et Jūnō, rēgīna deōrum, etiam putāvērunt sē *(they themselves)* pulcherrimās esse.
8. Hae trēs deae lēgērunt Paridem iūdicem *(as judge)* et ūnaquaeque *(each)* spērāvit Paridem dictūrum esse sē *("she")* pulcherrimam esse.
9. Paridī *(dative)* ūnaquaeque deārum prōmīsit magnum praemium: Minerva prōmīsit victōriam in bellō, Jūnō prōmīsit potestātem, sed Venus prōmīsit Paridem ductūrum esse in mātrimōnium fēminam in orbe terrārum *(in the world)* pulcherrimam.
10. Paris, putāns pulcherrimam uxōrem optimum *(the best)* praemium futūrum esse, lēgit Venerem.

11. Infēliciter nescīvit *(Unfortunately he did not know)* pulcherrimam fēminam in orbe terrārum esse Helēnam, iam uxōrem Menelāī *(the wife of Menelaus)*, rēgis Spartae *(of Sparta)*.

12. Posteā, Paris Helēnaque, captī amōre et īram Menelāī timentēs, ad Trōiam fūgērunt, spērantēs sē *(they)* in Trōiā sēcūrōs *(safe)* futūrōs esse.

13. Tum Menelāus auxilium Agamemnonis *(of Agamemnon, leader of all the Greeks)* petīvit, et cum magnā cōpiā mīlitum nāvigāvērunt ad Trōiam.

14. Poeta dīcit mīlle *(a thousand)* nāvēs ex omnibus partibus Graeciae dēductās esse *(were launched)*.

15. Itaque *(And so)* multī potuērunt dīcere bellum Trōiānum ob fēminam incipī.

Did You Know?

A visit to the public bath was an important part of the Roman day throughout the Empire. People went there not only to bathe, but also to exercise, socialize, relax, and perhaps have a snack. Bathing establishments, called **balneae** or **thermae,** ranged in size from small buildings to enormous complexes of huge vaulted rooms. The main areas of most baths were the **apodytērium** (locker or dressing room), **caldārium** (hot bath), **frīgidārium** (cold bath), **palaestra** (exercise ground), and **tepidārium** (warm bath). Remains of these popular structures can be found today in most former provinces.

Erich Lessing/Villa Romana del Casale, Piazza Armerina, Italy/Art Resource, NY

Near Piazza Armerina in Sicily is a luxurious Roman villa of the third and fourth centuries A.D. It may have been the hunting lodge of an owner much interested in sports, for it is filled with mosaics of wild animals, chariot races, hunting scenes, sea creatures, mythological creatures, and, most striking to modern eyes, ten bikini-clad gymnasts, two of whom are pictured here. Apparently, they are receiving prizes for their skill from their teacher *(left)*—note the wreaths and palm fronds.

WORD STUDY

Suffixes

The base of the Latin present participle is **-ant, -ent,** or **-ient**, according to the conjugation. This is used as a suffix in English, with the same meaning as the participial ending *-ing*.

A common mistake in the spelling of English words is due to the confusion of *-ant* and *-ent*. Reference to the Latin can help.

• Almost all English words derived from the first conjugation follow the Latin spelling with an *-a-: expectant, emigrant.*

• Most English words that are derived from the other conjugations follow the Latin spelling with an *-e-: regent, agent, efficient, expedient.*

• But some words in the latter group have an *-a-: tenant, defendant.*

Give eight English words with suffix *-ant* or *-ent* derived from Latin words previously studied. Explain the meanings and etymologies of *laboratory, omniscient, solvent, absolve, remunerate.*

LESSON LX

CORIOLĀNUS

LESSON OBJECTIVES
- To learn about the story of Coriolanus
- To learn the sequence of tenses in indirect statement

Mārcius, nōbilis Rōmānus, Coriolōs,[1] oppidum Volscōrum,[2] expugnāverat. Ob hoc mūnus "Coriolānus" appellātus est.

Post bellum plēbs,[3] ob variās causās īrā ācrī permōta, clāmāvit Coriolānum esse hostem. Is, sentiēns perīculum īnstāre, fūgit ad Volscōs quōs ipse superāverat. Volscī dīcuntur eum benignē[4] accēpisse, nam sēnsērunt eum esse ducem fortem ac iūstum et Rōmam nōn iam amāre. Etiam spērāvērunt eum contrā Rōmānōs pugnātūrum esse.

Mox Coriolānus, dux ā Volscīs lēctus, ad urbem Rōmam contendit, omnēs in itinere superāns. Rōmānī, castrīs eius ad urbem positīs, bellō īnstantī territī sunt. Lēgātī dē pāce ad Coriolānum missī sunt, sed ubi pervēnērunt ab 10 eō remissī sunt.

"Mātrem eius ad eum mittēmus," putāvērunt Rōmānī; "sī cūra urbis cor eius nōn tanget, ille amōre mātris certē tangētur et īra eius frangētur; tum fīnem labōrum nostrōrum inveniēmus." Itaque māter et uxor Coriolānī cum duōbus parvīs fīliīs ad castra hostium pervēnērunt. 15

Coriolānus, verbīs ācribus mātris permōtus et lacrimīs[5] omnium tāctus, dīcitur clāmāvisse: "Quid fēcistī, māter? Tū sōla Rōmam servāvistī sed mē vīcistī.[6]" Tum iussit Volscōs discēdere. Rōma lacrimīs,[5] nōn armīs, servāta erat. Coriolānī facta semper in memoriā omnium haerēbunt.

5

[1] *Cori´olī* (the names of ancient towns are often plural)
[2] *Volsci (Vol´sī)*
[3] *the common people* (nom. sing. fem.)
[4] *kindly*
[5] *by the tears*
[6] *have beaten*

Coriolanus, wearing the red cloak of a general, is moved by the tears of his gray-haired mother, the kiss of his wife, and the sight of his children in the arms of their nurse. The emissary from Rome kneels before him. A nineteenth-century painting by Rafaele Postiglione.

Archivo Inconografico, S.A./CORBIS

Questions

1. How did Coriolanus get his name?
2. Where did he go when exiled?
3. How did the Volsci receive Coriolanus, their former enemy?
4. Why did they make him their leader?
5. How were the Roman ambassadors received by Coriolanus?
6. What strategy did the Romans adopt next?
7. What did Coriolanus say to his mother?
8. By what means, according to the passage, was Rome saved?

▦ VOCABULARY

Nouns

ī´ra, -ae f. *anger*   (irate, irascible)
lēgā´tus, -ī m. *ambassador, envoy*   **[legō]**
*urbs, ur´bis, ur´bium f. *city*   (urbane, suburban)

Adjective

ā´cer, ā´cris, ā´cre *sharp, keen, fierce*   (acrid)

Verbs

hae´reō, haerē´re, hae´sī, hae´sus   (adhere, adhesive)
    stick, cling
īn´stō, īnstā´re, īn´stitī, — *threaten*   **[stō]**
perve´niō, pervenī´re, pervē´nī,   **[veniō]**
    perventū´rus *(come through), arrive*
sen´tiō, sentī´re, sēn´sī, sēn´sus *feel, realize* (sense, sensation)

▦ GRAMMAR

How the Indicative and the Infinitive Differ in Tense

Indicative tenses of the verb state facts relative to the present time, indicating that something happened in the past, is happening now in the present, or will happen in the future. Infinitive tenses, however, are translated according to their relation in time to the tense of the verb on which they depend. This is true in both Latin and English. Inspect these variations on the following sentence: *He is brave.*

1. *We think him to be brave.*
   We thought him to be brave.
   We will think him to be brave.

or 2. *We think that he is brave.*
   We thought that he was brave.
   We will think that he is brave.

or **3. Putāmus eum fortem esse.**
  Putāvimus eum fortem esse.
  Putābimus eum fortem esse.

Notice how the indirect statements in Group 3, like the sentences in Group 1, all use the present infinitive, because, at whatever time we do our thinking, present, past, or future, it is at that same time that our hero is brave. In Group 2, when we convert to indirect statement with *that* in English and as we shift to the past and change *think* to *thought,* we must also change *is* to *was,* so as to make sense. We cannot logically say *We thought* (yesterday) *that he is brave* (today).

The Sequence of Tenses

In Latin, the principle is that the present infinitive will refer to the same time as the verb upon which it depends, the perfect infinitive will refer to an earlier time, and the future infinitive will refer to a later time. The way in which the tense and sense of the infinitive must "follow" and be adjusted to the tense of the verb on which it depends is called the *sequence of tenses.*

4. Scīmus eam pulchram vocārī.	*We know she is called beautiful.*
5. Scīvimus eam pulchram **vocātam esse.**	*We knew she had been called beautiful.*
6. Dīcit eōs iūstōs esse.	*He says (that) they are just.*
fuisse.	*they were just.*
futūrōs esse.	*they will be just.*
7. Dīxit eōs iūstōs esse.	*He said (that) they were just.*
fuisse.	*they had been just.*
futūrōs esse.	*they would be just.*
8. Dīcet eōs iūstōs esse.	*He will say (that) they are just.*
fuisse.	*they were just.*
futūrōs esse.	*they will be just.*

In Example 7 above, it would make no difference in the sequence to substitute **dīcēbat** (imperfect) for **dīxit** (perfect), since both are past tenses. The meaning of the main verb would change slightly, however, from *he said* to *he used to say.*

Oral Practice

Give the Latin for the italicized words.
1. She knew *me to be* her friend.
2. He knew that *I was working* hard.
3. We saw that *we would* not *answer* in time.
4. He said that his *son was being taught* by new methods.
5. We hear that your *father has been sent* to Europe on a secret mission.

The subject of an infinitive in indirect statement must always be in the accusative and must always be expressed. Often you will need to supply a personal pronoun.

We knew that he was waiting.

Scīvimus *eum* **exspectāre.**

They thought we would like this.

Putāvērunt *nōs* **hoc amātūrōs/ās esse.**

🔲 *Exercises*

A. Translate the following sentences into English.
1. Omnēs sēnsimus perīculum īnstāre.
2. Puer nōn clāmāre potuit quod vōx haesit.
3. Quis dīxit socium meum sine frātre pervēnisse?
4. Servī spērāvērunt labōrem futūrum esse facilem.
5. Omnēs līberī certē sciunt Columbum ad Americam pervēnisse.
6. Rōmānī dīcēbant Caesarem esse ducem fortem et numquam superātum esse.
7. (a) Omnēs scīmus puellās nostrās esse ācrēs et fortēs.
   (b) Substitute **scīvimus** for **scīmus** in (a) and translate.

B. Translate the following sentences into Latin.
1. We can prove that our cause is just.
2. Who said that we would not arrive?
3. My mother wrote that the city was beautiful.
4. The boy thought that (his) father had been saved.
5. The envoy says that the soldiers of the provinces were brave.

Did You Know?

It was not until the beginning of the third century B.C. that the **plēbs,** the common people of Rome, achieved political equality with the **patriciī,** the patricians who had once been their patrons. Even then plebeians could not hold certain religious offices, but gradually a new aristocracy (**nōbilēs**) arose; it was comprised of the ruling political families from both the plebeians and patricians.

WORD STUDY

- **Suffixes** By adding the suffix **-ia** to the base of the present participle, a suffix **-antia** or **-entia** is formed which becomes *-ance, -ence, -ancy,* or *-ency* in English. Give eight English nouns with this suffix derived from Latin words previously studied. Explain the meanings and etymologies of *coherence, sensitive, consensus, intangible, dissension, inherent*. What is the difference between *adhesion* and *cohesion*?

- **Derivatives** Most of the names of American states are the result of Native American influence, but several of them are of Latin origin or form. Vermont means *green mountain* (**viridis mōns**), Pennsylvania is *Penn's woods* (**silva**), Virginia is the *maiden's* land (named after Queen Elizabeth I). Florida is the *flowery land* (**flōs, flōris**), Colorado is the land of the *colored* or *red* river, Montana is *mountainous* (**mōns**), Nevada is the land of *snow* (**nix, nivis**). Rhode Island is said to be named after the Greek island of Rhodes, meaning *rose*. New Jersey means "New Caesarea," named after the island of Jersey, one of many places named in honor of one of the Caesars. The titles *Kaiser* and *Czar* also came from **Caesar.**

  States whose endings (only) are Latin are Carolina (Charles II), Georgia (George II), Louisiana (Louis XIV), and Indiana.

- Here are more state mottoes.

  Salus populi suprema lex esto. *Let the safety of the people be the supreme law.* (Missouri)

  Crescit eundo. *She grows as she goes.* (New Mexico)

AGRICULTURE AND COMMERCE

In the early days of Rome nearly every man was a farmer, and farming remained the chief occupation of the Romans for centuries, as it had been for people in most countries. It is not surprising, therefore, that Cincinnatus left his plow to lead the Romans in war and upon his success he returned to his farm. In the early days many wars were won by the "embattled farmers." Nor is it surprising that agriculture was considered the foundation of Roman life and that the sturdy Roman character was largely shaped by the hard work on the farm.

At first, farms were small and were worked by the owner, his family, and perhaps one or two slaves. The work in the fields was done with the use of simple tools and intensive hand labor. The increased use of slaves on the farm led to the decline of free labor, and the destruction of land by war in southern Italy led to larger farms and a change in the attitude toward farming. Managing a farm then often became the domain of wealthy landowners who could afford large tracts of land and the slaves to work them.

Industry was not so highly developed among the Romans as it is among us. There were no large factories. Much of the work was done by hand either at home or in small shops. The spinning of thread and its weaving into cloth were often done at home by women. Even the Emperor Augustus wore clothing made by his household slaves under the direction of his wife, Livia. There were carpenters, metalworkers, masons and bricklayers, toolmakers, wagonmakers and brickmakers employed in ancient Rome. The making of bricks, red-glazed pottery, copper and bronze utensils, as well as the forging of ironwork came nearest to being industry in the modern sense.

The shops were very small; usually a room at the front of a private residence was used as a shop for goods made in the back rooms. The wares were often displayed outside the shops. Sometimes the shopkeepers cluttered up the sidewalks and streets so much that traffic was interfered with until some strict official prevented this practice—even as today.

In certain industries, the free workers—potters, dyers, gold and coppersmiths, carpenters, and tanners—were members of guilds or unions, whose chief purposes were to bring the members together for good fellowship and to provide burials for the members who died. Many slaves, too, came to be employed in industry.

Erich Lessing/Art Resource, NY

A shopkeeper selling fresh vegetables supplied an important part of the family meal. Here you can see that he has squashes, leeks, and several other varieties for sale.

Such were the occupations of the poorer classes. Rich men invested their money in wholesale trade, real estate, loans, government contracts, and foreign trade. Great profits could be made by buying from the government the right to collect the taxes in a province—everything collected over and above the cost of the contract went to the **pūblicānus** *(tax collector)*. The professions, with the exception of law, the army, architecture, and public life, were not well developed. Doctors and teachers were usually slaves or poorly paid freedmen, i.e., former slaves. Law and politics were reserved largely for the upper classes although both lawyers and politicians could not legally accept payment for their services.

QUESTIONS

1. What professions are highly respected today?
2. What percentage of people today are engaged in farming compared to the percentage of the Roman population who farmed?
3. How does mass production improve or degrade the life of the worker?

Department of Art & Archeology, Princeton University

In a mosaic from Antioch, Turkey, a shepherd tends his small flock. This Antioch (there were no less than eighteen Antiochs named for Antiochus, one of the three generals who succeeded to Alexander the Great's empire) became an important center of commerce and religion under Roman rule.

LESSONS LV–LX

VOCABULARY

Nouns

īra	mēnsis	vīs
labor	mūnus	vōx
lēgātus	urbs	

Adjectives

ācer	alter... alter	secundus
aliēnus	gravis	sōlus
alius	iūstus	tōtus
alius... alius	levis	ūllus
aliī... aliī	neuter	ūnus
alter	nūllus	uter

Verbs

cōnsistō	opprimō	putō
contendō	ostendō	sciō
haereō	perveniō	sentiō
īnstō	prohibeō	solvō

Conjunction

sī

GRAMMAR SUMMARY

Participles

IN LATIN	IN ENGLISH
1. Present active **(portāns)**	1. Present active *(carrying)*
2. No present passive	2. Present passive *(being carried)*
3. No perfect active	3. Past active *(having carried)*
4. Perfect passive **(portātus)**	4. Past passive *(having been carried)*
5. Future active **(portātūrus)**	5. No future active

The Present Participle

The nominative singular of the present participle is formed, for first and second conjugations, by adding **-ns** to the present stem; for third **-iō** and fourth conjugation by adding **-ēns** to the present stem. It is declined like a one-ending third declension adjective with **-ntis** as the genitive. Its action occurs at the same time as that of the main verb.

Audiēns hoc,	*Hearing this,*
consistere cupiēbam.	*I wanted to stop.*
Nūllōs līberōs in urbe	*I saw no children playing*
lūdentēs vīdī.	*in the city.*

The Future Active Participle

The future active participle is formed by adding **-ūrus, -ūra, -ūrum** to the stem of the fourth principal part. Like all participles, it agrees with the noun it modifies in gender, number, and case and represents an action as occurring after the time of the

main verb. Used in combination with a form of **sum**, it can substitute for the future tense.

Rēx verba factūrus est.	*The king is about to make a speech.*
Ad hanc urbem perventūrī sunt.	*They are going to arrive at this city.*

The Perfect Active Infinitive

The perfect active infinitive is formed by adding **-isse** to the perfect stem.

dedisse	*to have given*
iēcisse	*to have thrown*

The Perfect Passive Infinitive

The perfect passive infinitive is the fourth principal part (perfect passive participle) plus **esse.**

frāctus, -a, -um esse	*to have been broken*
prohibitus, -a, -um esse	*to have been prevented*

The Future Active Infinitive

The future active infinitive is formed by adding **-ūrus, -ūra, -ūrum** to the stem of the fourth principal part, plus **esse.**

captūrus, -a, -um esse	*(to be) going to take*
laudātūrus, -a, -um esse	*(to be) about to praise*

Direct and Indirect Statement

A direct statement quotes a person's words directly. An indirect statement is a report or mental perception of some action. In English, after verbs of *thinking, saying, knowing, perceiving,* etc., a clause often introduced by *that* is used. The subject is in the nominative, and the verb is indicative. In Latin, after similar verbs, an infinitive phrase is used instead of a clause. The subject of the infinitive is in the accusative.

Dīcit, "Amīcus meus tē vocat."	*He says, "My friend is calling you."*
Dīcit amīcum meum tē vocāre.	*He says that my friend is calling you.*

How the Indicative and Infinitive Differ in Tense

Indicative tenses are determined by their relation to present time: something is happening, has happened, or is going to happen. Infinitive tenses are determined by the time of the verb upon which they depend: the present infinitive for an action occurring at the same time as that of the verb; the perfect infinitive for a time before that of the verb; the future infinitive for a time after that of the verb.

Videō Annam adesse.	*I see that Anna is here.*
Vīdī Annam adesse.	*I saw that Anna was here.*
Vīdī Annam adfuisse.	*I saw that Anna had been here.*
Vīdī Annam adfutūram esse.	*I saw that Anna would be here.*

UNIT XI REVIEW

LESSONS LV–LX

UNIT PRACTICE

A. Do the following.

1. Decline **vōx ipsa, nūllus pēs, hic mēnsis.**

2. Give all tenses of the third person plural active voice of **timeō;** the third singular passive of **opprimō.**

3. Form the participles, active and passive, of **regō, iaciō, sciō,** and **prohibeō.**

4. Form the infinitives, active and passive, of **sentiō, intercipiō, ostendō,** and **mōnstrō.**

B. Give the Latin for the italicized words. Be careful to make each participle agree with the noun it modifies in gender, number, and case.

1. *Running* water is usually fresh.

2. We saw the boys *dragging* a big sled.

3. They heard the sound of men *approaching.*

4. Are they *going to remain* in this country?

5. She was *going to say* something to her friend.

6. *When these words had been heard*, he felt encouraged.

7. He forgot to mail the letter *after he had folded it.*

C. Give the Latin for the indirect statements. Then translate the sentences into English.

1. Sciō *(the boys are reading)* librōs.

2. Spērō *(the girls will read)* librōs.

3. Putō *(the boys have read)* librōs.

4. Dīxit *(the books were being read)* ā puerīs.

5. Dīxit *(the books had been read)* ā puerīs.

D. Which occupations would you like to follow? **Magister, medicus, iūriscōnsultus** *(lawyer),* **vir reīpūblicae perītus** *(politician),* **physicus** *(scientist),* **auctor, poēta, negōtiātor** *(business person),* **artifex** *(artist),* **pictor** *(painter),* **agricola, nauta, mīles, mercātor** *(merchant),* or something else? Why?

WORD STUDY

- Explain the following and give the Latin words from which they are derived: *omnipotent, alienate, vocal, expulsion, oppressive, diction, ostensible, prohibit.*

- Find and use in sentences as many English derivatives as possible from **dīcō** and **putō.**

- The first word in each of the following lines is a Latin word. From among the next five words in each line, pick the one which is an English derivative related to the first word.

scit	*skit*	*sky*	*sigh*	*scientific*	*sit*
tangō	*tangerine*	*tang*	*intangible*	*tango*	*tactics*
putātus	*putty*	*put*	*repute*	*potato*	*potable*
dīcere	*contradict*	*dixie*	*dice*	*decree*	*decent*
gravia	*graft*	*graveyard*	*gravity*	*engrave*	*gray*

UNIT XI ASSESSMENT

VOCABULARY

Choose the word that best completes each sentence.

1. Nūntium rēgis ē Graeciā ad urbem hōrā
   secundā _____ putāmus.
   a. haesisse
   b. pervēnisse
   c. prohibuisse
   d. sēnsisse

2. Hic fuit dominus _____, nam cūram aequam
   omnibus servīs ostendit.
   a. aliēnus
   b. iūstus
   c. levis
   d. nūllus

3. Pater Mārcō dīxit, " _____ fīlī labōrem prō
   familiā cōnficere est."
   a. Lēgātus
   b. Mēnsis
   c. Mūnus
   d. Vōx

4. Tibi ūllam pecūniam _____ nōn possum, sed
   multās grātiās agō.
   a. cōnsistere
   b. contendere
   c. īnstāre
   d. solvere

5. Duo mīlitēs fortēs trāns pontem ad salūtem
   cucurrērunt; hostis _____ prohibuit.
   a. alterum
   b. neutrum
   c. tōtum
   d. ūllum

GRAMMAR

Complete each sentence with the correct endings.

6. Ill___ mēnse pater eius tōt___ cōnsilium fugae
   fīliō alter___ nārrāvit, sed alterī verb___
   nūll___ dīxit.

7. Sī vōs amīcum nostr___ accēdent___ ad
   templum cum ali___ hominibus cernētis,
   vōcāte eum sōl___ ad cēnam sine ali___.

8. Tum nautae, timent___ potestāt___ deī,
   magn___ vī ventōrum ad īnsul___ redig___.

9. Urbem sine ūllō auxili___ mēns___ ācribus
   hiēmis contendisse et ab multīs host___
   oppress___ esse scīvimus.

10. Ventī īnstant___ terruērunt agricolās quī vōcēs
    nūll___ virōrum ali___ audīv___ dīcēbantur.

TRANSLATION

Translate the following sentences.

11. Ille lēgātus sōlus, vōce aliēnā ducis commōtus,
    in itinere cōnstitisse et mīlitēs aliōs relīquisse
    dīcitur.

12. Magister dīxit multōs librōs ā puellīs legī et eās
    verba omnium poētārum clārōrum cognitūrās
    esse.

13. Fīlia vestra vestem levem ā servīs cōnfectam
    esse putāvit; itaque labōrem eārum magnō cum
    studiō laudābat.

14. Mātrem ipsam hās litterās scrībere scīvī, et
    nunc nōs fābulam tōtam dē līberīs auditūrōs
    esse spērō.

15. Putātisne, sociī, hōc tempore vōs in marī lātō
    sine perīculō nāvigāre posse, nec undās altās
    futūrās esse causam iniūriae gravis.

INVESTIGATION

Find the answers to these questions from any lesson in Unit XI.

16. What is the **Āra Pācis Augustae,** and what can be seen on at least one part of it?

17. True or false? Julius Caesar reformed the calendar so well that it was used for over fifteen centuries before needing some adjustment.

18. Explain the meaning of the Greek word **Acropolis,** and name the most famous building found there.

19. What was the function of the following parts of the Roman bath complex?

apodytērium

frīgidārium

palaestra

20. When someone describes a person as another's *alter ego,* what does that expression mean literally?

CULTURE

Vērum aut Falsum? Indicate whether each statement is true or false.

21. Tax collectors, **pūblicānī,** were able to amass great personal fortunes in the provinces.

22. Many slaves worked in the numerous large factories throughout the Roman Empire.

23. Lawyers were able to accept large sums of money for defending their clients.

24. Private Roman homes often included small rooms that functioned as workshops.

25. The idea of workers' unions and the benefits of such groups were unknown to the Romans.

FROM LATIN TO ENGLISH

Apply your knowledge of Latin roots to determine the best meaning of the italicized words.

26. After the assembly everyone was speaking about the *urbane* visitor.

a. handsome

b. uncivilized

c. sophisticated

d. belligerent

27. The old woman in the village always tried to add a touch of *levity* to the situation.

a. instruction

b. frivolity

c. folklore

d. seriousness

28. Her friend lived in an *ostentatious* house at the end of the road.

a. neglected

b. historic

c. newly built

d. showy

29. The man outlined a *munificent* plan that would benefit the project.

a. generous

b. public

c. effective

d. private

30. Great clouds of *acrid* smoke rose from the site.

a. white

b. black

c. irritating

d. damp

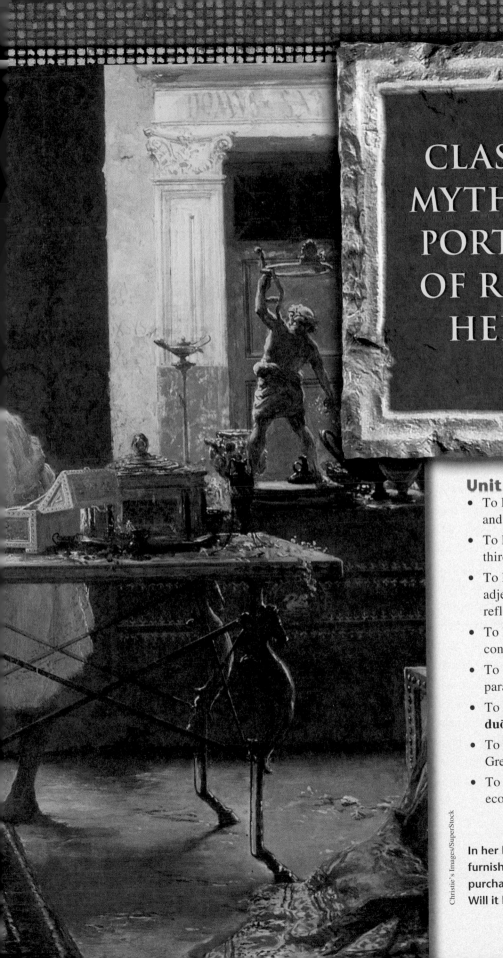

CLASSICAL MYTHS AND PORTRAITS OF ROMAN HEROES

Unit Objectives

- To learn the comparison of adjectives and adverbs
- To learn how to form adverbs from third declension adjectives
- To learn the third person reflexive adjective **suus, -a, -um** and the reflexive pronouns
- To learn the dative with adjectives construction
- To learn the use of **quam** with comparatives and superlatives
- To learn the declensions and uses of **duō, trēs, mīlle,** and **mīlia**
- To become familiar with well-known Greek and Roman legends
- To learn more about Roman social and economic conditions

In her luxurious home, filled with elaborate furnishings, a Roman matron considers the purchase of a beautiful necklace (**monīle**). Will it be hers or her daughter's?

LESSON OBJECTIVES

- To learn about the mythical ages of human evolution
- To learn the regular comparison of adjectives
- To learn the use of **quam** with comparatives

QUATTUOR AETĀTĒS

¹ *spring*
² *of milk*
³ *of bronze*
⁴ *again*
⁵ *better*
⁶ *are changed*
⁷ *both*

Antīquī dīxērunt prīmam aetātem esse auream. Sāturnus erat rēx deōrum hominumque. Illō tempore poenae lēgēsque aberant, quod omnēs hominēs iūstī erant. Nūllae nāvēs in marī erant, nec trāns mare lātum hominēs nāvigābant. Bellum numquam erat nec mīlitēs nec arma. In ōtiō vītam
5 hominēs agēbant, nam omnēs terrae concordiā et pāce ligātae sunt. Hominēs in agrīs nōn labōrābant; terra nōn culta ipsa frūmentum et omnia ūtilia dabat. Urbēs nōn erant. Neque hiems neque aestās erat; semper erat vēr¹. Flūmina lactis² et vīnī erant. Quod omnēs agrī commūnēs erant, terminī agrōrum nōn erant. Aliēnōs agrōs hominēs nōn cupiēbant.

10 Sāturnō expulsō, Iuppiter rēx erat. Nunc incipit secunda aetās, quae ex argentō est, dūrior quam prīma, grātior tamen quam tertia. Tum aestās et hiems esse incipiunt; quattuor sunt tempora annī. Tum prīmum in agrīs labōrāre hominēs incipiunt.

Tertia aetās ex aere³ erat. Dūrior erat quam secunda.

15 Quārta aetās, quae ex ferrō est, dūrissima omnium est. Poenae gravissimae statuuntur; hominēs tamen interficiunt et rapiunt. Nautae in omnī marī ad ultima loca nāvigant et ūtilia petunt quae in variīs terrīs continentur. Bellīs numquam intermissīs, hominēs terrās aliēnās vincere mātūrant. Nihil sacrum est; omnia rapiuntur. Hominēs in agrīs labōrant; nam labor omnia vincit.

20 Haec dīcunt auctōrēs clārissimī Graecī dē quattuor aetātibus. Vergilius, poēta Rōmānus, putābat iterum⁴ aetātem auream futūram esse. Etiam nunc multī putant vītam semper grātiōrem futūram esse. Putātisne fortasse condiciōnem fortūnamque populōrum antīquōrum meliōrem⁵ fuisse quam condiciōnem nostram? Quō modō statuistis hanc sententiam vērām esse?
25 Quae erit condiciō hominum post mīlle annōs? Aliī dīcunt: "Tempora mūtantur⁶, et nōs mūtāmur in illīs." Aliī respondent hominēs semper eōsdem fuisse et futūrōs esse. Quae est sententia vestra? Possuntne fortasse ambae⁷ sententiae vērae esse?

Questions

1. List the four ages and the basic characteristic of each.
2. Why didn't men work in the Golden Age?
3. When did they begin to toil?
4. When did crime first appear?
5. What age was the hardest of all?
6. Who ruled the gods in the first age?
7. When did wars first start?
8. What does the passage suggest about the motives of the sailors?
9. What belief did Vergil have about the Golden Age?
10. Write a short essay in response to the Latin questions that come at the end of the passage.

In this woodcut from a 1501 edition of Ovid, Prometheus creates man out of clay and sends him fire. Thus, the Golden Age was born. The Silver Age is represented by men working in the fields and building homes. Fighting started in the Bronze Age, but it became worse in the Iron Age when ships began putting to sea. A picture like this, which tells successive events in a single scene, is an example of narrative art.

VOCABULARY

Nouns

ae´tās, aetā´tis f. *age, time* — (eternal)

condi´ciō, condiciō´nis f. *condition, terms* — [dīcō]

Adjective

ū´tilis, -e *useful* — (utilitarian, utility)

Verbs

ra´piō, ra´pere, ra´puī, rap´tus — (rapacious, rapture)
carry off, steal

sta´tuō, statu´ere, sta´tuī, statū´tus — [stō]
(make stand), establish, determine, arrange

vin´cō, vin´cere, vī´cī, vic´tus *conquer* — (victor, invincible)

Conjunction

quam *than*

GRAMMAR

Comparison of Adjectives

Adjectives change form to show *degree*, i.e., a grade or measure of *comparison*. There are three degrees: *positive, comparative,* and *superlative*. The positive is the simple form of the adjective; the other two express successively greater degrees of the adjective's basic meaning. To compare an adjective is to change the form of the adjective in English or Latin to indicate those three degrees.

In English, the comparative is ordinarily formed by adding *-er (-r)* to the positive: *high-er, brave-r*. The superlative is formed by adding *-est (-st)* to the positive: *high-est, brave-st*. But adjectives of more than one syllable are often compared by the use of *more* and *most: more skillful, most skillful*.

In Latin, the comparative is formed by adding **-ior** (m. and f.), **-ius** (n.) to the base of the positive. The superlative is formed by adding **-issimus, -a, -um.**

Nota Bene

The comparative may often be translated using *more, too, rather;* the superlative, *most, very, exceedingly*. Thus, **altior,** *higher,* might also be translated *more high, rather high,* or even *too high*. Similarly, **altissimus** could be *very high* or *most high* as well as *highest*.

POSITIVE	COMPARATIVE	SUPERLATIVE
al´tus, -a, -um	**al´tior, al´tius**	**altis´simus, -a, -um**
high	*higher*	*highest*
for´tis, -e	**for´tior, for´tius**	**fortis´simus, -a, -um**
brave	*braver*	*bravest*

Classical antiquity provided endless subjects for Renaissance artists. This preliminary sketch of the Age of Iron by Pietro da Cortona shows how far man has fallen from the height of the Golden Age. The finished paintings are in a museum in Florence, Italy.

By adding the comparative endings to any first, second, or third declension adjective, its meaning changes to __-er or more __. Similarly, adding the superlative endings to the base of any first, second, or third declension adjective changes the meaning to __-est, most __, or very __.

The Declension of Comparatives

Note that although adjectives in the comparative degree are declined like adjectives of the third declension, they do not have **-ī** in the ablative singular, **-ium** in the genitive plural, or **-ia** in the nominative and accusative plural neuter. Thus, comparatives are not **i**-stems.

(Adjectives in the superlative degree are declined like first and second declension adjectives.)

	SINGULAR		PLURAL	
	M., F.	N.	M., F.	N.
Nominative	al´tior	al´tius	altiō´rēs	altiō´ra
Genitive	altiō´ris	altiō´ris	altiō´rum	altiō´rum
Dative	altiō´rī	altiō´rī	altiō´ribus	altiō´ribus
Accusative	altiō´rem	al´tius	altiō´rēs	altiō´ra
Ablative	altiō´re	altiō´re	altiō´ribus	altiō´ribus

Comparisons with *Quam*

When two nouns are compared in Latin, both are in the same case with **quam** *(than)* between them, but in English, *than* is often followed by the nominative, which can be taken as the subject of some omitted but easily understood verb.

Hic mōns est altior quam ille.	*This mountain is higher than that one (is).*
Fortiōrem virum quam illum nōn vīdī.	*I have not seen a braver man than he (is).*

Note in the second sentence that the accusative case **illum** is used (in the same case as **virum**), even though the nominative case *he* can be employed in English.

Oral Practice

1. Compare **grātus, nōbilis, clārus, levis, longus.**
2. Decline **tardus** in the comparative.
3. Decline **supplicium iūstius.**

▦ *Exercises*

A. Translate the following sentences.
1. Novissimum librum ad frātrem meum mittere statuī.
2. Quid est ūtilius grātiusque quam librōs bonōs semper legere?
3. Gallī vīribus corporis Rōmānōs superābant sed nōn erant fortiōrēs virī.
4. Condiciōnēs pācis ab hostibus victīs semper dūrissimae esse habentur.
5. Homō dē viīs mē rogāvit; ego respondī hanc esse plāniōrem quam illam.
6. Eī duo itinera ostendimus—alterum facile, alterum longius et incertius.

B. Translate the following sentences into Latin.
1. Nothing is more useful than water.
2. Why are the rivers of Italy not very long?
3. Does peace have nobler victories than war?
4. I know that that river is swift but not very wide.
5. More severe terms of peace than these will be established.

Did You Know?

The Romans knew of only eight metals: copper, gold, iron, lead, mercury, silver, tin, and zinc. Gold was as highly valued by the Romans as it is today and was used for jewelry and coins (the **aureus** and **solidus**). Iron was used to make axes, chains, scissors, razors, knives, javelins, darts, stakes, nails, styli, and swords. Lead was used in the construction of water pipes and pellets, and silver was used to make jewelry, serving dishes, and coins (the **dēnārius** and **sēstertius**).

WORD STUDY

Roots It is important to distinguish different words that come from the same stem. *Plain* and *plane* both come from **plānus,** *level, flat.* A *plain* is a level field; a *plain* person is not above the average level. A *plane* is a *flat* surface (hence *plane geometry*); it is also a tool that makes surfaces *flat.* The *flat* surfaces of an airplane (or hydroplane) enable it to glide through the air (or water). *Plane* is therefore used in a more literal sense than *plain.*

Take **corpus:** a *corpse* is a dead *body;* a *corps* (pronounced "core") is a *body* of individuals forming part of an army or other organization. The former is literal; the latter, figurative. A *corporation* is a *body* of individuals united for commercial or other purposes. A *corpuscle* is a little *body* in the blood. *Corporal* punishment is punishment inflicted upon the *body,* e.g., a whipping; something *corporeal* has a *body;* it is not imaginary. Similarly, a *principal* is the *leading* person in a school; a *principle* is a *leading* rule.

Explain in the same way *statue* and *statute; urban* and *urbane; sensory* and *sentiment; respiration* and *inspiration.*

LESSON
OBJECTIVES
• To learn the story of
  Baucis and Philemon
• To learn how to form
  and compare adverbs
  from third declension
  adjectives

BAUCIS ET PHILĒMŌN

¹ *sleep* (dat.)
² *Baucis (Bau´sis), Philē´mon*
³ *household* (pred. nom.)
⁴ *table*
⁵ *took,* i.e., *drank*
⁶ *mixing bowl*

Iuppiter et Mercurius per Phrygiam, quae in Asiā est, iter fēcērunt, sed nēmō in tōtā illā gente eōs cognōvit. Omnēs iūdicāvērunt eōs esse hominēs humilēs quod vestēs miserās gerēbant. Ad mīlle casās accessērunt; nam locum somnō¹ aptum petīvērunt. Sed omnēs, hīs vīsīs, casās celeriter
5 clausērunt. In tōtā regiōne ācriter repulsī sunt. Tamen ūna casa, parva et humilis, eōs nōn reppulit. Ibi Baucis et Philēmōn² multōs annōs ēgerant. Condiciōne humilī nōn affectī, paupertātem leviter ac fortiter sustinuērunt. Duo tōta domus³ fuērunt, et dominī et servī ipsī; nam nūllōs servōs habuērunt.

Cēnam humilem Baucis magnā dīligentiā celeritāteque parāvit; numquam
10 celerius labōrāverat. Tum, omnibus īnstrūctīs, deōs ad cēnam vocāvit. Mēnsa⁴, nōn pulchra sed ūtilis, paucīs sed bonīs cibīs īnstrūcta erat. Vīnum sūmpsērunt⁵, sed semper crāter⁶ vīnum continuit. Tum Philēmōn et Baucis, ad mēnsam sedentēs, clārē sēnsērunt deōs adesse. Tum Iuppiter, "Deī sumus," inquit. "Tōtam hanc gentem poenam solūtūram esse statuimus,
15 quod nēmō nōbīs auxilium dedit, sed vōs vīvētis. Ad montem prōcēdēmus."

Casa humilis deōs nōn reppulit. As Jupiter grandly announces that he and Mercury are gods, the aged couple piously kneel to apologize for the humble peasants' meal they are serving. Their plan to cook their only goose, the "watch-dog" of the household, fails because they are too old and feeble to catch it, and Jupiter orders it spared while Mercury looks on coolly. Note the tablecloth (!) and the basin in which the hosts washed their guests' feet.

Giraudon/The Bridgeman Art Library

Itaque Baucis et Philēmōn, hāc ōrātiōne permōtī, ad montem tardē prōcessērunt. Ibi cōnstitērunt et vīdērunt tōtam regiōnem sub aquā esse, casam suam[7] sōlam manēre. Dum spectant, casa eōrum in pulchrum templum vertitur.

Tum Iuppiter, "Quid cupitis?" inquit; "id quod petitis dōnābō." Philēmōn, [20] uxōre cōnsultā, respondit: "Iūdicāmus nūllum mūnus nōbīs grātius aptiusque esse quam esse sacerdōtēs[8] illīus templī et ē vītā eōdem tempore excēdere, quod in concordiā multōs annōs ēgimus." Post hanc ōrātiōnem hoc mūnus Iuppiter eīs permīsit.

Post multōs annōs, Philēmōn et uxor, aetāte gravēs, ante sacrum templum [25] stābant. Corpora eōrum in arborēs[9] tardē vertī incipiunt; vōcēs haerent; nōn iam spīrant nec vīvunt. Neuter ante alterum ē vītā excessit. Multōs annōs hae duae arborēs ante templum stābant.

[7] their own
[8] priests
[9] trees

Questions

1. How were the distinguished gods Jupiter and Mercury welcomed by most people and why?
2. Who finally admitted them?
3. What was their hosts' house like, and how many slaves did they have?
4. Describe the dinner given to the gods.
5. How did Philemon figure out that his guests were gods?
6. How were the neighbors of Philemon and Baucis punished?
7. How was this devout old couple rewarded for their piety?
8. How were they transformed in the end?

▦ VOCABULARY

Nouns

*gēns, gen´tis, gen´tium f. *people, nation* (gentle, gentry)

nē´mō, nē´minī (dat.), **nē´minem** (acc.) **[ne + homō]**
[no other forms], *no one*

ōrā´tiō, ōrātiō´nis f. *speech* (oration, oratory)

re´giō, regiō´nis f. *region* **[regō]**

Adjectives

ap´tus, -a, -um *fit, suitable* (with dat.) (adapt, aptitude)

hu´milis, -e *low, humble* (humiliate, humility)

Verbs

ĭn´struō, īnstru´ere, īnstrū´xī,   (instruction, instructor)
   īnstrūc´tus *arrange, set up*
iū´dicō, iūdicā´re, iūdicā´vī,   [iūs + dīcō]
   iūdicā´tus *judge*
repel´lō, repel´lere, rep´pulī, repul´sus   [pellō]
   drive back, repulse

GRAMMAR

Formation and Comparison of Adverbs

You will recall that adverbs formed from adjectives of the first and second declensions add **-ē** to the base. To form adverbs from adjectives of the third declension, you generally add **-iter** to the base.

Nota•Bene

Note that in the comparative degree the adverb always has the same form as the neuter accusative singular of the comparative adjective.

for´tis *brave*	**for´titer** *bravely*
ā´cer *sharp*	**ā´criter** *sharply*

The comparison of adverbs is very similar to that of adjectives: **-ius** is added to the base to obtain the comparative adverb *(more __ly)*, while **-issimē** is added to the base to obtain the superlative adverb *(most __ly)*.

POSITIVE	COMPARATIVE	SUPERLATIVE
al´tē *deeply*	**al´tius** *more deeply*	**altis´simē** *most deeply*
for´titer *bravely*	**for´tius** *more bravely*	**fortis´simē** *most bravely*

Oral Practice

Form and compare adverbs from the following adjectives: **longus, ūtilis, levis, clārus, firmus, gravis, vērus.**

▦ *Exercises*

A. Translate the following sentences.

1. Sciō hoc flūmen esse longius quam illud.
2. Pater meus omnia iūstē et celeriter iūdicat.
3. Praemiō acceptō, magister ōrātiōne aptā respondit.
4. Hī mīlitēs, ē castrīs ēductī, ad pugnam ā duce īnstruuntur.
5. Tardius pervēnimus quod reliquī puerī celerius cucurrērunt.
6. Hī hominēs, ab hostibus repulsī, in pāce vīvere statuērunt.

B. Translate the following sentences into Latin.

1. We shall breathe more easily.
2. No one approves a very long speech.
3. The battle was sharply fought, but few men received severe wounds.
4. We certainly hope that all nations will work more keenly for peace.

Did You Know?

The rose was among the favorite flowers of the Romans. Other popular garden flowers included lilies and violets. The conventional garden features of Roman villas were terraces, bordered walks, rows of statues, aviaries, fish ponds. Colonnades and hedges were made of scented shrubs, such as rosemary, myrtle, and laurel. Grapevines were trained to grow over trellises or arbors, and ivy hid foundations and retaining walls.

WORD STUDY

- **Suffixes**

  In Latin the suffix **-iō** is added to verb stems, usually to that of the past participle. Since this generally ends in **-t** or **-s,** words of this origin are likely to end in **-tiō** or **-siō.** The suffix indicates an act or the result of an act: **ōrātiō** is the act or result of speaking, i.e., a speech. Nouns with this suffix have **-iōnis** in the genitive and are regularly feminine. The stem ends in **-n.** The English form of the suffix, which is very common, is *-ion (-tion, -sion): region, oration, session.* It often has the force of the suffix *-ing.*

  Give and define ten English words with the suffix *-ion* derived from Latin verbs you have studied. Look up the origin and meaning of *gentle, gentile, genteel, jaunty.*

- Here are more state mottoes.

  Alis volat propriis.   *She soars on her own wings.* (Oregon)

  Cedant arma togae.   (Cicero) *Let arms yield to the toga, i.e., Let civil peace prevail over war.* (Wyoming)

DAEDALUS ET ĪCARUS

In īnsulā magnā Crētā Mīnōs[1] fuit rēx. Daedalus[2] cum fīliō parvō Īcarō[2] ibi captīvus fuit. Fugere nōn potuit quod mare prohibuit. "Neque per terram," inquit, "neque per mare fugere possum, sed caelum certē nōn clauditur. Illā viā difficillimā prōcēdēmus." Itaque ālās[3] parāvit, simillimās ālīs vērīs avium[4]. Partēs ālārum cērā[5] ligāvit. Īcarus ad patrem stābat, ālās levissimās 5 tangēbat, opus patris impediēbat. Tandem[6] fīnis labōris difficilis aderat; ālae parātae erant. Daedalus tempus aptum esse iūdicāvit. Tum ālās gracilēs[7] corporī gracilī fīlī iūnxit et eum hīs verbīs ācriter monuit:

"In mediō caelō prōcēdēmus; nam, sī humilius volābimus[8], undae ālās graviōrēs facient; sī altius volābimus, ignis ālās ūret[9] et in mare cadēmus. 10 Omnia nunc tibi explicābō."

Tum omnēs partēs ālārum fīliō ostendit et omnia in ōrdine explicāvit. Perīculum esse sēnsit et fīliō timuit, quī patrī dissimillimus erat. Ālīs propriīs īnstrūctus antecessit et fīlium post volāre iussit.

[1] *Mī´nos* (nom. sing.)
[2] *Daedalus (Dĕd´alus), Ic´arus*
[3] *wings*
[4] *of birds*
[5] *wax*
[6] *finally*
[7] *slender*
[8] *will fly*
[9] *will burn*

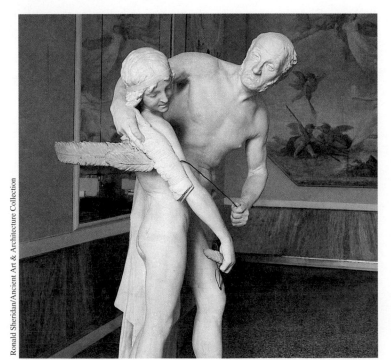

Ronald Sheridan/Ancient Art & Architecture Collection

The boy Icarus watches confidently as his father anxiously stitches the wings to his arms. To the ancients Daedalus represented the legendary master craftsman, architect, engineer, and artist. On Crete he designed the labyrinth for King Minos and elsewhere created temples with elaborate doors, steam baths, carpenters' tools, and hundreds of statues.

15   Agricolae territī ex agrīs eōs vīdērunt; multī putāvērunt eōs deōs aut deīs similēs esse. Celerrimē pater fīliusque āera[10] ālīs pepulērunt[11].

   Multās regiōnēs multāsque gentēs relīquērunt. Tum puer nōn iam timidus patrem ducem relīquit. Ōrātiōnem patris memoriā nōn tenuit et altius volāvit quod iūdicāvit nihil accidere posse. Sed multa accidērunt: celeriter sōl cēram
20 solvit; nōn iam ālae haesērunt. Puer miser praeceps in mare cecidit; nōn iam vīvit. Ab illō posteā hoc mare nōmen proprium "Īcarium" accēpit.

   Interim pater, nōn iam pater, in omnibus regiōnibus fīlium petēbat, nōmen fīlī clāmābat. Tandem alas Īcarī in undīs vīdit sed corpus eius numquam invēnit.

   Tum ipse ad Siciliam facile pervēnit et ibi multōs annōs ēgit. Sed fābula
25 ab aliīs dicta huic dissimilis est: scrībunt eum in Italiam volāvisse et ibi in templō ālās posuisse. Hōc modō deīs prō salūte grātiās ēgit.

   Prīmus omnium hominum Daedalus, Nātūrā victā, per caelum lātum volāvit, sī auctōrēs Graecī et Rōmānī vērum dīxērunt. Nunc multī hominēs facile volant, etiam per immēnsum[12], sed nēmō ālīs propriīs. Quod opus
30 hominibus difficilius[13] est?

Questions

1. Why did Daedalus wish to escape with his son from Crete?
2. What obstacle stood in his way, and how did Daedalus plan to overcome it?
3. Did Icarus help his father complete his work?
4. What warning did Daedalus give to Icarus?
5. What sort of additional instruction did he give?
6. What reaction did the farmers have to the sight?
7. What mistake did Icarus make, and what was the result?
8. What two versions are there for the end of the story?
9. Does the writer express any hestitation in believing the truth of this story? How?

[10] *air* (acc. sing.)
[11] *beat* (from **pellō**)
[12] *the immeasurable,* i.e., space
[13] See **Nota Bene,** p. 422.

Puer miser praeceps in mare cecidit. Some say Icarus' wings were made of wood, others that they were feathers; still others think that they represent the invention of sails, and that the pair escaped on a ship off which Icarus rashly jumped and was drowned. Here is the doomed Icarus on the door of the Wright Brothers' Memorial in Kitty Hawk, North Carolina, honoring their first airplane flight in 1903.

Ray Matthews

VOCABULARY

Nouns

*ig´nis, ig´nis, ig´nium m. *fire*   (ignite)
o´pus, o´peris n. *work, labor*   (opus, operate)
sōl, sō´lis m. *sun*   (solar)

Adjectives

diffi´cilis, -e *difficult*   [dis + facilis]
pro´prius, -a, -um *(one's) own*   (appropriate, proprietary)

si´milis, -e *like* (with dat.)   (similarity)
dissi´milis, -e *unlike* (with dat.)   [dis + similis]

Verbs

ca´dō, ca´dere, ce´cidī, cāsū´rus *fall*   (cadence, casualty)
ac´cidō, acci´dere, ac´cidī, —
    fall to, befall, happen (with dat.)   [cadō]
ex´plicō, explicā´re, explicā´vī,   [plicō]
    explicā´tus *unfold, explain*
iun´gō, iun´gere, iūn´xī, iūn´ctus   (joint, junction)
    join (to)

Adverb

fa´cile *easily* (formed irregularly)   [facilis]

GRAMMAR

Comparison of *-er* Adjectives and Their Adverbs

The comparative degree of all adjectives ending in **-er** is formed regularly from the base of the positive. But the superlative is formed by adding **-rimus, -a, -um** to the nominative singular masculine (not the base) of the positive.

POSITIVE	COMPARATIVE	SUPERLATIVE
lī´ber, lī´bera, lī´berum *free*	**lībe´rior, lībe´rius** *freer, too free*	**liber´rimus, -a, -um** *freest, most free*
ā´cer, ā´cris, ā´cre *sharp*	**ā´crior, ā´crius** *sharper, rather sharp*	**ācer´rimus, -a, -um** *sharpest, very sharp*
ce´ler, ce´leris, ce´lere *quick*	**cele´rior, cele´rius** *quicker*	**celer´rimus, -a, -um** *quickest*

The corresponding adverbs are compared as follows.

POSITIVE	COMPARATIVE	SUPERLATIVE
lī´berē	**lībe´rius**	**liber´rimē**
freely	*more freely*	*most freely*
ā´criter	**ā´crius**	**ācer´rimē**
sharply	*more sharply*	*very sharply*
cele´riter	**cele´rius**	**celer´rimē**
quickly	*more quickly*	*very quickly*

Oral Practice

1. Compare the adjectives **miser, pulcher, altus.** Form and compare the corresponding adverbs.
2. Decline **illa patria līberior.**

Adjectives with Superlative in *-limus*

The superlative of six adjectives ending in **-lis** is formed by adding **-limus, -a, -um** to the base of the positive. The comparatives are regular.

POSITIVE	COMPARATIVE	SUPERLATIVE
fa´cilis, -e	**faci´lior, faci´lius**	**facil´limus, -a, -um**
diffi´cilis, -e	**diffici´lior, diffici´lius**	**difficil´limus, -a, -um**
si´milis, -e	**simi´lior, simi´lius**	**simil´limus, -a, -um**
dissi´milis, -e	**dissimi´lior, dissimi´lius**	**dissimil´limus, -a, -um**
hu´milis, -e	**humi´lior, humi´lius**	**humil´limus, -a, -um**
gra´cilis, -e	**graci´lior, graci´lius**	**gracil´limus, -a, -um**

The superlative of other -lis adjectives, such as nōbilis, -e, ūtilis, -e, etc., is formed regularly—by adding -issimus to the base of the positive: nōbil-issimus, -a, -um.

The adverbs formed from these **-lis** adjectives are generally formed regularly, but the adverb from **facilis** is **facile.** In the superlative, the corresponding adverbs end in **-limē: facillimē.**

Dative with Adjectives

The dative case is often used with Latin adjectives whose English equivalents are followed by *to* or *for.* You are already familiar with many of them: **amīcus, inimīcus, similis, dissimilis, aptus, grātus, ūtilis.**

Hic liber est similis illī.	*This book is similar to that (like that) one.*
Ille homō est frātrī meō inimīcus.	*That man is unfriendly to my brother.*

Quam Plus the Superlative

Quam is used with superlative adjectives and adverbs to express *as . . . as possible.* In effect, it intensifies the superlative degree even further.

quam clārissimus, -a, -um	*as clear as possible*
quam facillimus, -a, -um	*as easy as possible*
quam celerrimē	*as quickly as possible*
quam facillimē	*as easily as possible*

Exercises

A. Translate the following sentences.
1. Hic equus similior meō est quam ille.
2. Deī Rōmānōrum dissimillimī deīs aliārum gentium erant.
3. Ille liber difficillimus est, nam pauca clārē explicat.
4. Homō humilis nec altē nec graviter cadere potest.
5. Nihil est nōbīs ūtilius quam liber bonus, nam est nōbilissimus amīcōrum.

B. Translate the following sentences into Latin.
1. This region is fit for some settlers, but not for others.
2. As the bad men approached, the boys ran more quickly.
3. The places in which our soldiers fell are most sacred.
4. The teacher, in a speech as beautiful as possible, unfolded the life of Caesar.

C. Many of the Greek and Roman myths are meant to explain a practice, a belief, a natural phenomenon, or a moral position. Work with a partner to write a short paragraph in Latin explaining what the Daedalus and Icarus story is intended to teach.

Did You Know?

As schoolboys, most Romans memorized the Twelve Tables of the law. This important law code was inscribed on bronze (originally wooden) tablets that were displayed in the Roman Forum. All physical remains of the tablets are gone, and our knowledge of their contents depends upon literary sources. Each tablet contained a number of detailed laws regulating, for example, the punishment of debtors, the gathering of fallen fruit, the power of a father over his sons, and the establishment of the rate of interest, property boundaries, etc.

WORD STUDY

- *Space* and *missile* terms are often taken from Latin and Greek. *Space* is from **spatium,** *missile* and *mission* from **mittō.** Others are *capsule* **(capiō),** which "holds" the crew, *circumlunar* **(circum,** *around,* **lūna,** *moon*), *core* **(corpus),** *fission* **(findō,** *split*), *fusion* **(fundō,** *pour, melt*), *gravity* **(gravis),** *intercontinental* **(inter, contineō),** *interstellar* **(inter, stēlla,** *star*), *jet* **(iaciō),** *orb, orbit* **(orbis,** *circle*), *propellant* **(prō, pellō),** *reaction* **(re, agō),** *supersonic* **(super, sonus,** *sound*), *trajectory* **(trāns, iaciō).**

- Missile names are often based on characters in myth: *Apollo, Atlas* (who held the earth on his shoulders), *Gemini, Jupiter, Mercury, Saturn, Titan.* Can you think of others?

- Lawyers are familiar with Latin because they use many Latin phrases in their daily activities. A few such phrases are:

    subpoena a summons to court *under penalty*
      for failure to attend

    in propria persona *in one's own person*
      (not through someone else)

    ex post facto *resulting after the fact;* as a law which
      makes punishable acts committed before its passage

    in forma pauperis *in the form* (or *manner*) *of a poor man;*
      to sue as a poor man and so avoid the costs of the suit

- One of the most important foundations of American and British civil liberties and justice is that of **habeas corpus,** *you must produce the body* (lit., *you should have the body*). By a writ of **habeas corpus** a judge compels a person who has detained or imprisoned another to show that the imprisonment was not illegal.

DĒ PYRRHŌ ET EIUS VICTŌRIĀ

Rōmānī, quī erant optimī mīlitēs, gentēs quae proximae urbī erant vīcerant et in ulteriōrēs partēs Italiae pervēnerant. Summā virtūte contrā maiōrem numerum hostium in extrēmīs ac difficillimīs regiōnibus Italiae bene pugnāverant. Posteā bellum novī generis, dissimile aliīs, cum Pyrrhō, duce summō et rēge maximō Ēpīrī[1], gessērunt.

Pyrrhus in Italiam īnferiōrem ā Tarentīnīs, gente pessimā, vocātus erat, quī eō tempore cum Rōmānīs pugnābant. Is in Italiam mīlitēs trānsportāvit et elephantōrum auxiliō Rōmānōs fortiter pugnantēs reppulit, quod Rōmānī elephantōs maximōs nōn ante vīsōs timuērunt. Peius[2] tamen Pyrrhō victōrī quam victīs Rōmānīs accidit, nam plūrimī mīlitēs Pyrrhī cecidērunt. Pyrrhus, ubi plūrima corpora Rōmānōrum interfectōrum in fronte vulnera habēre vīdit, haec verba fēcit: "Bene Rōmānī pugnāvērunt. Cum tālibus[3] mīlitibus tōtus orbis[4] facillimē ā mē vincī potest!" Familiāribus dē victōriā agentibus dīxit: "Sī iterum[5] eōdem modō vīcerō, miserrimē conficiar[6], et nūllōs mīlitēs ex Italiā īnferiōre in Ēpīrum redūcam." Nam hanc victōriam nōn ūtilem esse iūdicāvit quod plūrēs mīlitēs āmīserat.

5 [1] *Epirus (Epī´rus), a region in north-west Greece*
[2] *a worse thing*
[3] *such*
[4] *world* (nom.)
[5] *again*
[6] *ruined*

10

15

Gianni Dagli Orti/The Art Archive

This bust of a victorious general (note the wreath on his helmet) is now in a Naples museum and is said to be a portrait of Pyrrhus (318–272 B.C.). Pyrrhus' grand ambitions for an empire stretching from Epirus to Carthage were thwarted by the Romans in 279 B.C., even though they suffered a defeat. Now we call any success that is gained at a catastrophic cost to the winner a "Pyrrhic victory."

Questions

1. How good was the Roman army before encountering Pyrrhus?
2. How far did Roman dominion extend?
3. Who invited Pyrrhus into Italy, and what is the writer's attitude toward them?
4. What new weapon did Pyrrhus use against the Romans, and why did it work?
5. Although he had won the battle, why did Pyrrhus consider it a loss?
6. What did Pyrrhus say when he saw the fallen Roman soliders, and what was the point of his remark?
7. What do Pyrrhus' final remarks illustrate about the cost of his victory?

GRAMMAR

Irregular Comparison of Adjectives

In English, some adjectives have irregular comparative forms, such as *good, better, best; bad, worse, worst.* In Latin, the following adjectives, among others, have irregular comparative and superlative forms and should be memorized.

POSITIVE	COMPARATIVE	SUPERLATIVE
bo´nus, -a, -um	**me´lior, me´lius**	**op´timus, -a, -um**
good	*better*	*best*
ma´lus, -a, -um	**pe´ior, pe´ius**	**pes´simus, -a, -um**
bad	*worse*	*worst*
mag´nus, -a, -um	**ma´ior, ma´ius**	**ma´ximus, -a, -um**
large	*larger*	*largest*
par´vus, -a, -um	**mi´nor, mi´nus**	**mi´nimus, -a, -um**
small	*smaller*	*smallest*
mul´tus, -a, -um	**—, plūs**[7]	**plū´rimus, -a, -um**
much, many	*more (in quantity or number)*	*most*

The adverbs formed from the preceding adjectives are formed regularly in the comparative and superlative degrees, according to the rules given on page 428 (**-ius** in the comparative, **-ē** in the superlative). In the positive degree there are several exceptions, e.g., **bene** from **bonus,** which will be given to you in the notes or vocabularies as necessary.

---

[7] Gen. **plūris;** neuter sing. only; no dative singular. The plural is ***plūrēs, plūra,** gen. **plūrium,** etc. In the singular, use **plūs** as a neuter noun with the (partitive) genitive: **plūs cibi,** *more of food.*

This third-century B.C. theater in Epirus, now partially restored and still used for stage performances, once held seventeen thousand people and was only a part of a large complex of temples and buildings. It was from Epirus that Pyrrhus set off on his ill-fated conquest of Italy.

▓ VOCABULARY

In addition to the comparative and superlative forms of the irregular adjectives presented above, learn the following.

Adjectives

extrē´mus, -a, -um *farthest, last, end of*	(extremist)
īnfe´rior, īnfe´rius *lower*	(inferiority)
pro´ximus, -a, -um *nearest, next* (with dat.)	(proximity)
sum´mus, -a, -um *highest, top of*	(sum, summit)
ulte´rior, ulte´rius *farther*	(ulterior)
ul´timus, -a, -um *farthest*	(ultimatum)

Adverb

be´ne *well*	**[bonus]**

Adjectives Translated by Using Nouns

Some Latin adjectives indicating a location or a part of something are often best translated into English by using a noun. Study the following examples.

reliquī mīlitēs *the rest of the soldiers*
summus mōns *the top of the mountain*
in mediō flūmine *in the middle of the river*
in extrēmā ōrātiōne *at the end of the speech*
tōta Italia *the whole of Italy*

When used in this way, the adjective usually precedes its noun.

Oral Practice

Give the Latin for *more horses, the largest city, the farthest land, the lower field.*

📖 *Exercises*

A. Translate the following sentences into English.

1. Puerī puellaeque ad īnferiōrem partem flūminis quam celerrimē cucurrērunt.
2. Optimī cīvēs patriam semper optimē dēfendent.
3. Summus mōns ā nōbīs facillimē occupātus est.
4. Pessimī hominēs in ultimās regiōnēs expellī dēbent.
5. Hī septem puerī territī sunt quod perīculum maximum esse sēnsērunt.
6. Agricolae quī meliōrēs agrōs habent maiōrem cōpiam frūmentī habēbunt.
7. Nōnne spērās proximum mēnsem nōn futūrum esse dūriōrem quam hunc?

B. Translate the following sentences into Latin.

1. The smallest town is not the worst.
2. The largest (thing) is not the best (thing).
3. Can a horse run more swiftly than a man?
4. The smaller man fought more bravely than the larger.
5. We shall do this well and as quickly as possible without your aid.

Did You Know?

The Romans had many customs involving the celebration of victory and peace. The **laurea** was a wreath of laurel that was carried by victorious Roman generals and dedicated to Jupiter. The victorious Roman admiral was often presented with a **corōna classica,** or crown of victory, for his naval successes. To the Roman sailor who first boarded a captured enemy ship, a **corōna nāvālis** was presented. Then, as now, the olive branch (**olīva**) was a symbol of peace.

WORD STUDY

- A number of English words preserve the forms of the comparative and superlative of Latin irregular adjectives: *major* (cf. mayor), *maximum, minor, minus, minimum, plus, inferior, superior, ulterior, prior, anterior, posterior, interior, exterior, junior, senior*. What is the difference between a *majority* and a *plurality* vote? Between a *majority* and a *minority* report?

- Study the following English phrases that are borrowed from Latin, some of which are state mottoes.

E pluribus unum	*One (country) out of many (states)* (motto of the United States, found on all U.S. coins)
Excelsior!	*Higher!* (motto of the state of New York)
Esse quam videri	*To be rather than to seem (to be)* (motto of the state of North Carolina)
Semper paratus	*Always prepared* (motto of the Coast Guard)

- Translate **Labor omnia vincit** into English. It is the motto of Oklahoma, the University of Illinois, and the American Federation of Labor.

LESSON OBJECTIVES
- To learn the story of Fabricius
- To learn the forms and use of reflexive pronouns and adjectives

PYRRHUS ET FABRICIUS

[1] *Fabricius (Fabrish´us)*
[2] *course* (abl.)

Fabricius[1], quī erat īnferior genere quam aliī Rōmānī, tamen ab omnibus amātus est quod optimus fortissimusque mīles erat. Neque amīcōs neque inimīcōs suōs fallēbat. Praemia numquam sūmēbat. Itaque Rōmānī cīvitātis suae salūtem eī crēdidērunt et eum inter aliōs lēgātōs ad Pyrrhum mīsērunt.

5 Multa quae dē Fabriciō et eius summā honestāte Pyrrhus audīverat vēra esse crēdidit. Itaque hunc lēgātum in castrīs suīs cōnspectum bene accēpit. Ad extrēmum eī dīxit: "Cūr nōn in Ēpīrum mēcum venīs et ibi manēs? Tibi quārtam rēgnī meī partem tribuam." Sed Fabricius respondit sē neque partem rēgnī sibi tribuī cupere neque sūmptūrum esse.

10 Proximō annō Fabricius contrā Pyrrhum pugnāvit. Medicus rēgis mediā nocte ad eum vēnit et dīxit sē prō praemiō Pyrrhum interfectūrum esse. Fabricius, quī nēminem fefellerat, respondit sē nūllum praemium prōpōnere et iussit hunc ligātum ad dominum redūcī et Pyrrhō omnia dīcī. Ubi rēx medicum ligātum cōnspexit, maximē mōtus dīxit: "Ille est Fabricius quī 15 nōn facilius ab honestāte quam sōl ā cursū[2] suō āvertī potest!"

Questions
1. Why did the Romans have so much confidence in Fabricius?
2. What offer did Pyrrhus make to Fabricius?
3. What was Fabricius' reply?
4. What offer did the king's doctor make to Fabricius at a later time?
5. What was Fabricius' response?
6. What reason did Pyrrhus have for being grateful to Fabricius?
7. To what did Pyrrhus compare him?
8. What strength of character does the story of Fabricius illustrate?

Fabriclus stands before Pyrrhus. A painting by a Dutch artist of the seventeenth century. Presumably the bearded man seated on Pyrrhus' right is Cineas, the ever-faithful adviser.

VOCABULARY

Pronoun

su´ī reflexive, *of himself/herself/itself; of themselves,* etc.

Adjective

su´us, -a, -um (reflexive) *his own, her own, its own, their own*

Verbs

āver´tō, āver´tere, āver´tī, āver´sus *turn away*	[vertō]
cōnspi´ciō, cōnspi´cere, cōnspe´xī, cōnspec´tus *catch sight of, see, spot*	[spectō]
crē´dō, crē´dere, crē´didī, crē´ditus *believe, entrust* (with dat.)	(credible)
fal´lō, fal´lere, fefel´lī, fal´sus *deceive*	(fallacy, falsify)
sū´mō, sū´mere, sūmp´sī, sūmp´tus *take*	(resume, sumptuous)
tri´buō, tribu´ere, tri´buī, tribū´tus *grant*	(contribute, tribute)

Preposition

con´trā (with acc.) *against* (contradiction)

Reflexive Pronouns

In English, as we have seen (page 369), the emphatic pronouns *myself, ourselves,* etc., often, but not always, correspond to Latin **ipse: Ipse eum vīdī,** *I myself saw him.* These same English pronouns are used reflexively as objects of verbs or prepositions to refer to the subject of the verb: *I saw myself; He deceived himself.* The term *reflexive* is used because the action of the verb is reflected back upon the subject in these sentences.

In Latin, the personal pronouns of the first and second persons may be used reflexively to mean *myself, yourself, ourselves,* and *yourselves.* In the third person, however, Latin has a special reflexive pronoun, **suī,** which is declined the same way in both the singular and the plural.

Genitive	**suí**	*of himself, herself, itself, themselves*
Dative	**síbi**	*to/for himself, herself, itself, themselves*
Accusative	**sē (sé sē)**	*himself, herself, itself, themselves*
Ablative	**sē (sé sē)**	*with (from, etc.) himself, herself, itself, themselves*

The exact meaning (*himself, herself, itself,* or *themselves*) is regularly determined by the subject of the sentence or of the clause in which the reflexive occurs. Question: Why do reflexive pronouns have no nominative?

Use of Reflexive Pronouns

(ego) mē rogō	*I ask myself*
(tū) tē rogās	*you ask yourself*
(is)/(ea) sē rogat	*he asks himself; she asks herself*
(nōs) nōs rogāmus	*we ask ourselves*
(vōs) vōs rogātis	*you ask yourselves*
(eī)/(eae) sē rogant	*they ask themselves*
Mīles sē vulnerāvit.	*The soldier wounded himself.*
Nōs contrā hostēs dēfendimus.	*We defended ourselves against the enemies.*
Sē ob victōriam laudāvit.	*He/she praised himself/herself on account of the victory.*

Reflexive Possessive Adjectives and *Eius, Eōrum/Eārum*

Corresponding to **meus,** *my, my own,* **tuus/vester,** and *your, your own;* **noster,** *our, our own,* there is the *reflexive adjective* **suus, -a, -um,** *his own, her own, its own, their own,* derived from **suī.** Remember that **suus** always refers to the subject of the verb. Its case, number, and gender are determined by the thing possessed and not by the possessor. When *his, her, its,* and *their* do not refer to the subject, **eius** or **eōrum/eārum** (genitive forms of the pronoun **is, ea, id**) must be used instead. Unlike **suus,** they are not inflected to agree with the thing possessed. Note the difference in the following.

Anna (or **Mārcus**) **patrem suum vīdit.**	*Anna* (or *Marcus*) *saw her own* (or *his own*) *father.*
Anna (or **Mārcus**) **mātrem suam vīdit.**	*Anna* (or *Marcus*) *saw her own* (or *his own*) *mother.*
Anna (or **Mārcus**) **patrem eius vīdit.**	*Anna* (or *Marcus*) *saw his* (or *her*) *father* (i.e., someone else's).
Anna et Mārcus mātrem suam vīdērunt.	*Anna and Marcus saw their* (*own*) *mother.*
Mārcus patrem eōrum vīdit.	*Marcus saw their father* (i.e., of those men, not his own).
Anna mātrem eārum vīdit.	*Anna saw their mother* (i.e., of those women, not her own).

The Romans showed great adaptability in the development of armor and weapons, steadily altering them to meet different conditions, and often borrowing from their enemies. The metal helmet (**cassis**), of Greek origin, gave protection to the brow and neck and replaced the earlier leather **galea.** Over his tunic the soldier wore a leather breastplate (**lōrīca**), covered with segmented metal plates. The Gallic trousers (**brācae**) gave him mobility and protection from the cold. On his feet were leather sandals (**caligae**), tied on with thongs. The long rectangular shield (**scūtum**) was adopted from the Samnites; the pointed boss (**umbō**) projecting from the center could inflict a wound on its own. The principal offensive weapon was the **pīlum,** a seven-foot spear with a soft iron point which bent on contact and could not be extracted. At his right side, the legionary carried a short double-edged Spanish sword (**gladius**) better for stabbing at close quarters than for slashing; at his left, a dagger (**pūgiō**). Rigorously trained and well led, the Roman legionary was an awesome fighting machine.

Oral Practice

Give in all tenses, in the active voice, the first person singular forms and meanings of **līberō;** the second person plural of **fallō;** the third person singular of **expediō.** Use reflexive pronouns as direct objects with all verb forms.

📖 Exercises

A. Translate the following sentences into English.
   1. Frāter eius mātrem suam fefellit et posteā sē in mare iēcit.
   2. Tū tē ipsum fallere semper potuistī, sed mē numquam fefellistī.
   3. Mūnera pūblica optimīs, nōn pessimīs, cīvibus tribuī dēbent.
   4. Arma sūmēmus et nōs fortiter dēfendēmus contrā pessimōs hostēs.
   5. Puerum currentem cōnspexī, sed ille crēdidit sē ā mē nōn vīsum esse.

B. Give the Latin for the italicized words.
   1. We saw *his* brother.
   2. You will see *their* friends.
   3. The girl loved *her (own)* mother.
   4. The girl loved *her (own)* father.
   5. The girl loved *her (own)* horses.
   6. The girl loved *her (friend's)* horses.
   7. The girl liked *herself.*
   8. He wasted *his* money and *theirs.*
   9. They will defend *themselves* and *us.*
   10. We defend *ourselves* and you (sing.) must defend *yourself.*
   11. She spoke softly to *herself.*
   12. They gave *themselves* a lot of the credit.

C. Translate the following sentences into Latin.
   1. He says that he himself has four brothers.
   2. We always praise ourselves and say the worst (things) about others.
   3. Entrust yourselves and all your (possessions) to us.
   4. The leader of the enemy, having seen us *(use abl. abs.),* killed himself.

WORD STUDY

Derivatives In the fourteenth century there began a great revival of interest in the ancient Latin and Greek authors. This revival is known as the Renaissance (from **re-nāscor,** *be born again*). Beginning in Italy, it spread over Western Europe and reached England in the sixteenth century. Ever since then, many new words have been added to English from Latin and Greek. These new words are easily distinguished by their similarity to the Latin originals. Over ninety percent of the words in the works of Caesar and Cicero have English derivatives.

One result of the introduction of new words directly from Latin was the formation of a number of *doublets,* words that were derived at different times from a common Latin word but that have different meanings. Note the following (the earlier form precedes): *sample, example* (**exemplum**); *feat, fact* (**factum**); *Mr., master* (**magister**); *loyal, legal* (**lēx**); *mayor, major* (**maior**); *chance, cadence* (**cadō**). Show how these doublets got their meanings from the original Latin meaning. There is one set of quintuplets in English: *dais, desk, dish, disk,* and *discus,* all from **discus.** See page 430 for a quadruplet.

RĒGULUS

LESSON OBJECTIVES
- To learn the legend of Regulus
- To learn the declensions of **duo** and **trēs**
- To learn the declensions and uses of **mīlle** and **mīlia**

Contrā Carthāginiēnsēs quī partem Āfricae incoluērunt arma ā Rōmānīs sūmpta erant.[1] Rēgulus, dux Rōmānōrum, imperiō acceptō, ad Āfricam nāvigāvit et hostēs superāvit. Multa mīlia captīvōrum in Italiam mīsit sed ipse, opere difficilī nōn perfectō, in Āfricā remānsit. Contrā trēs Carthāginiēnsium
5 ducēs pugnāns victor fuit. Hostēs ā Rōmānīs pressī pācem petīvērunt. Quam[2] Rēgulus dīxit sē dūrissimīs condiciōnibus datūrum esse. Itaque Carthāginiēnsēs auxilium ā Lacedaemoniīs[3], quī Graeciam incoluērunt, petīvērunt. Dux quī ā Lacedaemoniīs missus erat cum quattuor mīlibus mīlitum et centum elephantīs contrā Rōmānōs prōcessit. Rōmānīs victīs, Rēgulus captus est.

10 Rēgulus in Āfricā mānsit sed quīntō annō Carthāginiēnsēs, graviter pressī, eum ad urbem Rōmam mīsērunt. Eum iussērunt pācem ā Rōmānīs obtinēre et permūtātiōnem[4] captīvōrum facere. Is dīxit, pāce nōn factā, sē ad eōs reversūrum esse. Illī crēdidērunt eum sē trāditūrum esse.

Itaque Rēgulus in Italiam pervēnit. Ductus in senātum Rōmānum dīxit sē
15 esse captīvum, nōn iam Rōmānum. Itaque etiam uxōrem, quae eum cōnspexerat et ad eum cucurrerat, ā sē remōvit. Dīxit hostēs, frāctōs multīs proeliīs, spem[5] nūllam nisi[6] in pāce habēre; nōn esse ūtile multa mīlia

[1] First Punic or Carthaginian War, 264–241 B.C. These wars were for domination of the Mediterranean. Carthage was in northern Africa, near present-day Tunis.

[2] In Latin, a relative is often used at the beginning of a sentence to connect with the preceding sentence. In English, a demonstrative is used instead. Translate: *this (peace treaty).*

[3] Spartans

[4] *exchange*

[5] *hope*

[6] *except (if not)*

Founded by Phoenicians in the ninth century B.C. at the narrowest passage through the Mediterranean, wealthy Carthage had an ideal site to control seaborne commerce. After defending herself for centuries against Etruscans and Greeks, she was finally destroyed by the Romans in 146 B.C. But the location was too valuable to lie unoccupied, and the Romans recolonized it in 46 B.C. The ruins shown here are of Roman baths of the third century A.D.

Nik Wheeler/CORBIS

captīvōrum prō sē ūnō, aetāte cōnfectō, hostibus reddī. "Captīvōs Rōmānōs aurō emere nōn dēbēmus," explicāvit; "nam virtūs eōrum āmissa est, nec vēra virtūs aurō emī potest." Senātus hōc cōnsiliō numquam ante datō permōtus 20 pācem cum hostibus nōn fēcit. Itaque Rēgulus, opere perfectō, Carthaginiēnsēs nōn fefellit sed in Āfricam revertit et sē Carthāginiēnsibus trādidit, ā quibus omnibus suppliciīs interfectus est. Posteā Rōmānī eī honōrēs tribuērunt.

Haec prīmō bellō Pūnicō accidisse dīcuntur. Posteā Rōmānī, pāce frāctā[7], duo alia bella cum eīsdem hostibus gessērunt et imperium suum maximē 25 auxērunt.

Questions

1. After Regulus' first victories, what was the fate of the defeated Carthaginians?
2. Why did Regulus remain in Africa?
3. How many Carthaginian generals did Regulus defeat?
4. What sort of peace terms did Regulus offer?
5. Who caused his later defeat?
6. Why was Regulus sent to Rome?
7. What did Regulus do when he saw his wife? Why?
8. Why did he urge the Romans not to make peace?
9. Did Regulus keep his promise with the Carthaginians?
10. How did the Carthaginians treat him?

[7] Regulus' return to Carthage after his mission to Rome took place ca. 249 B.C. However, the war lasted until 241 when the Romans prevailed and a treaty imposing very harsh conditions on Carthage was drawn up. Even then, hostilities did not entirely stop and in 218, with Hannibal's invasion of Spain, the Second Punic War (218–201) broke out in full force. Again Carthage was defeated, but fifty-five years later she again heroically tried to recover her once-proud position. Rome's might was too great, and at the end of the Third Punic War (149–146) the city of Carthage was utterly demolished. The story goes that the Roman general watched the destruction with tears in his eyes, reflecting that all great cities must have their end—Troy, Carthage, and perhaps someday Rome.

▓ VOCABULARY

Nouns

impe´rium, impe´rī n. *command, power* (imperial, empire)

*mī´lia, mī´lium n. pl. *thousands* [mīlle]

Adjectives

cen´tum (indeclinable) *hundred* (centennial, centipede)

du´o, du´ae, du´o *two* (duality, double)

mīl´le (indeclinable) *thousand* (millennium)

trēs, tri´a *three* (trio, triplet)

Verbs

e´mō, -ere, ē´mī, ēmp´tus *take, buy* (redemption)

in´colō, -ere, inco´luī, incul´tus *live, inhabit* [colō]

perfi´ciō, -ere, -fē´cī, -fec´tus *finish* [faciō]

trā´dō, -ere, trā´didī, trā´ditus
   give or *hand over, surrender* [dō]

▦ GRAMMAR

Declension of *Duo* and *Trēs*

The numbers from 4 to 100 are indeclinable in Latin. (For **ūnus** see p. 384.) **Duo,** *two,* and **trēs,** *three,* are declined as follows.

	M.	F.	N.	M., F.	N.
Nominative	du´o	du´ae	du´o	trēs	tri´a
Genitive	duō´rum	duā´rum	duō´rum	tri´um	tri´um
Dative	duō´bus	duā bus	duō´bus	tri´bus	tri´bus
Accusative	du´ōs	du´ās	du´ō	trēs	tri´a
Ablative	duō´bus	duā´bus	duō´bus	tri´bus	tri´bus

The Bridgeman Art Library

A Punic War monument of the third and second centuries B.C. in Mactar, Tunisia.

Note the forms **duōbus, duābus,** and **duo** (neuter nom. and acc.), which are irregular. **Trēs, tria** is declined as a third declension adjective. In Latin the numbers *one, two,* and *three* are adjectives. They must agree in gender, number, and case with the noun they modify: **duābus puellīs,** *for two girls;* **maximus trium ducum,** *greatest of the three leaders.*

Declension and Use of *Mīlle*

Mīlle, when used to mean *one thousand,* is an indeclinable adjective (like **centum**): e.g., **mīlle hominēs,** *one thousand men.* When it is used for two or more thousands, it is a neuter plural **i**-stem noun. The word used with the plural forms of **mīlle** must be in the genitive: **duo mīlia hominum** (lit., *two thousands of men*), *two thousand men.*

	SINGULAR	PLURAL
	one thousand	*thousands*
Nominative	mīl´le	mī´lia
Genitive	mīl´le	mī´lium
Dative	mīl´le	mī´libus
Accusative	mīl´le	mī´lia
Ablative	mīl´le	mī´libus

Oral Practice

Give in Latin *two boys, one hundred children, one thousand houses, two thousand citizens, by three thousand sailors, against five thousand soldiers.*

📖 *Exercises*

A. Translate the following sentences into English.
1. Nāvī frāctā, omnēs certē interficientur.
2. Duōs optimōs librōs ēmī quōs hāc aestāte legam.
3. Mīlle nautās cum tribus ducibus in maria ultima mīsimus.
4. Post duās pugnās hostēs cōnfectī nōn iam vim nostram sustinuērunt.
5. Centum mīlia agricolārum, agrīs suīs relīctīs, ad oppida contendērunt.

B. Translate the following sentences into Latin.
1. Anna was third in rank, but her brother was fifth.
2. Three men were killed, and two received wounds.
3. The lower part of this river is between two nations.
4. All the boys easily completed the work in three hours.

Did You Know?

In Roman society the **equēs** *(knight)* was the businessman of his day. **Equitēs** financed the public works of Rome by successfully bidding for government contracts. Knights also found the provinces to be sources of wealth by collecting taxes and financing provincial business operations. Grain, manufactured articles, ores, and wool could often be transported throughout the Roman Empire only with the money this class advanced.

WORD STUDY

- Much difficulty is caused in English spelling by silent or weakly sounded letters. This difficulty is often solved by referring to the Latin original: *labor·a·tory, rep·e·tition, lib·r·ary, sep·a·rate, auxil·i·ary, compar·a·tive, de·b·t, rei·g·n, recei·p·t.* The Latin original often helps with other spelling difficulties: *con·s·ensus, a·nn·uity, defi·c·it, acce·l·erate.* Define the above words and give their Latin originals.

- Much confusion is caused in English by the combinations *ei* and *ie.* Remember that the derivatives of compounds of **capiō** have *ei* as *receive, deceive,* etc.

ROMAN SOCIAL AND ECONOMIC CONDITIONS

Until the Romans could control the food supply of the empire they had conquered, their economic system was quite unstable. This economic instability was one of the principal causes of the political dissension that reached its peak in the first century B.C.

From time to time the common people of Rome suffered from lack of food when the wheat crop failed, as happens in modern times as well. According to tradition, at one such time the senate, which was the ruling body, obtained a large amount of wheat and was planning to give it away to the poor. It was in connection with this plan that the plebeians were angry at Coriolanus, as we have already read. He advised the senate not to give away free wheat and criticized the plebeians sharply. All this happened in the fifth century B.C.—nearly twenty-five hundred years ago.

In the time of the Gracchi (second century B.C.) economic conditions became especially bad. The rich nobles had acquired large farms by taking over public lands

A beautifully sculpted sheaf of wheat, the staple of Rome's agricultural economy and its civilization.

Archivo Iconografico, SA/CORBIS

and by forcing out the small farmers. These farmers wandered over Italy with their families, and many settled in Rome, where they found life difficult. They could not obtain work on the large farms because these were worked by slave labor. Tiberius Gracchus planned to force the large landowners to sell, at a reasonable price, all but five hundred acres of their lands. He then intended to cut this land up into small farms to be rented at a low cost to the veterans. He felt that the men who had fought for their country had as much right to a home as the wild animals in the forests.

After Tiberius' death, Gaius tried to carry out his brother's policies. In addition, he created road-building jobs for the unemployed, stored large amounts of wheat to avoid shortages, sold it to the poor well below cost, and established colonies to provide more land for farmers. His program was only moderately successful, but the idea persisted. Many of these measures have been tried in modern times; the Italian government has for some time tried to reduce poverty in southern Italy by dividing large estates into smaller farms.

The problems of breaking up the big estates, furnishing relief by making available cheap or free wheat, and of helping the landless mobs who had flocked to the city, continued to bother Roman leaders for another century after the death of the Gracchi. Julius Caesar, a popular leader who favored such measures, made himself dictator and laid the foundation of government by emperors. Under his successor, Augustus, a great peace was established that brought prosperity and better living conditions for two hundred years. But the people paid for these advantages by a loss of their liberties and privileges; free speech, political rights, and individual liberties of various sorts were gradually reduced.

QUESTIONS

1. Discuss the policy of the Gracchi in giving public lands and wheat to the poor and using the unemployed to build roads. Give some modern parallels.

2. In what European countries has a program of social and economic reform resembling that of the Gracchi led to dictatorship?

3. How can any nation get a maximum of social reform without abandoning important liberties?

Gianni Dagli Orti/Museo della Civiltà Romana, Rome/The Art Archive

The army, when not actually on a campaign, carried out many beneficial projects: building roads, constructing defenses, draining swamps, and helping in the fields. Here, while the man in the foreground cuts the grain with a sickle, others carry it off in baskets. The soldier in the background may be the centurion in charge of the work detail. This scene is from the column of Trajan in Rome.

VOCABULARY

Nouns

aetās	ignis	nēmō	regiō
condiciō	imperium	opus	sōl
gēns	mīlia	ōrātiō	

Pronoun

suī

Adjectives

aptus	maior	pessimus	trēs
centum	maximus	plūrimus	ulterior
difficilis	melior	plūs	ultimus
dissimilis	mīlle	proprius	ūtilis
duo	minor	proximus	
extrēmus	minimus	similis	
humilis	optimus	summus	
īnferior	peior	suus	

Verbs

accidō	explicō	perficiō	tribuō
āvertō	fallō	rapiō	vincō
cadō	incolō	repellō	
cōnspiciō	īnstruō	statuō	
crēdō	iūdicō	sūmō	
emō	iungō	trādō	

Adverbs

bene	facile

Preposition

contrā (+ acc.)

Conjunction

quam

GRAMMAR SUMMARY

Comparison of Regular Adjectives

The regular comparative of most adjectives is formed by adding **-ior, -ius** to the base. The comparatives are declined with ordinary third declension noun endings. **Quam** is used to say *than.*

Hoc flūmen est altius quam illud.	*This river is deeper than that (one).*

The superlative is formed by adding **-issimus, -a, -um** to the base.

Sēnsimus rēgīnam nostram esse iūstissimam.	*We felt that our queen was most just.*

Adjectives which end in **-er** add **-rimus, -a, -um** to the nominative singular masculine form to form the superlative. Six adjectives that end in **-lis** add **-limus** instead of **-issimus** to the base to form the superlative.

Illa pulcherrima est.	*That woman is very beautiful.*
Captīvī humillimī sunt.	*The captives are most humble.*

Quam is used with superlative adjectives to express *as . . . as possible,* **nauta quam miserrimus,** *a sailor as unhappy as possible.*

Formation and Comparison of Adverbs

Adverbs formed from third declension adjectives generally add **-iter** to the base to form the positive. The comparative adverb is formed by adding **-ius** to the base, and the superlative adverb adds **-issimē** to the base of the superlative adjective.

Nēmō fortiter pugnābat.	*No one fought bravely.*
Daedalus fīlium suum facilius exercuit, sed puer cecidit.	*Daedalus trained his son rather easily, but the boy fell.*
Omnēs celerrimē repulsī sunt.	*They all were driven back very quickly.*

Quam is used with the superlative adverb to say *as . . . as possible.*

Quam celerrimē ōrātiōnem explicāvimus.	*We explained the speech as quickly as possible.*

Comparison of Irregular Adjectives

Some adjectives have irregular comparative and superlative forms and must simply be learned as new vocabulary words.

In summā urbe plūrimī optimum opus perfēcērunt.	*In the highest part of the city, very many finished very good work.*
Victī sumus ab gentibus meliōribus quam nōbīs.	*We were beaten by people better than ourselves.*

The Dative with Adjectives

The dative is used after certain adjectives that often are followed by the word *to* or *for* in English.

Hās condiciōnēs pācis similēs illīs esse crēdidērunt.	*They believed these conditions of peace were similar to those.*
Hoc opus mihi aptissimum est, sed difficillimum.	*This task is very suited to me, but very difficult.*

Reflexive Pronouns

Reflexive pronouns are used when the object acted upon is the same as the subject of the verb. The first and second persons use the forms of the personal pronouns as reflexives. The third person, singular and plural, has a separate reflexive: **suī, sibi, sē, sē** (or **sēsē**). Its correct meaning *(himself, herself, itself,* or *themselves)* is determined by the subject, whether it is singular or plural, masculine, feminine, or neuter.

Ego mē vīdī.	*I saw myself.*
(Vōs) vōs fallitis.	*You deceive yourselves.*
Illa sē fefellit.	*That woman deceived herself.*
Is sē fefellit.	*He deceived himself.*
Lēgātī sē trādidērunt.	*The ambassadors surrendered (themselves).*

In an indirect statement construction, the meaning of **sē** changes to *he, she, it,* or *they,* depending on the subject.

Rēgulus dīxit sē reversūrum esse.	*Regulus said (that) he would return.*

Numerals

Numbers *one, two,* and *three* (**ūnus, duō, trēs**) are declined as adjectives; numbers *four* (**quattuor**) through *one hundred* (**centum**) are indeclinable. *One thousand* (**mīlle**) is an indeclinable adjective. *Thousands* (**mīlia,** pl.) is used as a declinable neuter noun followed by a word in the genitive.

Ūnum mūnus tibi et duo mūnera eīs ostendī.	*I showed one gift to you and two to them.*
Duās et trēs regiōnēs minimō tempore Caesar obtinuit.	*Caesar gained two and three regions in very little time.*
Erant plūs quam mīlle elephantī et duo mīlia mīlitum in illā regiōne.	*There were more than one thousand elephants and two thousand soldiers in that region.*

UNIT PRACTICE

A. Compare **aptus, celer, levis, iūstus.** Form and compare adverbs from **certus, ācer, humilis.**

B. Decline **ūtilior liber** and **melior aetās** in the singular.

C. Give in Latin in the singular and plural in the case indicated: *a most beautiful region* (nom.); *a worse time* (acc.); *a rather long journey* (dat.); *the smallest part* (abl.); *a larger ship* (gen.).

D. Give in Latin: *he deceives him and himself; they praise them and themselves; they will ask their friends and hers; he defends himself; we praise him; she will see her father.*

WORD STUDY

1. Give the Latin words suggested by the following English derivatives.

   accident, appropriate, conditional, conspicuous, credible, fallacious, instructive, opera, proximity, rapture, regional, redemptive, repulsive, centipede, millipede. .

2. From your knowledge of Latin, rearrange these French numerals in the proper sequence: *trois, sept, un, cinq, quatre, dix, huit, neuf, deux, six.*

3. Write sentences using as many English·derivatives as you can find from the Latin **nāvigō, doceō, vincō, sūmō.**

4. Complete each sentence. Follow the model.

   Perficiō is to *perfection* as **incipiō** is to *inception*.

   a. **Emō** is to *redemption* as _____ is to *repulsion*.

   b. *Creditor* is to **crēdo** as *instructor* is to _____.

   c. **Ūtilis** is to *utility* as _____ is to *humility*.

   d. *Statute* is to **statuō** as *status* is to _____.

   e. *Consistency* is to **cōnsistō** as _____ is to **currō**.

VOCABULARY

Choose the word that best completes each sentence.

1. Daedalus opus sine auxiliō fīlī suī _____ dīcēbātur.
   a. accidisse
   b. incoluisse
   c. perfēcisse
   d. vīxisse

2. Māter et ego in tōtā urbe librōs meliōrēs aut noviōrēs _____ nōn potuerāmus.
   a. cadere
   b. emere
   c. fallere
   d. repellere

3. Perīculō _____, nēmō ad portam gravem illīus templī sedēbat.
   a. explicātō
   b. incultō
   c. iūnctō
   d. raptō

4. Aenēās et reliquī Trōiānī cibum vīnumque magnō cum studiō _____.
   a. āvertērunt
   b. statuērunt
   c. sūmpsērunt
   d. vīxērunt

5. Rōmānī hostibus ā quibus in multīs proeliīs falsī erant nōn _____.
   a. accidērunt
   b. crēdidērunt
   c. iūdicāvērunt
   d. tribuērunt

GRAMMAR

Complete each sentence with the correct endings.

6. Domin___ servōs fortissim___ in agrōs ulteriōr___ cum tr___ equ___ mittere statuit.

7. Condiciōn___ pāc___ ā hōc duc___ prōpositae dūriōr___ quam eāe illīus rēg___ sunt.

8. Terra ipsa maxim___ cōpiam frūment___ auxili___ aptō sōlis aestāt___ proxim___ trādet.

9. In minim___ cas___ Baucis et Philēmōn quam humil___ vīxērunt, sed bon___ cēn___ du___ de___ parāt___ est.

10. Tr___ puellae dīcēbant sē et patrem su___ magnum ign___ in parte īnferiōr___ urbis cōnspex___.

TRANSLATION

Translate the following sentences.

11. Cognōscere linguam gentis alterius opus ūtilissimum et aptum cīvibus omnis aetātis est.

12. Nautae māteriam optimam obtinuerant, itaque nāvem pulcherrimam facile et celeriter fēcērunt.

13. Poēta in librō suō scrīpsit Rōmānōs plūrimās regiōnēs victūrōs esse et populōs imperiō iūstē rēctūrōs esse.

14. "Crēde mihi bene; numquam tē fefellī. Ex hīs centum virīs, amīcus tuus optimus sum," Mārcus sociō suō dubitantī narrāvit.

15. Itinere cōnfectō, dux cum quattuor mīlibus mīlitum ad summum montem stetit, et deīs grātiās ob salūtem virōrum suōrum ēgit.

INVESTIGATION

Find the answers to these questions from any lesson in Unit XII.

16. The great revival of interest in Latin and Greek authors, which began in Italy in the fourteenth century and spread throughout Western Europe, is known as the _____.

17. The Romans fought a series of _____ *(number?)* wars against _____, a city in North Africa, for domination of the Mediterranean Sea.

18. According to mythology, man fell from an ideal state through a series of four ages. Name these ages in descending order.

19. The flight of Icarus is part of the decoration on a monument dedicated to what famous American inventors?

20. To whom and for what action were the following prizes awarded?

corōna nāvālis   **corōna classica**

CULTURE

Vērum aut Falsum? Indicate whether each statement is true or false.

21. Tiberius Gracchus proposed land reform measures that would aid the poor.

22. Coriolanus proposed road building projects for the unemployed masses.

23. Rome experienced a great period of civil unrest during the years in which Augustus Caesar was emperor.

24. One of the plans of Gaius Gracchus was to create colonies for those whose land had been taken over by large estate owners.

25. Economic instability and political unrest in Rome reached a peak in the first century B.C.

FROM LATIN TO ENGLISH

Apply your knowledge of Latin roots to determine the best meaning of the italicized words.

26. The editorial contained some *pejorative* remarks about the local official.
  a. degrading
  b. informative
  c. favorable
  d. unimportant

27. The school handbook provided *explicit* rules for student conduct.
  a. unclear
  b. strict
  c. specific
  d. old-fashioned

28. Scientists were studying the *rapacious* nature of a certain species.
  a. gentle
  b. slow-moving
  c. stubborn
  d. predatory

29. No one clearly saw the *fallacy* in her side of the argument.
  a. anger
  b. error
  c. truth
  d. humor

30. A *sumptuous* dinner had been prepared by our hostess.
  a. traditional
  b. simple
  c. lavish
  d. hasty

ROMAN LEGENDS: PORTRAITS OF PERSEVERANCE, PATRIOTISM, AND COURAGE

Unit Objectives

- To learn how to express extent of time and space in Latin
- To learn the differences between **post, posteā,** and **postquam**
- To learn the fourth and fifth declensions
- To learn the genitive and ablative of description
- To learn stories of famous Roman historical figures
- To learn about the duties and privileges of being a Roman citizen

Caesar triumphāns. Seated on a sort of throne, the wreathed general is surrounded by his soldiers and bound foreign captives, while a young trumpeter calls attention to the celebration. A painting by Palma Vecchio (1480–1520), now in a Miami museum.

MARIUS ET SULLA

¹ *Jugur´tha*

² *Cimbri (Sim´brī), Teu´tons*

³ *laughing*

⁴ *from*

⁵ *necessary* (indeclinable)

⁶ *Mithridā´tēs*

⁷ *at Rome*

C. Marius, vir humilis generis, ob ēgregiam virtūtem cōnsul ā Rōmānīs factus est. Plūrimī cīvēs putāvērunt eum esse maximum imperātōrem aetātis suae.

Iugurthā¹, rēge Numidiae quae terra in Āfricā est, victō, Marius bellum
5 contrā Cimbrōs et Teutonēs² suscēpit. Hī, quī extrēmōs fīnēs Germāniae incoluerant, Cimbrīs sē iūnxerant. Multōs mēnsēs hae duae gentēs novās terrās petīverant et ad prōvinciam Rōmānam pervēnerant. Tribus ducibus Rōmānīs ā barbarīs repulsīs, Marius mīlitēs trēs annōs exercuit. Posteā Teutonēs sub Alpibus proeliō superāvit ac super centum mīlia interfēcit.

10 Cimbrī autem, quī nihil dē victōriā Rōmānōrum audīverant, per lēgātōs praemissōs ācriter sibi et Teutonibus agrōs petīvērunt. Marius rīdēns³, "Illī tenent," inquit, "semperque tenēbunt terram ā⁴ nōbīs acceptam." Proximō annō is cum mīlitibus bene exercitīs contrā eōs pugnāvit. Nec minor erat pugna cum uxōribus eōrum quam cum virīs. Illae quae supererant sē
15 līberōsque suōs interfēcērunt.

Multōs annōs Rōmānī hōs barbarōs īnstantēs timuerant, sed Alpēs post hanc victōriam Rōmam ā perīculō prohibēbānt.

Postquam Rōmānī intellēxērunt necesse⁵ esse bellum cum Mithridāte⁶ gerere, hoc negōtium Sullae commīsērunt. Sed postquam Sulla ex urbe
20 discessit, Marius, quī ipse cupīvit hoc negōtium super omnia suscipere, summam potestātem obtinuit. Posteā Sulla cum mīlitibus quōs circum sē habuit Marium in fugam dedit. Mīlitibus praemissīs, paucōs mēnsēs Rōmae⁷ Sulla mānsit. Postquam autem ad bellum discessit, Marius Rōmam occupāvit.

25 Quattuor annōs Sulla cum Mithridāte bellum gessit. Post mortem Marī in Italiam revertit. Omnēs hostēs prae sē agēns, circum multa oppida mīlitēs suōs dūxit. Dictātor factus, multa mīlia cīvium interficī iussit. Amīcus eum monuit: "Nōnne intellegis hoc nōn tibi ūtile esse? Sī omnēs interficiēs, et nēmō supererit, quōrum cīvium dictātor eris?"

Archivo Iconografico, SA/CORBIS

A portrait bust, now in a Roman museum, of Gaius Marius (157–86 B.C.), a plain-spoken man of the people. His military victories propelled him into great political influence and an unprecedented seven consulships. His power, however, and his program of reform in the tradition of the Gracchi (see pages 452–453) were consistently challenged by the aristocratic senatorial party whose champion was Sulla. Political conflict led to a brief period of open civil war (87–86 B.C.). After Marius' death, Sulla became the sole master of Rome, almost a king, and it was not until twenty-five years later that the popular party under Julius Caesar regained its influence.

Questions

1. What was the cause of the war with the Cimbri and Teutons?
2. Which did Marius defeat first? Where?
3. What natural barrier helped defend Rome from these nations?
4. How does the writer of this narrative imply that the Cimbri's decision to ask for lands from Rome was a mistake?
5. What was the point of Marius' cruel joke about the Teutons?
6. What did the Cimbrian women do after they lost the war against the Romans?
7. Who was put in charge of waging war against Mithridates?
8. What was the cause of the quarrel between Marius and Sulla?
9. What was the point that Sulla's friend tried to make to him?
10. Give some examples of men in modern times who, like Marius, rose to high positions from humble beginnings.

VOCABULARY

Noun

negō´tium, negō´tī n. *business*　　　　　　　[ōtium]

Verbs

exer´ceō, -ē´re, exer´cuī, exer´citus　　　(exercise)
　　keep busy, train

intel´legō, -ere, -lē´xī, -lēc´tus　　　　　[legō]
　　understand

praemit´tō, -ere, -mī´sī, -mis´sus　　　　[mittō]
　　send ahead

super´sum, -es´se, super´fuī,　　　　　　[sum]
　　superfutū´rus *be left (over), survive*

Prepositions

cir´cum with acc. *around*　　　　　　　(circumscribe)
prae with abl. *in front of, before*　　　　(president, prepare)
su´per with acc. *over, above*　　　　　　[superō]

Conjunctions

au´tem (never first word), *however*
post´quam *after*　　　　　　　　　　　[post + quam]

GRAMMAR

Accusative of Extent

Duōs annōs remānsit.	*He remained (for) two years.*
Flūmen decem pedēs altum est.	*The river is ten feet deep.*

Observe that:

> **Duōs annōs** answers the question *(for) how long?*
> **Decem pedēs** answers the question *how much?*
> Both express *extent* with the accusative. The first example is called the *accusative of the extent of time,* the second, the *accusative of the extent of space.* Neither uses a preposition in Latin. Do not confuse either with the direct object.

Oral Practice

Give the Latin for the following. Be careful to use the correct case and preposition for each, if required: *before that time, at that time, for a long time, for one year, around this region, for one thousand hours, one hundred feet deep, for three months, over the city.*

Post, Posteā, and *Postquam*

The conjunction **postquam,** meaning *after,* must be distinguished carefully from the adverb **posteā,** meaning *afterwards,* and the preposition **post,** meaning *after* (or *behind*). Examine the following.

Post **hunc mēnsem plūrēs librōs legam.**	*After this month I shall read more books.*
Posteā **multōs librōs lēgī.**	*Afterwards I read many books.*
Postquam **opus perfēcī, multōs librōs lēgī.**	*After I finished the work, I read many books.*

Observe that the addition of **quam** to **post** makes **postquam** a conjunction, which is followed by a verb, usually in the perfect indicative; **posteā** means literally *after that,* i.e., *afterwards.* The real confusion is not in Latin, but in the English use of *after* as both a conjunction and a preposition.

Postquam vidit quod *post*
sē erat, quinque milia
pedum cucurrit.

Words Often Confused

The words in the following groups closely resemble one another in form or sound and must be carefully distinguished.

accēdō, accidō	cīvis, cīvitās	ob, ab
aetās, aestās	gēns, genus	pars, pār, parō
alius, alter, altus	ibi, ubi	pōnō (posuī), possum
cadō, cēdō	liber, līber, līberī	vīs, vir

Tell the difference in meaning between each, consulting the Latin–English dictionary at the back of this book if necessary.

🔲 *Exercises*

A. Translate the following sentences into English.
1. Illī hominēs multōs mēnsēs sē exercuērunt.
2. Putō hunc montem esse mīlle pedēs altum.
3. Ego crēdō nōs in illō locō duōs annōs remānsisse.
4. Intellēximus autem hoc negōtium ab aliīs hominibus susceptum esse, nōn nostrīs.
5. Super tria mīlia Germānōrum, pāce factā, Rōmānīs sēsē iūnxērunt.
6. Postquam hostēs ā mīlitibus praemissīs victī sunt, paucī superfuērunt.
7. Postquam mīlitēs servōs cōnspexērunt, eōs circum viās prae sē ēgērunt.

B. Translate the following sentences into Latin.
1. In summer we hasten to the fields.
2. The greater part of the winter we remain in town.
3. After the boy fell into the river, his sister ran shouting to her mother.
4. My brother will arrive next year and remain with me (**mēcum**) the whole summer.
5. We understand that you have been training yourselves for many months.

Did You Know?

Roman women usually took the feminine form of their father's **nōmen;** thus **Mārcus Tullius Cicero** had a daughter **Tullia.** A first-born son was usually given his father's first name (**praenōmen**). Then came the name of the clan (**nōmen**), and finally the family name (**cognōmen**). Only eighteen **praenōmina** were in common use and they were regularly abbreviated, e.g. **C.** (spelled out **Gāius**), **L.** (**Lūcius**), **M.** (**Mārcus**), **P.** (**Pūblius**), **Q.** (**Quīntus**), **Sex.** (**Sextus**), **T.** (**Titus**), **Ti.** (**Tiberius**), to name eight of the most frequent.

WORD STUDY

Prefixes

- **Ne-** is sometimes used as a negative prefix in Latin: **nēmō (ne-homō), negōtium (ne-ōtium), neuter (ne-uter), nūllus (ne-ūllus).** We do the same thing in English with *no: nothing, none (no-one), neither (no-either).*

- **Circum, contrā, prae,** and **super** have their usual meaning when used as prefixes in Latin and English. In English **prae** becomes *pre-,* as *pre-pare, pre-fix;* **contrā** sometimes retains its form, sometimes becomes *counter-,* as *contra-dict, counter-act.* **Super** sometimes becomes *sur-* in English, which must be distinguished from assimilated **sub-:** *surplus, surmount* (**super**)*,* but *surreptitious* (**sub**).

- Find ten English words with these prefixes, compounded with Latin words which you have studied. Explain *intelligence, supervisor, surplus, precedent;* as well as *treason* and *tradition,* which are doublets derived from **trādō.**

treason

LESSON LXVIII

GRACCHĪ

**LESSON
OBJECTIVES**
- To learn about the
  Gracchi brothers and
  the social issues of
  their time
- To learn the fourth
  declension

[1] *grandsons.* Lesson LXIX will tell
you more about the great
Roman general *Scipio Africanus*
(Sip´io Afrikā´nus).

[2] The **tribūnus plēbis** was an official
elected by the common people to
protect their rights, property, and
lives. He could veto measures voted
by the Senate and other magistrates.
The election of Tiberius as tribune
in 133 B.C. and his attempts at
reform began a period of political
and military strife which ended
only when Augustus gained
supreme power in 27 B.C.
See p. 482.

[3] *Nasica (Nasī´ka)*

[4] *of the republic*

[5] *from* **supersum**

Ti. et C. Gracchī erant Scīpiōnis Āfricānī nepōtēs[1]. Dīligentiā Cornēliae
mātris puerī doctī sunt. Cornēlia crēdidit eōs certē summam potestātem
obtentūrōs esse. Quondam hospita, domō Cornēliae petītā, ōrnāmenta sua
pulcherrima manū prae sē tenēns dēmōnstrābat. Tum Cornēlia līberōs suōs,
5 quī cāsū aderant, manū tetigit atque eōs hospitae dēmōnstrāns dīxit: "Haec
sunt mea ōrnāmenta!"

  Tiberius iam vir plēbī amīcus erat. Tribūnus plēbis[2] factus populō agrōs
dare cupiēbat. Hī agrī pūblicī erant sed multōs annōs ā nobilibus occupātī
erant, quī dīxērunt sē eōs nōn redditūrōs esse. Tamen Tiberius populō eōs
10 reddidit. Tum senātus convocātus dē Tiberiō cōnsuluit. Multī eum
dēspicientēs interficere cupīvērunt. Tiberiō accēdente, Scīpiō Nāsīca[3], senātor,
clāmāvit: "Venīte mēcum sī reī pūblicae[4] salūtem cupitis." Tum ille et aliī quī
circum eum stantēs incitātī sunt, impetū factō, Tiberium interfēcērunt.

  Postēā in somnō Gāius dīcitur vīdisse frātrem suum dīcentem: "Cūr
15 dubitās, Gāī? Tū, quī superēs[5], hoc negōtium perficere et vītam tuam populō
dare dēbēs." Itaque Gāius opus Tiberī sē perfectūrum esse statuit neque eius
cōnsilia dēsertūrum. Tribūnus factus plēbī frūmentum dabat et cīvitātem

As the **paedagōgus** *(left)* waits
to take them to school, the two
Gracchi brothers are presented
to their mother Cornelia's
bejeweled and elaborately
dressed guest.

omnibus quī Italiam incolēbant. Mīlitēs autem exercēre nōn potuit et intellēxit sē sine exercitū nihil efficere posse. Ā multīs dēspectus et dēsertus et sine praesidiō fugere coāctus, interfectus est.   20

Itaque senātus mortem Gracchōrum effēcit. Sed cōnsilia hōrum mānsērunt, et Rōmānī multōs annōs eōs et eōrum cāsūs memoriā tenuērunt.

Questions

1. Who was the grandfather of the Gracchi?
2. Who was the teacher of the Gracchi?
3. What sort of jewels did Cornelia have, and why did she show them off?
4. What was the political policy of Tiberius Gracchus?
5. Who incited the senators to kill Tiberius? What justification did he allege?
6. Why, according to the passage, did Gaius pursue political and economic reforms?
7. What high political office did both brothers reach?
8. What two things did Gaius give the common people?
9. What prevented Gaius from completely enacting his reforms?
10. Why were the Gracchi important even after their death?

VOCABULARY

Nouns

cā´sus, -ūs m. *downfall, accident, chance, misfortune*	[cadō]
do´mus, -ūs[6] f. *house, home*	(domestic)
exer´citus, -ūs m. *(trained) army*	[exerceō]
im´petus, -ūs m. *attack*	[petō]
ma´nus, -ūs f. *hand*	(manual, manufacture)
senā´tus, -ūs m. *senate*	(senatorial)

Verbs

dēmōns´trō, -ā´re, -ā´vī, -ā´tus *show*	[mōnstrō]
dē´serō, -ere, dēse´ruī, dēser´tus *desert*	(desertion)
dēspi´ciō, -ere, dēspe´xī, dēspec´tus *look down on, despise*	[spectō]
red´dō, -ere, red´didī, red´ditus *give back, restore*	[dō]

---

[6] Usually has ablative singular **domō** and accusative plural **domōs**, forms drawn from the second declension.

GRAMMAR

Fourth Declension

As we have seen, the first declension is the **a**-declension, the second is the **o**-declension, and the third is the **consonant -stem** and **i**-stem declension. These three declensions, especially the third, include most of the nouns. A few nouns belong to the fourth declension, which is the **u**-declension. Most of these nouns are derived from verbs.

	ENDINGS		EXAMPLE	
	SINGULAR	PLURAL	SINGULAR	PLURAL
Nominative	**-us**	**-ūs**	cā´sus	cā´sūs
Genitive	**-ūs**	**-uum**	cā´sūs	cā´suum
Dative	**-uī**	**-ibus**	cā´suī	cā´sibus
Accusative	**-um**	**-ūs**	cā´sum	cā´sūs
Ablative	**-ū**	**-ibus**	cā´sū	cā´sibus

Most nouns of the fourth declension in **-us** are masculine; the only feminines in this book are **manus** and **domus.**

Oral Practice

1. Decline **exercitus noster, hic impetus fortis.**
2. Name the case or cases of each of the following words: **senātū, impetum, manibus, ōrātiōne, domuī, exercituum, condiciōnibus.**

 *Exercises*

A. Translate the following sentences into English.

1. Quid manū tuā tenēs?
2. Paucī cūrās cāsūsque vītae leviter dēspicere possunt.
3. Alter exercitus circum montem praemissus est, alter exercitus cāsū oppressus est.
4. Postquam cāsus ducī nūntiātus est, ille mortem manū suā petīvit.
5. Maiōrēs gentēs iūra minōrum populōrum dēspicere nōn dēbent.
6. Domūs dēsertae post impetum cīvibus ā senātū redditae sunt.

B. Translate the following sentences into Latin.

1. I determined to move into another house.
2. I found a suitable house and approached it.
3. The house was/had been deserted; no one was living in it.
4. I touched his/her/its head with my hand and cried out.
5. Next month I shall show you the author's great works and shall buy the best.

Four of the five declensions by size

WORD STUDY

Derivatives

In an earlier lesson (see page 139), we saw that many English words are simply the stem of a Latin noun, adjective, or verb, or the stem plus silent -*e*. A great many such words are derived from the Latin words in this book, for example, *facile, prime, just, cede, part*. In the case of verbs, the stem of the present indicative, present participle, or perfect participle, or of all three, may furnish an English word: *convene, convenient, convent; remove, remote; agent, act.*

As previously noted, there are sometimes changes in the base, such as the dropping of one of two final consonants, as in *remit, expel,* and also by the addition of a vowel to the main vowel of the word, as in the following: *p·e·ace, mo·u·nt, re·i·gn, rema·i·n. Cont·a·in, ret·a·in,* etc., are from compounds of **teneō.**

Find ten more words illustrating these principles. Explain *domestic, manual labor, manicure, despicable, impetuous.*

Manicure

SCĪPIŌ

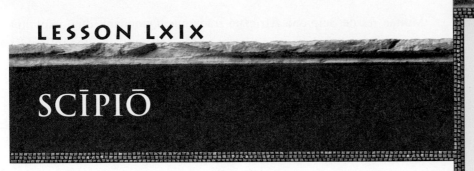

P. Cornēlius Scīpiō nōmen glōriamque meruit quod suum patrem, impetū hostium graviter vulnerātum, servāvit.[1] Tum, post pugnam Cannēnsem[2], in quā Rōmānī interclūsī et gravissimē victī erant, omnibus probantibus, Scīpiōnī, puerō vīgintī annōrum, summum imperium datum est. Ille spem salūtis Rōmānīs reddidit. Postquam sex annōs in Italiā exercituī 5 praefuit, Rōmānī eum exercituī Hispānō praefēcērunt. Ille urbem Carthāginem Novam diē quō vēnit expugnāvit; ita celer erat. Quīntō annō exercitūs hostium ex Hispāniā expulit. Dēmōnstrāverat cīvibus suīs potestātem Carthāginiēnsium frangī posse. Neque aurum rapuerat neque miserīs nocuerat. 10

Hispāniā victā, hic prīnceps in Āfricam prōcēdere mātūrāvit et ibi Carthāginiēnsēs victōriīs terruit. Tum senātus Carthāginiēnsium Hannibalem ad patriam revocāvit. Sed Scīpiō eum Zamae[3] vīcit, et ille, clārissimus et maximus omnium ducum quī contrā Rōmānōs pugnāvērunt, ex patriā suā fūgit. Scīpiō ob hanc victōriam Āfricānus[4] appellātus est. Nōn iam Hannibal, 15 cuius nōmen līberōs Rōmānōrum terruerat, īnstābat.

[1] In the Second Punic War (218–201 B.C.), greatest of the three wars against Carthage

[2] *of Cannae (Căn´ē),* 216 B.C. This Carthaginian tactic of encirclement, with the right and left flanks closing in around the enemy like pincers, was imitated with great success by both sides in World War II.

[3] *at Zama* (203 B.C.) in modern Tunisia

[4] Thus, with the addition of this honorary **cognōmen** (see page 467), his full name became **P. Cornēlius Scīpiō Āfricānus.**

Bettmann/CORBIS

Scipio Africanus the Elder (216–184/3 B.C.) returns to Rome in triumph after his victory over Hannibal (202 B.C.) in the Second Punic War. One can imagine that the woman with the garland is his wife Aemilia, and, skipping along beside her, their daughter Cornelia, mother of the Gracchi.

Multae rēs dē Scīpiōne Āfricānō trāduntur. Quondam, dum exercituī praeest, ille ad oppidum mūnītum in quō erant multī mīlitēs interclūsī exercitum addūxit. Scīpiō crēdidit oppidum capī posse, sed paucī eandem
20 spem habuērunt. Cāsū ūnus ē mīlitibus hominem ligātum, quī alterī mīlitī nocuerat, ad Scīpiōnem trāxit et rogāvit: "Quō diē locōque iubēs hunc hominem ad tē ad[5] supplicium venīre?" Tum Scīpiō manum ad oppidum ipsum tetendit et iussit eum hominem in illō oppidō tertiō diē esse. Ita rēs facta est; tertiō diē, impetū ācriter factō, oppidum expugnātum est eōdemque
25 diē ibi ille suppliciō hominem affēcit.

Saepe ante prīmam lūcem hic prīnceps populī Rōmānī domum relinquēbat et in Capitōlium veniēbat et ibi sōlus multās hōrās sedēbat. Aliī putāvērunt Scīpiōnem, deīs dēspectīs, hanc rem ad[5] speciem facere; aliī autem crēdidērunt eum dē salūte cīvitātis deōs cōnsulere.

[5] *for*

Questions

1. How old was Scipio when he went to Spain?
2. What did he accomplish there?
3. Why was Scipio called *Africanus?*
4. What did he force Hannibal to do?
5. What was Scipio's answer to the soldier who wanted to know when a prisoner would be punished? What was the point?
6. What explanations were given for Scipio's visits to the Capitol?

VOCABULARY

Nouns

di´ēs, diē´ī m. *day* — (diary, diurnal)
lūx, lū´cis f. *light* — (lucid, translucent)
prīn´ceps, prīn´cipis m. *leader, chief* — [**prīmus + capiō**]
rēs, re´ī f. *thing, matter, affair, situation* — (real)
spe´ciēs, speciē´ī f. *appearance* — [**spectō**]
spēs, spe´ī f. *hope* — [**spērō**]

Verbs

interclū´dō, -ere, -clū´sī, -clū´sus *cut off* — [**claudō**]
no´ceō, nocē´re, no´cuī, nocitū´rus — (innocent)
  do harm (to) (with dat.)
praefi´ciō, -ere, -fē´cī, -fec´tus — [**faciō**]
  put in charge of (with acc. and dat.)
prae´sum, -es´se, prae´fuī, praefutū´rus — [**sum**]
  be in charge of (with dat.)

▦ GRAMMAR

Fifth Declension

The last of the noun declensions includes comparatively few words. **Rēs** and **diēs,** however, occur constantly and should be memorized. Most other nouns of the fifth declension have no plural; all are feminine except **diēs,** which is usually masculine.

ENDINGS	SINGULAR	PLURAL
Nominative	-ēs	-ēs
Genitive	-ēī or ĕī	-ērum
Dative	-ēī or ĕī	-ēbus
Accusative	-em	-ēs
Ablative	-ē	-ēbus

EXAMPLES	SINGULAR	PLURAL	SINGULAR	PLURAL
Nominative	di´ēs	di´ēs	rēs	rēs
Genitive	diē´ī	diē´rum	re´ī	rē´rum
Dative	diē´ī	diē´bus	re´ī	rē´bus
Accusative	di´em	di´ēs	rem	rēs
Ablative	di´ē	diē´bus	rē	rē´bus

Observe that **-e-** appears in every ending; this is the **e**-declension. In **diēs** the **-ē-** is long in the genitive and dative singular, though it precedes a vowel, while in **reī** (genitive and dative singular) the **-e-** is short.[6] That is the only difference in the declension of these two words.

Oral Practice

1. Decline **rēs fortis** and **ūna spēs.**
2. Give each of the following in the form indicated: **diēs ultimus** (abl. pl.); **prīnceps noster** (acc. sing.); **speciēs nova** (dat. sing.); **impetus maior** (acc. pl.); **manus pulchra** (gen. pl.); **melior lūx** (abl. sing.).
3. Give the correct form in Latin for the following: *for one day, on that day, deceived hope* (acc.), *thing's, for the chief, in light, light cut off* (acc.), *to all appearances, more affairs* (nom.) *of the senate, a leader* (nom.) *put in charge of things.*

---

[6] In fifth declension nouns, the genitive and dative singular end in -ĕī instead of -ēī when a consonant precedes the ending; e.g., **rĕī**, but **speciēī**.

Developing "Word Sense"

Here are just a few of the English meanings that the single Latin word **rēs** can have in different contexts: *thing, matter, object, being, circumstance, affair, case, situation, condition, fortune, occurrence, deed, act, event, history, fact, reality, truth, substance, property, possessions, benefit, interest, profit, advantage, cause, reason, account, lawsuit,* etc. And when **rēs** is joined with adjectives, the list grows almost endlessly: **rēs secundae aut malae,** *prosperity or misery;* **rēs rūstica,** *agriculture;* **rēs dīvīna,** *sacrifice;* **rēs pūblica,** *state;* **rēs mīlitāris,** *warfare;* etc.

Memorize all these meanings? Never! Get the basic ones, inspect the context, and use common sense. Test case: what did the poet Ovid mean when he proudly described Rome as **caput rērum urbs Rōmāna?**

▦ *Exercises*

A. Translate the following sentences into English.
1. Amīcus certus in rē incertā cernitur.
2. Speciēs barbarōrum ācrium mē puerum terrēbat.
3. Virum quī huic operī praefuit illī urbī praeficiam.
4. Memoria diēī bene āctī est per sē magnum praemium.
5. Dēmōnstrāvī illum prīncipem nocuisse senātuī populōque Rōmānō.
6. Lēgātus Rōmānus dīxit exercitum suum domibus nōn nocitūrum esse.
7. Quid significant *(mean)* hae litterae, in signīs Rōmānīs vīsae, "S P Q R"? Rogā magistrum tuum (magistram tuam) sī nōn nōvistī.

B. Translate the following sentences into Latin.
1. Most (men) are deceived by the appearance of things.
2. Show (sing.) him your new books; he will not do harm to them.
3. By accident I heard our leader say that there was hope of peace.
4. We put a senator (**senātor**) in charge of our republic; he resolved (**statuō**) to send people to the moon (**lūna**). Now, that task (work) having been finished, we strive (**contendō**) to establish (**statuō**) a larger station (**statiō, -ōnis** f.) in space (**immēnsum, -ī** n.).

WORD STUDY

- English words which preserve the forms of the Latin fourth declension are: *census, consensus, impetus, prospectus, status, apparatus* (plural *apparatuses* or *apparatus;* the latter preserves the Latin plural). Note that *consensus* (from **sentiō**) is spelled with an *-s-* but *census* (from **cēnseō**) with a *-c-*. An ablative form of this declension is seen in *impromptu*.

  The fifth declension is represented by *rabies, series,* and *species.* The last two are used in the plural with no change of form (as in Latin).

  The accusative singular is represented by *requiem,* the ablative singular by *specie,* and the ablative plural by *rebus.*

  A.M., ante merīdiem, *before midday;* **P.M., post merīdiem,** *after midday.*

- Study the following English phrases borrowed from Latin.

bona fide	*in good faith*
casus belli	*an occasion for war*
prima facie	*on the first face (of it);* as in *prima facie* evidence
in statu quo	*in the situation in which (it was before)*
status quo	*the situation in which (it was before)*
sine die	*without a day (being set);* used of adjournment for an indefinite period by a parliamentary body

Explain **per diem, post mortem, sui generis.**

LESSON OBJECTIVES
- To learn about the conflict between Cato and Scipio
- To learn the genitive and ablative of description

CATŌ ET SCĪPIŌ

¹ *Antí´ochus*, a Syrian king
² **mihi... erat,** *I intended*
³ *tore in pieces*

M. Catō, vir humilī genere, ad summōs honōrēs per sē ascenderat. Hic Scīpiōnī, virō nōbilissimā familiā, inimīcus erat et eum dēspexit. Itaque familiārem suum Petīlium iussit in senātū explōrāre ratiōnēs pecūniae praedaeque captae in bellō cum Antiochō¹ ā Scīpiōne gestō. Hōc modō Catō,
5 cīvis magnae auctōritātis, senātum in duās partēs dīvīsit, alteram quae Scīpiōnī nocēre cupiēbat, alteram quae eum prīncipem maximae virtūtis esse crēdēbat. Tum Scīpiō, cuius īra ex speciē gravī frontis clārē cernī poterat, librum prae sē tenuit et dīxit:

"In hōc librō ratiōnēs scrīptae sunt omnis pecūniae omniumque rērum
10 quās accēpī. Hic est diēs quō mihi in animō erat² ratiōnēs apud vōs legere atque explicāre. Nunc autem, quod Petīlius eās explōrāre et mihi imperāre cupit, apud vōs eās nōn explicābō."

Hōc dictō, librum suīs propriīs manibus dīscidit³.

Cato the Elder *(right),* in his eighties, discusses the good and bad points of old age to an attentive audience. The two young men are C. Laelius the Younger and Scipio the Younger. Cato's feud with Scipio's adoptive grandfather, Scipio Africanus, has apparently been forgotten. In this illustration from a fifteenth-century French translation of Cicero's *Dē Senectūte,* the artist has added a dog, a servant *(left),* and another old man to the cast of characters.

Gianni Dagli Orti/Musée Condé Chantilly/The Art Archive

Questions

1. In what respect were Cato and Scipio unlike?
2. Who was Cato, and what was his attitude toward Scipio?
3. Who made an investigation, and what was it about?
4. How did the investigation divide the senate into two sides, and what opinions did each side have?
5. How was Scipio's anger revealed at first?
6. What importance did the book referred to have?
7. What reason did Scipio express for tearing the book in pieces?
8. Give an example of conduct by a public official from recent history that divided senate or parliament in this way.

▊ VOCABULARY

Nouns

*frōns, fron´tis, fron´tium f.   (frontal)
  forehead, front
ra´tiō, ratiō´nis f. *account, reason*   (rational, reason)

Verbs

ascen´dō, -ere, ascen´dī, ascēn´sus   [scandō, *climb*]
  climb (up), ascend
dī´vidō, -ere, dīvī´sī, dīvī´sus *divide*   (division)
explō´rō, -ā´re, -ā´vī, -ā´tus   [plōrō, *call out*]
  investigate, explore
im´perō, -ā´re, -ā´vī, -ā´tus   [imperium]
  command (with dat. of person)

Preposition

a´pud (with acc.) *among, in the presence of*

▊ GRAMMAR

Genitive and Ablative of Description

virī magnae virtūtis	*men of great courage*
spatium decem pedum	*a space of ten feet*
hominēs inimīcō animō	*people with* (or *of*) *an unfriendly spirit*

Observe that in English we may say *people of* or *with an unfriendly spirit*. Both are descriptive. Note also that description is similarly expressed in Latin, either by the genitive or the ablative, but only when modified by an adjective.

While the genitive and the ablative of description are translated alike, Latin uses the genitive chiefly for permanent qualities, such as measure and number, and the ablative for temporary qualities, such as personal appearance or behavior.

Oral Practice

1. Translate the following into English: **prīnceps magnā potestāte; manūs parvā vī; C. Marius, vir humilis generis; rēgīna summae virtūtis.**
2. Translate the following into Latin in two ways: *men of lower birth; no one with that appearance; people of the same age; Mercury, a god of great speed.*

🁣 *Exercises*

A. Translate the following sentences into English.
   1. Lēgātus Gallōrum fuit vir clārissimō genere.
   2. "Dīvide et imperā" erat cōnsilium Rōmānōrum.
   3. Ille erat puer magnā grātiā apud familiārēs suōs.
   4. Hāc aestāte ascendam montem decem mīlium pedum.
   5. Eum montem sōlī hominēs maximae virtūtis explōrāvērunt.
   6. Frontem huius montis ascendere nōn poterō, quod ea est praeceps et difficillima.

B. Translate the following sentences into Latin.
   1. The general was a man of great influence.
   2. Do you desire to climb a mountain which has never been explored?
   3. We know that Italy is divided from Gaul by very high mountains.
   4. After a journey of two days, we arrived at (**ad**) a very beautiful city.

WORD STUDY

Suffixes

The suffixes **-ilis** and **-bilis** are added to verb stems to form adjectives. They indicate what can be done: **facilis** is "doable," *easy*. The suffix **-ilis** usually becomes *-ile* in English: *facile, fertile*. The more common suffix **-bilis** becomes, *ble, able, -ible* in English: *amiable, comparable, credible, divisible, noble, visible*.

Several adjectival suffixes meaning *pertaining to* are added to nouns and adjectives: **-āris** (English *-ar*), **-ārius** *(-ary)*, **-ānus** *(-an, -ane)*, **-icus** *(-ic)*. Examples of their use in Latin and English are **familiāris, monētārius, Rōmānus, pūblicus;** *singular, ordinary, human, humane, generic*.

The suffix **-tūdō** (English *-tude*) is added to adjective stems to form nouns and means *state of being;* **magnitūdō,** *magnitude*.

Find fifteen other examples of these suffixes in English words derived from Latin words already studied.

ROMAN CITIZENSHIP AND ITS LEGACY

Library of Congress

The House of Representatives in Washington contains marble plaques of men who made important contributions to American law. Among the Romans are (*top*) Papinian (third century A.D.) and the Emperor Justinian (*bottom*).

According to tradition, Rome was founded in 753 B.C. April 21 is still celebrated as the birthday of Rome. The first rulers were kings, but the last king was driven out in 509 B.C. because he was a tyrant. The new government was headed by two consuls of equal power, one to be a check on the other. Their term of office was limited to a year. The Roman historian Livy saw this restriction as the origin of Roman liberty. Yet this government was not democratic, for it was in the control of a small group of noble families called *patricians* (from **patrēs**). For two hundred years the common people, (*plebeians,* **plēbs**) struggled for equality and justice and gradually won most of the rights of their more fortunate fellow citizens. At first they could not hold office and did not even have fair trials in court.

The plebeians' struggle for democracy and liberty is of great interest to us. First they secured the right to elect special officials, called tribunes, who could veto the acts of the patrician officials. Then in the fifth century B.C. they obtained a set of written laws, called the Twelve Tables, which served as a kind of constitution or bill of rights. In 326 B.C. imprisonment and slavery for debt were abolished. Livy called this step a second beginning of liberty for the plebeians. In 287 B.C. the plebeians succeeded in establishing the principle that a vote of the plebs should have the authority of law. Such a vote was called a **plēbiscītum,** from which we get our word *plebiscite*. In these ways a fairly democratic form of government was assured for some time.

While these struggles were going on inside the country, external wars were being fought and the foundations of Roman dominion were being formed. The heroic deeds of Horatius, Cincinnatus, Fabricius, Regulus, Scipio, and many others accounted for Roman success and developed the Roman virtues of courage, honesty, organizing ability, patriotism, devotion to family, strict justice, plain living, and the determination to persevere and never to give up. From all this grew the great system of Roman law and the ideal of stable government, one of the greatest things that modern society inherited from Rome.

The Romans organized law and government on a large scale. Their success in this may be compared to the growth of a modern government's power to regulate commerce, industry, transportation, communication, education, and issues of safety and social welfare. Europe and Latin America still use ideas from Roman law. English common law, the basis of the United States legal system, owes much to the law of the Romans.

No wonder the possession of Roman citizenship was highly prized and that people said with pride **"Cīvis Rōmānus sum."** This citizenship, bestowed in a solemn ceremony, brought the protection of Roman law everywhere in the world. It also brought the responsibility of protecting the Roman state against its enemies. Similarly, citizenship today in any country brings both advantages and duties.

The Roman concepts of liberty, representative government, the rule of law, patriotism, and the responsibilities of citizenship have been at work in Western civilization for two thousand years, and nowhere more than in the United States. As has been rightly said:

"It is clear that the spirit of '76 had a most diversified origin. . . . In listing the 'founding fathers,' it is not enough to include merely American patriots of the caliber of Jefferson, Franklin, and the Adamses . . . Demosthenes and Aristotle, Brutus, Cicero, and Tacitus belong there, as do many others of similar stamp and influence . . . In fact, they were often scarcely less significant as intellectual guides than such influential English standbys as Edward Coke and John Locke. Not less than the Washingtons and the Lees, these ancient heroes helped to found the independent American commonwealth."[1]

[1] Charles F. Mullet, *Classical Journal* 35 (1939), 104.

QUESTIONS

1. The Romans had two consuls as a check on each other. What system of checks and balances do we have in our government?
2. The restriction of the consulship to one year was regarded as the origin of Roman liberty. Do we have any similar restriction for our highest officials?
3. Are persons sometimes imprisoned for debt today? Have there been changes in our laws on the subject in the last one hundred years?
4. What are some of the privileges and duties of citizenship today?

C. Sherburne/PhotoLink/PhotoDisc

The reverse side of the Great Seal of the United States. (You can see both sides on a one dollar bill.) The Eye of Providence blazes in glory above a thirteen-step pyramid left unfinished. Why? MDCCLXXVI appears at its base. Why? The two mottoes are based on Vergil: "(He) has smiled on our undertakings" and "a new order of generations."

VOCABULARY

Nouns

cāsus	frōns	negōtium	senātus
diēs	impetus	prīnceps	speciēs
domus	lūx	ratiō	spēs
exercitus	manus	rēs	

Verbs

ascendō	exerceō	noceō	supersum
dēmōnstrō	explōrō	praeficiō	
dēserō	imperō	praemittō	
dēspiciō	intellegō	praesum	
dīvidō	interclūdō	reddō	

Conjunctions

autem	postquam

Prepositions

apud	prae
circum	super

GRAMMAR SUMMARY

Synonyms

We rarely find a word in any language that has exactly the same meaning as another word. Words which have almost the same meaning are called *synonyms*. **Homō** and **vir** both mean *man*, but **homō** sometimes means any *human being;* **vir,** a (male) *man, husband, hero,* etc.

The following synonyms have occurred in previous lessons.

ante = *before* (of time and place), adverb or preposition (with accusative)

prae = *before* (of position only), preposition (with ablative)

terra = *land* (as opposed to water), also some particular *land* or *country*

fīnēs = *borders,* therefore a *land* or *country* with reference to its boundaries

patria = *fatherland,* the *land* of one's birth

dux [dūcō] = a *leader* in any field, but often in a military sense

prīnceps [prīmus + capiō] = the *first* or *chief* man in a group—usually nonmilitary

videō = *see,* the most common word

cernō = *see clearly, discern*

cōnspiciō = *catch sight of, spot*

spectō = *look at*

labor = *hard work, toil, suffering*

opus = usually *a piece of work, task*

negōtium = *lack of leisure* [**ōtium**]*, business*

potestās = *power* in general

auctōritās = *influence*

rēgnum = *royal power*

imperium = *military power, command*

Accusative with Ad or In

When *to* implies literally *motion toward* a place or person, we have seen that the accusative after **ad** or **in** is used. This is true after the following motion verbs, which you have already learned.

accēdō, cēdō, contendō, dūcō, fugiō, mātūrō, mittō, moveō, nāvigō, portō, prōcēdō, prōdūcō, properō, redigō, redūcō, trānsportō, veniō

Dative of Indirect Object

When *to* does not imply actual motion but indicates the person to whom something is given, told, shown, etc., the dative is used. The following verbs are transitive and may have an accusative as the direct object and a dative as the indirect object: **committō, dīcō, dō, dōnō, iungō, mandō, mōnstrō, nūntiō, ostendō, permittō, prōpōnō, reddō, relinquō, respondeō, submittō, trādō, tribuō.** Some of these verbs have either a neuter pronoun or an infinitive as the direct object: **dīcō, respondeō, nūntiō.** With some other verbs, the dative is regularly used in Latin instead of a direct object: **noceō** (*do harm to*).

UNIT PRACTICE

A. Decline **senātus noster, diēs longior.**

B. Give the genitive and accusative singular and the genitive plural of **id negōtium, haec potestās, impetus fortis, īdem prīnceps, quae ratiō, rēs ipsa, cāsus peior, ūlla domus.**

C. Give in all tenses the third person singular active of **noceō;** the third person plural passive of **dēserō;** the first person plural active of **imperō;** the third person plural passive of **dēspiciō;** the second person singular active of **audiō.**

D. Identify these forms fully: **praemīsit, incoluisse, exercērī, interclūdēns, dēserunt, redde, dēmōnstrāte, explōrārī, dīvidī, imperāns, superestis, praeerimus, praeficiēmus, ascendam, vīvite, dīvīsus, interclūdentur, intellēctum est, permissūrus.**

WORD STUDY

1. Give the Latin words and prefixes suggested by the following English derivatives: *ascendancy, casualty, circumnavigate, demonstration, familiarity, indivisible, innocuous, intellectual, lucid, opponent, preview, subjunctive, superscription, transcend, virtue.*
2. Write sentences using as many English derivatives as you can find from the Latin **pōnō, veniō,** and **pellō.**

UNIT XIII ASSESSMENT

LESSONS LXVII–LXX

VOCABULARY

Choose the word that best completes each sentence.

1. Postquam līberī in _____ properāverant, sibi
   cēnam parātam invēnērunt.
   a. impetum
   b. exercitum
   c. domum
   d. cāsum

2. Rōmānī illam regiōnem in trēs partēs _____ et
   imperium suum sustinēre nōn potuērunt.
   a. dēmōnstrāre
   b. dēserere
   c. dēspicere
   d. dīvidere

3. Dominus servum doctissimum huic negōtiō
   tōtum mēnsem _____.
   a. praefēcit
   b. superfuit
   c. praefuit
   d. praemīsit

4. Pater dīxit sē _____ nōn āmīsisse, nam crēdidit
   fīliam suam vīvere.
   a. diem
   b. speciem
   c. rem
   d. spem

5. "_____ librum meum quem auctor clārus ipse
   mihi dōnāvit," poēta īnstāns iussit.
   a. Exercē
   b. Redde
   c. Nocē
   d. Interclūde

GRAMMAR

Complete each sentence with the correct endings.

6. Quīnque di___ circum mont___ altum tard___
   prōcesserant; loca praecipit___ autem in
   quibus perīcul___ maximum erat, explōrā___
   nōn potuērunt.

7. Puella ūnam vest___ pulchr___ manū su___
   di___ quīnt___ cōnfēcit, et eam mātr___ su___
   dedit.

8. Vir, qu___ in front___ vulnerāt___ ___, apud
   ali___ mīlit___ prae duc___nōbilī stetit.

9. Puer carmen scrīpsit dē quattuor equ___
   speci___ ēgregi___ quī ā sē et amīcō su___
   exercitī erant et decem ann___ superfu___.

10. Senāt___ convocāt___, patr___ intellēxērunt
    exercit___ Rōmānōs bellum difficillim___
    tempus longissim___ susceptūr___ esse.

TRANSLATION

Translate the following sentences.

11. Caesar mīlitem optimum castrīs praefēcit;
    reliquōs praemīsit ad flūmen centum pedēs
    lātum trāns quod pontem faciēbant.

12. Servus timidus pūtāvit sē fīliō suī dominī cāsū
    nocuisse, itaque in silvīs extrēmīs trēs diēs mānsit.

13. "Ratiōnem meam rērum omnium senātuī
    narrāvī," prīnceps superbē nūntiāvit, "et
    numquam plūs pecūniae solvam aut reddam."

14. Hominēs super oppidum agrōsque quōs
    dēseruerant stābant, et, iter incertum timentēs,
    cāsum pessimum dēspēxērunt.

15. Aestāte, lūdō et omnibus cūrīs relīctīs, mare
    explōrāre, ventum undāsque audīre, et tempus
    bonum cum amīcīs nostrīs paucōs diēs agere
    cupīmus.

INVESTIGATION

Track down the answers to these questions from any lesson in Unit XIII.

16. To an ancient Roman, what were the Twelve Tables?

17. Cicero wrote a famous essay entitled **Dē Senectūte,** in which Cato was one of the speakers. In English, what was the subject of this work?

18. What is the number of the declension which contains the greatest number of Latin nouns? The smallest number?

19. Give the correct Latin words and their translation for these common abbreviations.
    A.M.   P.M.   P.S.

20. According to the traditional rules, what would have been the Latin name of the daughter of Gaius Jūlius Caesar? Of Lūcius Cornēlius Sulla?

CULTURE

Vērum aut Falsum? Indicate whether each statement is true or false.

21. A solemn ceremony was held when a man became a Roman citizen.

22. The aristocratic, noble families of Rome were known as the plebeians.

23. The traditional founding date of Rome is in March, the month sacred to Mars.

24. In the Roman government a tribune was an official elected to represent the rights of the common people.

25. Roman legal and governmental ideas have been imitated in many present-day countries.

FROM LATIN TO ENGLISH

Apply your knowledge of Latin roots to determine the best meaning of the italicized words.

26. The executives were meeting to discuss their company's *ascendancy* in the field.
    a. reputation
    b. dominance
    c. collapse
    d. workforce

27. My cousin displayed his *impetuous* temperament in many situations.
    a. cautious
    b. generous
    c. rash
    d. evil

28. The biologist was studying the *diurnal* habits of a certain rare bird.
    a. eating
    b. daytime
    c. nesting
    d. nighttime

29. She offered a very *lucid* argument for her decision.
    a. weak
    b. forceful
    c. familiar
    d. clear

30. We thought the tone of the editorial was quite *innocuous.*
    a. unfriendly
    b. strong
    c. unexpected
    d. harmless

GRAMMAR APPENDIX

Pronunciation

Vowels

In Latin, as in English, the vowels are *a,e,i,o,u.*[1]

At one time the English vowels were pronounced like the Latin vowels, but the pronunciation of English has changed greatly. In French, Spanish, Italian, German, and other languages that have adopted the Latin alphabet, the vowels are still pronounced very much as in Latin.

Each of the Latin vowels may be pronounced long or short, the difference being one of time. This is called *quantity.* There is also a difference of sound between the long and the short vowels, except **a.** This is called *quality.* The pronunciation is approximately as follows.

LONG		SHORT		LONG AND SHORT
ā	as in *father*	a	as first *a* in *aha*	*Martha* (ā, ă)
ē	as in *they* or *a* in *late*	e	as in *let*	*lateness* (ē, ĕ)
ī	as in *police* or *ea* in *seat*	i	as in *sit*	*seasick* (ī, ĭ)
ō	as in *note*	o	as in *for*	*phonograph* (ō, ŏ)
ū	as in *rule* or *oo* in *fool*	u	as in *full*	*two-footed* (ū, ŭ)

In this book, long vowels are regularly marked with a long mark, called a **macron** *(may´kron)* ¯; short vowels are usually unmarked, but ˘ is sometimes used.

Be careful. It is very important to distinguish the sounds of the long and short vowels. To confuse ī and ĭ, or ē and ĕ in Latin is as bad a mistake as for a person to say, *I heard the din in the hall,* instead of *dean,* or *I forgot the debt,* instead of *date.*

The English equivalents of **e** and **o** are only approximate. Avoid pronouncing ŏ like *o* in *not* or in *note;* it sounds much like *aw.*

Quantity of Vowels

The quantity and quality of vowels must be learned as part of the word. There are, however, a few general rules.

1. A vowel is usually short before another vowel or **-h** (because **h** is weakly sounded).
2. A vowel is short before **-nt, -nd,** final **-m** and **-t,** and usually final **-r.**
3. A vowel is long before **-nf,** and **-ns.**

---

[1] And sometimes *y* (pronounced like French *u*). English too uses *y* as a vowel, as in *by,* but the *y* in *yes, young,* et al., is a consonant.

Diphthongs

The first three of the following diphthongs (two vowels making one sound) are the most common ones.

ae like *ai* in *aisle*   **ei** like *ei* in *freight*

au like *ou* in *out*   **eu** like *eh-oo* (pronounced quickly)

oe like *oi* in *oil*   **ui** like *oo-ee* (pronounced quickly);

       only in **cui** and **huic.**

Consonants

All letters other than vowels and diphthongs are consonants.

The Latin consonants have, generally speaking, the same sounds as in English. The following differences, however, should be noted.

b before **s** or **t** has the sound of **p**.

c is always hard as in *cat*, never soft as in *city*.

g is always hard as in *go*, never soft as in *gem*.

i (consonant) has the sound of *y* in *year*. **i** is a consonant between vowels and at the beginning of a word before a vowel. Some books use **j** for consonant **i**.

s always has the sound of *s* in *sin*; never of *s* in *these*.

t always has the sound of *t* in *ten*; never of *t* in *motion*.

v has the sound of *w* in *will*.

x has the sound of *x* in *extra*.

(ch=k; ph–p; th–t)

Doubled consonants are pronounced separately: **an-nus** .

In both English and Latin the combination **qu** forms a single consonant *(kw)*, and the **u** is not counted as a vowel. Occasionally in Latin **gu** (gw) and **su** (sw) are treated the same way, as in English *anguish* and *suave*.

English Pronunciation of Latin

Latin words that have become thoroughly English should be pronounced as English; for example in *terra firma*, the *i* is pronounced as in *mirth*, not as in *miracle;* in *alumni*, the *i* is pronounced as in *mile;* in *alumnae*, the *ae* is pronounced as *e* in *even*. Usage varies, especially in the pronunciation of anglicized proper names. Latin ŏ is often lengthened to ō in English, e.g. *bonus* from Latin **bŏnus.** Other examples: *bona fide (bohna fidee* or *bohna fīd* [ī = Eng. *eye*]), *ex officio (eks ohfishioh), modus operandi (mohdus operandī), sine die (sīnee dīee), vice versa (vīsa vursa* or *vīz vursa), viva voce (veeva vohsee* or *veeva vohchay* [Italian]*), Cato (Kaytoh* instead of *Katoh), Manilius (Manīlius* or *Manilius).*

Syllables

Every Latin word has as many syllables as it has vowels or diphthongs: **vir-tū-te, proe-li-um.**

A single consonant between two vowels or diphthongs is pronounced with the second: **fī-li-us, a-git.** Likewise, the double consonant **x [=ks]** is preferably joined to the following vowel: **dū-xī.** Compound words are divided into their component parts and are exceptions to this rule: **ad-es.**

When two or more consonants occur between vowels or diphthongs, the division is made before the last consonant: **por-tus, vīnc-tī, an-nus.** An exception to this rule occurs whenever a stop **(p, b, t, d, c, g)** is followed by a liquid **(l, r),** in which case the stop combines with the liquid and both are pronounced with the second vowel: **pū-bli-cus, cas-tra.**

The next to the last syllable of a word is called the *penult* (Latin **paene,** *almost*; **ultima,** *last*); the one before the penult (i.e., the third from the end) is called the *antepenult*.

Quantity of Syllables

Some syllables of course take longer to pronounce than others, just as some vowels are longer than others.

1. A syllable is *naturally* long if it contains a long vowel or a diphthong: **fā-mae.**
2. A syllable is *long by position* if it contains a short vowel followed by two or more consonants or the double consonant **x (=ks): sil-vīs, por-tō.**

Note. Exception is made in the case of a stop followed by a liquid. **H** is so weakly sounded that it does not help make a syllable long.

Caution. Distinguish carefully between long syllable and long vowel; in **ĕxĕmplum** the first two syllables are long, though the vowels are short.

Accent

The accented syllable of a word is the one that is pronounced with more stress or emphasis than the others; so in the word *an´swer,* the accent is on the first syllable. In Latin the accent is easily learned according to fixed rules.

1. Words of two syllables are accented on the first: **frā´ter.**
2. Words of three or more syllables are accented on the penult if it is long, otherwise on the antepenult: **lēgā´tus, exem´plum; dī´cĕre, sĭ´mĭlis.**

Note that the accented syllable is not necessarily long.

Basic Grammatical Terms

The material given here may be reviewed in connection with the lessons. For those who prefer to review basic grammar before beginning the lessons, a number of explanations are given here that are also in the body of the textbook. Teachers can easily devise English exercises for drill with classes that need it, or the sentences on these pages may be used for that purpose.

The Sentence: Subject and Predicate

A *sentence* is a group of words that completely expresses a thought. Every sentence consists of two parts—the *subject*, about which something is said, and the predicate, which says something about the subject.

> *The sailor* (subject) *saved*   **Nauta puellam servāvit.**
>   *the girl* (predicate).

A subject or predicate is said to be modified by those words that affect or limit its meaning.

Parts of Speech

The words of most languages are divided according to their use into eight classes called *parts of speech*. These are: nouns, adjectives, adverbs, conjunctions, pronouns, verbs, prepositions, and interjections.

Nouns

A *noun* (from Latin **nōmen,** *name*) is a word that names a person, place, thing, or concept: *Anna*, **Anna;** *island,* **īnsula;** *letter,* **littera;** *liberty,* **lībertās.**

Nouns may be classified as:

1. *common* (applies to any one of a group): *city,* **urbs;** *girl,* **puella.**
2. *proper* (applies to a particular one of a group and is always capitalized): *Rome,* **Roma;** *Julia,* **Iūlia.**

Pronouns

A *pronoun* (Latin **prō,** *for;* **nōmen,** *name*) is a word used in place of a noun. The noun whose place is taken by a pronoun is called an *antecedent* (Latin **ante,** *before;* **cēdō,** *go*).

1. *Personal* pronouns distinguish the three persons: the person speaking: *I*, **ego;** *we*, **nōs**–first person; the person spoken to: *you,* **tū, vōs**–second person; the person or thing spoken of: *he,* **is;** *she,* **ea;** *it,* **id;** *they,* **eī**–third person.
2. *Interrogative* pronouns are used to ask questions: *who?,* **quis?;** *what?,* **quid?**
3. *Relative* pronouns relate to a preceding word (antecedent) and join to it a dependent clause: *who, which, what, that,* **qui, quae, quod.**
4. *Demonstrative* pronouns point out persons or objects definitely—often accompanied with a gesture: *this,* **hic;** *that,* **ille;** *these,* **hī;** *those,* **illī.**

Adjectives

An *adjective* (Latin **adiectīvus,** *added to)* is used to describe a noun or pronoun or to limit its meaning.

1. *Descriptive* adjectives are either common or proper: *good,* **bonus;** *Roman,* **Rōmānus.** Proper adjectives begin with a capital letter.
2. *Limiting* adjectives can be divided into six groups.
   a. *Article*—definite: *the;* indefinite: *a, an.* There is no definite or indefinite article in Latin.
   b. *Numerals*—cardinals: *one, two, three, etc.,* **ūnus, duo, trēs,** etc.; ordinals: *first, second, third, etc.,* **prīmus, secundus, tertius,** etc.
   c. *Possessive* adjectives (formed from personal pronouns): *my, mine,* **meus;** *our, ours,* **noster;** *your, yours,* **tuus, vester;** *his, her, its,* **eius;** *their, theirs,* **eōrum.**

   Interrogative, relative, and demonstrative pronouns may be used as adjectives, in which case they are called respectively:

   d. *Interrogative* adjectives: **What** *street?* **Quae** *via?*
   e. *Relative* adjectives: *He spent a year in Italy, in* **which** *country he saw many beautiful things,* **Annum in Italiā ēgit, in** *quā* **terrā multa pulchra vīdit.**
   f. *Demonstrative* adjectives: *that road,* **illa** *via.*

   In English, the demonstrative adjectives are the only ones that have different forms in the singular and plural: *this, these; that, those.*

Verbs

A *verb* (Latin **verbum,** *word, verb*) tells what a subject does or is.

He *fought.*	**Pugnāvit.**
He *is* good.	**Bonus** *est.*

1. According to use, verbs are either *transitive* or *intransitive.*
   a. A *transitive* verb tells what a person or thing does to another person or thing (a direct object).

Anna **is carrying** *water.*	**Anna aquam** *portat.*

   b. An *intransitive* verb is one whose action is limited to the subject and has no direct object.

Anna **is working.**	**Anna** *labōrat.*

2. *Intransitive* verbs are either *complete* or *linking.*
   a. A *complete* verb is complete in meaning without an object or other word.

He **sails.**	*Nāvigat.*

   b. A *linking* verb links a noun or adjective to the subject.

They **are** *good.*	**Bonī** *sunt.*

The chief linking verbs in English are *be, appear, seem, become, feel, look, taste, smell, act,* etc.

3. An *auxiliary* verb (Latin **auxilium,** *help*) is one used in the conjugation of other verbs: *I am learning;* **Did** *you see? They* **have** *given.*

Adverbs

An *adverb* (Latin **ad,** *to;* **verbum,** *verb*) is used to modify the meaning of a verb, adjective, or other adverb.

> *He is working* **now.**   *Nunc* **labōrat.**

Prepositions

A *preposition* (Latin **prae,** *before;* **positiō,** *position*) is used to show the relation of a noun or pronoun, called its object, to some word (usually the verb) in the sentence.

> *He sails* **to** *the island.*   *Ad* **īnsulam nāvigat.**

Conjunctions

A *conjunction* (Latin **coniunctiō,** *a joining together*) is used to join words, phrases, and clauses. Conjunctions are classified according to their use.

1. *Coordinating conjunctions* connect words or sentences of equal rank (*and,* **et;** *but,* **sed;** *or,* **aut;** *nor,* **neque**).
2. *Subordinating conjunctions* connect a subordinate clause of a sentence with the principal clause (*if,* **sī;** *while,* **dum;** *because,* **quod,** etc.).
3. *Correlative conjunctions* are used in pairs (*both . . . and,* **et... et;** *neither . . . nor,* **neque... neque,** etc.).

Interjections

An *interjection* (Latin **interiectiō,** *a throwing between*) is used to show emotion. It has no direct relation to any other word in the sentence: *O!, Alas!, Ah!, Oh!* (For several Latin interjections, see page 177.)

Inflection

The change of form that words undergo to indicate differences in their use is called *inflection: boy, boys,* **puer, puerī;** *see, saw, seen,* **videō, vīdī, vīsus.** The inflection of nouns, pronouns, and adjectives is called *declension.* They are declined to indicate change in number, case, and sometimes gender. Personal pronouns also indicate person. The inflection of verbs is called *conjugation.*

Number

A noun or pronoun is *singular* when it refers to one person or thing: *girl,* **puella;** *house,* **casa;** *mouse,* **mūs;** *tooth,* **dēns.** It is *plural* when it refers to more than one: *girls,* **puellae;** *houses,* **casae;** *mice,* **mūrēs;** *teeth,* **dentēs.**

Gender

Gender is a distinction in the form of words corresponding to a distinction of sex. It is shown by change of word, by change of ending, or by use of a prefix: *father—mother,* **pater—māter,** *master—mistress,* **dominus—domina;** *he-goat—she-goat,* **caper—capra.** The first words given in each group are *masculine,* the second are *feminine.* Most nouns in English have no gender and are therefore *neuter* (neither masculine nor feminine). In Latin, however, many such nouns are masculine or feminine. The gender of the noun must be memorized as part of the basic form.

Case

Case is the change in form of a noun, pronoun, or adjective to show its use.

She (subject) *is here.*	***Ea* adest.**
*I saw **her*** (object).	***Eam* vīdī.**

Subject and Object

1. The *subject* of a verb is that about which something is said.

2. The *direct object* is that which is directly affected by the action indicated in the transitive active verb.

*Anna carries **water**.*	**Anna *aquam* portat.**

3. The *indirect object* indicates that which is indirectly affected by the action of the verb.

*She gave the gift **to me**.*	**Ea *mihi* dōnum dedit.**

4. The term *object* is also applied to a word dependent upon a preposition.

Names and Uses of the Cases

1. *Nominative.* A noun or pronoun used as the subject of a verb is in the *nominative* case.

*The **farmer** calls.*	***Agricola* vocat.**

2. *Genitive.* Possession is expressed by the *genitive* case: *the **boy's** book,* **puerī liber.** It serves to make one noun modify another: *signs **of peace**,* **signa *pācis*—**peaceful *signs.*

3. *Dative*. The noun or pronoun that indicates *to* or *for whom* the direct object is given, shown, or told is called the *indirect object* and is put in the *dative* case.

> *I gave **him** a book.*   **Eī librum dedī.**

4. *Accusative* (objective). A noun or pronoun used as the object of a verb or preposition is in the *accusative* (or objective) case.

> *I sent a **book** to **him**.*   **Ad *eum librum* mīsī.**

5. *Ablative*. The *ablative* case is used with or without prepositions to express separation, means, association, place, and time.

6. *Vocative*. The *vocative* case is used to address someone directly.

> ***Marcus,** are you coming?*   **Vēnisne, *Mārce*?**

7. *Locative*. The *locative* case is used to express *place where: at Rome,* **Rōmae;** *at home,* **domī.**

Conjugation

The inflection of verbs is called *conjugation* (Latin **coniugātiō**, *connection*). Verbs are conjugated by combining the various parts that indicate *person, number, tense, voice,* and *mood.*

Person and Number

A verb must agree with its subject in person and number.

> *The girl **is** good.*   **Puella *est* bona.**
> *The girls **are** good.*   **Puellae *sunt* bonae.**

Tense

Tense (Latin **tempus**) means *time.* There are six tenses in Latin.

1. The *present* represents an act as taking place now: *He **goes.***

2. The *perfect* represents an act as having already taken place: *He **went** yesterday.* This can also be translated as an action complete in the past: *He **has gone**.*

3. The *future* represents an act that will occur later: *He **will go** tomorrow.*

4. The *imperfect* represents an act in the past as incomplete or repeated: *He **was going**; He **used to go**.*

5. The *pluperfect* represents an act as completed at some definite time in the past (before something else occurred): *He **had gone**.*

6. The *future perfect* represents an act as completed at or before some definite time in the future: *He **will have gone*** (before something else will occur).

Interrogative, Negative, Emphatic, and Progressive Verb Forms

The first three types are verbs that ask, negate, or provide emphasis, usually with some form of the auxiliary *do*. They are used only in the present and past. Progressive verb forms express an action as being in progress.

1. Used in questions: ***Do (did)*** *you* ***know*** *this?*
2. Negative: ***I do (did)*** *not* ***know*** *it.*
3. Emphatic: ***I do (did) believe*** *it.*
4. Progressive: *I am walking; I was writing; I will be coming.*

For these four types of English verb forms, Latin does not use separate words or phrases.

Voice

A transitive verb is in the *active voice* (Latin **vox**) when it represents the subject as the doer or agent.

*Anna **loves** Clara.*	**Anna Clāram** *amat*.

A transitive verb is in the *passive voice* when it represents the subject as the receiver of the action.

*Clara **is loved.***	**Clāra** *amātur*.

Intransitive verbs are used only in the active voice in English.

Mood

1. The *indicative* mood (Latin **modus**, *manner*) is used to state a fact or to ask a question.

*Rome **is** a great city.*	**Rōma** *est* **magna urbs.**
*Where **is** Anna?*	**Ubi** *est* **Anna?**

2. The *imperative* mood is used to express commands.

***Look** at the waves.*	***Spectā** undās.*

Infinitive

The *infinitive* (Latin **infinitīvus**, *unlimited*) is a verbal noun considered neuter singular. It is a form of the verb to which *to* is usually prefixed in English: ***to go, to sing***. It has tense and voice but not person, or mood.

Participle

The *participle* (Latin **particeps**, *sharing* [some qualities of a verb]) is a verbal adjective. As an adjective it modifies a noun or pronoun: *a **losing** fight*. As a verbal form it may have an object or adverbial modifiers: *Suddenly **losing** his balance, he fell off.* It has three forms in Latin:

PRESENT ACTIVE	**vidēns**	*seeing*
PERFECT PASSIVE	**vīsus/a/um**	*seen, having been seen*
FUTURE ACTIVE	**vīsūrus/a/um**	*about to see, going to see*

Phrase

A *phrase* (Greek **phrāsis,** *speech*) is a group of words without subject and predicate. One important kind of phrase is the prepositional phrase, that is, a preposition together with its object: *in great danger,* **in magnō perīculō.**

Clauses

A *clause,* (Latin **clausus,** *closed*) like a phrase, is a part of a sentence but differs from a phrase in having a subject and a predicate. There are two ways to classify clauses.

1. *Main*—the principal or independent statement in a sentence, which can stand alone as a complete thought.

   > **The girl** *whom you saw on the street* **is my sister.**
   > **Puella** *quam in viā vīdistī* **soror mea est.**

2. *Subordinate*—a dependent statement modifying the main clause, which cannot stand alone.

   > The girl **whom you saw on the street** *is my sister.*
   > Puella *quam in viā vīdistī* soror mea est.

Sentences

1. A *simple* sentence (Latin **sententia,** *thought*) contains one main clause.

   > *My friend, the farmer, has many horses.*
   > **Amīcus meus, agricola, multōs equōs habet.**

2. A *compound* sentence contains two or more main clauses connected by a coordinate conjunction, such as *and, but*, etc.

   > *My friend, the farmer, has many horses, but I have not seen them.*
   > **Amīcus meus, agricola, multōs equōs habet, sed eōs nōn vīdī.**

3. A *complex* sentence contains one main clause to which one or more subordinate clauses are joined by subordinate conjunctions or by relative or interrogative pronouns.

   > *My friend, the farmer, has many horses, which I have not seen.*
   > **Amīcus meus, agricola, multōs equōs habet quōs nōn vīdī.**

Basic Forms

Nouns

First Declension
via, viae, f. *road*

	SINGULAR	PLURAL
NOM.	via	viae
GEN.	viae	viārum
DAT.	viae	viīs
ACC.	viam	viās
ABL.	viā	viīs
VOC.[2]		

Second Declension
servus, servī, m. *slave*

	SINGULAR	PLURAL
NOM.	servus	servī
GEN.	servī	servōrum
DAT.	servō	servīs
ACC.	servum	servōs
ABL.	servō	servīs
VOC.		serve

Second Declension

ager, agrī, m. *field*

	SING.	PL.
NOM.	ager	agrī
GEN.	agrī	agrōrum
DAT.	agrō	agrīs
ACC.	agrum	agrōs
ABL.	agrō	agrīs

puer, puerī, m. *boy*

	SING.	PL.
NOM.	puer	puerī
GEN.	puerī	puerōrum
DAT.	puerō	puerīs
ACC.	puerum	puerōs
ABL.	puerō	puerīs

signum, signī, n. *sign*

	SING.	PL.
NOM.	signum	signa
GEN.	signī	signōrum
DAT.	signō	signīs
ACC.	signum	signa
ABL.	signō	signīs

Third Declension

mīles, mīlitis, m. *soldier*

	SING.	PL.
NOM.	mīles	mīlitēs
GEN.	mīlitis	mīlitum
DAT.	mīlitī	mīlitibus
ACC.	mīlitem	mīlitēs
ABL.	mīlite	mīlitibus

lēx, lēgis, f. *law*

	SING.	PL.
NOM.	lēx	lēgēs
GEN.	lēgis	lēgum
DAT.	lēgī	lēgibus
ACC.	lēgem	lēgēs
ABL.	lēge	lēgibus

corpus, corporis, n. *body*

	SING.	PL.
NOM.	corpus	corpora
GEN.	corporis	corporum
DAT.	corporī	corporibus
ACC.	corpus	corpora
ABL.	corpore	corporibus

Third Declension I-Stems

cīvis, cīvis, m. or f. *citizen*

	SINGULAR	PLURAL
NOM.	cīvis	cīvēs
GEN.	cīvis	cīvium
DAT.	cīvī	cīvibus
ACC.	cīvem	cīvēs (-īs)
ABL.	cīve	cīvibus

mare, maris, n. *sea*

	SINGULAR	PLURAL
NOM.	mare	maria
GEN.	maris	marium
DAT.	marī	maribus
ACC.	mare	maria
ABL.	marī	maribus

[2]The vocative forms have been omitted from these paradigms unless they differ from the nominative. In the second declension singular, the vocative of -**us** nouns ends in -**e**; of -**ius** nouns, in -**i**.

Fourth Declension
cāsus, cāsūs, m. *chance*

	SING.	PL.
NOM.	cāsus	cāsūs
GEN.	cāsūs	cāsuum
DAT.	cāsuī	cāsibus
ACC.	cāsum	cāsūs
ABL.	cāsū	cāsibus

Fifth Declension
diēs, diēī, m. *day*

	SING.	PL.
NOM.	diēs	diēs
GEN.	diēī	diērum
DAT.	diēī	diēbus
ACC.	diem	diēs
ABL.	diē	diēbus

rēs, reī, f. *thing*

	SING.	PL.
NOM.	rēs	rēs
GEN.	reī	rērum
DAT.	reī	rēbus
ACC.	rem	rēs
ABL.	rē	rēbus

Irregular Nouns
vīs, –, f. *strength*

	SING.	PL.
NOM.	vīs	vīrēs
GEN.	——	vīrium
DAT.	——	vīribus
ACC.	vim	vīrēs (-īs)
ABL.	vī	vīribus
(LOC.)		

nēmō, m. or f. *no one*

	SING.
NOM.	nēmō
GEN.	(nūllīus)
DAT.	nēminī
ACC.	nēminem
ABL.	(nūllō)

domus, domūs, f. *house*

	SING.	PL.
NOM.	domus	domūs
GEN.	domūs (-ī)	domuum (-ōrum)
DAT.	domuī (-ō)	domibus
ACC.	domum	domōs (-ūs)
ABL.	domō (-ū)	domibus
(LOC.)	(domī)	

Adjectives
First and Second Declensions

	SINGULAR			PLURAL		
	M.	F.	N.	M	F.	N.
NOM.	magnus	magna	magnum	magnī	magnae	magna
GEN.	magnī	magnae	magnī	magnōrum	magnārum	magnōrum
DAT.	magnō	magnae	magnō	magnīs	magnīs	magnīs
ACC.	magnum	magnam	magnum	magnōs	magnās	magna
ABL.	magnō	magnā	magnō	magnīs	magnīs	magnīs
VOC.[3]	magne					

	SINGULAR			SINGULAR		
NOM.	līber	lībera	līberum	noster	nostra	nostrum
GEN.	līberī	līberae	līberī	nostrī	nostrae	nostrī
DAT.	līberō	līberae	līberō	nostrō	nostrae	nostrō
ACC.	līberum	līberam	līberum	nostrum	nostram	nostrum
ABL.	līberō	līberā	līberō	nostrō	nostrā	nostrō

Plural, **līberī, līberae, lībera,** etc.   Plural, **nostrī, -ae, -a,** etc.

[3]The vocative form is the same as the nominative except in adjectives of the second declension masculine ending in **-us.** There it ends in **-e;** in **-ius** adjectives it ends in **-ie.**

Third Declension

THREE ENDINGS

	SINGULAR			PLURAL		
	M.	F.	N.	M.	F.	N.
NOM.	ācer	ācris	ācre	ācrēs	ācrēs	ācria
GEN.	ācris	ācris	ācris	ācrium	ācrium	ācrium
DAT.	ācrī	ācrī	ācrī	ācribus	ācribus	ācribus
ACC.	ācrem	ācrem	ācre	ācrēs (-īs)	ācrēs (-īs)	ācria
ABL.	ācrī	ācrī	ācrī	ācribus	ācribus	ācribus

TWO ENDINGS

	SINGULAR		PLURAL	
	M., F.	N.	M., F.	N.
NOM.	fortis	forte	fortēs	fortia
GEN.	fortis	fortis	fortium	fortium
DAT.	fortī	fortī	fortibus	fortibus
ACC.	fortem	forte	fortēs (-īs)	fortia
ABL.	fortī	fortī	fortibus	fortibus

ONE ENDING

	SINGULAR		PLURAL	
	M., F.	N.	M., F.	N.
NOM.	pār	pār	parēs	paria
GEN.	paris	paris	parium	parium
DAT.	parī	parī	paribus	paribus
ACC.	parem	pār	parēs (-īs)	paria
ABL.	parī	parī	paribus	paribus

Present Participle

	SINGULAR		PLURAL	
	M., F.	N.	M., F.	N.
NOM.	portāns	portāns	portantēs	portantia
GEN.	portantis	portantis	portantium	portantium
DAT.	portantī	portantī	portantibus	portantibus
ACC.	portantem	portāns	portantēs (-īs)	portantia
ABL.	portante (-ī)	portante (-ī)	portantibus	portantibus

Comparison of Adjectives and Adverbs

POSITIVE		COMPARATIVE		SUPERLATIVE	
ADJ.	ADV.	ADJ.	ADV.	ADJ.	ADV.
altus	altē	altior	altius	altissimus	altissimē
fortis	fortiter	fortior	fortius	fortissimus	fortissimē
līber	līberē	līberior	līberius	līberrimus	līberrimē
ācer	ācriter	ācrior	ācrius	ācerrimus	ācerrimē
facilis	facile[4]	facilior	facilius	facillimus	facillimē

[4]This form is slightly irregular.

Irregular Comparison of Adjectives

POSITIVE	COMPARATIVE	SUPERLATIVE
bon**us, -a, -um**	mel**ior, -ius**	opt**imus, -a, -um**
mal**us, -a, -um**	pe**ior, -ius**	pess**imus, -a, -um**
magn**us, -a, -um**	ma**ior, -ius**	max**imus, -a, -um**
parv**us, -a, -um**	min**or, -us**	min**imus, -a, -um**
mult**us, -a, -um**	—, plūs	plūr**imus, -a, -um**

Declension of Comparatives

	SINGULAR		PLURAL		SINGULAR	PLURAL	
	M., F.	N.	M., F.	N.	N.	M., F.	N.
NOM.	altior	altius	altiōr**es**	altiōr**a**	plūs	plūr**ēs**	plura
GEN.	altiōr**is**	altiōr**is**	altiōr**um**	altiōr**um**	plūr**is**	plūr**ium**	plūr**ium**
DAT.	altiōr**ī**	altiōr**ī**	altiōr**ibus**	altiōr**ibus**	——	plūr**ibus**	plūr**ibus**
ACC.	altiōr**em**	altius	altiōr**ēs (-īs)**	altiōr**a**	plūs	plūr**ēs**	plūr**a**
ABL.	altiōr**e**	altiōr**e**	altiōr**ibus**	altiōr**ibus**	plūr**e**	plūr**ibus**	plūr**ibus**

Declension of Numerals and Pronominal Adjectives

	M.	F.	N.	M.	F.	N.
NOM.	ūn**us**	ūn**a**	ūn**um**	duo	du**ae**	duo
GEN.	ūn**īus**	ūn**īus**	un**īus**	du**ōrum**	du**ārum**	du**ōrum**
DAT.	ūn**ī**	ūn**ī**	ūn**ī**	du**ōbus**	du**ābus**	du**ōbus**
ACC.	ūn**um**	ūn**am**	ūn**um**	du**ōs**	du**ās**	duo
ABL.	ūn**ō**	ūn**ā**	ūn**ō**	du**ōbus**	du**ābus**	du**ōbus**

	M., F.	N.	M., F., N. *(adj.)*	N. *(noun)*
NOM.	tr**ēs**	tr**ia**	mīlle	mīl**ia**
GEN.	tr**ium**	tr**ium**	mīlle	mīl**ium**
DAT.	tr**ibus**	tr**ibus**	mīlle	mīl**ibus**
ACC.	tr**ēs (-īs)**	tr**ia**	mīlle	mīl**ia**
ABL.	tr**ibus**	tr**ibus**	mīlle	mīl**ibus**

Like **ūnus** are **alius, alter, neuter, nūllus, sōlus, tōtus,** and **ūllus.** The nominative and accusative singular neuter of **alius** is **aliud;** for the genitive singular, **alterius** is generally used.

Numerals

	ROMAN NUMERALS	CARDINALS	ORDINALS
1	I	ūnus, -a, -um	prīmus, -a, -um
2	II	duo, duae, duo	secundus (alter), -a, -um
3	III	trēs, tria	tertius, -a, um
4	IIII *or* IV	quattuor	quārtus, etc.
5	V	quīnque	quīntus
6	VI	sex	sextus
7	VII	septem	septimus
8	VIII	octō	octāvus
9	VIIII *or* IX	novem	nōnus
10	X	decem	decimus
11	XI	ūndecim	ūndecimus
12	XII	duodecim	duodecimus
13	XIII	tredecim	tertius decimus
14	XIIII *or* XIV	quattuordecim	quārtus decimus
15	XV	quīndecim	quīntus decimus
16	XVI	sēdecim	sextus decimus
17	XVII	septendecim	septimus decimus
18	XVIII	duodēvīgintī	duodēvīcēsimus
19	XVIIII *or* XIX	ūndēvīgintī	ūndēvīcēsimus
20	XX	vīgintī	vīcēsimus
21	XXI	vīgintī ūnus *or* ūnus et vīgintī	vīcēsimus prīmus *or* ūnus et vīcēsimus
30	XXX	trīgintā	trīcēsimus
40	XXXX *or* XL	quadrāgintā	quadrāgēsimus
50	L	quīnquāgintā	quīnquāgēsimus
60	LX	sexāgintā	sexāgēsimus
70	LXX	septuāgintā	septuāgēsimus
80	LXXX	octōgintā	octōgēsimus
90	LXXXX *or* XC	nōnāgintā	nōnāgēsimus
100	C	centum	centēsimus
101	CI	centum (et) ūnus	centēsimus (et) prīmus
200	CC	ducentī, -ae, -a	ducentēsimus
300	CCC	trecentī, -ae, -a	trecentēsimus
400	CCCC	quadringentī, -ae, -a	quadringentēsimus
500	D	quīngentī, -ae, -a	quīngentēsimus
600	DC	sescentī, -ae, -a	sescentēsimus
700	DCC	septingentī, -ae, -a	septingentēsimus
800	DCCC	octingentī, -ae, -a	octingentēsimus
900	DCCCC	nōngentī, -ae, -a	nōngentēsimus
1000	M	mīlle	mīllēsimus
2000	MM	duo mīlia	bis mīllēsimus

Pronouns

Personal

	SING.	PL.	SING.	PL.	M.	F.	N.
NOM.	**ego**	**nōs**	**tū**	**vōs**	**is**	**ea**	**id**
GEN.	**meī**	**nostrum** (**nostrī**)	**tuī**	**vestrum** (**vestrī**)	(Used as third person pronoun. For full declension see **Demonstratives** below.)		
DAT.	**mihi**	**nōbīs**	**tibi**	**vōbīs**			
ACC.	**mē**	**nōs**	**tē**	**vōs**			
ABL.	**me**	**nōbīs**	**tē**	**vōbīs**			

Reflexive

	FIRST PERSON SING. AND PL.	SECOND PERSON SING. AND PL.	THIRD PERSON SING. AND PL.
GEN.	Decline like	Decline like	**suī**
DAT.	**ego** above.	**tū** above.	**sibi**
ACC.			**sē (sēsē)**
ABL.			**sē (sēsē)**

Reflexives are not used in the nominative and therefore have no nominative form.

Demonstrative

	SINGULAR			PLURAL		
	M.	F.	N.	M.	F.	N.
NOM.	**hic**	**haec**	**hoc**	**hī**	**hae**	**haec**
GEN.	**huius**	**huius**	**huius**	**hōrum**	**hārum**	**hōrum**
DAT.	**huic**	**huic**	**huic**	**hīs**	**hīs**	**hīs**
ACC.	**hunc**	**hanc**	**hoc**	**hōs**	**hās**	**haec**
ABL.	**hōc**	**hāc**	**hōc**	**hīs**	**hīs**	**hīs**
NOM.	**is**	**ea**	**id**	**eī (iī)**	**eae**	**ea**
GEN.	**eius**	**eius**	**eius**	**eōrum**	**eārum**	**eōrum**
DAT.	**eī**	**eī**	**eī**	**eīs (iīs)**	**eīs (iīs)**	**eīs (iīs)**
ACC.	**eum**	**eam**	**id**	**eōs**	**eās**	**ea**
ABL.	**eō**	**eā**	**eō**	**eīs (iīs)**	**eīs (iīs)**	**eīs (iīs)**

	SINGULAR			PLURAL		
	M.	F.	N.	M.	F.	N.
NOM.	**īdem**	**eadem**	**idem**	**eīdem**	**eaedem**	**eadem**
GEN.	**eiusdem**	**eiusdem**	**eiusdem**	**eōrundem**	**eārundem**	**eōrundem**
DAT.	**eīdem**	**eīdem**	**eīdem**	**eīsdem**	**eīsdem**	**eīsdem**
ACC.	**eundem**	**eandem**	**idem**	**eōsdem**	**eāsdem**	**eadem**
ABL.	**eōdem**	**eādem**	**eōdem**	**eīsdem**	**eīsdem**	**eīsdem**

	SINGULAR			PLURAL		
	M.	F.	N.	M.	F.	N.
NOM.	ille	illa	illud	illī	illae	illa
GEN.	illīus	illīus	illīus	illōrum	illārum	illōrum
DAT.	illī	illī	illī	illīs	illīs	illīs
ACC.	illum	illam	illud	illōs	illās	illa
ABL.	illō	illā	illō	illīs	illīs	illīs

	SINGULAR			PLURAL		
	M.	F.	N.	M.	F.	N.
NOM.	ipse	ipsa	ipsum	ipsī	ipsae	ipsa
GEN.	ipsīus	ipsīus	ipsīus	ipsōrum	ipsārum	ipsōrum
DAT.	ipsī	ipsī	ipsī	ipsīs	ipsīs	ipsīs
ACC.	ipsum	ipsam	ipsum	ipsōs	ipsās	ipsa
ABL.	ipsō	ipsā	ipsō	ipsīs	ipsīs	ipsīs

Relative

	SINGULAR			PLURAL		
	M.	F.	N.	M.	F.	N.
NOM.	quī	quae	quod	quī	quae	quae
GEN.	cuius	cuius	cuius	quōrum	quārum	quōrum
DAT.	cui	cui	cui	quibus	quibus	quibus
ACC.	quem	quam	quod	quōs	quās	quae
ABL.	quō	quā	quō	quibus	quibus	quibus

Interrogative

	SINGULAR			PLURAL		
	M., F.	N.		M.	F.	N.
NOM.	quis?	quid?		quī?	quae?	quae?
GEN.	cuius?	cuius?		quōrum?	quārum?	quōrum?
DAT.	cui?	cui?		quibus?	quibus?	quibus?
ACC.	quem?	quid?		quōs?	quās?	quae?
ABL.	quō?	quō?		quibus?	quibus?	quibus?

Verbs

First Conjugation

PRINCIPAL PARTS: **portō, portāre, portāvī, portātus**

<table>
<tr><td></td><td colspan="2" align="center">ACTIVE</td><td colspan="2" align="center">PASSIVE</td></tr>
<tr><td colspan="5" align="center">INDICATIVE</td></tr>
</table>

PRESENT — *I carry*, etc. / *I am carried*, etc.

portō	portāmus	portor	portāmur
portās	portātis	portāris	portāminī
portat	portant	portātur	portantur

IMPERFECT — *I was carrying*, etc. / *I was (being) carried*, etc.

portābam	portābāmus	portābar	portābāmur
portābās	portābātis	portābāris	portābāminī
portābat	portābant	portābātur	portābantur

FUTURE — *I shall (will) carry*, etc. / *I shall (will) be carried*, etc.

portābō	portābimus	portābor	portābimur
portābis	portābitis	portāberis	portābiminī
portābit	portābunt	portābitur	portabuntur

PERFECT — *I carried, have carried*, etc. / *I was carried, have been carried*, etc.

portāvī	portāvimus		
portāvistī	portāvistis		
portāvit	portāvērunt		

portātus (-a, -um) { sum / es / est }   portātī (-ae, -a) { sumus / estis / sunt }

PLUPERFECT — *I had carried*, etc. / *I had been carried*, etc.

portāveram	portāverāmus		
portāverās	portāverātis		
portāverat	portāverant		

portātus (-a, -um) { eram / erās / erat }   portātī (-ae, -a) { erāmus / erātis / erant }

FUTURE PERFECT — *I shall (will) have carried*, etc. / *I shall (will) have been carried*, etc.

portāverō	portāverimus		
portāveris	portāveritis		
portāverit	portāverint		

portātus (-a, -um) { erō / eris / erit }   portātī (-ae, -a) { erimus / eritis / erunt }

INFINITIVE

	ACTIVE	PASSIVE
PRESENT	portāre, *to carry*	portārī, *to be carried*
PERFECT	portāvisse, *to have carried*	portātus esse, *to have been carried*
FUTURE	portātūrus esse, *to be going to carry*	

PARTICIPLE

	ACTIVE	PASSIVE
PRESENT	portāns, *carrying*	
PERFECT		portātus *(having been) carried*
FUTURE	portātūrus, *going to carry*	

IMPERATIVE

PRESENT — *carry*

portā	portāte

Second Conjugation

PRINCIPAL PARTS: **doceō, docēre, docuī, doctus**

INDICATIVE

PRESENT   *I teach*, etc.   *I am taught*, etc.

doceō	docēmus	doceor	docēmur
docēs	docētis	docēris	docēminī
docet	docent	docētur	docentur

IMPERFECT   *I was teaching*, etc.   *I was (being) taught*, etc.

docēbam	docēbāmus	docēbar	docēbāmur
docēbās	docēbātis	docēbāris	docēbāminī
docēbat	docēbant	docēbātur	docēbantur

FUTURE   *I shall (will) teach*, etc.   *I shall (will) be taught*, etc.

docēbō	docēbimus	docēbor	docēbimur
docēbis	docēbitis	docēberis	docēbiminī
docēbit	docēbunt	docēbitur	docēbuntur

PERFECT   *I taught, have taught*, etc.   *I was taught, have been taught*, etc.

docuī	docuimus		**sum**		**sumus**
docuistī	docuistis	doctus	**es**	doctī	**estis**
docuit	docuērunt	**(-a, -um)**	**est**	**(-ae, -a)**	**sunt**

PLUPERFECT   *I had taught*, etc.   *I had been taught*, etc.

docueram	docuerāmus		**eram**		**erāmus**
docuerās	docuerātis	doctus	**erās**	doctī	**erātis**
docuerat	docuerant	**(-a, -um)**	**erat**	**(-ae, -a)**	**erant**

FUTURE   *I shall (will) have taught*, etc.   *I shall (will) have been taught*, etc.
PERFECT

docuerō	docuerimus		**erō**		**erimus**
docueris	docueritis	doctus	**eris**	doctī	**eritis**
docuerit	docuerint	**(-a, -um)**	**erit**	**(-ae, -a)**	**erunt**

INFINITIVE

PRESENT	docēre, *to teach*	docērī, *to be taught*
PERFECT	docuisse, *to have taught*	doctus esse, *to have been taught*
FUTURE	doctūrus esse, *to be going to teach*	

PARTICIPLE

PRESENT	docēns, *teaching*	
PERFECT		doctus, *(having been) taught*
FUTURE	doctūrus, *going to teach*	

IMPERATIVE

PRESENT   *teach*

docē	docēte

| ACTIVE | PASSIVE |

Third Conjugation

PRINCIPAL PARTS: **pōnō, pōněre, posuī, positus**

INDICATIVE

PRESENT

I put, place, etc.		*I am placed*, etc.	
pōnō	pōnimus	pōnor	pōnimur
pōnis	pōnitis	pōneris	pōniminī
pōnit	pōnunt	pōnitur	pōnuntur

IMPERFECT

I was placing, etc.		*I was (being) placed*, etc.	
pōnēbam	pōnēbāmus	pōnēbar	pōnēbāmur
pōnēbās	pōnēbātis	pōnēbāris	pōnēbāminī
pōnēbat	pōnēbant	pōnēbātur	pōnēbantur

FUTURE

I shall (will) place, etc.		*I shall (will) be placed*, etc.	
ponam	pōnēmus	pōnar	pōnēmur
pōnēs	pōnētis	pōnēris	pōnēminī
pōnet	pōnent	pōnētur	pōnentur

PERFECT

I placed, have placed, etc.		*I was placed, have been placed*, etc.			
posuī	posuimus	positus	sum	positī	sumus
posuistī	posuistis	(-a, -um)	es	(-ae, -a)	estis
posuit	posuērunt		est		sunt

PLUPERFECT

I had placed, etc.		*I had been placed*, etc.			
posueram	posuerāmus	positus	eram	positī	erāmus
posuerās	posuerātis	(-a, -um)	erās	(-ae, -a)	erātis
posuerat	posuerant		erat		erant

FUTURE PERFECT

I shall (will) have placed, etc.		*I shall (will) have been placed*, etc.			
posuerō	posuerimus	positus	erō	positī	erimus
posueris	posueritis	(-a, -um)	eris	(-ae, -a)	eritis
posuerit	posuerint		erit		erunt

INFINITIVE

PRESENT	pōnere, *to put, place*	pōnī, *to be placed*
PERFECT	posuisse, *to have placed*	positus esse, *to have been placed*
FUTURE	positūrus esse, *to be going to place*	

PARTICIPLE

PRESENT	pōnēns, *placing*	
PERFECT		positus, *(having been) placed*
FUTURE	positūrus, *going to place*	

IMPERATIVE

PRESENT *place*

pōne	pōnite

Third Conjugation -iō Verbs

PRINCIPAL PARTS: **capiō, capĕre, cēpī, captus**

INDICATIVE

PRESENT *I take,* etc.   *I am taken,* etc.

capiō	capimus	capior	capimur
capis	capitis	caperis	capiminī
capit	capiunt	capitur	capiuntur

IMPERFECT *I was taking,* etc.   *I was (being) taken,* etc.

capiēbam	capiēbāmus	capiēbar	capiēbāmur
capiēbās	capiēbātis	capiēbāris	capiēbāminī
capiēbat	capiēbant	capiēbātur	capiēbantur

FUTURE *I shall (will) take,* etc.   *I shall (will) be taken,* etc.

capiam	capiēmus	capiar	capiēmur
capiēs	capiētis	capiēris	capiēminī
capiet	capient	capiētur	capientur

PERFECT *I took, have taken,* etc. *I was taken, have been taken,* etc.

cēpī	cēpimus		sum		sumus
cēpistī	cēpistis	captus	es	captī	estis
cēpit	cēpērunt	(-a, -um) { est	(-ae, -a) { sunt

PLUPERFECT *I had taken,* etc.   *I had been taken,* etc.

cēperam	cēperāmus		eram		erāmus
cēperās	cēperātis	captus	eras	capti	erātis
cēperat	cēperant	(-a, -um) { erat	(-ae, -a) { erant

FUTURE *I shall (will) have taken,* etc. *I shall (will) have been taken,* etc.

PERFECT

cēperō	cēperimus		erō		erimus
cēperis	cēperitis	captus	eris	capti	eritis
cēperit	cēperint	(-a, -um) { erit	(-ae, -a) { erunt

INFINITIVE

PRESENT capere, *to take*   capī, *to be taken*
PERFECT cēpisse, *to have taken*   captus esse, *to have been taken*
FUTURE captūrus esse, *to be going to take*

PARTICIPLE

PRESENT capiēns, *taking*
PERFECT   captus, *(having been) taken*
FUTURE captūrus, *going to take*

IMPERATIVE

PRESENT *take*
     cape   capite

		ACTIVE		PASSIVE	

ACTIVE   PASSIVE

Fourth Conjugation

PRINCIPAL PARTS: mūniō, mūnīre, mūnīvī, mūnītus

INDICATIVE

PRESENT   *I fortify*, etc.   *I am fortified*, etc.

mūniō	mūnīmus	mūnior	mūnīmur
mūnīs	mūnītis	mūnīris	mūnīminī
mūnit	mūniunt	mūnītur	mūniuntur

IMPERFECT   *I was fortifying*, etc.   *I was (being) fortified*, etc.

mūniēbam	mūniēbāmus	mūniēbar	mūniēbāmur
mūniēbās	mūniēbātis	mūniēbāris	mūniēbāminī
mūniēbat	mūniēbant	mūniēbātur	mūniēbantur

FUTURE   *I shall (will) fortify*, etc.   *I shall (will) be fortified*, etc.

mūniam	mūniēmus	mūniar	mūniēmur
mūniēs	mūniētis	mūniēris	mūniēminī
mūniet	mūnient	mūniētur	mūnientur

PERFECT   *I fortified, have fortified*, etc.   *I was fortified, have been fortified*, etc.

mūnīvī	mūnīvimus
mūnīvistī	mūnīvistis
mūnīvit	mūnīvērunt

mūnītus (-a, -um)	{ sum es est }	mūnītī (-ae, -a)	{ sumus estis sunt }

PLUPERFECT   *I had fortified*, etc.   *I had been fortified*, etc.

mūnīveram	mūnīverāmus
mūnīverās	mūnīverātis
mūnīverat	mūnīverant

mūnītus (-a, -um)	{ eram erās erat }	mūnītī (-ae, -a)	{ erāmus erātis erant }

FUTURE PERFECT   *I shall (will) have fortified*, etc.   *I shall (will) have been fortified*, etc.

mūnīverō	mūnīverimus
mūnīveris	mūnīveritis
mūnīverit	mūnīverint

mūnītus (-a, -um)	{ erō eris erit }	mūnītī (-ae, -a)	{ erimus eritis erunt }

INFINITIVE

PRESENT	mūnīre, *to fortify*	mūnīrī, *to be fortified*
PERFECT	mūnīvisse, *to have fortified*	mūnītus esse, *to have been fortified*
FUTURE	mūnītūrus esse, *to be going to fortify*	

PARTICIPLE

PRESENT	mūniēns, *fortifying*	
PERFECT		mūnītus, *(having been) fortified*
FUTURE	mūnītūrus, *going to fortify*	

IMPERATIVE

PRESENT   *fortify*

mūnī	mūnīte

Irregular Verbs

PRINCIPAL PARTS: **sum, esse, fuī, futūrus**

INDICATIVE

PRESENT — *I am, you are*, etc.

su**m**	su**mus**
es	es**tis**
es**t**	su**nt**

IMPERFECT — *I was, you were*, etc.

er**am**	er**āmus**
er**ās**	er**ātis**
er**at**	er**ant**

FUTURE — *I shall (will) be*, etc.

er**ō**	er**imus**
er**is**	er**itis**
er**it**	er**unt**

PERFECT — *I was*, etc.

fu**ī**	fu**imus**
fu**istī**	fu**istis**
fu**it**	fu**ērunt**

PLUPERFECT — *I had been*, etc.

fu**eram**	fu**erāmus**
fu**erās**	fu**erātis**
fu**erat**	fu**erant**

FUTURE PERFECT — *I shall (will) have been*, etc.

fu**erō**	fu**erimus**
fu**eris**	fu**eritis**
fu**erit**	fu**erint**

INFINITIVE

PRESENT	es**se**, *to be*
PERFECT	fu**isse**, *to have been*
FUTURE	fut**ūrus esse**, *to be going to be*

PARTICIPLE

FUTURE	fut**ūrus**, *going to be*

IMPERATIVE

PRESENT — *be*

es	es**te**

PRINCIPAL PARTS: **possum, posse, potuī, ——**

INDICATIVE

PRESENT — *I am able, I can*, etc.

pos**sum**	pos**sumus**
pot**es**	pot**estis**
pot**est**	pos**sunt**

IMPERFECT — *I was able, I could*, etc.

pot**eram**	pot**erāmus**
pot**erās**	pot**erātis**
pot**erat**	pot**erant**

FUTURE — *I shall (will) be able*, etc.

pot**erō**	pot**erimus**
pot**eris**	pot**eritis**
pot**erit**	pot**erunt**

PERFECT — *I was able, I could,* etc.

pot**uī**	pot**uimus**
pot**uistī**	pot**uistis**
pot**uit**	pot**uērunt**

PLUPERFECT — *I had been able*, etc.

pot**ueram**	pot**uerāmus**
pot**uerās**	pot**uerātis**
pot**uerat**	pot**uerant**

FUTURE PERFECT — *I shall (will) have been able*, etc.

pot**uerō**	pot**uerimus**
pot**ueris**	pot**ueritis**
pot**uerit**	pot**uerint**

INFINITIVE

PRESENT	pos**se**, *to be able*
PERFECT	pot**uisse**, *to have been able*
FUTURE	——

PARTICIPLE

PRESENT	pot**ēns** *(adj.)*, *powerful*

Basic Syntax

Agreement

1. *Adjectives.* Adjectives and participles agree in gender, number, and case with the nouns they modify. Adjectives standing alone are often used as nouns.

2. *Verbs.* Verbs agree in person and number with their subjects. When two subjects are connected by **aut, aut... aut, neque... neque,** the verb agrees with the nearer subject.

3. *Relative Pronouns.* A relative pronoun agrees in gender and number with its antecedent, but its case depends upon its use in its own clause.

4. *Appositives.* Appositives regularly agree in case with the nouns or pronouns they describe and usually follow them.

Noun Syntax

Nominative

1. *Subject.* The subject of a verb is in the nominative.

2. *Predicate.* A noun or adjective used in the predicate after a linking verb (*is, are, seem*, etc.) to complete its meaning is in the nominative.

Genitive

1. *Possession.* The possessor is expressed by the genitive.

2. *Description.* The genitive, if modified by an adjective, may be used to describe a person or thing.

3. *Partitive.* The whole of which something is a part is in the genitive.

Dative

1. *Indirect Object.* The indirect object of a verb is in the dative. It is used with verbs of giving, reporting, telling, etc.

2. *With Special Verbs.* The dative is used with a few intransitive verbs, such as **noceō.**

3. *With Adjectives.* The dative is used with certain adjectives, as **amīcus, pār, similis,** and their opposites.

Accusative

1. *Direct Object.* The direct object of a transitive verb is in the accusative.

2. *Extent.* Extent of time or space is expressed by the accusative.

3. *Place to which.* The accusative with **ad** *(to)* or **in** *(into)* expresses *place to which.*

4. *Subject of Infinitive.* The subject of an infinitive is in the accusative.

5. *With Prepositions.* The accusative is used with the prepositions **ad, ante, apud, circum, contrā, inter, ob, per, post, super,** and **trāns;** also with **in** and **sub** when they show the direction toward which a thing moves.

Ablative

1. *Place from which.* The ablative with **ab, dē,** or **ex** expresses *place from which.*
2. *Agent.* The ablative with **ā** or **ab** is used with a passive verb to show the person (or animal) *by whom* something is done.
3. *Accompaniment.* The ablative with **cum** expresses *accompaniment.*
4. *Manner.* The ablative of manner with **cum** describes *how* something is done. **Cum** may be omitted if an adjective is used with the noun.
5. *Means.* The means by which a thing is done is expressed by the ablative without a preposition.
6. *Description.* The ablative without a preposition is used (like the genitive) to describe a person or thing.
7. *Place where.* The ablative with **in** expresses *place where.*
8. *Time when. Time when* is expressed by the ablative without a preposition.
9. *Respect.* The ablative without a preposition is used to tell *in what respect* the statement applies.
10. *Absolute.* A noun in the ablative used with a participle, adjective, or other noun in the same case and having no grammatical connection with any other word in its clause is called an *ablative absolute.*
11. *With Prepositions.* The ablative is used with the prepositions **ab, cum, dē, ex, prae, prō, sine;** also with **in** and **sub** when they indicate *place where.*

Vocative

The *vocative* is used in addressing a person.

Locative

The *locative* is used in certain nouns to express *place in* or *at which.*

Verb Syntax
Tenses

1. *Imperfect.* Repeated, customary, or continuous action in the past is expressed by the imperfect.
2. *Perfect.* An action completed in the past is expressed by the perfect. It is translated by the English simple past or present perfect.

Participles

1. The tenses of the participle (present, perfect, future) indicate time present, past, or future *from the standpoint of the main verb.*
2. Perfect participles are often used as simple adjectives and, like adjectives, may be used as nouns.
3. The Latin participle is often a one-word substitute for a subordinate clause in English introduced by *who* or *which*, *when* or *after*, *since* or *because*, *although*, and *if.*

Infinitive

1. The infinitive is a verbal indeclinable singular neuter noun, and as such it may be used as the subject of a verb.
2. The infinitive, like other nouns, may be used as the direct object of many verbs.
3. The infinitive object of some verbs, such as **iubeō** and **doceō,** often has a noun or pronoun subject in the accusative.
4. Statements that convey indirectly the thoughts or words of another, used as the objects of verbs of *saying, thinking, knowing, hearing, perceiving,* etc., require verbs in the infinitive with subjects in the accusative.

LATIN FORMS AND PHRASES IN ENGLISH

You will be reminded daily that Latin is a living language. Almost every time you open a book, a magazine, or even a newspaper you will find an abbreviation or a phrase in Latin. A knowledge of the forms on these pages, their meanings, and how to use them correctly is one of the marks of an educated person. Partial lists are given below of 1) Latin phrases, mottoes, and quotations; 2) Latin abbreviations; 3) unchanged Latin forms in English; 4) bases of the Latin words used in English; 5) bases plus -e used in English. The last three groups especially represent only a small part of the total number. The figure after each phrase or word gives the page on which it is treated. The words without numbers are not specifically mentioned in the lessons.

Phrases, Mottoes, Quotations

ab ovo usque ad mala, **338**

ad astra per aspera (Kansas), **149**

ad infinitum, **149**

ad maiorem Dei gloriam, *to the greater glory of God*

ad nauseam, **69**

Alis volat propriis. (Oregon), **430**

Alma Mater, **355**

alter ego, **385**

Amantium irae amoris integratio est. **11**

amicus curiae, **184**

Anno Domini, **355**

Annuit coeptis. **483**

ante bellum, *before the (Civil) war* **291**

aqua et ignis, **69**

argumentum ad hominem, *argument to the man,* i.e., one that uses prejudice for or against an individual

Arma non servant modum. **335**

Ars longa, vita brevis. *Art is long, time is fleeting.*

Audemus iura nostra defendere. (Alabama), **335**

Audi et alteram partem. *Hear the other side too.*

aut Caesar aut nihil, **355**

auxilio ab alto, **164**

bona fide, **477**

Carpe diem!, **51**

casus belli, **477**

Cave canem! *Beware of the dog!*

Cedant arma togae. (Wyoming), **430**

consilio et armis, **184**

corpus delicti, *the body of the crime*, i.e., the facts of the crime

Crescit eundo. (New Mexico), **409**

cui bono? **265**

cum grano salis, *with a grain of salt*

cum laude, *with honor*

de facto, **291**

De gustibus non est disputandum. *About taste there is no disputing.*

de jure, **322**

de novo, **129**

Dei gratia, **235**

Deo gratias, **235**

Dirigo. (Maine), **355**

Disciplina (est) praesidium civitatis. *Discipline is the protection of the state.* **331**

Ditat Deus. (Arizona), **335**

Divide et impera. **480**

Dominus providebit. **335**

dramatis personae, *characters of the play*

Dulce et decorum est pro patria mori. **398**

Dum spiro spero. (South Carolina), **360**

Dux femina facti. **283**

Elizabeth regina, *Elizabeth the Queen*

Ense petit placidam sub libertate quietem. (Massachusetts), **335**

E pluribus unum, **441**

Errare est humanum. **128**

Abbreviations

Latin Forms in English[1]

abacus	Cornelius	Julius	quietus
actor	corona	junior	Quintus
addendum	curriculum	labor	rabies
affidavit	datum (data)	larva	radius
agenda	deficit	Lavinia	ratio
alibi	delirium	Leo	rebus
Alma	dictum	locus	recipe
alumna	discus	major	regalia
alumnus	doctor	mandamus	requiem
amanuensis	duplex	Marcia	rostrum
amoeba	erratum (errata)	maximum	Rufus
antenna	excelsior	medium	saliva
anterior	exterior	memorandum	scintilla
apex	facsimile	militia	senior
apparatus	factor	minimum	September, etc.
appendix	fibula	minister	series
arbiter	focus	minor	simile
area	formula	minus	simplex
arena	forte	minutiae	sinister
atrium	forum	miser	specie
Augustus	fungus	monitor	species
aurora	genius	nausea	specimen
axis	genus	nebula	spectrum
bacillus	gladiolus	neuter	stamen
bacterium	gratis	nostrum	status
basis	habitat	nova	Stella
bonus	honor	octavo	stimulus
camera	ignoramus	omnibus	stratum
campus	impedimenta	onus	superior
cancer	impetus	opera	Sylvester
candelabrum	impromptu	opus	tenet
Cecilia	index	papilla	terror
census	inertia	par	ulterior
circus	inferior	pauper	vertebra
Clara	insignia	penna	vertex
Claudia	insomnia	plus	vesper
codex	integer	posterior	veto
consensus	interceptor	prior	via
consul	interior	prospectus	victor
copula	inventor	pupa	viscera
Cornelia	Julia	quarto	

[1]This is only a partial list. For a list of 7000 Latin words in English see *Classical Journal,* 48 (1952), pp. 85–108.

English Words From Latin Base[2]

accept	deception	instant	rapt
act	defend	intellect	ration
agent	desert	intercept	region
alien	duct	invent	remiss
apt	effect	just	script
ascend	excess	laud	sermon
audit	expedient	oration	session
client	export	part	sign
consist	familiar	perfect	tangent
consult	firm	pomp	tend
contend	form	position	timid
convenient	fort	press	urban
convent	front	prohibit	verb
credit	habit	prospect	
cult	habitat	public	
debit	incipient	quart	

English Words From Latin Base Plus -*e*[3]

Belle	explore	mode	response
cause	extreme	nature	senate
cede	facile	plane	sense
commune	false	prime	sole
conserve	fame	probe	solve
convene	fortune	produce	statue
cure	grave	pulse	statute
defense	legate	reduce	tribute
discipline	liberate	remote	urbane
divide	mandate	remove	verse

[2]There are many other words with suffixes -*al, -an, -ant, -ar, -ent, - ic, -id, -ion*.
[3]There are many other words derived from the present stem and perfect participle of verbs; there are also many more nouns and adjectives with suffixes -*tude, -ure, -ile, -ane, -ive, -ose*.

The Star-Spangled Banner

Ōh, potestne cernī, praefulgente diē,
Salūtātum signum circā noctis adventum?
Lātī clāv(ī) et stēllae, dēcertant(e) aciē,
Glōriōsē cingunt oppidī mūnīmentum!
Iaculumque rubēns, globus sūrsum rumpēns
Per noctem mōnstrant vexillum fulgēns.
Stēllātumne vexillum volāns tegit nōs,
Patriam līberam fortiumque domōs?

Tr. F. A. Geyser

Adeste Fidēlēs[4]

Adeste, fidēlēs,
Laetī triumphantēs;
Venīte, venīte in Bethlehem;
Nātum vidēte
Rēgem angelōrum;
Venīte adōrēmus, venīte adōrēmus,
Venīte adōrēmus Dominum.

Cantet nunc "Iō!"
Chorus angelōrum;
Cantet nunc aula caelestium:
"Glōria, glōria
In excelsīs Deō!"
Venīte, etc.

Ergō quī nātus
Diē hodiernā,
Iēsū, tibi sit glōria;
Patris aeternī
Verbum carō factum!
Venīte, etc.

[4]Also known as "The Portuguese Hymn"; sung to the same tune as its translation, "O Come, All Ye Faithful."

The greatest of all medieval student songs.
*In 1860 the composer Brahms used its
melody in the glorious climax to his
"Academic Festival Overture."*

GAUDEAMUS IGITUR

Student Song

1. Gau-de-a-mus i-gi-tur, Iu-ve-nes dum
2. Vi-vat a-ca-de-mi-a, Vi-vant pro-fes-
3. Vi-vat et res pu-bli-ca Et qui il-lam

su - mus; Post iu-cun-dam iu-ven-tu-tem,
so - res, Vi-vat mem-brum quod-li-bet,
re - git; Vi-vat nos-tra ci-vi-tas;

Post mo-les-tam se-nec-tu-tem, Nos ha-be-bit
Vi-vant mem-bra quae-li-bet, Sem-per sint in
Vi-vat haec so-da-li-tas Quae nos huc col-

hu - mus, Nos ha-be-bit hu - mus.
flo - re, Sem-per sint in flo - re.
le - git, Quae nos huc col-le-git.

INTEGER VITAE

Horace, Odes I. 22 (ca. 25 b.c.)   Dr. F. F. Flemming, ca. 1811

1. In - te - ger vi - tae sce - le - ris - que
2. Si - ve per Syr - tes i - ter aes - tu -
3. Nam - que me sil - va lu - pus in Sa -

pu - rus Non e - get Mau - ris ia - cu - lis ne -
o - sas, Si - ve fac - tu - rus per in - hos - pi -
bi - na, Dum me - am can - to La - la - gen et

qu(e) ar - cu Nec ve - ne - na - tis gra - vi - da sa -
ta - lem Cau - ca - sum vel quae lo - ca fa - bu -
ul - tra Ter - mi - num cu - ris va - gor ex - pe -

git - tis, Fus - ce, pha - re - tra,
lo - sus Lam - bit Hy - das - pes.
di - tis, Fu - git in - er - mem.

The theme of this ode is that the virtuous man needs no defense. The poem was later converted into a Christian hymn; the idea was one that Christians also accepted.

DICTIONARY

Latin–English

Proper names are not included unless they are spelled differently in English or are difficult to pronounce in English. Their English pronunciation is indicated by a simple system. The vowels are as follows: ā as in *hate*, ă as in *hat*, ē as in *feed*, ĕ as in *fed*, ī as in *bite*, ĭ as in *bit*, ō as in *hope*, ŏ as in *hop*, ū as in *cute*, ŭ as in *cut*. In the ending *ēs* the *s* is soft as in *rose*. When the accented syllable ends in a consonant, the vowel is short; otherwise it is long. The reference numbers after each entry indicate the lesson in which the word is introduced.

A

ā, ab, *(prep. w. abl.)* away from, from, by **13**

absum, abesse, āfuī, āfutūrus, be away, be absent **30**

ac, (*see* **atque**)

accēdō, -ere, accessī, accessūrus, approach **19**

accidō, -ere, accidī, —, *(w. dat.)* fall to, befall, happen **63**

accipiō, -ere, accēpī, acceptus, receive **20**

ācer, ācris, ācre, sharp, keen, fierce **60**

ad, *(prep. w. acc.)* to, toward, for, near **6**

addūcō, -ere, addūxī, adductus, lead to, influence **43**

adiuvō, -āre, -ūvī, -ūtus, help

adōrō, -āre, -āvī, -ātus, worship

adsum, -esse, adfuī, adfutūrus, be near, be present **34**

adulēscentulus, -ī, *m.*, young man

aeger, aegra, aegrum, sick, ill

Aegyptiī, -ōrum, *m. pl.* the Egyptians

Aegyptus, -ī, *f.*, Egypt

Aenēās, -ae, *m.*, Aeneas (Enē′as)

Aeolus, -ī, *m.*, Aeolus (E′olus)

aequus, -a, -um, even, just, calm **18**

āēr, āeris, *m.,* air

aes, aeris, *n.,* copper, bronze

aestās, -ātis, *f.,* summer **51**

aetās, -ātis, *f.*, age, time **61**

Aetna, -ae, *f.*, (Mt.) Etna

afficiō, -ere, affēcī, affectus, affect, afflict with **23**

Āfricānus -ī, *m.*, Africā′nus

ager, agrī, *m.,* field **14**

agō, -ere, ēgī, āctus, do, drive, discuss, live, spend time **19**; **grātiās agō,** thank; **vītam agō,** lead a life

agricola, -ae, *m.*, farmer **3**

āla, -ae, *f.,* wing

albus, -a, -um, white

aliēnus, -a, -um, another's, unfavorable **57**

aliquandō, *(adv.)* sometimes

alius, alia, aliud, other, another; **alius... alius,** one . . . another; **aliī... aliī,** some . . . others **56**

Alpēs, -ium, *f. pl.,* the Alps

alter, altera, alterum, the other; **alter... alter,** the one . . . the other **56**

altus, -a, -um, high, tall, deep **12**

ambō, -ae, -ō, both

ambulō, -āre, -āvī, -ātus, walk

Americānus, -a, -um, American; **Americānus, -ī,** *m.*, an American

amīcitia, -ae, *f.*, friendship **11**

amīcus, -a, -um, friendly **14**; **amīcus, -ī,** *m.*, **amīca, -ae,** *f.*, friend **7**

āmittō, -ere, āmīsī, āmissus, let go, lose **29**

amō, -āre, -āvī, -ātus, love, like **3**

amor, -ōris, *m.,* love

amphitheātrum, -ī, *n.,* amphitheater

Anglicus, -a, -um, English

anima, -ae, *f.,* breath, spirit

animus, -ī, *m.*, mind, courage, spirit **15**

annus, -ī, *m.*, year **16**

ante, *(adv.)* before; *(prep. w. acc.)* before (of time or place) **39**

antecēdō, -ere, -cessī, -cessūrus, go before, go earlier **41**

antīquus, -a, -um, old, ancient

aperiō, -īre, -uī, -tus, open, uncover

appellō, -āre, -āvī, -ātus, call, name **28**

Appius, -a, -um, *(adj.)* of Appius, Appian; **Appius, -pī,** *m.,* Appius

aptus, -a, -um, fit, suitable *(w. dat.)* **62**

apud, *(prep. w. acc.)* among, in the presence of **70**

aqua, -ae, *f.,* water **1**

aquaeductus, -ūs, *m.,* aqueduct

Aquītānus, -ī, *m.,* an Aquitā´nian

arbor, -is, *f.* tree

Arcadia, -ae. *f.,* a region in Greece

arcus, -ūs, *m.,* arch, bow

arēna, -ae, *f.,* arena, sand, desert, seashore

argentum, -ī, *n.,* silver

arma, -ōrum, *n. pl.* arms, weapons **17**

ascendō, -ere, ascendī, ascēnsus, climb (up), ascend **70**

Athēna, -ae, *f.,* a Greek goddess = Minerva

atque (ac), *(conj.)* and, and even **38**

ātrium, ātrī, *n.,* atrium, entry hall

auctor, -ōris, *m.,* maker, author, writer **48**

auctōritās, -ātis, *f.,* authority, influence **49**

audācia, -ae, *f.,* boldness

audāx, audācis *(gen.),* bold, daring

audiō, -īre, -īvī, -ītus, hear **24**

augeō, -ēre, auxī, auctus, increase **10**

aureus, -a, -um, golden

aurum, -ī, *n.,* gold

aut, or; **aut... aut,** either . . . or **28**

autem, *(conj.)* however *(never first word)* **67**

autumus, -ī, *m.* autumn, fall

auxilium, -lī, *n.,* aid, help; *pl.* reinforcements **17**

āvertō, -ere, āvertī, āversus, turn away **65**

avis, avis, avium, *f.,* bird

avus, -ī, *m.,* grandfather

B

barbarus, -a, -um, *(adj.),* foreign; **barbarus, -ī,** *(noun) m.,* foreigner, barbarian **16**

Belgae, -ārum, *m. pl.,* the Belgians; the Belgian people

bellum, -ī, *n.,* war **17**

bene, *(adv.)* well **64**; *(comp.)* **melius,** better; *(superl.)* **optimē,** best, very well

beneficium, -cī, *n.,* kindness, benefit **33**

benignus, -a, -um, kind

bonus, -a, -um, good **2**; *(comp.)* **melior, melius,** better; *(superl.)* **optimus, -a, -um,** best

brevis, -ē, short, brief, small

Britannia, -ae, *f.,* Britain

Britannus, -ī, *m.,* a Briton

C

C., *abbreviation for* **Gāius**

cadō, -ere, cecidī, cāsūrus, fall **63**

Caecilius, -lī, *m.,* Caecilius (Sēsil´ius)

caecus, -a, -um, blind

caelum, -ī, *n.,* sky

Caesar, -aris, *m.,* Caesar

campus, -ī, *m.,* field

canis, -is, *m.* or *f.,* dog

canō, -ere, cecinī, cantus, sing

capiō, -ere, cēpī, captus, take, seize **20**; **cōnsilium capiō,** adopt a plan

Capitōlium, -lī, *n.,* the Capitol, temple of Jupiter at Rome; the Capitoline Hill

captīvus, -ī, *m.*; **captīva, -ae,** *f.,* prisoner **13**

caput, capitis, *n.,* head **45**

carmen, -minis, *n.,* song **45**

carrus, -ī, *m.,* cart, wagon **4**

Carthāginiēnsēs, -ium, *m. pl.,* the Carthaginians (Carthajin´ians)

Carthāgō, -ginis, *f.,* Carthage (a city in Africa); **Carthāgō Nova,** New Carthage (in Spain)

casa, -ae, *f.,* house **12**

castra, -ōrum, *n. pl.* camp **16**

cāsus, -ūs, *m.,* downfall, accident, chance, misfortune **68**

causa, -ae, *f.,* cause, reason, case **18**

cēdō, -ere, cessī, cessūrus, move (away from), retreat, yield, give way **19**

celebrō, -āre, -āvī, -ātus, celebrate, honor

celer, celeris, celere, swift, quick **47**

celeritās, -tātis, *f.,* swiftness, speed **49**

Celtae, -ārum, *m. pl.,* Celts, a people of Gaul

cēna, -ae, *f.,* dinner **13**

centum, *(indeclinable)* hundred **66**

cēra, -ae, *f.* wax

Cerēs, -eris, *f.,* Ceres (Sē´rēs), goddess of agriculture

cernō, -ere, crēvī, crētus, discern, see **42**

certus, -a, -um, fixed, sure, certain **42**

cibus, -ī, *m.,* food **5**

Cicerō, -ōnis, *m.,* Cicero (Sis´ero)

Circē, -ae, *f.,* Circe (Sir´sē), a sorceress

circum, *(prep. w. acc.)* around **67**

circus, -ī, *m.,* circle, circus (esp. the Circus Maximus at Rome)

cīvis, cīvis, cīvium, *m.* or *f.,* citizen **46**

cīvitās, -ātis, *f.,* citizenship, state **48**

clam, *(adv.)* secretly

clāmō, -āre, -āvī, -ātus, shout, cry out **40**

clāmor, -ōris, *m.,* noise, shouting **45**

clārus, -a, -um, clear, famous **5**

claudō, -ere, clausī, clausus, close **45**

cliēns, -ntis, *m.,* client, dependent

cognōmen, -minis, *n.,* surname, nickname

cognōscō, -ere, -nōvī, -nitus, learn; have learned, *(perf.)* know **39**

cōgō, -ere, coēgī, coactus, drive together, collect, compel **38**

colō, -ere, coluī, cultus, till, cultivate, worship, inhabit **54**

colōnus, -ī, *m.,* settler, colonist **15**

Colossēum, -ī, *n.,* the Colisé´um (an amphitheater at Rome)

committō, -ere, -mīsī, -missus, join together, commit, entrust **27; proelium committō,** begin battle **27**

commodus, -a, -um, suitable, convenient **22**

commoveō, -ēre, -mōvī, -mōtus, disturb, alarm **42**

commūnis, -e, common **52**

comprehendō, -ere, -hendī, -hēnsus, understand

concordia, -ae, *f.,* harmony **17**

condiciō, -ōnis, *f.,* condition, terms **61**

cōnficiō, -ere, -fēcī, -fectus, complete, exhaust, do thoroughly, do in **46**

cōnfīdō, -ere, cōnfīsus sum, have confidence in

cōnfirmō, -āre, -āvī, -ātus, make firm, encourage, establish **49**

cōnservō, -āre, -āvī, -ātus, save, preserve **37**

cōnsilium, -lī, *n.,* plan, advice **16**

cōnsistō, -ere, cōnstitī, cōnstitūrus, stand still, stop **58**

cōnspiciō, -ere, -spexī, -spectus, catch sight of, see, spot **65**

constituō, -ere, -uī, -ūtus, determine, decide

cōnsul, -ulis, *m.,* consul (the highest elected Roman official)

cōnsulō, -ere, -suluī, -sultus, consult **43**

contendō, -ere, -tendī, -tentus, struggle, hasten **57**

contineō, -ēre, -uī, -tentus, hold together, contain **24**

contrā, *(prep. w. acc.)* against **65**

conveniō, -īre, -vēnī, -ventūrus, come together **25**

convocō, -āre, -āvī, -ātus, call together **25**

cōpia, -ae, *f.,* supply, abundance **5**

cor, cordis, *n.,* heart **51**

corium, corī, *n.,* skin, leather

corōna, -ae, *f.,* crown

corpus, -poris, *n.,* body **45**

crās, *(adv.)* tomorrow **6**

crātēr, -is, *m.* large bowl

crēdō, -ere, -didī, -ditus, *(w. dat.)* believe, entrust **65**

Crēta, -ae, *f.,* Crete

cum, *(prep. w. abl.)* with **23**

Cupīdō, -inis, *m.,* Cupid (the god of love)

cupiō, -ere, cupīvī, cupītus, desire, wish, want **31**

cūr, *(adv.)* why **36**

cūra, -ae, *f.,* worry, care, concern **5**

cūrō, -āre, -āvī, -ātus, care for, cure

currō, -ere, cucurrī, cursūrus, run **50**

currus, -ūs, *m.,* chariot

cursus, -ūs, *m.* running, course, voyaging

D

dē, *(prep. w. abl.)* from, down from, about, concerning **13**

dea, -ae, *f.,* goddess **22**

dēbeō, -ēre, dēbuī, dēbitus, ought, owe **17**

decem, ten

decimus, -a, -um, tenth

dēfendō, -ere, dēfendī, dēfēnsus, defend **19**

dēlecto, -āre, -āvī, -ātus, please

dēligō, -ere, dēlēgī, dēlēctus, select

dēmōnstrō, -āre, -āvī, -ātus, show **68**

dēpōnō, -ere, dēposuī, dēpositus, put down, lay aside

dēscendō, -ere, dēscendī, dēscēnsus, descend

dēserō, -ere, dēseruī, dēsertus, desert **68**

dēsiliō, -īre, dēsiluī, dēsultus, jump down, dismount

dēspiciō, -ere, dēspexī, dēspectus, look down on, despise **68**

deus, -ī, *m.,* god **22**

dēvorō, -āre, -āvī, -ātus, swallow

dīcō, -ere, dīxī, dictus, say, tell **22**

dictātor, -ōris, *m.,* dictator

dictum, -ī, *n.,* word

diēs, diēī, *m.,* day **69**

difficilis, -e, difficult **63**

digitus, -ī, *m.,* finger

dīligentia, -ae, *f.,* diligence **35**

dīmittō, -ere, dīmīsī, dīmissus, let go, send away **31**

discēdō, -ere, -cessī, -cessūrus, go away, depart **32**

disciplīna, -ae, *f.,* training, instruction **10**

discipulus, -ī, *m.,* **discipula, -ae,** *f.,* student learner, pupil

dissimilis, -e, unlike *(w. dat.)* **63**

dīvidō, -ere, dīvīsī, dīvīsus, divide **70**

dō, dare, dedī, datus, give **35; poenam dō,** pay the penalty

doceō, -ēre, docuī, doctus, teach **10**

dominus, -ī, *m.,* master **18; domina, -ae,** *f.,* mistress

domus, -ūs, *f.,* house, home **68**

dōnō, -āre, -āvī, -ātus, give, present to (as a gift) **7**

dormiō, -īre, -īvī, -ītus, sleep

dubitō, -āre, -āvī, -ātus, hesitate, doubt **31**

dūcō, -ere, dūxī, ductus, lead, draw **21**

dulcis, -e, sweet

dum, *(conj.)* while **52**

duo, -ae, -o, two **66**

duodecim, twelve

dūrus, -a, -um, hard, harsh **2**

dux, ducis, *m.,* leader, general **40**

E

ē, ex, *(prep. w. abl.)* out from, from, out of **13**

ea, *(see* **is**)

ecce, *(interj.)* look, here!

edō, esse, ēdī, ēsus, eat

ēdūcō, -ere, ēdūxī, ēductus, lead out **34**

efficiō, -ere, effēcī, effectus, bring about, produce, effect **21**

ego, meī, *m.* or *f.,* I **31**

ēgregius, -a, -um, distinguished, excellent **33**

eius, his, her, its; **eōrum,** their, *(see* **is**) **52**

elephantus, -ī, *m.,* elephant

emō, -ere, ēmī, ēmptus, take, buy **66**

Ēpīrus, -ī, *f.,* Ēpī´rus, a province in Greece

equēs, -itis, *m.,* horseman, knight

equus, -ī, *m.,* horse **4**

ērumpō, -ere, ērūpī, ēruptus, burst forth

et, *(conj.)* and, even **1; et… et,** both . . . and **28**

etiam, *(adv.)* also, even, too **32**

Etrūscī, -ōrum, *m. pl.,* the Etruscans

Eumaeus, -ī, *m.,* Eumaeus (Ūmē´us)

Eurōpa, -ae, *f.,* Europe

ēvādō, -ere, ēvāsī, ēvāsus, go out, escape

ēvocō, -āre, -āvī, -ātus, call out, summon **16**

excēdō, -ere, excessī, excessūrus, depart **19**

exclāmo, -āre, -āvī, -ātus, shout

exemplum, -ī, *n.,* example **33**

exerceō, -ēre, exercuī, exercitus, keep busy, train **67**

exercitus, -ūs, *m.,* (trained) army **68**

expediō, -īre, -īvī, -ītus, set free **44**

expellō, -ere, expulī, expulsus, drive out **50**

explicō, -āre, -āvī, -ātus, unfold, explain **63**

explōrō, -āre, -āvī, -ātus, investigate, explore **70**

expugnō, -āre, -āvī, -ātus, capture by assault **53**

exspectō, -āre, -āvī, -ātus, look out for, await **19**

exstinguō, -ere, exstīnxī, exstīnctus, extinguish

extrā, *(prep. w. acc.)* outside, beyond

extrēmus, -a, -um, farthest, last, end of **64**

F

fābula, -ae, *f.,* story

facile, *(adv.)* easily **63**

facilis, -e, easy, doable **47**

faciō, -ere, fēcī, factus, do, make **20; verba faciō,** speak, make a speech

factum, -ī, *n.,* deed **42**

fallō, -ere, fefellī, falsus, deceive **65**

fāma, -ae, *f.,* report, fame **2**

familia, -ae, *f.,* family **2**

familiāris, -e, *(noun) m.,* friend (familiar); *(adj.)* of the family, friendly **49**

fāmōsus, -a, -um, famous, notorious

fātum, -ī, *n.,* fate; *(often personified)* the Fates

fēmina, -ae, *f.,* woman, wife

ferio, -īre, -īvī, -ītus, hit, strike

ferrum, -ī, *n.,* iron

festīno, -āre, -āvī, -ātus, hurry

fīdus, -a, -um, faithful, reliable, loyal

fīlius, -lī, *m.,* son **14; fīlia, -ae,** *f.,* daughter **9**

fīnis, fīnis, fīnium *m.,* end; *pl.* borders, territory **46**

fīnitimus, -a, -um *(adj.)* neighboring **27**

fīnitimus, -ī, *m.,* neighbor **27**

firmus, -a, -um, strong, firm **23**

fluctus, -ūs, *m.,* wave

flūmen, flūminis, *n.,* river **45**

fluō, -ere, flūxī, fluxus, flow

focus, -ī, *m.,* hearth

fōrma, -ae, *f.,* shape **5**

fortasse, *(adv.)* perhaps **41**

fortis, -e, strong, brave **47**

fortūna, -ae, *f.,* fortune, luck **2**

forum, -ī, *n.,* market place; Forum (at Rome)

frangō, -ere, frēgī, frāctus, break **54**

frāter, frātris, *m.,* brother **54**

frīgidus, -a, -um, cold

frōns, frontis, frontium, *f.,* forehead, front **70**

frūmentum, -ī, *n.,* grain **16**

fuga, -ae, *f.,* flight **43; in fugam dō,** put to flight, cause to run away, make run **43**

fugiō, -ere, fūgī, fugitūrus, run away, flee **22**

fulmen, -minis, *n.,* lightning

futūrus, *(see* **sum**)

G

Gāius, -ī, *m.,* Gā´ius

Gallia, -ae, *f.,* Gaul, ancient France

Gallicus, -a, -um, Gallic

Gallus, -a, -um, Gallic (from Gaul); *(noun) m.,* a Gaul

gaudium, -dī, *n.,* joy, gladness

genius, -nī, *m.,* inborn spirit

gēns, gentis, gentium, *f.,* people, nation **62**

genus, generis, *n.,* birth, kind **53**

Germānia, -ae, *f.,* Germany

Germānus, -ī, *m.,* a German

gerō, gerere, gessī, gestus, carry on, wage **23**

gladiātor, -ōris, *m.,* gladiator

gladius, -dī, *m.,* sword

glōria, -ae, *f.,* glory **11**

glōriōsus, -a, -um, glorious

gracilis, -ē, slender, graceful

Graecia, -ae, *f.,* Greece

Graecus, -a, -um, Greek; **Graecus, -ī,** *m.,* a Greek

grammaticus, -ī, *m.,* school teacher

grātia, -ae, *f.,* gratitude, influence **11; grātiam habeō,** feel grateful; **grātiās agō,** thank *(w. dat.)*

grātus, -a, -um, pleasing, grateful **7**

gravis, -e, heavy, severe **57**

gustus, -ūs, *m.,* taste

H

habeō, -ēre, habuī, habitus, have, hold **10; grātiam habeō,** feel grateful *(w. dat.);* **ōrātiōnem habeō,** deliver an oration

habitō, -āre, -āvī, -ātus, live, dwell **15**

haereō, -ēre, haesī, haesus, stick, cling **60**

Hannibal, -alis, *m.,* Hannibal (a Carthaginian general)

herba, -ae, *f.,* herb, plant, grass

Hibernia, -ae, *f.,* Ireland

hic, haec, hoc, this, these; *(pron.)* he, she, it **50**

hiems, hiemis, *f.,* winter **51**

Hispānia, -ae, *f.,* Spain

Hispānus, -a, -um, Spanish

historia, -ae, *f.,* story, history

hodiē, *(adv.)* today

homō, hominis, *m.,* man, person, human being **40**

honestās, -tātis, *f.,* honor, honesty

honor, -ōris, *m.,* honor, office

hōra, -ae, *f.,* hour **9**

hospes, -itis, *m.,* stranger, guest/host

hospita, -ae, *f.,* guest/hostess

hostis, hostis, hostium, *m.,* enemy *(usually pl.)* **46**

humilis, -e, low, humble **62**

I

iaciō, -ere, iēcī, iactus, throw, hurl, cast **45**

iam, *(adv.)* already, now **30; nōn iam,** no longer

ibi, *(adv.)* there **11**

id, *(see* **is)**

īdem, eadem, idem, *(adj.)* the same **53;** *(pron.)* the same man, woman, thing

ignis, -is, ignium, *m.,* fire **63**

ille, illa, illud, that, those; *(pron.)* he, she, it **50**

impedīmentum, -ī, *n.,* hindrance **44**

impediō, -īre, -īvī, -ītus, hinder, obstruct **44**

imperātor, -ōris, *m.,* commander, general

imperium, -rī, *n.,* command, power **66**

imperō, -āre, -āvī, -ātus, *(w. dat.)* command **70**

impetus, -ūs, *m.,* attack **68; impetum faciō in** *(prep. w. acc.)* make an attack against

in *(prep. w. acc.)* into, onto, to, against **15;** *(prep. w. abl.)* in, on **11**

incertus, -a, -um, uncertain **52**

incipiō, -ere, incēpī, inceptus, take on, begin **23**

incitō, -āre, -āvī, -ātus, excite, stir up, incite **8**

incolō, -ere, incoluī, incultus, live, inhabit **66**

īnferī, -ōrum, *m.* inhabitants of the Underworld

īnferior, īnferius, lower **64**

inimīcus, -a, -um *(adj.)* unfriendly, hostile **30; inimīcus, ī,** *m.,* enemy

iniūria, -ae, *f.,* injustice, wrong, injury **8**

iniūriōsus, -a, -um, harmful

inquit, he, she said

īnstō, -āre, institī, —, threaten **60**

īnstruō, -ere, īnstrūxī, īnstrūctus, arrange, *set up* **62**

īnsula, -ae, *f.,* island **1**

integer, -gra, -grum, fresh, whole, untouched **31**

intellegō, -ere, -lēxī, -lēctus, understand **67**

inter, *(prep. w. acc.)* between, among **35**

intercipiō, -ere, -cēpī, -ceptus, intercept, cut off, catch **53**

interclūdō, -ere, -clūsī, -clūsus, cut off **69**

interficiō, -ere, -fēcī, -fectus, kill **34**

interim, *(adv.)* meanwhile

intermittō, -ere, -mīsī, -missus, stop, interrupt, let go **37**

inveniō, -īre, invēnī, inventus, find, come upon **20**

iō, *(interj.)* hurrah!

ipse, ipsa, ipsum, -self, the very **54**

īra, -ae, *f.,* anger **60**

is, ea, id, *(pron.),* he, she, it **31;** *(adj.)* this, that **52**

ita, *(adv.)* so, yes **22**

Ītalia, -ae, *f.,* Italy

Italus, -a, -um, Italian; **Italī, -ōrum,** *m.,* the Italians

itaque, *(adv.)* and so, therefore, and as a result

iter, itineris, *n.,* journey, route, march **46**

iterum, *(adv.)* again, a second time

iubeō, -ēre, iussī, iussus, order **32**

iūdicō, -āre, -āvī, -ātus, judge **62**

Iūlius, -lī, *m.,* Julius; **Iūlia, -ae,** *f.,* Julia

iungō, -ere, iūnxī, iūnctus, join (to) **63**

Iūnō, -ōnis, *f.,* Juno (a goddess, wife of Jupiter)

Iuppiter, Iovis, *m.,* Jupiter (king of the gods)

iūs, iūris, *n.,* right **47**

iūstus, -a, -um, just **59**

L

labor, -ōris, *m.,* work, hardship **59**

labōrō, -āre, -āvī, -ātus, work **3**

lac, lactis, *n.,* milk

lacrima, -ae, *f.,* tear

lacrimō, -āre, -āvī, -ātus, weep

lapis, lapidis, *m.,* stone

Lār, Laris, *m.,* Lar (a household god)

Latīnus, -a, -um, Latin, belonging to Latium; **Latīnī, -ōrum,** *m.,* the Latins

Latīnus, -ī, *m.,* Latī´nus (king of Latium)

lātus, -a, -um, wide **18**

laudō, -āre, -āvī, -ātus, praise **4**

lavō, -āre, lāvī, lautus, wash, bathe

lēgātus, -ī, *m.,* ambassador, envoy **60**

legō, -ere, lēgī, lēctus, gather, choose, read **26**

levis, -e, light (in weight) **58**

lēx, lēgis, *f.,* law **40**

līber, -era, -erum, *(adj.)* free **14; līberō, -āre, -āvī, -ātus,** *(verb)* free **12**

liber, librī, *m.,* book **24**

līberī, -ōrum, *m. pl.* children **34**

lībertās, -tātis, *f.,* freedom, liberty **47**

ligō, -āre, -āvī, -ātus, bind, tie **44**

lingua, -ae, *f.,* tongue, language **10**

littera, -ae, *f.,* letter (of the alphabet), a letter (epistle), *pl.* letters *(if modified by an adjective such as **multae**)* **7**

locus, -ī, *m.,* (*pl.* **loca, locōrum,** *n.*), place **21**

longus, -a, -um, long **3**

lūdō, -ere, lūsī, lūsus, play

lūdus, -ī, *m.,* game, play, show, school **35**

Lūsitānia, -ae, *f.,* Portugal

lūx, lūcis, *f.,* light **69**

M

M., abbreviation for **Mārcus**

mactē, *(interj.)* well done!

magister, -trī, *m.* **14; magistra, -ae,** *f.,* teacher

magnus, -a, -um, large, great, big **2;** *(comp.)* **maior, maius,** greater; *(superl.)* **maximus, -a, -um,** greatest, very great

maior, *see* **magnus**

malus, -a, -um, bad **4;** *(comp.)* **peior, peius,** worse; *(superl.)* **pessimus, -a, -um,** very bad, worst; **malum, -ī,** *n.,* trouble

mandō, -āre, -āvī, -ātus, entrust, give to (to keep safe) **7**

maneō, -ēre, mānsī, mānsūrus, remain **11**

manus, -ūs, *f.,* hand **68**

Mārcius, -cī, *m.,* Marcius (Mar´shus)

mare, maris, marium, *n.,* sea **46**

marītus, -ī, *m.,* husband

Marius, -rī, *m.,* the Roman general Marius

Mārs, Mārtis, *m.,* Mars (god of war)

māter, mātris, *f.,* mother **50**

māteria, -ae, *f.,* matter, timber **11**

mātrimōnium, -nī, *n.,* marriage

mātūrō, -āre, -āvī, -ātūrus, hasten **17**

maximē, *(adv.)* very greatly, especially

maximus, *see* **magnus**

medicus, -ī, *m.,* doctor

Mediterrāneum (Mare), Mediterranean Sea

medius, -a, -um, middle, middle of **25**

mel, mellis, *n.,* honey

melior, *see* **bonus**

memoria, -ae, *f.,* memory **8; memoriā teneō,** remember

mēnsa, -ae, *f.,* table

mēnsis, -is, -ium, *m.,* month **58**

mercātor, -ōris, *m.,* merchant

Mercurius, -rī, *m.,* Mercury

mereō, -ēre, meruī, merits, deserve, earn **12**

meus, -a, -um, my, mine **9**

migrō, -āre, -āvī, -ātūrus, depart, migrate **15**

mīles, mīlitis, *m.,* soldier **40**

mīlia, mīlium, *n.,* thousands **66**

mīlle, *(adj.) (indeclinable)* thousand **66**

Minerva, -ae, *f.,* a goddess

minimē, *(adv.)* not at all, no **3**

minimus, minor, *see* **parvus**

miser, -era, -erum, unhappy, poor **29**

Mithridātēs, -is, *m.,* Mithridates (king of Pontus)

mittō, -ere, mīsī, missus, let go, send **19**

modus, -ī, *m.,* manner, way **38**

moneō, -ēre, -uī, -itus, remind, warn **38**

mōns, montis, montium, *m.,* mountain **46**

mōnstrō, -āre, -āvī, -ātus, point out, show to **7**

mors, mortis, mortium, *f.,* death **51**

mōs, mōris, *m.,* custom

moveō, -ēre, mōvī, mōtus, move **13**

mox, *(adv.)* soon

mulier, mulieris, *f.,* woman

multus, -a, -um, much **3**; *pl.,* many; *(comp.)*
   plūrēs, plūra, more; *(superl.)* **plūrimus, -a,**
   -um, most

mundus, -ī, *m.,* world

mūniō, -īre, -īvī, -ītus, fortify **20; viam mūniō,**
   build a road

mūnus, mūneris, *n.,* duty, service, gift **59**

mutātus, -a, -um, changed

mūtō, -āre, -āvī, -ātus, change

N

nam *(conj.)* for **38**

nārrō, nārrāre, nārrāvī, nārrātus, tell, relate **21**

nātō, -āre, -āvī, -ātus, swim

nātūra, -ae, *f.,* nature **36**

nauta, -ae, *m.,* sailor **6**

nāvigō, -āre, -āvī, -ātus, sail **6**

nāvis, nāvis, nāvium, *f.,* ship **46**

-ne, *(introduces questions)* **18**

nec, *see* **neque**

neglegentia, -ae, *f.,* negligence

negōtium, -tī, *n.,* business **67**

nēmō, *(dat.)* **nēminī,** *(acc.)* **nēminem** *(no other*
   forms), no one **62**

Neptūnus, -ī, *m.,* Neptune (god of the sea)

neque (or **nec**), and not, nor **28; neque… neque,**
   neither . . . nor **28**

nesciō, -īre, -īvī, -ītus, not know

neuter, -tra, -trum, neither (of two) **56**

nihil, *n.,* nothing *(indeclinable)* **51**

nōbilis, -e, noble **53**

nōbīscum = cum nōbīs

noceō, -ēre, nocuī, nocitūrus, *(w. dat.)* do harm
   to **69**

nōmen, nōminis, *n.,* name **45**

nōn, *(adv.)* not **1; nōn iam,** no longer **43**

nōs, nostrum, we *(pl. of* **ego) 31**

nōscō, -ere, nōvī, nōtus, learn; *(perf.)* have learned,
   know **30**

noster, -tra, -trum, our **14**

nōtus, -a, -um, known, familiar **42**

novem, nine

novus, -a, -um, new, strange **3**

nox, noctis, noctium, *f.,* night

nūllus, -a, -um, no, none **56**

numerus, -ī, *m.,* number **5**

numquam, *(adv.)* never **26**

nunc, *(adv.)* now **4**

nūntiō, -āre, -āvī, -ātus, announce, report to **7**

nūntius, -tī, *m.,* messenger **17**

O

ob, *(prep. w. acc.)* facing toward, on account of,
   for, because of **35**

obtineō, -ēre, obtinuī, obtentus, hold, obtain **37**

occupō, -āre, -āvī, -ātus, seize hold of **8**

Ōceanus, -ī, *m.,* ocean

octō, eight

oculus, -ī, *m.,* eye

officium, -cī, *n.,* duty **19**

ōlim, *(adv.)* formerly, once (upon a time) **31**

omnis, omne, all, every **47**

oportet, -ēre, -tuit, it is fitting, it is necessary
   (w. acc. of person + inf.)

oppidum, -ī, *n.,* town **18**

opprimō, -ere, oppressī, oppressus, overcome,
   surprise **57**

optimē, *see* **bene**

optimus, *see* **bonus**

opus, operis, *n.,* work, labor **63**

ōrātiō, -ōnis, *f.,* speech **62**

ōrātor, -ōris, *m.,* orator

orbis, -is, -ium, *m.,* world, circle, ring

ōrdō, ōrdinis, *m.,* order, rank, row **45**

ōrnāmentum, -ī, *n.,* jewel, costume

ostendō, -ere, ostendī, ostentus, show, stretch
   out before, present **58**

ōtiōsus, -a, -um, leisurely, idle

ōtium, ōtī, *n.,* leisure, peace **22**

P

P., *abbreviation for* **Pūblius**

paedagōgus, -ī, *m.,* an escort for children

paene, *(adv.)* almost **9**

pār, paris *(gen.)* equal, equal to **47**

parātus, -a, -um, prepared, ready **42**

parō, -āre, -āvī, -ātus, get, get ready, prepare **3**

pars, partis, partium, *f.,* part, direction, side **52**

parvus, -a, -um, small, little **2**; *(comp.)* **minor,**
   minus, less; *(superl.)* **minimus, -a, -um,** least

passus, -ūs, *m.,* pace

pāstor, -ōris, *m.,* herdsman, shepherd **46**

pater, patris, *m.,* father **48**

paterfamiliās, patrisfamiliās, *m.,* father of the
   household

patria, -ae, *f.,* fatherland, country **10**

patricii, -orum, *m.,* patricians

patrōnus, -ī, *m.,* patron
paucī, -ae, -a, a few, few **27**
paupertās, -tātis, *f.,* poverty, humble circumstances
pāx, pācis, *f.,* peace **40**
pecūnia, -ae, *f.,* money **6**
peior, *see* **malus**
pellō, -ere, pepulī, pulsus, beat, drive, defeat, drive out **48**
Penātēs, -ium, *m.,* the Penā´tēs (household gods)
Pēnelopē, -ae, *f.,* Penĕl´ope (wife of Ulysses)
per, *(prep. w. acc.)* through, by **33**
perficiō, -ere, -fēcī, -fectus, finish **66**
perīculum, -ī, *n.,* danger **29**
permittō, -ere, -mīsī, -missus, let go through, allow, permit, entrust *(w. dat.)* **34**
permoveō, -ēre, -mōvī, -mōtus, move (deeply), upset **37**
permūtātiō, -ōnis, *f.,* exchange
perpetuus, -a, -um, constant **23**
persōna, -ae, *f.,* character
perveniō, -īre, -vēnī, -ventūrus, (come through), arrive **60**
pēs, pedis, *m.,* foot **44; pedibus,** on foot
pessimus, *(see* **malus)**
petō, -ere, petīvī, petītus, seek, ask **36**
Philippus, -ī *m.,* Philip
philosophia, -ae, *f.,* philosophy
Phrygia, -ae, *f.,* Phrygia (Frij´ia) (a country of Asia Minor)
pictūra, -ae, *f.,* picture
pila, -ae, *f.,* ball
pius, -a, -um, loyal
plācō, -āre, -āvī, -ātus, please, calm
plāgōsus, -a, -um, fond of whipping
plānus, -a, -um, level, flat **5**
plēbs, plēbis, *f.,* common people, plebians
plēnus, -a, -um, full **24**
plicō, -āre, -āvī, -ātus, fold **39**
plūrēs, plūra, more, *(see* **multus)**
plūrimus, *(see* **multus)**
plūs, *(see* **multus)**
Plūtō, -ōnis, *m.,* Plū´tō
poena, -ae, *f.,* punishment, penalty **8**
poēta, -ae, *m.,* poet **26**
Polyphēmus, -ī, *m.,* Polyphē´mus (a man-eating giant)
pompa, -ae, *f.,* parade, procession
pōnō, -ere, posuī, positus, put, place **19; castra pōnō,** pitch camp
pōns, pontis, pontium, *m.,* bridge **54**
pontifex, -ficis, *m.,* priest
Pontus, -ī, *m.,* Pontus (a country in Asia Minor)

populus, -ī, *m.,* people **18;** *pl.,* peoples, nations
porta, -ae, *f.,* gate (of a city or a camp) **32**
portō, -āre, -āvī, -ātus, carry **3**
portus, -ūs, *m.,* harbor
possum, posse, potuī, —, can, be able **42**
post, *(adv. and prep. w. acc.)* behind *(of place);* after *(of time)* **48**
posteā, *(adv.)* afterwards **48**
postquam, *(conj.)* after **67**
potēns, potentis *(gen.)* powerful
potestās, -tātis, *f.,* power **54**
prae, *(prep. w. abl.)* in front of, before **67**
praeceps, praecipitis *(gen.)* headfirst, steep, straight (down) **50**
praeda, -ae, *f.,* loot, booty **7**
praeficiō, -ere, -fēcī, -fectus, put in charge of **69**
praemittō, -ere, -mīsī, -missus, send ahead **67**
praemium, -mī, *n.,* reward **16**
praesidium, -dī, *n.,* guard, protection **28**
praesum, -esse, -fuī, -futūrus, be in charge of **69**
praetextus, -a, -um, (woven in front), bordered; **toga praetexta,** crimson-bordered toga
premō, -ere, pressī, pressus, press, press hard **40**
pretium, -tī, *n.,* price **21**
prīmō, *(adv.)* at first
prīmum, *(adv.)* for the first time
prīmus, -a, -um, first **34**
prīnceps, -cipis, *m.,* leader, chief **69**
prō, *(prep. w. abl.)* in front of, before, for, in behalf of **29**
probō, -āre, -āvī, -ātus, test, prove, approve **7**
prōcēdō, -ere, -cessī, -cessūrus, go forward, advance **30**
procus, -ī, *m.,* suitor
prōdūcō, -ere, -dūxī, -ductus, lead out **30**
proelium, -lī, *n.,* battle **27**
proelium committō, *begin battle* **27**
prohibeō, -ēre, -hibuī, -hibitus, prevent, keep from **58**
prope, *(adv. and prep. w. acc.)* near, nearby, almost
properō, -āre, -āvī, -ātūrus, hasten, hurry **27**
prōpōnō, -ere, -posuī, -positus, put forward, offer **33**
proprius, -a, -um, (one's) own **63**
prōvideō, -ēre, -vīdī, -vīsus, foresee, see ahead **43**
prōvincia, -ae, *f.,* province **8**
proximus, -a, -um, nearest, next *(w. dat.)* **64**
pūblicus, -a, -um, *m.,* public **18**
Pūblius, -lī, *m.,* Pub´lius
puella, -ae, *f.,* girl **2**
puer, puerī, *m.,* boy **14**

pugna, -ae, *f.*, battle, fight **8**

pugnō, -āre, -āvī, -ātus, fight **8**

pulcher, -chra, -chrum, beautiful **20**

Pūnicus, -a, -um, Punic, Carthaginian

pūpa, -ae, *f.*, doll, little girl

putō, -āre, -āvī, -ātus, think, suppose **59**

Pyrrhus, -ī, *m.*, Pyr´rhus (king of Epirus)

Q

quam, *(conj.)* than **61**; *(adv. with superl.)* as . . . as possible **63**

quartus, -a, -um, fourth

quattuor, four **41**

-que *(joined to second word),* and **26**

quī, quae, quod, *(rel. pron.)* who, which, what, that **36**; *(interrog. adj.)* what? which? **38**

quid?, what? **18, 38**

quīndecim, fifteen

quīnque, five

quīntus, -a, -um, fifth **9**

quis? quid? *(interrog, pron.)* who? what? **18, 38**

quō modō, how (in what manner)

quod, *(conj.)* because, since **4**

quondam, *(adv.)* once (upon a time) **53**

quot? *(adv.)* how many?

R

rāmus, -ī, *m.*, branch

rāna, -ae, *f.,* frog

rapiō, -ere, rapuī, raptus, carry off, steal **61**

ratiō, -ōnis, *f.*, account, reason **70**

recipiō, -ere, recēpī, receptus, take back, recover **32**

reddō, -ere, reddidī, redditus, give back, restore **68**

redigō, -ere, redēgī, redāctus, drive back, reduce **32**

redūcō, -ere, redūxī, reductus, lead back **25**

rēgia, -ae, *f.*, palace

rēgīna, -ae, *f.*, queen **5**

regiō, -ōnis, *f.*, region **62**

rēgnum, -ī, *n.,* kingdom, realm **44**

regō, -ere, rēxī, rēctus, rule, guide **20**

relinquō, -ere, relīquī, relictus, leave (behind), abandon **41**

reliquus, -a, -um, remaining, rest (of) **26**

remaneō, -ēre, remānsī, remānsūrus, stay behind, remain **34**

remedium, -dī, *n.,* remedy

remittō, -ere, remīsī, remissus, relax, send back, (let back) **52**

removeō, -ēre, remōvī, remōtus, remove, move back **32**

repellō, -ere, reppulī, repulsus, drive back, repulse **62**

rēs, reī, *f.*, thing, matter, affair, situation **69**; **rēs pūblica, reī publicae,** public affairs, government

respondeō, -ēre, respondī, respōnsus, answer, reply **49**

restō, -āre, restitī, —, remain

retineō, -ēre, retinuī, retentus, hold back, keep **30**

reverentia, -ae, *f.*, respect

revertō, -ere, revertī, reversūrus, return

rēx, rēgis, *m.*, king **44**

Rhēnus, -ī, *m.*, the Rhine river

rīdeō, -ēre, rīsī, rīsus, laugh (at)

rogō, -āre, -āvī, -ātus, ask, ask for **42**

Rōma, -ae, *f.*, Rome

Rōmānus, -a, -um, *(adj.)* Roman; **Rōmānus, -ī,** *m.,* a Roman

ruīna, -ae, *f.*, downfall, collapse; *pl.* ruins

S

saccus, -ī, *m.*, sack, bag

sacer, -cra, -crum, sacred **14**

sacerdōs, -ōtis, *m.* or *f.*, priest, priestess

sacrificō, -āre, -āvī, -ātus, sacrifice, sacrifice to *(+ dat.)*

saepe, *(adv.)* often

salūs, salūtis, *f.*, health, safety **40**

salūtō, -āre, -āvī, -ātus, greet

salvē, *sing.,* **salvēte,** *pl.,* (good) health to you, hail, hello

sānus, -a, -um, sound, sane

sapientia, -ae, *f.*, wisdom

Sāturnālia, -ōrum, *n. pl.,* Saturnalia (a winter festival in honor of the god Saturn)

Sāturnus, -ī, *m.*, Saturn (a god)

saucius, -a, -um, wounded, hurt

saxum, -ī, *n.,* rock

scēptrum, -ī, *n.,* scepter

schola, -ae, *f.*, school

scientia, -ae, *f.*, knowledge, science

sciō, -īre, scīvī, scītus, know **59**

Scīpiō, -ōnis, *m.*, Scipio (Sip´io)

scrībō, -ere, scrīpsī, scrīptus, write **26**

sēcum = cum sē

secundus, -a, -um, second **59**

sēcūrus, -a, -um, free of care, safe

sed, *(conj.)* but **1**

sedeō, -ēre, sēdī, sessūrus, sit **54**

semper, *(adv.)* always **9**

senātor, -ōris, *m.,* senator

senātus, -ūs, *m.,* senate **68**

sententia, -ae, *f.,* feeling, opinion, motto **25**

sentiō, -īre, sēnsī, sēnsus, feel, realize **60**

sēparō, -āre, -āvī, -ātus, separate

septem, seven

sepulchrum, -ī, *n.,* tomb

sermō, -ōnis, *m.,* talk, conversation

servō, -āre, -āvī, -ātus, save, guard **8**

servus, -ī, *m.;* **serva, -ae,** *f.,* slave **4**

sex, six

sī, *(conj.)* if **59**

sīc, yes, thus, so **3**

Sicilia, -ae, *f.,* Sicily (Sis´ily)

signum, -ī, *n.,* sign, standard, signal **16**

silva, -ae, *f.,* forest, woods **1**

similis, -e, like *(w. dat.)* **63**

sine, *(prep. w. abl.)* without **30**

singulī, -ae, -a, *(always pl.)* one at a time, one by one **13**

socius, -cī, *m.,* ally, comrade **12**

sōl, sōlis, *m.,* sun **63**

sōlus, -a, -um, alone **56**

solvō, -ere, solvī, solūtus, loosen, pay **59**

somnus, -ī, *m.,* sleep

sordidus, -a, -um, dirty

soror, -ōris, *f.,* sister **54**

spatium, -tī, *n.,* space, time **43**

speciēs, speciēī, *f.,* appearance **69**

spectō, -āre, -āvī, -ātus, look (at), watch **3**

spērō, -āre, -āvī, -ātus, hope for, hope that **52**

spēs, speī, *f.,* hope **69**

spīrō, -āre, -āvī, -ātus, breathe **52**

spondeō, -ēre, spopondī, spōnsus, promise, engage

sportula, -ae, *f.* small gift basket

statua, -ae, *f.,* statue

statuō, -ere, statuī, statūtus, establish, determine, arrange **61**

stella, -ae, *f.* star

stō, stāre, stetī, stātūrus, stand, stand up **41**

studiōsus, -a, -um, eager, studious

studium, -dī, *n.,* eagerness, interest, studies **22**

sub, *(prep. w. acc. with verbs of motion; w. abl. with verbs of rest or position)* under, close up to **33**

submittō, -ere, -mīsī, -missus, let down, furnish **35**

suī, *(reflex. pron.)* of himself, herself, itself, themselves **65**

sum, esse, fuī, futūrus, be **15**

summus, -a, -um, highest, top of **64**

sūmō, -ere, sūmpsī, sūmptus, take **65**

super, *(prep. w. acc.)* over, above **67**

superbia, -ae, *f.,* pride, arrogance **34**

superbus, -a, -um, proud, arrogant **34**

superō, -āre, -āvī, -ātus, excel, overcome, surpass, conquer **49**

supersum, -esse, -fuī, -futūrus, be left (over), survive **67**

supplicium, -cī, *n.,* punishment **53**

suscipiō, -ere, -cēpī, -ceptus, undertake, take up, start **33**

sustineō, -ēre, -tinuī, -tentus, hold up, maintain, endure **36**

suus, -a, -um, *(reflex.)* his, her, its, their; his own, her own, its own, their own **65**

T

taberna, -ae, *f.,* shop, tavern

tablīnum, -ī, *n.,* study, den

tamen, *(adv.)* nevertheless **34**

tandem, *(adv.)* at last, finally

tangō, -ere, tetigī, tāctus, touch **53**

tardus, -a, -um, late, slow **24**

Tarentīnī, -ōrum, *m. pl.,* the people of Tarentum

tēcum = cum tē

Tēlemachus, -ī, *m.,* Telĕm´achus

tēlum, -ī, *n.,* weapon

templum, -ī, *n.,* temple **20**

tempus, -oris, *n.,* time **45**

tendō, -ere, tetendī, tentus, stretch **47**

teneō, -ēre, tenuī, tentus, hold, keep **12; memoriā teneō,** remember

terminus, -ī, *m.,* end, boundary **21**

terra, -ae, *f.,* earth, land **2**

terreō, -ēre, terruī, territus, scare, frighten **10**

tertius, -a, -um, third **42**

texō, -ere, texuī, textus, weave

theātrum, -ī, *n.,* theater, amphitheater

Ti., *abbreviation for* **Tiberius**

Tiberis, -is, *m.,* the Tī´ber (a river in Italy)

Tiberius, -rī, *m.,* Tībē´rius

timeō, -ēre, timuī, —, fear, be afraid of **51**

timidus, -a, -um, shy **43**

Tīrō, -ōnis, *m.,* Tī´rō

toga, -ae, *f.,* toga (cloak)

tōtus, -a, -um, whole, entire **56**

trādō, -ere, -didī, -ditus, give/hand over, surrender **66**

trādūcō, -ere, dūxī, -ductus, lead across **41**

trahō, -ere, trāxī, tractus, draw, drag **24**

trānō, -āre, -āvī, -ātus, swim across

trāns, *(prep. w. acc.)* across **39**

trānsportō, -āre, -āvī, -ātus, transport, carry across **41**

trēs, tria, three **66**

tribūnus, -ī, *m.,* tribune, a Roman official

tribuō, -ere, tribuī, tribūtus, grant **65**

trīgintā, thirty

triumphō, -āre, -āvī, -ātus, triumph

triumphus, -ī, *m.,* triumph

Trōia, -ae, *f.,* Troy

Trōiānus, -a, -um, *(adj.)* Trojan; **Trōianus, -i,** *m.,* a Trojan

tū, tuī, you, *of you (sing.)* **31**

tum, *(adv.)* then, next **6**

tuus, -a, -um, your, yours *(referring to one person)* **9**

U

ubi, *(adv.)* where? **4**; when? **18**

Ulixēs, -is, *m.,* Ūlys´sēs

ūllus, -a, -um, any **56**

ulterior, ulterius, farther **64**

ultimus, -a, -um, farthest, last **43**

unda, -ae, *f.,* wave **6**

ūnus, -a, -um, one **56**

Uranus, -ī, *m.,* Ū´ranus (god of the Sky)

urbs, urbis, urbium, *f.,* city **60**

ūsus, -ūs, *m.,* use, custom

uter, -ra, -rum, which (of two)

uterque, utraque, utrumque, each (of two)

ūtilis, -e, useful **61**

uxor, -ōris, *f.,* wife **47**

V

valeō, -ēre, valuī, valitūrus, be well, be strong **22**; *(impv.)* **valē** *(sing.),* **valēte** *pl.,* farewell, good-bye

vāllum, -ī, *n.,* wall

varius, -a, -um, changing, various **22**

veniō, -īre, vēnī, ventūrus, come **20**

ventus, -ī, *m.,* wind **27**

Venus, -eris, *f.,* Vēnus (goddess of love and beauty)

vēr, vēris, *n.,* spring

verbōsus, -a, -um, wordy

verbum, -ī, *n.,* word **24**; **verba faciō,** make a speech

Vergilius, -lī, *m.,* Vergil

vertō, -ere, vertī, versus, turn **44**

vērus, -a, -um, true, real, not false **18**

Vesta, -ae, *f.,* Vesta (goddess of the hearth); **Vestālis, -e,** of Vesta

vester, -tra, -trum, your, yours *(referring to two or more persons)* **18**

vestis, -is, -ium, *f.,* garment, clothes **46**

via, -ae, *f.,* road, way, street **1**

victor, -ōris, *m.,* conqueror, victor

victōria, -ae, *f.,* victory **8**

videō, -ēre, vīdī, vīsus, see **11**

vīgintī, twenty

vīlla, -ae, *f.,* country home

vincō, -ere, vīcī, victus, conquer **61**

vīnum, -ī, *n.,* wine

vir, virī, *m.,* man, hero **14**

virgō, -ginis, *f.,* virgin, maiden

virīlis, -e, of a man

virtūs, -tūtis, *f.,* manliness, courage **49**

vīs, vīs, vīrium, *f.,* force, violence; *pl.* strength **58**

vīta, -ae, *f.,* life **2**

vīvō, -ere, vīxī, vīctus, live, be alive **41**

vīvus, -a, -um, alive, living

vix, *(adv.)* scarcely

vocō, -āre, -āvī, -ātus, call **13**

volō, -āre, -āvī, -ātus, fly

vōs, vestrum, you, of you *(pl.)* **31**

vōx, vōcis, *f.,* voice, remark **57**

Vulcānus, -ī, *m.,* Vulcan (god of fire)

vulnerō, -āre, -āvī, -ātus, wound **40**

vulnus, vulneris, *n.,* wound **45**

DICTIONARY

English–Latin

A

abandon, relinquō, -ere, relīquī, relictus **41**
able (be), possum, posse, potuī, — **42**
about, dē *(w. abl.)* **13**
above, super *(w. acc.)* **67**
abundance, cōpia, -ae, *f.* **5**
absent (be), absum, abesse, āfuī, afutūrus **30**
accident, cāsus, -ūs, *m.* **68**
account, ratiō, -ōnis, *f.* **70**
across, trāns *(w. acc.)* **39**
advance, prōcēdō, -ere, -cessī, -cessūrus **30**
advice, cōnsilium, -lī, *n.* **16**
affair, rēs, reī, *f.* **69**
affect, afficiō, -ere, affēcī, affectus **23**
afflict with, afficiō, -ere, affēcī, affectus **23**
afraid (be), timeō, -ēre, timuī, — **51**
after, post *(w. acc.)* **48;** *(conj.)* postquam **67;**
  (use abl. abs.)
afterwards, *(adv.)* posteā **48**
against, contrā *(w. acc.)* **65**
age, aetās, -ātis, *f.* **61**
aid, auxilium, -lī, *n.* **16**
alarm, commoveō, -ēre, -mōvī, -mōtus **42**
all, omnis, -e **47**
allow, permittō, -ere, permīsī, permissus **34**
ally, socius, -cī, *m.* **12**
almost, paene **9**
alone, sōlus, -a, -um **56**
already, iam **30**
also, etiam **32**
always, semper **9**
ambassador, lēgātus, -ī, *m.* **60**
among, inter *(w. acc.)* **35;** apud *(w. acc.)* **70**
and, et **1,** -que **26,** atque (ac) **38; and not,** neque
  (nec) **28**
anger, īra, -ae, *f.* **60**
announce, nūntiō, -āre, -āvi, -ātus **7**
another, alius, -a, -ud **56**
another's, aliēnus, -a, -um **57**
answer, respondeō, -ēre, respondī, respōnsus **49**
any, ūllus, -a, -um **56**
appearance, speciēs, speciēī, *f.* **69**
approach, accēdō, -ere, accessī, accessus
  (w. ad) **19**

approve, probō, -āre, -āvī, -ātus **7**
arms (weapons), arma, -ōrum, *n. pl.* **17**
army, exercitus, -ūs, *m.* **68**
around, circum *(w. acc.)* **67**
arouse, incitō, -āre, -āvī, -ātus **8**
arrange, statuō, -ere, statuī, statūtus **61;** īnstruō,
  -ere, īnstrūxī, īnstrūctus **62**
arrive, perveniō, -īre, -vēnī, -ventūrus **60**
arrogance, superbia, -ae, *f.* **34**
arrogant, superbus, -a, -um **34**
as, quam
ascend, ascendō, -ere, ascendī, ascēnsus **70**
attack, impetus, -us, *m.* **68**
ask (for), petō, -ere, petīvī, petītus **36;** rogō, -āre,
  -āvī, -ātus **42**
author, auctor, -ōris *m.* **48**
authority, auctōritās, -ātis, *f.* **49**
await, exspectō, -āre, -āvī, -ātus **19**
away (be), absum, -esse, āfuī, āfutūrus **30**

B

bad, malus, -a, -um **4**
barbarian, barbarus, -i, *m.* **16**
battle, pugna, -ae, *f.* **8;** proelium, -lī, *n.* **27**
be, sum, esse, fuī, futūrus **15**
beautiful, pulcher, -chra, -chrum **20**
because, quod **4** *(use particip. or abl. abs);*
  because of, ob *(w. acc.)* **35**
befall, accidō, -ere, accidī, — *(w. dat.)* **63**
before, prō *(w. abl.)* **29;** ante *(adv. or prep.*
  w. acc.) **39;** prae *(w. abl.)* **67**
begin, incipiō, -ere, -cēpī, -ceptus **23; begin**
  battle, proelium committō **27**
behind, post *(w. acc.)* **48**
believe, crēdō, -ere, -didī, -ditus **65**
benefit, beneficium, -cī, *n.* **33**
between, inter *(w. acc.)* **35**
big, magnus, -a, -um **2**
bind, ligō, -āre, -āvī, -ātus **44**
birth, genus, generis, *n.* **53**
body, corpus, corporis, *n.* **45**
book, liber, librī, *m.* **24**
booty, praeda, -ae, *f.* **7**
border, fīnis, fīnis, fīnium, *m.* **46**
both . . . and, et... et **28**
boundary, terminus, -ī, *m.* **21**

boy, puer, puerī, *m.*

brave, fortis, -e **47**

break, frangō, -ere, frēgī, frāctus **54**

breathe, spīrō, -āre, -āvī, -ātus **52**

bridge, pōns, pontis, pontium, *m.* **54**

bring about, efficiō, -ere, effēcī, effectus **21**

brother, frāter, frātris, *m.* **54**

business, negōtium, -tī, *n.* **67**

but, sed **1**

buy, emō, -ere, ēmi, ēmptus **66**

by, ā, ab *(w. abl.)* **13**

C

call, vocō, -āre, -āvī, -ātus **13;** appellō, -āre, -āvī, -ātus **28; call out,** ēvocō **16; call together,** convocō **25**

calm, aequus, -a, -um **18**

camp, castra, -ōrum, *n.* pl. **16**

can, possum, posse, potuī, — **42**

cannot, nōn possum

capture (by assault), expugnō, -āre, -āvī, -ātus **53**

care, cūra, -ae, *f.* **5; carefully,** cum cūrā

carry, portō, -āre, -āvī, -ātus **3; carry off,** rapiō, -ere, rapuī, raptus **61; carry on,** gerō, -ere, gessī, gestus **23**

cart, carrus, -i *m.* **4**

case, causa, -ae, *f.* **18**

cast, iaciō, -ere, iēcī, iactus **58**

catch, intercipiō, -ere, -cepī, -ceptus

catch sight of, cōnspiciō, -ere, -spexī, -spectus **65**

cause, causa, -ae, *f.* **18**

certain, certus, -a, -um

chance, cāsus, -ūs, *m.* **68**

changing, varius, -a, -um **22**

charge of, (be in) praesum, -esse, -fuī, -futurus **69;** **(put in)** praeficiō, -ere, -fēcī, -fectus **69**

chief, prīnceps, -cipis, *m.* **69**

children, līberī, -ōrum, *m.* **34**

choose, legō, -ere, lēgī, lēctus **26**

citizen, cīvis, cīvis, cīvium, *m.* or *f.* **46**

citizenship, cīvitās, -ātis, *f.* **48**

city, urbs, urbis, urbium, *f.* **60**

clear, clārus, -a, -um **5**

climb (up), ascendō, -ere, ascendī, ascēnsus **70**

cling, haereō, -ēre, haesī, haesus **60**

close, *(verb),* claudō, -ere, clausī, clausus **45; close up to,** *(prep.)* sub *(w. acc. or abl.)* **33**

clothes, vestis, -is, -ium, *f.* **46**

collect, cōgō, -ere, -ēgī, -āctus **38**

colonist, colōnus, -ī, *m.* **15**

come, veniō, -īre, vēnī, ventūrus **20; come through,** perveniō, -īre, -vēnī, -ventūrus **60; come together,** conveniō **25; come upon,** inveniō **20**

command, *(noun)* imperium, -rī, *n.* **66;** *(verb)* imperō, -āre, -āvī, -ātus *(w. dat.)* **70**

commit, committō, -ere, -mīsī, -missus **27**

common, commūnis, -e **52**

common people, plebs, -bis, *f.*

compel, cōgō, -ere, coēgī, coactus

complete, cōnficiō, -ere, -fēcī, -fectus **46**

comrade, socius, -cī, *m.* **12**

concern, cūra, -ae, *f.* **5**

concerning, dē *(w. abl.)* **13**

condition, condiciō, -ōnis, *f.* **61**

conquer, superō, -āre, -āvī, -ātus **38;** vincō, -ere, vīcī, victus **61**

constant, perpetuus, -a, -um **23**

consult, cōnsulō, -ere, -suluī, -sultus **43**

contain, contineō, -ēre, -uī, -tentus **24**

convenient, commodus, -a, -um **22**

country, patria, -ae, *f.* **10**

courage, animus, -ī, *m.* **15;** virtūs, -tūtis, *f.* **49**

cry out, clāmō, -āre, -āvī, -ātus **40**

cultivate, colō, -ere, coluī, cultus **54**

cut off, interclūdō, -ere, -clūsī, -clūsus **69**

D

danger, perīculum, -ī, *n.* **29**

daughter, fīlia, -ae, *f.* **9**

day, diēs, diēī, *m.* **69**

death, mors, mortis, mortium, *f.* **51**

deceive, fallō, -ere, fefellī, falsus **65**

deed, factum, -ī, *n.* **42**

deep, altus, -a, -um **12**

defeat, pellō, -ere, pepulī, pulsus **48**

defend, dēfendō, -ere, dēfendī, dēfēnsus **19**

depart, excēdō, -ere, excessī, excessūrus **19;** migrō, -āre, -āvī, ātūrus **15;** discēdō **32**

desert, dēserō, -ere, dēseruī, dēsertus **68**

deserve, mereō, -ēre, meruī, meritus **12**

desire, cupiō, -ere, cupīvī, cupītus **31**

despise, dēspiciō, -ere, dēspexī, dēspectus **68**

determine, statuō, -ere, statuī, statūtus **61**

difficult, difficilis, -e, **63**

diligence, dīligentia, -ae, *f.* **35**

dinner, cēna, -ae, *f.* **13**

direction, pars, partis, partium, *f.* **52**

discern, cernō, -ere, crēvī, crētus **42**

discipline, disciplīna, -ae, *f.*

discuss, agō, -ere, ēgī, āctus **19**

dismiss, dīmittō, -ere, dīmīsī, dīmissus

distinguished, ēgregius, -a, -um **33**

disturb, commoveō, -ēre, -mōvī, -mōtus **42**

divide, dīvidō, -ere, dīvīsī, dīvīsus **70**

do, agō, -ere, ēgī, āctus **19;** faciō, -ere, fēcī, factus **20; do harm to,** noceō, -ēre, nocuī, nocitus (w. dat.) **69; do in,** conficiō, -ere, -fēcī, -fectus **46**

doable, facilis, -e **47**

doubt, dubitō, -āre, āvī, ātus **31**

downfall, cāsus, -ūs, m. **68**

drag, dūcō, -ere, dūxī, ductus **21;** trahō, -ere, trāxī, tractus **24**

draw, trahō, -ere, trāxī, tractus

drive, agō, -ere, ēgī, āctus **19;** pellō, -ere, pepulī, pulsus **48; drive back,** redigō **32;** repellō **62; drive out,** expellō **50; drive together,** cōgō **38**

duty, officium, -cī, n. **19;** mūnus, mūneris, n. **59**

dwell, habitō, -āre, -āvī, -ātus **15**

E

each (of two), uterque, utraque, utrumque **56**

eagerness, studium, -dī, n. **22**

earn, mereō, -ēre, meruī, meritus **12**

earth, terra, -ae, f. **2**

easily, facile **63**

easy, facilis, -e **47**

effect, efficiō, -cre, effēcī, effectus **21**

either . . . or, aut... aut **28**

encourage, cōnfirmō, -āre, -āvī, -ātus **49**

end, fīnis, fīnis, fīnium, m. **46;** terminus, -ī, m. **21**

endure, sustineō, -ēre, -tinuī, -tentus **36**

enemy, (personal) inimīcus, -ī, m.; (national) hostis, -is, -ium, m. (usually pl.) **46**

entire, tōtus, -a, -um **56**

entrust, mandō, -āre, -āvī, -ātus **7;** committō, -ere, -mīsī, -missus **27;** permittō **34;** crēdō, -ere, -didī, -ditus **65**

equal, pār, paris (gen.) **47;** aequus, -a, -um **18**

establish, cōnfirmō, -āre, -āvī, -ātus **49;** statuō, -ere, statuī, statūtus **61**

even, (adj.) aequus, -a, -um **18;** (adv.) etiam **32**

every, omnis, -e **47**

envoy, lēgātus, -ī, m. **60**

example, exemplum, -ī, n. **33**

excel, superō, -āre, -āvī, -ātus **49**

excellent, ēgregius, -a, -um **33**

excite, incitō, -āre, -āvī, -ātus **8**

exhaust, cōnficiō, -ere, -fēcī, -fectus **46**

explain, explicō, -āre, -āvī, -ātus **63**

explore, explōrō, -āre, -āvī, -ātus **70**

F

facing (toward), ob (w. acc.) **35**

fall, cadō, -ere, cecidī, cāsūrus **63**

fame, fāma, -ae, f. **2**

familiar, nōtus, -a, -um **42**

family, familia, -ae, f. **2**

famous, clārus, -a, -um **5**

farmer, agricola, -ae, m. **3**

farther, ulterior, ulterius, **64**

farthest, ultimus, -a, -um **43, 64;** extrēmus, -a, -um **64**

father, pater, patris, m. **48**

fatherland, patria, -ae, f. **10**

fear, timeō, -ēre, timuī, — **51**

feel, sentiō, -īre, sēnsī, sēnsus **60; feel grateful,** grātiam habeō

feeling, sententia, -ae, f. **35**

few, paucī, -ae, -a (pl.) **27**

field, ager, agrī, m. **14**

fierce, ācer, ācris, ācre **60**

fifth, quīntus, -a, -um **9**

fight, (noun) pugna, -ae, f. **8;** proelium, -lī, n. **27;** (verb) pugnō, -āre, -āvī, -ātus **8**

find, inveniō, -īre, invēnī, inventus

finish, perficiō, -ere, -fēcī, -fectus **66**

fire, ignis, -is, -ium, m. **63**

firm, firmus, -a, -um **23**

first, prīmus, -a, -um **34**

fit, aptus, -a, -um **62**

fixed, certus, -a, -um **42**

flat, plānus, -a, -um **5**

flee, fugiō, -ere, fūgī, fugitūrus **22**

flight, fuga, -ae, f. **43**

fold, plicō, -āre, -āvī, -ātus **39**

food, cibus, -ī, m. **5**

foot, pēs, pedis, m. **44; on foot,** pedibus

for, (conj.) nam **38;** (prep.) prō (w. abl.) **29;** (prep.) ob (w. acc.) **35**

force, prōvideō, -ēre, -vīdī, -vīsus **43**

foreign, barbarus, -a, -um **16**

foreigner, barbarus, -ī, m. **16**

foresee, prōvideō, -ēre, -vīdī, -vīsus

forest, silva, -ae, f. **1**

formerly, ōlim **31**

fortify, mūniō, -īre, -īvī, -ītus **20**

fortune, fortūna, -ae, f. **2**

four, quattuor **41**

free (adj.), līber, -era, -erum **14;** (verb), līberō, -āre, -āvī, -ātus **12;** expediō, -īre, -īvī, -ītus **44**

freedom, lībertās, -tātis, f. **47**

fresh, integer, -gra, -grum **31**

friend, amīcus, -ī, *m.* **7;** amīca, -ae, *f.*; familiāris, -e **49**

friendly, amīcus, -a, -um **14**

friendship, amīcitia, -ae, *f.* **11**

frighten, terreō, -ēre, terruī, territus **10**

from, out from, ē, ex *(w. abl.)* **13; away from,** ā, ab *(w. abl.)* **13; down from,** dē *(w. abl.)* **13**

full, plēnus, -a, -um **24**

furnish, submittō, -ere, -mīsī, -missus **35**

G

game, lūdus, -i, *m.* **35**

garment, vestis, -is, -ium, *f.* **46**

gate porta, -ae, *f.* **32**

gather, legō, -ere, lēgī, lēctus **26**

Gaul, Gallia, -ae, *f.*; **a Gaul,** Gallus, -ī, *m.*

general, dux, ducis, *m.* **40**

get, get ready, parō, -āre, -āvī, -ātus **3**

gift, mūnus, mūneris, *n.* **59**

girl, puella, -ae, *f.* **2**

give, dō, dare, dedī, datus **35; (as a gift)** dōnō, -āre, -āvī, -ātus **7; (to keep safe)** mandō, -āre, -āvī, -ātus **7; give back,** reddō, -ere, reddidī, redditus **68**

glory, glōria, -ae, *f.* **11**

go away, discēdō, -ere, -cessī, -cessūrus **32; go before,** antecēdō **41; go forward,** prōcēdō **30**

god, deus, -ī, *m.* **22**

goddess, dea, -ae, *f.* **22**

good, bonus, -a, -um **2**

good-bye, valē *(sing.),* valēte *(pl.)*

grain, frūmentum, -ī, *n.* **16**

grant, tribuō, -ere, tribuī, tribūtus **65**

grateful, gratus, -a, -um **7; (be** *or* **feel)** grātiam habeō

gratitude, grātia, -ae, *f.* **11**

great, magnus, -a, -um **2**

guard, *(noun)* praesidium, -dī, *n.* **28;** *(verb)* servō, -āre, -āvī, -ātus **8**

guide, regō, -ere, rēxī, rēctus **20**

H

hand, manus, -ūs, *f.*; **hand over,** trādō, -ere, -didī, -ditus **66**

happen (to someone), accidō, -ere, accidī, — *(w. dat.)* **63**

hard, dūrus, -a, -um **2**

hardship, labor, -ōris, *m.* **59**

harm, do harm to, noceō, -ēre, nocuī, nocitus *(w. dat.)* **69**

harmony, concordia, -ae, *f.* **17**

harsh, dūrus, -a, -um

hasten, mātūrō, -āre, -āvī, -ātus **17;** properō, -āre, -āvī, -ātūrus **27;** contendō, -ere, -tendī, -tentus **57**

have, habeō, -ēre, habuī, habitus **10**

he, is; hic; ille **31, 52** *(often not expressed)*

head, caput, capitis, *n.* **45**

headfirst, praeceps, praecipitis *(gen.)* **50**

health, salūs, salūtis, *f.* **40**

hear, audiō, -īre, -īvī, -ītus **24**

heart, cor, cordis, *n.* **51**

heavy, gravis, -e **57**

help, auxilium, -lī, *n.* **17**

her *(poss.)* eius; *(reflex.)* suus, -a, -um **65** *(often not expressed)*

herdsman, pāstor, -ōris, *m.* **46**

herself, *(intens.)* ipsa; *(reflex.)* suī **65**

hero, vir, virī, *m.* **14**

hesitate, dubitō, -āre, -āvī, -ātus **31**

high, altus, -a, -um **12; highest,** summus, -a, -um **64**

himself, *(intens.)* ipse; *(reflex.)* suī **65**

hinder, impediō, -īre, -īvī, -ītus **44**

hindrance, impedīmentum, -ī, *n.* **44**

his *(poss.)* eius; *(reflex.)* suus, -a, -um **65** *(often not expressed)*

hold, habeō, -ēre, habuī, habitus **10;** teneō, -ēre, tenuī, tentus **12;** obtineō **37; hold back,** retineō **30; hold together,** contineō **24; hold up,** sustineō **36**

home, domus, -ūs, *f.* **68**

hope, spēs, speī, *f.* **69; hope for/that,** spērō, -āre, -āvī, -ātus **52**

horse, equus, -ī, *m.* **4**

hostile, inimīcus, -a, -um **30**

hour, hōra, -ae, *f.* **9**

house, casa, -ae, *f.* **11;** domus, -ūs, *f.* **68**

how (in what manner), *(adv.)* quō modō

however, *(conj.)* autem **67**

human being, homō, hominis, *m.* **40**

humble, humilis, -e **62**

hundred, centum **66**

hurl, iaciō, -ere, iēcī, iactus **45**

I

I, ego, meī **31** *(often not expressed)*

if, sī *(or use abl. abs.)*

in, in *(w. abl. or acc.)* **11, 15; in front of,** prō *(w. abl.)* **29;** prae *(w. abl.)* **67; in the presence of,** apud *(w. acc.)* **70**

incite, incitō, -āre, -āvī, -ātus **8**

increase, augeō, -ēre, auxī, auctus **10**

influence, *(noun)*, grātia, -ae, *f.* **11**; auctōritās, -ātis, *f.* **49**; *(verb)* addūcō, -ere, addūxī, adductus **43**

inhabit, colō, -ere, coluī, cultus **54**; incolō **66**

injury, iniūria, -ae, *f.* **8**

injustice, iniūria, -ae, *f.* **8**

instruction, disciplīna, -ae, *f.* **10**

intercept, intercipiō, -ere, -cēpī, -ceptus **53**

interest, studium, -dī, *n.* **22**

interrupt, intermittō, -ere, -mīsī, -missus **37**

into, in *(w. acc.)* **15**

investigate, explōrō, -āre, -āvī, -ātus **70**

island, īnsula, -ae, *f.* **1**

it, is, ea, id **31**; hoc **50**; illud **50**; *(often not expressed)*

its (own), suus, -a, -um **65**

itself, *(intens.)* ipsum **54**; *(reflex.)* suī **65**

J

join, iungō, -ere, iūnxī, iūnctus **63**

join together, committō, -ere, -mīsī, -missus **27**

journey, iter, itineris, *n.* **46**

judge, iūdico, -āre, -āvī, -ātus **62**

just, aequus, -a, -um **18**; iūstus, -a, -um **59**

K

keen, ācer, ācris, ācre **60**

keep, teneō, -ēre, tenuī, tentus **12**; retineō, -ere, retinuī, retentus **30**; **keep busy,** exerceō, -ēre, exercuī, exercitus **67**; **keep from,** prohibeō, -ere, -hibuī, -hibitus **58**

kill, interficiō, -ere, -fēcī, -fectus **34**

kind, genus, generis, *n.* **53**

kindness, beneficium, -cī, *n.* **33**

king, rēx, rēgis, *m.* **44**

kingdom, regnum, -ī, *n.* **44**

know, *(perf. tense of)* nōscō, -ere, nōvī, nōtus **30**; cognōscō, -ere, -nōvī, -nitus **39**; sciō, -īre, scīvī, scītus **59**

known, nōtus, -a, -um **42**

L

labor, opus, operis, *n.* **63**

land, terra, -ae, *f.* **2**; **native land,** patria, -ae, *f.* **10**

language, lingua, -ae, *f.* **10**

large, magnus, -a, -um **2**

last, ultimus, -a, -um **43**; extrēmus, -a, -um **64**

late, tardus, -a, -um **24**

law, lēx, lēgis, *f.* **40**

lead, dūcō, -ere, dūxī, ductus **21**; **lead across,** trādūcō **41**; **lead a life,** vītam agō; **lead back,** redūcō **25**; **lead out,** ēdūcō **34**, prōdūcō **30**; **lead to,** addūcō **43**

leader, dux, ducis, *m.* **40**; prīnceps, -cipis, *m.* **69**

learn, nōscō, -ere, nōvī, nōtus **30**; cognōscō, -ere, -nōvī, -nitus **39**

leave (behind), relinquō, -ere, relīquī, relictus **41**

leisure, ōtium, otī, *n.* **22**

let down, submittō, -ere, -mīsī, -missus **35**

let go, mittō, -ere, mīsī, missus **19**; amittō **29**; dīmittō **31**; intermittō **37**

let through, permittō, -ere, -mīsī, -missus **34**

letter (of alphabet) littera, -ae, *f.* **7**; **(epistle,** *usually pl.)* litterae, -arum, *f.* **7**

level, plānus, -a, -um **5**

liberty, lībertā, -tātis, *f.* **47**

life, vīta, -ae, *f.* **2**

light, lūx, lūcis, *f.* **69**

light (in weight), levis, -e **58**

like, amō, -āre, -āvī, -ātus **3**; **similar,** similis, -e **63**

little, parvus, -a, -um **2**

live, habitō, -āre, -āvī, -ātus **15**; agō, -ere, ēgī, āctus **19**; vīvo, -ere, vīxī, vīctus **41**; incolō, -ere, incoluī, incultus **66**; **live a life,** vītam agō

long, longus, -a, -um

look (at), spectō, -āre, -āvī, -ātus **3**; **look down on,** despiciō, -ere, dēspexī, dēspectus **68**; **look out for,** exspectō, -āre, -āvī, ātus **19**

loosen, solvō, -ere, solvī, solūtus **59**

loot, praeda, -ae, *f.* **7**

lose, āmittō, -ere, āmīsī, āmissus **29**

love, amō, -āre, -āvī, -ātus **3**

low, humilis, -e **62**

lower, īnferior, īnferius **64**

luck, fortūna, -ae, *f.* **2**

M

maintain, sustineō, -ēre, -tinuī, -tentus **36**

make, faciō, -ere, fēcī, factus **20**; **make firm,** cōnfirmō, -ārē, -āvī, -ātus **49**

maker, auctor, -ōris **48**

man, vir, virī, *m.* **14**; homō, hominis, *m.* **40**

manliness, virtūs, -tūtis, *f.* **49**

manner, modus, -ī, *m.* **38**

many, multī, -ae, -a **3**

march, iter, itineris, *n.* **46**

master, dominus, -ī, *m.* **18**

matter, māteria, -ae, *f.* **11**; rēs, reī, *f.* **69**

memory, memoria, -ae, *f.* **8**

messenger, nūntius, -tī, *m.* **17**

middle (of), medius, -a, -um **25**

migrate, migrō, -āre, -āvī, -ātūrus **15**

mind, animus, ī, *m.* **15**

mine, *(poss.)* meus, -a, -um **9**

misfortune, cāsus, -ūs, *m.* **68**

money, pecūnia, -ae, *f.* **6**

month, mēnsis, -is, -ium, *m.* **58**

most, plūrimī, -ae, -a **64**

mother, māter, mātris, *f.* **50**

motto, sententia, -ae, *f.* **25**

mountain, mōns, montis, montium, *m.* **46**

move, moveō, -ēre, mōvī, mōtus **13**; migrō, -āre, -āvī, -ātūrus; **move away from,** cēdō, -ere, cessī, cessūrus **19; move back,** removeō **32; move deeply,** permoveō **37**

much, multus, -a, -um **3**

my, meus, -a, -um **9**

myself, *(intens.)* ipse, ipsa, **54;** *(reflex.)* mei **65**

N

name, *(noun)* nōmen, nōminis, *n.* **45;** *(verb)* appellō, -āre, -āvī, -ātus **28**

nation, gēns, gentis, gentium, *f.* **62**

native land, patria, -ae, *f.* **10**

nature, nātūra, -ae, *f.* **36**

near, ad *(w. acc.)* **6; (be) near,** adsum, adesse, adfuī, adfutūrus **34**

nearest, proximus, -a, -um **64**

neighbor, finitimus, -ī, *m.* **27**

neighboring, fīnitimus, -a, -um **27**

neither (of two) *(adj. or pron.)* neuter, -tra, -trum **56**

neither . . . nor *(conj.)* neque… neque **28**

never, numquam **26**

nevertheless, tamen **34**

new, novus, -a, -um **3**

next, tum, **6;** proximus, -a, -um **64**

no, minimē **3;** nūllus, -a, -um **56**

no longer *(adv.)* nōn iam **43**

no one, nēmō, nēminī *(dat.),* nēminem *(acc.)* *(no other forms)* **62**

noble, nōbilis, -e **53**

noise, clāmor, -ōris, *m.* **45**

none, nūllus, -a, -um **56**

nor, neque **28**

not, nōn **1**

not at all, minimē **3**

nothing, nihil *(indeclinable)* **51**

now, nunc **4;** iam **30**

number, numerus, -ī, *m.* **5**

O

obtain, obtineō, -ēre, obtinuī, obtentus **37**

offer, prōpōnō, -ere, -posuī, -positus **33**

offering, mūnus, mūneris, *n.* **59**

on in *(w. abl.)* **11, 15; on account of,** ob *(w. acc.)* **35**

once (upon a time), ōlim **31;** quondam **53**

one, ūnus, -a, -um **56**

one at a time, one by one, singulī, -ae, -a **13;**

one . . . another, alius... alius **56**

one . . . the other, alter... alter **56**

onto, in *(w. acc.)* **15**

opinion, sententia, -ae, *f.* **25**

or, *(conj.)* aut **28**

order, *(noun)* ōrdō, ōrdinis, *m.* **45;** *(verb)* iubeō, -ēre, iussī, iussus **32**

other, alius, -a, -ud **56; the other (of two),** alter, -era, -erum **56**

ought, dēbeō, -ēre, dēbuī, dēbitus **17**

our, noster, -tra, -trum **14**

ourselves *(intens.),* ipsī, ipsae, **54;** *(reflex.),* nostrum **65**

out of, ē, ex *(w. abl.)* **13**

over, super *(w.acc.)* **67**

overcome, superō, -āre, -āvī, -ātus **38;** opprimō, -ere, oppressī, oppressus **57**

owe, dēbeō, -ēre, dēbuī, dēbitus **17**

own (one's), proprius, -a, -um **63**

P

part, pars, partis, partium, *f.* **52**

pay, solvō, -ere, solvī, solūtus **59**

peace, pāx, pācis, *f.* **40;** ōtium, ōtī, *n.* **22**

penalty, poena, -ae, *f.* **8**

people, populus, -ī, *m.* **18;** gēns, gentis, gentium, *f.* **62**

perhaps, fortasse **41**

person, homō, hominis, **40**

pitch camp, castra pōnō

place, *(noun)* locus, -ī, *m.*; pl. loca, -ōrum, *n.* **21;** *(verb)* pōnō, -ere, posuī, positus **19**

plan, cōnsilium, -lī, *n.* **16**

play, lūdus, -ī, *m.* **35**

pleasing, grātus, -a, -um **7**

poor, miser, -era, -erum **29**

poet, poēta, -ae, *m.* **26**

point out, mōnstrō, -āre, -āvī, -ātus **7**

power, potestās, potestātis, *f.* **54;** imperium, -rī, *n.* **66**

praise, laudō, -āre, -āvī, -ātus **4**

prepare, parō, -āre, -āvī, -ātus **3**

prepared, parātus, -a, -um **42**

present (be), adsum, esse, adfuī, adfutūrus **34**

present (as a gift), dōnō, -āre, -āvī, -ātus **7**; prōpōnō, -ere, -posuī, -positus **33**

preserve, servō, -āre, -āvī, -ātus **8**; cōnservō **37**

press (hard), premō, -ere, pressī, pressus **40**

prevent, prohibeō, -ēre, -hibuī, -hibitus **58**

price, pretium, -tī, *n.* **21**

pride, superbia, -ae, *f.* **34**

prisoner, captīvus, -ī, *m.* **13**

produce, efficiō, -ere, effēcī, effectus **21**

protection, praesidium, -dī, *n.* **28**

proud, superbus, -a, -um **34**

prove, probō, -āre, -āvī, -ātus **7**

provide, īnstruō, -ere, īnstrūxī, īnstrūctus **62**

province, prōvincia, -ae, *f.* **8**

public, pūblicus, -a, -um, *m.* **18**

punishment, poena, -ae, *f.* **8**; supplicium, -cī, *n.* **53**

put, pōnō, -ere, posuī, positus **19; put forward,** prōpōnō, -ere, -posui, -positus **33; put in charge of,** praeficiō, -ere, -fēcī, -fectus **69; put to flight,** in fugam dō **43**

Q

queen, rēgīna, -ae, *f.* **5**

quick, celer, celeris, celere **47**

R

rank, ōrdō, ōrdinis, *m.* **45**

rather *(expressed by comparative degree)*

read, legō, -ere, lēgī, lēctus **26**

ready, parātus, -a, -um **42; get ready,** parō, -āre, -āvī, -ātus

real, vērus, -a, -um **18**

realize, sentiō, -īre, sēnsī, sēnsus **60**

reason, causa, -ae, *f.* **18**; ratiō, -ōnis, *f.* **70**

receive, accipiō, -ere, accēpī, acceptus **20**

recover, recipiō, -ere, recēpī, receptus **32**

reduce, redigō, -ere, redēgī, redāctus **32**

region, regiō, -ōnis, *f.* **62**

reinforcements, auxilia, -ōrum, *n.* **17**

relate, nārrō, -āre, -āvī, -ātus **21**

relax, remittō, -ere, remīsī, remissus **52**

remain, maneō, -ēre, mānsī, mānsūrus **11**; remaneō **34**

remaining, reliquus, -a, -um **26**

remember, memoriā teneō

remark, vōx, vōcis, *f.* **57**

remind, moneō, -ēre, -uī, -itus **38**

remove, removeō, -ēre, remōvī, remōtus **32**

report, *(noun)* fāma, -ae, *f.* **2;** *(verb)* nūntiō, -āre, -āvī, -ātus **7**

reply, respondeō, -ēre, respondī, respōnsus **49**

repulse, repellō, -ere, reppulī, repulsus **62**

rest (of), reliquus, -a, -um **26**

restore, reddō, -ere, reddidī, redditus **68**

retreat, cēdō, -ere, cessī, cessūrus **19**

reward, praemium, -ī, *n.* **16**

right, iūs, iūris, *n.* **47**

river, flūmen, flūminis, *n.* **45**

road, via, -ae, *f.* **1**

row, ōrdō, ōrdinis, *m.* **45**

rule, regō, -ere, rēxī, rēctus **20**

run, currō, -ere, cucurrī, cursūrus **50; run away,** fugiō, -ere, fūgī, fugitūrus **22**

S

sacred, sacer, -cra, -crum **14**

safety, salūs, salūtis, *f.* **40**

sail, nāvigō, -āre, -āvī, -ātus **6**

sailor, nauta, -ae, *m.* **6**

same, īdem, eadem, idem **53**

save, servō, -āre, -āvī, -ātus **8**; cōnservō **37**

say, dīcō, -ere, dīxī, dictus **22**

scare, terreō, -ēre, terruī, territus **10**

school, lūdus, -ī, *m.* **35**

sea, mare, maris, marium *n.* **46**

second, secundus, -a, -um **59**

see, videō, -ēre, vīdī, vīsus **11**; cernō, -ere, crēvī, crētus **42**; cōnspiciō, -ere, -spexī, -spectus **65**

seek, petō, -ere, petīvī, petītus **36**

-self, *(intens.)* ipse, ipsa, ipsum **54** *(or use reflexives)* **65**

seize, occupō, -āre, -āvī, -ātus **8**; capiō, -ere, cēpī, captus **20**

senate, senātus, -ūs, *m.* **68**

send, mittō, -ere, mīsī, missus **19; send ahead,** praemittō **67; send away,** dīmittō **31; send back,** remittō **52**

service, mūnus, mūneris, *n.* **59**

set free, expediō, -īre, -īvī, -ītus **44**

settler, colōnus, -ī, *m.* **15**

severe, gravis, -e **57**

shape, fōrma, -ae, *f.* **5**

sharp, ācer, ācris, ācre **60**

sharply, ācriter

she, ea; haec; illa **31, 52** *(often not expressed)*

shepherd, pāstor, -ōris, *m.* **46**

ship, nāvis, nāvis, nāvium, *f.* **46**

shout, clāmō, -āre, -āvī, -ātus **40**

shouting, clāmor, -ōris, *m.* **45**

show, mōnstrō, -āre, -āvī, -ātus **7**; dēmōnstrō **68**; ostendō, -ere, ostendī, ostentus **58**

shy, timidus, -a, -um **43**

side, pars, partis, partium *f.* **52**

sight of, (catch) cōnspiciō, -ere, -spexī, -spectus

sign, signum, -ī, *n.*; **signal,** signum, -ī, *n.* **16**

since, *(use abl. abs.) (conj.)* quod

sister, soror, sorōris, *f.* **54**

sit, sedeō, -ēre, sēdī, sessūrus **54**

situation, rēs, reī, *f.* **69**

slave, servus, -ī, *m.* **4**

slow, tardus, -a, -um **24**

small, parvus, -a, -um **2**

so, *(adv.)* ita **22**

soldier, mīles, mīlitis, *m.* **40**

some . . . others, aliī... aliī **56**

son, fīlius, -lī, *m.* **14**

song, carmen, -minis, *n.* **45**

space, spatium, -tī, *n.* **43**

speech, ōrātiō, -ōnis, *f.* **62**; **make a speech,** verba faciō

speed, celeritās, -tātis, *f.* **49**

spend time, agō, -ere, ēgī, āctus **19**

spirit, animus, -ī, *m.* **15**

spot, cōnspiciō, -ere, -spexī, -spectus **65**

stand, stō, stāre, stetī, stātus **41**; **stand still,** cōnsistō, -ere, cōnstitī, cōnstitūrus **58**

standard, signum, -ī, *n.* **16**

star, stella, -ae, *f.*

start, suscipiō, -ēre, -cēpī, -ceptus **33**

state, cīvitās, -ātis, *f.* **48**

stay behind, remaneō, -ēre, remānsī, remānsūrus **34**

steal, rapiō, -ere, rapuī, raptus **61**

steep, praeceps, praecipitis *(gen.)* **50**

stick, haereō, -ēre, haesī, haesus **60**

stir up, incitō, -āre, -āvī, -ātus **8**

stop, intermittō, -ere, -mīsī, -missus **37**; cōnsistō, -ere, cōnstitī, cōnstitūrus **58**

straight down, praeceps, praecipitis *(gen.)* **50**

strange, novus, -a, -um **3**

street, via, -ae, *f.* **1**

strength, vīs, vīs, vīrium **58**

stretch, tendō, -ere, tetendī, tentus **47**; **stretch out,** ostendō, -ere, ostendī, ostentus **58**

strong, firmus, -a, -um **23**; fortis, -e, **47**

struggle, contendō, -ere, -tendī, -tentus **57**

studies, studia, -ōrum, *n.* **22**

suitable, commodus, -a, -um **22**; aptus, -a, -um **62**

summer, aestās, -ātis, *f.* **51**

summon, evocō, -āre, -āvī, -ātus **16**

sun, sōl, sōlis, *m.* **63**

supply, cōpia, -ae, *f.*

suppose, putō, -āre, -āvī, -ātus **59**

sure, certus, -a, -um **42**

surprise, opprimō, -ere, oppressī, oppressus **57**

surrender, trādō, -ere, -didī, -ditus **66**

survive, supersum, -esse, -fuī, -futūrus **67**

swift, celer, celeris, celere

swiftness, celeritās, -tātis, *f.* **49**

T

take, capiō, -ere, cēpī, captus **20**; sūmō, -ere, sūmpsī, sūmptus **65**; emō, -ere, ēmi, ēmptus **66**; **take back,** recipiō, -ere, recēpī , receptus **32**; **take on,** incipiō **23**; **take up,** suscipiō **33**

tall, altus, -a, -um **12**

teach, doceō, -ēre, docuī, doctus **10**

teacher, magister, -trī, *m.* **14**; magistra, -ae, *f.*

tell, nārrō, -āre, -āvī, -ātus **21**; dīco, -ere, dīxī, dictus **22**

temple, templum, -ī *n.* **20**

terms, condiciō, -ōnis, *f.* **61**

territory, fīnis, fīnis, fīnium, *m.* **46**

test, *(verb)* probō, -āre, -āvī, -ātus **7**

than, *(conj.)* quam **61**

thank, grātiās agō *(w. dat.)*

that *(dem.)* ille, illa, illud **50**; is, ea, id **52**; *(rel. pron.)* quī, quae, quod **36**

their, eōrum, eārum, eōrum; **(own)** suus, -a, -um **65**

themselves *(intens.)* ipsī, -ae, -a; *(reflex.)* suī **65**

then, tum **6**

there, ibi **11**

they, eī, eae, ea; hī, hae, haec; illī, illae, illa **52**; *(often not expressed)*

thing, rēs, reī, *f.* **69**

think, putō, -āre, -āvī, -ātus **59**

third, tertius, -a, -um **42**

this, *(dem.)* hic, haec, hoc **50**; is, ea, id **52**

those, ille, illa, illud **50**

thousand, *(indeclin. adj.)* mīlle **66**; **thousands,** *(pl. noun)* mīlia, mīlium **66**

threaten, īnstō, -āre, īnstitī, — **60**

three, trēs, tria **66**

throw, iaciō, -ere, iēcī, iactus **45**

through, per *(w. acc.)* **33**

tie, ligō, -āre, -āvī, -ātus **44**

till, colō, -ere, coluī, cultus **54**

timber, māteria, -ae, *f.* **11**

time, tempus, -oris, *n.* **45**; aetās, -ātis, *f.* **61**; spatium, -tī, *n.* **43**; **one at a time,** singulī, -ae, -a

to, ad *(w. acc.)* **6** *(dat. of indir. obj.)*
tomorrow, crās **6**
tongue, lingua, -ae **10**
too *(expressed by comparative)*
top (of), summus, -a, -um **64**
touch, tangō, -ere, tetigī, tactus **53**
toward, ad *(w. acc.)* **6**
town, oppidum, -ī, *n.* **18**
train, exerceō, -ēre, exercuī, exercitus **67**
training, disciplīna, -ae, *f.* **10**
transport, trānsportō, -āre, -āvī, -ātus **41**
true, vērus, -a, -um **18**
turn, vertō, -ere, vertī, versūrus **44; turn away,**
　āverto **65**
two, duo, duae, duo **66**

U

uncertain, incertus, -a, -um **52**
under, sub *(w. acc. or abl.)* **33**
understand, intellegō, -ere, -lēxī, -lēctus **67**
undertake, suscipiō, -ere, -cēpī, -ceptus **33**
unfavorable, aliēnus, -a, -um **57**
unfold, explicō, -āre, -āvī, -ātus **63**
unfriendly, inimīcus, -a, -um **30**
unhappy, miser, -era, -erum **29**
unlike, dissimilis, -e **63**
untouched, integer, -gra, -grum **31**
upon, in *(w. abl. or acc.)*
upset, permoveō, -ēre, -mōvī, -mōtus **37**
urge on, incitō, -āre, -āvī, -ātus
useful, ūtilis, -e **61**

V

various, varius, -a, -um **22**
very *(expressed by superlative)*
victory, victōria, -ae, *f.* **8**
violence, vīs, vīs, vīrium, *f.* **58**
voice, vōx, vōcis, *f.* **57**

W

wagon, carrus, -ī, *m.* **4**
wait, exspectō, -āre, -āvī, -ātus
want, cupiō, -ere, cupīvī, cupītus **31**
war, bellum, -ī, *n.* **17**
warn, moneō, -ēre, -uī, -itus **38**
watch, spectō, -āre, -āvī, -ātus **3**

water, aqua, -ae, *f.* **1**
wave, unda, -ae, *f.* **6**
way, via, -ae, *f.* **1;** modus, -ī, *m.* **38**
we, nōs, nostrum **31** *(often not expressed)*
weapons, arma, -ōrum, *n. pl.* **17**
well *(adv.)* bene **64; (be),** valeō, -ēre, valuī,
　valitūrus **22**
what *(interrog. pron.)* quis? quid? **18, 38;** *(adj.)*
　quī, quae, quod **38**
when, ubi **18**
where, ubi **4**
which, quī, quae, quod **36**
while *(conj.)* dum **52**
who *(rel. pron.)* quī, quae, quod **36;** *(interrog.*
　pron.) quis? quid? **18, 38**
whole, integer, -gra, -grum **31;** tōtus, -a, -um **56**
why, cūr **36**
wide, lātus -a, -um **18**
wind, ventus, -ī, *m.* **27**
winter, hiems, hiemis, *f.* **51**
wish, cupiō, -ere, cupīvī, cupītus **31**
with, cum *(w. abl.)* **23**
without, sine *(w. abl.)* **30**
woman, fēmina, -ae, *f.;* mulier, mulieris, *f.*
woods, silva, -ae, *f.* **1**
word, verbum, -ī, *n.* **24**
work *(noun),* opus, operis, *n.* **63;** labor, -ōris, *m.*
　59; *(verb),* labōrō, -āre, -āvī, -ātus **3**
worse, peior, peius; **worst,** pessimus, -a, -um
worry, cūra, -ae, *f.* **5**
worship, colō, -ere, coluī, cultus **54**
wound *(noun)* vulnus, vulneris, *n.* **45;** *(verb)*
　vulnerō, -āre, -āvī, -ātus **40**
write, scrībō, -ere, scrīpsī, scrīptus **26**
wrong, iniūria, -ae, *f.* **8**

Y

year, annus, -ī, *m.* **16**
yes, sīc **3**
yield, cēdō, -ere, cessī, cessūrus **19**
you, tū, tuī *(sing.);* vōs, vestrum *(pl.)* **31** *(often not*
　expressed)
your, tuus, -a, -um **9;** vester, -tra, -trum, pl. **18;**
　(often not expressed)
yourself *(intens.)* ipse, ipsa, **54;** *(reflex.)* tuī

SUBJECT INDEX

Artemis, Temple of, 45
Ascanius, *see* Iulus
Asia Minor, 173, 182, 362, 372
astrologers, 373
astronomy, 207
Athena, 250, 383
Athens, 268, 271; *383*
athletics, 151, 164, 304f.; *204f.; see also*
   games, sports
atrium, 139, 236; *134, 136, 139, 236*
Atrium Vestae, 352
Atropos, 229
Atticus, T. Pomponius, 386f.
augures (augurs), 373
Augusta, Empress, 84
Augustus Caesar, 30, 38f., 76f., 92,
   117, 164, 213, 230, 261, 304, 379,
   383, 410, 453, 468; *213*
Aurelian, Emperor, 77
auspices, 373
Austria, 52
Aventine Hill, 76, 304
axes, 425

B

Baalbek, Lebanon, *250*
Babylonia, 372
Bacchus, 152, 346, 362; **Temple of,** *250*
bakery, *336*
banking and finance, 57, 361, 411, 435,
   451; *see also* commerce
barbarians, 196, 357; *165, 267*
barbers, 86, 363
bars, *337*
Bath, England, *49*
baths, 77, 403; *49, 284, 288, 448*
Baucis, 426f.; *426*
beards, 97, 196; *97*
Belgium, 66, 208
books, 182, 209, 270; *8, 87, 117, 386*
boundary stone, 346
bowling, *306*
Boys from Syracuse, 305
Brahms, Johannes, 520
bread, 317, 336ff.
breakfast, 337
Brennus, 68
bricks, 410

bridges, *368*
Britain, 15, 49, 51f., 89, 91, 117, 266,
   268, 284f., 293, 296; *v, 49, 91, 284*
Bronze Age, 420; *421*
bronze, 410, 420
Brundisium, (Brindisi, Italy), 33, 38
Brutus, M. Junius, 291, 483
building, 421, *421*
Bulgaria, 7
bulla, *379, 468*
bullfights, 53, 306
burials, 410
business, 410f., 451; *see also* commerce
busts, *89, 384, 386, 437, 463*

C

Caedicius, Q., 353
Caelian Hill, 76
Caesar, C. Julius, 3, 9, 11, 17, 53, 66,
   76, 89, 143, 221, 266, 291ff., 368,
   383, 396, 409, 447, 453, 463; *89, 143*
calendar, 396
Calypso, 314
Camillus, M. Furius, 68; *68*
Campania, 38, 295
Campo Vaccino, 356
camps, 287
Campus Martius, 76
Cannae, Battle of, 473
Capernaum, *152*
Capitol Building (Washington, D.C.),
   76; *88*
Capitoline Hill, 13, 76; *17, 68*
Capitolium, 76, 197, 474
captives, 99; *400, 460f.*
Capua, 33, 38; *130*
Caron, Antoine, 213
carriages and carts, 33, 38; *33, 400*
Carthage, 20, 191ff., 205f., 208, 437,
   448f., 473; *158f., 193, 448*
Carthaginians, 448f.
cartoons, *18, 23, 25, 27, 58, 63, 75, 102,*
   110, 148, 167, 177, 181, 184, 187,
   195, 218, 249, 261, 300, 322, 341,
   366, 375, 397, 465, 467, 471f.
Castor and Pollux, Temple of, *12f., 20,*
   76, 356

Cato, M. Porcius the Elder, 478; *478*
cavalry, *114, 222, 267, 332*
censor, *346;* census, 346; *346*
centurion, *221, 453*
Cerberus, *350*
Ceres, 160–63, 346, 372; *xii, 162f., 372*
chariots and races, 19, 76, 164, 304f., 403; *46, 160, 162*
Chedworth, England, *284*
Cherchel, Tunisia, 315
children, 11, 60, 94, 246, 270f., 304, 435, 462; *8, 23, 43, 70, 101, 169, 172, 196f., 246, 268, 306, 378f., 405, 468, 473*
Chinese writing, 5ff.
Christianity, 11, 39, 77, 373
Churchill, Winston, 11
Cicero, M. Tullius, 3f., 9, 83, 117, 382, 384, 386f., 430, 447, 467, 478, 483; *xiii, 384, 386*
Cicero, Q. Tullius, 386f., 392
Cimbri, 462
Cincinnati, Society of, 395, 397
Cincinnatus, L. Quinctius, 393, 395f., 410, 482; *393, 395*
Cineas, 332f.; *443*
Circe, 297, 300, 314; *x, 298, 300*
Circus Maximus, 76, 304; *46*
citizenship, 106, 196, 346, 383, 482f.
Civil War, 89, 230, 463
Claudius, Emperor, 117
clients, 134f.
Clio, *174*
clothing, 196ff., 235; *82f., 158f., 196f., 271, 378f., 405*
Clotho, 229
codex, 182
cognomen, 367, 405, 467
coins, 76, 425; U. S. coins, 57; *57*
Coke, Edward, 483
Coliseum (Colosseum), 13, 130, 245, 257, 306; *ix, 12f., 46, 76, 244f., 257*
colonists, 108, 208, 284f.
colors, 198
Columbus, Christopher, 59, 296
columns, 13, 38, 257f.; *12f., 17, 20, 38, 45, 88, 114, 134, 136, 141, 208, 213,*

236, 250, 252, 257ff., 259, 347, 356, 383, 453
comedy, 305
commerce, 39, 45, 152, 207, 250, 410f., 451, 482; *411*
communication, means of, 33, 38, 268
Comum (Como, Italy), 288
Concordia, 380
Constantine, Emperor, 11, 373
Constitution of the United States, 3
Consualia, 373
consuls, 356, 384, 463, 482
Consus, 373
Continental Army (United States), 397
cooking, 43, 86, 302; *see also* food and meals
copper, 410, 425
Corinthian order, 257f.; *12f., 17, 133, 236, 257f.*
Coriolanus, C. Marcius, 405, 452; *405*
Cornelia, 468, 473; *468, 473*
cornucopia, *xii, 350, 372*
corona, classica, 441; navalis, 441
Cortona, Pietro da, 216, 423
cosmetics, 196f.
Crane, Walter, 363
Crete, 173, 348, 431
Creusa, 211; *viii, 211*
Cupid, 192; *344*
Curius, 382
cursus honorum, 384
Cyclopes, 278f., 297; *278*
Cyrillic alphabet, 7

D

Dacia (Romania), 114
Daedalus, 431f., *431*
daily life, 150ff., 384; *151*
Danube River, 368
Dardanelles, 173
Darius, 105
De Senectute, 478
debt, 435
Declaration of Independence, 3, 392
Delos, 231
Delphi and Delphic oracle, 231
Demeter, 163, 372; *163*

lead, 425
Lee, Robert E., 483
Leeds, England, 328
legion, 287
Lepcis Magna, Libya, *84*
letters, 266, 268, 288, 292, 382, 384
libraries, 45, 182, 288; *386*
lighthouses, 255
Lincoln's Gettysburg Address, 11
Lindum (Lincoln, England), 285
linen, 197
literacy, 172
Livia, 30, 410
Livy, 222, 405, 482
Locke, John, 483
logographic writing, 6
Londinium (London, England), 285
loom, *x, 300, 319*
Lotus-eaters, 279, 297
Louvre, Paris, *165, 213*
Lower World, 162, 209, 211f., 277,
    350; *276f., 344f.*
ludi circenses, 164; **gladiatorii,** 151,
    164, 257, 261; **ludi scaenici**
    (plays), 164
lunch, 338
Lusitania, *see* Portugal
lustrum, 346; *346*
Lyso, 382

M

Macedonia, 104f.
Mactar, Tunisia, *450*
magic, 103, 368
Magna Carta, 51; *51*
Mantua, Italy, 178
manuscripts, *51, 230, 293, 478*
maps of Italy, *14;* Roman Empire,
    54f.; Sicily, *175;* the World (15th
    cent.), *59*
marble, *383, 482*
Marius, C., 462f.; *463*
market, *151*
marriage, 31, 195, 292, 322; *31*
Mars, 126, 328, 345f., 372; *344*
Marsus, Gaius Vibius, 84
Martial, 304
Marygold, 363; *363*

masks, 305; *82f., 174*
matron, 195; *116, 196*
meals, 336f., 372; *426*
medicine, 103, 231, 382f.
Mediterranean Sea, 140, 184, 208, 250,
    255; *448*
Melpomene, *174*
Menelaus, 403
merchants, *see* commerce
Mercury, 161, 206f., 297, 346, 426;
    207, 426
mercury, 425
messengers, *33*
metals, 425
Metamorphoses, 426; *426*
Metropolitan Museum of Art, New
    York, 325
Midas, 362f.; *363*
Middle Ages, 3, 9, 76f.
Middle East, 116
Milan, Italy (Mediolanum), 288
milestones, 38; *152;* Roman mile, 152
milk, 337, 420
milliarium aureum, *38*
Minerva, 112, 320, 346, 372, 402; *316*
Minos, King of Crete, 431
Minucius, 393, 396
mirror, *196*
Mithras, 372
Mithridates, 462
model of ancient Rome, *46*
monotheism, 372
months, names of, 361
mosaics, *2, 82f.,101, 124f., 136, 169,*
    172, 174,178, 186, 315, 328, 403, 411
mosques, 45
mottoes of states, *see* state mottoes
Mt. Etna, 185
Mt. Olympus, 348
Mt. Vesuvius, 150, 295
multiplication, 271
Muses, 174; *174, 345*
museums, 373
musical instruments, 83; *82f., 267;*
    flute, *82, 315;* **lyre,** *31, 521;*
    panpipe, *278;* **trumpet,** *267, 460*
musicians, 116; *83*
mystery religions, 372

N

Naples, Italy, 27, 83, 150, 323, 437
Narcissus, 117
Native Americans, 5, 59, 287
Nausicaa, 314; *96, 316*
naval battles, 245
navigation, *421*
Neptune, 125, 185f., 314, 346, 348; *vii, 125, 186, 191*
Nîmes, France, 53, 65; *iv, 53*
Niobe, 231f.
nobiles, 408
nomina, 467
Normans, 371
North Africa, 92
Numa Pompilius, 126
numerals, 25, 502
Numicus (River), 225
Numidia, 462
Numitor, 328f.
nurses, 43, 383; *405*
nymph, *70*
nymphaeum, *124*

O

oars, 326; *61*
Odysseus, 278; *323; see also* Ulysses
Odyssey, 270, 276–83, 297, 300, 313–16, 319f., 323ff.; *96, 276f., 298, 300, 312f., 315f., 319, 323, 325*
olive branch, 441; *57;* oil, 138, 337
Olympian gods, 348; *344f.*
oracles, 231
orators, 384; *271*
Orbilius, 169f.
orchestra, 259; *259*
Ostia, 92, 151
Ovid, 160, 162, 225, 420f., 426

P

Pactolus, River, 362
paedagogus, 270; *468*
palace, *158f.*
palaestra (exercise ground), 403
Palatine Hill, 30, 76, 238, 304; *1, 46, 76, 141*

Pales, 76, 373
Palestine, 372
Palilia, 373
Pallanteum, 216f.; *216*
Pallas, 216f.; *216*
Palma Vecchio, 460f.
Pantheon, 77
pantomimes, 305
Papinian, *482*
papyrus, 182, 209, 270
parades, 257, 304, 393
Parcae, 229
parchment, 182, 270
Paris, France, 165, 379
Paris, Prince of Troy, 402
Parthenon, 250; *383*
Parthians, 7
Pater Patriae, *57*
paterfamilias, 23, 347, 380; **patria potestas,** 435
patres (senators), 356
patricians, 408, 452, 482
patrons, 134f.
Pax, 380
Pecunia, 380
pediment, 133; *133*
Penates, 173, 176f., 211, 372, 380; *176*
Penelope, 277, 319f., 323ff.; *319, 325*
perfumes, 197
Pergamum, 45, 182
peristylium, 139, 237; *139*
Persia, 105, 372
Petilius, 478
Phaeacia, 96, 313f.; *312f.*
Philemon, 426f.; *426*
Philip II of Macedon, 104f.
philosophy, 214; **philosophers,** 104f., 150, 271
Phoenicians, 6, 448
Phrygia, 362, 426f.
physical fitness, 271
Piazza Armerina (Sicily), *403*
pictographic writing, 5
pig Latin, 150
place names, U.S., 36, 115, 177, 190, 195, 224, 283, 287, 296, 318, 352, 397, 409

turret, *61*

Twelve Tables, 270, 435, 482

Twinkle, Twinkle Little Star, 10

U

U.S. Capitol, *88;* House of Representatives, 482; Presidents, 393; Supreme Court Building, *133*

Ulysses, 112, 276–80, 297f., 300, 313–16, 319f., 323ff., 327; *xf., 96, 276f., 278, 280, 300, 312, 315f., 319, 323, 325*

Underworld, *see* Lower World

uniforms, *398, 405, 443, 460f.*

unions, 410

Uranus, 348

utensils, eating, 338

V

Vaga, Pierino del, 344f.

vases, 280; *x,116, 280, 300, 316*

Vatican City, 9; Museum and Library, 11, 61

vegetables, 336; *410*

Venus, 17, 173, 191f., 211, 225, 345f., 372, 402; *vii, 191;* Temple of Venus Genetrix, *iii, 17;* Temple of Venus and Rome, *12f.*

Vergil, 3, 11, 150, 159, 173f., 177ff., 205, 225, 230, 277, 392, 420, 483; *174, 178, 230*

Vespasian, Emperor, 1

Vesta, 372f., 380; Temple of, 352; *vi, 12, 76, 141*

Vestals, 126, 141, 245, 352

veterans, 230

Vetulonia, Italy, *34, 39*

Via Appia, *see* Appian Way; Via Lata, 74; Via Sacra, *see* Sacred Way

Victoria, 380

Victorius, Petrus, 386

victory crown, 441; *143*

Vienna, 379

vigiles, 77

villas, 39, 238, 403, 429; *284, 403;* villa of Cicero, 83

Viminal Hill, 76

Virtus, 380

Volscians, 405

Vulcan, 224, 346

Vulgate, 335

W

wall paintings, 138, 237; *27, 30, 43, 96, 136, 146, 176, 225, 268*

walls, 38, 77; *v, 91, 398*

warfare, 361, 398f., 410, 420f.; *221, 421; see also* weapons

warship, *61*

Washington, D.C., 76, 398, 482; *88, 133*

Washington, George, 483; *57*

water supply, 29, 425; *29*

weapons, 220, 224, 323f., 410, 425, 445; *61, 116, 158, 165, 221, 263, 267, 332, 395, 445, 461*

weaving, 410; *x, 116, 300, 319*

Western civilization, 482f.

wheat, 92, 452f.; *452f.*

wines, 57, 295, 337f., 420

Winged Victory, *225*

women, 195, 197, 234, 410, 467; *23, 27, 116, 146, 151, 162, 197, 389, 405, 418, 468, 473*

wooden tablets, *270*

wool, 197, 451

wreaths, 441; *27, 43, 83, 89, 143, 372, 378f., 403, 437, 461*

Wright Brothers' Memorial (Kitty Hawk, NC), *432*

writing, 5–8; writing implements, 9, 270; *5, 9, 172, 246, 268, 270, 386*

Z

Zama, Battle of, 473

Zeus, 348, 372; *344*

zinc, 425

Zodiac, *344*

Zoroaster, 372

GRAMMAR INDEX

The numbers in roman type refer to page numbers in the book; those in italic refer to illustrations on the page referenced.

A

a-declension, 17f., 73, 470; *471*

ā, *ab,* 100–103, 110, 193, 340, 512; *102, 366;* as prefix, 103

ablative case, absolute, 299ff., 308, 512; accompaniment, 167, 200, 260, 340, 375, 512; *167, 366;* agent, 193f., 200, 340, 375, 512; description, 479f., 512; manner, 259f., 273, 375, 512; means, 67f., 79, 167, 193f., 200, 260, 340, 375, 512; *167;* respect, 334, 340, 375, 512; time when, 354, 374f., 512; place from which, 101f., 118, 512; *102, 366;* place where, 90, 110, 354, 375, 512; *110, 366;* with prepositions, 90, 101f., 110, 118, 340, 512; *102, 110, 366;* summary of uses, 78, 340, 495, 512

absolute, ablative, 299ff., 308, 512; **nominative** in English, 299, 308

accent, 10, 95, 113, 132, 490

accompaniment, ablative of, 167, 200, 260, 340, 375, 512; *167, 366*

accusative case, direct object, 22f., 62, 78, 485, 495, 511; extent, 464, 511; place to which, 110, 119, 485, 511; *110, 366;* subject of infinitive, 223, 395, 401, 408, 511, 513; with prepositions, 62f., 110, 119, 485, 495, 511; *63,110, 366;* summary of uses, 511

active voice, 187, 496; *187*

ad, 62f., 110, 119, 485, 511; *63, 110, 366;* as prefix, 107

adjectives, 21ff., 40, 491f., 499–504; agreement of, 21ff., 35, 40, 73, 106, 114, 119, 281, 511; as nouns, 113, 207, 239, 289, 439, 511; comparison of, 422ff., 433ff., 438, 454f., 500f.; dative with, 434, 455, 511; declension of comparatives, 423, 438, 501; demonstrative, 349ff., 359, 364, 374, 492, 503f.; first and second declension, 21f., 72f., 105f., 114, 119, 281, 499; intensive, 369f., 374, 504; interrogative, 263f., 272, 492, 504; numerals, 286, 309, 384, 450, 492, 501f.; participles as, 226, 388, 500; position of, 23, 40, 147; possessive, 219, 240, 445, 492; predicate, 21f., 128; pronominal ("irregular"), 383f., 501; reflexive, 445; relative, 492, 504; third declension, 325f., 340, 388, 500

adverbial clause, ablative absolute as, 299

adverbs, 493; formation of, 166, 199, 428; comparison of, 428, 433ff., 438, 455, 500

agent, ablative of, 193f., 200, 340, 375, 512

agō, different meanings of, 144

agreement, of adjectives, 21f., 35, 40, 72f., 106, 119, 219, 281, 445, 450, 511; of appositives, 137f., 511; of participles, 226f., 294, 307, 389f., 401; of relative pronouns, 253ff., 511; of verbs, 28f., 41, 194, 495, 511

alius and *alter,* 384

antecedent, 491; of demonstrative pronoun, 359; of relative pronoun, 253ff.

antepenult, 490

appositives, 137f., 154, 511

articles, 16, 492

assimilation, 107, 111, 168, 229, 249, 364, 385

auxiliary verbs, 29, 227f., 493

B

bases, of adjectives, 428, 433; of nouns, 18, 280, 307; *see also* **stems**

basic forms, 498–510; **grammar,** 490–97; **syntax,** 511ff.

C

case, 16, 21ff., 40, 494f.; summary of uses, 511f.; *see also* **nominative,** etc.

clauses, 253, 294, 358, 497

comparison, of adjectives, 422ff., 433ff., 438, 454f., 500f.; of adverbs, 428, 433ff., 438, 455, 500; irregular, 438f.

complementary infinitive, 290

complex sentence, 254, 497

compound forms, of infinitives, 401

compound sentence, 497

conjugation, 29, 153f., 493, 495; first, 29, 247, 285, 505; second, 85f., 258, 506; third, 135ff., 147, 153, 267f., 507; third -iō, 142, 153, 162, 199, 508; fourth, 142, 154, 171, 199, 286, 509; *see also* **irregular verbs**

conjunctions (coordinating, subordinating, correlative), 493

connecting relative, 448

consonants, 6ff., 489

contraction of vowels, 95, 101, 113

cum, (preposition), accompaniment, 167, 219, 512; *167, 366;* manner, 259f., 512; omission of, 260; as prefix, 168

D

dative, indirect object, 61f., 78f., 485, 495, 511; *63;* with adjectives, 434, 455, 511; with transitive (special) verbs, 485, 511

dē, 101f.; *102;* as prefix, 103

declension, 17, 47, 73, 118, 493; *471;* first, nouns and adjectives, 17f., 70ff., 498f.; second, nouns and adjectives, 35, 70ff., 105f., 113f., 118, 147, 498f.; third, nouns and adjectives, 280f., 307, 316, 321, 325f., 339f., 423, 498, 500; fourth, 470, 499; fifth, 475, 499; irregular, 394, 427, 469, 499

demonstratives, 349ff., 358f., 364, 374, 491f., 503f.

derivatives, *see* **Word Study**

description, ablative and genitive of, 479f., 511f.

Developing Word Sense, *see* **Reading and Translation Hints**

diphthongs, 489f.

direct object, 22f., 30f., 61f., 78, 147f., 223, 485, 494f., 511, 513; *148*

direct statement, 401, 413

dō, 247

domus, 469, 499

dum, 358

duo, 450, 501

E

ē, ex, 101f., 110; *102;* as prefix, 103

e-declension, 475

emphatic verb forms, 29, 389, 496

enclitics, 132, 154, 179

extent of time or space, accusative of, 464, 511

F

fifth declension, 475, 499

first conjugation, 29, 56, 96, 135, 188f., 239, 247f., 285, 505

first declension, 17f., 35, 48, 71f., 498f.; *471*

fourth conjugation, 142, 154, 171, 199, 286, 509

fourth declension, 470, 499; *471*

future tense, 56, 79, 85f., 119, 127, 153, 162, 171, 189, 199, 495; future active infinitive and participle, 232, 390, 400, 406f., 412f.; future passive infinitive, 400

future perfect tense, *see* perfect system

G

gender, 16f., 21, 35, 40, 47, 113f., 280f., 325, 470, 475, 494; **grammatical,** 35; **natural,** 35

genitive case, 16, 18, 47ff., 78f., 95, 113, 118, 147, 494, 511; of description, 479f., 511; of possession, 47ff., 78, 494, 511; of the whole (partitive), 219, 450, 511

grammar, basic, 490–97; **summaries,** 40f., 78f., 118ff., 153f., 199f., 239f., 272f., 307f., 339f., 374f., 412f., 454ff., 484f.

H

hic, 349ff., 359, 374, 503

Hints for Understanding Latin, *see* **Reading and Translation Hints**

I

īdem, 364, 374, 503

idioms, 175

ille, 349ff., 359, 369, 374, 504

imperative mood, 73, 79, 142, 153, 496

imperfect tense, 180ff., 188f., 200, 495; *181*

in, 90, 110, 119, 512; *110, 366;* as a prefix, 111

indicative mood, 73, 406f., 413, 496

indirect object, 61ff., 78f., 147f., 485, 494f., 511; *63, 148*

indirect statement, 401ff., 406ff., 413, 455, 513

infinitives, 28f., 73, 153f., 290, 406ff., 413, 496, 513; as nouns, 128, 207, 223, 234, 239f.; complementary, 290; future active and passive, 400, 407, 413; in indirect statement, 401ff., 407, 413, 513; perfect active and passive, 394f., 400, 407, 413; present active and passive, 28f., 73, 153f., 231, 240, 401ff., 407; with subject accusative, 223, 401, 513

inflection, 16, 22f., 29, 493; *23*

intensives, 369f., 374, 444, 504; suffix *-ce,* 350

interjections, 177, 493

interrogatives, 131, 154, 263f., 272, 491f., 496, 504

intransitive verbs, 193, 200, 232, 390, 492

-iō verbs (third conjugation), 142, 153, 171, 199, 508

ipse, 374, 379f., 444, 504

irregular, adjectives, 383f., 501; comparison of adjectives and adverbs, 438f., 455, 501; nouns, 394, 427, 469, 499; verbs, 510; *see also* **sum, possum**

is, 217f., 358f., 374, 503

i-stem nouns, 321f., 325, 339f., 498

L

linking verbs, 18, 109, 147, 187, 492f.

liquid consonants, 490

locative case, 495, 512

M

macrons, 282

manner, ablative of, 259f., 273, 375, 512

means, ablative of, 67f., 79, 167, 193f., 200, 260, 340, 375, 512; *167*

medius, use of, 439

mille, declension and use of, 450, 501f.

mood, 73, 496; *see also* **imperative, indicative**

N

-ne, 132, 154

nēmō, declension of, 427, 499

nominative case, 16–19, 21, 23, 29, 47, 78, 316, 494, 511; absolute in English, 299

nonne, 132

nouns, 16–19, 40, 491, 498f.; irregular, 394, 424, 469, 499; *see also* **first declension,** etc.

nūllus, nihil, nēmō, 384

number, 16f., 21, 29, 40f., 494f.

numerals, 25, 286, 309, 384, 450, 456, 492, 501f.; *25;* **cardinal,** 502; **ordinal,** 502

O

o-declension, 73, 470

object, direct, 22f., 30f., 61ff., 78, 147f., 223, 485, 494f., 511, 513; *148;* indirect, 61ff., 78f., 147f., 485, 494f., 511; *63, 148;* infinitive as, 128, 153, 223, 513

objective case, 22f., 47, 78, 223, 495

order of words, *see* **word order**

P

participles, 226, 232, 248, 259, 267, 269, 289, 388ff., 412f., 430, 496f., 500, 513; in ablative absolute, 299ff., 308; tenses of, 513; used as adjectives and nouns, 289, 301, 308, 531; used as clauses, 294, 307f., 513

partitive genitive, 219, 450, 511

parts of speech, 491

passive voice, 187ff., 193, 200, 227f., 234, 496; *187*

past perfect (pluperfect) tense, *see* **perfect system**

penult, 490

perfect system, future perfect tense, 213, 227f., 239f., 495; past perfect (pluperfect) tense, 213, 227, 239f., 495; perfect infinitives, active and passive, 394f., 400, 407, 413; perfect participle, 226, 232, 248, 259, 267, 269, 289, 294, 299ff., 430, 513; perfect stem, 95f., 135ff., 213, 248; perfect tense, 95f., 98, 120, 127, 137, 142, 153f., 200, 213, 227, 240, 495, 512, distinguished from imperfect, 181f., 200; *181*

person, 28f., 41, 495

personal endings, 28f., 96, 188f., 213

personal pronouns, 28, 218f., 239f., 351, 359, 491, 503

phrase, 497; prepositional, *366*

place, from which, 101f., 118, 512; *102, 366;* to which, 62f., 110, 119, 485, 511; *63, 110, 366;* where, 90, 110, 512; *110, 366; see also* **locative case**

pluperfect, *see* **perfect system**

plūs, 438, 501

possession, genitive of, 47ff., 78, 494, 511

possessive adjectives, 219, 240, 445, 492

possum, 290, 307, 388, 510

post, posteā, postquam, 465; *465*

predicate, 18, 28, 147, 491; adjectives and nouns, 18, 22, 109, 128, 511

prefixes, *see* **Word Study**

prepositions, 67, 493; ablative with, 90, 101f., 110, 118, 340, 512; *102, 110, 366;* accusative with, 62f., 110, 119, 485, 495, 511; *63, 110, 366; see also* **prefixes**

present system, active participle, 388ff., 404, 412, 500; imperatives, 73, 79, 86, 137, 142, 147, 153, 496; infinitives, active, 27f., 407; passive, 234, 240, 400; present stem, 29, 136, 142, 248; present tense, 27ff., 85f., 109, 119, 137, 142, 188; *see also* **future** and **imperfect tense**

principal parts, 27, 85, 95, 135, 162, 232, 239, 247f., 258f., 267f., 272, 285f.

progressive verb forms, 29, 109, 182, 187, 389, 496

pronominal adjectives, 383f., 501

pronouns, 207, 491, 503f.; demonstrative, 349ff., 358f., 364, 374, 491f., 503f.; intensive, 369f.,

374, 444, 504; interrogative, 263f., 272, 491f., 504; personal, 28, 218f., 239f., 351, 359, 491, 503; reflexive, 444, 455, 503; relative, 251–55, 272, 491, 504, 511

Q

quality of vowels, 488

quam, with comparative, 424, 454; with superlative, 435, 454

quantity of syllables, 490; **of vowels,** 488

questions, 131f., 147, 154, 263

quī, declension of, 251f., 504

quis, declension of, 263f., 504

R

Reading and Translation Hints, 16, 30f., 50, 62, 67f., 91, 120, 144, 180, 233, 254f., 282, 294, 301, 330, 389ff., 422, 476, 484

reflexives, 444f., 455, 503

relative clauses, 250–55, 294

relative pronouns, 251–55, 272, 491f., 504, 511; as connective, 448

reliquus, use of, 439

respect, ablative of, 334, 340, 375, 512

roots, *see* **Word Study**

S

second conjugation, 85f., 96, 119, 258f., 506

second declension, 35, 48, 71ff., 95, 101, 105f., 113f., 118, 147, 498f.

sentences, 18, 147f., 491, 497; *148*

sequence of tense, 407, 413

special verbs, dative with, 485, 511

stems, adjective, 114, 340; noun, 18, 85, 105f.; participle, 248, 388, 412; verb, 29, 85, 95f., 135ff., 142, 153f., 213, 248, 413

subject, 18, 22f., 28f., 491, 494, 511,
513; of infinitive, 223, 401, 408, 413,
511

subordinate clauses, 254f., 497

substantives, 113, 128, 153, 207, 239,
289, 389, 513

suffixes, *see* **Word Study**

suī, 444, 503

sum, 109, 120, 127, 153, 181, 187, 213,
290, 388, 510

summus, use of, 439

superlatives, 422f., 428, 433ff., 438f.,
454

suus, 445

syllables, 6, 16, 489f.

synonyms, 484

syntax, basic, 511ff.

T

temporal clauses, 294

tense, 28, 406f., 413, 495, 512f.;
sequence of, 407, 413; signs, 56, 180,
213; *see also* **present system,** etc.

third conjugation, 135ff., 147, 153f.,
162, 188f., 267f., 507; -iō verbs, 142,
153f., 171, 188f., 199, 267f., 508

third declension, adjectives, 325f., 340,
500; nouns, 280f., 307, 316, 324, 339,
498; -i stems, 321, 339, 498

time when, ablative of, 354, 374f., 512

tōtus and *omnis,* distinguished, 384

transitive verbs, 193, 200, 492

Translation Strategies, *see* **Reading
and Translation Hints**

U

u-declension, 470

ūnus, 383f., 501

V

verbs, 28f., 41, 492f.; agreement with
subject, 28f., 41, 194, 495, 511;
auxiliary, 29, 227f., 493; complete,
492; emphatic, 496; interrogative
forms, 496; intransitive, 193, 200,
232, 390, 492; irregular, 109, 120,
127, 153, 181, 187, 213, 290, 307,
388, 510; linking, 18, 109, 187, 492f.;
negative forms, 496; number of, 29;
personal endings, active, 28f., 96,
passive, 188f; position of, 147f., *148;*
progressive forms, 29, 496; transitive,
193, 200, 492; summary of forms,
505–10, of syntax, 512; *see also*
**conjugation, infinitive, participle,
perfect system, present system,
principal parts, stems, voice**

vīs, 394, 499

vocative case, 101, 119, 316, 495, 498f.,
512

voice, 187ff., 193, 496; *187*

vowels, 6, 8, 10, 488f.

W

whole, genitive of the, 219, 450, 511

word order, 16, 19, 21ff., 31, 40, 48,
62, 68, 101, 147f., 180, 223, 260,
351; *148*

Word Study

abbreviations, 51, 195, 331, 355, 366,
477, 516

assimilation, 107, 111, 168, 229,
249, 385

doublets, 447

French influence, 111, 371

importance of verb, 269, 273; of third
declension, 352

intensive prefixes, 256